VIATOR

Medieval and Renaissance Studies

VOLUME 9

VIATOR

MEDIEVAL AND RENAISSANCE STUDIES

Volume 9 (1978)

PUBLISHED UNDER THE AUSPICES OF
THE CENTER FOR MEDIEVAL AND RENAISSANCE STUDIES
UNIVERSITY OF CALIFORNIA, LOS ANGELES

UNIVERSITY OF CALIFORNIA PRESS

BERKELEY, LOS ANGELES, LONDON 1978

VIATOR

Medieval and Renaissance Studies

Manuscripts should be addressed to the Editors, Center for Medieval and Renaissance Studies, University of California, Los Angeles, California 90024, U.S.A. *Viator* is open to contributions from all sources. The Editors are particularly interested in considering intercultural and interdisciplinary articles. Texts, illustrations, maps, diagrams, musical examples, and the like, will be published when they are necessary to documentation. Articles that have been, or soon will be, printed elsewhere in any language in substantially the same form are not acceptable.

Inquiries concerning subscriptions and earlier volumes should be addressed to the University of California Press, 2223 Fulton Street, Berkeley, California 94720, U.S.A.

University of California Press
Berkeley and Los Angeles, California
University of California Press, Ltd.
London, England

CONTENTS

Ecology and Economy in Early Medieval Frisia   1
WILLIAM H. TE BRAKE

An Iconographic Explanation of *The Wanderer,* Lines 81b—82a   31
GEORGE HARDIN BROWN

Legend, History and Artifice in *The Battle of Maldon*   39
A. N. DOANE

The Formation of the Salzburg Ministerialage in the Tenth and
Eleventh Centuries: An Example of Upward Social Mobility in
the Early Middle Ages   67
JOHN B. FREED

Periculosus homo: Pope Gregory VII and Episcopal Authority   103
IAN STUART ROBINSON

The Early *Ars dictaminis* as Response to a Changing Society   133
WILLIAM D. PATT

The Foundation of the Confraternity of Tarragona by Archbishop
Oleguer   157
LAWRENCE J. MC CRANK

A Twelfth-Century Concept of the Natural Order   179
RICHARD C. DALES

The Performing Self in Twelfth-Century Culture   193
MARTIN STEVENS

The Indian Tradition in Western Medieval Intellectual History   213
THOMAS HAHN

New Light on the Transmission of Donatus's *Commentum
Terentii*   235
M. D. REEVE and R. H. ROUSE

Narrative Anomalies in *La Chançun de Willame*   251
JOHN D. NILES

"Of Heigh or Lough Estat": Medieval Fabulists as Social
Critics   265
    ARNOLD CLAYTON HENDERSON

Magisterium and License: Corporate Autonomy against Papal
Authority in the Medieval University of Paris   291
    ALAN E. BERNSTEIN

Aristotle and the French Monarchy, 1260-1303   309
    THOMAS RENNA

Religious Careers and Religious Devotion in Thirteenth-Century
Metz   325
    CHARLES MC CURRY

The Netherlands Herring Fishery in the Late Middle Ages: The
False Legend of Willem Beukels of Biervliet   335
    RICHARD W. UNGER

The Community of Law and Letters: Some Notes on Thomas
Usk's Audience   357
    MAY NEWMAN HALLMUNDSSON

Piers Plowman and Holychurch   367
    MARGARET JENNINGS, C.S.J.

Contributions of Foreigners to Dubrovnik's Economic Growth
in the Late Middle Ages   375
    BARIŠA KREKIĆ

The Lübeckers Bartholomäus Ghotan and Nicolaus Bülow in
Novgorod and Moscow and the Problem of Early Western
Influences on Russian Culture   395
    DAVID B. MILLER

Viator Style Sheet   413

ECOLOGY AND ECONOMY IN EARLY MEDIEVAL FRISIA

•

by William H. TeBrake

During the early Middle Ages, the Frisians were able to expand their territory and political influence significantly southward along the North Sea coast. They met little resistance until the sixth century when, in the Rhine delta, they encountered the northward-pushing Franks. For much of the following two centuries these groups engaged in a protracted struggle over possession of the delta and surrounding territories, with the fortunes of warfare varying widely from one side to the other. Under the leadership of Charles Martel, however, the Franks were finally able to gain the initiative. By the middle of the eighth century, in the wake of the death in 719 of the Frisian king Redbad, Charles was able to conquer most of Frisia within what is now the Netherlands. Charlemagne completed the Frisian conquest in the last years of the eighth century by defeating both the Frisians and the Saxons and pushing the frontier of his empire to the Elbe river. From then on Frisia was part of the political world of the Franks.

The Frankish conquest of Frisia brought a number of very important changes. Not only were political alignments altered by the new administration, but the establishment of the Frankish church under the bishops of Utrecht gradually undermined many of the old Frisian cultural ties. In other respects, however, the Frankish conquest of Frisia was rather superficial. Contrary to what one might expect, for example, the relatively great wealth and commercial success of the Frisians was not adversely affected. Frisia did not become an occupied land, nor were the lucrative functions of trade assumed by the Franks. Rather, the period from 750 to 850 comprised the golden age of Frisian commerce. Similarly, the general subsistence patterns of the Frisian districts continued to develop along pre-conquest lines. In short, what might be termed a Frisian way of life, stemming ultimately from a peculiar set of man-environment interrelationships that had evolved over more than a millennium in the coastal areas, persisted after the conquest. The preponderant economic role of the Frisians in the early Middle Ages cannot be properly understood apart from these ecologic or man-environment considerations. A close look at the human ecology of the Frisian districts, therefore, will help explain how the Frisians were able to maintain their economic vitality despite Frankish conquest. At the same time, an examination of essential Frisian-Frankish ecologic differences will show how Frisian patterns of economic development remained essentially distinct from dominant Frankish patterns of material culture until the later Middle Ages.[1]

That there were fundamental differences between the Frisians and the Franks was recognized by observers in the early Middle Ages already. In the first half of the ninth century an anonymous biographer of Saint Boniface described the Frisians as a people who lived in water like fish and rarely traveled outside their own territory unless they could do so by boat. Because they lived in what seemed to the writer a remote region, cut off from ready contact with other people, he considered them stupid and barbaric.[2] The author, a priest at Utrecht on the Frisian-Frankish frontier, was a great admirer of Saint Boniface who had been killed seventy-five years earlier by recalcitrant, pagan Frisians.[3] He deliberately painted a gloomy picture in an attempt to show that the Frisians lacked the civilizing and socializing influences of Christianity until they were converted by missionaries like the martyred saint.

If the obvious cultural bias of this observer is stripped away, however, a certain amount of truth remains. The people he was describing in fact were separated physically from mainland Europe. The Frisians lived on the *terpen* or dwelling mounds[4] that they had raised on the flat surface of the treeless salt marsh along the Friesland-Groningen coast (see map). This marsh consisted of marine clays, deposited some time earlier by the sea, covered by a vegetation of various salt-tolerant grasses, rushes, and sedges. Though there was a series of low, sandy barrier ridges at the coast, they formed no unbroken defense against the influence of the sea. The entire

[1] J. G. D. Clark, *Prehistoric Europe: The Economic Basis* (London 1952) 6: "The economic life of early man can most fruitfully be considered in relation to the wider economy of nature." To speak of man-environment interrelationships is to speak in ecological terms. See, for example, the recent statement by John W. Cole and Eric R. Wolf, *The Hidden Frontier: Ecology and Ethnicity in an Alpine Valley*, Studies in Social Discontinuity (New York 1974) 119-121, as well as a review of ecological approaches in recent anthropological research by Robert Netting, "The Ecological Approach in Cultural Study," *Addison-Wesley Modular Publications in Anthropology* 6 (1971). The importance of looking for and analyzing differences as well as similarities while doing comparative history was pointed out fifty years ago by Marc Bloch, "A Contribution Towards a Comparative History of European Societies," in *Land and Work in Medieval Europe: Selected Papers by Marc Bloch*, trans. J. S. Anderson (New York 1969) 58.

[2] "At primum Frisonibus, quibus jam antea praedicaverat, navigio revectus est; qui fere, quemadmodum et pisces, morantur in aquis, quibus ita undique concluduntur, ut raro ad exteras regiones accessum habeant, nisi navibus subvehantur. Hos remotos a ceteris nationibus, ideoque brutos ac barbaros, coelestis semini verbius adiit"; Anonymous of Utrecht, *II vita S. Bonifacii auctore presbyterro S. Martini Ultrajecti* chap. 1. 9, in AS June 1.471.

[3] The probable author of this piece was Frederik, bishop of Utrecht (ca. 820-835); see D. P. Blok, *De Franken in Nederland*, ed. 2, Grote Fibula Serie (Bussum 1974) 114; and J. Romein, *Geschiedenis van de Noord-Nederlandse geschiedschrijving in de Middeleeuwen: Bijdrage tot de beschavingsgeschiedenis* (Haarlem 1932) no. 2.

[4] *Terp* (plural, *terpen*) is a Frisian word, originally meaning village, that has come into common use to describe the elevated dwelling mounds of the coastal clay regions of the modern province of Friesland. In the province of Groningen the word most used is *wierde*, while across the Ems in Germany the most common word is *Wurt*. Other forms, such as -*werd*, -*wird*, or -*ward*, appear widely in both the Netherlands and Germany as place-name endings. See H. T. Waterbolk, "Terpen, milieu en bewoning," in *Terpen — Mens en milieu*, ed. J. W. Boersma, Triangelreeks (Haren, Groningen 1970) 7.

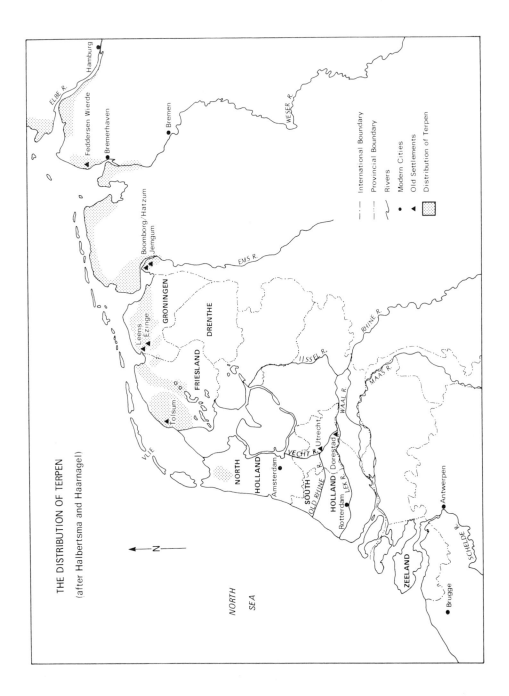

THE DISTRIBUTION OF TERPEN
(after Halbertsma and Haarnagel)

landscape was intersected by a network of tidal creeks and gullies. Twice each day the tides would force salt water up these creeks and gullies and into the salt marsh; at low tide the waters would flow out to sea once again.[5] The *terpen* that were thrown up on this landscape were not intended to change the flow of waters as later dikes were. They were established, instead, as a defensive reaction to the postglacial rise in sea level[6] and to the storm surges associated with the periodic transgressive phases of the sea.[7] They provided a high and dry base on which to construct dwellings, a place

[5] W. A. van Es, "Friesland in Roman Times," *Berichten van de Rijksdienst voor het Oudheidkundig Bodemonderzoek* 15/16 (1965/1966) 37-39; L. J. Pons, "De zeekleigronden," in *De Bodem van Nederland: Toelichting bij de bodemkaart van Nederland, schaal 1:200,000,* Stichting voor Bodemkaartering (Wageningen 1965) 26-34, 62-63; *Bodemkaart van Nederland, schaal 1:200,000,* Stichting voor Bodemkaartering (Wageningen 1961) sheets 1-2; H. Halbertsma, *Terpen tussen Vlie en Eems: Een geografisch-historische Benadering,* Vereniging voor Terpenonderzoek (Groningen 1963) 2, 99; P. C. J. A. Boeles, *Friesland tot de elfde eeuw: Zijn voor en vroege geschiedenis,* ed. 2 (The Hague 1951) 81-82; and T. Edelman, "Oude Ontginningen van de veengebieden in de Nederlandse kuststrook," *Tijdschrift voor economische en sociale geografie* 49 (1958) 239-240. See also D. P. Blok, "Histoire et toponymie: l'example des Pays-Bas dans le haut moyen âge," *Annales: Économies, sociétés, civilisations* 24 (1969) 919, 922; and J. M. G. van der Poel, "De Landbouw in het verste verleden," *Berichten van de Rijksdienst voor het Oudheidkundig Bodemonderzoek* 10/11 (1960/1961) 174-175. For the geographical distribution of *terpen,* see Halbertsma 2, 99. In the area of the modern province of Friesland, many of the earliest settlements were built directly on the marshes, without *terpen,* indicating that the sea was not a constant threat to human occupation; Boeles 75, 81-83. Occupation of the marine marsh region may have begun as early as 600 B.C. with the first *terpen* erected by 500 B.C.: L. P. Louwe Kooijmans, *The Rhine/Meuse Delta: Four Studies on its Prehistoric Occupation and Holocene Geology,* Analecta praehistorica leidensia 7 (Leiden 1974) 43-44.

[6] G. D. van der Heide, "Dijkbouw door de eeuwen heen," in *Antiquity and Survival* 2 nos. 5-6: *Honderd Eeuwen Nederland,* ed. J. E. Bogaers, et al. (The Hague 1959) 266. The rise in sea level has been more or less continuous since the most recent glaciation, though the pace has gradually diminished. By 6000 B.C. it was about 20 meters below the present level. Between 6000 and 3000 B.C. the level of the sea rose by an average of 50 centimeters per century; between 3000 and 1000 B.C. the rate was about 15 centimeters per century. By the beginning of our era the level of the sea was about a meter below what it is today. There have been many attempts to plot this postglacial sea level rise, and many of these are represented and carefully discussed in Louwe Kooijmans 50-69; and S. Jelgersma, *Holocene Sea Level Changes in the Netherlands,* Mededelingen van de Geologische Stichting, ser. C-VI, Monografiën: Reeks behandelende de uitkomsten van nieuwe geologisch-palaeontologische onderzoekingen van de ondergrond van Nederland 7 (Maastricht 1961) 10-12 and chap. 4. The final curve in Louwe Kooijmans 68 perhaps best incorporates the most recent scholarship; it is a curve corrected to solar years of the relative rise in Mean High Water (MHW) level since 5000 B.C. Human occupation always took place above MHW; *ibid.* 64.

[7] Though the sea level rise was continuous since the last glaciation, MHW fluctuated considerably, due to alternating transgressive and regressive phases of the sea: the former were periods of great storm activity that would produce storm surges or unusually high water levels; the latter were periods in which the sea was relatively calm with few or no storm surges. Some eleven transgressive phases have been identified, of which the following have a bearing on the salt marsh areas occupied by the Frisians: 400-100 B.C., A.D. 250-600, and A.D. 800-1000. See William H. TeBrake, "The Making of a Humanized Landscape in the Dutch Rijnland, 950-1350: Ecological Change in a Coastal Lowland," Ph.D. diss. (University of Texas at Austin 1975) 55. The dates given should be considered nothing more than wide limits between which heightened storm activity occurred.

of security for livestock, and space for a well or a small pond or pool in which to collect precipitation for use as potable water.[8] As the ninth-century observer suggested, however, the inhabitants of this landscape were actually separated from mainland Europe by a lower lying band of lagoons and occasional brackish to freshwater peat growth, traversable only by boat along natural waterways.[9]

The priest from Utrecht was partially correct in at least one other respect. As he intimated, the Frisians in fact differed culturally from the inhabitants of the more inland areas. He was wrong, however, in automatically assuming that these differences could be removed simply by converting them to Christianity and integrating them into the political sphere of the Franks. The cause of the cultural variance was much more fundamental than that, ultimately rooted in the peculiar man-environment interrelationships or human ecology that had evolved in the coastal areas over a period of some twelve centuries. Because natural conditions in force there were quite different from those pertaining elsewhere, especially in the inland portions of the Frankish world, the results of the man-environment equations were considerably different as well.[10]

NATURAL CONDITIONS AND TERP-BUILDING

A wide variety of evidence clearly shows that the people who became the Frisians began to move into the coastal marshes of the northern Netherlands before the middle of the last millennium B.C. A few of the new residents may have come from the marine clay areas to the west, the northeastern part of the modern province of North Holland, as well as from the coastal dunes of South and North Holland. Most, however, came from the south and east, as part of a larger movement of peoples from the middle Weser valley towards the west. Many of the latter stayed in the sandy regions of the modern province of Drenthe where they mixed with the already ancient population there, while others moved down onto the newly emerged clay soils of the coast of Friesland and Groningen. This first occupation of the Friesland-Groningen coast began during a regression phase of the sea, a period in which the mean high water level was lower than before, thus reducing temporarily the danger of

[8] Boeles 69, 194-195; Halbertsma 99: and J. A. Brongers, et al., "Prehistory in the Netherlands: An Economic-Technological Approach," *Berichten van de Rijksdienst voor het Oudheidkundig Bodemonderzoek* 23 (1973) 14.

[9] Pons (n. 5 above) 27-34, 62-63; *Bodemkaart van Nederland* (n. 5 above) sheets 1-2; Halbertsma (n. 5 above) 2, 99; Boeles (n. 5 above) 81-82; and Edelman (n. 5 above) 239-240.

[10] A satisfactory solution to complicated man-environment equations is not easily achieved. Ideally, the data concerning the human ecology of a particular region would be of such quantity and quality that it could be subjected to sophisticated statistical manipulation. But, for many areas of northwestern Europe including Frisia in the early Middle Ages, still essentially straddling the boundary between the prehistoric and the historic, the data are so scanty that one can only hope to draw some of the main lines of man-environment relationships.

flooding. Settlement was also possible at this time in the Rhine estuary and along the lower courses of the Ems, Weser, and Elbe rivers (see map).[11]

The earliest habitation sites along the North Sea in Friesland and Groningen were built on the flat marsh surface itself.[12] They consisted of small collections of farm units that included long, narrow farm houses with an east-west orientation, granaries or storage pits, and occasionally worksheds.[13] That conditions were temporarily favorable for settlement is indicated by the fact that salt-intolerant crops at times could be grown on the flat marsh surface behind the coastal ridges, suggesting that a certain amount of desalination of the marine clay could occur, particularly during regression phases of the sea.[14]

[11] A. Russchen, "Origin and Earliest Expansion of the Frisian Tribe," *It Beaken: Tydskrift fan de Fryske Akademy* 30 (1968) 143, 149 map 7; *idem*, "Tussen Aller en Somme," *It Beaken: Tydskrift fan de Fryske Akademy* 29 (1967) 95; H. T. Waterbolk, "The Occupation of Friesland in the Prehistoric Period," *Berichten van de Rijksdienst voor het Oudheidkundig Bodemonderzoek* 15/16 (1965/1966) 25-26; W. Haarnagel, "De prähistorischen Siedlungsformen in Küstengebiet der Nordsee," in *Beiträge zur Genese der Siedlungs- und Agrarlandschaft in Europa*, Geographische Zeitschrift: Beihefte (Wiesbaden 1968) 68, 71; Blok (n. 5 above) 919, 922; and van der Poel (n. 5 above) 174-175.

[12] There were a number of distinct zones within the coastal marsh area that supported characteristic vegetation complexes. On the lower marsh, daily flooded and exposed by the tides, were *Salicornietum strictae*, consisting mostly of *Salicornia herbacea* and occasionally *Suaeda maritima*. Next there was a zone flooded regularly at certain times, but not on a daily basis, that contained *Puccinellietum maritimae*, including *Puccinellia maritima, Limonium vulgare, Spergularia marginata, Perapholis strigosa*, and perhaps some *Suaeda maritima*. The highest part of the marsh was flooded only during times of extremely high water such as the storm surges associated with transgression phases of the sea and during spring tides. The principal vegetation complex here consisted of *Juncetum gerardii*, including *Juncus gerardii, Glaux maritima, Ameria maritima*, as well as *Plantago maritima*. Along the tidal creeks that cut through the marsh *Scirpetum maritimi* grew, including *Scirpus maritimus, Scirpus tabernaemontani*, and *Phragmites communis*. If the raised creek banks were quite sandy, they could support *Statice limonium* and *Artemisia maritima* as well. The first two zones were usually rather narrow, but the third and highest zone of the marsh could extend for many kilometers inland. The first residents of the Frisian-Groningen coastal marshes settled in the broad, highest zone. See W. van Zeist, "De Plantengroei in het terpengebied," in *Terpen – Mens en milieu* (n. 4 above) 27-30; and *idem*, "The Environment of 'Het Torp' in its Early Phases," *Berichten van de Rijksdienst voor het Oudheidkundig Bodemonderzoek* 23 (1973) 351-352.

[13] Waterbolk (n. 11 above) 33; van Es (n. 5 above) 42, 44-46; Boeles (n. 5 above) 93-96; Haarnagel (n. 11 above) 68, 70, 72; W. A. van Es, "Excavations at Dorestad: A Pre-Preliminary Report, 1967-1968," *Berichten van de Rijksdienst voor het Oudheidkundig Bodemonderzoek* 19 (1969) 202, 204-206; *idem*, "Die neuen Dorestad-Grabungen 1967-1972," in *Vor- und Frühformen der europäischen Stadt im Mittelalter: Bericht über ein Symposium in Reinhausen bei Göttingen vom 18. bis 24. April 1972*, Abhandlungen der Akademie der Wissenschaften in Göttingen, philologische-historische Klasse, ser. 3, 83-84 (Göttingen 1973) 1.212-214; and H. Parker, "Feddersen Wierde and Vallhagar: A Contrast in Settlements," *Medieval Archaeology* 9 (1965) 2-3.

[14] Van Es (n. 5 above) 38, 40-41. Not all food consumed in the coastal areas was produced there. Some cereals, in particular, would have been imported. Enough evidence has accumulated, however, to show that crop raising was possible in the *terp* landscape: the remains of stalks, hulls, pods, and other organic material points to this as well as the occasional discovery of fossilized plough traces in the soil. Perhaps some was grown on the edges of the *terpen* themselves, but most would have come from the higher-lying portions of the marsh (the *Juncetum gerardii*

During the fifth century B.C. a new transgression phase of the sea began, causing the abandonment of settlement sites in the Ems, Weser, and Elbe marshes, while most inhabitants of the clay soils in the Rhine estuary retreated into the nearby coastal dunes.[15] In Friesland and Groningen, however, occupation continued; here the reaction to higher mean high water levels because of the new transgression was one of building artificial dwelling mounds, the first *terpen*.[16] Initially, individual dwelling sites were raised, forming small *terpen* with one or a few farm units on them. Through time these mounds fused together to make a number of large *terpen* that were further raised uniformly by deliberate action or by the gradual, unconscious accumulation of debris. With the growth of individual raised dwelling sites into large *terpen*, a new settlement pattern emerged, the radial *terp* village. In contrast to the previous stage, in which the long axis of a house was almost invariabley oriented in an east-west direction, the new villages consisted of a circular arrangement of farmhouses with their long axes converging on an open space in the center. The most thoroughly investigated radial *terp* village from this period is Ezinge, Groningen; by the beginning of the first century A.D., this village contained approximately fifteen farmsteads arranged in a circle on a *terp* that had a diameter of 150 meters and was raised 2.8 meters above present sea level.[17]

Meanwhile, the pre-Roman transgression of the sea had ended by the last century B.C., and, until the fourth or fifth century A.D., conditions for human occupation of the coastal marshes were quite favorable once again. While the radial *terp* villages continued to be inhabited, many new farmsteads were established along coastal or tidal creek ridges and on the flat marsh surface of Friesland and Groningen and in the

---

zone – see n. 12 above), even in slightly saline soils. Recent experiments of planting a variety of food plants by U. Körber-Grohne on undiked salt marsh in northwestern Germany (1960 and 1961) and by W. van Zeist and others on unprotected salt marsh in Groningen (since 1969) have confirmed this. Oats, barley, flax, gold-of-pleasure (an oil-producing plant), celtic bean, millet, and bread wheat were planted. Preliminary results show that, if no flooding by salt water occurred during the growing season, all but millet and bread wheat could give good results. Flooding in the seedling stage or in certain later stages of development, however, would kill many plants if they were immersed for a few hours during several successive high tides. At other times, short immersions were less damaging but could reduce yields. See W. Van Zeist, "Palaeobotanical Studies of Settlement Sites in the Coastal Area of the Netherlands," *Palaeohistoria: Acta et communicationes Instituti bio-archaeologici Universitatis Groninganae* 16 (1974) 364-366; and *idem*, "De Plantengroei" (n. 12 above) 32-35.

[15] Jemgum and Boomborg/Hatzum, for example, on the left bank of the lower Ems, were both abandoned around 400 B.C. They subsequently were buried under a meter of marsh soils; see Haarnagel (n. 11 above) 70-71; and H. Jankuhn, *Vor- und Frühgeschichte vom Neolithikum bis zur Völkerwanderungszeit*, Deutsche Agrargeschichte 1 (Stuttgart 1969) 130.

[16] *Terpen* are found only in the southern part of the North Sea – the Netherlands, Germany, and a small corner of Denmark – even though there are coastal marshes and mudflats of a similar nature elsewhere that presumably could have been inhabited but never knew *terpen*. It was not simply a particular type of environment, therefore, that caused the raising of *terpen*. The peculiar living habits of a certain group of people were crucial. The *terpen* culture covered an area almost identical to the area of Frisian language at its largest extent. See Waterbolk (n. 4 above) 10-11.

[17] Waterbolk (n. 11 above) 26, 30, 33-34; van Es (n. 5 above) 42; and Boeles (n. 5 above) 85-93.

estuaries of the Maas, Rhine, Ems, Weser, and Elbe rivers. With the onset of the post-Roman transgression of the sea in the late third century, however, the new settlements on the flat marshes were increasingly threatened with flooding. The responses to deteriorating conditions were similar to those of the fifth century B.C.: many habitation sites on the coastal marshes between the Maas and the Elbe were gradually abandoned, while others, particularly in Friesland and Groningen, were transformed into new *terpen*. These latter, as before, were first developed as small *terpen* supporting one or a few farmsteads; eventually they fused into larger and fewer dwelling mounds on which radial *terp* villages came into existence.[18]

A third generation of coastal marsh settlements began during the eighth and ninth centuries after the conclusion of the post-Roman transgression. Until the onset of the Carolingian or Ottonian transgression in the late ninth century, small collections of individual farmsteads were established along low ridges or on marsh surfaces throughout the coastal regions from Flanders to southern Denmark. Renewed flooding, however, caused the abandonment of many of these, while others were replaced once again by small *terpen*. Ultimately, many of the latter, in turn, fused into radial *terp* villages, not only in Friesland and Groningen, but also in a number of areas between the Ems and southern Denmark.[19]

With the beginning of dike building in the eleventh century, *terp* construction came to an end. Since then occupation of the low, North Sea coast has been possible without dwelling mounds during regression as well as transgression phases of the sea. Nevertheless, in the approximately fifteen centuries of *terp*-building, from the fifth century B.C. to the tenth century A.D., thousands of *terpen* were raised. In Friesland and Groningen alone, 1190 *terpen* have been identified, excluding those which were at some time covered by marine sedimentation. Many were dug away in the nineteenth and twentieth centuries and spread over agricultural lands to increase soil fertility, but enough of them remain to indicate that they ranged in area from less than one hectare, large enough for one or a few farmsteads, to a maximum of twenty-four hectares. Some *terpen* were raised five to seven meters above the surrounding landscape by the eleventh century.[20]

The most critical time in the development of Frisian culture was the period between 400 and 200 B.C., during the pre-Roman transgression of the sea. In the face of increasing danger of floods, small *terpen* were constructed which evolved into larger

[18] Van Es (n. 5 above) 40, 44; and Haarnagel (n. 11 above) 67, 72, 79. Some flooding began in Friesland around A.D.250; Louwe Kooijmans (n. 5 above) 45.

[19] Haarnagel (n. 11 above) 67, 79; and van Es (n. 5 above) 40. Het Torp, a *terp* in North Holland near Den Helder, was from the Carolingian phase; it achieved its ultimate size and shape between the eleventh and fourteenth centuries. See W. A. van Es, "Terp Research: With Particular Reference to a Medieval Terp at Den Helder, Province of North Holland," *Berichten van de Rijksdienst voor het Oudheidkundig Bodemonderzoek* 23 (1973) 337-345.

[20] Halbertsma (n. 5 above) 25, 99, 265-271; Boeles (n. 5 above) 69-71, 81-83; van der Poel (n. 5 above) 174-175; van Es (n. 5 above) 40; Haarnagel (n. 11 above) 67, 83; and B.H. Slicher van Bath, "The Economic and Social Conditions of the Frisian Districts from 900 to 1500," *A. A. G. Bijdragen* 13 (1965) 98.

radial *terp* villages, while a complete and successful adaptation was made to an environment dominated by the sea.[21] Succeeding regression and transgression periods saw a considerable expansion and contraction of the geographical extent of coastal marsh settlement outside of Friesland and Groningen, but little change occurred in the broad patterns of occupation in the Frisian heartland. New generations of settlements simply went through the same developmental sequence as did the original habitation sites.

The earliest written descriptions of the *terp* districts came after this initial development of Frisian culture:[22] one of the best of these reports was incorporated in Pliny the Elder's *Natural History,* based on his own observations made while taking part in a Roman military expedition through the northern Netherlands into northwestern Germany in the middle of the first century A.D. He reported seeing large expanses of treeless, coastal marsh that were alternately flooded and exposed by the tides, making it difficult to determine where the land ended and the sea began. On mounds raised above the bleak plain, the inhabitants had built their dwellings which at high tide seemed to resemble ships at sea. According to Pliny, these people had no visible means of subsistence besides fishing; they used a sort of dried mud for fuel; and in general they seemed so miserable that to conquer them and include them in the Roman Empire would be doing them a great service.[23] That a representative of Roman civilization and a native of northern Italy accustomed to having firm, dry soil under his feet should have no appreciation of the life style of these far-off people is, of course, understandable. Despite this cultural bias, however, Pliny's comments constitute a valuable early description of the physical geography of the coastal marshes along the North Sea and provide an idea of the spatial and cultural remoteness of the people who lived there. His condescending tone also rather accurately sums up the attitude that the outside world generally held concerning the *terp* dweller and his way of life.[24]

[21] Waterbolk (n. 11 above) 26, 34.

[22] It was termed "Proto-Frisian" by Boeles (n. 5 above) 69-108; see also Waterbolk (n. 11 above) 29.

[23] Plinius Secundus, *Naturalis historia* 16.2-5. See the helpful biographical and geographical notes in *Excerpta Romana: De Bronnen der Romeinsche geschiedenis van Nederland* 1: *Teksten,* ed. A. W. Byvanck, Rijks geschiedkundige Publicatiën 73 (The Hague 1931) 132, 133, 150-151. What Pliny most likely saw were temporary dwelling mounds used by fishermen in the summer only; the permanent settlements were further into the marshes where other means of subsistence prevailed; see W. Jappe Alberts and H. P. H. Jansen, *Welvaart in wording: Sociaal-economische Geschiedenis van Nederland van de vroegste tijden tot het einde van de middeleeuwen* (The Hague 1964) 10; Boeles (n. 5 above) 83; Halbertsma (n. 5 above) 11-12; and I. H. Gosses, *Handboek tot de staatkundige geschiedenis der Nederlanden* 1: *De Middeleeuwen,* rev. ed. R. R. Post (The Hague 1959) 12-14.

[24] Though Pliny was speaking specifically of the land of the Chauci, a group which at that time inhabited the coastal marshes between the Ems and Weser rivers, the later Ostfriesland, his comments concerning physical features apply as well to the land of the Frisians west of the Ems. For the location of the Chauci and Frisians at the beginning of our era, see the map in Jankuhn (n. 15 above) 130. The general problem of Roman attitudes toward barbarians was recently reexamined by Gerhart B. Ladner, "On Roman Attitudes Toward Barbarians in Late Antiquity," *Viator* 7 (1976) 1-26.

FRISIA AND THE OUTSIDE WORLD

The Frisians first mounted the historical stage when the Romans pushed their empire into the Rhine delta. In 12 B.C. the Roman commander Drusus sailed down the Rhine and northeastward along the North Sea coast in a campaign against the Chauci, the new occupants of the coastal regions between the Ems and Weser since the end of the pre-Roman transgression.[25] On his way he defeated the Frisians as well, requiring them to pay a tribute in cowhides. Tiberius in A.D. 5 and Germanicus in A.D. 16 also sent expeditions through the Frisian districts on their way to the east and north. The Frisians remained rather friendly towards Rome until their revolt of A.D. 28 in protest against the unreasonable demands of a Roman official in charge of collecting the hide tribute; after initial Frisian successes, the revolt ended indecisively. They were defeated once again around A.D. 47 by an expedition under Corbulo in which Pliny the Elder took part, but orders were soon sent from Rome telling local commanders to desist from attempting to extend the empire beyond the Rhine. Attention was to be lavished instead on conquering Britain, while Frisians thereafter began to appear as cohorts in the Roman armies. The great rebellion of the Batavians under Julius Civilis in A.D. 69-70 carried with it the Frisians as well as neighboring coastal groups: the Cananefaten to the south and the Chauci to the northeast. After A.D. 70 the Frisians for the most part disappeared from surviving Roman sources except for the report that they visited Roman markets as cattle vendors.[26]

Due at least in part to the onset of the post-Roman transgression of the sea, resulting in serious marine and river flooding, the Roman occupation of the Rhine delta abruptly ended during the second half of the third century A.D.[27] Some

[25] Precisely who the Chauci were and who they were to become is not clearly known. Lucien Musset, *The Germanic Invasions: The Making of Europe A.D. 400-600*, trans. Edward and Columba James (London 1975) 97, suggests that some of them broke away to form the Saxons in the early Middle Ages. Blok (n. 3 above) 15 believes that some of them may have been the original Franks.

[26] See, for example, C. W. Vollgraff, "Eene Romeinsche Koopacte uit Tolsum," *De Vrije Fries: Tijdschrift uitgegeven door het Friesch Genootschap van Geschied-, Oudheid- en Taalkunde* 25 (1917) 71-101; P. C. J. A. Boeles, "De Terpencultuur tot omstreeks 400," in *Algemene Geschiedenis der Nederlanden* 1 (Utrecht 1949) 195-199; Gosses (n. 23 above) 9-19; and Jappe Alberts and Jansen (n. 23 above) 14-15. Tacitus described the Frisian revolt of A.D. 28 in his *Annales* 4.72-73.

[27] Until rather recently, it was thought that this withdrawal stemmed from internal administrative and political problems or from external pressures applied by barbarian tribes. It seems, however, that the Roman retreat from the Rhine delta may have been caused at least in part by deteriorating drainage conditions, phenomena for which the Romans apparently had no response. In any case, archaeologists have found the remains of some Roman occupation sites near the mouth of the Old Rhine covered by marine sediments. See Blok (n. 3 above) 19; H. Sarfatij, "Friezen-Romeinen-Cananefaten: Balans van tien jaar oudheidkundig bodemonderzoek (1960-1970) in de provincies Noord- en Zuid-Holland," *Holland: Regionaal-historisch tijdschrift* 3 (1971) 175; *idem*, "Middeleeuwse Mens en eeuwig water: Veranderingen in landschap en bewoning aan de monden van Rijn en Maas gedurende de middeleeuwen," *Zuid-Holland* 14 (1968) 20; R. G. den Uyl, "Dorpen in het rivierkleigebied," *Bulletin van de Koninklijke Nederlandse Oudheidkundige Bond*, ser.6, 11 (1958) 101; and Jappe Alberts and Jansen (n. 23 above) 16.

flooding also occurred in the Frisian districts with the subsequent loss of some settlement sites,[28] although in many instances a second generation of *terpen* came into being. For the next several centuries, however, very little is known from written records concerning events in northwestern Europe.

When documents began to flow again during the Merovingian era, the Frisians figured prominently in the affairs of northwestern Europe. The *Lex Frisionum*,[29] the earliest compilation of Frisian law carried out at the command of Charlemagne in the beginning of the ninth century, recognized three main divisions of Frisia that together encompassed the entire North Sea coast from northern Flanders to the Weser river in northwestern Germany: "inter Fli et Sincfalam,"[30] "inter Laubachi et Wiseron,"[31] and "inter Laubachi et Flehi."[32] The last of these was the Frisian heartland, while the first two were areas into which the Frisians had expanded. [33] Whether this expansion occurred through outright conquest, colonization, or the simple merger of a number of discrete groups into a sort of confederation is not clear. Perhaps it was a combination of all three. In general, the territorial expansion of the Frisians in the early Middle Ages should be seen as part of the widespread migrations that took place throughout Europe on the heels of the collapse of the Roman Empire.[34] At any rate, by the early Middle Ages the word Frisian had

[28] Louwe Kooijmans (n. 5 above) 45; Waterbolk (n. 4 above) 18; and Waterbolk (n. 11 above) 33.

[29] *Lex Frisionum*, ed. Karl von Richthofen, MGH Legum nationum Germanicarum 3.656-682.

[30] All of the western Netherlands from the Vlie in the north to the Sincfal near Brugge in Flanders, often designated as Westfriesland or West Frisia. This is not to say, however, that Frisians settled the entire coast as far south as Flanders. Rather, they exercised strong political and economic influence there. The southern limit of concentrated Frisian settlement according to Blok was in the vicinity of The Hague or the area of the mouth of the Maas river. He places it there on the basis of his researches into the distribution of toponyms betraying peculiarly Frisian characteristics as well as his discovery that this area formed the southern limit of the diffusion of the *aasdom*, the typically Frisian manner of administering justice and regulating inheritance. See D. P. Blok, "Plaatsnamen in Westfriesland," *Philologia Frisica anno 1966* 319 (1968) 15-18; *idem*, "De Vestigingsgeschiedenis van Holland en Utrecht in het licht van de plaatsnamen," in M. Gysseling and D. P. Blok, *Studies over de oudste plaatsnamen van Holland en Utrecht*, Bijdragen en Mededelingen der Naamkunde-Commissie van de Koninklijke Nederlandse Akademie van Wetenschappen 17 (Amsterdam 1959) 15, 24; *idem*, "Holland und Westfriesland," *Frühmittelalterliche Studien: Jahrbuch des Instituts für Frühmittelalterforschung der Universität Münster* 3 (1969) 348-350; and *idem*, "Opmerkingen over het aasdom," *Tijdschrift voor rechtsgeschiedenis* 31 (1963) 243-274. See also S. J. Fockema Andreae, "Friesland van de vijfde tot de tiende eeuw," in *Algemene geschiedenis der Nederlanden* 1 (Utrecht 1949) 394-395; and S. van Leeuwen, *Costumen, Keuren ende ordinnatien van het baljuschap ende lande van Rijnland* (Leiden 1667) 13, 231.

[31] Between the Lauwers — essentially the boundary between the provinces of Friesland and Groningen — and the Weser river in northwestern Germany.

[32] The modern Netherlands province of Friesland.

[33] See the *Lex Frisionum* (n. 29 above) throughout, as well as such studies as Blok, "Holland und Westfriesland" (n. 30 above) 347; and H. Halbertsma, "The Frisian Kingdom," *Berichten van de Rijksdienst voor het Oudheidkundig Bodemonderzoek* 15/16 (1965/1966) 73-74.

[34] However, unlike the other migrating groups of the period, who left their old places of residence to occupy new lands, the Frisians never abandoned their heartland. According to J. F. Niermeyer, *De Wording van onze volkshuishouding: Hoofdlijnen uit de economische geschiedenis der noordelijke Nederlanden in de middeleeuwen*, Sevire's Encyclopaedie, afdeeling

become a collective designation much like Frank or Saxon that reflected the commonality of political, social, economic, and linguistic interests of many groups formerly considered separate.[35]

The Frisians who expanded into neighboring coastal areas during the fifth and sixth centuries, however, were part of a larger interaction sphere that included linguistic, cultural, and economic similarities and connections. During the fifth century, Anglo-Saxons moved into and through Frisia. That some hostilities between the newcomers and the old residents may have occurred is suggested by a layer of ashes found in many *terpen*. In general, however, there was a peaceful mixing and partial merging of two already quite similar groups of people. Somewhat later, many of these same Anglo-Saxons and similar groups from elsewhere in northern Europe, including some Frisians, took part in the better known Anglo-Saxon invasion of England, while many others stayed in Frisia, helping to create a revitalized Frisian culture.[36] Those who went on to England, however, continued to maintain close contacts with their places of origin across the North Sea.[37]

The new North Sea ties were expressed first of all in linguistic similarities. Old Frisian, Old English, to a lesser extent Old Saxon, as well as some of the dialects of

---

geschiedenis B-3/2 (The Hague 1946) 13, the Frisians were the only group beyond the Roman frontier that survived the period of the great migrations in essentially the same locality.

[35] Blok (n. 3 above) 12-17. Gosses (n. 23 above) 23-24, 28; C. Verlinden, "De Frankische kolonisatie," in *Algemene Geschiedenis der Nederlanden* 1 (Utrecht 1949) 249; and Musset (n. 25 above) 11-12, 69.

[36] Boeles (n. 5 above) 207-258; Gosses (n. 23 above) 28; Jappe Alberts and Jansen (n. 23 above) 17, 22; Halbertsma (n. 5 above) 67-69, 71; Dirk Jellema, "Frisian Trade in the Dark Ages," *Speculum* 30 (1955) 16, 24; Musset (n. 25 above) 97-100; and A. Russchen, "Keramiek en ritueel in de vijfde eeuw," *It Beaken: Tydskrift fan de Fryske Akademy* 32 (1970) 129.

[37] Blok (n. 3 above) 27; Musset (n. 25 above) 97, 108-109, 208; and David Wilson, *The Anglo-Saxons*, ed. ? (Harmondsworth 1971) 27. A body of water like the North Sea offered no real difficulties for communications. Once in possession of ships and navigation skills, it was much easier for groups like the Anglo-Saxons or Frisians to travel by water than by land; see *De "Noordzeecultuur": Een Onderzoek naar de culturele relaties van de landen rond de Noordzee in de vroege middeleeuwen*, University of Amsterdam, Albert Egges van Giffen Instituut voor Prae- en Protohistorie, Working Paper 2: Project middeleeuwse archeologie 1972-1974 (Amsterdam 1975) 5. Close connections existed between the British Isles and the Continent at least since the Bronze Age; see J. J. Butler, *Bronze Age Connections Across the North Sea: A Study in Prehistoric Trade and Industrial Relations between the British Isles, the Netherlands, North Germany and Scandinavia, c. 1700-700 B.C.*, Palaeohistoria: Acta et communicationes Instituti bio-archaeologici Universitatis Groninganae 9 (Groningen 1963). The nature of political boundaries in the early Middle Ages further illustrates this point. It was common for dense woods, difficult for armies to penetrate, to serve as buffer zones between political entities; see J. K. de Cock, *Bijdrage tot de historische geografie van Kennemerland in de middeleeuwen op fysisch-geografische grondslag* (Groningen 1965) 22, 52; W. Gordon East, *The Geography Behind History* ed. 2 (London 1965) 100; Richard Koebner, "The Settlement and Colonization of Europe," in *The Cambridge Economic History of Europe* 1: *The Agrarian Life of the Middle Ages*, ed. 2 M. M. Postan (Cambridge 1966) 21; and H. C. Darby, "The Fenland Frontier in Anglo-Saxon England," *Antiquity* 8 (1934) 185-201. Rivers, in contrast, served rather unsatisfactorily as political boundaries; see, for example, S. J. Fockema Andreae, "Stein: Het Ontstaan van een vrije hooge heerlijkheid op de grenzen van Holland en van hare bestuursorganen," *Tijdschrift voor geschiedenis* 47 (1932) 403-404.

Holland, Zeeland, and Flanders belonged to the North Sea or Coastal Germanic group of languages.[38]

Further, the archaeological record of the early Middle Ages shows there were broad commercial connections between Scandinavia, England, and Frisia based on extensive water-borne trade. Attacks by Avars and Slavic groups in central Europe around 550 severed the old commercial routes between the Baltic and Mediterranean Seas. New connections were sought westward along the Rhine river and the Alpine passes and after 570, in response to Langobard attacks in northern Italy, along the Maas river-Marseille route. After 620 the Rhine-Alps connection was restored, marking the real beginning of the emergence of Dorestad, the Netherlands, as the preeminent international commercial center. Since the sixth century, Anglo-Saxons, Scandinavians, and especially the Frisians had capitalized on those new routes.[39]

Finally, there were various cultural similarities between the North Sea lands. These were expressed in similar forms of pottery and jewelry from England, Frisia, and Scandinavia.[40] The existence of close cultural relations between the coastal areas on all sides of the North Sea appeared as well in such sagas as *Beowulf,* in which a Frisian king named Finn is mentioned alongside other figures like Beowulf and Hygelac as leaders of groups of Angles, Saxons, Danes, Jutes, Frisians, and others fighting out their endless battles.[41]

The North Sea interaction sphere may have had its greatest influence on the affairs of northern Europe, however, by virtue of its being vibrantly pagan. Near the end of the sixth century, the Frankish church experienced a series of serious setbacks. The bishopric of Tournai (Doornik), for example, was moved southward to

[38] Blok (n. 3 above) 27; B. H. Slicher van Bath, "Problemen rond de Friese middeleeuwse geschiedenis," in his *Herschreven Historie: Schetsen en studiën op het gebied der middeleeuwse geschiedenis* (Leiden 1949) 266; A. Russchen, "Jutes and Frisians," *It Beaken: Tydskrift fan de Fryske Akademy* 26 (1964) 30; Musset (n. 25 above) 7; and *"Noordzeecultuur"* (n. 37 above) 20-23.

[39] Blok (n. 3 above) 27, 29-30; Slicher van Bath (n. 19 above) 260, 269-270; Edith Ennen, *Die europäische Stadt des Mittelalters,* ed. 2 (Göttingen 1975) 46; H. Jankuhn, "Der fraṅkisch-friesische Handel zur Ostsee im frühen Mittelalter," *Vierteljahrschrift für Sozial- und Wirtschafts-geschichte* 40 (1953) 202-209; *"Noordzeecultuur"* (n. 37 above) 138; Archibald R. Lewis, *The Northern Seas: Shipping and Commerce in Northern Europe, A.D. 300-1100* (Princeton 1958) 110-178; Jellema (n. 36 above) 16-24; Georges Duby, *The Early Growth of the European Economy: Warriors and Peasants from the Seventh to the Twelfth Century,* trans. H. B. Clarke (Ithaca 1974) 102-107; R. Grand and R. Delatouche, *L'agriculture au moyen âge de la fin de l'Empire au XVIe siècle* (Paris 1950) 11. Actually, however, the trade routes via the Alpine passes and the Rhine were not new in the early Middle Ages. They, as well as overland routes further east, were already in use in the early second millennium B.C.; see Stuart Piggott, *Ancient Europe from the Beginnings of Agriculture to Classical Antiquity* (Edinburgh 1965) 120. For the results of recent archaeological investigations at Dorestad, see van Es, "Excavations at Dorestad" (n. 13 above) 183-207; and *idem,* "Die neuen Dorestad-Grabungen" (n. 13 above) 202-217.

[40] Slicher van Bath (n. 38 above) 265; Jellema (n. 36 above) 17-18; Russchen (n. 38 above) 32; and *"Noordzeecultuur"* (n. 37 above) 38-122, 142, 143.

[41] H. Halbertsma, "De cultuur van het noordelijk kustgebied," in *Honderd Eeuwen Nederland* (n. 6 above) 196; and Blok (n. 3 above) 116. For an account of a Frisian who sang old songs glorifying the exploits of the Frisian kings and people, see D. A. Stracke, "Bernlef," *Historisch Tijdschrift* 4 (1925) 59-70, 150-169.

Noyon in 577, while about the same time the bishopric of Arras (Atrecht) was combined with that of Cambrai (Kamerijk). Previously, the bishop of Tongeren (Tongres) had been forced to seek refuge in the *castellum* at Maastricht; around 590 the bishopric of Tongeren was temporarily combined with the archbishopric of Cologne. This retreat of the Frankish church may have been linked to the renewal of the cremation of the dead in the Netherlands, Belgium, and western Germany during the sixth and seventh centuries. Apparently a powerful and still viable pagan culture arrayed around the North Sea was able to stimulate a pagan resurgence deep into the Merovingian kingdom for a time. That it was partly carried out by force is suggested by the report that Chilperic, king of the West Franks (561-584), was one of the few able to turn back a raid of Frisians and Suevi.[42]

While linguistic and commercial ties between Anglo-Saxons, Frisians, and Scandinavians remained in force for some time, the North Sea interaction sphere was only a temporary affair. The first step in its demise occurred with the conversion of the Anglo-Saxons to Christianity in the seventh century and the second with the conquest and forced conversion of Frisia by the Franks during the eighth century supported by Anglo-Saxon missionaries.[43] This conquest and conversion of Frisia was completed, however, only after a struggle of some 150 years' duration.

During the sixth century, the southward migration of Frisians along the North Sea coast encountered a northward expansion of Franks.[44] The region at the mouth of the Rhine was captured by the Franks during that century, but by the early seventh century the Frisians had once again acquired it. The fortification of Utrecht, however, remained in Frankish hands until the death of Dagobert I in 639. For nearly a century thereafter, the Frisians prevented further Frankish penetration northward; it was during this period that "Greater Frisia" achieved its maximum extent, stretching along the North Sea from northern Flanders to the Weser in Germany. The Frisians also gained control of the Rhine and its tributaries as far upstream as Dorestad, because it was reported that the Frisian king Aldgisl was ruler of this emporium in 678.[45]

Shortly before 690, Franks under Pepin II counterattacked and won a significant battle at Dorestad against Frisians under King Redbad, Aldgisl's successor. By 696 Pepin was in possession of the fort at Utrecht and was minting Frankish coins at

[42] Blok (n. 3 above) 28; Jellema (n. 36 above) 16; Musset (n. 25 above) 13; and *"Noordzee-cultuur"* (n. 37 above) 31-37.

[43] Musset (n. 25 above) 208 suggests the Anglo-Saxon mission to the Continent was evidence of a continued feeling of ethnic solidarity with old confederates across the North Sea.

[44] For an excellent recent treatment of the Franks, from their first appearance until the collapse of the Carolingian empire, see Blok (n. 3 above) throughout.

[45] F. L. Ganshof, "Het Tijdperk van de Merowingen," in *Algemene Geschiedenis der Nederlanden* 1 (Utrecht 1949) 258; Jappe Alberts and Jansen (n. 23 above) 23; Blok (n. 3 above) 32-38; Boeles (n. 5 above) 269-273; Gosses (n. 23 above) 29-31; and J. F. Niermeyer, "Het midden-Nederlands Rivierengebied in de Frankische tijd op grond van de *Ewa quae se ad Amorem habet,*" *Tijdschrift voor geschiedenis* 66 (1953) 154-155.

Dorestad, though the coast to the west and north of Utrecht remained under Frisian control. It was then that Saint Willibrord, consecrated the first bishop of Utrecht in 695, made his initial attempts to convert the Frisians to Christianity. Those who would be converted were promised the special protection of Pepin II. Because such missionary activities were so closely tied to Frankish expansion interests, however, the notions "Christian" and "Frank" assumed rather similar meanings for many Frisians. Consequently, Christianity made little progress in areas not under direct Frankish control.[46]

Pepin's death in 714 and the resulting struggle over succession within the Frankish kingdom gave the Frisians the opportunity to reconquer most of the former territory of "Greater Frisia"; in 716 Redbad sailed his fleet up the Rhine and even threatened the city of Cologne. By 717, however, Charles Martel had emerged as leader of the Franks. He defeated his Frisian rival in a battle that yielded Utrecht in 718. The death of Redbad the following year finally made possible the conquest of most of Frisia within what is now the Netherlands by 734. Once again missionaries, this time both Saint Willibrord and Saint Boniface, attempted to convert the Frisians. Only very slowly, however, did the Frisians adopt the new religion. Boniface was killed by pagan Frisians in 754 within territory under Frankish control.[47]

Toward the end of the eighth century Charlemagne defeated the Frisians and the Saxons, thereby pushing the frontier of his empire to the Elbe and eventually the Eider river in northern Germany. Consequently, Frisia ceased to be a disputed border area and slowly became integrated into the larger sphere of western Europe. In the first place, by accepting conversion, the Frisians came into contact with the ideas and perspectives transmitted by the international culture of Christianity. Secondly, through conquest, the long arm of imperial power came to be felt by virtue of royal possessions, the wilderness *regalia* (royal rights to the disposal of unexploited land and water), and legal and political administration (through the counts and other appointees of the royal court). Because there is no information available specifically for Frisia, one could assume the situation there was similar to that pertaining to some other areas.[48] In many respects, however, this may be an erroneous assumption. It was under Frankish rule, after all, that the essential ecological differences between the Frisians and the Franks became obvious.

[46] Ganshof (n. 45 above) 26-61; Blok (n. 3 above) 40; Gosses (n. 23 above) 31-32; Boeles (n. 5 above) 270-278; Niermeyer (n. 45 above) 155; Halbertsma (n. 33 above) 71; and Wilhelm Levison, *England and the Continent in the Eighth Century* (Oxford 1946), esp. 45-69 for early Frisian missions.

[47] Blok (n. 3 above) 46-54; Ganshof (n. 45 above) 261; Gosses (n. 23 above) 31-32; Boeles (n. 5 above) 71-75.

[48] See Blok (n. 3 above) 60-130; F. L. Ganshof, "Het tijdperk van de Karolingen tot de grote Noormanneninval, 751-879," in *Algemene geschiedenis der Nederlanden* 1 (Utrecht 1949) 306-366; *idem* (n. 45 above) 269-270, 272-274; Boeles (n. 5 above) 382-386; 405-515; Gosses (n. 23 above) 33-42; H. van der Linden, *De Cope: Bijdrage tot de rechtsgeschiedenis van de openlegging der Hollands-Utrechtse laagvlakte* (Assen 1955) 81; and de Cock (n. 37 above) 260.

FRISIAN-FRANKISH ECOLOGICAL DIFFERENCES

The *terpen* on which the Frisians lived had served them extremely well. First of all, they provided a stable place of dwelling, some of them for nearly twelve centuries before the Frankish conquest.[49] Secondly, they were able to support a surprisingly large population. This was already the case during the Roman period,[50] and by the early Middle Ages the *terp* districts of the northern Netherlands were among the most populous areas of western Europe. The most careful estimates of total population of the *terpen* in Friesland and Groningen alone suggest there were 35,600 inhabitants by A.D. 900, with densities of up to twenty per square kilometer. In western Europe only the Paris basin and parts of Flanders were more densely occupied at that time.[51]

A population of such size and density required a substantial food base. The average adult male living in western Europe during the ninth century, it is estimated, required a minimum intake of approximately 3000 calories each day, while the average adult female needed about 2400 calories.[52] The average for an entire

---

[49] According to Niermeyer (n. 34 above) 13, the Frisians were the only group beyond the Roman frontier able to survive the period of barbarian migrations in essentially the same locality. There was, of course, an influx of Anglo-Saxons in the fifth century; see *ibid.* 13-14; Boeles (n. 5 above) 207-258; Gosses (n. 23 above) 28; and Jappe Alberts and Jansen (n. 23 above) 17, 22. But as Halbertsma (n. 5 above) 67-69, 71, and Russchen (n. 36 above) 129 point out, the Frisian lands were not entirely put to the sword and flame. There is no evidence to suggest that the Frisians were at any time displaced; rather, they were able to absorb the newcomers and form a revitalized Frisian culture. See also Jellema (n. 36 above) 16; and van Es (n. 5 above) 65-66.

[50] H. Halbertsma, "Enkele Aantekeningen bij een verzameling oudheden afkomstig uit een terpje bij Deinum," *Jaarverslag van de Vereniging voor Terpenonderzoek* 33-37 (1948) 243, estimates that Westergo alone, the northwest corner of the province of Friesland, may have had a population of at least 20,000 during the first century of our era, a density of 27 people per square kilometer. While Slicher van Bath (n. 20 above) 100, thinks this figure may be somewhat too high, van Es (n. 5 above) 53 considers it realistic. Such high population densities among relatively "backward" groups need not catch one too much by surprise. William S. Cooter, "Preindustrial Frontiers and Interaction Spheres: Aspects of the Human Ecology of Roman Frontier Regions in Northwest Europe," Ph.D. diss. (University of Oklahoma 1976) 47, has made an excellent case for saying that even quite "primitive" agricultural societies "lacking states, bureaucracies, kings, or socio-economic classes" can often equal and even surpass complex societies in agricultural production and population density.

[51] Van Es (n. 5 above) 52-53; B. H. Slicher van Bath, "De paleodemografie," *A. A. G. Bijdragen* 15 (1970) 191; *idem*, "Le climat et les récoltes en haut moyen âge," in *Agricoltura e mondo rurale in Occidente nell'alto medioevo*, Settimane di studio del Centro italiano di studi sull'alto medioevo 13 (Spoleto 1966) 421-422; and especially *idem* (n. 20 above) 98-102, 131-133. In this last study, this author assessed the total population in 900 at 42,500 for the area of the present provinces of Friesland and Groningen, including the higher Pleistocene sands to the south. If the higher-lying areas are eliminated from this total, the estimate for the *terpen* in Friesland and Groningen (i.e., Westergo, Oostergo, Westerkwartier, Hunsego, and Fivelgo) is 35,600.

[52] These are the estimates supplied by M. Rouche, "La faim à l'époque carolingienne: Essai sur quelques types de rations alimentaires," *Revue historique* 508 (1973) 314-315, though he suggests that those engaged in heavy labor may have required as much as 4500 and 3000 calories per day respectively. W. Abel, *Geschichte der deutschen Landwirtschaft vom frühen Mittelalter bis zum 19. Jahrhundert*, Deutsche Agrargeschichte 2, ed. 2 (Stuttgart 1967) 23-25, assumes an

population may have been similar to that calculated for the late Bronze Age of West Friesland (the northeast section of North Holland): 12,000 calories per day for a family of six with a per capita requirement of something on the order of 2000.[53] The exact proportions of foodstuffs that were actually consumed to meet these caloric minima naturally varied from place to place and from season to season; yet, it is possible to reconstruct what might have been some common diets.[54]

The discovery of some early medieval cooking pots containing food remnants in one of the *terpen* at Leens, Groningen, has provided a valuable glimpse of the dietary habits of the people who lived in the coastal marshes of the northern Netherlands and northwestern Germany in the early Middle Ages. Analysis of the food showed it to consist of a mixture of oats, rye, wheat, undefinable vegetables, and a large proportion of fat, presumably derived from meat.[55] In fact, meat and dairy products seem to have been staples in the coastal areas and had been since the earliest occupation. The long, rectangular houses that occur in all occupation layers of excavated *terpen* combined living quarters at one end with a byre at the other, having space for twenty or more head of cattle in separate stalls. Assuming all their stalls were filled, the residents of the *terp* at Feddersen Wierde, near Bremerhaven, Germany, apparently consumed 100 kilograms of meat and 1000 kilograms of milk products per person annually. These items alone accounted for nearly 1600 of the 2000 to 3000 calories that the average person needed each day.[56]

---

average daily adult requirement of 3200 calories, while Eric Wolf, *Peasants*, Foundations of Modern Anthropology Series (Englewood Cliffs, N.J. 1966) 6, estimates the caloric minima of peasant groups to lie between 2000 and 3000 calories per day. Richard Roehl, "Patterns of Structure and Demand, 1000-1500," in *The Fontana Economic History of Europe* 1: *The Middle Ages*, ed. Carlo M. Cipolla (London 1972) 112, speaking of a later period, suggests that an average of 2000 to 2200 calories per day may have been enough to keep an adult alive and able to do his work, though not enough to keep him in the peak of health.

[53] See R. W. Brandt, "Landbouw en veeteelt in de late bronstijd van West-Friesland," *Westerheem* 25 (1976) 59, 64.

[54] These will be of necessity very general, with great local variance; yet the following two seem to have been the main types.

[55] W. von Stokar, "De Analyse van de spijsresten," *Jaarverslag van de Vereniging voor Terpenonderzoek* 20-24 (1935-1940) 91-93. See as well Boeles (n. 5 above) 455; Slicher van Bath (n. 20 above) 104; van der Poel (n. 5 above) 181; A. T. Clason, *Animal and Man in Holland's Past: An Investigation of the Animal World Surrounding Man in Prehistoric and Early Historical Times in the Provinces of North and South Holland*, Palaeohistoria: Acta et communicationes Instituti bio-archaeologici Universitatis Groninganae 13 (Groningen 1967) 204-205; and Louwe Kooijmans (n. 5 above) 26, 277-278.

[56] Abel (n. 52 above) 23-24, bases these quantities on his reconstruction of the average herds of livestock that he believes were housed in the stalls on the *terp*. The total capacity was 20 to 25 head: 6 or 7 cows older than 3.5 years, 2 heifers 2.5 years old, 1 ox or steer of 3.5 years, and 11 to 14 young cattle and calves. He concluded that by butchering 1 calf, 2 or 3 steers or oxen, and 2 cows each year, 420 to 520 kilograms of beef were made available; he added another 80 kilograms of mutton or pork to bring the total to 500 or 600 kilograms of meat for a 5 or 6 member family. At Ezinge, Groningen, the herds may have contained 30 to 50 head of cattle and horses; see Jankuhn (n. 15 above) 142. Archaeologists have found the remains of churns and cheese molds in the *terpen* that date from the Roman period and the Middle Ages; see van der Poel (n. 5 above) 181, 183. For cereal production, see *ibid*, 175-179, as well as Clason (n. 55 above) 203-206. Louwe Kooijmans (n. 5 above) 26; van Es (n. 5 above) 50-51; and n. 14 above.

The remaining calories were provided by varying amounts of fish, game, vegetables and cereals.[57]

The most common diet within the more inland portions of the Frankish empire during the eighth and ninth centuries, on the other hand, seems to have consisted of a preponderance of cereals in the form of bread, the *companaticum* or accompaniment to bread, and liberal quantities of beer and wine. The cereals, mostly rye, spelt, barley, and oats, were sometimes made into a thick gruel or porridge to which the *companaticum* was added.[58] The latter was the most varied part of the menu. It could consist of fresh or dried legumes, nuts, fruits, vegetables, fish, meat, dairy products, or eggs, with honey for sweetening and rather large quantities of salt and spices for preserving as well as for making the food palatable. The salt and spices, in turn, would cause tremendous thirsts that were quenched by a thick beer (brewed from cereals and likely having the consistency of soup) or wine. In some cases as much as two-thirds to three-quarters of the caloric intake for the inhabitants of the higher-lying parts of the Frankish empire in the early Middle Ages was provided by the consumption of cereals alone.[59]

The differences between the dietary habits of the residents of the North Sea coastal regions and those of the people who lived on the higher and drier soils within the Frankish empire can be explained in part by differences in physical geography. People like the Frisians were prevented from relying predominantly on cereals because such could be cultivated only in certain places in the coastal marshes. During regressions of the sea, barley, flax, beans, and possibly oats could be planted directly on the flat marsh surface, while transgressions would restrict crop-raising to the very

---

[57] Slicher van Bath (n. 20 above) 104; *idem*, "De Paleodemografie" (n. 51 above) 187; van der Poel (n. 5 above) 181; Halbertsma (n. 5 above) 61-63; and Boeles (n. 5 above) 192. On the significance of hunting both terrestrial and marine animals and fresh- and saltwater fishing, see A. T. Clason, "De dierenwereld van het terpenland," in *Terpen – Mens en milieu* (n. 4 above) 37; Boeles (n. 26 above) 213-214; and van Es (n. 5 above) 51.

[58] Though most peasants raised some wheat, they probably ate very little of it; it essentially served either as a cash crop or as something with which to discharge manorial or feudal obligations. Wheat was for the most part a commodity that only the upper classes of society consumed with regularity. Presumably it was something the lower classes wished they could have on their tables; see, for example, Roehl (n. 52 above) 115; Georges Duby, *Rural Economy and Country Life in the Medieval West*, trans. Cynthia Postan (London 1968) 90; and Duby (n. 39 above) 118-119.

[59] Based on the reconstruction of a typical early medieval household in Buckigau in northwestern Germany by Abel (n. 52 above) 24 and average ratios of bread calories to total calories consumed in eight diets analyzed by Rouche (n. 52 above) 315, table V. In addition, see the many comments concerning medieval nourishment in Lynn White, jr., *Medieval Technology and Social Change* (Oxford 1962) 75-76, 158 n. 6; P. Riché, *La vie quotidienne dans l'empire carolingien* (Paris 1973) 205-212; R. Delatouche, "Agriculture médiévale et population," *Les études sociales*, n. s. 28 (1955) 13-23; *idem*, "Le poisson d'eau douce dans l'alimentation médiévale," *Comptes-rendus de l'Académie d'agriculture de France* (1966) 793-798; Duby (n. 39 above) 17-24; *idem* (n. 58 above) 8-10, 66, 90-91; Grand and Delatouche (n. 39 above) 291-355, 361-410, 477-618; Jankuhn (n. 15 above) 141-160; Roehl (n. 52 above) 112-116; B. H. Slicher van Bath, *Agrarian History of Western Europe, A.D. 500-1850*, trans. O. Ordish (London 1963) 84; and *idem*, "De Paleodemografie," (n. 51 above) 180-189.

highest zones of the marsh or to the *terpen* themselves. The inhibiting factors were excess water and high concentrations of salts in the soils. Most cereals require relatively dry conditions during ripening stages, and all but barley are very salt-intolerant.[60] On the other hand, the Frisians were literally surrounded by extensive grasslands, consisting of halophytic or salt-loving grasses, rushes, and sedges that could be successfully grazed by livestock.[61] From the very beginning of settlement, therefore, the economy of the inhabitants of the coastal marshes of the Netherlands and Germany corresponded to physical conditions: animal husbandry, supplemented by fishing, hunting, and locally important cultivation.[62]

The people who lived in the inland portions of the Frankish empire, however, where soils were naturally better drained and did not have high concentrations of salts, were not inhibited from relying predominantly on cereals for their nourishment. Yet, there were no natural conditions that forced them to do so. In humid, temperate Europe north and west of the Alps, both pastoral and arable agriculture could be successfully practiced almost everywhere except in the coastal lowlands. In fact, the prehistoric rural economy of northwestern Europe was a mixed one, with the primary emphasis on pastoral rather than on arable exploitation of the land.[63] The Frisians, therefore, were closer to the traditional patterns of land use and food consumption. The overwhelming reliance on cereals, in contrast, stemmed from a relatively recent importation of a dietary tradition and rural economy that had its origins in the Middle East and the Mediterranean world. It was first introduced into

[60] Van der Poel (n. 5 above) 175-177; van Es (n. 5 above) 50; and W. van Zeist, "Prehistoric and Early Historic Food Plants in the Netherlands," *Palaeohistoria: Acta et communicationes Instituti bio-archaeologici Universitatis Gronginganae* 14 (1968) 155, 157, 160, tables 64, 65, 66 respectively. For the results of modern experiments in crop raising on undiked salt marsh, see n. 14 above. In much of the area between the Vlie southward to the Sincfal in Flanders, territory into which the Frisians expanded during the early Middle Ages, conditions were somewhat different. The coast of the modern provinces of North and South Holland was protected, and still is, by a series of sand dune ridges which sheltered the freshwater swamp behind from the direct influence of the sea. Only at the mouths of the great rivers were high salt concentrations found; elsewhere there were extensive freshwater peat bogs which we.. ..o wet for cultivation. Such could be practiced only in isolated elevated places along the dune ridges or on some of the natural clay levees of the rivers and large creeks; see TeBrake (n. 7 above) 43-70.

[61] Mostly of the *Juncetum gerardii* complexes: see van Zeist, "Environment of 'Het Torp' " (n. 12 above) 350; *idem*, "De Plantengroei" (n. 12 above) 27-30; and Boeles (n. 26 above) 211-212. Along the coasts of North and South Holland, halophytes grew only near the mouths of the great rivers, with freshwater species outside the areas of direct marine influence.

[62] Boeles (n. 5 above) 82, 191-192, 412; van Es (n. 5 above) 50-51; den Uyl (n. 27 above) 100; Niermeyer (n. 34 above) 19-21; van der Poel (n. 5 above) 175-179; Edelman (n. 5 above) 239-240; S. Jelgersma et al., "The Coastal Dunes of the Western Netherlands: Geology, Vegetational History and Archaeology." *Mededelingen van de Rijks Geologische Dienst*, n. s. 21 (1970) 132; and Clason (n. 55 above) 9-26.

[63] Piggott (n. 39 above) 235-236, 243; Duby (n. 39 above) 23-24; Rouche (n. 52 above) 313; C. F. W. Higham, "Stock Rearing as a Cultural Factor in Prehistoric Europe," *Proceedings of the Prehistoric Society* 33 (1967) 83-106; Carl O. Sauer, "The Agency of Man on Earth," in *Man's Role in Changing the Face of the Earth*, ed. William L. Thomas, Jr., et al. (Chicago 1956) 58-59; and Cooter (n. 50 above) 232. The Franks preferred stock-raising to cultivation until some time after they had entered Gaul; White (n. 59 above) 55.

northern and western Europe by the Romans, but it was greatly reinforced by the gradual northward diffusion of Christianity, a religion that had made bread and wine the symbols of divine nourishment in its holiest rite.[64] By the seventh century, a diet of bread, *companaticum*, and beer or wine had become the hallmark of cultural advancement.[65]

Because eating habits are so visible, observers like the Utrecht priest were undoubtedly aware of the cultural implications of the two dietary traditions. This knowledge must have played an important role in his rather low assessment of the life styles of people like the Frisians.[66] What such critics did not realize, however, is that the "unfortunate barbarians" they were describing were not necessarily less well nourished than their "civilized" contemporaries who often consumed very little besides cereals. In fact, there is some evidence to suggest that the reverse may have been the case.

Recent examinations of early medieval nourishment for the inland portions of the Frankish world show that diets could often be inadequate. Particularly in the late eighth and early ninth centuries, famines and starvation were serious enough to cause Charlemagne to take measures designed to minimize the consequences of such occurrences in the future.[67] The root of the problem lay in an agricultural economy that produced appallingly low crop yields, at times so low that a substantial portion of the harvest had to be set aside as seed for the next planting. Of course, not every year saw a crop failure; some harvests could be quite plentiful. The average level of productivity, however, was often so close to bare subsistence levels that relatively minor annual or seasonal fluctuations in temperature or rainfall could spell the difference between feast or famine.[68]

[64] Duby (n. 39 above) 17-21; and Rouche (n. 52 above) 313. It is not at all uncommon for conquering, colonizing groups to take their agricultural regimes and traditional diets with them to new environments. This was done by early European colonists in the Americas, for example; see Alfred W. Crosby, Jr., *The Columbian Exchange: Biological and Cultural Consequences of 1492*, Contributions in American Studies 2 (Westport, Conn. 1972) 64-121.

[65] Duby (n. 39 above) 18.

[66] The fifth-century Gallo-Roman, Sidonius Appollinaris, for example, was quite appalled by the eating habits of his "barbarian" neighbors; this no doubt only reinforced him in his opinions of their barbarism; see Duby (n. 39 above) 17.

[67] A. E. Verhulst, "Karolingische Agrarpolitik: Das Capitulare de Villis und die Hungersnöte von 792/93 und 806/07," *Zeitschrift für Agrargeschichte und Agrarsoziologie* 13 (1965) 179-185; Riché (n. 59 above) 63, 294-295, suggests many more famines throughout the ninth century.

[68] Slicher van Bath, "Le climat et les récoltes" (n. 51 above) 403-414, 423, and the discussion 443-447; Duby (n. 58 above) 26-27; Duby (n. 39 above) 28-29, 81-82; Riché (n. 59 above) 63-64, 305. Duby suggests that an extensive rather than intensive approach to land use, coupled with a rather primitive technology, was still characteristic of the cultivation system in the Frankish Empire during the first half of the ninth century. Population growth without an attendant expansion of the food base resulted in some relative overpopulation that only began to be relieved in the period beginning with the second half of the ninth century. The reasons for the appallingly low yields of early medieval cereal production have been examined in detail by Cooter (n. 50 above) 34-59. Swidden agriculture (the clearing of fields by felling and burning trees) could be an amazingly productive system on the brown-earth soils of temperate deciduous forests, yet it would not be particularly destructive as long as the cycle for the regeneration of

During the course of the ninth century, however, agricultural productivity in parts of the Frankish empire began to increase, gradually relieving some of the pressures of population upon food supply. A number of changes were made in agricultural technology and organization that not only gradually increased the quantity of food produced per agricultural unit, but eventually produced a more balanced diet as well.[69] These beneficial effects were not felt immediately in all places, however. One study has shown that eight of nine Carolingian rations examined far exceeded the estimated daily caloric requirements.[70] Yet, complaints of hunger and famine were frequently voiced in the very areas in which these diets were consumed, stemming presumably from the fact that the caloric intake, though quite plentiful, was not

---

vegetation and soil (the fallow period) were sufficiently long (perhaps something under 100 years: pp. 45, 233). If the cycle were significantly shortened, however, a process of degeneration would begin, resulting in a degradation in the structure and fertility of the soil. Expressed in terms of ratios of yield to seed of cereals, Cooter argues that yields 16:1 to 20:1 were possible under a long-term swidden or forest-fallow agricultural system in prehistoric Europe. By the late Iron Age, however, millennia of shorter fallow periods had taken their toll. Yields by the early Middle Ages were commonly on the order of 5:1 or 6:1 (perhaps as low as 3:1 or worse at times) — p. 42. Thus, what has often been viewed as a revolutionary increase in yields in the seventeenth and eighteenth centuries to ratios of 16:1 or greater was nothing more than overcoming millennia of ecological abuse by better management and husbandry and reachieving the production capabilities of prehistoric, long-fallow, swidden agriculture. See also Paul B. Sears, "The Processes of Environmental Change by Man," in *Man's Role in Changing the Face of the Earth* (n. 63 above) 475. In a short period of time, yields of wheat on land newly cleared from deciduous hardwood forest in southern Ontario in the nineteenth century declined significantly; contemporary observers noted changes from thirty-five or forty bushels per acre to twenty-five, although they did not seem to connect this decline to a depletion of soil fertility; see Kenneth Kelly, "Wheat Farming in Simcoe County in the Mid-Nineteenth Century," *Canadian Geographer* 15 (1971) 105-106. Professor Kelly feels that Cooter's findings with regard to yield declines on brown, forest soils are quite realistic (personal communication).

[69] White (n. 59 above) 39-78 argues for an early medieval agricultural revolution, the components of which had been essentially assembled by 800; see also Lynn White, jr., "The Expansion of Technology 500-1500," in *Fontana Economic History of Europe* 1 (n. 52 above) 146-153; and *idem*, "Food and History," in *Food, Man, and Society*, ed. Dwain N. Walcher et al. (New York 1976) 13-15. The new three-field crop rotation system, in particular, encouraged the raising of some legumes, the amino-acids of which would often combine with the limited amounts of proteins in cereals to provide for most protein requirements. Higher protein sources such as fish also became more commonly consumed in certain places — see White, "Food and History" (this note) 16-19; *idem* (n. 59 above) 76, 158-159; Delatouche, "Agriculture médiévale et population" (n. 59 above) 13-23; *idem*, "Le poisson d'eau douce" (n. 59 above) 793-798; and G. Bertrand, "Pour une histoire écologique de la France rurale," in *Histoire de la France rurale*, ed. G. Duby and A. Wallon, 1: *La formation des campagnes françaises des origines au XIVe siècle* (Paris 1975) 66, 68. There is evidence to suggest that the new agricultural regime was beginning to be applied on the lands of some large abbeys as early as the reign of Charlemagne (White [n. 59 above] 78; and *idem*, "The Expansion of Technology 500-1500" 146), but the total effects of it were probably not felt until the tenth century and after; see Georges Duby, "La révolution agricole médiévale," *Revue de géographie de Lyon* 29 (1954) 361-363; White, "The Expansion of Technology 500-1500" 153; and *idem*, "Food and History" 13-21. On the other hand, Cooter (n. 50 above) 42-43, 201-203, calls the entire early medieval agricultural revolution into serious question.

[70] They ranged from 1767 to 6882 calories per day and averaged more than 5200 for adult males; see Rouche (n. 52 above) 315-316.

always properly supplemented by proteins, vitamins, and minerals. An overdependence on carbohydrates could cause gastric and intestinal disturbances that might well feel like constant hunger, while a shortage of the necessary supplementary substances over long periods of time would have dire consequences on health. [71] Though dietary conditions were beginning to improve, resulting in some renewed population growth in parts of the Frankish realm by the late ninth century, [72] the twin dangers of hunger and malnutrition were still real for many.

In comparison with their inland contemporaries, who subsisted on a diet often consisting overwhelmingly of carbohydrates and occasionally deficient in the necessary supplemental substances, the Frisians fared quite well. By obtaining most of their calories from meat, milk products, and fish, they were well supplied with a large proportion of the proteins, vitamins, and minerals needed for maintaining good health. [73] Not only was the population of the *terpen* one of the densest in Europe in the early Middle Ages, but it was, relatively speaking, rather well nourished as well.

The livestock that formed the basis of nourishment for the inhabitants of the North Sea coasts consisted overwhelmingly of cattle. Exhumations of domesticated animal bones from six widely scattered *terpen* east of the Ems in northwestern Germany have revealed that cattle greatly outnumbered all other species of domesticated animals combined; [74] the same situation prevailed in Friesland and Groningen. [75] In the coastal regions of the provinces of North and South Holland, cattle remains were far more numerous than those of all other domesticated species

---

[71] Rouche (n. 52 above) 316-320; and Slicher van Bath (n. 59 above) 84. In the long run, it was the quality and not the quantity of food that most affected the size and composition of early medieval populations in Europe. Though food shortages or actual famine periodically brought high mortality from simple starvation (insufficiency of calories), inadequate amounts of supplemental proteins, vitamins, or minerals in the diet operated in a much more insidious manner. Such deficiencies would cause chronic weakness and listlessness and generally bring on lower life expectancies by weakening an individual's resistance to diseases that were not necessarily fatal to well-nourished populations. There is every reason to believe that it was improperly balanced diets rather than simple starvation that kept mortality rates high throughout the Middle Ages and particularly aided in the contagion and fatality of disease during times of epidemic and famine. See White, "Food and History" (n. 69 above) 12; Slicher van Bath (n. 59 above) 84, 89-90; and Rouche (n. 52 above) 316, 318-320. At times, however, especially after periods of exceptionally high mortality such as a plague or famine, life expectancies could be quite good: better than for the Roman Empire, early modern Europe, and some less developed areas of the world today; see J. C. Russell, "Population in Europe, 500-1500", in *Fontana Economic History of Europe* 1 (n. 52 above) 46. Presumably, the standard of living of the survivors would greatly improve as the lands and wealth of the deceased would be realloted and any pressures of population against the carrying capacity of the land would be relaxed. Consequently, there was often a trend towards a more varied diet, towards a greater consumption of foods containing animal proteins in particular; see Carlo M. Cipolla, *Before the Industrial Revolution: European Society and Economy, 1000-1700* (New York 1976) 200-201; White, "Food and History" (n. 69 above) 21; and Slicher van Bath (n. 59 above) 84.

[72] Duby (n. 39 above) 82-93; and White, "Food and History" (n. 69 above) 20-21.

[73] See White, "Food and History" (n. 69 above) 12; and Rouche (n. 52 above) 313, 317-319.

[74] Based on an estimate of the numbers of individuals represented by each species, the following proportions were calculated: 63 percent cattle, 17 percent sheep and goats, 10 percent swine, 9 percent horses, and about 1 percent dogs, cats, and poultry; Jankuhn (n. 15 above) 145.

[75] Van Es (n. 5 above) 50; and Clason (n. 57 above) 38.

at every one of twenty-two excavated settlements dating from the late Neolithic through the Middle Ages (about 2500 B.C. to the fifteenth century A.D.).[76]

Not only did livestock supply most of the food consumed by the Frisians, they also formed the basis of their entire economy. After the Roman conquest of parts of Frisia, the people who lived there were required to pay a tribute in cattle hides. In addition, the Frisians sold livestock and livestock products directly to the Romans.[77] Indeed, active trade with neighboring groups, which continued into and through the Middle Ages, provides an essential key to the proper evaluation of the human ecology of the Frisian districts.

If the physical geography of the coastal regions of the Netherlands and north-western Germany prevented the Frisians from being primarily cultivators of the soil, it nevertheless offered a number of distinct advantages that more than made up for the lack of choice. A predominantly arable peasant economy binds the agriculturalist to the soil and forces on him a very rigorous regimen of work that is dictated by times of plowing, planting, and harvesting.[78] Given a certain set of tools and techniques, production can be increased essentially by greater inputs of labor alone. The pastoralist, in contrast, is much less bound to the soil and his regimen of work is much less rigorous.[79] People like the Frisians who subsisted on a pastoral economy,

[76] At 15 of the 22 settlements, sheep and goats were the second most numerous, with swine the third; at the remaining 7, swine outnumbered the small ruminants: see Clason (n. 51 above) 9-26, 203-204; Louwe Kooijmans (n. 5 above) 26; and van Es (n. 5 above) 50. Along the North Sea coasts, generally, there was an inverse proportion of sheep and goats to swine. The small ruminants were second only to cattle in those areas where grass was plentiful and woods lacking; swine outnumbered sheep and goats in those areas near higher-lying woods where oak and beech mast was easily available; see Jankuhn (n. 15 above) 146; Abel (n. 52 above) 25; D. Brothwell, "Diet, Economy and Biosocial Change in Late Prehistoric Europe," in *Economy and Settlement in Neolithic and Early Bronze Age Britain and Europe*, ed. D. D. A. Simpson (Leicester 1971) 81; Jappe Alberts and Jansen (n. 23 above) 58-59; and Clason (n. 57 above) 38-40. Other animals included horses, dogs, cats, and chickens; see Clasen 40-41; and van Es (n. 5 above) 50.

[77] A wood tablet from the late first century A.D. found at Tolsum recorded the sale of cattle to some Romans; see Vollgraff (n. 26 above) 71-101; as well as van der Poel (n. 5 above) 181; Clason (n. 55 above) 105; and Boeles (n. 5 above) 129-130.

[78] See, for example, Diana Shard, "The Neolithic Revolution: An Analogical Overview," *Journal of Social History* 7 (1973/1974) 165-170; Netting (n. 1 above) 17; and B. H. Slicher van Bath, "Volksvrijheid en democratie," in his *Herschreven Historie: Schetsen en studiën op het gebied der middeleeuwse geschiedenis* (Leiden 1949) 305-315.

[79] The most serious problem associated with a pastoral economy is the danger of overgrazing. In the water-rich environments of the North Sea coasts, however, this was not a serious consideration. Salt marshes are perhaps the most productive biomes of the entire ecosphere, while mesotrophic and eutrophic plant associations, so common in the peat bogs of the coastal regions of North and South Holland before reclamation, are only slightly less productive. On the relations between changes in labor input and arable agricultural productivity, see Ester Boserup, *The Conditions of Agricultural Change: The Economics of Agrarian Change Under Population Pressure* (Chicago 1965); *idem*, "Environnement, population et technologie dans les sociétés primitives," *Annales: Économies, sociétés, civilisations* 29 (1974) 538-552; and Cole and Wolf (n. 1 above) 141. See also B. H. Slicher van Bath, "Les problèmes fondamentaux de la société pré-industrielle en Europe occidentale: Une orientation et un programme," *A. A. G. Bijdragen* 12 (1965) 14-17, 20; *idem* (n. 78 above) 305-315; and Netting (n. 1 above) 12-17. Cooter (n. 50 above) 44, 233, calculates that the return on labor for livestock-raising was at least five times that of cereal production.

therefore, were not only well nourished, but they also had a certain amount of time on their hands. Along with locally very high population densities, this produced an early functional differentiation among them. In addition to herding and locally important cultivation, hunting, and fishing, such activities as industry, shipping, and commerce became significant ways of life in the coastal regions of the Netherlands and northwestern Germany by the early Middle Ages.[80]

Living as they did where salt water first met land, separated from the continent by wide, difficult to traverse peat bogs and lagoons, the Frisians had become accustomed over many centuries to traveling by water; in fact, it was the only way they could effectively move through their surroundings. As the priest of Utrecht described them in the ninth century, they lived in water like fish, and all evidence suggests that they were extremely competent boatmen and sailors.[81] Further, the Frisians resided at the juncture of the most important river routes of northwestern Europe and the sea. It was only natural, therefore, that they should take an active role in both river and sea trade, especially since they were primarily pastoralists who were not as closely tied to the soil as their inland neighbors.

Not only was it easy and possible for many Frisians to engage in trade; by doing so they filled a function that most of their inland contemporaries did not. The Franks, like the Romans before them, organized their commercial activities along networks of roads that for the most part were quite inadequate for year-round wagon traffic.[82] The Frisians' only real competition in trade came from other constituents of the North Sea world. Because the Frisians controlled the Rhine-Maas-Schelde delta, however, and thereby access into the European interior, they had advantages that Scandinavian and English traders did not have. Until the onset of Viking attacks in the ninth century, therefore, the Frisians played the predominant role in the trade of northwestern Europe.[83]

The Frisians not only traded to secure items that were not available in sufficient

[80] Slicher van Bath (n. 20 above) 104, 106.

[81] See Anonymous of Utrecht (n. 2 above) 471; as well as Niermeyer (n. 34 above) 13, 25; and Slicher van Bath (n. 38 above) 260, 279.

[82] Slicher van Bath (n. 38 above) 269; *idem* (n. 59 above) 33; and Robert Latouche, *The Birth of Western Economy: Economic Aspects of the Dark Ages*, trans. E. M. Wilkinson (London 1967) 132-135. For transport in general see the discussions of Robert S. Lopez, "The Evolution of Land Transport in the Middle Ages," *Past and Present* 9 (1965) 17-29; and Albert C. Leighton, *Transport and Communication in Early Medieval Europe, A.D. 500-1100* (Newton Abbot 1972).

[83] For the North Sea interaction sphere, see above. On the significance and extent of Frisian trade in the Middle Ages, see Jellema (n. 36 above) 15-36; Niermeyer (n. 34 above) 18-28; Latouche (n. 82 above) 134-135, 231; Jappe Alberts and Jansen (n. 23 above) 20-38; Boeles (n. 5 above) 394-405; W. Haarnagel, "Die Grabung Feddersen Wierde und ihre Bedeutung für die Erkenntnisse der bäuerlichen Besiedlung im Küstengebiet in dem Zeitraum vom 1. Jahrhundert vor bis 5. Jahrhundert nach Chr.," *Zeitschrift für Agrargeschichte und Agrarsoziologie* 10 (1962) 152-153; *idem* (n. 11 above) 81, 83; Jankuhn (n. 39 above) 193-243; M. M. Postan, "The Trade of Medieval Europe: The North," in *The Cambridge Economic History of Europe* 2: *Trade and Industry in the Middle Ages*, ed. M. M. Postan and E. E. Rich (Cambridge 1952) 119-124, 155-156, 169-170, 176-178; Slicher van Bath (n. 59 above) 33; and Wilson (n. 37 above) 87-88. For a time in the early Middle Ages the North Sea was known as the Frisian Sea; see Jappe Alberts and Jansen (n. 23 above) 24; and "*Noordzeecultuur*" (n. 37 above) 17.

quantities locally, but they also acted as middlemen between other groups. Because cereals could be raised on only a limited scale in Frisia, some were normally imported. Similarly, because the coastal marshes were treeless, some wood was imported.[84] In exchange, Frisian merchants offered such local products as hides, parchment, leather, articles made of bone and wood, livestock, wool, woollen products, and salt.[85] They also dealt in cloth, tin, and lead from England, cloth from Flanders, armaments and glasswork from northern France, armaments, glass, wine, pottery, and millstones from the German Rhineland, and slaves from wherever they could be found.[86]

Such trade, as well as occasional acts of piracy,[87] made the Frisians relatively prosperous, shown most dramatically by archaeological research throughout north-western Europe. In the first place, all layers of the *terpen*, from the Roman period onward, contained large numbers of imported luxury goods.[88] Secondly, excavations in the *terp* districts have disclosed substantial hoards of coins from all over the then known world, while finds in other places included large numbers of coins of possible

[84] Postan (n. 81 above) 120-121, 155-156; Slicher van Bath (n. 57 above) 37; and *idem* (n. 19 above) 106. See also n. 14 above.

[85] Brongers et al. (n. 8 above) 14-35; Haarnagel (n. 11 above) 72-73, 78-79, 83; *idem* (n. 83 above) 152-153; van Es, "Die neuen Dorestad Grabungen" (n. 13 above) 215-217; Parker (n. 13 above) 4-6, 9; C. A. R. Radford, "The Saxon House: A Review and Some Parallels," *Medieval Archaeology* 1 (1957) 37; and Blok (n. 3 above) 101, 103-104, 106. After decades of discussion concerning certain "pallia Fresonica" mentioned from the reigns of Charlemagne and Louis the Pious, most scholars are now agreed that the cloth could have come from Frisia as well as from England and Flanders, and were all termed "Frisian" because they were brought by Frisian merchants; see the discussion of this in Jellema (n. 36 above) 32 n. 57. Recent archaeological discoveries have convincingly shown that the Frisian industry was just as capable of producing such luxury items of cloth as any other; see van Es, "Die neuen Dorestad Grabungen" (n. 13 above) 215; Ennen (n. 39 above) 52; Jappe Alberts and Jansen (n. 23 above) 34; Brongers et al. (n. 8 above) 21-23; and Clason (n. 57 above) 38-39. For an interesting and readable account of early wool-production and processing, see J. P. Wild, "Prehistoric and Roman Textiles," in *The Wool Textile Industry in Great Britain*, ed. J. Geraint Jenkins (London 1972) 3-18.

[86] See, among others, Slicher van Bath (n. 20 above) 105-106; Jellema (n. 36 above) 15-36; Jappe Alberts and Jansen (n. 23 above) 20-38; and Jankuhn (n. 39 above) 193-229.

[87] As Philip Grierson, "Commerce in the Dark Ages: A Critique of the Evidence," *Transactions of the Royal Historical Society*, ser. 5, 9 (1959) 130-139, and Duby (n. 39 above) 42, 44, 48-57, 75-76, 105, 112-120, have made clear, pillage or piracy, the exchanging of gifts, the payment of tribute, as well as the types of activities we are likely to call trade or commerce all represented different and supplementary ways of circulating wealth and were often carried out by the same individuals in the early Middle Ages. See also Musset (n. 25 above) 12; and Ennen (n. 39 above) 46. The Frisians, too, were not above occasional piracy; see Postan (n. 83 above) 170; Jappe Alberts and Jansen (n. 23 above) 38; Slicher van Bath (n. 38 above) 279; and Blok (n. 3 above) 28. They most likely behaved much like the Vikings who, in addition to plundering, also carried on trade; see Anton C. F. Koch, "Phasen in der Entstehung von Kaufmannsnieder-lassungen zwischen Maas und Nordsee in der Karolingerzeit," in *Landschaft und Geschichte: Festschrift für Franz Petri zu seinem 65. Geburtstag am 22. Februar 1968*, ed. Georg Droege et al. (Bonn 1970) 317, 323-324; Latouche (n. 82 above) 231; Jappe Alberts and Jansen (n. 23 above) 37-38; and Halbertsma (n. 33 above) 79-80. This easy alternation between trade and piracy was already common in Europe as early as the second millenium B.C.; see Piggott (n. 39 above) 158.

[88] See for example, van Es (n. 5 above) 51; Jankuhn (n. 39 above) 193-229; and Haarnagel (n. 11 above) 73, 79.

and certain Frisian origin. In short, the inhabitants of the coastal areas of the Netherlands and northwestern Germany continued to use money throughout the Middle Ages, while in many portions of inland Europe money declined greatly in significance.[89]

The most striking Frisian-Frankish contrasts, however, were revealed by differences in the social and economic organization of society. It was among the Franks that the institutions known as feudalism and manorialism came to their fullest expression, with their close personal ties between vassals or peasants and lords, their tendencies toward local self-sufficiency, and their transactions in kind or personal services. The Frisian districts, on the other hand, never saw the manorialization and feudalization so characteristic of the inland, cereal-growing regions of the Frankish empire.[90] No single cause for these differences can be identified; one can only suggest that the peculiar human ecology of the Frisian districts — expressed in a pastoral economy, the need to import some cereals, extensive trading connections, an early craft specialization, and the continued use of money — created conditions unfavorable to the establishment of such institutions.

CHANGES IN THE FRISIAN NICHE

The various distinctions that have been drawn between the Frisians and their more inland contemporaries in the early Middle Ages represented two contrasting ways of life that ultimately stemmed from different sets of ecological or man-environment relationships. Each way of life betrayed a fundamentally distinct approach to the natural environment that had vast economic, social, cultural, political and attitudinal implications.[91]

---

[89] See, for example, Jellema (n. 36 above) 21-24, 29-30, 35-36; Niermeyer (n. 34 above) 21-22; Slicher van Bath (n. 20 above) 105-106; idem (n. 38 above) 279; idem (n. 59 above) 33-35; Musset (n. 25 above) 208; Karl F. Morrison, "Numismatics and Carolingian Trade: A Critique of the Evidence," Speculum 38 (1963) 408-409, 427-432; P. C. J. A. Boeles, "De Karolingsche Muntvondsten in Friesland," De Vrije Fries: Tijdschrift uitgegeven door het Friesch Genootschap van Geschied-, Oudheid- en Taalkunde 24 (1916) 159-164; Carlo M. Cipolla, Money, Prices, and Civilization in the Mediterranean World, Fifth to Seventeenth Century (Princeton 1956) 10, 12; and Jankuhn (n. 39 above) 209-212.

[90] There is no evidence of extensive institutions of this sort either in the Frisian heartland or in areas of Frisian expansion. See B. H. Slicher van Bath, "Hoven op de Veluwe," in Ceres en Clio: Zeven Variaties op het thema landbouwgeschiedenis, Agronomisch-historische bijdragen 6 (1964) 168-169; idem, "De Nederlanden in West-Europa gedurende de Middeleeuwen," in his Herschreven Historie (n. 78 above) 111-112; idem (n. 19 above) 104-106; idem (n. 38 above) 259-280; idem (n. 59 above) 36-37; Niermeyer (n. 34 above) 30-31; Marc Bloch, Feudal Society, trans. L. A. Manyon (Chicago 1961) 445; Blok (n. 3 above) 93, 98-99, 101; and Jappe Alberts and Jansen (n. 23 above) 20-38.

[91] Recent anthropological research has suggested that there are statistically significant differences in group character that seem to be linked to different systems of environmental exploitation. Robert B. Edgerton, " 'Cultural' vs. 'Ecological' Factors in the Expression of Values, Attitudes, and Personality Characteristics," American Anthropologist 67 (1965) 442-447, found the following differences in attitudes and personality characteristics between groups of herders and cultivators in East Africa: cultivators put great value on hard work while herders did not;

Stated somewhat differently, the two groups occupied and exploited different ecological niches.[92]

It is not surprising, therefore, that the Frankish conquest of Frisia in the eighth and ninth centuries had little or no effect on the Frisian way of life.[93] The Franks were among the most advanced cereal cultivators of their day,[94] but, until extensive reclamations were carried out some centuries later, most of the coastal areas of the Netherlands and northwestern Germany remained too soggy for such exploitation. Livestock-keeping and thriving industry and trade continued as before in the Frisian districts. Becoming part of the Frankish empire actually may have brought greater wealth to the Frisians through expanded trade contacts with the European interior under imperial protection.[95]

---

cultivators tended to consult one another and work in a communal fashion while herders tended to act individually; cultivators were generally more suspicious of and hostile toward their fellows than were herders; cultivators tended toward indirectness, abstraction, anxiety, emotional and impulsive behavior, and often engaged in fantasy, while herders tended toward directness and openness, kept their emotions under control and were more realistic; and finally, those groups that were the most thoroughly pastoral put the greatest value on independence of action for the males of the group. See also Robert B. Edgerton, *The Individual in Cultural Adaptation: A Study of Four East African Peoples*, Studies in Culture and Ecology (Berkeley 1971), esp. 167-197, 271-294; and Piggott (n. 39 above) 181-182. In some respects, Frisian-Frankish differences may also have resembled those that existed earlier between the Romans and barbarians; see Andreas Alföldi; "The Moral Barrier on the Rhine and Danube," in *The Congress of Roman Frontier Studies 1949*, ed. Eric Birley, proceedings of a congress held at Newcastle upon Tyne, 11-14 July 1949 (Durham 1952) 1-16.

[92] A species survives by virtue of its niche. This is not a spatial concept, but one used to describe the complex of activities of a species and the relationships between that species and its organic and inorganic environment. A given habitat or natural landscape will contain many niches, that is, many species will inhabit the same geographical area and develop within that area unique life styles based on specialized adaptations to natural conditions.

[93] The same local environment offers one set of possibilities and limitations to a group of pastoralists and another set to a group of cultivators. See Boeles (n. 5 above) 248; as well as Bengt Anell, "The Ecological Factor," *Folk: Dansk Etnografisk Tidsskrift* 6.1 (1964) 7-8; and Richard Yarnell, "Reciprocity in Cultural Ecology," *Economic Botany* 17 (1963) 333-336. Fredrik Barth, "Ecologic Relationships of Ethnic Groups in Swat, North Pakistan," *American Anthropologist* 63 (1956) 1079-1089, attempting to utilize some concepts from ecology, especially the concept of the niche, to delimit culture areas, came to the following conclusions: 1) the distribution of ethnic groups is not determined by objective or fixed "natural areas" but rather by the distribution of discrete niches that different groups can exploit; 2) differing groups often establish themselves in stable co-residence, often including symbiotic economic ties, if they can exploit different niches; 3) if two groups exploit the same niche fully, the one more powerful militarily will replace the weaker in most cases, and 4) if two or more groups exploit the same niche but the weaker one can better utilize marginal environments, the groups may co-reside in one area.

[94] For the improvements in agriculture among the Franks between the Loire and the Rhine, see, for example, White (n. 57 above) 39-78.

[95] These contacts in many ways seem to have resembled the symbiotic economic ties that Barth found in certain parts of North Pakistan between groups occupying different niches; see Barth (n. 93 above) 1079-1089. Jellema (n. 36 above) 25-34 maintains that during the period 750 to 850 Frisian trade reached its greatest extent with a whole network of Frisian trading colonies along the Rhine in Germany, in England, and in Scandinavia. See also Blok (n. 3 above) 101, 103-104, 106; Koch (n. 87 above) 316-317, 323-324; and "*Noordzeecultuur*" (n. 37 above) 19.

Gradually, however, some changes began to occur in the coastal regions. The progress of Christianity among the Frisians brought them into contact with and eventually integrated them into the culture of the rest of Europe at the expense of the North Sea culture, while some ecclesiastical foundations received properties, rights, and incomes in Frisian territory.[96] Furthermore, there was some Frankish colonization of conquered lands, particularly in the central portions of the Netherlands along the great rivers and in the dunes along the coast of North and South Holland.[97] Nevertheless, the Franks were quite incapable of affecting the ratio of pastoral to arable agriculture in Frisian lands; natural conditions continued to dictate a preponderance of livestock-keeping. The coastal regions of the Netherlands and northwestern Germany remained outposts of settlement in a watery environment with contacts to the interior only along natural waterways. The Frisians persisted as the negotiators of these routes, and they continued to reside in the settlements built on the *terpen* in the coastal marshes.

Eventually the Frisian way of life changed dramatically, and it did so quite apart from the Franks. During the ninth and early tenth centuries the Frisian dominance in the trade of northwestern Europe was partially destroyed, by Viking predations. Further, the sea-faring Vikings, by combining piracy and trade in a particularly aggressive fashion, were able to outcompete the Frisians in their own maritime niche.[98] While Frisian trade in general made a significant recovery after the Viking retreat, it never again achieved its former dominance. By that time, other maritime peoples had also begun to play important economic roles, particularly in the Hansa towns and in coastal Flanders.[99] Most importantly, however, the Frisians began to embank and drain some of their lands around the year 1000. This amounted to creating new ecological niches requiring a stable, resident population to maintain the drains and earthworks as well as to cultivate some of the new lands. Gradually, therefore, many Frisians began to resemble more and more their contemporaries elsewhere, though pastoralism, industry and trade continued to be important occupations in the coastal marshes of the Netherlands and northwestern Germany. [100]

[96] For example, Blok (n. 3 above) 46, 60-72; and Jappe Alberts and Jansen (n. 23 above) 40-43. See also Barth's third conclusion (n. 93 above).

[97] Niermeyer (n. 45 above) and Blok (n. 3 above) 43-46, 72-81, 99, 101.

[98] See, for example, Fockema Andreae (n. 30 above) 403, 405; Jellema (n. 36 above) 34-35; and Latouche (n. 82 above) 137.

[99] Jappe Alberts and Jansen (n. 23 above) 40-56; and Jellema (n. 36 above) 36.

[100] In some of the areas into which the Frisians expanded during the early Middle Ages, particularly along the coast of North and South Holland and along the major rivers as far upstream as Dorestad, changes in natural conditions aided in destroying the traditional Frisian niche. Between 800 and 1000, the mouth of the Old Rhine silted shut while the Lek and Waal branches of the Rhine became the chief tributaries. Consequently, many inhabitants of the western and central Netherlands lost their ready contact with the maritime world. See TeBrake (n. 7 above) 52, 136-137; Louwe Kooijmans (n. 5 above) 120; D. P. Blok, "Probleme der Flussnamenforschung in den alluvialen Gebieten der Niederlande," in *Namenforschung: Festschrift für Adolf Bach zum 75. Geburtstag am 31. Januar 1965*, ed. Rudolf Schützeichel and Matthias Zender (Heidelberg 1965) 222; S. J. Fockema Andreae, "De Oude Rijn: Eigendom van

Finally, reclamation in a sense removed the element of remoteness that the priest from Utrecht mentioned in the early ninth century, by creating a land bridge between the Frisian districts and the continental interior.

Department of History
University of Maine at Orono
Orono, Maine 04473, U.S.A.

---

openbaar water in Nederland," in *Rechtskundige Opstellen op 2 November 1935 door oud-leerlingen aangeboden aan Prof. Mr. E. M. Meijers* (Zwolle 1935) 699-700; Koch (n. 87 above) 323; and W. C. Braat, "Early Medieval Glazed Pottery in Holland," *Medieval Archaeology* 15 (1971) 113. Such changes in relative location acted as a strong encouragement to reclaim the peat bogs of the western Netherlands and become farmers. Particularly in the coastal regions of North and South Holland, reclamation was accompanied by a strong de-Frisianization; during the course of the eleventh century, the people of the western Netherlands replaced their Frisian language by Frankish or proto-Dutch. Changed ecological relationships had undermined old Frisian connections and cemented new ones to the Frankish interior. See TeBrake (n. 7 above) 186-189.

AN ICONOGRAPHIC EXPLANATION OF "THE WANDERER," LINES 81b–82a

•

by George Hardin Brown

The highly rhetorical lines 78-84 of *The Wanderer* present neither syntactical nor metrical problems:

> Woriað þa winsalo,   waldend licgað
> dreame bidrorene,   duguþ eal gecrong
> wlonc bi wealle.   Sume wig fornom,
> ferede in forðwege: sumne fugel oþbær
> ofer heanne holm;   sumne se hara wulf
> deaðe gedælde;   sumne dreorighleor
> in eorðscræfe   eorl gehydde.[1]

However, the meaning of parts of the passage has been the topic of considerable scholarly controversy for over a century. Lines 81b-82a, *sumne fugel oþbær / ofer heanne holm*, has particularly distressed editors and critics. Thorpe, apparently skeptical that even a very large bird could carry off a man over the sea and no doubt recalling the description of a ship as *fugle gelicost* (*Beowulf* 218), queried in a note: "fugel = ship?"[2] Thorpe's suggestion proved attractive to a number of scholars: Wülker sanctioned it, Brooke augmented it to "war-ship," and Krapp and Kennedy's edition, followed by Krapp and Dobbie's standard text in *Anglo-Saxon Poetic*

---

[1] George Philip Krapp and Elliott Van Kirk Dobbie, eds., *The Exeter Book*, Anglo Saxon Poetic Records (ASPR) 3 (New York 1936) 136; however, following T. P. Dunning and A. J. Bliss, eds., *The Wanderer* (New York 1969), I have used no comma at the end of line 79 and a colon in line 81 rather than a comma, as giving better sense. J. W. Bright, "*The Wanderer* 78-84," *Modern Language Notes* 13 (1898) 351, first proposed this punctuation. Dunning and Bliss emend *woriað* to *woniað*, although "the manuscript reading is clearly *woriað*, and the form has not been emended by previous editors." About the reading of that word, however, there has been some confusion, as Fred C. Robinson has called to my attention. Israel Gollancz, *The Exeter Book* 1, Early English Text Society (EETS) o.s. 104 (London 1895) 290, prints *woriað* but claims that the MS reads *woniað*; and Friedrich Kluge, *Angelsächsischen Lesebuch*, ed. 3 (Halle 1902) 142, notes "Gollancz liest *woniað*." Furthermore, the argument used by Dunning and Bliss that *wonað* occurs in "what seems to be a similar context" in *The Ruin* 12, is vitiated by the fact that the MS reading of *Ruin* 12 is clearly *worað*, as R. F. Leslie correctly prints it in his edition of *Three Old English Elegies* (Manchester 1966) 51. See Stanley B. Greenfield's careful critique of Dunning and Bliss's edition in *Notes and Queries* n.s. 17 (1970) 113-116, in which he notes these and other discrepancies.

[2] Benjamin Thorpe, ed., *Codex Exoniensis* (London 1842) 291 n.

Records, gave the proposal wider approbation than it deserves.[3] J. E. Cross, however, has convincingly argued against this meaning:

> Even recently scholars have still noted as a possibility Thorpe's conjecture that *fugel* means ship. This is a mere contextual speculation, for never is O.E. *fugel* in either simplices or compounds anything other than bird. It is used as a comparison for a ship but never as a *heiti* and one supposes that the conjecture arose because it appears from the poem that a single bird could carry a dead man over the high sea. At face value the statement is fanciful and is best explained by parallels which reveal the allusion.[4]

One would expect such linguistic evidence to have laid the nautical conjecture to rest; but in 1971 Kispert undauntedly opined that "possibly it is a figurative expression for 'ship.'"[5] Nonetheless, Cross's point seems incontrovertible, and I believe that an examination of the context and of the topos of the bird and wolf adds further weight to his objection.

The occurrence in ancient and medieval folktales and literatures of huge birds capable of carrying off men might suggest "mythical bird" as a possible meaning for our *fugel*. Grein proposed a griffin (*Greif*), others a roc or an enormous eagle.[6] Such huge birds, capable of carrying a man, occur in many ancient and medieval folktales and literatures. Classical bird-myths had been brought to England. At Bignor Villa, Sussex, was found a large fourth-century mosaic showing the rape of Ganymede, who is "being carried up to heaven by a very large and naturalistically rendered yellow

[3] Richard Wülker, *Grundriss zur Geschichte der angelsächsischen Literatur* (Leipzig 1885) 206, rejects the proposals of Grein (who suggests *Greif*, "griffin") and of Rieger (who suggests an eagle carrying off a child), and concludes: "Deshalb fasse ich mit Thorpe *fugel*=Schiff, womit das Meer sehr gut stimmt." Stopford Augustus Brooke, *History of Early English Literature* (New York 1892) 366 n. asserts that "*Fugel* is the warship"; Bright (n.1 above) 352 cites this as one plausible interpretation; and so do George Philip Krapp and Arthur Garfield Kennedy, *An Anglo-Saxon Reader* (New York 1929) 203, and Krapp and Dobbie (n. 1 above) 290. Marjorie Anderson and Blanche Williams, *Old English Handbook* (Cambridge, Mass. 1935) 350, remark "*fugel*: This has been taken figuratively to mean ship, or literally to mean eagle." "Eagle" hardly seems literal.

[4] J. E. Cross, "On *The Wanderer* Lines 80-84: A Study of a Figure and a Theme," *Vetenskaps-Societetens i Lund Årsbok* (1958-1959) 92.

[5] Robert J. Kispert, *Old English: An Introduction* (New York 1971) 210. Despite Marijane Osborn's contention in "The Finnsburg Raven and *Guðrinc Astah*," *Folklore* 81 (1970) 192 n. 22, that "G. V. Smithers thought that the bird referred to a death ship," for which she cites his entire "The Meaning of *The Seafarer* and *The Wanderer*," *Medium Ævum* 26 (1957) 137-153, and 28 (1959) 1-22, I have not found any such statement in that article.

[6] C. W. M. Grein, ed., *Bibliothek der angelsächsischen Poesie* 1 (Leipzig 1857) 240: "Ich beziehe es auf den Vogel Greif (vergl. die Jugendgeschichte Hagens in der *Gudrun*)." Wülker (n. 3 above) 206 pointed out that the Anglo-Saxon poet was not likely to have known about Hagen's childhood experience. See also Friedrich Panzer, *Hilde-Gudrun: Eine sagen- und literargeschichtliche Untersuchung* (Halle 1901) 190-193. Grein might also have mentioned another, late example of a man being carried off by a bird over the sea, in a version of the Danish ballad *Germand Gladensvend*, in Svend Grundtvig, ed., *Danmarks Gamle Folkeviser* (Copenhagen 1856) 1-3.

eagle."[7] Marvelous birds are well attested in Scandinavian as well as Celtic, Pictish, and Hiberno-English pre-Conquest art. According to Wyatt, "Craigie points out that there is an example of a bird carrying off a man on one of the Celtic stones at Meigle in E. Perthshire."[8] Presumably Craigie's reference is to Meigle Stone No. 9, which represents "a bird seizing a man by the neck, and with the legs of the bird interlaced with the limbs and body of a man";[9] but the bird is not in flight. Craigie could also have cited the very similar Monifieth Stone No. 3, on which is sculpted "a long necked bird seizing a man with its beak by the back of the neck, the legs of the bird being interlaced with the limbs and the body of the man."[10] Such motifs are reminiscent of the zoomorphic interlaces in Hiberno-English art, as in the Lindisfarne Gospels. However, the likelihood that any such mythical bird was in the mind of the Anglo-Saxon poet seems very remote; the substance of the lines really precludes a wondrous bird. A mythical bird, as Cross has noted, would be out of place with a real wolf, real war, and real burial.[11] But Marijane Osborn has recently proposed that the *fugel* is a psychopompos: "It is of course no ordinary bird, but the chooser of the slain, and it is not the warrior's body, but his soul that is borne away."[12] Although the psychopompal motif is undeniably present in some other English works (*Andreas* 862-866; Æthelwulf's *De abbatibus* 174-182 and 576-578),[13] the context of these lines of *The Wanderer* militates against such an allegory here. War, bird, wolf, and sad-faced warrior have dealt with dead men's bodies, not their souls. The beasts are scavengers, as in *Beowulf* 3024b-3027:

> ac se wonna hrefn
> fus ofer fægum   fela reordian,
> earne secgan,   hu him æt æte speow,
> þenden he wið wulf   wæl reafode.

Instances of this realism are to be found in Celtic and Anglo-Saxon art too. Indeed, another northern stone can be cited as iconographic evidence that realistic as well as mythic representations of birds were in sculpture, as in literature. The back of the Pictish Aberlemno Stone No. 2 depicts in the lower right corner a man, wounded or dead with his targe fallen from his hand, being attacked by a bird of prey. The bird is obviously not transporting a soul. This stone seems to commemorate a Danish

---

[7] J. M. C. Toynbee, *Art in Roman Britain* (London 1962) 200 no. 190, and pl. 224.

[8] Alfred J. Wyatt, *An Anglo-Saxon Reader* (Cambridge 1919, repr. 1962) 264 n. 81.

[9] John Romilly Allen, *The Early Christian Monuments of Scotland* (Edinburgh 1903) 330.

[10] *Ibid.* 230 and fig. 243a.

[11] Cross (n. 4 above) 92 n. 57.

[12] Osborn (n. 5 above) 192. This is a suggestive article, but the argumentation makes unwarranted leaps, as, for instance, linking the Finnsburg fragment's raven with the woman of the *Beowulf* digression. There is no element of prophecy or summoning of the bird-psychopomp in the fragment or the digression. See also her "The Inscription on the Franks Casket," *Neuphilologische Mitteilungen* (NM) 72 (1971) 33-34 n. 5.

[13] George Philip Krapp, *The Vercelli Book*, ASPR 2 (New York 1932) 27; Æthelwulf, *De abbatibus*, ed. Alistair Campbell (Oxford 1967) 17, 47.

defeat by the Picts.[14] Similarly, large carrion birds alight to feast on fallen warriors, or to make off with them, on two Gotland picture-stones at Lärbro, the one at Sankt Hammars and the other at Tängelgårda (see fig. 1). On the latter, the bird is enormous, larger than the fallen warrior whose leg it grasps. In the same scene two other great birds wing across the sky.[15]

It has been tempting to identify the presence of the bird and wolf in the lines of *The Wanderer* with the "beasts of battle" convention, found in Old English and in Old Norse. Magoun, who rather uncritically examined this motif as a recurrent oral theme in Old English poetry, cites nine poems and twelve occasions where the animals occur.[16] However, numerous appearances of predatory birds and wolves in Old English literature, as listed by G. Neckel, E. G. Stanley, and F. C. Robinson,[17] indicate that the motif was used to express a more generic concept of violent death, under various circumstances, rather than of battle-death alone. In addition to the poetic descriptions of bodily dismemberment by birds and wolves, such as in *The Battle of Brunanburh* 60-65a, Klaeber first called attention also to two homiletic texts to which *The Wanderer* passage bears "an unmistakable resemblance": Blickling Homily 7 has "þeah þe hie [þa lichoman] ær eorþe bewrigen hæfde, oþþe on wætere adruncan, oþþe wildeor abiton, oþþe fuglas tobæron"; Pseudo-Wulfstan 40 has "eorþe ær forswealh oððe fyr forbærnde and sæ besencte and wilde deor fræton and fugelas tobæron."[18] In both these examples burial is juxtaposed or contrasted to the violent deaths symbolized by the carrion animals. Adding further instances found in Hatton MS 116 Homily 3, Vercelli Homily 2, and CCCC MS 162 Homily 39, Cross had argued against Kershaw, Whitelock, and Magoun that in lines 80-81 of *The Wanderer* it "seems certain that the O.E. poet here recalls a common Christian theme and that the wolf and the bird should not be linked with the beasts and birds which appear in O.E. poetic battle-scenes."[19] Instead, Cross hypothesizes

---

[14] See Allen (n. 9 above) 211 and fig. 227b; also Herbert Coutts, *Ancient Monuments of Tayside* (Dundee 1970) pl. 11; Stewart Cruden, *The Early Christian and Pictish Monuments of Scotland* (Edinburgh 1964) pl. 10; and Isabella Anderson, *The Picts* (London 1967) pl. 41.

[15] Sune Lindqvist, *Gotlands Bildsteine* 1 (Stockholm 1941) taf. 27 (fig. 81), taf. 31 (fig. 86).

[16] Francis P. Magoun, Jr., "The Theme of the Beasts of Battle in Anglo-Saxon Poetry," NM 56 (1965) 81-90. Old Norse examples are in the "Eiríksdrápa" of Thord Kolbeinsson, sts. 12-14, and in "Knútsdrápa" by Ottar the Black, st. 11; cited in Dorothy Whitelock, ed., *English Historical Documents* 1 (London 1968) 307-308.

[17] Gustav Neckel, "Der kriegerische Kultur der heidnischen Germanen," *Germanisch-romanische Monatsschrift* 7 (1915-1919) 26-27; E. G. Stanley, "Old English Poetic Diction and the Interpretation of *The Wanderer, The Seafarer* and *The Penitent's Prayer*," *Anglia* 73 (1955) 442-443; Fred C. Robinson, "Notes on the Old English *Exodus*," *Anglia* 80 (1972) 366 n. 1.

[18] Friedrich Klaeber, "Notes on Old English Poems," *JEGP* 12 (1913) 259; R. Morris, ed., *The Blickling Homilies*, EETS o.s. 73 (London 1880) 95; Arthur Napier, ed., *Wulfstan: Sammlung der ihm zugeschriebenen Homilien* (Berlin 1883; repr. Dublin 1967) 183.

[19] Cross (n. 4 above) 93. Neither Klaeber nor Cross mention Vercelli Homily 21, the second part of which closely parallels Homily 2; on fol. 115 it reads: "7 þonne ealle arisað swa-hwæt-swa eorþe forswealh 7 fyr forbærnde 7 sæ besencte 7 wildeor fræton 7 fugelas tobæron, eall þæt on ðam dæge arist." Furthermore, Cross says nothing about the soul's vituperative address to the body in Vercelli Homily 4, "Eala, ðu wyrma ge-ców 7 wulfes ge-slit 7 fugles ge-ter" (ed. Förster, lines 294-295), in which the body's resurrection is here not at issue.

that the use of the animals in these homilies and in *The Wanderer* has its source in patristic reports of arguments by heretics against the Christian dogma of the resurrection of the body. Cross provides two dozen examples from Christian writings from the second to the eleventh century, in which beasts and birds, along with some other ways of bodily destruction, are associated with arguments for the resurrection of the flesh in spite of bodily dismemberment.

Just as Bonjour and Cross contend that Magoun was too categorically narrow in his analysis of the Old English use of the birds and beasts motif, so it can be argued that Cross himself seems too constrictive in confining the Christian use of the ways of bodily destruction to the specific topic of the resurrection. He holds that "at l. 80 the list of ways of bodily destruction reflects the heretical objection to resurrection of the flesh."[20] But this section of the poem is treating of modes of grim death, and there is neither an overt nor a covert statement in the poem as a whole about the resurrection of the flesh. The most that can be said, according to the ending of the poem, is that in the face of destruction it is well to turn to the security of God. This sentiment is biblical, one found especially in the Psalms, but not thematically united with the Christian doctrine of bodily resurrection. A more important objection still to Cross's hypothesis is that the theme of predatory beasts and birds associated with violent deaths as opposed to peaceful demise is a universal one, common to Near Eastern, biblical, classical, Celtic, and Germanic traditions. Cross may well be correct in asserting that Christian Latin works provided the models for lines 80ff. of *The Wanderer*, but the Christian Latin writers themselves do not employ the theme only in relation to the dogma of the resurrection. The passage of Revelation, 19.17-20, certainly contains no reference to the resurrection:

> Et vidi unum angelum stantem in sole, et clamavit voce magna, dicens omnibus avibus quae volebant per medium caeli: Venite et congregamini ad coenam magnam Dei; ut manducetis carnes regum, et carnes tribunorum, et carnes fortium, et carnes equorum et sedentium in ipsis. . . . Et omnes aves saturatae sunt carnibus eorum.

And Prudentius in the *Psychomachia* is drawing upon classical tradition as he describes beasts and birds devouring Discordia, hacked down on the battlefield.[21] (The "beasts of battle" theme, at least with unspecified birds and animals, is obviously not solely a Germanic motif.) Poets like Prudentius had a goodly number

---

Adrien Bonjour genially remonstrated in "*Beowulf* and the Beasts of Battle," *PMLA* 72 (1957) 562-573, that Magoun's oral-formulaic categorization ignored the great artistic diversity amongst the uses of the "beasts of battle" theme. See also Stanley (n. 17 above) 442-443, 466.

[20] See also R. F. Leslie, ed., *The Wanderer* (Manchester 1966) 93-94. Dunning and Bliss (n. 1 above) 120 argue that "against this hypothesis is the fact that both *The Wanderer* and the two homilies [Blickling 7 and Pseudo-Wulfstan 40] include burial among the three fates; in *The Wanderer*, indeed, burial seems to occupy a climactic position." J. E. Cross has countered in *The Literate Anglo-Saxon — On Sources and Disseminations*, Gollancz Lecture 1972 (Oxford 1972) 24-25 n. 4, that the element of burial is no obstruction to his thesis about the resurrection, since "a buried body needs to be made whole at resurrection."

[21] *Psychomachia* 716-725, in H. J. Thomson, ed., *Prudentius* 1 (Cambridge, Mass. 1949) 328.

of classical precedents for the theme of wild animals and violent death: the dogs and birds which feast on the corpses in *Iliad* 1.5 and 22.354, are found in *Ilias latina* 4-5 and 992-993, a work known at least in late eleventh-century England;[22] in the *Aeneid* 9.587, desired burial is opposed to being destroyed by predatory birds of the sea; Seneca's *Epistle* 92 says it does not matter whether the body is laid out peacefully in burial or has suffered violent death, being devoured by birds and beasts; in Propertius's *Elegy* 3.7-20, the drowned Paetus is addressed: "Sed tua nunc volucres astant super ossa marinae,/ nunc tibi pro tumulo Carpathium omne mare est"; and in Lucan's *Civil War* 7.835-846, Bistonian wolves, obscene dogs, and greedy birds prey on the fallen dead at Pharsalia.[23] Another Christian example: Rufinus tells how the holy Apollonius exhorted a pagan to make peace with his Christian neighbor or else "nullus enim alius praeter te perimetur, sed et congruum honori tuo tibi sepulcrum fiet, non terra sed bestiarum et vulturum ventres."[24] Aldhelm in his version of the story reports Apollonius as saying, "Insuper nefandum cadaver nequaquam ut ceteros mortales sepulcri sarcofagus receptet, sed volucrum rostris laceratus et bestiarum rictibus corrosus communi sepultura carebis!"[25] Ælfric in his description of the Martyrdom of Saint Vincent relates that the impious Datianus commanded his minions to cast the corpse of the martyr into a field as food for wild birds and beasts: "Awyrpað nu his lic on anum widgillum felda . fugelum to æse . & fulum hundum to mete."[26] In these and similar instances in Christian Latin writings known in Anglo-Saxon England, there is surely no reference to resurrection of the body. Instead, predatory birds and beasts are used conventionally to depict violent death as opposed to, or juxtaposed with, burial. Hence, rather than to suppose that the lines in *The Wanderer* derive from the patristic disputations concerning the resurrection, it seems more likely that the Old English poet, like the Fathers themselves, had drawn upon a common topos to express modes of death.

In lines 80-81 of *The Wanderer*, then, we have a reference to these beasts of prey.

[22] *Liber Omeri*, fols. 6-27 of Oxford, Bodleian Library MS Rawlinson G. 57 (Ker #350); the *Ilias latina* is edited by E. Baehrens, *Poetae latini minores* 3 (Leipzig 1881). Of course, Greek literature is replete with the topos of carrion birds and dogs: cf. also, *Iliad* 2.393; 8.379; 12.395, 453-454; 13.831; 22.335-336; 24.411; *Odyssey* 3.259, 321; 14.133; Empedocles 21.11, 130.2 (ed. H. Diehls, *Poetarum graecorum fragmenta* 3.1: *Poetarum philosophorum fragmenta* [Berlin 1901] 74); Aeschylus, *Seven Against Thebes* 1025; Sophocles, *Antigone* 29, 205, 696-698; *Ajax* 830.

[23] *Virgil*, ed. H. R. Fairclough, 2 (Cambridge, Mass. 1934) 152; Seneca, *Ad Lucilium epistulae morales*, ed. Richard M. Gummere, 2 (London 1920) 468; Propertius, *Elegies*, ed. H. E. Butler (London 1912) 196; Lucan, *Civil War*, ed. J. D. Duff (London 1928) 430. Jakob Grimm, *Deutsche Rechtsalterthumer*, ed. 3 (Göttingen 1881) 40-42, gives a number of ancient Germanic judicial sentences condemning, with formulaic variants, the guilty man's "leib und fleisch den thieren in den wäldern, den vögeln in den lüften," etc.

[24] Rufinus Aquileiensis Presbyter, *Historia monachorum* cap. 7, PL 21.416.

[25] Aldhelm, *De virginitate (prosa)* cap. 38, in *Aldhelmi Opera*, ed. Rudolph Ehwald, MGH Auctores antiquiores 15 (Berlin 1919) 289.

[26] Walter W. Skeat, ed., *Ælfric's Lives of Saints* 2, EETS o.s. 114 (Oxford 1900; repr. 1966) no. 37, "Passio sancti Vincentii," lines 234-235; cf. 261-262, where his body is thrown into the sea for the fish to eat.

The bird is not a ship but a bird. It is one bird, like the lone wolf and the individual victims (*sumne . . . sumne*) in the same passage, and represents a "thematic bird," which, as Sedgefield, Leslie, Campbell and Rosier, and Cross have suggested, is presumably carrying off the victim piecemeal.[27] A large bird of prey, such as the Gray Sea Eagle (*Haliaëtus albicilla*) or kite, could carry off very large portions indeed; but the poet is not specific. Thus I find fault with R. K. Gordon's and Kevin Crossley-Holland's translaticns of *fugel* as "raven," and to some extent with Burton Raffel's exaggeration in "Some the monstrous sea-bird/ Bore over the sea."[28] The choice of *fugel* instead of *earn* or *hræfn* may well be not just a question of alliterative exigency. The poet does not use topoi such as "the beasts of battle" and "the fates of men" simplistically, as the fascinating expression of 83a, *deaðe gedælde,* confirms. *Fugel* seems both generic and suggestive, freeing the imagination but keeping it within physical, realistic bounds.

This interpretation, that we have here a general but artistically employed topos of bird and beast associated with violent death, can be corroborated from Anglo-Saxon iconography. For example, in the *Bury Saint Edmunds Psalter*, ca. 1035, the illustration on fol. 87v can exemplify equally well the Psalm verse and the lines in *The Wanderer.*[29] In the upper left quadrant are depicted a bird and a beast sharing human carnage (see fig. 2). The image is used to illustrate Psalm 78.2: "Posuerunt morticina servorum tuorum, escas volatilibus caeli; carnes sanctorum tuorum bestiis terrae." The big bird is flying off with parts of the upper body (head, arm), while the wolf-creature is rending another part, apparently the legs. Surely this is a realistic illustration of a *fugel* and a *wulf* at work, as we find recalled in *The Wanderer.*

Remarking on the singular form, *fugel*, in line 81, Dunning and Bliss suggest that "the homilies may preserve a more original form of the concept, since in them *fug(e)las* is plural, and the prefix *to-* in *tobæron* means 'asunder.' "[30] Interestingly, also in the *Bury Saint Edmunds Psalter* the many birds in the text (*volatilibus*) are reduced by the artist to one schematic bird, and he does the same for the beasts (*bestiis terrae*), represented by the one vicious animal. By way of contrast, in the illustration of this Psalm in the earlier *Utrecht Psalter*, which served as the model for

[27]W. J. Sedgefield, *An Anglo-Saxon Verse Book* (Manchester 1922) 155; Leslie (n. 20 above) 16-17, 84; Jackson J. Campbell and James L. Rosier, eds., *Poems in Old English* (New York [1962]) 67; Cross (n. 4 above) 92-93. Concerning the type of bird meant, see Frederic G. Cassidy and Richard N. Ringler, eds., *Bright's Old English Grammar and Reader*, ed. 3 (New York 1971) 327 and 166, note to *Brunanburh* 63a; and Charles Huntington Whitman, "The Birds of Old English Literature," *JEGP* 2(1898-1899) 168.

[28]R. K. Gordon, *Anglo-Saxon Poetry* (London 1954) 74; Kevin Crossley-Holland and Bruce Mitchell, *The Battle of Maldon and Other Old English Poems* (London 1967) 110; Burton Raffel, *Poems from the Old English*, ed. 2 (Lincoln, Nebr. 1966) 61

[29]See Robert Mark Harris's excellent dissertation on the illustrations of the Psalter, "The Marginal Drawings of the *Bury St. Edmunds Psalter* (Rome Vatican Library MS Reg. Lat. 12)," Ph.D. diss. (Princeton 1960), and specifically 298-300 and nn. for the bird drawing.

[30]Dunning and Bliss (n. 1 above) 120. However, an examination of the uses of *toberan* and *opberan* given in Bosworth-Toller, *Anglo-Saxon Dictionary* and Toller, *Supplement*, suggests that

the *Bury Saint Edmunds Psalter*, a number of birds and beasts are making off with pieces of human bodies.[31] Perhaps the poet has simplified as has the artist.

Besides these examples from Psalter illustrations, we find in other religious works, known to the early Middle Ages, artistic descriptions of strikingly large birds carrying off human bodies. The text of Revelations 19.17, 18, and 20 afforded such a pictorial opportunity. In the Ottonian *Bamberger Apocalypse* the artist reduces the plurality of birds to two for the scene, somewhat as the artist of the *Bury Saint Edmunds Psalter* reduces them to one.[32] However, the later (early twelfth-century) representation of these verses in Haymo of Auxerre's *Commentary on the Apocalypse* depicts eight birds, generally larger than the human corpses that they are dismembering and bearing off (see fig. 3). Similarly, among the numerous illustrations of Prudentius's *Psychomachia* 5.719-721, mentioned above as an example of the birds and beasts theme, we note that the artists have imaginatively portrayed the birds as nearly the size of their victims.[33]

These illustrations, particularly that of the *Bury Saint Edmunds Psalter*, help confirm these points: that in literature and art the bird and beast of prey are linked with *violenti et improvisa morte*, with burial of the body or lack of it for the hapless victim; that these animals are associated with various feared deaths often but not always associated with battle; and that the appearances of these beasts on the death scene in early medieval Christian literature does not necessarily involve the dogma of the resurrection of the flesh. All these examples help to clarify the intent of the lines 81b-82a, *sumne fugel oþbær/ ofer heanne holm*.

Department of English
Stanford University
Stanford, California 94305, U.S.A.

---

both verbs in various early and late contexts mean "to carry off, bear away," so that it seems unjustified to affirm that *tobæron* indicates "a more original form" of the concept.

[31] See E. T. DeWald, ed., *The Illustrations of the Utrecht Psalter* (Princeton [1932]) 36 and fol. 46v; and M. R. James, ed., *The Canterbury Psalter* (London 1935) 30 and fol. 141. Another example of this reduction of numerous birds and victims described in the text to a single bird and carcass pictured in an illustration can be seen in the Beatus *Commentary on the Apocalypse*, MS of the Archives of Urgel Cathedral (ca. 970), fol. 82v, bottom, where a carrion bird, more than half the size of a man, devours a corpse.

[32] See fol. 48v of the *Ottonian Bamberger Apokalypse*, ed. Alois Faber (Munich 1958), Tafel 45.

[33] See Richard Stettiner, *Die illustrierten Prudentiushandschriften*, Inaugural-Dissertation, Strassburg (Berlin, 1895) 379-386, and pls. 105, 4; 123, 2.

FIG. 1. Lärbro Tängelgårda I, detail from Sune Lindqvist, *Gotlands Bildsteine* 1 (Stockholm 1941) fig. 86.

FIG. 2. Detail of Vatican MS Reg. lat. 12, fol. 87v; courtesy of the Biblioteca Apostolica Vaticana.

FIG. 3. Detail of Oxford MS Bodley 352, fol. 11; courtesy of the Bodleian Library.

LEGEND, HISTORY AND ARTIFICE IN
"THE BATTLE OF MALDON"

•

by A. N. Doane

Views of *The Battle of Maldon* as an historical poem have had a tendency to divide into two well-defined camps. On the one hand are those who regard the poem as a more or less accurate historical document whose details reflect what actually took place near the estuary of the Blackwater River on the afternoon of 11 August 991. This group, much the older, going back to Freeman and Liebermann, receives its modern warrant from the researches of Laborde and still attracts adherents.[1] Positions within this group range from those who regard the poem as merely one among a number of useful historical documents relating to the battle and the life of Byrhtnoth, to those who would read it as a realistic record of details of action, topography, tide, landscape and personnel, presenting the battle in terms of intelligible military tactics, with accurate reportorial detail derived from eyewitness accounts, even to the extent that the poem's integrity, vividness and heroic ideology depend on its supposed historical truth and accuracy. On the other hand is the more recently emerging group that stresses the artificial, traditional nature of the poem:

> That *The Battle of Maldon* and Hallfreth's *Óláfsdrápa* are probably true in the main is not their virtue . . . ; they are no more truthful than they should be. As is clearer in the Norse piece than in the English one, they are historical poems from a markedly artificial tradition, poems which brilliantly demonstrate the virtues of their genre, the heroic panegyric, within the subtypes of narrative and court lyric.[2]

According to the critics who may be said to have adopted a stance similar to this one, and this includes nearly all of the serious writing on *Maldon* in the last fifteen

[1] Edward A. Freeman, *The History of the Norman Conquest of England* (Oxford 1876-1879) 1.271-277; Felix Liebermann, "Zur Geschichte Byrhtnoths, des Helden von Maldon," *Archiv* 101 (1898) 15-28; E. D. Laborde, "The Site of the Battle of Maldon," *English Historical Review* 11 (1925) 161-173. Recent elaborations of the literal accuracy of the poem as history are W. A. Samouce, "General Byrhtnoth," *JEGP* 62 (1963) 129-135 and A. D. Mills, "Byrhtnoth's Mistake in Generalship," *Neuphilologische Mitteilungen* (NM) 67 (1966) 14-27. The topographical evidence is reexamined with scientific precision by a geologist and a literary scholar in George R. Petty, Jr., and Susan Petty, "Geology and *The Battle of Maldon*," *Speculum* 51 (1976) 435-446.

[2] Jess B. Bessinger, "*Maldon* and the *Óláfsdrápa*: An Historical Caveat" in *Studies in Old English Literature in Honor of Arthur G. Brodeur*, ed. Stanley B. Greenfield (Eugene 1963) 24.

years, the historical event behind the poem is virtually irrelevant, for the poet is merely working up some much less developed account of the battle for his own artistic purposes, to give a generalized picture of ancient heroic values,[3] praise heroes and condemn cowards,[4] or, conversely, to travesty the old epic virtues.[5]

The two positions threaten to harden into a set antithesis, preventing a realization of the strengths and limitations of both, and crystalizing opinion about the poem around a few increasingly threadbare topics, such as Byrhtnoth's *ofermod* and Panta's *west*. Already such a polarity has been tacitly accepted as natural by at least one writer, O. D. Macrae-Gibson, himself of the "historical" persuasion:

> The present article hopes to contribute usefully to the discussion by the following line of approach: I shall assume provisionally that the poem does offer reliable evidence of what took place. On this basis, and putting beside the evidence of the poem some other evidence not hitherto used [viz. topographical evidence], I shall try to reconstruct in as much detail as possible the events of the battle, both as Byrhtnoð intended that it should go and as it actually did go. If the attempt leads to contradictions or implausibility, the non-historical view is supported; if on the contrary everything falls neatly into place, the "historical" view is supported.[6]

But either position, carried to its extreme, as here, involves a partial view which leads us away, both as historians and literary critics, from what the main issues ought to be. For both positions are surely "right" as far as they go, but each favors only one side of what is really a three-sided issue: (1) the poem's relation to some actual outside event, (2) the poet's technical and aesthetic procedures in presenting his understanding of that event, (3) the assumptions which underlie those procedures, both conscious and unconscious.[7] To put it another way: the question that both the

---

[3] Edward B. Irving, Jr., "The Heroic Style in *The Battle of Maldon*," *Studies in Philology* 58 (1961), 457-67. The "increasing use of epic diction [in the later parts of the poem] is very much related to the meaning of the poem. A real historical event is being raised to a higher level of significance; the actions thus become increasingly symbolic; the ordinary identifiable men of Essex approach and enter the world of heroes, the world of legend" (460).

[4] George Clark, "*The Battle of Maldon*: A Heroic Poem," *Speculum* 43 (1968) 52-71. The poet "intends to praise heroes and condemn cowards" (57).

[5] Michael J. Swanton, "*The Battle of Maldon*: A Literary Caveat," *JEGP* 67 (1968) 441-50. The poem is ironic, undercutting the values of the leaders by showing the nobility of peasants, cowardice of lords, cynicism and pomp of Byrhtnoth, rationality of the Vikings, etc. "The poet has let slip that he was really very well aware of the actual nature of 10th century society. At the same time this has ironically cut away the entire basis of the subsequent assumptions on which Byrhtnoth dies, and the more faithful of his followers strut and puff to their deaths. The whole is seen to have been built up on false foundations, a travesty of antique heroic values" (448).

[6] O. D. Macrae-Gibson, "How Historical is The Battle of Maldon?" *Medium Ævum* 39 (1970) 89.

[7] The "historical" view implies that what determines the ordering and detail of the poem is what happened "out there," that events control the poem. The "artistic" view implies that while something did happen "out there" it is of no importance to the poem beyond the bare fact of its historicity, if that. Both positions ignore obvious elements: On the one hand, the poet is at work ordering events into clear, sequential blocks, at the very least bringing narrative order out of the chaos of events. However simply, any historical record of an event must reflect the mind and

historical view and the artistic view ask of the poem is, "Is *Maldon* historical?" The one group answers "yes," the other "no," and each goes on from there. But the real questions must cast their nets more widely: According to what historical presuppositions was *Maldon* written? What are the artistic effects of such presuppositions? What is the purpose of such historical writing?

To make an attempt to answer these interrelated questions will require some consideration of the historical and artistic milieus of the late tenth and early eleventh centuries, the span of time in which the poem could have been composed. But I would like to stress at the outset that at the center of the issue is *The Battle of Maldon*'s isolation, its uniqueness. It is isolated in time, even from most of the Chronicle poems, by its attested late date. Even more, it is isolated by certain unusual literary features, namely its extremely paratactic style, going beyond the already considerable paratactic tendencies inherent in the O.E. poetic style of most older poetry, and as a concomitant of this style, its self-conscious symmetry and clarity of structure unparalleled in other O.E. poems. Any consideration of the poem must keep in mind its isolation and fully take into account and try to explain its unique qualities of style and structure.

Severely articulated parts, down to the smallest details, are carefully arranged so as to achieve a coherent, balanced structural effect, an effect of simplicity and limpid cohesiveness which makes the poem so attractive and yet, it seems, so deceptive. For far from regarding this bright simplicity as the product of a complex art, still less springing from a complex intent, there has always been a tendency to read the poem literally, as a straightforward attempt to relate a straightforward historical situation straightforwardly – the poem's simplicity reflecting the starkness of the event; or, on the technical level, even among the group of critics concentrating on the poem's art, to regard such complexities as are seen as merely the result of the masterly use of traditional devices, the toughness that resides under the smooth surface of all "simple" art produced by long traditions; or, on the ideological level, to see in the poem no more than the old "heroic ethic" revived for one last time. Now there is something deeply true in all three assumptions, and with the first two I have no quarrel, except to say they are not stopping places, but starting places. As for the third, while not denying the heroic tone and intent that the poem obviously has, I must confess that the "sunset glow" cast over the poem by such critics as regard it solely in this way strikes me as rather banal, denying as it does much of the sinewy

---

presuppositions of the recorder. On the other hand, the poet is concerned to reify the details of the battle in the mind of the audience, even if he is inventing out of whole cloth, so that the prevailing fiction of the poem is that it "records" an actual event in a true way. As for the "third thing," I think we must grant that the poet thinks he is conveying what actually happened "out there" or wants us to think so (the mistake is in thinking that we can reconstruct the historical actuality from a single document, however circumstantial); but in order to do this he is ordering, inventing, calling attention to repetitions, echoes, dysfunctions. He is doing this for some purpose, to bring out some coherent statement more abstract and universal than the mere reportage of a single engagement. Even panegyric exists on the third level, though *Maldon*'s purpose is more comprehensive than praise of the good leader.

complexity that the light of noonday, not to say, of eternity, reveals about it.[8] We really can do better by *Maldon* by taking into account more than Tacitus and the Laws of Cnut.[9] And one should not shunt aside the fact that, if *Maldon* really is an unmixed "heroic" poem composed after 991, its existence in such a pure state is the most complex and bewildering question of all.

Since we can date the poem within three-quarters of a century, and we do know quite a lot about certain external circumstances relating to the event and the persons that the poem purports to sing, it seems for once that we can turn to the historical milieu from which it came to help explain the actual responses that its specific stylistic and structural features evoke and to enrich those responses. By "historical milieu" I mean not so much the narrow event which is the immediate occasion of the poem, the battle of 991, but the general intellectual and literary environment of the rather long span during which the poem may have developed. Within this period of three-quarters of a century certain prevalent and fairly steady norms governing historical writing may be perceived; and it seems not unreasonable to begin by considering the poem as influenced by the normal thought-processes, interests and methods of the time that produced it, rather than of a relatively remote "Germania."

What strikes one immediately about the period in question is that historical and fictive narrative are not markedly distinct. Poetry, history, encomium, hagiography tend to merge into a single all-pervasive method of narrative which I will call "legendary." The legendary method is on its surface historical, and all narrative claims to be historical, since fiction has little status. It is turned predominantly to the uses of hagiography and royal panegyric, the two genres tending to merge in the series of politico-religious *Lives* of Anglo-Saxon kings, and of their adjutants, the bishops and archbishops of the English church, a tendency continuing and strengthening into Norman times. In such writing historical events must conform to established ideological, typological, anagogical ways of looking at them. All means of writing, whether derived from the old artistic heroic tradition of narrative poetry, itself looking back to a sort of "history", or derived from history writing such as Bede's, itself derived ultimately from early hagiography, refer to an inner world of

---

[8] Cf. the concluding remarks of Cecily Clark, "Byrhtnoth and Roland: A Contrast," *Neophilologus* 51 (1967) 292: "This war, unlike that in *Roland,* is not between religions but between Germanic tribes, and what is at stake is not faith, but land and gold, or, at most, martial honour . . . . The slightness and vagueness of [the poet's] references to [Christianity] compel us to the conclusion that he was playing it down, in order to depict Germanic heroism with the more purity." For all their authority and charm, Tolkien's remarks on *Maldon* amount to little more than this (J. R. R. Tolkien, "The Homecoming of Beorthnoth Beorthelm's Son," *Essays and Studies,* n.s. 6 [1953] 1-18).

[9] Cf. Clark (n. 4 above) 60. Swanton (n. 5 above) 444, probably overestimates the anachronistic quality of *Maldon*; the old values of the *comitatus* transferred easily and were pretty handy to the system of vassalage evolving under the late Anglo-Saxon kings. Hollister seems to take the military tactics and organization described in the poem as normal for its time (C. Warren Hollister, *Anglo-Saxon Military Institutions on the Eve of the Norman Conquest* [Oxford 1962] 93, 115-17, and passim). On the survival of "heroic" values into the final period see Dorothy Whitelock, "Anglo-Saxon Poetry and the Historian," *Transactions of the Royal Historical Society* ser. 4, 31 (1949) 75-94.

ideal patterns (patterns revealed historically by the life of Christ) informing outward events. The individual event was not regarded as important in itself, nor analyzed in terms of individual causes and effects, but scrutinized, read, as it were, in such a way as to reveal its conformity to a world of ideas. It was the common task of poet and historian to show how events in the secular world manifested the eternal events of which they were the shadowiest part. Hagiography and history fall together, cannot be separated, while, in the eleventh century, both were tinged with the violent hues of those heroic ideals which had survived as functional and realistic components of a politics accustomed to anarchy and warfare.

What follows, then, assumes, initially on the basis of the unique qualities of its style and structure, and on a consideraton of the age in which it was composed, that *Maldon*, while utilizing the material of a past heroic age, and casting a nearly contemporary event in an antique mold, has as its purpose, or motivating force, an explication of larger issues than the literal ones that exercise the heroes of the poem, as their struggle in a moment of time and fragment of space becomes a simulacrum of all worldly struggles. It is set in a larger cosmic framework, showing a pattern for all historical events. The issues central to the poem are those of social order and its relation to individual and general salvation within the divine plan, with special reference to the English of the late Anglo-Saxon period. The characters look to the past for their inspiration, implicitly comparing themselves to heroes of old, and behaving like them, while the poet looks upward and inward, to a more general standard, valid for all Christians, at the same time providing a mirror for Christian princes, who must still fight their battles, political and military, within a secular framework. As a literary product the poem harkens not so much back to the likes of *Finnesburh* and *Hildebrand*, but forward to the *Roland*, with which it shares a concern for correct heroic action within an all-encompassing spiritual-ethical frame-work, and which in both manifests itself by the stylistic traits of parallelism and hierarchical structuring. Although the development of the genre in England was truncated by events, and despite all the differences between the Frankish epic and the English "lay," *Maldon* is England's first and only "chanson de geste."[10]

I hope it is obvious by now how I differ from those who would read the poem as purely "historical" as we understand the word, or purely heroic. I am equally anxious, after what I have just said, to disclaim any intention of reading *Maldon* as a specifically religious poem, allegory or saint's life. Byrhtnoth may be a *figura*; he is not a saint. Yet several suggestions along these lines have been put forward. N. F.

---

[10] The comparison between *Roland* and *Maldon* has been frequently made, most notably by W. P. Ker, *Epic and Romance* (New York 1957 [1896]) 51-57; Frederick Whitehead, "Ofermod et desmesure," *Cahiers de civilisation médiévale* 3 (1960) 115-117; Clark (n. 8 above): all these emphasize the differences between the two works, as well as superficial similarities. The most enlightening piece in this regard for the student of *Maldon* is Erich Auerbach's profound analysis of the style of *Roland,* to which the following pages owe not a little; for it is in matters of style and structure, rather than subject, that *Maldon* most resembles the *chansons de geste* (Erich Auerbach, *Mimesis: The Representation of Reality in Western Literature,* trans. Willard R. Trask [Princeton 1953] 96-122).

Blake compares Byrhtnoth's death to that of Ælfric's Saint Edmund.[11] More recently, in an interesting and ingenious article that contains many good points, but whose general thesis not many will be able to accept, W. F. Bolton sees in the trials of Byrhtnoth the temptations of the world, the flesh and the devil.[12] Against suggestions of this stripe, occasioned in fact by several much more modest essays in this direction,[13] J. E. Cross, himself by no means unsympathetic to "patristics" in the criticism of Old English literature, has shown the difference between the overt motivations that governed Saint Oswald in Ælfric's *Life* and Byrhtnoth; he concludes,

> All the emphasis of the poet that has been distinguished from his own words, illuminated, I trust, with relevant contrasts and comparisons from his own age, confirms the view of older scholars that this is a secular poem about Englishmen who are historically Christian but with the aim of illustrating secular virtues and motives. May we therefore now return to the view held by W. P. Ker that "the poem of *Maldon*, late as it is, has uttered the spirit and essence of the Northern heroic literature in its reserved and simple story and its invincible profession of heroic faith."[14]

Cross is right to emphasize the "secular" nature of *Maldon*. It obviously is not concerned with the life of a saint, or the Church, or much involved with doctrine. Certainly it is no such stone-built bulwark of piety as will yield to the direct assault of Robertsonian methods. Yet Cross's view of the poem as "secular" is too narrowly drawn. In the time when *Maldon* could have been composed — the reigns of Kings Ethelred II to William I — nothing was only secular, of this world, cut off completely from other realities and higher spheres. Every worldly action implied an action in an unseen world. Hero and saint are not mutually exclusive categories, nor are their activities divided into rigidly separated areas. The virtues and activities specific to each are available and necessary to the other. Byrhtnoth himself, while never canonized, was the object of at least private veneration for a time, and though his cult did not survive, his memory as "vir religiosus" did.[15] It would be remarkable if one of the great benefactors and protectors of monasticism, memorialized in a poem

---

[11] N. F. Blake, "The Battle of Maldon," *Neophilologus* 49 (1965) 332-345.

[12] W. F. Bolton, "Byrhtnoð in the Wilderness," *Modern Language Review* (MLR) 64 (1969), 481-490.

[13] Morton W. Bloomfield, "Patristics and Old English Literature: Notes on Some Poems," in *Brodeur Studies* (n. 2 above) 37-38, suggests that *Maldon* 175-180 alludes to the familiar concept of angels and devils struggling for the soul of a dying person. Bernard F. Huppé, *Doctrine and Poetry: Augustine's Influence on Old English Poetry* (New York 1959) 237-238 calls attention to the "Christian spirit" of Byrhtnoth's dying speech "which most completely illumines the entire poem."

[14] J. E. Cross, "Oswald and Byrhtnoth: A Christian Saint and a Hero Who is Christian," *English Studies* 46 (1965), 93-109. This article appeared simultaneously with Blake's (n. 11 above), so neither could refer to the other: they coincidentally present almost the same evidence but arrive at diametrically opposed conclusions.

[15] Cf. Florence of Worcester, *Chronicon ex chronicis,* ed. Benjamin Thorpe (London 1848-1849) 1.144. Florence (d. 1118) is here following the *Vita sancti Oswaldi* (written before

written in an age of all-pervasive, rigid, official piety, should not be presented to some extent in the guise of a saint. But however this may appear to various readers, it is not the main thrust of *The Battle of Maldon*.

* * *

The most familiar document relating to the battle other than our poem is the Anglo-Saxon Chronicle. The A (Parker) version is the fullest for this event, but the E (Laud) text expresses it in the most uncompromising terms:

> 991. Her was G[ypes]wic ge hergod. 7 æfter þam swiðe raðe wæs Brihtnoð ealdorman of slægen æt Mældune. 7 on þam geare man ge rædde þ man geald ærest gafol Deniscan mannum. for þam mycclan brogan þe hi worhtan be þam sæ riman. þ wæs ærest ·x· þusend punda. þæne ræd ge rædde Siric arceb.[16]

The first impression of this is of an irreducible, opaque lumping of facts into a paratactic mass. Its "truth" appears to be its undeniable "having-happenedness." Its very colorlessness persuades. One thing happened, and then another, and another, in a single, uncomplicated line of physical sequence. No event stands out, or has particular significance. The annalist's dry comment that at this time "man geald ærest gafol" yields to us more pointed irony than its author intended because we hear Byrhtnoth's words:

> Gehyrst þu, sælida,   hwæt þis folc segeð?
> Hi willað eow to gafole   garas syllan,
> ættrynne ord   and ealde swurd,
> þa heregeatu   þe eow æt hilde ne deah. (45-48)[17]

In fact, the lack of comment is only apparent when the entry is isolated, for the whole section of the Chronicle concerned with the reign of Ethelred is marked by a consistent pattern of horror expressed at the excesses of the invaders and disgust for the cowardice and treachery of the English. A practical and shrewd political ideology is exhibited by the author of the annals in the C version after 997, but he is only making explicit an attitude inferable in the other versions and earlier.[18] Nevertheless,

---

1005); see n. 21 below. After the battle, Byrhtnoth's body was recovered by the monks of Ely and buried there. His bones were transferred to a new grave in the Norman cathedral in 1154, and his fame lived on, if for no other reason than the great tapestry, since perished, which hung there depicting his deeds (see E. D. Laborde, *Byrhtnoth and Maldon* [London 1936] 32-33). See n. 32 below.

[16] Charles Plummer and John Earle, *Two of the Saxon Chronicles Parallel* (Oxford 1892). All citations of the Anglo-Saxon Chronicle (ASC) are from this edition.

[17] All citations of O.E. poetry are from George Philip Krapp and Elliott Van Kirk Dobbie, *The Anglo-Saxon Poetic Records,* 6 vols. (New York 1931-1953). *The Battle of Maldon* is edited by Dobbie in vol. 6, *The Anglo-Saxon Minor Poems* (1942) 7-16; the standard separate edition is E. V. Gordon, *The Battle of Maldon* (London 1937).

[18] For an excellent characterization of this part of the Chronicle see Margaret Ashdown, *English and Norse Documents relating to the Reign of Ethelred the Unready* (Cambridge 1930) 14-17.

it is true that the Chronicle is concerned to present an event only in one dimension, in an ungraded linear sequence, without subordination.

But the Chronicle has been in various places subjected to a "legendary" reworking of some of its entries, resulting in several semi-metrical treatments of events which have caught the imagination of revisors. These metrical passages tend to generalize events, to decrease their singularity as individual occurrences in the secular sphere, and to bring out their participation in more universal patterns. Thus, under 1011, the Laud version has a reworked entry for the captivity of Archbishop Ælfeah of Canterbury, presenting it in the form of a popular lament, so generalized that it is recognizable as a secular event only by its context in the Chronicle next to the prose:

> 7 þa hi hæfdon þa burh ealle asmeade. wendon him þa to scipon. 7 læddon þone arcb mid him;

> > Wæs ða ræpling   .   se þe ær wæs
> > Angel cynnes headfod .   7 Xpēndomes.
> > þær man mihte þa ge seon earmðe
> > þær man ær ge seah blisse
> > on þære ærman byrig.   þanon us com ærest
> > Xpēndom.   7 blisse for Gode.   7 for worulde.

> 7 hi heafdon þone arcb mid him swa lange oð þone timan þe hi hine ge martyredon.

The lament is not for an English lord only, but for all the children of the Church; the wretched city is Jerusalem, and the lamentation is raised as it were by the daughters of Zion beside the waters of Babylon. The capture of the archbishop is an event, like all the others in a series, but here suddenly providing a glimpse into an eternal state. The statesman-bishop of the chronicler (incidentally, one of the first, according to a note in the A version, to agree to pay tribute to the Danes, after the fall of Byrhtnoth) is subsumed in the saint.

In the entry for 975, the expulsion of the Mercian monks in favor of secular canons by Ealdorman Ælfhere, an event in which Byrhtnoth himself was an important participant on the side of the monastic party,[19] we can see a development of the treatment of the event from the most annalistic to a fairly high degree of legendary complication in different versions. The Laud version (E) for 975 merely says "Ælfere ealdorman het towurpon swyðe manig munuc lif þe Eadgar cyng het ær þone halgan biscop Aðelwold ge staðelian." The D version has an intermediate popularized metrical version which appears to be worked up from some longer prose account than E. It remains on the level of events, being paratactic and linear, adding little more than a kind of meter and irregular rhyme to the significance of the entry. The Parker version (A, also B and C) has a fully legendary treatment worked up into

---

[19] See Laborde (n. 15 above) 24-28; Gordon (n. 17 above) 19.

fairly regular verse, where universal patterns once again replace the unique event, though keeping it localized:

> Ða wæs on Myrceon ,   mine gefræge ,
> wide 7 wel hwær . Waldendes lóf.
> afylled on foldan.   fela wearð tó dræfed .
> gleawra Godes ðeowa.   þ wæs gnornung micel
> þam þe on breostum wæg   byrnende lufan
> Metodes ón mode.   Þa wæs mærða Fruma .
> to swiðe forsewen   .   sigora Waldend .
> rodera Rædend ,   Þa man his riht tó bræc.

The poetic formulas, borrowed laboriously from various literary sources, so that the poem is almost pure cento, increase the sense of an event held in a pattern larger than the mere historical context — the "heroic" wordhoard, for nearly the last time, coming to the aid of a legendary thought-world diametrically opposed to its original spirit. The pillaged formulas all point upwards and outwards away from the ostensible object of interest: *Waldendes lof, gleawra godes ðeowa, sigora Waldend, rodera Rædend.*[20] But these are all expected, and part of the automatic legendary apparatus. There are no architechtonics here, hardly even any independent ideology.

The Chronicle does not stand alone with the poem as the only record of the battle of Maldon. Within a few years of Byrhtnoth's death, perhaps well before the poem even began to take form, an account of the event was composed by the anonymous author of a *Life of Saint Oswald* between 995 and 1005 at Ramsey Abbey (Hunts.), a house where Byrhtnoth had been personally known and remembered respectfully as a benefactor.[21] In this version Byrhtnoth is explicitly brought within the ambit of hagiography, though not himself a saint, yet living and dying according to a saintly model, as a man of holiness and a *miles Christi* whose actions are guided by a stronger hand and greater strategy than his own. He is treated here as a son of the Church, surpassing, because of his faith, the heroes of the Old Testament, yet like them a *figura* of the militant saints. His patterned life exceeds the ordinary in bravery and moral worth just as his stature does; he is protected by the supernatural armor of the sacraments, surrounded by a heavenly light emanating from his own venerable white head. Each literal, historical action is cast in a form which reveals behind it the inner significance, the physical action illuminated by its spiritual double.

> Stabat ipse, statura procerus, eminens super caeteros, cujus manum
> non Aaron et Hur sustentabant, sed multimoda pietas Domini fulciebat,
> quoniam ipse dignus erat. Percutiebat quoque a dextris, non reminiscens
> cigneam canitiem sui capitis, quoniam elemosinae et sacrae Missae eum

[20] The line "þam þe on breostum wæg byrnende lufan" has special interest; it resembles a line in *Genesis A* where the devotion of the unfallen Adam and Eve to God is described: "ac him drihtnes wæs / þam on breostum byrnende lufu" (190b-191).

[21] *Vita sancti Oswaldi auctore anonymo,* ed. James Raine, *The Historians of the Church of York and its Archbishops* 1, Rolls Series 71.1 (London 1879). The dating is Liebermann's (n. 1 above) 23 n. 52; on Byrhtnoth's patronage of Ramsey and Ely see Gordon (n. 17 above) 18-19.

confortabant. Protegebat se a sinistris debilitationem oblitus sui corporis, quem orationes et bonae actiones elevabant. Cumque pretiosus campi ductor cerneret inimicos ruere et suos viriliter pugnare, eosque multipliciter caedere, tota virtute coepit pro patria pugnare. Ceciderunt enim ex illis et nostris infinitus numerus, et Byrihtnothus cecidit, et reliqui fugerunt. Dani quoque mirabiliter sunt vulnerati, qui vix suas constituere naves poterant hominibus.[22]

Like *Maldon*, this account is circumstantial, the use of the right arm and the left, the charge of the enemy, the fierce fight, the flight of the retainers. Some of these details may have been derived from some early version of the poem, as Liebermann suggests,[23] but some of the details in the poem could just as well be derived from the *Vita* or some common source. Both texts are formulaic and generalizing about Byrhtnoth's personal features, though in fact the *Vita* seems to show more personal knowledge of Byrhtnoth the man than *The Battle of Maldon* does. But it is the stylistic treatment of the historical battle which deserves notice and gives it significance for the present purpose. The "flowery" language which Liebermann so vociferously deplores[24] is the typical efflorescence of hagiography. It is primarily by this "high" style that a distancing and generalizing effect is achieved that lends the event its religious significance. Byrhtnoth's heroic defense of his ealdormanry is thereby brought within a certain stylistic world in which saints operate. And the passage shows another hagiographical feature that we shall have occasion to refer to again. That is, the story is built on two intersecting lines, the horizontal historical line, recounting the actual or imagined events as they took place on the ground, in time, and a vertical typological line referring Byrhtnoth's actions to an eternal pattern of Christian action, in which God directly intervenes ("Not Aaron nor Hur strengthened his arm, but the love of the Lord so variously manifested"). One may conclude from the *Vita sancti Oswaldi* that, at the very least, some of Byrhtnoth's contemporaries chose to view and present his death as a kind of martyrdom.[25]

[22] Raine 456; this passage is given by Gordon (n. 17 above) 6.

[23] Liebermann (n. 1 above) 24; Gordon (n. 17 above) 6 lists the correspondences: "Byrhtnoth in the thick of the fight, inciting his followers to the front of battle (4, 127, 170); his white hair (169); his piety (170f.); his carelessness of his own bodily weakness (168); and the widespread flight following his death ... (185, 195, 239-243). Two details not in the poem are added, Byrhtnoth's great stature, and the bloody slaughter on both sides."

[24] Liebermann (n. 1 above) 24: "Stilistische Redensart des schwülstige Ausschmückung liebenden und theologisch wie klassisch wohl belesenen Pedanten sind die meisten inhaltsleeren Sätze dieser Seite über Byrhtnoth."

[25] There is a longer account of the battle in the so-called *Liber Eliensis,* ed. D. J. Stewart (London 1848: only volume 1, containing Books 1 and 2, was ever published). The purpose of this is to list the donations of Byrhtnoth to Ely, and partially, to explain his supposed preference for the Ely establishment over that of Ramsey; but with it is a detailed, slightly fabulous version of the battle. Actually there are two battles, one at a "bridge" where the Vikings are totally defeated and another four years later, where he is killed. He hurries to the second battle on a forced march from Northumbria, fights fourteen days, almost routs the Vikings, but at the last moment they make a final desperate charge and cut off his head in the heat of battle (2.62; Stewart 180-183). The *Liber Eliensis* was written about 1150 by one Thomas of Ely and this

Some time later, once *The Battle of Maldon* had assumed its ultimate form, the final compiler viewed it as conformable to hagiography, or at least worthy of it; for in the manuscript, Cotton Otho A. XII, the poem stood with several saints' lives related to *Maldon* by subject and period. The manuscript itself was burnt in the famous Ashburnham House fire in 1731, but before the fire the contents had been recorded by Thomas Smith in his catalog of the Cottonian Library. This is what he lists: (1) Asser's *Life* of King Alfred, "charactere antiquo"; (2) "Exorcismus super-stitiosus adversus febres, Latine, praemissis & intermixtis Saxonicus"; (3) *Maldon* ("Fragmentum quoddam Historicum de Eadrico, &c.");[26] (4) "Vita & Passio S. Ælphegi, Archiepiscopi Cantuariensis & martyris, per Osbernum, Monachum Cantuariensem"; (5) "Translatio S. Ælphegi" (also by Osbern); (6) "Vita S. Odonis, Cantuariensis Archiepiscopi, per Osbernum, Monachum Cantuariensem."[27] Smith lists seven more items following, which must, however, have formed a manuscript originally distinct from the one which contained the first six items.[28] The part con-

---

chapter may be derived from an earlier chronicle by Richard of Ely (ca. 1130); unlike the Ramsey account, this is no hagiographical portrayal, but an unadorned adventure story in a romance or ballad style. Gordon (n. 17 above) 7-9 points out certain resemblances that the Ely account has to the poem, which may be more than accidental: most striking is the phrase "ne hostilis exercitus saltem unum passum pedis se absente occuparet" (Stewart 181; cf. *Maldon* 247). It is interesting to note the relative precision with which Byrhtnoth's memory was preserved at Ely 150 years after his death, particularly the detailed lists of estates and church ornaments bequeathed by him to St. Etheldred's. His chapter in *Liber Eliensis* is headed "De venerabili duce Brihtnotho . . .". The whole passage, minus place-names and gifts, is given in translation by Walter John Sedgefield, *The Battle of Maldon and Short Poems from the Saxon Chronicle* (Boston 1904) xviii-xx.

[26] Referring to *Maldon,* line 11.

[27] Thomas Smith, *Catalogus librorum bibliothecae Cottonianae* (1696) 67. But not too much confidence can be placed in Smith's descriptions, at least of items in English. His description of MS Vitellius A. XV, for example, lists six items, but nothing for *St. Christopher* or *Beowulf*; and of MS Nero A. X he notes merely, "Poema in lingua veteri Anglicana, in quo sub insomnii figmento, ad religionem, pietatem, & vitam probam hortatur auctor . . ." with no mention of separate items. Humphrey Wanley, generally more to be trusted than Smith, differs slightly but not materially in his description, though he is not concerned with the Latin items; after Asser's *Life* he lists: "I Exorcismus contra Melancholiam; II Exorcismus prolixior contra frigora & febres; III Fragmentum capite & calce mutilum, sex foliis constans, quo Poetice & Stylo Caedmoniano celebratur virtus bellica *Beorhtnoth,* Ealdormanni Offae & aliorum Anglo-Saxonum, in praelio cum Danis" (*Antiquiae literaturæ septentrionalis . . .* [Oxford 1705] 2.232). The manuscript being lost, modern editions of the poem depended on the *editio princeps,* Thomas Hearne, *Johannis confratris et monachi Glastoniensis . . .* (Oxford 1726) 2.570-577. This was based on a transcript of the poem made some years earlier by John Elphinston. The Elphinston transcript was rediscovered about 1935 by N. R. Ker and formed the basis of the editions of Gordon (1937) and Dobbie (1942). See Gordon (n. 17 above) 34-37 and Dobbie (n. 17 above) xxvii for details of the transcript.

[28] According to Thomas James, Bodley's librarian, who described MS Otho A. XII when it was in Lord Lumley's library, this manuscript contained 107 leaves in 1600. Elphinston noted that *Maldon* occupied folios 57a-62b. It is reasonable therefore to assume that the remaining 45 folios contained the three texts by Osbern (which occupy 35 double-columned quarto pages in Wharton's print), and that the following seven items, much later works, were part of a distinct manuscript, which was bound together with the earlier one as MS Cotton Otho A. XII after James had seen it. This is confirmed by an annotated copy of Smith's *Catalogue* in the Bodleian

taining Asser's *Life* of Alfred appears to have been in an earlier hand than that containing *Maldon* and items 4 through 6, but *Maldon* and the three pieces by Osbern formed a single unit written in one hand − at least there is no evidence to the contrary.[29] From the date of Osbern's works, composed after 1070,[30] and the evidence of handwriting in several tiny fragments surviving from items 4 and 5, the manuscript which contained *Maldon* must be dated in the final quarter of the century.[31]

It appears, then, that *Maldon* stood between an early eleventh-century copy of Asser's *Life* and the three Canterbury texts of the last quarter of the century. Leaving out *Maldon,* what these texts have in common is their quasi-historical, legendary treatment, whether in the secular or religious sphere, of a saintly heroic struggler against the country's enemies, the "Danes". The series Alfred, Byrhtnoth, Alphege, Odo is striking. The three works of Osbern form an even more unitary group than at first meets the eye: both Alphege (Ælfeah) and Odo were archbishops of Canterbury notable for their military and political efforts against the Danish marauders. Saint Odo was present with Athelstan at the battle of Brunanburh, and Saint Alphege was murdered by Vikings while being held for ransom after the sack of Canterbury in the winter of 1011-1012. The general harmony of the death of Byrhtnoth with the subjects of the other two works is apparent. Even the short piece on the Translation of Saint Alphege's relics is instructive, reminding us as it does of the attitude of the new Norman ecclesiastical class towards the easy-going canonization procedures of their Anglo-Saxon predecessors.[32] Byrhtnoth is in with his own

Library (classed as MS Bodl. Add. D 82), based apparently on observations by Wanley; it is noted that Otho A. XII was a quarto containing 155 leaves. That is, before 1696, 48 leaves had been added to the MS. described by James (see W. H. Stevenson, *Asser's Life of King Alfred* [Oxford 1904] xxxii-li "Description of the Lost Manuscript," esp. xxxviii, n. 1 and xliv, n. 2; also Gordon, ed. cit., 32-33).

[29] In the edition of Asser's *Life* published by Francis Wise (Oxford, 1722) appears a crude facsimile of the opening of the text, in Latin and O.E. Stevenson xxxii (reproduction of Wise's facsimile facing) uncertainly identifies it as a hand of the early eleventh century. According to Wise, Wanley estimated the date of the handwriting of the Asser text to be "1000 or 1001" (see Stevenson xliv f.).

[30] C. L. Kingsford (*Dictionary of National Biography,* s.v. "Osbern") gives a *floruit* of 1090. This seems rather late. Osbern was certainly writing during the reign of Archbishop Lanfranc (1070-1089), and was dead before 1093.

[31] Gordon (n. 17 above) 32.

[32] Canonization was an informal procedure, beginning with a strictly local cult, centralized around a "saint's" tomb, certified loosely by stories of miracles, authorized by the local bishop and ratified by a "translation" of the relics into the cathedral church. Ælfeah's cult was immediately national because of his importance as archbishop, his "political" career, patriotic death and the location of his tomb at London. The translation of Ælfeah, which marked his canonization, was carried out with great ceremony at the order of King Cnut, his remains being removed from St. Paul's, where many miracles had occurred (ASC "E" anno 1012), to Christ Church, Canterbury (ASC "D" anno 1023, a very elaborate entry; the *Historia de translatione corporis S. Elphegi* gives the same facts, with much more rhetorical elaboration). The first Norman archbishop of Canterbury, Lanfranc, undertook the purging of at least the Christ Church calendar of a plethora of native saints and feasts, only St. Augustine and Ælfeah surviving, the latter only by the intercession of Anselm. Not even Dunstan remained. Lanfranc's objection to Ælfeah was that he had not died as a martyr to Christ, but as a political hostage. Anselm argued

kind here. All three were great men involved in the affairs of state through the latter half of the tenth century, and each in his way was an exemplary figure — hero, statesman, saint — standing out among their contemporaries during the dismal time of Ethelred, raised up by the enthusiasm of popular piety and brought together by the diligence of official scribal procedures.

As in the Ramsey account of Byrhtnoth examined above, what is outstanding in Osbern's *Lives* of Alphege and Odo is their historical foundation, following the individual events of the biographies as found in charters, chronicles and other memorials in greater detail and with an appearance of greater historical accuracy than is found in the English and Latin *vitae* of native saints of the previous century and earlier.[33] This greater commitment to circumstantiality is combined with the customary legendary treatment, so that while actual historical details appear in great number, and the length of the *vitae* has increased correspondingly, these details are always being transmuted into something universal. The saint must work out his destiny in history, in time; but he exhibits while doing this his ideal self, so that, as is true of hagiography in all ages, the life of the saint is an imitation of the life of Christ and follows the pattern of the lives of all saints. Thus, like Saint Lawrence, Alphege "hides" the treasure of the Church from the persecutors, that is, he refuses ransom

---

that he had died for justice (see F. A. Gasquet and E. Bishop, *The Bosworth Psalter* [London 1908] 31-34). The "martyrdom" of Byrhtnoth raises exactly the same question, and contemporary answers may be reflected in the cultic preservation of his memory at Ely and the "translation" of his body from the Saxon church to the new Norman cathedral in 1154. The solemn recovery of his remains after the battle of Maldon by the abbot and monks of Ely (Stewart [n. 25 above] 183) and their careful transportation thither, no doubt with some pomp, must have resembled the canonical "translation" of a saint. However, no miracles are reported for him and his cult died out — at least he never entered the calendar of saints at Ely.

[33] The text of the *Lives* used here is Henry Wharton, ed., *Anglia Sacra* 2 (London 1691): *Vita Odonis,* 78-87; *Vita S. Elphegi,* 122-142; *Historia de translatione corporis S. Elphegi,* 143-147. Wharton unfortunately did not use MS Otho A. XII, though he mentions it (p. x), and notes that the ascription of the *Vita Odonis* to Osbern is in a later hand. He follows rather a very late manuscript, Lambeth Palace Q.8 (E. ŋ. 3), a paper and vellum manuscript written by Richard Stone at Christ Church Canterbury in 1507, with later additions (M. R. James, *A Descriptive Catalogue of the MSS in the Library of Lambeth Palace,* Part 2 [Cambridge 1931] 248-256 no. 159). The authenticity of Osbern's *Vita Elphegi* is attested by his successor, Eadmer of Canterbury, in chap. 29 of his *Vita Anselmi* (Wharton 2.ix). But Wharton cast doubt on the authorship of the *Vita Odonis* in the Lambeth manuscript because it departed considerably from William of Malmesbury's summary of Osbern's version (*Gesta pontificum anglorum* 1.14, ed. N. E. S. A. Hamilton, Rolls Series 52 [London 1870; repr. 1964]. 20ff.); hence, Wharton attributed it to Eadmer, since he found that the Lambeth text agreed with a *Vita Odonis* included among the undoubted works of Eadmer in a Cambridge, Corpus Christi College manuscript (CCC 15.1 [T. James 338]; M. R. James, *A Descriptive Catalogue of the MSS in Corpus Christi College, Cambridge* [Cambridge 1912] 2.210-214 no. 371; the manuscript, described as "cent. xi-xii in an excellent Christ Church hand," bears the general title "Opuscula Edmeri Cantoris"; *Vita Sancti Odonis* is item 9). It appears that Osbern's version perished with the Cotton MS. However, Eadmer was commissioned by Anselm to revise several of Osbern's works, and his *Vita Odonis* must have largely followed Osbern's, though in soberer fashion. However this may be, it is certain from William's summary that Osbern's *Vita Odonis* contained an account of Brunanburh similar to Eadmer's (i.e., the one printed by Wharton and followed by us). See p. 52 and note 37 below.

from his people who are already groaning under burdens of tribute.[34] Like Stephen he dies by *stoning*, though in all probability he was accidentally killed by being pelted with bones during the Vikings' barbarous ship-board revels.[35] The stones are like those rejected by the workman, but made the cornerstone of the Temple. Secular events are generalized, their individuality not lost, but giving way to a greater reality. Thus, the burning of Canterbury is as impressive as the Neronian burning of Rome or the destruction of Troy, but, like those cities, is just another example of the fragility of this world and of human wantonness, one of an endless series of such dreary, warning events.[36]

The convergence of the historical, the heroic and the hagiographic in these texts is strikingly illustrated in the *Life* of Odo. Odo was present at the battle of Brunanburh as personal chaplain to King Athelstan. Though the Chronicle poem may have been known to Osbern, it appears to have had no influence on his story of "the greatest of all battles since the English came over the sea." It is not a story of a hero's strength and personal valor in victory, but of man's weakness; and it is an example of how the victory is given to those who possess God's mercy. God, or his agent Odo, interferes directly in the natural events of the battle, a clear vertical line of intervention from above intersecting the horizontal line of history. The story, as Eadmer tells it, no doubt following Osbern closely, is that at the height of the battle the king, surrounded by enemies, breaks his sword. As the enemy rush in, Odo, some distance off, praying for his lord's safety, hears a sudden cry break out from heaven. Flying to the king, Odo points out a sword hanging by his side that no one had noticed before and he admonishes him to draw it and fight, the strong hand of the Lord being with him. Suddenly, with these words, all those standing nearby can see the sword that had not been seen before. Drawing it, the king rallies his forces and overthrows the enemy on all sides.[37]

Unlike the heroic, antiquarian *Battle of Brunanburh,* which is not at all concerned with the sequence of actual events which took place on that day, but only with a general enthusiastic impression of the princes who "ealdorlangne tir / geslogon æt sæcce sweorda ecgum" (3b-4), Osbern-Eadmer's version is particular both about the historicity of these events, that they did take place in this world, and about who accomplished them. The history is recited and the glory is returned to the saint and to God, at the expense of a slightly confused and ineffectual hero-king who stood helpless without his saintly bishop.

The view of history that we have to deal with in these texts goes back to the roots

[34] Wharton 2.138.

[35] *Ibid.* 141. Cf. ASC "E" anno 1012: "7 hine þa þær oftorfodon mid banum. 7 mid hryðera heafdum. 7 sloh hine þa an heora mid anre æxe yre on þet heafod. þet he mid þam dynte niðer asah. 7 his halige blod on ða eorðan feoll. 7 his þa haligan sawle to Godes rice asende"; also Thietmar of Merseburg, *Chronicon* 7.29 (PL 139.1384-1385).

[36] Wharton 2.135.

[37] *Ibid.* 80-81. Cf. William of Malmesbury (n. 33 above) 1.14 (Hamilton 21).

of Christian historiography and cannot be more than briefly indicated here.[38] It rests on the idea that history, which from the Creation had been the record of man's prideful rejection and gradual recognition of God's plan, was permanently altered when God entered the historical arena as Man. He entered historical events in order to remake and redeem them by powerful intervention, and to set up a visible Church which would preside over and regularize His future interventions. This happened once and for all at the Incarnation, and continues in the life of the Church and the saints. As events are controlled from outside and above they tend to reflect back their maker and controller. The uniqueness of the historical event is not denied, but it is seen as conforming to broad general patterns. Each man is working towards his own unique salvation or damnation, but he has to do this through events, that is in history; and at the same time each historical man is seen according to patterns which align him with universal Christ-like and king-like forms. The individual event is of manifest importance, but in the literary treatment of it its individuality tends to be deemphasized. The importance of history is concentrated on one all-important factor, its relation to the individual's end: over nothing else does he have control.

> The Judaeo-Christian world view denies to blind chance any role in shaping human destiny, and therefore implicitly denies human freedom from the providential control of God, who, moreover, makes all men and events in accordance with his nature, which is absolutely good. Even as hagiography glorifies the Christian as isolated from or opposed to his environment (the world, or *saeculum*), it still rests on the notion of the church's corporate personality in Christ. The Christian hero may free himself from the evils of the world by withdrawal to the desert or by death in the arena, but he can never free himself from history, which, like his soul, belongs to God. We may almost say that, in early Christian thought, history controls the individual to the point where the concept of individuality disappears. All human destinies are narrowed to two alternatives — salvation or damnation; all society is divided into two groups — the wheat and the chaff, the wise and foolish virgins.[39]

Hence, any human action must be regarded not in isolation, but from several large perspectives, and it must be judged according to its end. It must be regarded from the perspective of time, in which it happens, and the perspective of eternity, whither it eventually leads. Pertinent to any historical act are two dimensions, a horizontal dimension of time-progression, consisting of numberless events in an indeterminate series, perceived only blindly by its participants, and in successive order by our senses and memory when it is history, and a vertical dimension consisting of direct interventions of the divine into the historical line, and perceived by us as the layered

---

[38] The following paragraph depends heavily on Robert W. Hanning, *The Vision of History in Early Britain from Gildas to Geoffrey of Monmouth* (New York 1966) 5-20 ("Christianity and History").

[39] *Ibid.* 15-16.

hierarchical order of correspondences in history which is called typology. The horizontal line is the line of the chronicle or annals. The historian must take this line into account as the basic structure of his work; but he must also bring out the vertical line, where one event may reflect another, or figure another, so that historical order is a reflection of divine order. The divine intervention must not be perceived or recounted merely as an event on the horizontal level, though to human eyes, say Livy's, it may appear so; it must be fully accounted for by reference to a scheme that extends up and out of this world, in a scheme clear to the mind. The commonest instance of divine intervention, or should we say, of that moment when the horizontal and vertical lines intersect, is the death of a man.

When we regard *Maldon* as a history poem from the perspective of the idea of history outlined above, and remember its external connections with hagiographically conceived historical texts, certain perceptions arise. Certainly the poem is not exactly the same as these texts, but it is closer in spirit to them than it is to, say, *Brunanburh.* This is not to deny that *Maldon* is made up of heroic materials, presented in an archaizing epic spirit, and on one level is concerned with the historical event of a battle that was the stuff of many a "pure" heroic poem. But unlike the nostalgic *Brunanburh,* which smells more of the lamp than the camp in any case, and still more unlike the *Finnesburh, Maldon* has a "legendary" element transcending the heroic. That is, it not only presents a certain historic event as a process in time, using the thought- and word-patterns of Germanic antiquity, but also presents this event as related to a pattern of events neither heroic nor historical, but religious, structured according to the hierarchical assumptions of the official ecclesiastical thought of the time. Byrhtnoth fights for his own honor and the defense of his ealdormanry in response to a unique occasion, fights in a particular way, with words and swords, and makes a particular mistake, clearly disapproved of by the poet: "se eorl ongan for his ofermode / alyfan landes to fela laþere ðeode."[40] But ultimately the poet is not really concerned with Byrhtnoth's intent or culpability in this secular matter, and it is a mistake to see the poem centering around it. Byrhtnoth is fighting in what is perceived as a more permanent state: he fights, like Roland, within the structure of a divinely determined social order, which is the means for carrying out earthly action to prove social value and personal worth, to be sure, but more, to determine one's final destination. The chaos of battle is the type and the finest expression of order, an order determined not by events, by history, the past, but by the nature of things as they were ordained from the beginning by God. And the order which hierarchically proceeds from nameless peasants of the *fyrd,* to the "ceorl" Dunnere, through the *heorðweorod,* to Byrhtnoth himself, and

---

[40] Much ink has been spilt trying to mitigate Byrhtnoth's miscalculation, e.g., Irving (n. 3 above) 462; R. W. V. Elliot, "Byrhtnoth and Hildebrand: A Study in Heroic Techniques," in *Brodeur Studies* (n. 2 above) 59, and especially Clark (n. 4 above) 52-71, but the sense of the text is plain: the Vikings were smarter than he. Tolkien's translation is sensible: "Then the earl in his overmastering pride actually yielded ground to the enemy as he should not have done" (n. 8 above) 13; cf. also F. J. Battaglia, "Notes on *Maldon*: Towards a Definitive *ofermod,*" *English Language Notes* 2 (1965) 247-249.

on up to his lord Ethelred, to Christ is stable and effective whether the actor in the framework perform ill or well. That Byrhtnoth makes a mistake and fails is not his blame, but part of the order, for his fall must precede his rise. The mode of action is secular, "heroic", within the *comitatus* structure; but its end is sacramental, the salvation of societies and the individuals in it through good action and right orientation. The poem assumes without discussion just such an ordered society, with the triumphant Christ reigning over all, and indeed, the poet goes to some trouble to order the poem so that such a structure emerges. Its particular subject is the action of one part of this whole society, the Essex *fyrd* led by the illustrious Byrhtnoth. A segment of the whole is presented by which all may be inferred. Through his fate in historical time we are to understand his eternal destination, and through him his men's and our own. Byrhtnoth's fall is a patterned "tragedy" by a poet who, like the *Wanderer*-poet, is conditioned to be pessimistic about the effects of political and military actions, but optimistic about the outcome of spiritual heroism.

So while it is a mistake to read allegories into *Maldon*, and shortsighted to see no more than the martyrdom of Byrhtnoth as its subject, it is equally off the mark to see only the death of a hero, like Garulf of old *Finnesburh,* whose death is a meaningless event against an unilluminated background, given dignity by the personal value of the protagonists. Nor is it enough to see the ideology of the poem as completed by the simple creed of Byrhtnoth's followers. A personal history built partly on secular heroic values is being fought out against a vast backdrop of eternal values, and the action is structured to show a definite pattern. There lies the reason on the one hand for the poem's concern with the particular exact details of Byrhtnoth's death (no matter for the poem whether they be historically true, at least by our standards), and on the other its concern for setting those details into an elaborate structured pattern. The uniqueness of the event is important, for each soul is unique and important, saved in time, once and for all; but the salvation takes place according to normative patterns which hold good for all events, validated for all men by Christ's life and death. As a mirror for heroes, the poem is cast so that warrior-craft fits into the largest religious mold.

If the "legendary" milieu may be accepted as pertinent to *Maldon,* its unusual literary features take on a profoundly functional aspect and we are in a position to understand its isolation as more than an accident of time and preservation of manuscripts. Its unusual features, and their significance in a "legendary" reading of the poem may be quickly summarized: a generalizing moral tone, consisting of explicit comments by author and protagonists, as well as the slanting of countless details, providing a rigid, uncompromising, unambiguous point of view emphasizing intellectual understanding and recognition rather than sympathy and pathos; a style of extreme parataxis, extending from the grammar up to the ordering of the narrative units of the whole, providing an unbroken "horizontal" line of temporal action; a symmetrical pyramidal overall structure which conveys the sense of the "vertical" spiritual action informing the temporal events. The real "action" of the poem is the intersection of the horizontal and vertical at the moment of Byrhtnoth's death, on the horizontal line a heroic death as demanded by the old code, on the vertical line a victorious entry into heaven and release of a soul, in the manner of a saint's victory. Earthly defeat and heavenly victory coincide and interact at this moment, commenting on each other.

* * *

The stylistic world of *Maldon* is still fundamentally that of the old heroic poetry, and it is from the reflexes and built-in attitudes of its traditional techniques of composition that much of the poem's flavor comes.[41] But the *Maldon*-poet's mentality has been formed by the legendary literature of his own time. The poet looks back, not with nostalgia, but with a keen critical eye to the ideals of the past, bringing them forward with a consciousness of purpose not evident in the earlier poetry. Only here, in *Maldon* and in Tacitus's *Germania,* does the old *comitatus* ideal receive such explicit expression. It seems that, standing far enough outside the living tradition, the poet is able to use this expression of the old ideal, purified, idealized, politicized, identified with the forces of justice and order as a model of good action in the secular world *par excellence.*

But the level of significance has changed; the heroic battle has achieved a unity of action and spirit because all heroic greatness is seen as the product of soul, and each soul as part of a harmonious divine network. Heroic exertion is the visible part of a universal process of upward striving, personal and communal, in a multi-dimensional world. This perception is not unique to the *Maldon*-poet, it is a product of his time and, probably, of his training; but the adjustment of the old code to contemporary requirements is his own achievement. I feel that the *Maldon*-poet was a less complex and meditative man than the *Beowulf*-poet, but he lived in a more intellectually rigid and demanding time, in an age of official dogma and piety, where doubt and speculation took second place to the necessity for clear-cut expression of ideas.

The increased sense of purpose in *Maldon* is evidenced by its completely unproblematical moral system. Unlike true heroic poetry it takes sides, makes simple moral distinctions which are given as self-evident and determined by outside standards, by a moral system tacitly shared by poet and audience, and different from that of the protagonists.

Everyone agrees, of course, that the *Beowulf*-poet is a moralist. But his moralizing concerns itself with the conflicts and doubts tied up in a man's fate, the unclear and insecure place a man occupies in a cloudy and ambiguous universe, where there are no clear channels by which a man may find his way out of the coils of fate. God rules, is wise and mighty, gives just judgment to the wicked, but he does not intervene. A man's virtue avails for little; after all, Beowulf dead gets the heathen's

---

[41] A thorough but old-fashioned study is E. D. Laborde, "The Style of 'The Battle of Maldon,'" MLR 19 (1924) 401-417; instructive are the remarks on the poem's "plain style" alternating with an "epic style" by Irving (n. 3 above) 460; on its stylistic "austerity", Elliot (n. 40 above) 56.

portion and no more. The past gives clear examples of bad action (Cain, Heremod), but the poet does not narrate in order to judge. He has no rigid moral system to guide him. Judgments emerge only through deeds, and deeds themselves need to be weighed and tested according to their results. Grendel is evil through his lineage, but the fact of his evil emerges through his own history of evil deeds. Hnæf is not set above Finn because of lineage or nationality or creed, but because his actions are nobler. In the end, the object of the Finn episode is not apportionment of blame and praise, but sympathy for the suffering that deeds bring about. That Unferth in his malice allows himself to tell the Breca story with an unjust purpose, the slandering of the guest Beowulf, is his chief bad deed in the poem: this above all else establishes his inferiority to Beowulf, it is this fault which Beowulf corrects and rebukes in his retelling of the same story in a way which celebrates himself and his opponent Breca. His added attack on Unferth, scornfully advertizing the fratricide, his prediction that the slayer will land in hell, is authorized only by what we have already seen of Unferth through his deeds. The later apparently peaceful, even cordial relations between Beowulf and Unferth must be explained in terms of the lack of moral tension in the poet's posture towards these characters — he does not take up rigid, fixed moral positions in regard to individuals.[42]

Such wavering, or forgetfulness, would be unthinkable on the part of the *Maldon*-poet. Moral alignments are at the center of the poem, tense, imperative and unchanging, without national or personal bitterness. Tendentiousness is so ingrained as to appear casual — the participation of everything in a moral system consisting of oppositions is not stressed, but everywhere assumed.

> Ða hine heowon   hæðene scealcas
> and begen þa beornas   þe him big stodon,
> Ælfnoð and Wulmær   begen lagon,
> ða onemn hyra frean   feorh gesealdon. (181-184)

> . . . he gehleop þone eoh   þe ahte his hlaford,
> on þam gerædum   þe hit riht ne wæs . . . (189-190)

> He bræc þone bordweall   and wið þa beornas feaht,
> oðþæt he his sincgyfan   on þam sæmannum
> wurðlice wrec,   ær he on wæle læge. (277-279)

Passage after passage telegraphs the message of Christian loyalty opposed to the desolation of heathen savagery. The few whom we must love, surrounded by "heathen men," are set apart with their lord in attitudes of loyalty to the death. Life is opposed to virtue. To survive, one must abandon the common good. All this is explicit, and the reader's assent is assumed. The actions are heroic, but the attitude towards them is not. A coward is not found to be in the wrong by his deeds alone, by

---

[42] To an even greater extent this is true of the *Finnesburh Fragment:* it is confusing not only because the fragmentary action lacks a context, but because the poem has no clear moral point of view to give perspective to the situation. We therefore do not know how to read anything, whether e.g. *styrde* (18b) is mocking, ironic or sympathetic, hostile or friendly.

something we instinctively recoil from, but by the author's remark. A thane's sacrifice for his treasure-giver is not only felt to be a virtue, but said to be. All through the poem deeds are named and labled, in a one-sided, unwavering onset of intellectual judgment.

For the other side, the Vikings, no concern is shown one way or the other:

> Forlet þa drenga sum   daroð of handa,
> fleogan of folman,   þæt se to forð gewat
> þurh ðone æþelan   Æþelredes þegen. (149-151)
>
> Ða wearð borda gebræc.   Brimmen wodon,
> guðe gegremode;   gar oft þurhwod
> fæges feorhhus. (295-297)

However brave, cunning, resourceful the Vikings may be as heroes, their exploits hold no interest, except insofar as they affect "our" side, and "ðone æþelan Æðelredes þegen," an epithet for Byrhtnoth which sums up the whole hierarchical system of good action with which the poem is concerned. The Vikings are props, mere *wælwulfas,* of no moral interest in themselves, while on the English side everything done is significant, even when wrong, foolish or rash.[43] Byrhtnoth's *ofermod* and the cowards' flight are worthy of particular moral judgment, and ultimately they are right or wrong as individuals in their own understood world of values from which the Vikings, mere forces of destiny, are excluded. Good can only come from one side, significance can only reside within the Christian framework; so there are no surprising sidelights on human courage, strength and evil, no tears, no irony. Everything is given value, is judged. It is not for the audience to judge again. Such a presentation reflects assurance about a world of realities outside of and larger than the events depicted. There is no room for doubt about man's fate, or even wonder at the fate of a man, no great dragon lies dead next to his slayer, no hero faces the serpents harp in hand – everything is clear, explicit, has its place, and reinforces what we knew and will always know about God's ways to men. Our attention fastens on ends, not means, on eschatology, not psychology.

The brightness and definition of the moral world of *Maldon* is paralleled by the style. The unstated assumptions governing the explicit moral alignments appear also to govern the linguistic structure, which is more rigorously paratactic than that of any other Old English poem. Of course all Old English poetry tends towards a great degree of grammatical parataxis, but never to such an extent as with *Maldon,* where not only the clausal structure is predominantly paratactic, but also the larger structural units of statements, actions and scenes.[44] Elements of progress and change

---

[43] The opposite opinion, i.e., that the Vikings are typologically meaningful as devils, is expressed by Blake (n. 11 above) 337. On their heroic role in the poem see Clark (n. 4 above) 64ff.; on their lack of differentiation see G. C. Britton, "The Characterization of the Vikings in *The Battle of Maldon," Notes and Queries* n.s. 12 (1965) 85-87.

[44] The standard work is Alarik Rynell, *Parataxis and Hypotaxis as a Criterion of Syntax and Style, especially in Old English Poetry* (Lunds Universitets Årsskrift, N.F. Avd. 1, 48.3 [1952]).

are not mingled and subordinated, controlling ideas and pictures do not maintain themselves behind technically paratactic clauses, statements and actions, but even the larger intellectual and narrative elements remain severely isolated into articulated parts, each one foregrounded, so that nothing, from the smallest details of clausal structure, to the largest structural elements of the whole, impinges on anything else. The sense is of one thing occurring after the last has finished, each in its turn, each complete in itself. Our mind bends itself to one thing at a time, impassive, un-perturbed by shades of meaning, by that back-and-forth weaving effect which enriches *Beowulf* all the time, where, however paratactic the grammar is, the overall structure of any sequence is of subordination, ideas and actions interpenetrating, combining, giving new values and orderings to familiar material.[45] In *Maldon* the controlling parataxis isolates each element, so that each attains its own definite meaning, hardly modified by anything around it. There is no room for ambiguity in each clear-cut, brightly separated part, and more important, perhaps, there is no doubt that each thing, separated as it is, does have its own definite encoded meaning.[46] The young man at the beginning of the poem is not commanded to leave his horse *and* hawk, nor does he himself decide to renounce horse *and* hawk, being commanded; the configuration is not *het / let* (2a, 7a), *hors / hafoc* (2b, 8a). Rather, the natural rhythmical, phonetic, notional pairs are separated so that they do not concatenate: *het / hors* and *let / hafoc,* setting up a sequence of actions further separated by the intercalated comment by the poet: "Þa þæt Offan mæg ærest onfunde, / þæt se eorl nolde yrhðo geþolian." This set-up enforces the "reading" of the preceding and following segments: the young man is commanded to renounce ideas of safety and retreat, and he voluntarily relinquishes peaceful pleasures, while the poet's comment tells us that this is as it should be.

The clarity and linearity of the poem is partly a product of the fact that there are no "atmospherics", since the nuance of one passage does not linger to color another. The river, for instance, does not evoke some feeling of fear or possession or doom, as Grendel's fens and moors exhale Grendel's own personality and meaning. It is not even a scenic constant, tying the poem together by topographical hypotaxis. Rather it is a functional actor at particular points, and is either foregrounded or forgotten. At one point the tide comes in, "lucon lagustreamas" (65a), temporarily preventing the battle, then, at another point, the tide goes out, "se flod ut gewat" (71a), exposing the "bridge" and allowing movement to the next stage of action.

Contrast the movement of *Finnesburh.* There, although grammatical parataxis predominates, things do not fall into clear, separable sections. Everything is mixed together and subordinated to an overall effect. Incidents and speeches do not yield clear pictures or statements. A feeling of confusion and mystery prevails, going beyond that resulting from the poem's fragmentary state (*Maldon* is a fragment, but does not produce a fragmentary effect since each part is self-contained, self-

[45] See, e.g., *Beowulf* 2771a-2782.

[46] See the excellent discussion of the symbolic significance of parataxis, with further refer-ences, by Angus Fletcher, *Allegory: The Theory of a Symbolic Mode* (Ithaca 1964) 162-171.

explanatory and complete within itself). Even things on their face perfectly clear have in reality the most cryptic effect:

> Ne ðis ne dagað eastan.   ne her draca ne fleogeð,
> ne her ðisse healle   hornas ne byrnað.
> Ac her forþ berað;   fugelas singað,
> gylleð græghama,   guðwudu hlynneð,
> scyld scefte oncwyð.   Nu scyneð þes mona, [etc.] (*Finnesburh* 3-7)

The relation of the dawn, the flying dragon, the burning gables, if those are what is being evoked, the relation of their presence, or absence even, to the action being exhorted or predicted, is entirely symbolic and magical. "Fugelas singað," probably a reflex of the "beast of battle" theme, is vague in function, but clearly subordinate to the overall theme "battle is impending" implicit in these lines, but never clearly put. Later the "beast" motif is recalled once again (34b-35a, "Hræfen wandrode, / sweart and sealoburn") but still mixed with other actions and motifs. The function of these phrases is theme-reinforcement, involving neither orderly statement, co-ordinant with other "statements" of the theme of battle, nor scenic entity. They evoke a "feeling" of battle subordinate to the main theme, the confrontation of the individual warriors.

The ravens of *Maldon,* on the other hand, are explicit harbingers of an action about to begin, placed logically in their place in the narrative leading up to the battle, and in combination with explicit statements to this effect, so that theme and statement unmistakably coincide:

> Þa wæs feohte neh, ‖
> tir æt getohte. ‖   Wæs seo tid cumen ~
> þæt þær fæge men   feallan sceoldon. ‖
> þær wearð hream ahafen, ‖   hremmas wundon, ‖
> earm æses georn; ‖   wæs on eorþan cyrm. (103b-107)

The paratactic placing of the segment, its independence and lack of subordination, is extended downward, into its internal structure, for it consists almost entirely of principal clauses, the only hypotaxis being the *þæt*-clause in line 105, and may be cut into even smaller segments: "The fight was near." "Glory in battle (is near)." "The time had come when men had to fall." "A cry arose." "Ravens circled." "Ravens eager for prey (circled)." "There was an outcry on earth." As with any paratactic series, these segments imply grammatical relationships which can be hypotactically restated: "The fight which gives glory is near. The time had come ... a cry was lifted as ravens circled, being eager for prey." The unity of the whole segment is revealed, without, however, lifting the paratactic cover, only in the last half-line, "wæs on eorþan cyrm," when the cry of battle mingles with the screech of the birds.

Causality is seldom made explicit, but it is always plain because of the sequence of events, which gives the clear sense of one thing happening before another. Each event occupies its own phrase, line, sentence, scene. The whole poem is divided into a series of carefully articulated events, the place and function of each detail, its ordering and relations, elegantly transparent. The whole battle is presented not only as a series of single combats, as has often been noticed, but as a series of separate incidents, carefully arranged to form a multiple statement on a single abstract theme.

Byrhtnoth's last fight illustrates the linearity of the distinct, articulated action. Ostensibly a single action, it breaks down into many equal parts, causality and subordination formally minimized. The parts exist side by side, without, as it were, acknowledging their relationship.

[a]   Sende ða se særinc   suþerne gar, ~
        þæt gewundod wearð   wigena hlaford; ‖

[b]   he sceaf þa mid ðam scylde, ~   þæt se sceaft tobærst, ‖

[bb]   and þæt spere sprengde, ~   þæt hit sprang ongean. ‖

[c]   Gegremod wearð se guorinc; ‖   [d] he mid gare stang
        wlancne wicing, ~   þe him þa wunde forgeaf. ‖

[e]   Frod wæs se fyrdrinc; ‖   [f] he let his francan wadan
        þurh ðæs hysses hals, ‖   [ff] hand wisode ~
        þæt he on þam færsceaðan   feorh geræhte. ‖

[g]   Ða he oþerne   ofstlice sceat, ~
        þæt seo byrne tobærst; ‖   [h] he wæs on breostum wund
        þurh ða hringlocan, ‖   [hh] him æt heortan stod
        ætterne ord. ‖   [i] Se eorl wæs se bliþra, ‖

[ii]   hloh þa, modi man, ‖   [j] sæde metode þanc
        ðæs dægweorces   þe him drihten forgeaf. (134-148)

In this fifteen-line segment there are ten distinct movements, four of which involve repetition. Hypotaxis occurs within some of the movements but there are no grammatical connections between the movements, which are short and of uniform length throughout the poem. The causal and subordinate functions must be inferred. Each movement is foregrounded and isolated so that each is exactly equal to the preceding and following ones. A simple linear sequence is thus set up, serving to stress the reality and presentness of each stage of the action, as though there were no possibility of memory or foresight. It is true that movements are repeated, but they are formally as unrelated as any other two, and can be interpreted as separate actions or a single one repeated (for example, c/e, d/f). Either way, the narrative structure does not concede that a repetition has taken place. This quality of the poem is so strong that it stands out when the poet does look back to the central event after Byrhtnoth's fall (202ff.). We are left with the effect of a purely physical action moving forward in a simple time-dimension.

Related to this effect, emerging from it, is a strong sense of discrete units, well-articulated and absolute. It is the apparently careful ordering of these units by the poet which produces the well-defined structural form of *Maldon,* so different from that of any other Old English poem, so atypically clear and unproblematical in itself. Though consisting of many parts, the structure is regular, clear and simple. I would venture to call this structure "Romanesque" because of its symmetrical arrangement of more or less equal, non-impinging parts arranged towards a central point. The effect of the parts is not cumulative, but strictly sequential, the significance arising not from interaction of parts, but strictly from within the part itself. Overall the poem may be likened to a nave comprising bays of regular arches in tiers, leading equally from two sides to a large central arch towards which the eye moves. The "arches" are the segments of paratactically separated clauses, actions, scenes, and so on, detachable units which may be taken away, added or rearranged without disturbing the essential overall order of the poem, as long as symmetry and ideology are maintained. The "central arch" is the central scene, Byrhtnoth's last fight and death (134-184).

The attention inevitably is caught by the death scene, first of all because of its simple centrality in the poem. There are 133 lines before the death scene and 141 after it. This is partly fortuitous, of course, since the poem is fragmentary at beginning and end; but it seems just right, and appears to maintain an essential balance in the poem that was always there, especially, as seems reasonable, if we can assume an equal and not significant loss at each end of the poem, perhaps of only one leaf. But more important, the scene fixes our attention because, whatever the original state of things, this is the fulcrum of the poem on which all the action turns. Our eye is led *up* to Byrhtnoth's death, and *back* to it. All the action of the first 133 lines is leading to it, and all the 141 lines following are a consequence of it. Ideologically the death scene vindicates Byrhtnoth's career, and provides the impetus for his followers' subsequent actions. Thus there are two overall movements in the poem, the paratactic linear movement in which each scene progresses to the next one without impingement, and an all-encompassing larger movement which is "hypo-tactic," by which our minds subordinate all the action to a central event. This "hypotactic" movement is elliptical, rising to the death scene and then moving down and away, with the death of Byrhtnoth occurring at the peak of the curve. The rising curve is focused on the good action of a leader and his men where temporal victory is the goal. The explicit ideology of the noble life is held in reserve, while Byrhtnoth is before us. He also provides the chief example of heroic weakness within the secular value-system. After his death the scenes lead away not only with examples of how and how not to behave in the face of temporal defeat, but with repeated explicit statements of the ideology behind this behavior. Before his death, everything is focused on Byrhtnoth's visible figure and his commanding words; afterwards on his memory, and his words as precepts. At the very peak of the action, when everything is for one moment focused, forwards and back, Byrhtnoth dies, leaving the action as his body falls to earth, to be pillaged, and his soul flies up, following the initial curve of the action, into the arms of angels.[47]

[47] Most critics see the poem hingeing on two crises, the initial mistake of letting the Vikings across, and the flight of the cowards, thus a three-part structure. My view of the structure is similar to that of George Clark, "The Battle in *The Battle of Maldon*," NM 69 (1968) 374-379; cf. the analysis of the death scene by Bolton (n. 12 above) 486: "Up to his death, the poem depicts Byrhtnoð's confrontation with his adversary; thereafter, his retainers' confrontation with

It is apparent that the long description of the battle is structured to form a statement larger than any explicit ideological utterance which appears, and to recount a battle more important than the one fought on the saltings and clay-lands of Maldon that day. Instead of chance, blind historical events, produced and resisted by the old-fashioned valor of the English forces, the battle emerges as a resolute moral encounter, patterned around the actions and words of one man, and seen from above and outside, where the invisible dimension of historical events may be perceived. This battle is not what it is because the characters think or deem it so, but because all events fall into such patterns. Thus the characters may make mistakes (Byrhtnoth's *ofermod*) and moral failures may occur (the flight of the cowards), without disqualifying the heroism and success of individuals or the rightness of the English side. Even these two lapses, balancing each other symmetrically on either side of the death scene, reinforce the patterned meaningfulness of the whole.

But the human relationship is not the main fulfillment. Lineally, the death scene looks across, towards its result, the cowards' flight and the English defeat, and at the same time it points up, to the eternal result of that death. Byrhtnoth is part of a hierarchy that extends not only downwards, a theme that the poem exhausts, but upwards into the heavenly *comitatus* that is headed by Christ, the invisible world that the death-speech indicates briefly, but which the structure of the whole heavily implies. When the possibility of further action in this world is taken from him, after the most valiant human efforts, Byrhtnoth ceases to act and, for one moment, looks up. For the only time in the poem a speech is directed not to the action on the horizontal plane, but to a static vertical, where being is more important than doing. Here, at the middle point, for a brief moment the vertical dimension is revealed, otherwise hidden in the linear thrust of the horizontal action:

> . . . ne mihte þa on fotum leng   fæste gestandan.
> He to heofenum wlat:
> "Geþancie þe,   ðeoda waldend,
> ealra þæra wynna   þe ic on worulde gebad.
> Nu ic ah, milde metod,   mæste þearfe
> þæt þu minum gaste   godes geunne,
> þæt min sawul to ðe   siðian mote
> on þin geweald,   þeoden engla,
> mid friþe ferian.   Ic eom frymdi to þe
> þæt hi helsceaðan   hynan ne moton." (171-180)

The human action is stilled, the hortatory tone ceases and the optative takes over. For the first time, one may look back in reflection and forward in hope, but here back is "down" and forward is "up". The action extends up and down, involving

---

their duty. Both halves retell temporary setback and ultimate victory. The tactical situation – the Tacitean *donum* – is only selectively involved in the confrontations and in their outcomes, and even then often in a literary rather than a historical way. Byrhtnoð's prayer consistently identifies the tactical with the moral situation, through specialized use of language which equates God's role in the moral sphere with Byrhtnoð's in the military."

unseen armies who fight in an invisible dimension not for a field of ground but for a man's soul. The perishing hero leaves his horizontal battle, where he exerted himself to become spoils in a vertical battle, and where he can no longer exert himself for his own victory, his life being over.[48] But, put another way, the lower battle, with its own importance and significance, is suddenly seen as only a testing ground pertaining to the eternal battle extending upwards, evoking its own loyalties and exertions.

The death-speech of Byrhtnoth is hypotactically constructed. For the only time in the poem there is an idea to which everything else is subordinated, in which levels and interrelations, rather than contiguity and sequence, are important. And it is this speech which, though only a few lines long, by its centrality and its sudden transformation of the "grammar" of earthly battle, forces us to see the whole battle with new eyes. At this moment occurs the critical junction between the horizontal line of the present — the battle itself, which is not really interrupted while Byrhtnoth breathes his last — and a vertical line, representing an eternal world which is obtruding into a temporal event. Such a junction, the intersection of history and mystery, occurs always at the point of death.

Thus the strong convergence of the predominant line, the horizontal secular line of action, paratactically constructed, with the sudden vertical line of Byrhtnoth's death, implies the universal intervention into the life of everyman which occurs at the time of death. On the horizontal level moves the visible action, impassive, events unconnected with each other, causes of action apparently the result of blind chance or erring human will, where bad and good are clearly differentiated, but where the triumph of evil and controlling force of human weakness are all that is apparent. In this perspective actions are redeemed only by the bleak standards of the old heroic *dom*, and a man's actions, ratified by his relations with a temporal lord, are doomed to failure. At the crucial point of this action, where it seems most hopeless, a vertical line suddenly intervenes, seen as both projected by the protagonist's mind and descending from above, causing all action to be seen as related through a hierarchy of causes (men and angels) to the highest cause, which is also the highest *dom*. Here good and bad are not only differentiated, but controlled, with the good victorious. Here a man's actions are ratified by his relations with his eternal lord. This sudden intervention, ascent and descent, causes us to see the poem not merely linearly, but hypotactically, from the simultaneous point of view, where structure, not action, predominates; for, in the end, *Maldon* is written from an historical viewpoint which sees history not as action but as structure, in which all events are endless repetitions of the same Christ-dominated event of history, where each event is a testing-place for the individual soul striving through action for salvation.

To summarize: *Maldon* is structured on two lines. First, there is a line of parataxis, where the action is presented as a simple unbroken horizontal, without highlights or backgrounding, where each action takes place on an idealized temporal

---

[48] Cf. Bloomfield (n. 13 above) 37-38, on the battle for the soul of Byrhtnoth between angels and devils here; in the *Vita Oswaldi* angels and devils fight for the soul of King Eadweard (Raine [n. 21 above] 1.451-452).

plane. Each action is part of a chronological sequence necessarily implying causality and succession but not stating it, still less explaining; and this series is entirely impassive, mechanical and blind. Events cause things to come to pass, bring them to where they are in the history of the world; each secular event is an undeniable but unremarkable entity. But as these events pass in review, they are seen by a narrator who lends them moral significance entirely from outside — dividing all forces and actions into good and bad, giving them a moral tone, generalizing them. Events are neutral insofar as they happen of themselves, affecting only the world; but insofar as they provide the occasion for the testing of souls they are significant, and as seen from a purely human standpoint, as history, they confirm the eternal patterns of society and cosmos that lie behind them.

The horizontal line consists of events. These events are placed in a carefully arranged structure pointing upwards, and forwards and back to Byrhtnoth's death. The poem thus assumes an overall vertical dimension, which becomes explicit at the moment of Byrhtnoth's death, when his soul shoots up out of the temporal event. The death-speech opens briefly a window on eternity; for a moment the horizontal line is broken, and light is shed over all the events. The horizontal structure is entirely temporal, physical, palpable, all there is to see, while the vertical structure is a product of contemplation, being spiritual, eternal and typological. At the moment of Byrhtnoth's death there is a powerful intersection of these two lines, and secular and eternal meet. The significance of earthly events is suddenly, once and for all made clear. Loyalty to the victorious lord pulls the action towards the fateful point; the desire for vengeance for the dead lord pushes memory and desire back to that point. All things order themselves around the greater design. The famous cry of the "eald geneat" Byrhtwold contains it all:

> "Hige sceal þe heardra,   heorta þe cenre,
> mod sceal þe mare,   þe ure mægen lytlað.
> Her lið ure ealdor   eall forheawen . . . ." (312-314, etc.)

Spirit increases as prosperity decreases: seen one way, it is the valiant resolution of the old customary code, ready to meet death squarely; seen another, it is the joyful recognition of the true meaning of the end of life, present simultaneously as examples in the figure of the dead lord (as in the *Wanderer*), old age ("ic eom frod feores," 317a) and violence ("wigplegan," 316a). Byrhtnoth's death is not only the example of heroic dying for the other warriors, but also the eternal type; and we can see that their deaths have the same spiritual dimension that is explicit in the case of his. We see that each has his struggle, and we understand that each has his unseen victory. Byrhtnoth's spirit, flying upward after earthly *dom* has been assured, is the mediator between earth and heaven, time and eternity, carrying our minds up from the glory in battle to glory in heaven: in this function, at least, Byrhtnoth *is* saint-like.

Morally, however, the poem is about right action in the secular arena, what that means and where it leads. The poet has deliberately selected a difficult case in point, a famous battle in which a great hero is easily defeated by a hated perennial enemy, proverbially unjust. This archaic action stands as an equivalent for all good secular behavior. Byrhtnoth's death is the exemplary death of the world-man, and so it is his soul which goes up, but as type and example of us all; for each of us reaches the struggle and crisis sooner or later, and must choose to stand or flee on the threshing-floor of this world. At this point the historical and eternal meet in all of us, and to all of us is thus appointed the special ambiance of the hero and the saint.

Department of English
University of Wisconsin
Madison, Wisconsin 53706, U.S.A.

THE FORMATION OF THE SALZBURG MINISTERIALAGE IN THE TENTH AND ELEVENTH CENTURIES: AN EXAMPLE OF UPWARD SOCIAL MOBILITY IN THE EARLY MIDDLE AGES

•

by John B. Freed

I. THE STATE OF THE PROBLEM

The sudden appearance around 1100 of the ministerials, key instruments in the efforts of the Hohenstaufen to restore the power of the German monarchy after the Investiture Conflict and of the princes to develop their nascent territorial states, has long puzzled scholars.[1] The ministerials, the ancestors of many of Germany's most distinguished noble and patrician families, are usually mentioned for the first time when their rights were codified in a *Dienstrecht* (the oldest code, that of the ministerials of the bishops of Bamberg, was written in about 1060)[2] or when they appeared in a list of witnesses as members of a distinct estate. The first reference to the ministerials of the archbishops of Salzburg as witnesses only occurs, for instance, in an entry from the *Traditionsbuch* of the Benedictine monastery of Admont, purportedly drafted sometime between 1074 and 1088, but which was edited in the twelfth century.[3] In spite of the fact that the *Dienstrechte* and many twelfth-century documents clearly point to the servile ancestry of the ministerials,[4] many older

I wish to thank Professors Joseph R. Strayer of Princeton, Herwig Wolfram of Vienna, and Rhiman A. Rotz of Indiana University Northwest, Dr. Heinz Dopsch of Salzburg, and my colleagues, Roy Austensen, David MacDonald, and Lawrence Walker, who read earlier drafts of this article and whose criticisms clarified my own thoughts. I would also like to thank the staff of the *Salzburger Landesarchiv* for their assistance.

[1] The following abbreviations will be used in this article: *Cod. Bald., Codex Balduuini; Cod. Fri., Codex Fridarici; Cod. Hart., Codex Hartuuici; Cod. Odal., Codex Odalberti; Cod. Tiet., Codex Tietmari;* MGSL, *Mitteilungen der Gesellschaft für Salzburger Landeskunde;* SUB, *Salzburger Urkundenbuch,* ed. Willibald Hauthaler and Franz Martin, 4 vols. (Salzburg 1898-1933); *Trad. Dom., Die Traditionscodices des Domcapitels;* and *Trad. St. Peter, Traditionen von St. Peter.*

[2] Wilhelm Altmann and Ernst Bernheim, *Ausgewählte Urkunden zur Erläuterung der Verfassungsgeschichte Deutschlands im Mittelalter,* ed. 4 (Berlin 1909) no. 77.

[3] SUB 2 no. 105a. See below p. 92.

[4] Archbishop Conrad II was involved, for instance, in 1167 in a dispute with Admont about a bequest made to the monastery by Matilda, the daughter of Albert, the archiepiscopal judge in Friesach, Carinthia, and the wife of the archiepiscopal chamberlain Bernhard, both of whom were identified in another document as *ministeriales sancti Rudberti* (SUB 2 no. 196). Conrad asked

German scholars refused to accept this evidence and devised ingenious theories to prove that the ancestors of the later lower nobility had been of free origin; but after nearly a century and a half of controversy, historians have generally agreed that the ministerials were indeed of servile ancestry.[5]

There remains, however, some disagreement about the precise social stratum from which the lords recruited their servile retainers. In his study of the evolution of Bavarian rural society between the late ninth and the mid-thirteenth century, Philippe Dollinger maintained that the lords selected their reeves (*villici, Meier*), household officials, and servile warriors from the children of mixed marriages between serfs and free individuals and, above all, from the *servi casati* or *servi manentes,* the wealthier serfs who possessed their own quasi-hereditary tenures. The ministerials' privileged position depended not only on the prestigious services which they performed for their lords, but also on their personal status as the richest peasants.[6] In other words, the lords perceived the better economic condition of the *servi manentes* as proof of their superior ability and potential talents. Karl Bosl, among whose best-known works is his study of the imperial ministerialage, *Die Reichsministerialität der Salier und Staufer* (Stuttgart 1950-1951), has repeatedly argued that the ancestors of the ministerials should rather be sought among the lowliest element of the servile population, the *servi proprii,* the serfs who did not possess their own tenures, but who worked every day in the lord's household or on his demesne in exchange for room and board. He contended that the *servi proprii* had daily personal contacts with their lord who was able to judge their abilities on a first-hand basis, were at the lord's complete disposal, and most important, unlike the *servi manentes,* who were tied to the soil and who continued to be peasants, had freedom of movement, a crucial factor in medieval social mobility.[7] The paucity of the extant information from the tenth and eleventh centuries, when the future ministerialage was being formed and before the ancestors of the later ministerials had

---

his vassals if "aliquod ęcclesię nostrę proprium mancipium" could dispose of an allod purchased with the proceeds of his office without the concurrence of the archbishop. The vassals ruled that such a person could not do so (SUB 2 no. 384).

[5] John B. Freed, "The Origins of the European Nobility: The Problem of the Ministerials," *Viator* 7 (1976) 215-225.

[6] Philippe Dollinger, *L'évolution des classes rurales en Bavière depuis la fin de l'époque carolingienne jusqu'au milieu du XIIIe siècle,* Publications de la Faculté des lettres de l'Université de Strasbourg 112 (Paris 1949) 291-292. F. Keutgen, "Die Entstehung der deutschen Ministerialität," *Vierteljahrschrift für Sozial – und Wirtschaftsgeschichte* 8 (1910) 483, and Edmund E. Stengel, "Ueber den Ursprung der Ministerialität," *Papsttum und Kaisertum: Forschungen zur politischen Geschichte und Geisteskultur des Mittelalters, Paul Kehr zum 65. Geburtstag dargebracht,* ed. Albert Brackmann (Munich 1926) 182, likewise argued that the ministerials were recruited from the upper strata of the servile population.

[7] Karl Bosl, "Über soziale Mobilität in der mittelalterlichen 'Gesellschaft': Dienst, Freiheit, Freizügigkeit als Motive sozialen Aufstiegs," *Frühformen der Gesellschaft im mittelalterlichen Europa: Ausgewählte Beiträge zu einer Strukturanalyse der mittelalterlichen Welt* (Munich 1964) 174-179; "Freiheit und Unfreiheit: Zur Entwicklung der Unterschichten in Deutschland und Frankreich während des Mittelalters," *Frühformen* 198-200; and "Das ius ministerialium: Dienstrecht und Lehnrecht im deutschen Mittelalter," *Frühformen* 301-308.

attained a position of prominence within Germanic society, has thus forced scholars to speculate about the origins of the institution.

Günther Flohrschütz has shed considerable light on this complex problem by a careful scrutiny of the names and titles of the transactors and witnesses in the notices recorded in the *Traditionsbücher* of the bishops and ecclesiastical foundations of Freising in the ninth, tenth, and eleventh centuries.[8] The bishops' advisers were initially drawn from the free vassals and the clergy. In the middle of the tenth century individuals who belonged to the *familia,* which was composed of the dependent members of the episcopal household, joined the vassals and the clergy as witnesses. The members of the *familia* who appeared as witnesses were in turn divided into two separate components: the *clerici proprii,* free families who had commended themselves along with their property to the church as hereditary clerics and who had come to be considered a part of the *familia,* and the *servi proprii* themselves. Bishop Abraham (957-993), in whose episcopate it became customary to seek the advice of the *clerici proprii* and the *servi proprii,* stopped enfeoffing the vassals with ecclesiastical property. Under his successor Gotschalk (994-1005) the transactions recorded in the *Traditionsbücher* involving members of the *familia* outnumbered those in which the vassals participated. The vassals ceased to be mentioned altogether after 1039 in spite of the fact that such families survived in the diocese until well into the twelfth century. At the same time the titles by which the members of the *familia* were designated became more prestigious, though the designation *servus* persisted for a long time: *proprius servus* (ca. 920), *servus* (ca. 970), *famulus* (ca. 1039), *serviens* and *quidam de familia* (ca. 1080), *ministerialis* (ca. 1130), and occasionally by 1180 even *dominus.*[9] The persistence of the same first names or the components of names among the members of the *familia* and the later ministerials in an era noted for its multiplicity of names, as well as the continuity in property holdings between the two groups, leaves little doubt that the twelfth-century ministerials of the bishops of Freising were indeed, as Bosl had argued on theoretical grounds, the descendants of the earlier *servi proprii* and the *clerici proprii* with whom the former had intermarried. The crucial factors in the formation of the Freising ministerialage and in the ministerials' rapid upward social mobility in the tenth century, most notably under Bishop Abraham, were the desperate need for warriors to fight the Hungarian invaders after the Bavarians' disastrous defeat at Bratislava in 907 and the military obligations imposed upon the German church by the Saxon dynasty.

This article will examine the extant *Traditionsbücher,* the codices of traditions, of the archdiocese of Salzburg, which has, next to Freising, the most extensive collection of such codices, to see what additional evidence they can provide about the formation of the ministerialage in the tenth and eleventh centuries. The

---

[8] Günther Flohrschütz, "Die Freisinger Dienstmannen im 10. und 11. Jahrhundert," *Beiträge zur altbayerischen Kirchengeschichte* 25 (1967) 9-79.

[9] *Ibid.* 70.

Traditionsbücher of five archbishops, who were the metropolitans of the Bavarian church, have survived: Odalbert (923-935), Frederick (958-991), Hartwig (991-1023), Thietmar II (1025-1041), and Baldwin (1041-1060). In addition the *Traditionsbuch* of the Benedictine monastery of Saint Peter's, an archiepiscopal proprietary foundation, whose abbot was until 987 the archbishop himself, is also available. This codex covers the period between 987, when the abbey's endowment was separated from the archbishopric's, and 1259.[10] The *Traditionsbücher* contain notices about the archbishopric's or the monastery's acquisition of property and people. The entries in the older codices, most notably in the *Codex Odalberti,* are largely summaries of now lost archiepiscopal charters. No formal written documents were ever drafted about most of the transactions recorded in the later *Traditions-bücher.* These later notices were simply a device to record the identity of the individuals who had witnessed a particular transaction and who could be summoned to the public court to give oral testimony if the proceedings were ever challenged; the *Traditionsbücher* themselves had no legal validity. The character of the codices is perhaps best illustrated by the frequently used formula which introduces the witness lists: "Isti sunt testes per aures adtracti" — a box on the ear had replaced, figuratively speaking at least, a charter as legal proof.[11]

There are a number of serious problems in using the *Traditionsbücher.* Most of the entries cannot be more precisely dated than the tenure in office of a particular archbishop or abbot. This is a formidable obstacle if one keeps in mind that Archbishop Frederick ruled for thirty-three years or that Abbot Tito (987-1025), the first abbot after the monastery's endowment was separated from the archbishopric's, served for thirty-eight. Moreover, the codices contain a bewildering number of first names. There are more than 600 different personal names, for instance, in 102 notices in the *Codex Odalberti.*[12] As was true in the rest of Germany, the nobles and the ministerials in the Salzburg area only started to adopt surnames toward the end of the eleventh century. To compound the problem, only the counts — and there are some exceptions even here[13] — are normally identified among the witnesses. The estate to which the other witnesses belonged is indicated in only five entries written before 1060.[14] Contemporaries who consulted the *Traditionsbücher* required no additional identification of the witnesses. It is thus extremely difficult to assign

[10] The archiepiscopal and abbatial *Traditionsbücher* were published by Willibald Hauthaler in the first volume of the *Salzburger Urkundenbuch.* All references are to this edition. The codex of the cathedral chapter, which was started after the introduction of the Augustinian Rule in 1121, is published in the same volume.

[11] For information about the *Traditionsbücher,* see Wilhelm Erben, "Untersuchungen zu dem Codex traditionum Odalberti," MGSL 29 (1889) 454-480; Willibald Hauthaler and Eduard Richter, "Die salzburgischen Traditionscodices des X. und XI. Jahrhunderts," *Mittheilungen des Instituts für oesterreichische Geschichtsforschung* (MIOG) 3 (1882) 63-95, 369-385; Oswald Redlich, "Ueber bairische Traditionsbücher und Traditionen," MIOG 5 (1884) 1-82; and Josef Widemann, "Die Traditionen der bayerischen Klöster," *Zeitschrift für bayerische Landesgeschichte* 1 (1928) 225-243.

[12] Josef Dittrich, "Personennamen im Codex Odalberti," MGSL 61 (1921) 55.

[13] See below p. 89.

[14] *Cod. Fri.* no. 12; *Cod. Tiet.* no. 17; and *Trad. St. Peter* nos. 19, 48, 51a.

individuals to specific families or to distinguish between contemporaries who belonged to different estates, but who bore the same name, or between the members of successive generations with identical first names. Under the circumstances there is an element of doubt involved in many identifications.

Nevertheless, it is possible to identify specific individuals with a fair degree of accuracy. The *Traditionsbücher* cover a distinct geographic region, the archdiocese of Salzburg, especially that section now located in Upper Bavaria, and deal with a restricted group of individuals, namely those people with personal, familial, feudal, servile, and/or spiritual ties to the archbishops or the monastery of Saint Peter's. Since distinctive first names were clearly a device to identify people in a period which lacked surnames — hence the multiplicity of personal names — it is highly probable in most cases that all the occurrences of a given name within a specific time period, for example, the episcopate of a particular archbishop, and especially among the members of a definite stratum of society, such as the archiepiscopal *familia*, are references to the same person. Some names such as Rupert, the patron saint of the archdiocese, or Aribo, a *Leitname* within the so-called Aribonen clan which dominated the archdiocese in the tenth century, admittedly recur frequently and were undoubtedly borne by several different individuals of diverse estates at the same time; but most of the names in the codices were sufficiently rare to refer to only a single individual in any given time period. While the legal and social status of the witnesses was not normally indicated in the entries, this information was usually provided in the case of the transactors and their relatives. By comparing the names of the transactors and their kinsmen with the names of the witnesses, especially the rare names in a particular codex, which are most likely to refer to the same individual, and by keeping in mind the context in which persons are mentioned, for example, the specific geographic region, it is possible to identify a good many people with a reasonable degree of certainty and to determine the estate of the witnesses in many of the entries. There will undoubtedly be questionable or erroneous identifications in any prosopographical study of obscure, legally unfree individuals who lacked surnames; but one of the chief reasons for employing this type of methodology is to compensate for the limitations imposed by the evidence.

These difficulties in using the *Traditionsbücher*, along with older German scholars' general reluctance to acknowledge the servile ancestry of the ministerials and their commitment to a legalistic and philological rather than a prosopographical, proprietary, and genealogical methodology,[15] may help to explain why comparatively little use has been made of this otherwise abundant source material in studying the origins of the Salzburg ministerialage. There has been only one monograph specifically devoted to the Salzburg ministerialage, the unpublished doctoral dissertation of Dominik Müller, "Die salzburgische Ministerialität im 12. und 13. Jahrhundert" (University of Innsbruck 1904).[16] All other discussions of the Salzburg ministerial-

[15] Freed (n. 5 above) 215-222.

[16] Unfortunately, the University of Innsbruck cannot locate its copy; and neither the *Salzburger Landesarchiv* nor the University of Salzburg, which have large collections devoted to local history, including unpublished dissertations, possesses a copy. Judging by the time-span

age have appeared in studies devoted to larger topics.[17] Special mention should be made of Karl Schwarzenberg's "Die Hörigkeit in der Erzdiözese Salzburg bis auf die Zeit Eberhards II. nach den Quellen des Salzburger Urkundenbuchs."[18] He examined the various terms which were used in the *Traditionsbücher* to designate the future ministerials and their transformation by the middle of the thirteenth century into the lower nobility of the nascent ecclesiastical principality. Unlike Flohrschütz, Schwarzenberg made no attempt to use the names in the transactions and the witness lists to identify specific individuals and to trace their genealogies or to explain the formation of an elite group within the *familia* in the tenth and eleventh centuries.

In spite of these problems, this article will show that it is possible to trace the movement of a segment of the servile population into the ministerialage in Salzburg between the tenth and the early twelfth century. The nature of the evidence makes the argument unavoidably somewhat technical and tentative, but a careful examination of the formulas used in the codices and of the identity of the transactors and of the persons who witnessed the traditions reveals a gradual but distinct change in the composition of the archiepiscopal entourage in the tenth and eleventh centuries, in which servile retainers replaced nobles and/or free vassals as the large noble clan

---

indicated in the title, Müller would have had little reason to use the *Traditionsbücher*. He was able to identify 126 Salzburg ministerial families, whose names have been published in Hans Widmann's *Geschichte Salzburgs,* 3 vols., Deutsche Landesgeschichte 9 (Gotha 1907-1914) 1.374-381.

[17] Richard Mell, "Abhandlungen zur Geschichte der Landstände im Erzbistume Salzburg," MGSL 43 (1903) 122-173 dealt with the ministerials as the precursors of the knightly estate in his investigation of the Salzburg estates prior to 1620. Paul Kluckhohn, *Die Ministerialität in Südostdeutschland vom zehnten bis zum Ende des dreizehnten Jahrhunderts,* Quellen und Studien zur Verfassungsgeschichte des Deutschen Reiches in Mittelalter und Neuzeit 4 (Weimar 1910) mentioned the Salzburg ministerialage; but Kluckhohn was more concerned with the Austrian, Bavarian and Styrian ministerials. Wilhelm Erben's "Beiträge zur Geschichte der Ministerialität im Erzstift Salzburg," MGSL 51 (1911) 185-208 clarified a number of specific points which Müller, Mell, and above all Kluckhohn had made in regard to the Salzburg ministerials. Mell, Kluckhohn, and Eber were deeply influenced by the then fashionable theories about the origins of the ministerials, largely designed to disprove or at least to diminish the significance of the ministerials' servile ancestry; and their work is primarily of historiographical interest today.

More recently, Helga Schedl, "Gericht, Verwaltung und Grundherrschaft im bayerischen Salzach-Saalach Grenzland unter der Herrschaft der salzburger Erzbischöfe," Ph.D. diss. (Munich 1956) 156-199, as part of her examination of the administrative and judicial structure of the area, identified the ministerial families who lived in the twelfth and thirteenth centuries in the so-called Rupertiwinkel, the section of the old ecclesiastical principality which was assigned to Bavaria after the Congress of Vienna. She relied heavily on the outdated views of older scholars for her conceptual framework. Ernst Klebel, *Der Lungau: Historisch-politische Untersuchung* (Salzburg 1960) 111-177, identified the few ministerial families who resided or who had property holdings in the Lungau. Finally, Heinz Dopsch, "Ministerialität und Herrenstand in der Steiermark und in Salzburg," *Zeitschrift des historischen Vereines für Steiermark* 62 (1971) 3-31, esp. 7-15, briefly discussed the origins and development of the ministerialage in Salzburg in explaining why the most powerful Styrian ministerials formed in the later Middle Ages a separate estate of dynasts, whereas the ecclesiastical principality of Salzburg only had a single estate of knights, which included the few surviving ministerial families.

[18] Karl Schwarzenberg, "Die Hörigkeit in der Erzdiözese Salzburg bis auf die Zeit Eberhards II. nach den Quellen des Salzburger Urkundenbuchs," MGSL 99 (1959) 1-79.

composed of the archbishops' kinsmen broke up into distinct lineages. By the mid-eleventh century there are definite signs that these servile retainers had coalesced with the clerical members of the *familia* to form a self-conscious, hereditary estate, later known as the ministerialage. This paper, then, will present an example of upward social mobility in the early Middle Ages and will seek to explain the circumstances under which such mobility occurred.

The year 1060 has been selected as the terminal date of this study for a number of reasons, beyond the obvious one that the archiepiscopal codices end in that year. The episcopate of Archbishop Gebhard (1060-1088), who was in exile for most of the time after 1077, was a decisive turning point in the history of the archdiocese. Salzburg became for a century a major center of opposition to the Salian-Hohenstaufen monarchy and of the religious reform movement which swept across Europe in the wake of the Investiture Conflict.[19] The ministerials, who became deeply involved in the turbulent politics of the archbishopric during the Gregorian Era, started around 1100, like the old free nobility, to form into distinct lineages named after a castle or village. The connection between the religious reform movement and the ministerials' increasing self-consciousness of their political and social importance, as is reflected in their adoption of surnames and in their patronage of and entrance into the new religious orders, merits a separate study.[20]

II. THE ARISTOCRATIC WORLD OF THE EARLY TENTH CENTURY

The *Codex Odalberti* presents a picture of an aristocratic world similar to that described by Karl Schmid in his analysis of the Carolingian and Ottonian *Libri memoriales.* This society was composed of large noble clans whose members could claim kinship, however remote, with a powerful magnate, lay or ecclesiastical, and which were associated with the possession of a particular bishopric, duchy, or county. Both paternal and maternal relatives were considered to be kinsmen, and

[19] For information, see Renate Bucher, "Das Erzstift Salzburg vom Investiturstreit bis zum Frieden von Venedig," Ph.D. diss. (Graz 1961); Ch. Dereine, "Les chanoines réguliers dans l'ancienne province ecclésiastique de Salzbourg d'après les travaux récents," *Revue d'histoire ecclésiastique* 55 (1960) 902-916; Leopold Grill, *Erzbischof Eberhard I. von Salzburg (um 1087 bis 1164, 22. Juni.)* (Stift Rein, Styria 1964); Franz Martin Mayer, *Die östlichen Alpenländer im Investiturstreite* (Innsbruck 1883); Stefan Weinfurter, *Salzburger Bistumsreform und Bischofspolitik im 12. Jahrhundert: Der Erzbischof Konrad I. von Salzburg (1106-1147) und die Regularkanoniker,* Kölner historische Abhandlungen 24 (Cologne 1975); Widmann (n. 16 above) 1.202-278; and Kurt Zeillinger, *Erzbischof Konrad I. von Salzburg 1106-1147,* Wiener Dissertationen aus dem Gebiete der Geschichte 10 (Vienna 1968).

[20] The connection between the religious reform movement and the old nobility has often been studied. See, for instance, Werner Goez, "Reformpapsttum, Adel und monastische Erneuerung in der Toscana," *Investiturstreit und Reichsverfassung,* ed. Josef Fleckenstein, Vorträge und Forschungen herausgegeben vom Konstanzer Arbeitskreis für mittelalterliche Geschichte 17 (Sigmaringen 1973) 205-239; Joachim Wollasch, "Reform und Adel in Burgund," *Investiturstreit* 277-293; and Karl Schmid, "Adel und Reform in Schwaben," *Investiturstreit* 295-319.

enates could be more important than agnates if they were more distinguished in their ancestry, wealth, and social position. In the absence of surnames, first names helped to identify the members of a particular clan. The same names or components of names, often the name of the clan's alleged famous or notorious common ancestor, recurred within the group. It is this repetition of names or components of names which is a key tool in isolating and in identifying the members of a particular clan. When the clan lost control of the ecclesiastical or secular office with which it was associated, it disintegrated as the individual nobles who composed the clan regrouped around different figures. This could easily occur since each individual member of a clan, except for brothers, possessed different sets of paternal and maternal relatives. Kinship was thus largely conceived of in horizontal rather than vertical terms in the ninth and early tenth century, that is, one's relationship to other people within one's own generation, in particular to a powerful magnate, was more important than descent in the agnate line from a particular ancestor.

As office-holding tended to become hereditary, however, in the tenth century, greater emphasis was placed upon agnate descent, a fact which is reflected in the increasing use of the same first names, inherited in the male line, in successive generations. This phenomenon can first be observed in royal houses, for example, the use of the names Otto and Henry by the Saxon dynasty. This practice was eventually imitated by the rest of the nobility and culminated in the adoption in the late eleventh century of surnames, usually the name of the family's most important castle or other possession. A fundamental change thus occurred in the structure of the nobility during the course of the tenth and eleventh centuries as the great amorphous clans of the Carolingian and early Ottonian periods, crystalizing around different magnates in each generation, were replaced by distinct dynasties, highly conscious of their lineage, with their own characteristic first names repeated in each generation and eventually identified by their surnames.[21]

Judging by the transactors and by the witness lists in the *Codex Odalberti,* Archbishop Odalbert (923-935) was surrounded by a large entourage composed of his kinsmen and/or nobles. He belonged to the powerful clan of the Aribonen, whom modern historians have named after Aribo, the margrave of the Danubian counties

---

[21] Karl Schmid, "Die Mönchsgemeinschaft von Fulda als sozialgeschichtliches Problem," *Frühmittelalterliche Studien: Jahrbuch des Instituts für Frühmittelalterforschung der Universität Münster* (FS) 4 (1970) 173-200; "Neue Quellen zum Verständnis des Adels im 10. Jahrhundert," *Zeitschrift für die Geschichte des Oberrheins* (ZGORh) 108 (1960) 185-232; "Religiöses und sippengebundenes Gemeinschaftsbewusstsein in frühmittelalterlichen Gedenkbucheinträgen," *Deutsches Archiv für Erforschung des Mittelalters* 21 (1965) 18-81; "Über das Verhältnis von Person und Gemeinschaft im früheren Mittelalter," FS 1 (1967) 225-249; "Über die Struktur des Adels im früheren Mittelalter," *Jahrbuch für fränkische Landesforschung* 19 (1959) 1-23; and "Zur Problematik von Familie, Sippe und Geschlecht, Haus und Dynastie beim mittelalterlichen Adel: Vorfragen zum Thema, 'Adel und Herrschaft im Mittelalter,'" ZGORh 105 (1957) 1-62; and Karl Schmid and Joachim Wollasch, "Die Gemeinschaft der Lebenden und Verstorbenen in Zeugnissen des Mittelalters," FS 1 (1967) 365-405. For a recent application of Karl Schmid's methodology to the study of the Bavarian nobility, see Wilhelm Störmer, *Früher Adel: Studien zur politischen Führungsschicht im fränkisch-deutschen Reich vom 8. bis 11. Jahrhundert,* Monographien zur Geschichte des Mittelalters 6 (Stuttgart 1973), esp. 29-69.

from 871 until his death shortly after 909;[22] Odalbert had been married to Rihni, who became a nun after his selection as archbishop. She was a relative of Margrave Luitpold (d. 907), the father of Dukes Arnulf the Bad (907-937) and Berthold (938-947) of Bavaria. Odalbert and Rihni had at least three sons, Counts Bernhard, Diotmar, and Otachar; four daughters, the nuns Himmiltrude and Rihni, another Rihni, and Heilrat, the widow of the archiepiscopal vassal Diotrih; and a grand-daughter Willa, who was married to Count Sighard IV, the brother of Archbishop Frederick.[23] The advocate Hartwig, whom most historians have identified as Odalbert's brother, was described as the archbishop's closest relative (*proximus suus*) (*Cod. Odal.* nos. 17, 83).[24] The archbishop's relatives frequently appear in the codex as witnesses. Many other individuals who are mentioned in the codex were also related to the archbishop. The deacon Reginolt gave, for instance, an allod to the archbishop for the benefit of the souls of Archbishop Pilgrim (907-923), Odalbert's predecessor, and Odalbert himself (no. 9). Since Margrave Aribo was the brother-in-law of Archbishop Pilgrim[25] and the uncle or grandfather of Odalbert[26] and since such arrangements were customarily made by relatives,[27] it is possible to conclude that Reginolt was the archbishops' kinsman.[28] The remaining transactors, laymen and clerics, men and women, who cannot now be identified as Odalbert's relatives,

[22] Michael Mitterauer, *Karolingische Markgrafen im Südosten: Frankische Reichsaristokratie und bayerische Stammesadel im österreichischen Raum,* Archiv für österreichische Geschichte 123 (Vienna 1963) 188-203. For additional information on the Aribonen, see Gertrud Diepolder, "Die Herkunft der Aribonen," *Zeitschrift für bayerische Landesgèschichte* 27 (1964) 74-119. The following older studies of the Aribonen, though they have not yet been completely replaced, are largely outdated: Jos. Egger, "Das Aribonenhaus," *Archiv für österreichische Geschichte* 83 (1897) 385-525; Eduard Richter, *Untersuchungen zur historischen Geographie des ehemaligen Hochstifts Salzburg und seiner Nachbargebiete* (Innsbruck 1885) 41-65; and Heinrich Witte-Hagenau, "Genealogische Untersuchungen zur Rechtsgeschichte unter den salischen Kaisern," *Mittheilungen des Instituts für oesterreichische Geschichtsforschung* supp. 5 (1896-1903) 371-474.

[23] Heinz Dopsch, "Der bayerische Adel und die Besetzung des Erzbistums Salzburg im 10. und 11. Jahrhundert," MGSL 110/111 (1970-1971) 128-132, 135. Störmer (n. 21 above) 105-109 has challenged the prevalent opinion that Rihni was a member of the Luitpoldingian clan. Instead, he links her to Oda, the wife of Arnulf of Carinthia and the mother of Louis the Child.

[24] Mitterauer (n. 22 above) 196. To avoid the repetition of too many similar footnotes, citations to specific entries in the codices will be made in the text itself.

[25] Dopsch (n. 23 above) 126-128.

[26] Dopsch (n. 23 above) 131 identifies Odalbert as Aribo's grandson, while Mitterauer (n. 22 above) 196-197 identifies him as Aribo's nephew.

[27] Schmid, "Neue Quellen" (n. 21 above) 211-223; "Struktur" (n. 21 above) 7-10; and "Religiöses Gemeinschaftsbewusstsein" (n. 21 above) 18-81; and Schmid and Wollasch (n. 21 above) 365-405.

[28] Abbot Hauthaler, the editor of the *Salzburger Urkundenbuch,* also suspected that Reginolt was a kinsman of Archbishops Pilgrim and Odalbert (*Cod. Odal.* no. 4, explanatory note). This in turn suggests that the archiepiscopal advocate Reginbert, who appears 62 times in that capacity and who served both archbishops (no. 21, explanatory note), and that the noble and vassal Reginhart, who is mentioned 30 times as a witness and twice as an advocate (no. 8, explanatory note), were also related, as is revealed by the common component *Regin-* in their names, to Reginolt and the two archbishops.

were described in the entries as *nobiles viri* (*feminae*) (*Cod. Odal.* nos. 4, 8, 15, 20, 22, 23, 25, 26, 28, 30, 32, 41-46, 48-53, 55-65, 67, 68, 71, 76-83, 85, 86, 88, 89, 92-98, 100). Since men who are identified in the traditions as nobles appear in different positions in the witness lists of various notices,[29] there can be little doubt that all the witnesses were also nobles. Archbishop Odalbert was the central figure in a noble clan which controlled the archdiocese in the first half of the tenth century.

Such ties of kinship were more important than feudal bonds in tenth-century Salzburg. The transactors possessed extensive allodial holdings. Fiefs (*beneficia*), owned by laymen (nos. 6-8, 23, 32, 39, 55, 65, 73, 82, 83, 85, 88, 101), by clerics (nos. 3, 11-13, 31, 36, 37, 40, 48, 54, 61, 69, 97), and even by nuns (nos. 59, 74), were normally only mentioned in the *Codex Odalberti* when their noble holders converted them into allods. The more precise term *foedum* never appears in the archiepiscopal or abbatial *Traditionsbücher*. Only seven individuals were identified in the *Codex Odalberti* as archiepiscopal *vassi*. These men were powerful noblemen, often, like the archbishop's son-in-law Diotrih, kinsmen of the archbishop.[30] *Vassus*,

---

[29] For example, the *nobilis vir* Graman (*Cod. Odal.* no. 20) was the sixth witness out of 16 in no. 6, twenty-fourth out of 40 in no. 12, twentieth out of 24 in no. 33, thirteenth out of 39 in no. 41, eleventh out of 73 in no. 44, seventh out of 20 in no. 73, twenty-fifth out of 41 in no. 77, and third out of 18 in no. 89b.

[30] The archiepiscopal *vassi* were: Diotrih (*Cod. Odal.* no. 44), who served as an envoy of Duke Arnulf (no. 44) and who was the son-in-law of Archbishop Odalbert (no. 41, explanatory note); the *nobilis vir* Eberhard (no. 97), who may have been identical with the Eberhard, who was the son of Rafolt (no. 82), who is mentioned as a witness 60 times (no. 7, explanatory note) and whom Mitterauer (n. 22 above) 150, 152 linked to Witagowo, a count in Upper Styria in 860; Heimo, who served as the archbishop's advocate in a tradition with the bishop of Regensburg (no. 66) and whom Mitterauer 152 also linked with Count Witagowo; Reginhart (no. 26), who is mentioned as a witness 30 times (no. 8, explanatory note) and who probably was a kinsman of the archbishop (n. 28 above); the *nobilis vir* Willihalm (no. 28), the son of Reginhart (no. 28, explanatory note), whom Mitterauer 184 associated with the clan of the Wilhelminer, who held a number of counties in the eastern marks in the ninth century; a Wolfperht (no. 101), who cannot be further identified; and Zuentipolch (no. 98), who Mitterauer 150, 152 also connected with Count Witagowo.

Karl Pivec, "Servus und Servitium in den frühmittelalterlichen Salzburger Quellen," *Südost-Forschungen* 14 (1955) 61 maintains that the word *vassus* was not used at all in the Salzburg sources before 1000 and that *servus* was employed, therefore, as a substitute for *vassus*. As the examples cited above indicate, the words *vassus* and *vassalus* occasionally appear in the Salzburg sources before 1000. Pivec's evidence that *servus* was used as a synonym for *vassus* is not very convincing. As proof Pivec cites the "servus sancti Rudberti episcopi nomine Tonazan, et alter vocabatur Ledi servus ipsius ducis [Duke Theodo of Bavaria]" (*Breves notitiae* 3, SUB 1.20), who discovered in 711/712 the Maximilianszelle in Bischofshofen, the Pongau. Pivec states that Tonazan and Ledi, whom Herwig Wolfram, "Libellus Virgilii: Ein quellenkritisches Problem der ältesten Salzburger Güterverzeichnisse," *Mönchtum, Episkopat und Adel zur Gründungszeit des Klosters Reichenau*, ed. Arno Borst, Vorträge und Forschungen 20 (Sigmaringen 1974) 191-193 identified as members of the noble clan of the Albina, were military vassals of St. Rupert and Duke Theodo. Störmer (n. 21 above) 18-21 has shown, however, that such *servi principis* occupied an intermediary position as a privileged group within the lower strata of society between the *nobiles* and the *servi*. Störmer 212-213 believes that either the Albina underwent a phenomenal social rise in the eighth century or the designation of Tonazan and Ledi as *servi* was a deliberate falsification in order to strengthen Salzburg's claim to the Maximilianszelle. In any case, this use of the word *servus* for a vassal, if this is the correct interpretation of this passage, the most common designation for a vassal in western Europe, was never employed in the later *Traditionsbücher;* and only one individual, the Bavarian count-palatine Aribo I, the son of Count Chadelhoh, was described as a *vassalus* in a later codex (*Cod. Fri.* no. 15). The same entry in the *Codex Fridarici,* written in about 976, used, however, the word *milicia* in opposition to *familia,* indicating the continued existence in the archdiocese of legally free individuals who owed the archbishop military service. These free vassals and holders of fiefs were undoubtedly included among the *fideles* whose advice and consent Odalbert repeatedly sought and who witnessed the transactions. "Cum consultu fidelium suorum clericorum atque laicorum" is a typical formula (*Cod. Odal.* no. 65).

Fideles was an ambiguous word with a wide range of possible meanings. It could simply mean the Christian faithful, and it was employed in this sense in the notification clauses of the entries. A typical notification clause stated: "Notum sit omnibus Christi fidelibus" (*Cod. Odal.* no. 3). This phrase was used interchangeably with such expressions as: "Et est etiam omnibus christianitatis cultoribus agnoscendum" (no. 47); "Quapropter omnis, qui christiano profitetur nomine, agnoscat" (no. 83); and "Notum sit igitur omnibus christicolis" (no. 92). In this context *fideles* merely referred to the Christian faithful of the archdiocese, but in tenth-century Freising *fideles* was also the technical term for the free vassals.[31] Since it does not seem very likely that the archbishop sought the advice of all the Christian faithful, regardless of their social and legal position, before engaging in a transaction, it is possible to conclude that *fidelis* was also used in Salzburg as a synonym for *vassus*. The absence of specific technical terms to distinguish the archbishops' lay vassals, some of whom owed their lord military service, from the clerical vassals, and to differentiate the fiefs held by laymen from the benefices of clerics, and the fact that the transactors, including the holders of fiefs, were normally described as nobles rather than as archiepiscopal vassals, suggest, however, that the feudal system was never very deeply entrenched in the archbishopric. This basic weakness of the feudal system helps to explain why the German princes, like the archbishops of Salzburg, were forced to turn to their servile dependents for faithful retainers when the great noble clans composed of their kinsmen disintegrated into distinct noble dynasties.[32]

---

points to the lowly status of a vassal at the beginning of the eighth century; and it is hardly likely that such a term would be applied later on to vassals of noble origin. Pivec's other examples are drawn from the second half of the tenth century or the early eleventh century. The peculiar transaction in which the noble Chunihoh freed his sons from *servilium* (*Cod. Fri.* no. 18) appears to refer to a noble's redemption of his illegitimate sons from servitude rather than from vassalage (Pivec's translation of *servilium*), which was not so onerous in Salzburg as to require manumission. The other *servi* cited by Pivec (*Cod. Fri.* nos. 8, 19 and *Cod. Hart.* nos. 7, 35) were members of the archiepiscopal *familia,* the precursors of the later ministerials. *Servus* in this context referred to their status as non-free *familiares,* not to their status as vassals. *Fideles* was the standard designation for the vassals in the Salzburg sources (see below, p. 77).

[31] Flohrschütz (n. 8 above) 11-13. Störmer (n. 21 above) 264 states that *fidelis* was the standard designation after the ninth century for a vassal in Bavaria.

[32] Bosl, "Über soziale Mobilität" (n. 7 above) 158-169; and "Das ius ministerialium" (n. 7 above) 291-296.

The use of the word *ministerialis* in the *Codex Odalberti* requires special scrutiny. The term, which had referred in late Antiquity to the imperial household slaves, was applied under the Carolingians to a great variety of state, court, and domestic officials, that is, to a count or a bishop as well as to a stableboy, and did not designate the members of a particular estate.[33] In the following example the term was clearly being applied to men of relatively low social standing who could be given away. In 908 Louis the Child gave to the church of Salzburg the royal manor at Salzburghofen, two tolls, and the royal revenues from the gold, salt, and animals in Bad Reichenhall and the territory located between the Saalach and the Salzach Rivers. Three *ministeriales homines,* Kerolt, Stinno, and Engilwan, and their wives, children, and property were included in the gift.[34] The three men were probably charged with the administration of the manor and/or with the collection of the tolls and the other royal revenues. There was a tendency in the late Carolingian period, however, as the next example illustrates, to use the term as an honorific for high-ranking officials of noble origin.[35] In 888 King Arnulf of Carinthia freed the allods located in the Bavarian eastern mark which belonged to his butler, the *ministerialis* Heimo, the son of Count Witagowo, from comital jurisdiction.[36] This charter is in fact one of the rare surviving examples of the grant of an immunity to a layman.[37] The *ministerialis* Heimo was obviously a powerful nobleman and the social superior of Kerolt, Stinno, and Engilwan.

This late Carolingian usage of *ministerialis* as an honorific for noble office-holders persisted in the *Codex Odalberti.* Five of the six men who are specifically identified in the codex as ministerials were nobles. Rafolt, who witnessed sixty traditions,[38] was called, for instance, both a noble and a ministerial.[39] The sixth man, the

---

[33] Karl Bosl, "Vorstufen der deutschen Königsdienstmannschaft: (Begriffsgeschichtlich-prosopographische Studien zur frühmittelalterlichen Sozial- und Verfassungsgeschichte)," *Frühformen* (n. 7 above) 232-238, 250-255.

[34] SUB 2 no. 40. Otto I confirmed the charter in 940; SUB 2 no. 42.

[35] Bosl (n. 33 above) 252-255.

[36] SUB 2 no. 30. Heimo was called Arnulf's butler in a later forgery, SUB 2 no. 32, but there appears to be no question about the basic accuracy of the document. For information on the family, see Mitterauer (n. 22 above) 144-153.

[37] Georg Waitz, *Deutsche Verfassungsgeschichte,* ed. 3 (Graz 1955) 4.457-458.

[38] *Cod. Odal.* no. 7, explanatory note.

[39] Rafolt was specifically called a *nobilis vir* in *Cod. Odal.* no. 71, a revised version of no. 7. In the tenth-century table of contents to the codex, SUB 1.63, 65, he was described as a *ministerialis* in the headings for both entries. The *ministeriales* Jacob and his father Ruodgoz exchanged property in the Pinzgau with the archbishop (*Cod. Odal.* no. 73). Jacob was probably identical with the *nobilis vir* Jacob who had engaged in another transaction with the archbishop (no. 25). Diepolder (n. 22 above) 87-88 and 111-112 argues that the noble Jacob (no. 25) was the son or nephew of Margrave Aribo, but categorically denies that he could have been identical with the ministerial. I suspect that she simply associated the term *ministerialis* with a person of servile origin and thus excluded the possibility that the noble Jacob could have been identical with the ministerial. While it is impossible to prove that they were identical, the cases of Heimo and Rafolt clearly prove that a noble could be called a ministerial in the tenth century. The *ministerialis* Gotabert gave Odalbert his allod at Herioltinga (now unidentifiable) and received in exchange as an allod his fief located at Letting, south of Saalfelden (no. 6). The only other

archiepiscopal ministerial and chamberlain (*camerarius*) Deganbert, who was involved in four separate transactions with Odalbert (*Cod. Odal.* nos. 35-38), poses more of a problem. Deganbert is described as the archbishop's freeman (*cum quodam homine suo libero Deganperht*) (no. 37) rather than as a noble, is never listed among the witnesses, and in two of the four transactions (nos. 35, 36) required, like a woman or a cleric, the services of an advocate. Karl Schwarzenberg in his study of the servile population in the archdiocese cited Deganbert as an example of a person of servile origin who attained freedom in the archbishop's service.[40] A more likely explanation is that the archiepiscopal chamberlain was in fact a cleric. The chamberlain Diotbald, who employed his brother Otachar as his advocate (no. 3), was specifically described in another entry as a *nobilis clericus* (no. 15). In this context *ministerialis* apparently meant a cleric who held an important household office although it is not clear whether Deganbert, like Diotbald, was also of noble origin. It was this use of the same word *ministerialis* for both high-ranking officials of noble ancestry in the late Carolingian and early Ottonian periods and for the twelfth-century estate of legally unfree individuals which caused some older German scholars to conclude that the twelfth-century ministerials, in spite of the restrictions upon their liberty, were in fact the descendants of free men and even of nobles who had entered into a position of dependency.[41] While it is possible to understand how some of the descendants of men like Kerolt, Stinno, and Engilwan might have been included in the later ministerialage, it is impossible to imagine under what circumstances the offspring of such obviously powerful men like Heimo and Rafolt could ever have been numbered among the servile population. The origins of the later ministerialage must be sought elsewhere, namely, among the serfs.

Mancipium, which simply meant the inhabitant of a hide (*mansus*), was by far the most common designation for a serf in the *Codex Odalberti.* Such *mancipia* were merely objects to be traded along with the land on which they dwelled. In one transaction no less than 212 *mancipia* were exchanged (*Cod. Odal.* no. 85). The term was used in Bavarian sources, including the archiepiscopal *Traditionsbücher,* for both the *servi manentes,* the wealthier serfs who possessed their own quasi-hereditary tenures, and the *servi proprii,* the propertyless serfs who were at their lord's complete disposal.[42] Both categories of serfs were meant when the archbishop granted the noble Marchwart a village "cum aedificiis et mancipiis tunc inibi manentibus exceptis

---

layman in the codex with a similar name, Kotaperht, witnessed an exchange of property between Archbishop Odalbert and, significantly enough, Bishop Gotabert, who was serving as an auxiliary bishop in Carinthia (no. 1). It is possible to surmise that the ministerial and the auxiliary bishop named Gotabert were kinsmen. Finally, the *ministerialis* Erchanbald, who witnessed one tradition (no. 87), exchanged property in the valley of the Sempt River in Bavaria with the archbishop (no. 39). Störmer (n. 21 above) 344 linked Erchanbald to Bishop Erchanbald of Eichstätt (882?-912), whose clan controlled the bishopric. These ministerials were undoubtedly of noble origin.

[40] Schwarzenberg (n. 18 above) 10.

[41] Mell (n. 17 above) 123-127 cited, for example, Rafolt and Deganbert as examples of free men who became ministerials in the tenth century.

[42] Dollinger (n. 6 above) 265 and 280; and Schwarzenberg (n. 18 above) 21.

duobus, et si forte aliquid exinde in servitio dei domus tunc foret occupatum pretermisit..." (no. 83). *Servus* could simply be employed as a synonym for *mancipium.* One entry (no. 82) referred, for example, to "mancipia V n[ominata] Hugipold et Ermpurgam uxorem eius cum filiis tribus et ipsum servum cum uxore domui dei reliquit." The terms *servi casati* or *servi manentes* were not used in the *Codex Odalberti,* but a few *servi proprii* are mentioned. In one transaction (no. 81) the archbishop's son Bernhard gave his brother Diotmar in Odalbert's presence a *servus proprius* named Goteschal and received in return another *servus proprius* Ruozo, whom he then gave to his father. The transactors tended to distinguish, however, between the *servi* whose names were stated in the notices and the great mass of the *mancipia* who often remained anonymous. Archbishop Odalbert granted his son Bernhard and his daughter Himmiltrude, for example, various properties in the Tyrol and in Bavaria "cum mancipiis omnibusque pertinentibus," three boatmen (*nautae*), and a saltpan in Bad Reichenhall with the *servus* Scrutolf and his wife and sons, Uualtrih, Azo, Strulli, and Vuano (no. 76). Scrutolf may have been responsible for the operation of the saltpan. These *servi* who were singled out by name seem already to have been the beneficiaries of a process of selection which had started to separate them from and to raise them above the other inhabitants of the manor, but the Salzburg sources do not reveal whether they were *servi proprii* or *manentes.* It is probably foolish to draw too rigid distinctions between the two categories of serfs since a lord undoubtedly found his servants wherever he could in the turbulent tenth century; but as the later *Traditionsbücher* indicate, the twelfth-century ministerials were the descendants of men who had risen out of the ranks of the dependent population.

III. The Emergence of the "Familia" in the Later Tenth Century

At first glance the aristocratic world depicted in the *Codex Fridarici* appears to be very similar to that portrayed in the *Codex Odalberti.* The central figures were Archbishop Frederick (958-991), his brother Count Sighard IV, who exercised comital jurisdiction in the Salzburggau, his sister-in-law Willa, and his nephews Engelbert III, Nordbert, and Bishop Pilgrim of Passau (971-991) (*Cod. Fri.* nos. 1, 2, 14, 24). The archbishop and his brother were the sons of Count Sighard III who, along with his brothers Nordbert and Engelbert, had frequently witnessed notices in the *Codex Odalberti* (nos. 61, 82, 84). While Archbishop Frederick belonged to the so-called clan of the Sighardinger, his sister-in-law Willa, the granddaughter of Archbishop Odalbert and Rihni, was a member of the Aribonen clan.[43] Some of the other transactors, like the Bavarian count-palatine Aribo I (d. 1000), an archiepiscopal vassal (*Cod. Fri.* no. 15) and a descendant of Margrave Aribo, could also claim kinship with the archbishop or his brother's family. Since the eighteen witnesses in

[43] Dopsch (n. 23 above) 134-136.

one transaction (no. 12) are specifically identified as *nobiles viri,* the initial impression is that the social structure of the archdiocese had not changed since the death of Archbishop Odalbert.

Yet the differences between the two codices are more significant than the apparent similarities. The first and most obvious difference, as is revealed by Table 1,[44] is the reduction in the number of witnesses per tradition, a trend which continued in the later *Traditionsbücher.* The best explanation for this is that the great noble clans which had dominated the archbishopric in the first half of the tenth century and which had grouped around the archbishops had started to separate into distinct lineages conscious of their descent in the agnate line. The repetition of such obvious family names as Sighard, Engelbert, and Nordbert in successive or alternate generations among Archbishop Frederick's immediate relatives provides evidence for this. It is this use of the same first names inherited in the agnate line which, it will be recalled, Karl Schmid takes as a sign of the breakup of the large noble clan into dynasties. Through his son Engelbert III, Archbishop Frederick's brother Count Sighard IV was in fact the common ancestor of the later counts of Tengling, Peilstein, Burghausen, and Schala, who lived in the archdiocese until their extinction in the twelfth or thirteenth century.[45] The gradual dissolution of the large noble clan surrounding the archbishop and its replacement by separate dynasties would thus help to explain the progressive reduction in the size of the archbishops' entourage.

Second, Archbishop Frederick, like his suffragan Abraham of Freising (957-993), had started to seek the advice of the members of the *familia.* The consent clause in thirteen of the twenty-four transactions in the *Codex Fridarici* (nos. 1, 3-7, 9-11, 14, 17, 19, 21), at least in its wording, is similar to that in the *Codex Odalberti.* It states that the archbishop had sought the advice and/or consent of his *fideles,* clerical and lay. In four of the transactions, however, it is stated that he had also sought the

TABLE 1

Number of Witnesses Per Tradition

Codex	*Maximum Number*	*Minimum Number*	*Average*
Odalberti	74	5	22.3
Fridarici	33	4	16.7
Hartuuici	11	2	6.5
Tietmari	11	2	5.2
Balduuini	16	5	9.6

[44] The table is taken from Hauthaler and Richter (n. 11 above) 376.

[45] Dopsch (n. 23 above) 135; Richter (n. 22 above) 46-79; Franz Tyroller, *Genealogie des altbayerischen Adels im Hochmittelalter,* Genealogische Tafeln zur mitteleuropäischen Geschichte, ed. Wilhelm Wegener 4 (Göttingen 1962) 98-101; and Witte-Hagenau (n. 22 above) 371-409.

advice and/or consent of his non-noble vassals or the members of the *familia,* that is, the dependent members of the archiepiscopal household: "assensus et consilium fuit omnium suorum fidelium clericorum ac laicorum nobilium atque ignobilium" (no. 2); "secundum consilium suorum fidelium clericorum ac laicorum utriusque conditionis" (no. 8); "cum consultu fidelium suorum clericorum scilicet et laicorum nobilium et ignobilium" (no. 13); and "cum consilio tocius cleri tociusque miliciae familiaeque omnis" (no. 15). The remaining seven entries (nos. 12, 16, 18, 20, 22-24) contain no consent clause. There does not appear to be any pattern to the use or the non-use of the consent clause or to the choice of the particular formulation; for example, consultations with the non-noble vassals were not limited to transactions which involved their social peers. The four transactions in which the archbishop specifically sought the advice of his non-noble vassals or the members of the *familia* involved his sister-in-law Willa (no. 2); a *servus* of Saints Peter and Rupert (no. 8); the noble cleric and archdeacon Richer (no. 13); and the count-palatine Aribo (no. 15). On the other hand, in two other traditions with his sister-in-law the archbishop consulted only with his *fideles* (no. 14) or sought no advice at all (no. 24); and in an exchange of property with another *servus* Wolfperht, Frederick acted merely upon the advice of his *fideles,* clerical and lay (no. 19).

Since the consent clause in three of the entries (*Cod. Fri.* nos. 2, 8, 13) clearly indicates that non-nobles could be included among the *fideles,* this raises the question whether the term *fideles* in the remaining notices where there is no qualifying phrase such as *nobilium et ignobilium* or *utriusque conditionis* might also have encompassed the archbishop's servile vassals. Unfortunately, the estate of the witnesses is indicated in only one entry, where they are specifically identified as *nobiles viri* (no. 12). This notice, which contains no consent clause, involved an exchange of property between Frederick and the noble archdeacon Liutfrid; and the identification of the witnesses as nobles may be an indication that this was no longer always the case. On the other hand, an Adaluni, presumably the same person as the Adaluni who was identified as the father of the *servus* Wolfperht (no. 19), appeared as a witness in one transaction where Frederick had consulted with his non-noble vassals (no. 2) and as the tenth of thirty witnesses in one notice where only the *fideles* without a qualifying phrase are mentioned (no. 14). Wolfperht himself served as the twenty-first of twenty-five witnesses in one of the transactions in which the archbishop sought the advice of his non-noble vassals (no. 13). There is thus at least some evidence to suggest that *servi* occasionally acted as witnesses under Archbishop Frederick, even when it was not explicitly stated in the consent clauses; but this evidence is too fragmentary to draw any firm conclusions about how frequently and under what circumstances this occurred. But the notices leave no doubt that non-nobles had joined the archiepiscopal entourage, perhaps even replacing members of the nobility, and that Archbishop Frederick, at least on occasion, sought their advice and consent.

The identity of these non-noble vassals is revealed by two traditions. In about 963 "quidam servus sancti Petri sanctique Ruodberti n[ominatus] Diotrih" gave to the archbishop his allod of three hides (*hobae*) and twelve yokes (*iugera*) in Meggenthal, near Tittmoning in Upper Bavaria, and received in return an equal amount of land at Lanzing, also situated near Tittmoning, which he and his posterity were to possess in perpetuity (*Cod. Fri.* no. 8). The exchange was witnessed by twenty individuals, the first two of whom were identified as counts. In the other instance (no. 19), "quidam familiae servus n[ominatus] Wolfpreht" gave to the archbishop on 1 August 976 in Regensburg one hide located at Aich; the noble Erchanger, as the advocate of Wolfperht's wife, handed over forty yokes of arable land and fields situated at Deissenbach, northwest of Mühldorf in Upper Bavaria. In exchange Wolfperht received in perpetuity whatever lands his father Adaluni had previously held in fief at Saxinga (now unidentifiable) which he could dispose of as he wished. This transaction was witnessed by nineteen individuals whose societal position is not indicated; but the first two of them can be identified as the archbishop's nephew Nordbert and the count-palatine Aribo.

There are several things that should be pointed out about these two transactions. The first is that they occurred at all. There is not the slightest evidence that Archbishop Odalbert had ever exchanged property with a member of his household. In the *Codex Odalberti, mancipia* were merely appurtenances of the land on which they dwelled; they did not engage in property dealings with their lord. Second, these *servi* already owned allods and had been holding fiefs from the archbishops for at least two generations (Adaluni and Wolfperht), that is, since at least 950. While it is impossible to establish any genealogical or proprietary connection between Diotrih, Adaluni, and Wolfperht and the few *servi*, like Scrutolf, who had been singled out for special mention in the *Codex Odalberti* thirty or forty years earlier, such a link may very well have existed although Archbishop Frederick was undoubtedly also free to select additional retainers from the ranks of the servile population. Third, there is some evidence to indicate that these *servi* may have had personal ties to the Sighardinger clan. Count Sighard IV, the archbishop's brother, also possessed an allod in Meggenthal (*Cod. Fri.* no. 1). The advocate Erchanger (we presume that he too was a kinsman of the archbishop) owned an allod in Aich (no. 21). This possible personal acquaintance with prominent nobles, particularly with close relatives of the archbishop, may explain why these *servi* in particular had been singled out for preferment.

Finally, and perhaps most interesting of all, is that Wolfperht should have traded property with the archbishop in Regensburg in the summer of 976. King Otto II and the German magnates were meeting in Regensburg after a successful siege of that city in July, in which Wolfperht may have participated as one of Frederick's warriors, to discuss the fate of the Bavarian duchy after the suppression of the revolt of Otto's cousin, Duke Henry the Wrangler of Bavaria (955-976, 985-995). They made a number of crucial decisions: Margrave Leopold, the first of the Babenberg rulers of Austria, was enfeoffed with the eastern mark which his descendants were destined to govern until their extinction in 1246; Carinthia was separated from Bavaria and elevated to the rank of an independent duchy; and Otto II's nephew, Duke Otto of

Swabia, was installed as the new duke of Bavaria.[46] The archbishop clearly valued Wolfperht's services if, in the midst of deliberating about such weighty matters of state, he and his kinsmen concerned themselves with the disposition of a few acres owned by a *servus*. All of the evidence – the presence of members of the *familia* in the archiepiscopal entourage, including at the Regensburg Diet; the archbishop's consultation with them; their hereditary possession of both allods and fiefs; their exchange of property with their lord; and their possible testificatory function – indicates that a small segment of the servile population had experienced rapid upward social mobility in the second half of the tenth century in Salzburg, as it had in Freising under Frederick's contemporary and suffragan, Bishop Abraham.

IV. THE DOMINANCE OF THE "FAMILIA"
IN THE FIRST HALF OF THE ELEVENTH CENTURY

The clerical and lay members of the *familia,* to judge by the identity of the transactors and of the witnesses in the *Traditionsbücher,* gradually replaced the archbishops' kinsmen and free vassals as the prelates' most frequent companions in the first half of the eleventh century. Archbishop Hartwig (991-1023), the son of the count-palatine of Bavaria, Hartwig I (953-ca. 985), was related in a way that can no longer be precisely defined to Archbishop Odalbert's brother, the advocate Hartwig. He was connected through his sister Adala, who had married the count-palatine Aribo I (d. 1000) and Count Engelbert III (d. 1020), Archbishop Frederick's nephew, to both the Aribonen and the Sighardinger.[47] Another sister, Wichburg, the founder of the Benedictine nunnery of Sankt Georgen am Längsee in Carinthia, was the widow of Count Otwin of the Lurngau and the Pustertal.[48] A number of Hartwig's other relatives still held important positions in the archdiocese during his archiepiscopate or exchanged property with him: his nephew Hartwig, the chancellor (*primicerius*) of the church of Salzburg and subsequently bishop of the suffragan diocese of Brixen (1022-1039) (*Cod. Hart.* no. 14); his nephews Count Sighard and the deacon Frederick, the sons of his sister Adala and brother-in-law Count Engelbert (no. 28);[49] and the advocate Odalscalch (nos. 6-12, 14, 36), whose name is reminiscent of Archbishop Odalbert's and who gave an allod to Saint Peter's for the benefit of Hartwig's soul (*Trad. St. Peter* no. 37). In 1058 Frederick, the son of Eberhard, the count along the Isar and Vils Rivers in Bavaria, gave the Friulian village of San Odorico with its chapel to the cathedral chapel in memory of his kinsman (*cognatus*) Archbishop Hartwig (*Trad. Dom.* no. 1). On the other hand, no known relative of Hartwig's successors, Thietmar II (1025-1041) and Baldwin (1041-1060), is even mentioned in their codices of traditions; and the identities of their families are in fact unknown. Baldwin's name, which was rare in this period in Bavaria,

[46] Max Spindler, *Handbuch der bayerischen Geschichte* (Munich 1967) 1.222-224.
[47] Dopsch (n. 23 above) 137-144.
[48] SUB 2 no. 65.
[49] Richter (n. 22 above) 46-48.

suggests that he came from northwestern Germany.[50] Even if some of the transactors were Thietmar's and Baldwin's kinsmen, it is noteworthy that they were no longer being identified as such. The noble clan centered around the archbishops had disappeared.

The change in the archbishops' relations with the nobility of the archdiocese is most clearly revealed by an examination of the social origins, where they are known, of the transactors in the five archiepiscopal *Traditionsbücher.* The transactors have been classified in Table 2 in eight categories: noblemen, noble clerics, noblewomen, freemen, lay members of the *familia,* clerical members of the *familia,* female members of the *familia,* and unknown. Individuals who engaged in more than one transaction with the archbishop have been listed only once. The women who have been listed in the table acted either alone or in conjunction with their husbands.

TABLE 2

Social Origins of the Transactors

Codex	Noble-men	Noble clerics	Noble-women	Free-men	Lay members of familia	Clerical members of familia	Female members of familia	Un-known
Odalberti	42	11	20	2	0	0	0	8
Fridarici	9	4	3	0	2	0	1	4
Hartuuici	6	2	0	1	19	1	0	4
Tietmari	2	1	0	1	21	7	1	3
Balduuini	7	2	1	1	9	3	0	4

The most striking thing which is revealed by Table 2 is the sharp decline in the number of noble transactors, male or female, starting with the episcopate of Archbishop Frederick, and the concomitant rise in the transactors drawn from the *familia* in the first half of the eleventh century. This does not mean that the nobility had completely disappeared from the archdiocese, since a number of nobles are still mentioned among the benefactors of the monastery of Saint Peter's in the period between 987 and 1060 (*Trad. St. Peter* nos. 2, 4, 6, 13, 18, 20, 25, 34-38, 40, 43, 45, 47, 50-52). The slight rise in the number of noble transactors under Archbishop Baldwin can be attributed in part to his efforts to obtain the payment of the canonical tithe on agricultural products in those parts of the archdiocese, Carinthia in particular, which had previously been required to pay only a smaller fixed amount in order to facilitate the conversion of the pagan Slavic population to Christianity.[51]

[50] Dopsch (n. 23 above) 144-145.

[51] Dominikus Lindner, "Vom mittelalterlichen Zehntwesen in der Salzburger Kirchenprovinz," *Zeitschrift der Savigny-Stiftung für Rechtsgeschichte,* Kanonistische Abteilung 46 (1960) 291-293.

Some of these nobles gave Baldwin property to free their remaining possessions from the archbishop's new financial exactions (*Cod. Bald.* nos. 11, 12). Their appearance in the *Codex Balduuini* may thus not have been entirely voluntary. The decrease in the total number of entries in the *Traditionsbücher* – 102 in the *Codex Odalberti,* 24 in the *Codex Fridarici,* 38 in the *Codex Hartuuici,* 36 in the *Codex Tietmari,* and 28 in the *Codex Balduuini* – is probably due to the fact that members of the nobility, who presumably owned far more property than the members of the *familia,* had ceased, as was also the case in Freising, to engage in transactions with the archbishops.

The other thing which Table 2 shows is the emergence of the clerical members of the *familia* to positions of prominence in the first half of the eleventh century, particularly under Archbishops Thietmar and Baldwin. Unlike Freising, the term *clericus proprius* was not used in the Salzburg sources; but the frequent designation of a cleric or a priest as a *nobilis vir* (*Cod. Odal.* nos. 48, 59-62) indicates by itself that not all members of the clergy were of noble ancestry. In one notice in the *Codex Fridarici* (no. 13), the cleric Reginolt headed the list of *mancipia* who were given to the church of Salzburg. Starting in the *Codex Hartuuici,* members of the clergy were specifically described as "quidam ex familia clericus" (*Cod. Hart.* no. 14) or "prespiter (sic) sancti Ruodberti" (no. 37). No attempt was made to disguise the fact that many of these clerics were married and had children. These clerical members of the *familia* should not be confused with the cathedral canons who were variously described as nobles, canons, and/or members of the church of Salzburg (*Cod. Hart.* no. 14; *Cod. Tiet.* no. 27; and *Cod. Bald.* nos. 6, 17). The notices themselves carefully distinguished between the two. The same entry in the *Codex Hartuuici* (no. 14) referred to "quidam nobilis clericus Iuuauensis ecclesię primicerius," the archbishop's nephew and namesake, and to Starchand, "quidam ex familia clericus." These clerical members of the household, the counterparts of the *clerici proprii* in Freising, may have been the descendants of clerics like Reginolt who were given to the church or of priests like Engilhart, who gave himself and his church and all the allods which he possessed at Tacherting on the left bank of the Alz, north of Trostberg, Bavaria, and at Mögling, southwest of Trostberg, to the church of Salzburg in the eighth century.[52] As was also the case in Freising in the first half of the eleventh century, the clerical and lay members of the *familia* had replaced the free vassalage and nobility as transactors in Salzburg.

An examination of the consent clauses and of the witness lists in the *Codices Hartuuici, Tietmari,* and *Balduuini* indicates that the members of the *familia* had also replaced the nobles and free vassals as the archbishops' advisers and as witnesses. There is a consent clause in twenty-four of the thirty-eight entries in the *Codex Hartuuici* (nos. 1, 5, 6, 10-15, 17, 18, 20, 23, 25, 28-37), notices concerning both nobles and servile transactors; it is absent in traditions involving both nobles (nos. 2, 3) and members of the *familia* (nos. 4, 7, 9, 16, 19, 26, 27, 38). In three cases,

[52] *Breves notitiae* 18, SUB 1.47.

involving the noble Thietmar (no. 1), an unknown individual (no. 13), and Count Sighard and his brother, the deacon Frederick (no. 28), it is specifically indicated that the archbishop had sought the consent of both the free vassalage (*militia*) and the *familia*. In nineteen entries Hartwig is merely said to have acted upon the advice of the *fideles*, clerical and lay; and in two instances (nos. 10, 11), both concerning *servi* of Saint Rupert's, it is specifically stated that he acted "secundum placitum (conplatitationem) totius familiae." While the majority of the entries in the *Codices Tietmari* and *Balduuini* likewise only mention the approval of the *fideles* (*Cod. Tiet.* nos. 1, 3, 4, 7, 14, 18, 19, 22; *Cod. Bald.* nos. 19, 24), the clergy and laity (*Cod. Tiet.* nos. 5, 8-13, 15, 21, 23, 24, 26, 28, 33-35; *Cod. Bald.* nos. 1-3, 6, 10, 17, 18, 20, 21), or the clergy and people (*populus*) (*Cod. Tiet.* no. 20), a number of other traditions state that the archbishop acted with the consent of the *familia* (*familia conlaudante*) (*Cod. Tiet.* nos. 2, 6, 17), the clergy and the *familia* (*conlaudante clero et familia*) (*Cod. Tiet.* nos. 29, 30, 32; *Cod. Bald.* nos. 7, 8, 23), or the clergy and laity of the *familia* (*cum consensu clericorum ac laicorum supradictę familię*) (*Cod. Bald.* no. 16). It is thus clear that in at least some transactions, particularly those where the transactor belonged to the *familia*, Archbishops Hartwig, Thietmar, and Baldwin consulted only with the clerical and lay members of their households. This again raises the question whether in the other traditions, especially those where the transactor himself belonged to the *familia*, the terms *fideles, clerici,* and *laici* without the addition of a qualifying phrase like *de familia* in the consent clause also referred to the members of the archiepiscopal household rather than to the free vassalage and the noble clergy.[53] This question can only be answered by a careful scrutiny of the witness lists.

It can safely be assumed that the witnesses in the two transactions in the *Codex Hartuuici* (nos. 10, 11), in which the archbishop sought the consent only of the *familia*, were members of the household. If it can be demonstrated that these same individuals also served as witnesses in transactions where only the *fideles* without any qualifying phrase are mentioned in the consent clause, there can be no further doubt that Archbishop Hartwig's servile retainers also acted as his advisers and as witnesses in those entries in which the archbishop's advisers were not specifically identified as belonging to the *familia*. The first notice (*Cod. Hart.* no. 10) was witnessed by three individuals: Ozi, Hugo, and Engilschalch. An Ozi was called the owner of half a servile hide in a notice in which the section identifying the transactor has been destroyed (no. 20). He served as a witness for the chancellor Hartwig (no. 14) and for the *ministerialis vir* Raban (no. 36); in both cases only the *fideles*, clerical and lay, are said to have consented. While Hugo was also the name of a contemporary noble (*Trad. St. Peter* no. 45), the Hugo, who appeared as a witness in five other entries in the *Codex Hartuuici* (nos. 26, 29-31, 33) in which *servi* were transactors and in one notice where a *prespiter sancti Ruodberti* exchanged property with the archbishop (no. 37), was almost certainly identical with the member of the *familia*, Hugo, who

---

[53] See above, p. 82.

witnessed no. 10. In five of these six traditions the archbishop is merely said to have consulted with his *fideles*. An Engilschalch appears as a witness in only one other transaction in the codex. This is the entry (no. 13) concerning the unknown individual in which the archbishop sought the advice of both the free vassalage and the *familia*. Since this Engilschalch headed the witness list, preceding a Sizo, a nickname of Count Sighard IV (no. 21), he cannot have been the same man who witnessed the transaction of a fellow *servus*.

The second notice (*Cod. Hart.* no. 11) was witnessed by four persons: Adalbert, Wezil, Hartwig, and Engilram. The first three were extremely common names borne by a number of roughly contemporary individuals, but even here it is possible to distinguish between the various men. Adalbert was the name of a noble (*Trad. St. Peter* no. 34a) and of a *ministerialis vir* under Hartwig's successor Thietmar (*Cod. Tiet.* no. 7); it was probably the latter who witnessed notice no. 11. An Adalbert appeared as a witness in twelve other transactions in the *Codex Hartuuici* (nos. 6, 9, 15, 17-19, 25, 26, 28, 30, 31, 35), nine of which involved members of the *familia;* in seven of these entries only the *fideles* or the laity gave their consent (nos. 15, 17, 18, 25, 30, 31, 35). In one of the remaining three notices (no. 28), where an Adalbert was the fourth of eleven witnesses, the archbishop acted with the advice of both the *militia* and the *familia*. The Adalbert who witnessed so many traditions where the transactor belonged to the archiepiscopal household was almost certainly a *servus* himself and not a nobleman. A Wezil is mentioned as a witness in only one other entry (no. 6), where the transactor was a noble, but where the archbishop acted "cum . . . consensu communi." Since this Wezil again follows Adalbert as a witness, he probably was identical with the Wezil who witnessed entry no. 11 and may have been a relative of Adalbert, with whom he was associated in the two witness lists. Hartwig was the name of the archbishop's nephew, the chancellor of the church of Salzburg (*Cod. Hart.* no. 14); of the count-palatine, Hartwig II (*Cod. Tiet.,* no. 3); and of a *servitor sancti Ruodberti* (*Trad. St. Peter* no. 19), this last in all probability the man who witnessed entry no. 11. A Hartwig served as a witness in twelve other transactions in the *Codex Hartuuici* (nos. 1b, 1c, 7, 14, 15, 17, 18, 20, 25, 31, 33, 36), seven of which concerned members of the *familia*. In two of the remaining traditions (nos. 1b, 1c), where Hartwig appears as the last of ten witnesses, the archbishop specifically sought the advice of the clergy and laity of either condition. Since it is highly improbable that either the archbishop's nephew or the count-palatine of Bavaria would have appeared in random positions without any further identification in the witness lists of entries where the transactor belonged to the *familia*, let alone have been named last in a tradition witnessed by people of free and servile status, the witness Hartwig can only have been the *servitor sancti Ruodberti,* Hartwig. Finally, an Engilram acted as a witness in three other notices whose transactors were *servi* (nos. 26, 27, 31); the *fideles* consented in one entry (no. 31).

This examination of the witness lists in the *Codex Hartuuici* indicates that by the year 1000 the witnesses were normally recruited from the *familia* in the entries where the transactor belonged to the *familia*, and that *fideles, clerici,* and *laici,* with or without the addition of a qualifying phrase like *de familia,* referred in this context to the members of the archiepiscopal household rather than to the free vassalage and the noble clergy. The members of the *familia* undoubtedly also served, as the entries themselves reveal, as witnesses for noble transactors; but it is impossible to separate the nobles and the *servi* in such cases. Indeed, it may very well be that in the three notices in the *Codex Hartuuici* (nos. 1, 13, 28), at least two of which involved nobles (nos. 1, 28), in which the archbishop consulted with both the free vassalage and the *familia,* it was the presence of the noble vassals and not that of the *familia* which was exceptional. One word of caution must, however, be added. In a number of entries a man with the name of a count who resided in the archbishopric, for example, Aribo (no. 38), Chadelhoh (nos. 4, 7), and Pabo (no. 4), headed the witness lists. These men should probably be classified as counts, even if they were not specifically designated as such, as was the case in a number of other traditions (nos. 2, 3, 5, 9, 21, 28). Nevertheless, it is possible to conclude that members of the *familia* usually served as witnesses for their social peers and that nobles, except for the counts, were normally only mentioned in transactions which concerned their fellow nobles.

This conclusion is supported by two other pieces of evidence. First of all, it is clear that this was the pattern in the abbatial *Traditionsbuch* under Hartwig's contemporary, Abbot Tito (987-1025). The gift of the *servitor sancti Ruodberti,* Hartwig, to the abbey for the benefit of his relatives' souls was witnessed, for instance, by sixteen individuals, the first of whom was his son Sigiboto (*Trad. St. Peter* no. 19). It is highly unlikely that nobles would have been listed after a person who was legally unfree. On the other hand, ten individuals witnessed the noble Herideo's gift of twelve *mancipia* to the abbey (no. 13). The witnesses were: Adalbert, Engildio, Adalbert, Weriant, Einhart, Hartwig, Voccho, Pubo, Adalbert, and Waltunc. An Adalbert was a kinsman (*cognatus*) of the noble Engildio (*Trad. St. Peter* no. 34a); the noble Einhart was described as a close relative (*propinquus*) of Waltunc (no. 18); the noble Pubo had a son named Hartwig (no. 20); and Weriant may have been related to the deceased Count Weriant (no. 2). These men who were related to one another and who, we may safely assume, were nobles witnessed each other's transactions in the abbatial *Traditionsbuch.* Second, the witness list in one transaction between Archbishop Thietmar and the *servus* Hartwig (*Cod. Tiet.* no. 17) was introduced with the words: "familia sancti Ruodberti id conlaudante et testimonio istorum approbante." This formula removes any lingering doubts that the witnesses were recruited from the *familia* in traditions involving their social peers, the type of transaction which composes the overwhelming majority of the entries in the *Codices Hartuuici, Tietmari,* and *Balduuini.*

This unavoidably detailed analysis of the consent clauses and witness lists in the eleventh-century *Traditionsbücher* has shown that the members of the *familia* replaced the archbishops' kinsmen and free vassals not only as transactors in the first half of the eleventh century in Salzburg, but also as witnesses and as the archbishops' advisers. While Archbishop Odalbert, and to a lesser extent Archbishop Frederick as well, had been surrounded by an entourage composed of relatives and/or noble vassals, the clerical and lay members of the *familia* were the most frequent companions of Archbishops Hartwig, Thietmar II, and Baldwin, both in Salzburg and in their journeys through the archdiocese. The dominance of the *familia* in the first half of the eleventh century was a direct consequence of the breakup of the large noble clans into separate dynasties.

V. FROM "SERVUS" TO "MINISTERIALIS": THE FORMATION OF THE NEW ESTATE

The growing importance of the lay members of the archiepiscopal household in the first half of the eleventh century is reflected in the increasingly more prestigious titles by which they were designated. While *servus* itself or equivalent expressions like *quidam servilis conditionis* (*Cod. Hart.* no. 35) remained by far the most common designation, *quidam de familia* or *ex familia sancti Ruodberti* appeared already in the *Codex Hartuuici* (nos. 21, 25, 26, 30-32, 38), more than a half century earlier than in Freising, and *quidam vir de familia* (no. 19), *minister* (no. 17 and Anhang), and *serviens* (no. 17) in the *Codex Balduuini*. These variations in terminology were adopted, at least in part, for literary purposes to avoid the repetition of the same word or phrase in a notice. Thus a certain Rupert was called both a *serviens* and a *minister* in an entry in which Archbishop Baldwin was titled *archiepiscopus, archipraesul,* and *archipontifex* (*Cod. Bald.* no. 17). *Servitor sancti Ruodberti* was used before 1025 in the abbatial *Traditionsbuch* for the archbishop's men (*Trad. St. Peter* no. 19), but never in the archiepiscopal codices. The abbey's own retainers were referred to under Abbot Tito as *fidelis servus* (*ancilla*) (nos. 5,10), *fidelis vir* (*femina*) (nos. 24, 27), and *servitor sancti Petri* (no. 46.)[54]

The further development in the use of the word *ministerialis* requires closer examination. While the term had been employed in the late Carolingian period and in the *Codex Odalberti,* as we have already seen,[55] primarily as an honorific for noble office-holders, by the first half of the eleventh century it was being applied exclusively to members of the *familia* who held a variety of domestic, manorial, or administrative posts. It is not completely clear when this change in usage occurred in the Salzburg sources. Two transactors, Liuther and Waltker, were identified in about 976 in the *Codex Fridarici* as *ministeriales viri* (nos. 16, 20). Since no men with these names are mentioned in any other entry in that codex as transactors or witnesses, it is impossible to tell whether *ministerialis* in this context referred to people of noble or servile ancestry. The first official who definitely was of servile origin was the *ministerialis vir* Raban, who sometime between 991 and 1023 gave Archbishop

---

[54] That *fidelis vir* referred to a servile retainer of the abbey rather than to a free vassal can be demonstrated by the following example. An Engilpero was called both a *fidelis servus* (*Trad. St. Peter* no. 5) and a *fidelis vir* (no. 29). After 1025 two men named Engilpero, perhaps the father and his son, appeared in two entries as witnesses separated from individuals who were identified as nobles (nos. 48, 51a).

[55] See above, pp. 78-79.

Hartwig his allod of fifty-three yokes situated at Grödig, south of Salzburg, and who received in return an equal amount of land at Halberstätten, northeast of the city (*Cod. Hart.* no. 36). In another entry Raban followed in a witness list an individual who was identified as the son of a *servitor sancti Ruodberti* (*Trad. St. Peter* no. 19) and he himself was called a *servus sancti Ruodberti* (*Cod. Tiet.* no. 4). In about 1041 the *vicedominus* Raban, presumably still the same person, traded some serfs with Abbot Rupert II of Saint Peter's (*Trad. St. Peter* no. 49a). While *vicedominus* became the title in the twelfth and thirteenth centuries of high-ranking officials in Salzburg, Friesach, and Leibnitz, who were selected from the ranks of the cathedral canons and the archiepiscopal ministerials and who were charged with the management of the financial affairs of the archdiocese,[56] it seems more likely that the *ministerialis vir* and *vicedominus* (an isolated use of the word in the eleventh century) Raban was merely a manorial or household official.

A number of entries in the *Codices Tietmari* and *Balduuini* leave no doubt that *ministerialis* still meant in the middle of the eleventh century an official of servile origin rather than the member of a particular estate. Odalbert, who received from Archbishop Thietmar II fifty yokes at Weisspriach near Mauterndorf in the Lungau in exchange for an equal amount of land at Saaldorf, about eight miles northwest of Salzburg in Upper Bavaria, was described as "quidam de familia sancti Ruodberti [nomine] Ódalpreht ministerialis fratrum canonicorum" (*Cod. Tiet.* no. 36). Some time later Odalbert gave Archbishop Baldwin another twelve yokes near Saaldorf for land at Weisspriach (*Cod. Bald.* no. 18). Odalbert presumably administered some of the property in the Lungau, including land at Weisspriach, which King Henry II gave to Archbishop Hartwig in 1002 and which passed upon the latter's death to the cathedral chapter.[57] A similar use of the word *minister* for a local administrator or reeve occurred in about 1050 in an exchange of property along the Inn River between Count Chadelhoh III and Archbishop Baldwin, in which the archbishop gave the count "quicquid ad ministerium Liutfridi pertinet . . . cum ministris in eodem ministerio habitantibus et inde beneficium habentibus" (*Cod. Bald.,* Anhang). In the last example, Totili, who was still serving in 1077 as the archiepiscopal butler (*Trad. St. Peter* no. 71), was described in the same entry in the *Codex Balduuini* as a *ministerialis vir* and a *servus* (no. 21).

This exclusive use of the word *ministerialis* for officials of servile origin rather than for members of the nobility, as had been the case at the beginning of the tenth century, explains why it had become by the middle of the twelfth century the most common designation for the estate itself. Thus when Bishop Altmann of Trent (1124-1149) gave in 1142 the Carinthian castle of Hohenburg with its appurtenances, including the ministerials, to the church of Salzburg, he stipulated that the ministerials

---

[56] Josef Karl Mayr, "Geschichte der salzburgischen Zentralbehörden von der Mitte des 13. bis ans Ende des 16. Jahrhunderts," MGSL 64 (1924) 9-12. Liutwin, who was *vicedominus* of Salzburg from 1121 until 1151, was described as "Liutuuinus qui et nummos accepit et dedit" (*Trad. Dom.* no. 51b).

[57] SUB 2 no. 64; and Klebel (n. 17 above) 55-64.

assigned to the castle were to live there in accordance with the law of the Salzburg ministerials ("ut ministerialium iure inibi vivant");[58] and in 1146 a cathedral
canon was described as "quidam clericus istius ecclesie nomine Pabo de ordine
ministerialium" (*Trad. Dom.* no. 51a). It is not altogether clear when *ministerialis*
acquired this technical meaning in Salzburg. Sometime between 1074 and 1088
a group of individuals who were identified as *ministeriales prefati archiepiscopi*
followed a group of nobles in a witness list in an entry from the *Traditionsbuch* of
the Benedictine monastery of Admont.[59] While *ministerialis* in this context referred
to the members of an estate rather than to archiepiscopal officials, the notice itself
was edited in the twelfth century. Most of the witnesses in this tradition also appear
in the so-called foundation charter of Admont. In this document, drafted sometime
between 1130 and 1135 and included in the Admont codex of traditions, Archbishop Conrad I (1106-1147) confirmed the donations which Archbishop Gebhard
(1060-1088) had made to Admont and listed the individuals who had witnessed
Gebhard's gifts. The *ministeriales Salzpurgensis ecclesie* appear at the end of the
list.[60] It seems virtually certain that this terminology reflects the usage of the
post-Investiture-Conflict era rather than the late eleventh century, since the word
ministerialis was not employed in this sense in any other document prior to the
1120s. Thus the term *servitor sancti Ruodberti* continued to be used in the
Traditionsbuch of Saint Peter's for the archbishop's men until the second decade of
the twelfth century (*Trad. St. Peter* nos. 71, 72, 123, 137a, 142, 145, 151, 152,
154). Indeed, as late as 1136, Henry of Seekirchen, the castellan of Salzburg between
1130 and 1139, was described in this way (no. 192). Nevertheless, it is significant
that the scribes of the twelfth century in editing or drafting these two entries from
the Admont codex regarded the servile retainers of Gebhard's episcopate as identical
with the ministerials of their own age.

As the so-called foundation charter of Admont of the early 1130s indicates,
ministerialis only acquired its technical meaning as the designation for an estate after
Archbishop Conrad's return from exile in 1121. *Ministerialis sancti Ruodberti* first
appeared in the abbatial codex in a notice written in the 1120s (*Trad. St. Peter* no.
144). Archbishop Conrad's purchase of the bridge over the Vöckla in Upper Austria
in 1134 was witnessed "ex viris illustribus tam ingenuis quam ministerialibus";[61] and
Wernhard of Julbach renounced his claims in the 1130s to property which had been
given to Berchtesgaden in the presence of Archbishop Conrad and "sub attestatione
multorum nobilium virorum ac honoratorum ministerialium Salzburgensis
ęcclesię."[62] The use of the adjectives *illustris* and *honoratus* to describe the ministerials speaks for itself for the status that these descendants of serfs had attained in
the archdiocese by the 1130s. The shift from *servitor* to *ministerialis* as the standard

[58] SUB 2 no. 207.
[59] *Ibid.* no. 105a.
[60] *Ibid.* no. 140.
[61] *Ibid.* no. 159.
[62] *Ibid.* no. 153.

designation is nicely illustrated by the following example. Sometime between 1104 and 1116 Auram, a *servitor sancti Ruodberti,* received from Saint Peter's whatever property the monks possessed at Kirchisen, north of Mühldorf, Upper Bavaria (*Trad. St. Peter* no. 142). Approximately twenty-five years later Auram of Kirchisen, *ministerialis ecclesię Salzburgensis,* gave all the allods which he owned at Kirchisen to the Augustinian canons at Gars.[63] *Ministerialis* had thus become by about 1130, approximately the same time as in Freising, the customary designation for the estate, a fact which undoubtedly reflects Archbishop Conrad's reliance on the ministerials in restoring order in the archdiocese after the turmoil of the Investiture Contest.

The recurrence of the same names or components of names among the archbishops' servile retainers in the first half of the eleventh century and the concentration of their property holdings in the same general area within the archdiocese are a clear indication, however, that the estate itself had formed by the middle of the eleventh century. Nineteen individuals are specifically identified as lay members of the *familia* in the *Codex Hartuuici,* twenty-four in the *Codex Tietmari,* and ten in the *Codex Balduuini.* If the persons who acted as witnesses for clerical and lay members of the *familia* are added to this core group of known *servi* under the assumption that the individuals who witnessed transactions involving *familiares* were normally recruited from the household, the total number of servile retainers mentioned in the three *Traditionsbücher* becomes sixty-four, eighty-one, and eighty-six, respectively.

There is a striking repetition of names or components of names, for example, *Adal-, Liut-,* and *Wolf-* or *-bero, -izili,* and *-rich,* among the men who have been singled out in this manner. Twenty-nine of the sixty-four names in the *Codex Hartuuici* reappear in the *Codex Tietmari,* and forty-two of the eighty-one names in the *Codex Tietmari* recur in the *Codex Balduuini.* This is all the more noteworthy if one keeps in mind that a vast number of possible names could be formed by combining the different components — more than 600 names are mentioned, after all, in the *Codex Odalberti.* There are two possible explanations, not mutually exclusive, for this recurrence of names. The first is that the same man served more than one archbishop. The archbishops may in fact have deliberately selected young men, as well as the most prominent members of the *familia,* to witness a transaction to insure that someone could testify about it for a considerable length of time. For instance, a presumably young Totili, a fairly rare name, first appeared before 1041 as the ninth of ten witnesses in a tradition of Archbishop Thietmar (*Cod. Tiet.* no. 35), headed the witness list in one of Baldwin's notices (*Cod. Bald.* no. 24), and served as the archiepiscopal butler, one of the four major court offices, in about 1077 (*Trad. St. Peter* no. 71). The other obvious explanation is that the same name or component of a name was often borne by successive or alternate generations. An Adaluni followed, for example, a Wolfperht and a Tagaperht as a witness in a transaction of Archbishop Hartwig (*Cod. Hart.* no. 16). These names are reminiscent of the *servus*

---

[63] *Ibid.* no. 179.

Wolfperht, who had received the fief of his father Adaluni approximately twenty-five years earlier (*Cod. Fri.* no. 19).[64] The Adaluni in Hartwig's notice probably was the grandson of the earlier Adaluni. The recurrence of the same names or components of names among the individuals who have been identified as members of the *familia* indicates that they already formed by the middle of the eleventh century a fairly stable, quasi-hereditary group who served the church of Salzburg rather than a particular prelate.

This conclusion is supported by the additional piece of evidence that the property of the members of the *familia* was concentrated in two distinct regions where the church of Salzburg had been richly endowed by the Agilulfinger dukes of Bavaria in the eighth century:[65] the immediate vicinity of the city of Salzburg, roughly the area bounded by Bad Reichenhall in the southwest, Traunstein in the west, Laufen in the north, and Seekirchen in the northeast; and the immediate vicinity of Mühldorf in Upper Bavaria, roughly the area bounded by Au am Inn in the southwest, Obertaufkirchen in the west, Neumarkt-Sankt Veit in the north, and Ötting in the east. They possessed only scattered holdings, judging by the traditions in the codices, in most of the territory which composes the modern Austrian province of Salzburg, namely in the mountainous Pinzgau, Pongau, and Lungau. In other words, the archbishops recruited their servile retainers from their oldest and most settled domains. If it is safe to conclude that individuals with identical or similar names holding fiefs or owning allods in the same general area and belonging to the same social stratum were kinsmen, then the archbishops' servile retainers had coalesced by the middle of the eleventh century into a distinct estate. It was precisely at this time, it should be recalled, that the special rights of the ministerials of the bishops of Bamberg were being codified in the oldest extant *Dienstrecht.*

It also appears probable that the clerical and lay members of the *familia,* who are mentioned so frequently together in the *Codices Tietmari* and *Balduuini,* inter-married and coalesced, like the *clerici* and *servi proprii* in Freising, to form the later estate of the ministerials. The following example may provide some proof for this hypothesis. Archbishop Thietmar gave to Chuno, a clerical member of the *familia,* and to his posterity a hide and seven yokes of land in Ringham, south of Petting, northwest of Salzburg (*Cod. Tiet.* no. 5). In 1147 Egilolf, a "ministerialis sancti Ruodberti," who was about to leave on the Second Crusade and whose wife was taking the veil, gave to the monastery of Saint Peter's his property at Ringham (*Trad. St. Peter* no. 296). It is at least possible that either Egilolf or his wife was a descendant of Chuno.

The persistence of the same names among the *servi* of the eleventh century and the ministerials of the twelfth, and the fact that ministerials like Egilolf owned property in places where clerical and lay members of the *familia* like Chuno had once possessed allods or fiefs, point to the continuity between the two groups. Unfortu-

---

[64] See above, pp. 82-83.
[65] Spindler (n. 46 above) 1.355.

nately, few documents survive from the period between 1077, when Archbishop Gebhard was forced to flee from the archdiocese, and 1121, when Archbishop Conrad returned in triumph to Salzburg; and this, as well as the lack of surnames before 1100, makes it difficult to trace the genealogies of noble, as well as ministerial, families prior to 1121. Nevertheless, three examples will help to illustrate the connection between the earlier members of the archiepiscopal household and the twelfth-century ministerials. Odalbert, a member of the *familia* of Saint Rupert's and an official of the cathedral chapter, received, as we have already seen,[66] property at Weisspriach near Mauterndorf in the Lungau from Archbishops Thietmar and Baldwin (*Cod. Tiet.* no. 36; and *Cod. Bald.* no. 18). A century later Trunt, a "ministerialis beati R[oudberti]," gave his property in Weisspriach to the cathedral canons (*Trad. Dom.* no. 117). Interestingly enough, a Drunt had witnessed the transaction between Archbishop Thietmar and Odalbert, the only time a man with that name is mentioned in the *Codex Tietmari*. The evidence points to the conclusion that Trunt was a descendant of either Odalbert and/or his kinsman and/or neighbor Drunt, especially since few ministerial families owned property in the Lungau.[67]

Second, among the prominent archiepiscopal ministerials in the first half of the twelfth century were two brothers, Adalbero and Wezil of Dietraming, who are first mentioned in the early 1090s (*Trad. St. Peter* no. 123) (see Table 3). Dietraming, the modern Diebering, is located between Hallwang and Eugendorf, northeast of Salzburg. Adalbero was the archiepiscopal seneschal (*dapifer*) and castellan of Werfen, a fortress situated south of Pass Lueg, a narrow mountain gorge through

TABLE 3
Dietraming

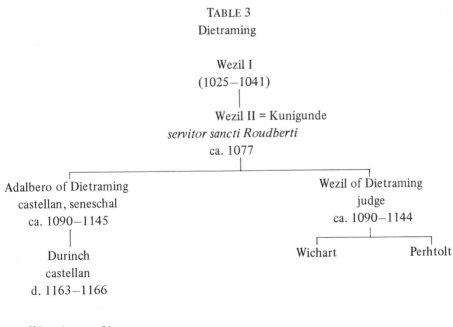

Wezil I
(1025–1041)
|
Wezil II = Kunigunde
servitor sancti Roudberti
ca. 1077

Adalbero of Dietraming
castellan, seneschal
ca. 1090–1145
|
Durinch
castellan
d. 1163–1166

Wezil of Dietraming
judge
ca. 1090–1144

Wichart   Perhtolt

[66] See above, p. 91.
[67] Klebel (n. 17 above) 111-138.

which the Salzach flows, and which controlled access to the city of Salzburg from the Pongau. Adalbero was succeeded as castellan by his son Durinch, who died sometime between 1163 and 1166. Adalbero's brother Wezil served as the archiepiscopal judge at Hallwang. The last known members of the family were Wezil's sons, Wichart and Perhtolt.[68] Adalbero and Wezil were the sons of Wezil II, a *servitor sancti Ruodberti,* who was listed sometime between 1074 and 1088 among the archiepiscopal ministerials in the *Traditionsbuch* of Admont[69] and who before 1077 gave to the monastery of Saint Peter's a number of different properties for the benefit of his soul and those of his relatives and of his wife Kunigunde (*Trad. St. Peter* nos. 66, 71, 72). Among the properties which Wezil II gave to the abbey were a mill on the Fischach, a stream north of Hallwang and Eugendorf (no. 66), and his allods at Fenning and Farmach, northeast of Eugendorf, and at Gausbach, southeast of Eugendorf (no. 71). The proximity of these properties to Dietraming is virtually positive proof that Wezil II was the father of the later Salzburg ministerials who adopted the name of that particular village as their surname. Wezil II may in turn have been a son or kinsman of the "quidam de familia sancti Ruodberti n[omine] Wezil," who exchanged forty yokes of land located in the vicinity of Anger, west of Salzburg, with Archbishop Thietmar sometime between 1025 and 1041 (*Cod. Tiet.* no. 30). It should be pointed out in this regard that Wezil II also possessed an allod at Geiselprechting, southwest of Vachendorf, about fourteen miles west of Anger (*Trad. St. Peter* no. 66).

The final example which demonstrates that the ministerials were the descendants of the *servi* of the eleventh century is the genealogy of two families of prominent Salzburg ministerials, the Kröpfel-Traunsdorf and the Haberland-Siegsdorf, whose common ancestor was named Etzo (see Table 4). In about 1077 Reginhart, the son of Etzo, handed over to Saint Peter's a number of properties on behalf of the *servitor sancti Ruodberti* Wezil, who was identified in the previous example as the father of

TABLE 4

Kröpfel-Traunsdorf and Haberland-Siegsdorf

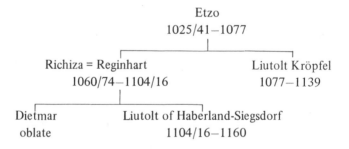

[68] Franz Valentin Zillner, "Salzburgische Geschlechterstudien 3: Die Werfener Burggrafen," MGSL 21 (1881) 25-37.

[69] SUB 2 no. 105a.

Adalbero and Wezil of Dietraming. Etzo and his son Liutolt headed the list of witnesses (*Trad. St. Peter* no. 66). This Etzo, the father of Reginhart and Liutolt, first served as a witness for a member of the archiepiscopal household sometime between 1025 and 1041 (*Cod. Tiet.* no. 35) and then appeared as a witness in a number of other notices until about 1077 (*Cod. Bald.* no. 5b; *Trad. St. Peter* nos. 65, 67). Etzo's son Reginhart witnessed a number of entries in the abbatial *Traditions-buch* between 1060/74 and 1104/16 (nos. 54, 69, 79, 84a, 84c, 128, 132, 150), and was listed among the *ministeriales Salzpurgensis ecclesie* in the so-called foundation charter of Admont.[70] Sometime between 1104 and 1116 Reginhart's widow Richiza, who had become a nun, gave an allod at Ernsting, Upper Austria, located approximately five miles southeast of Tittmoning, Upper Bavaria, to Saint Peter's on behalf of her deceased husband and her son Dietmar, an oblate in Saint Peter's (*Trad. St. Peter* no. 129). Since Reginhart and his son Dietmar headed the list of witnesses in another transaction (no. 150), there can be no doubt that the same Reginhart was involved in the various transactions.

Liutolt, another son of Reginhart, first appeared as a witness before 1116 in a transaction involving property at Lanzing, situated, significantly enough, southwest of Tittmoning, the same general area in which his mother Richiza had also owned property. A Liutolt Kröpfel preceded him as a witness (*Trad. St. Peter* no. 137a). Between 1125 and 1130 a Liutolt of Haberland, who was listed immediately after Liutolt Kröpfel, witnessed a number of entries on behalf of the Augustinian canons at Herrenchiemsee.[71] This Liutolt of Haberland was more commonly known as Liutolt of Siegsdorf after a village located on the Traun, south of Traunstein, Upper Bavaria,[72] and was being called *dominus,* a title hitherto reserved for the nobility, as early as 1135 (*Trad. St. Peter* no. 521), a half-century before such predicates were given to ministerials in Freising. That Liutolt of Haberland-Siegsdorf, who appeared as a witness between 1125/30 and 1160,[73] was the same person as Liutolt, the son of Reginhart, is proved not only by his position on the witness lists immediately after Liutolt Kröpfel, but also by the fact that Liutolt of Haberland was among the witnesses in 1139, when the noble Wichart of Ernsting gave Saint Peter's the church of Saint Bartholomew's in Ernsting (*Trad. St. Peter* no. 229), the very place where Reginhart's widow Richiza had once given property to the abbey. The Liutolt Kröpfel, with whom Liutolt of Haberland-Siegsdorf was associated and who is mentioned as a witness between 1090/95 (*Trad. St. Peter* no. 123) and 1139,[74] can only have been Liutolt of Haberland's paternal uncle Liutolt, the son of Etzo and the brother of Reginhart (*Trad. St. Peter* no. 66). This conclusion receives additional support from the fact that Liutolt Kröpfel's descendants also called themselves Traunsdorf after a village located west of Traunstein, about four miles from

---

[70] *Ibid.* no. 140.

[71] *Ibid.* nos. 132a, 132b, 210c.

[72] That Liutolt of Siegsdorf was the same person as Liutolt of Haberland is revealed by *Trad. St. Peter* no. 356b, where Liutolt of Siegsdorf conditionally gave Haberland to St. Peter's.

[73] SUB 2 nos. 132a, 346.

[74] *Ibid.* no. 196.

Siegsdorf, where the other descendants of Etzo had their chief residence.[75] Both
Liutolt Kröpfel and his nephew Liutolt of Haberland-Siegsdorf were specifically
identified as Salzburg ministerials.[76] The genealogies of these two families, the
Kröpfel-Traunsdorf and the Haberland-Siegsdorf, as well as that of the Dietramings,
the castellans of Werfen, provide conclusive proof that the archiepiscopal ministerials
of the twelfth century did not suddenly appear in 1100, but were the direct
descendants, in these two cases in the male line, of the *servi* who had attained such
prominence in the first half of the eleventh century.

VI. Causes of Upward Social Mobility in
Tenth-Century Salzburg

This study of the formation of the Salzburg ministerialage indicates that the
episcopate of Archbishop Frederick (958-991), when members of the *familia* first
started to replace the free vassals as the archbishop's companions, was the decisive
moment in the development of the new estate. A number of factors contributed to
the rapid upward social mobility of a segment of the servile population in the second
half of the tenth century. The most obvious was the threat posed by the Hungarians.
The Magyars, driven west from their Black Sea homeland by the Petchenegs, made
their first incursion into Bavaria in 900, a year after the death of King Arnulf of
Carinthia, who had employed them as mercenaries in his campaigns against the
Moravians in the 890s. After a number of raids had been repulsed in the following
years, a Bavarian force under the leadership of Arnulf's kinsman, Margrave Luitpold,
who had assumed control of the duchy during the minority of Louis the Child,
advanced into Pannonia and was annihilated at Bratislava. Margrave Luitpold and
Archbishop Thietmar I of Salzburg (874-907) were among the dead. Luitpold's son,
Duke Arnulf the Bad (907-937), defeated several bands of marauders between 909
and 913. This show of force halted further Hungarian attacks until 926. At the end
of that year Archbishop Odalbert was forced to seek refuge in Zell am See (*Cod.
Odal.* nos. 21, 22), deep in the Austrian Alps. The *Codex Odalberti* mentions
abandoned land located in a wide arc stretching from the immediate vicinity of
Salzburg (Siezenheim) toward the Inn in the northwest and across the Salzach in the
northeast (nos. 10, 60, 63, 93). Arnulf managed to reestablish peaceful relations with
the Magyars in the following year. Hostilities resumed under his brother, Duke

---

[75] A Rudolph of Traunsdorf, who I believe was the son of Liutolt Kröpfel (*Trad. St. Peter*
no. 167), was married in approximately 1122 to Adelheid, the sister of two prominent Salzburg
ministerials, Hartnit of Fischach, the castellan of Salzburg between 1151 and 1167, and
Marchwart of Itzlingen, the archiepiscopal seneschal (no. 476). A Rudolph Kröpfel, who could
only have been the son of Rudolph of Traunsdorf and Adelheid, was variously described in the
1150s and 1160s as the *cognatus* (no. 392), the *consobrinus* (no. 569), and, most significantly, as
the *sororius,* the sister's son (SUB 2 no. 397, explanatory note), of Hartnit and Marchwart.

[76] Liutolt Kröpfel was identified as a ministerial of the church of Salzburg in SUB 2 nos. 187,
196, and Liutolt of Haberland-Siegsdorf in SUB 2 no. 238 and *Trad. St. Peter* no. 222c.

Berthold, in the 940s. Although Otto I decisively defeated the Hungarians at the Lechfeld, outside of Augsburg, on 9 August 955, there were occasional Hungarian forays until the end of the century.[77] As the owners of extensive domains situated on the exposed border between the Christian and pagan worlds, the tenth-century archbishops undoubtedly appreciated and rewarded men, whatever their social origins, who knew how and were willing to fight.

After the Hungarian danger started to subside in mid-century, the increasing military burdens which the German rulers imposed upon the Bavarian church provided the servile retainers with further opportunities to demonstrate their martial skills. In 980 or 981 Otto II ordered Archbishop Frederick, for instance, to send seventy heavily armed cavalrymen (*loricati*) to Italy to join the emperor's ill-fated campaign. In comparison, the archbishops of Mainz and Cologne and the bishops of Augsburg and Strasbourg were ordered to send one hundred men, the archbishop of Trier and the duchy of Alsace seventy, the bishops of Liège, Verdun, and Würzburg sixty, the bishop of Eichstätt fifty, the bishops of Chur, Constance, Freising, and Worms forty, the bishop of Toul and the abbot of Saint-Gall twenty, and the bishop of Cambrai twelve.[78] Archbishop Frederick, in whose episcopate the large noble clan had clearly started to disintegrate,[79] could only have fulfilled such imperial commands by employing members of the *familia*. The servile warriors who survived such campaigns were no doubt rewarded and gained in personal prestige and social standing.

Finally, the efforts of the German monarchs to curb the autonomy of the Luitpoldingian duchy of Bavaria created a situation highly conducive to the rise of a class of servile warriors.[80] The archbishops of Salzburg as the heads of the Bavarian church and as members of the Aribonen or Sighardinger clans were inevitably drawn into the conflict. Indeed, it is possible to see the history of tenth-century Bavaria as a struggle between the Luitpoldingian dukes and the Aribonen and Sighardinger archbishops with the king as an external third party. The rivalry between the Aribonen and the Luitpoldingians may date to the late ninth century when the two margraves, Luitpold and Aribo, jockeyed for power in the disintegrating Carolingian Empire. For instance, after Arnulf of Carinthia deprived Aribo's enemies, the Wilhelminer, of their offices in the eastern marks in 893, he gave the county of Pannonia Superior, though it had been assigned to Aribo from 871 to 887, as well as the mark of Carantania, to Luitpold. In fact, Luitpold, who was also granted the Bavarian Nordgau in 895, may have become Aribo's superior.[81] Luitpold's triumph over Aribo, which was due in part to his kinship with the emperor Arnulf,[82]

---

[77] Spindler (n. 46 above) 1.203-234.

[78] "Epistolae Bambergenses," *Monumenta Bambergensia,* Bibliotheca rerum Germanicarum, ed. Philipp Jaffé (Berlin 1869) 5.471-472, no. 1.

[79] See above, pp. 80-81.

[80] For general information on the history of Bavaria in the tenth century, see Spindler (n. 46 above) 1.206-227.

[81] Mitterauer (n. 22 above) 165-167, 180-181, 188-189.

[82] *Ibid.* 239-243.

facilitated his son's assumption of the Bavarian ducal dignity after the margrave's death at Bratislava in 907.

In 914 King Conrad I forced Duke Arnulf the Bad to flee to Hungary. After an unsuccessful attempt to regain power in 916, Arnulf reconquered Bavaria the following year. The Bavarian episcopate under the leadership of Archbishop Pilgrim, the brother-in-law of Margrave Aribo,[83] sided with Conrad. In 921 Arnulf, who had been elected king after Conrad's death in 918, reached an agreement with the new German monarch, Henry the Fowler. In exchange for Arnulf's recognizing Henry as his overlord, the king granted Arnulf extensive royal rights in his duchy, including the right to appoint bishops. It is not clear whether Odalbert, the nephew or grandson of Margrave Aribo and former husband of Arnulf's kinswoman Rihni,[84] owed his preferment to Arnulf's intervention or whether Odalbert was elected archbishop in opposition to the duke, though the latter seems more probable.[85]

After the death of Arnulf's brother Berthold (938-947), Otto I named his own brother Henry, who had married Arnulf's daughter Judith, as duke. The Luit-poldingians naturally resented this change of dynasties. In 953 the Bavarian nobility under the leadership of the count-palatine Arnulf, the son of Duke Arnulf, joined the revolt of Otto's son Liudolf against his father. Duke Henry I (947-955) suppressed the revolt with the utmost severity. The Luitpoldingian archbishop Herold (939-955), the son of Duke Arnulf's cousin,[86] who had joined the rebellion, was captured by Duke Henry at the battle of Mühldorf, blinded, and deposed. Arch-bishop Frederick, a Sighardinger, who was connected to the Aribonen through his sister-in-law Willa, Odalbert's granddaughter, was ordained in his stead.[87] At the same time Hartwig I, the father of Frederick's successor, Archbishop Hartwig, and the father-in-law of the first Aribonen count-palatine, Aribo I,[88] replaced the Luitpoldingians as the count-palatine, the second most important secular office in the duchy. Duke Henry the Wrangler (955-976, 985-995), who succeeded his father at the age of four, was reared by his mother Judith in the traditions of the Luitpoldingian house. He joined a conspiracy against his royal cousin Otto II and was imprisoned after its detection. Escaping from captivity at the beginning of 976, he stirred up a revolt in Bavaria, which ended with Otto's capture of Regensburg in July and Henry's flight to Bohemia. Archbishop Frederick and his relatives once more supported the king.[89]

During the eleventh century when Bavaria was more closely tied to the empire than at any other time in its history — for fifty-three years between 995 and 1096

---

[83] Dopsch (n. 23 above) 126-128.

[84] *Ibid.* 131; and Mitterauer (n. 22 above) 196-197.

[85] Dopsch (n. 23 above) 129; and Spindler (n. 46 above) 1.299.

[86] Dopsch (n. 23 above) 132-134.

[87] *Ibid.* 134-136; and SUB 2 nos. 49, 50, 51.

[88] Dopsch (n. 23 above) 137-143.

[89] Otto II thanked Archbishop Frederick and his relatives for their services and devotion on 21 July 976, when he granted the archbishop and his successors a permanent residence in Regensburg; SUB 2 no. 55.

the duke was either the king himself, his wife, or one of his children[90] — the emperors deliberately selected non-Bavarians as archbishops. Archbishop Gunther (1023-1025) was a Saxon; Baldwin probably belonged to a noble family from northwestern Germany; Gebhard was a Swabian; and Thietmar II's origins are unknown.[91] The king no longer needed or wanted an archbishop with familial ties to counterbalance the power of the duke.

These internecine feuds contributed to the dissolution of the large noble clans which dominated the archdiocese at the beginning of the tenth century by forcing the archbishops' kinsmen and/or vassals, who could often claim kinship with the dukes as well, to choose between the Luitpoldingian dukes and count-palatines who stood for the continued autonomy, if not the independence, of Bavaria, and the archbishops who sided with the alien Saxon dynasty. Ties of kinship had always been more important, as we have already seen,[92] than feudal obligations in the arch-diocese. The sundering of the bonds of kinship thus forced the archbishops to turn to the subservient *familia* as the only reliable alternative. The formation of a new class of warriors, bound to their lord by servile as well as feudal ties, was a deliberate attempt to create a more dependable substitute for the free vassalage; but as Karl Bosl has rightly pointed out, the performance of honorable and esteemed services for a great lord has always tended to elevate the man who performs them.[93] The decrease in the size of Archbishop Frederick's noble entourage and the simultaneous emergence of the servile retainers to positions of prominence and trust were closely linked to the rivalry between the archbishops and the dukes and the German monarchy's suppression of the tribal duchy.[94] The non-Bavarian archbishops of the eleventh century, who had no kinsmen in the duchy and who were thus even more dependent than their predecessors on their servile entourage, were in no position to reverse the trend.

We are inclined to perceive the early Middle Ages as an essentially static period, but as the careers of the archbishops' servile retainers reveal, upward social mobility was possible for specific groups of individuals under the right set of circumstances. In tenth-century Salzburg the threat posed by the Magyar invaders, the increasing military burdens imposed upon the Bavarian church by the monarchy, and the gradual disintegration of the noble clan centered around the archbishop provided a segment of the servile population with the opportunity to rise above their fellow serfs. Some of their remote progeny were eventually accepted as members of the lower nobility. But there were distinct limits to such upward social mobility. Marc

[90] Spindler (n. 46 above) 1.227.

[91] Dopsch (n. 23 above) 144-147.

[92] See above, p. 76.

[93] Bosl, "Uber soziale Mobilität" (n. 7 above) 156-179.

[94] Erben (n. 17 above) 187-192, who had observed the simultaneous decline in the arch-bishops' noble entourage and the emergence of the servile retainers, concluded that the Bavarian nobles had been attracted to the service of the emperor and of the Bavarian branch of the imperial family; but as we have seen, it was the archbishops with their kinsmen and their servile retainers, rather than the nobility as a whole, who supported the Saxon dynasty.

Bloch has argued that Europe lacked a true nobility, defined as a hereditary, legally-privileged social class, until at least the twelfth century when the descendants of the Carolingian imperial aristocracy and local landowners coalesced with warriors of varied social origins into a single class sharing a common knightly life style. The nobles of Europe were, in other words, the offspring of the warrior elite created by the military revolution of the eighth century, in which the heavy cavalry had replaced the infantry as the main fighting force.[95] The evidence from Salzburg clearly contradicts this theory. After two centuries of fighting, the ministerials, some of whom were the remote descendants of Archbishop Odalbert's *servi,* were still being carefully distinguished from the nobility in the so-called foundation charter of Admont drafted in the 1130s, and continued to be for decades to come.[96] The ministerials had risen far above their servile ancestors by the beginning of the twelfth century; but the chasm which separated them from the nobles, the surviving descendants of the clans which had dominated the archbishopric in the late Carolingian and early Ottonian periods, remained unbridged.

Department of History
Illinois State University
Normal, Illinois 61761, U.S.A.

[95] Marc Bloch, *Feudal Society,* trans. L. A. Manyon, 2 vols. (Chicago 1964) 2.283-331.
[96] See, for instance, SUB 2 nos. 465, 479, 497.

"PERICULOSUS HOMO": POPE GREGORY VII AND EPISCOPAL AUTHORITY

•

by Ian Stuart Robinson

The attempt to depose Pope Gregory VII which opened the great conflict of *regnum* and *sacerdotium* in the later eleventh century was the work not only of King Henry IV of Germany but also of a majority of the bishops of the imperial territories. Henry IV's attempts in 1076 and 1080 to depose the pope at a distance – not as his father had done in 1046 by personal intervention in Italy – necessarily involved an alliance with the episcopate: the papal deposition could only be made effective by influencing "public opinion" within the Church. The bishops of Germany and Lombardy were, however, by no means passive partners in this alliance. The decree of the synod of Worms of January 1076, in which two archbishops and twenty-four bishops renounced their obedience to "Brother Hildebrand" – the first "anti-Gregorian" polemic of the Investiture Contest – was concerned solely with the grievances of the episcopate against the pope.[1] It was not Gregory VII's attacks on the "honor" and the "hereditary dignity" of the kingship (the theme of Henry IV's own propaganda of 1076)[2] which preoccupied the bishops at Worms, but the pope's maltreatment of the episcopate. Gregory had "robbed the bishops of every power conferred on them by the grace of the Holy Spirit," reserving to himself the power of binding and loosing in all cases and giving over "the control of ecclesiastical affairs to the ravening frenzy of the mob." This charge, restated at the synod of Brixen in June 1080,[3] was regularly reiterated in the polemical writings of the late eleventh century. Hildebrand had "trodden underfoot the rulers of holy Church, the archbishops, bishops and priests;"[4] he had "reviled the priests of the Lord, the bishops and archbishops, with filthy names"[5] and had acted "in contempt and to the prejudice of

---

I am indebted to Miss Beryl Smalley for her advice in the preparation of this article. I must also express my thanks for the kindness and encouragement shown to me by Professor Stephan Kuttner and by Professor Horst Fuhrmann, the influence of whose Pseudo-Isidorean studies appears very clearly in this article.

[1] Decree of the synod of Worms: *Die Briefe Heinrichs IV.,* ed C. Erdmann, MGH Deutsches Mittelalter, kritische Studientexte 1 (Leipzig 1937) 65-68 (hereafter cited as Erdmann).

[2] *Ibid.* nos. 11-13

[3] Brixen decree: *ibid.* 71.

[4] *Ibid.* no. 12.

[5] Wenrich of Trier, *Epistola,* MGH Libelli de lite 1 (Hanover 1891) 286.

the metropolitans and bishops" of Germany.[6] According to the pope's enemies, therefore, the pontificate of Gregory VII witnessed a violent attack on the traditional rights of the episcopate which had "thrown into confusion the inmost *ordo* of the Church."[7]

A very different picture of Gregory VII's attitude towards the episcopate is suggested by the pope's own pronouncements. Many of Gregory's letters contain expressions of reverence for the episcopal office which it is possible to interpret as an acceptance of the traditional episcopal *ordo* of the Church.[8] "For as we desire due honor to be paid to the Roman church by other churches, so also we desire to preserve for each church its own right (*proprium ius*)," concludes the papal letter of 1073 concerning the right of the bishop of Verona to receive the *pallium*.[9] This theme recurs in a letter of 1077 concerning the *proprium ius* of the archbishop of Vienne: "As we desire that the rights and dignities of the holy Roman and apostolic church should be preserved, so we consider it necessary and most worthy that her members, namely the other churches, be preserved by her provision and authority."[10] Here, however, the papal solicitude for the rights of the local churches is more clearly set within the framework of the Roman primacy: "the other churches" are the *membra* of the Roman church and their rights can only be guaranteed by her *providentia* and *auctoritas*. There can be no doubt that Gregory VII considered the bishop to be the key figure in Christian society. "The order and careful management of the Christian religion," he informed Duke Boleslav II of Poland, "depends very much, after God, upon the pastors and rulers of the Lord's flock." Hence the church in Poland ought to be organized along the same lines — with bishops having definite dioceses and owing obedience to a metropolitan — as the rest of Christendom.[11] The episcopal dignity was "instituted by divine piety"[12] in order to "rule the Christian people in the love of Christ"[13] and therefore the bishop could expect to be obeyed by the faithful as their "spiritual father."[14] "Show reverence and obedience to bishops as to your fathers," wrote Gregory to the pious layman, Count Centullus of Béarn.[15] Such papal admonitions were particularly necessary in the case of newly converted regions on the margins of Western Christendom (where filial obedience to

---

[6] *Liber de unitate ecclesiae conservanda, ibid.* 2 (Hanover 1892) 241.

[7] Wenrich 287.

[8] It is in this sense that Gregory VII's conception of the episcopal role is discussed by L. F. J. Meulenberg, *Der Primat der römischen Kirche im Denken und Handeln Gregors VII.,* Mededelingen van het Nederlands Hist. Inst. te Rome 33 (The Hague 1965) 53-79. See the reviews of this work by A. M. Stickler in *Zeitschrift für Kirchengeschichte* 81 (1970) 103-107 and D. Lindner in *Zeitschrift der Savigny-Stiftung für Rechtsgeschichte, Kan. Abt.* 84 (1967) 368-372,

[9] *Gregorii VII Registrum,* ed. E. Caspar, MGH Epistolae selectae (Berlin 1920-1923) 1.24 (41) (hereafter cited as *Registrum*).

[10] *Ibid.* 4.16 (321), concerning the archbishop's rights over the abbey of Romans.

[11] *Ibid.* 2.73 (233-235).

[12] *Ibid.* 4.2 (295).

[13] *Ibid.* 2.49 (189).

[14] *Ibid.* 9.16 (597).

[15] *Ibid.* 6.20 (432).

bishops was to be demonstrated above all by the payment of tithes);[16] but the command to clergy and people to be "subject and obedient to your bishop" recurs in papal letters directed throughout the West.[17] For the flock to neglect their duty of obedience and to rebel against their pastor was "irregular, evil, criminal, . . . contrary to divine and human laws."[18] The sufferings of Archbishop Cyriacus of Carthage among the Saracens – at which some of the Christian population of Carthage had connived – drew from Gregory an exalted defense of the episcopal dignity. In the person of the archbishop "Christ is taken prisoner once more and condemned by false accusers and false witnesses."[19] The pastor had the right to expect an unlimited and unconditional obedience from the faithful. Thus the pope admonished an unidentifiable Count C., the persecutor of his bishop, who had condemned C.'s consanguineous marriage: "You ought to obey him, even if he had passed an unjust sentence on you."[20]

The *ordo ecclesiasticus* of the "pre-Gregorian" Church, as it is presented in the *Collectio Isidori Mercatoris,* attributed a most extensive authority to the episcopate. The texts of Pseudo-Isidore protect the person and the privileges of bishops, respect the boundaries of dioceses, assert the inviolability of episcopal property and forbid the bringing of accusations against bishops by subordinates.[21] This Pseudo-Isidorean language of episcopal authority –typifying the Church order of the West before the impact of the reforming papacy had been felt – can also be identified in the letters of Gregory VII. When, for example, Gregory asserted the primacy of the archbishopric of Lyons over the provinces of Rouen, Tours and Sens, he did so by means of a lengthy extract from the Pseudo-Isidorean letter of Pope Anacletus, defining the rights of the primatial and the metropolitan dignities.[22] Elsewhere Gregory emphasized the significance of the role of the metropolitan in the hierarchy, reminding the bishop of Poitiers that the archbishop of Bordeaux was his *magister,*[23] and, in the decrees of the Roman synod of Lent 1080, accentuating the supervisory function of the metropolitan in episcopal elections.[24] The preoccupation of the Pseudo-Isidorean collection with the protection of prelates against accusation by subordinates is also reflected in the papal correspondence. A letter of 1081 warned the clergy and people of Chartres, in terms reminiscent of the Pseudo-Isidorean texts of Zephyrinus, Fabian and Stephen, against assailing their bishop "with false accusations,

---

[16] E.g., *ibid.* 9.14 (593; to the kings of Sweden).

[17] E.g., *ibid.* 1.69 (99: Die); 1.74 (106: Beauvais); 1.80 (114: Le Puy)

[18] *Ibid.* 1.65 (94-95: to the clergy and people of Ragusa).

[19] *Ibid.* 1.22 (38).

[20] *Ibid.* 9.23 (604).

[21] See, for example, O. Capitani, *Immunità vescovili ed ecclesiologia in età "pregregoriana" e "gregoriana": L'avvio alla "restaurazione,"* Biblioteca degli studi medievali 3 (Spoleto 1966) esp. 1-51.

[22] *Registrum* (n. 9 above) 6.35 (451-452), citing *Epistola Anacleti* c. 26, ed. P. Hinschius, *Decretales Pseudoisidorianae* (Leipzig 1863) 79.

[23] *Registrum* 2.2 (125).

[24] *Ibid.* 7.14a, c. 6 (482).

as is the custom of some men, to defile prelates with slanderous suspicions."[25] The statements in Gregory VII's letters concerning ecclesiastical government seem to defend, in traditional language, the traditional structure of the Church. Yet the complaint brought against Gregory VII by the German bishops in 1076 was precisely that he had shown contempt for the traditional hierarchy of the Church and sought to destroy the privileges of the bishops. The bishops' charge, as summarized by Henry IV in 1076, was that

> not only have you not feared to "touch the Lord's Anointed" – the rulers of holy Church, namely the archbishops, bishops and priests – but you have even trodden them under your feet like slaves who "know not what their lord does;" and in so doing you have won for yourself the acclaim of the mob . . . . You have armed subjects against prelates; while as for our bishops who received the call from God, you (who were not called) have taught that they must be held in contempt and you have unlawfully conferred their authority over priests upon laymen.[26]

A central preoccupation of the episcopal polemic of 1076 was that major concern of the *Collectio Isidori Mercatoris,* the right of the bishop to the obedience of the faithful – that right frequently affirmed in the letters of Gregory VII's *Register* and the right which, according to his opponents, Gregory VII had consistently undermined.

It is instructive to reexamine the ecclesiology implicit in Gregory VII's pronouncements in the light of the episcopal polemic of 1076; and in particular to analyze those letters which show a "positive" attitude towards the traditional *ordo ecclesiasticus.* At the outset, it is clear that Gregory's most vehement defenses of episcopal rights were made in the context, not of a discussion of the structure of the Church, but of a confrontation of the claims of *regnum* and *sacerdotium.* Gregory's fullest exposition of the extent of the episcopal dignity occurs in his letter of 1083 complaining of William the Conqueror's imprisonment of Bishop Odo of Bayeux. Here the pope applied to priests the language of Psalm 104.15 (exactly as Henry IV's letter of 1076 had done): priests were "the Lord's Anointed" and the apple of God's eye (Zachariah 2.8). Gregory reminded the Conqueror of the reverence which the emperor Constantine I had shown the bishops at the Council of Nicaea; and he concluded with the *sententia* of Saint Ambrose, "The episcopal honor and sublimity are incomparable."[27] These same texts were cited in the pope's doctrinal letters of 1076 and 1081 to Bishop Herman of Metz, in which he justified the excommunication of Henry IV and defended the thesis that "the priests of Christ are to be accounted the fathers and masters of kings and princes and all the faithful."[28] In

---

[25]*Ibid.* 9.16 (596). Cf., e.g., *Epistola Zephyrini* c. 3.4; *Epistola Fabiani* c. 21; *Epistola Stephani* c. 12 (Hinschius [n. 22 above] 131, 165, 186).

[26]Erdmann (n. 1 above) no. 12 (citing Psalm 104.15; John 15.15).

[27]*Registrum* (n. 9 above) 9.37 (631) citing Ambrose, *De dignitate sacerdotali* 2, PL 17.569.

[28]*Ibid.* 4.2 (295-296); 8.21 (553-555).

these instances, Gregory's expressions of reverence for the episcopal dignity can be seen, not as a comment on the *interior ordo* of the Church, but as an indication that, in the face of aggression from a secular prince, there were no limits to the pope's exaltation of the claims of the *sacerdotium*.

Secondly, an examination of the papal correspondence suggests that when Gregory VII affirmed the rights of bishops in Pseudo-Isidorean terms, he did so only in the case of bishops who were proven supporters of papal policies. The most famous instance is that of Lucca in 1079, when the pope intervened to excommunicate the clergy of the cathedral of San Martino, who were resisting their bishop's efforts to impose on them the *vita communis* of regular canons.[29] For his letter of 1079 condemning these rebels against episcopal authority, Gregory obtained from his advisers the Pseudo-Isidorean "authority of the blessed martyrs and popes Fabian and Stephen."[30] This Pseudo-Isidorean *auctoritas*, outlawing conspiracies of the clergy against their bishop, is found in a number of canonical collections compiled under the inspiration of the reforming papacy; and it is relevant to mention here its appearance in the *Collectio canonum* compiled about 1083 by Anselm of Lucca.[31] For Bishop Anselm II of Lucca, "the tireless fellow-worker of Pope Hildebrand"[32] and papal legate in northern Italy, was the bishop on whose behalf Gregory VII intervened in 1079. Gregory VII was naturally prepared to defend the authority of a bishop who was so trusted a supporter of Gregorian policies (so trusted indeed that the pope would, on his deathbed, designate Anselm as his successor).[33] The reform, moreover, which the bishop of Lucca was seeking to impose in 1079 — the regular, communal life for canons — was a reform in which the pope had long been keenly interested.[34] Gregory's acting upon the authority of popes Fabian and Stephen in 1079, therefore, can certainly not be interpreted as a simple papal vindication of the Pseudo-Isidorean principle that the clergy owe *obedientia* to their bishop.[35]

---

[29] Cf. E. Kittel, "Der Kampf um die Reform des Domkapitels in Lucca im 11. Jahrhundert," *Festschrift A. Brackmann dargebracht* (Weimar 1931) 218-247; M. Giusti, "Le canoniche della città e diocesi di Lucca al tempo della riforma gregoriana," *Studi Gregoriani* 3 (Rome 1948) 321-367.

[30] *Registrum* (n. 9 above) 7.2 (461), citing *Epistola Fabiani* c. 21, *Epistola Stephani* c. 12 (Hinschius [n. 22 above] 165, 186).

[31] *Anselmi Lucensis Collectio canonum,* ed. F. Thaner. (Innsbruck 1915) 7.150 (Fabian c. 21). Cf. *Collectio in LXXIV titulos,* ed. J. Gilchrist (Vatican City 1973) nos. 67 (Fabian c. 21), 68 (Stephen c. 12). See also Polycarpus 4.31, (32) 15 (Fabian c. 21) (cited after E. Friedberg, *Corpus Iuris Canonici* 1 [Leipzig 1879] note on Gratian, *Decretum* C. 11 q. 1 c. 31).

[32] Sigebert of Gembloux, *Chronica* a.1086, MGH Scriptores 6, 365.

[33] See the version of Gregory VII's last words preserved in the Hildesheim letter collection (ed. C. Erdmann, *Briefsammlungen der Zeit Heinrichs IV.,* MGH Die Briefe der deutschen Kaiserzeit 5 [Weimar 1950] 75), in the chronicle of Hugh of Flavigny (MGH Scriptores 8, 466) and in the *Vita Gregorii VII* of Paul of Bernried (ed. J. M. Watterich, *Pontificum romanorum vitae* 1 [Leipzig 1862] 539).

[34] See especially C. Dereine, "Vie commune, règle de saint Augustin et chanoines réguliers au XIe siècle," *Revue d'histoire ecclésiastique* 41 (1946) 365-406.

[35] Cf. Meulenberg (n. 7 above) 59, who interprets *Registrum* 7.2 as a general defense of episcopal authority.

A similar case is presented by the papal letter of 1074 which summons the laity of the diocese of Die to show "obedience and favor" to their new bishop and to submit to being "instructed in spiritual disciplines under his rule."[36] The new bishop was Hugh, a man in whom the pope had great confidence. Hugh had been consecrated in Rome on 16 March 1074[37] and there he had doubtless been subjected to the Gregorian proselytizing arts which were exercised upon so many visitors from beyond the mountains during the pontificate of Gregory VII;[38] so that the pope could write of Hugh as early as 1075, "There is no one in whom we may more fully trust; for we find that he has faithfully performed all the duties which we have imposed on him."[39] Hugh's career, as bishop of Die (1074-1082), archbishop of Lyons (1082-1106) and papal legate in France, was fully to justify Gregory VII's early confidence in him. But at the outset of his episcopal career, Hugh faced serious difficulties. Immediately after his election as bishop of Die, he encountered the hostility of Count William of Die who, during the bishop-elect's absence early in 1074, took punitive action against the clergy.[40] It was in this situation that Gregory VII intervened with his command to the laity of Die to show "obedience and favor" to Bishop Hugh. The papal letter of 1074 reveals not an abstract ideal of obedience to episcopal authority, but a concern lest the reforming efforts of a useful agent should be rendered ineffective by lay opposition. In similar vein, Gregory's letter of 1076 to Dol illustrates the most common motive for a papal admonition to obedience. The clergy and people of Dol were required to "show obedience in all things, as to a father and ruler" to Ivo, who was not the candidate whom they had elected as their bishop. Gregory had consecrated Ivo in place of the preferred candidate of the electors, Gilduin, whom the pope considered to be too young.[41] A special papal summons to show obedience to a new bishop was the characteristic signal that the election of the clergy and people had been set aside, and Gregory's candidate substituted. So it was in the bishopric of Le Puy in 1074;[42] and similarly in the bishopric of Orléans in 1078.[43] The situation in this latter case — the election of Sanzo in Orléans in place of Bishop Rainerius, whom the pope had deposed as an intruder, a simoniac and a rebel against the Holy See[44] — became increasingly familiar in the latter years of Gregory's pontificate. In December 1080, for example, in the archbishoprics of Narbonne[45] and Reims[46] and the antipope Wibert's archsee

[36] Registrum (n. 9 above) 1.69 (99).

[37] Hugh of Flavigny, Chronicon, MGH Scriptores 8.412.

[38] See, for example, the case of Abbot William of Hirsau, who became an "ultra-Gregorian" during his sojourn in Rome in 1075–1076: H. E. J. Cowdrey, The Cluniacs and the Gregorian Reform (Oxford 1970) 203.

[39] The Epistolae Vagantes of Pope Gregory VII no. 12, ed. H. E. J. Cowdrey (Oxford 1972) 28 (hereafter cited as Epistolae Vagantes).

[40] Registrum (n. 9 above) 1.69 (100).

[41] Ibid. 4.4 (300-301).

[42] Ibid. 1.80 (114).

[43] Ibid. 5.14 (367-368).

[44] Ibid. 5.8, 9 (358-361).

[45] Ibid. 8.16 (537-538).

[46] Ibid. 8.17-20 (538-543).

of Ravenna[47] the faithful were informed by papal letters of the deposition of their former pastor and his replacement by a worthier candidate. Each of these letters demanded that the faithful should render all possible assistance to their new archbishop; and each forbade the faithful to "show any reverence" to the man who had formerly occupied the office of "father and ruler."

Gregory VII's attitude to the privileges of the episcopal office, was, therefore, determined by the response of particular holders of that office to papal reforming initiatives. "If he leans to the right, we shall rejoice exceedingly," Gregory observed of an episcopal candidate about whose dependability he was still uncertain; "but if – which Heaven forbid! – he leans to the left, we shall be very sorry: but we shall never consent to impiety out of respect or favor for any one."[48] Bishops who consistently "leaned to the right" were most cordially welcome to play their part in the government of Christian society. For, as a papal letter of 1077 expressed it, bishops "ought to be pillars in the Church of God":[49] they should participate in papal reforming councils and enforce the decisions of these councils in their own dioceses. There seems at first sight to be nothing novel in this conception. The image of bishops as "pillars in the Church of God" is Pseudo-Isidorean;[50] and the idea that the local churches throughout Christendom should be reformed by their bishops in accordance with the decrees of papal councils had been actively canvassed for at least a quarter of a century. Pope Leo IX's council of Mainz in October 1049 provides an early example: here the great archbishop Adalbert of Bremen heard decrees pronounced against simony and clerical unchastity; "and when he returned home, he did not remain silent about them."[51] The change of emphasis which the pontificate of Gregory VII gave to this central preoccupation of the papal reform movement becomes clear from the papal letter directed to Archbishop Adalbert's successor, Liemar of Bremen, in December 1074. Liemar had failed to hold a local reforming synod; the pope therefore suspended him from his office and summoned him to answer for his conduct at the coming Lenten synod in Rome. The papal letter of December 1074 which announced this suspension also contains a Gregorian statement of the duties of the episcopal office. A bishop should be "an impregnable wall

---

[47] *Ibid.* 8.14 (534-535).

[48] *Ibid.* 1.11 (19: the reference to "right" and "left" is modelled on Jonah 4.11). The suspect bishop elect in this letter of 1073 was, ironically, Anselm II of Lucca, who was to prove to be the most steadfastly "Gregorian" of Italian bishops. Anselm was suspect in the summer of 1073 because of his intention of receiving investiture from Henry IV at a time when the king was communicating with his excommunicate counsellors. Cf. *Registrum* (n. 9 above) 1.21, 35 and G. B. Borino, "Il monachato e l'investitura di Anselmo vescovo di Lucca," *Studi Gregoriani* 5 (1956) 361-374.

[49] *Epistolae Vagantes* (n. 39 above) no. 19 (52).

[50] Cf. *Epistola Anacleti* c. 19 (Hinschius [n. 22 above] 76).

[51] Adam of Bremen, *Gesta Hammaburgensis ecclesiae pontificum* 3.30 in *Quellen des 9. und 11. Jahrhunderts zur Geschichte der Hamburgischen Kirche und des Reiches,* Ausgewählte Quellen zur deutschen Geschichte des Mittelalters 11 (Darmstadt 1973) 364. Unfortunately Adalbert's interpretation of the reforming decrees of 1049 seems to have deviated from the ideal pronounced by the pope; since, according to the author of *scholia* 76 on the *Gesta Hammaburgensis ecclesiae,* the archbishop's advice to the unchaste clergy of the archdiocese was: *si non caste, tamen caute.*

in defense of the Roman Church (over which we, although unworthy, preside) and in defense of us: [a bishop] ought, if necessary, to take up the shield of the faith and the sword of Christ on our behalf and on behalf of our successors, by virtue both of [his] office and of [his] debt to the holy Roman Church."[52] In this characteristic Gregorian pronouncement, the episcopal office is presented merely as an adjunct of the Roman primacy: a bishop is an agent of the pope and his usefulness in Christian society must be judged by his relative assiduity in carrying out papal commands. This new emphasis in the papal attitude towards the episcopate is immediately apparent in the contrast between the intended synod of 1074, involving Liemar of Bremen, and the reforming decrees which his predecessor had issued in his archdiocese under the inspiration of Leo IX's council of Mainz. Archbishop Adalbert's attempts to reform his church had links (as his biographer, Adam of Bremen, pointed out) with the local reforming tradition of the earlier archbishops, Liawizo II (1029-1032) and Alebrand-Bezelin (1035-1043):[53] Adalbert's reforms were an expression of the prelate's long-established power of correcting the lives of his clergy. In the case of Archbishop Liemar in 1074, however, the initiative was taken out of the prelate's hands. For Gregory VII sent two legates, the cardinal bishops of Ostia and Palestrina, to northern Germany early in 1074, "in order to summon together archbishops, bishops, abbots and clerks, so that, relying on our authority and standing in our place, they might correct whatever needed correction."[54] These legates officiously demanded that Liemar assist them in holding a synod in his province and when he showed reluctance, they commanded him "on [his] obedience to the apostolic see, either to do their will by calling a synod or to come to Rome to give an account [of himself]."[55] In the demands of the legates Archbishop Liemar accurately perceived a startling intrusion upon the traditional authority of a metropolitan and a novel extension of papal authority over the Church, in the name of reform. The confrontation between the archbishop of Bremen and the papal legates in 1074 illustrates the distinctive "Gregorian" ecclesiology which had already emerged at the beginning of the pontificate.

Gregory VII's conception of episcopal duties received its earliest expression in the papal letters concerning the Lenten synods held in Rome in 1074 and 1075. The purpose of these synods was "to find some relief and remedy, so that we may not see in our time the irreparable ruin and destruction of the Church";[56] and the pope commanded the attendance of the bishops "by apostolic authority" in order "to exercise the solicitude proper to your order and to our office, in divine and ecclesiastical affairs."[57] When these synodal deliberations had produced reforming

[52] *Registrum* (n. 9 above) 2.28 (160-161).
[53] Adam of Bremen 3.30 (364). Cf. *scholia* 42, 53.
[54] *Registrum* 2.28 (161). On the case of Archbishop Liemar, see C. Erdmann, *Studien zur Briefliteratur Deutschlands im elften Jahrhundert,* Schriften der MGH 1 (1938) 265ff.
[55] Letter of Liemar of Bremen: *Hildesheimer Briefe* no. 15, ed. Erdmann (n. 33 above) 34.
[56] *Registrum* (n. 9 above) 1.42 (65).
[57] *Ibid.* 1.43 (66). Cf. *ibid.* 2.29 (162).

decrees, it became the duty of the episcopate to implement these decrees throughout Christendom. So, for example, Archbishop Siegfried of Mainz was informed in 1075 that, "since your clergy and people are spread far and wide, and your suffragans are very many and dispersed, we have decided to impose on you this office of obedience: that through your own efforts and those of your fellow-bishops you should zealously force this decree of the Roman Church upon all the clergy."[58] The same duty was simultaneously imposed on Bishop Otto of Constance, "so that the Roman Church may be able to rejoice over you as a most dear brother and zealous fellow-worker."[59] It was not enough, considered Gregory VII, to leave the reform of the local churches to the initiative of the bishops, exercising their power of correction over the clergy. Reform could only be assured if bishops would "obey our commands and drive out simoniacal heresy and the pollution of lust from the sanctuary of the Lord."[60] The key word in Gregory VII's discussion of the responsibilities of bishops is *obedientia*. The biblical quotation which recurs most frequently in Gregory's letters is I Samuel 25.22-23, "Obedience is better than sacrifices, and to hearken, than the fat of rams: for rebellion is as the sin of witchcraft and stubbornness is as iniquity and idolatry";[61] and this text was generally cited in order to elucidate the duty of bishops towards the pope. Gregory usually cited in conjunction with this text the exposition of I Samuel 25.22-23 given by Pope Gregory I in his *Moralia*: obedience is "that alone which possesses the merit of faith; since if a man is without it, he is proved to be unfaithful, even though he seems to be faithful."[62] To Gregory I *obedientia* signified the voluntary subjection of the human will to the divine will. To Gregory VII, however, *obedientia* had come to mean the subjection of the bishops and clergy to the commands of the pope. Gregory VII's interpretation of I Samuel 25.22-23 appears, for example, in a letter of 1080 referring to a bishop who "has disagreed with, and been disobedient towards, the apostolic see." Here the text from Samuel is coupled with a *sententia* attributed to Saint Ambrose: "He who does not agree with the Roman Church is held to be a heretic."[63] A bishop's competence in his pastoral office and his orthodoxy in religion were equally to be assessed by his readiness to obey papal instructions. This Gregorian idea of obedience is fully expounded in a letter written in the last year of Gregory's pontificate by his legate, Odo, cardinal-bishop of Ostia (the future Pope Urban II). The letter reproves the bishop of Hildesheim for abandoning the Gregorian cause:

> You remember that you were ordained in the catholic obedience of our
> lord the pope; you remember how much you owe him as a Christian, and
> how much more you owe him, and have promised him, as a bishop. It is

[58] *Epistolae Vagantes* (n. 39 above) no. 6 (14). On the date of this letter, see the discussion in Cowdrey's edition, 160-161.

[59] *Ibid.* no. 8 (18).

[60] *Ibid.* no. 9 (21).

[61] Cf. the *Quellenverzeichnis* of Caspar's edition of the *Registrum* (n. 9 above) 644; and *Epistolae Vagantes* (n. 39 above) 169.

[62] Pope Gregory I, *Moralia in Iob* 35.28 (PL 76.765).

[63] *Registrum* (n. 9 above) 7.24 (504-505).

with grief that I say, with the prophet Samuel: you have fallen into the wickedness of idolatry.[64]

Having equated the special relationship of the bishop vis-à-vis the pope with the *obedientia* demanded in I Samuel 25.22-23, Gregory VII drew the obvious conclusion that disobedience on the part of a bishop disqualified him from exercising his episcopal authority. The earliest statement of this conclusion is found in a papal letter directed late in 1075 to the clergy and people of the diocese of Constance, dealing with the case of their bishop, Otto. Bishop Otto of Constance had been informed by the pope early in 1075 of the decisions of the Roman synod condemning simony and clerical unchastity.[65] He had subsequently held a council in his diocese in order to acquaint his clergy with the papal decrees; but the lower clergy had shown themselves so hostile to the decree concerning clerical marriage that the Constance council had thrown it out and Bishop Otto had acquiesced in his clergy's expression of their prejudice.[66] Gregory VII's assessment of this situation was that the bishop of Constance had incurred "the guilt not only of disobedience but also of rebellion; as we have heard that he has openly tolerated in his clergy things entirely contrary to our command — or rather, the command of Saint Peter." Otto had failed to honor his mother, the holy apostolic see, and his father, Saint Peter; and "it is quite obvious that a man who does not honor his mother or father should rightfully neither expect nor ask their faithful sons to yield obedience to himself." The clergy and people of the diocese of Constance were therefore absolved by apostolic authority from their duty of obedience to their bishop: "So long as he is a rebel against God and the apostolic see, you are bound to pay him no fealty."[67] In 1075, therefore, Gregory VII was driven by the obstructive behavior of the bishop of Constance to declare invalid the familiar Pseudo-Isidorean proposition, that the faithful must remain obediently subject to their pastor. The pope was evidently aware that he was overturning the traditional ecclesiological assumptions of the clergy and people of Constance whom he was now commanding to rebel, since he took pains to provide them with a scriptural and patristic justification of his command:

> Do not think that this endangers your souls . . . . How perilous and how far removed from Christ's law it is, not to show obedience to the apostolic see above all, you can recognize from the words of the blessed prophet Samuel, which the most holy pope Gregory undertook to expound in the last book of the *Moralia*. We have set them down in writing. . .so that you may know beyond doubt that what we are saying to you is no new doctrine, but the ancient teaching of the holy fathers.

[64] *Hildesheimer Briefe* no. 7, ed. Erdmann (n. 33 above) 26.

[65] *Epistolae Vagantes* (n. 39 above) no. 8 (16-18).

[66] The only evidence for the holding of this council in the diocese of Constance is the reference of Bernhard of Hildesheim, in his letter of 1076 to former colleagues in the cathedral chapter of Constance, to "your synod which, I hear, [was held] last year by 3,600 of the clergy" (*De damnatione scismaticorum,* MGH Libelli de lite 2.45).

[67] *Epistolae Vagantes* (n. 39 above) no. 10 (22-24).

This teaching was presented in a generalized form in Gregory VII's letter directed late in 1075 "to all the clergy and laity of the kingdom of Germany," warning them against bishops who condoned clerical unchastity: "We command you in no way to obey these bishops...just as they do not obey the commands of the apostolic see."[68] Thereafter this injunction became a commonplace of Gregory's letters. The basic bond of loyalty in the Church was, according to the vision of Gregory VII, to be that of *obedientia* to the apostolic see, instead of the traditional submission of the faithful to their bishop, which was preached in the *Collectio Isidori Mercatoris* and reiterated, for example, in the influential canonical collection of Burchard of Worms.[69]

The campaign against simony and clerical concubinage which had been launched in the Lenten synods of 1074 and 1075 revealed almost immediately to Gregory VII that the traditional ecclesiastical hierarchy, instead of insuring the rapid and effective implementation of papal reforming directives, furnished unlimited opportunities for obstruction. Papal decrees could be frustrated, for example, by the attitude of a bishop like Otto of Constance, who bowed to the will of his clergy rather than stir up dissension in his diocese by enforcing clerical celibacy. The furthering of reform by means of local councils presided over by papal legates could be hindered by the uncooperative behavior of a metropolitan like Liemar of Bremen. Liemar's explanation of his failure to cooperate with the legates in 1074 was that he considered it ill-advised to summon a synod before he had time to consult with the bishops in his province.[70] A decorous episcopal consensus seemed to him more important than the pope's impatient onslaught against abuses in the German Church. The attitude of Archbishop Siegfried of Mainz to the papal campaign of 1074 was, according to the chronicler Lampert of Hersfeld, that "it required no small effort to uproot a custom [clerical marriage] which had become implanted over so long a period, and to reform an aging world according to the principles of the early Church. He therefore acted with greater moderation towards [his clergy]."[71] It was this tendency of the episcopate to compromise, to tone down the papal decrees which were sent to them, which defeated Gregory VII's first reforming campaign and which prompted him to find alternative instruments to implement his reforms. Two important papal letters of January 1075 reveal the workings of Gregory's mind, as he sought more amenable agents of reform — agents whom he would exhort to actions which were detrimental to episcopal authority. The letter of 22 January 1075 to Abbot Hugh of Cluny contains a bitter complaint about the inadequacy of the rulers of Western Christendom,

---

[68] *Ibid.* no. 11 (26).

[69] Burchard, *Decretum* (in the Paris edition of 1549 = PL 140) 1.132-139, citing Pseudo-Isidorean extracts under the rubric, "That bishops must not be rebuked by their subjects."

This contrast between the Pseudo-Isidorean view of the Church and that of the "Gregorian" reform movement has recently been made by H. Fuhrmann in an article which challenges many of the traditional assumptions about the papal reform: "Über den Reformgeist der 74-Titel-Sammlung," *Festschrift für Hermann Heimpel* 2 (Göttingen 1972) 1101-1120.

[70] *Hildesheimer Briefe* no. 15, ed. Erdmann (n. 33 above) 34.

[71] Lampert, *Annales* a. 1074, *Lamperti Opera,* ed. O. Holder-Egger, MGH Scriptores rerum germanicarum in usum scholarum 38.199.

both secular princes and bishops: "When in my mind's eye I look over the Western lands, whether to north or south, I find hardly any bishops who conform to the law either in their appointment or in their way of life, and who rule the Christian people in the love of Christ and not for worldly ambition." Since the ecclesiastical and the secular rulers were failing to give guidance to the Christian people, the pope must look elsewhere for allies in the work of reform: "I wish to know more precisely who are truly faithful to [Saint Peter] and who love that heavenly prince for the sake of heavenly glory no less than they love those to whom they are subject for the sake of miserable earthly rewards." [72]

It was therefore to the subjects rather than to the rulers that Gregory considered entrusting the reform of the Church. Subjects could be summoned to assume a political role, forcing their princes to accept reform; [73] or they could be mobilized to purify the churches of Western Christendom by removing simoniac or unchaste clergy from the service of the altar. This latter function is the subject of the papal letter of 11 January 1075 addressed to Rudolf of Rheinfelden, duke of Swabia, Duke Berthold of Carinthia and Duke Welf IV of Bavaria — a letter which, to judge from the unusually large number of late eleventh-century and twelfth-century copies which survive, must have had a considerable impact on Gregory VII's contemporaries. [74] This papal letter to the south German dukes begins by stating the central proposition of Pope Gregory I's writings on secular and pastoral rule: that rulers are to be held directly responsible for the morals of their subjects. "The good or evil of subjects originates in the leadership of those who have taken up either worldly dignities or spiritual rule. While rulers seek nothing save the glory and the pleasures of this world. . .they loosen the reins of sin to others by their example." [75] From this premiss Gregory I had deduced the urgent necessity for rulers to repent of their sins, for the sake of their subjects' salvation. From this same premiss Gregory VII drew the conclusion — totally inimical to the "political thought" of Gregory I [76] — that subjects should disregard sinful rulers and resist their authority. The dukes of Swabia, Carinthia and Bavaria were therefore instructed by Gregory VII in the correct

---

[72] *Registrum* (n. 9 above) 2.49 (189-190). Cf. similar complaints against the bishops in a letter written three months earlier, *Registrum* 2.11 (142-143).

[73] Cf. I. S. Robinson, "Gregory VII and the Soldiers of Christ," *History* 58 (1973) 174-177.

[74] *Registrum* (n. 9 above) 2.45 (182-185). The letter is cited by Hugh of Flavigny (n. 37 above) 428, Paul of Bernried c. 39 (n. 33 above) 1.493-495, Pope Urban II (Jaffé-Loewenfeld 5743, *Epistolae Urbani II papae* no. 273, PL 151.532B) and Cardinal Deusdedit (*Kanonessammlung* 4.186, ed. V. Wolf von Glanvell [Paderborn 1905] 491) and is also found in the codices Sélestat, Bibliothèque municipale 13, fol. 42v, and Munich, Clm 16085, fol. 11v. The address to Welf of Bavaria is not recorded in the Register, but is found in the versions of Hugh of Flavigny, Paul of Bernried and the Sélestat codex.

[75] *Registrum* 2.45 (183). Cf. Gregory I, *Moralia in Iob* 2.16: "praepositis voluptati servientibus subditis frena laxantur" (PL 75.568). On the moral character of government according to Gregory I, see also *Moralia* 4.29, 11.13, 24.38.

[76] The most succinct survey of Gregory I's teaching of "non-resistance" is that written ca. 1090 by an anonymous monk of Hersfeld: *Liber de unitate ecclesiae conservanda,* MGH Libelli de lite 2.199-200, 226-227.

behavior to be adopted towards an ecclesiastical hierarchy which had failed to obey the apostolic decrees concerning simony and clerical marriage:

> Since we know that the people are being led astray by [bishops] who despise apostolic commands. . .and encourage the wickedness of their subjects by their criminal forbearance, it is fitting that we (on whom, before all others, falls the care of the Lord's flock) should guard against these evils by some other method. For it seems to us far better to reestablish divine justice by means of new counsels than to allow the souls of men to perish along with the laws which they have neglected. Therefore we now turn to you and to all in whose loyalty and devotion we trust, asking and admonishing you by apostolic authority that – whatever bishops may say or may not say about it – you should in no way recognize as priests those whom you know either to have been promoted and ordained simoniacally or to be accused of fornication. You are bound by your obedience to publish and urge these [commands] both in the king's court and elsewhere, in the diets of the kingdom; and, to the utmost of your power, you are to prevent such men from administering the sacred mysteries – even, if necessary, by violence. But if any persons begin to babble at you that this is none of your business, tell them this: that they are not to hinder your salvation and that of the people, but are to come to us to discuss the obedience which we have enjoined on you.

The "new counsels" (*nova consilia*) by means of which Gregory VII sought to compensate for the negligence of the bishops, therefore, involved the forcible ejection of delinquent priests from their altars by the faithful laity. This instruction was given to those of the pope's secular allies who disposed of sufficient political power to carry it out effectively – to the south German dukes and to Count Robert I of Flanders.[77] The humble *populus* meanwhile was expected to exert pressure on any bishop under papal displeasure. The clergy and people of Constance, for example, were given precisely this task, "so that, forced by this exigency if nothing else, [Bishop Otto] may learn to go back to the path of righteousness."[78] The new role of the laity in the Church was written into the decrees of the Lenten Synod of 1075: "Those who are not corrected through the love of God and the dignity of their office may be brought to their senses through the shame of the world and the rebuke of the people."[79] This was the papal policy which elicited the severest censures in Henry IV's deposition letter of 1076: "You have armed subjects against prelates. . . you have taught that [our bishops] must be held in contempt and you have unlawfully conferred their authority over priests upon laymen, so that laymen may

[77] *Registrum* (n. 9 above) 4.10, 11 (309-311).

[78] *Epistolae Vagantes* (n. 39 above) no. 10 (24).

[79] As reported in the papal letter to Siegfried of Mainz, *Epistolae Vagantes* no. 6 (14). Cf. the similar formula recorded in *Registrum* 2.66 (222).

depose and condemn those to whom they themselves have been committed by the hand of the Lord."[80] It was the "new counsels" which Gregory VII brought to the work of reform which turned the distinguished scholar and monk Sigebert of Gembloux into an "anti-Gregorian" polemicist. Sigebert, like many of the churchmen who would eventually adhere to the party of Henry IV in the Investiture Contest, sympathized with the reforming ideals of the papacy: "If one returns to the principles, what is more lovely and more profitable to Christianity than to make holy orders subject to the laws of chastity, to determine ecclesiastical promotions not by a financial arrangement but by personal merit?" Where the pope had erred, however, was in trying to implement these reforms in blatant disregard of *iustitia* and *ordo* — that is, the traditional rights of the ecclesiastical hierarchy. In consequence, "if you look now for the fruits [of papal policy], you see the Lord's flock miserably scattered and their shepherds inciting the wolves against them."[81]

The papal letters of 1074-1075 reveal the formation of a hostile attitude to the episcopate and a desire to neutralize episcopal authority. This attitude is summarized in the *Dictatus papae* — the twenty-seven *sententiae* concerning the powers of the papacy, which have the appearance of the *capitula* of a short canonical collection,[82] and which are found in the *Register* of Gregory VII between the letters of the third and the fourth of March 1075. Twelve of the *sententiae* comment on the relationship of the papacy with the episcopate;[83] and many of these *sententiae* serve as a commentary on Gregory's disillusioning experiences of 1074-1075. "That [the pope] can depose and reconcile bishops without a synod's meeting" (25) and "That he who does not agree with the Roman Church is not held to be a catholic" (26) reecho the admonitions concerning *obedientia* in the papal letters directed to German bishops during the first two years of the pontificate. "That [the pope] can absolve subjects from fealty to wicked men" (27) may well refer to the subjects of bishops as much as to the subjects of kings. This *sententia* is more probably a reflection of the case of Bishop Otto of Constance — to whose subjects the pope wrote, "For so long as he is a rebel against Almighty God and the apostolic see, you are bound to pay him no fealty"[84] — than a prognostication of the case of King Henry IV in 1076. Of the *sententiae* of the *Dictatus papae* which reflect the papal-episcopal relations of 1074-1075, three are noteworthy as directly contradicting canon law as it was

[80] Erdmann (n. 1 above) no. 12.

[81] Sigebert, *Apologia contra eos qui calumniantur missas coniugatorum sacerdotum*, MGH Libelli de lite 2.438.

[82] The hypothesis of G. B. Borino ("Un' ipotesi sul *Dictatus papae* di Gregorio VII," *Archivio della R. Deputazione romana di storia patria* 67 [1944] 237-252) that the *Dictatus papae* are the *capitula* of a canonical collection, is still perhaps the most satisfactory explanation of this document. See also the additional comments of S. Kuttner, "*Liber canonicus:* A Note on *Dictatus Papae* c. 17," *Studi Gregoriani* 2 (1947) 387-401; and, most recently, H. Mordek, "*Proprie auctoritates apostolici sedis:* Ein zweiter *Dictatus papae* Gregors VII.?" *Deutsches Archiv* 28 (1972) 105-132.

[83] *Registrum* (n. 9 above) 2.55a, cc. 3-5, 13-15, 20, 21, 24-27 (202-208).

[84] *Epistolae Vagantes* (n. 39 above) no. 10 (24)

generally understood in the 1070s. These *sententiae* did not long remain "lawless"; for, like most of the statements of the *Dictatus papae*, they were provided with *pièces justificatives* by the distinguished canonists — notably Anselm of Lucca and Cardinal Deusdedit — whom Gregory VII encouraged to defend his reforming measures in their canonical collections.[85] Nevertheless, in presenting texts to support these controversial claims of the *Dictatus papae,* the canonists were obliged to distort the sense of their canonical authorities. (Anselm of Lucca and Cardinal Deusdedit were indeed denounced by the "anti-Gregorians" among the cardinals as "perverters of the scriptures" and authors of "fraudulent compilations.")[86] For the first of the "lawless" *sententiae,* "That [the pope's] legate takes precedence over all bishops in a council, even [if he is] of inferior rank; and he can give sentence of deposition against them" (4), Anselm and Deusdedit provided in their canonical collections the *auctoritas* of a single case mentioned in the *Register* of Pope Gregory I. This the canonists cited out of context, giving it a generalized import which is not present in the original.[87] In this way the activities of Gregory VII's legates in Germany, which had so offended Archbishop Liemar of Bremen and Bishop Burchard II of Halberstadt in 1074,[88] were given legal justification. *Sententiae* 5 and 24 of the *Dictatus papae* — "That the pope can depose men in their absence" and "That by [the pope's] command and permission, subjects are allowed to bring accusations [against superiors]" — presented even greater difficulties. In support of the former claim, Anselm and Deusdedit were able to find the case (not entirely to the purpose) of Bishop Dioscorus, condemned in his absence for his contumacy at the Council of Chalcedon.[89] On the subject of *sententia* 24, the canonists were silent. Both these claims, which Gregory VII had put into effect in his relations with the German bishops in 1074, were explicitly opposed by traditional canon law. The *Collectio Isidori Mercatoris* had frequently reiterated the canonical rules that no man can be judged in his absence, and that superiors cannot be accused by inferiors; and Pseudo-Isidorean materials on this subject were transmitted by the *Decretum* of Burchard of Worms.[90] These two canonical principles were also carefully preserved in the canonical collections produced by, and reflecting the aims of, the papal reform movement. For example, the "Collection in Seventy-four Titles" has as its thirteenth title, "That no one may be judged in his absence," and as its seventh title, "That those of inferior degree cannot accuse their superiors," both titles presenting Pseudo-

[85] Cf. P. Fournier, "Un tournant de l'histoire du droit," *Nouvelle revue historique de droit français et étranger* 41 (1917) 142-143. On the role of the *Dictatus papae* in the works of the "Gregorian" canonists, see K. Hofmann, *Der Dictatus Papae Gregors VII.: Eine rechtsgeschichtliche Erklärung,* Görres-Gesellschaft, Veröff. der Sektion für Rechts- und Staatswissenschaft 63 (Paderborn 1933).

[86] *Cardinalium schismaticorum scripta,* MGH Libelli de lite 2.399-400.

[87] Anselm (n. 31 above) 1.25 (17); Deusdedit (n. 74 above) 1.206 (121).

[88] *Registrum* (n. 9 above) 2.12, 28 (143-144, 160-161).

[89] Anselm (n. 31 above) 3.92 (173); Deusdedit (n. 74 above) 1.36 (46)

[90] Burchard (n. 69 above) 1.177, 16.13-14 ("Ut nemo absens dijudicetur"); 1.136-139 ("Episcopos a suis ovibus non reprehendendos").

Isidorean material.[91] The same material was reproduced in the third book of the *Collectio canonum* of Anselm of Lucca[92] and was eventually absorbed into the *Decretum* of Master Gratian of Bologna.[93] The *Collectio* of Anselm and, to a lesser extent, the "Collection in Seventy-four Titles" have often been categorized as "Gregorian" collections; but in these two instances of judicial procedures, they had clearly not been persuaded by the Gregorian ecclesiology of the *Dictatus papae* to deviate from the canonical principles of Pseudo-Isidore.

Gregory VII's ecclesiology took as its starting point the doctrine of the papal primacy, as it had developed, impelled by the needs of the papal reform movement, since the mid-eleventh century. The reform movement had exploited the "Roman" interpretation of the three crucial Petrine texts of the New Testament, Matthew 16.18–19, Luke 22.32 and John 21.15–17. In patristic writings and in the works of the Carolingian period, the commission of Christ to Saint Peter recorded in these texts is generally interpreted as the foundation of the Church, in the sense that the power of the keys was conferred on a *sacerdotalis ordo* in the person of Peter: the power granted to Peter was symbolically granted to the whole episcopate.[94] In the writings of the papal reform movement of the eleventh century, however, the Petrine commission is interpreted exclusively as the foundation of the *Roman* church.[95] The ecclesiology of the papal reform movement takes as the basis of the organization of Christian society, not the concept of *ecclesia,* but the authority of the Roman church,[96] the *caput et cardo* by which all other churches are regulated.[97] This view of Roman authority was initially developed, in the early 1050s, in the context of papal negotiations with the Eastern church. Faced with an intransigent patriarch of Constantinople, Pope Leo IX had appealed to the privilege which the "Donation of Constantine" supposedly conferred on the Roman church: "That throughout the whole world, priests shall have [the pope] as their head, as all *iudices* [obey] the king."[98] Leo IX here referred to the passage of the "Donation of Constantine" which represented the Roman pontiff as superior in authority to the four Eastern patriarchs of Alexandria, Antioch, Jerusalem and Constantinople, and as "*princeps* over all priests throughout the whole world."[99] This conception of the papal

[91] *Collectio in LXXIV titulos* (n. 31 above) 13, 7 (71-73, 54-56).

[92] Anselm (n. 31 above) 3.28, 36, 43, 52, 57, 58, 86, 87.

[93] Gratian, *Decretum,* ed. Friedberg (n. 31 above) esp. C.3 q.9 c.1-15; C.3 q.7 c.10-13.

[94] Y. M.-J. Congar, *L'ecclésiologie du haut moyen-âge* (Paris 1968) 138-149.

[95] Y. M.-J. Congar, "Der Platz des Papsttums in der Kirchenfrömmigkeit der Reformer des 11. Jahrhunderts," in *Sentire ecclesiam,* ed. J. Daniélou and H. Vorgrimler (Freiburg 1961) 196-217.

[96] Cf. H. M. Klinkenberg, "Der römische Primat im 10. Jahrhundert," *Zeitschrift der Savigny-Stiftung für Rechtsgeschichte, Kan. Abt.* 41 (1955) 1-57.

[97] *Collectio in LXXIV titulos* (n. 31 above) 2 (20).

[98] Leo IX, *Epistola I ad Cerullarium* c. 10 (C. Will, *Acta et scripta quae de controversiis ecclesiae Graecae et Latinae saeculo undecimo composita extant* [Leipzig 1861] 70b). On the authorship of this letter, see A. Michel, *Humbert und Kerullarios: Quellen und Studien zum Schisma des XI. Jahrhunderts* 1, Quellen und Forschungen aus dem Gebiete der Geschichte herausgegeben von der Görres-Gesellschaft 21 (Paderborn 1924) 45-52.

[99] *Constitutum Constantini,* ed. H. Fuhrmann, MGH Fontes iuris germanici antiqui in usum scholarum 10 (1968) 82-83. On the use of the "Donation" in the letter of Leo IX, see H.

primacy over the priesthood *in toto orbe* was inherited by Gregory VII; and traces of Leo IX's elaboration of the privilege accorded by the "Donation of Constantine" are found in *sententiae* 2 and 8 of the *Dictatus papae*. Gregory VII, however, applied this Leonine conception of the Roman primacy not to his relations with Byzantium, but to his relations with the churches of Western Christendom. From Leo IX's analogy of the obedience due to the pope with that due to a king, Gregory deduced the idea of a papal monarchy with bishops as its officials. This was the assumption behind his precept to bishops to act as "an impregnable wall in defence of the Roman church. . .and of us";[100] and from this assumption derived his demand that bishops show *obedientia* to the apostolic see.

The corollary of Gregory VII's notion of ecclesiastical governance – that disobedient bishops lose the privileges guaranteed to them by Pseudo-Isidore: that they cease to be protected from the accusations of inferiors and indeed are no longer to be obeyed by their subjects – seems similarly to derive from an exposition composed earlier in the history of the papal reform. The Gregorian assault on the judicial immunity of the episcopate was anticipated in a letter written between 1065 and 1071 and addressed to Pope Alexander II by Peter Damian, cardinal bishop of Ostia, the great Italian ascetic and reformer. Peter Damian complained to the pope: "The statement, 'It is not permissible for a son of any church to bring charges against his own bishop . . . before a greater church,' is too incongruous and utterly contrary to ecclesiastical discipline."[101] Damian's formulation of this concept of judicial immunity may be a reflection of a contemporary *cause célèbre* in which he was involved as papal legate: the campaign of the monks of Vallombrosa against the simoniacal bishop of Florence, Peter Mezzabarba. The bishop of Florence was supported by most of his fellow bishops and his conviction was secured in 1068 only through his accuser's undergoing the ordeal of fire. (His triumphant accuser was the Vallombrosan monk Peter "Igneus," that hero of the reform movement who in 1072 became cardinal bishop of Albano.)[102] The theory of episcopal immunity from accusation which had protected Peter Mezzabarba until 1068 was declared by Peter Damian to be a "pernicious custom."[103] In his letter to Alexander II, Damian referred to two of the principal Pseudo-Isidorean texts defending this immunity: texts of Pseudo-Fabian and Pseudo-Anacletus which reappear in the "Collection in Seventy-four Titles" and in the *Collectio canonum* of Anselm of Lucca and, finally, in the *Decretum* of Master Gratian.[104] This Pseudo-Isidorean tradition Damian

Fuhrmann, "Konstantinische Schenkung und abendländisches Kaisertum: Ein Beitrag zur Überlieferungsgeschichte des Constitutum Constantini," *Deutsches Archiv* 22 (1966) 109ff.

[100] *Registrum* (n. 9 above) 2.28 (160-161).

[101] Peter Damian, *Epistolae* 1.12 (PL 144.215D).

[102] Cf. G. Miccoli, *Pietro Igneo: Studi sull' età gregoriana,* Studi storici 40-41 (Rome 1960) 42ff.

[103] Peter Damian, *Epistolae* 1.12 (PL 144.218C).

[104] *Epistola Fabiani* c. 22, *Epistola Anacleti* c. 39 (Hinschius [n. 22 above] 165, 85); identified in Damian's letter by J. J. Ryan, *Saint Peter Damiani and his Canonical Sources,* Pontifical Institute of Mediaeval Studies 2 (Toronto 1956) 129. Cf. *Collectio in LXXIV titulos* (n. 31 above) 78, 74; Anselm (n. 31 above) 3.31, 37; Gratian, *Decretum* C.2 q.7 c.12.

wished to discard, replacing it by a judicial procedure which would enhance the authority of Rome: "Let this cunning subterfuge be abolished, so that. . .[no one] may enjoy immunity for the sins which he has committed. Let free access be permitted to just grievances and complaints be made at the primatial see." In this letter of 1065–1071 it is easy to see the origin of *sententia* 24 of *Dictatus papae,* "That by [the pope's] command and permission, subjects are allowed to bring accusations"; and in the case of Peter Mezzabarba, the simoniac to whom Pseudo-Isidore permitted immunity from accusation, it is easy to perceive the origins of the attack on the Pseudo-Isidorean privileges of the episcopate in the early years of Gregory VII's pontificate.

It is significant that Peter Damian should have been associated with those policies of the early papal reform movement which first caused the papacy to intervene in areas of episcopal jurisdiction. Firstly, Peter Damian's journey to France, as legate of Alexander II, in 1063 marks a turning point in the papal policy of exempting monasteries from the spiritual authority of bishops. With this legatine mission of 1063 the granting of papal privileges of exemption (a tradition which can be traced back to the pontificate of Nicholas I) began to be reinforced by active papal intervention in the affairs of dioceses on behalf of the exempt houses.[105] At the legatine council of Châlon-sur-Saône of 1063, in the face of the bitter opposition and the "secret machinations" of the neighboring bishops, Peter Damian defended the monastery of Cluny against the assertions of the bishop of Mâcon and compelled the bishop to do public penance.[106] This practice of protecting favored monasteries and restricting the rights of bishops over them was a recurrent feature of papal activity in Gregory VII's pontificate. His *Register* contains warnings to bishops against infringing the rights guaranteed by the pope both to houses of the Cluniac connection, like Saint-Gilles in the diocese of Nîmes and Saint-Sernin in Toulouse,[107] and to houses of the Lotharingian reform, like Saint-Mihiel in the diocese of Verdun and Saint-Hubert-en-Ardennes.[108] Secondly, Peter Damian's legatine mission to Milan in 1059 made an important contribution to that central policy of the reforming papacy, the subjection of the Milanese archbishopric to Roman jurisdiction.[109] The Milanese claim that "the Ambrosian church ought not to be subject to Roman laws and no right of judging or of ordering affairs in that see belongs to the Roman pontiff"[110] was refuted by Damian in his treatise *Actus Mediolani,* describing his proceedings in Milan in 1059 and recording in detail the *sermo ad populum* by means of which he sought to persuade the Milanese to obey the Roman church. Damian's *opusculum,* expounding fully the extent and the implications of the *privilegium*

[105] Cowdrey (n. 38 above) 47-51.

[106] *De Gallica Petri Damiani profectione et eius ultramontano itinere,* MGH Scriptores 30.1044-1046.

[107] *Registrum* (n. 9 above) 1.68 (97-99); 9.30 (615-617).

[108] *Ibid.* 1.81 (115-116); 2.61 (216).

[109] Cf. F. Dressler, *Petrus Damiani: Leben und Werk,* Studia Anselmiana, fasc. 34 (Rome 1954) 143ff.; H. E. J. Cowdrey, "The Papacy, the Patarenes and the Church of Milan," *Transactions of the Royal Historical Society* ser. 5, 18 (1968) 25-48.

[110] Peter Damian, *Opusculum V. Actus Mediolani,* PL 145.90C.

Romanae ecclesiae, was addressed to Archdeacon Hildebrand, that staunch defender of the Roman primacy who (according to the exordium of the *Actus Mediolani*) had often requested the compilation of a canonical collection on the subject of the primacy. The papal policy of crushing Milanese independence was continued by Hildebrand, after his elevation to the papacy, through the devices of inciting the suffragans of Milan to disobey their archbishop "in order to restore the honor of your mother, the Milanese church"[111] and encouraging the violent resistance of the lay opponents of the archbishop of Milan, the knights Herlembald, Henry, Arderic and Wifred, whom the pope saluted as "vassals of the holy apostolic see and legitimate sons of the Milanese church."[112]

The exalted view of the Roman primacy contained in Peter Damian's *Actus Mediolani* was likewise perpetuated in the pronouncements and the actions of Gregory VII. For example, Damian's insistence that the Roman church, unlike the Milanese and all the other churches of Christendom, was divinely instituted without any human intermediary — "[Christ] himself alone founded the Roman church and raised it upon the rock of the nascent faith" — reappears in the first *sententia* of the *Dictatus papae* of Gregory VII: "That the Roman church was founded by the Lord alone."[113] Another idea which frequently recurs in the censures which Gregory VII addressed to bishops first appears in this treatise of Peter Damian: "He who seeks to take away the privilege conferred on the Roman church by the supreme head of all churches, undoubtedly falls into heresy: . . . he is to be called a heretic. He who acts against the mother of the faith, certainly violates the faith." This is the idea contained in *Dictatus papae* 26, "That he who does not agree with the Roman Church is not held to be a catholic," and in the formula which Gregory VII used to demand obedience of bishops, "He who does not agree with the Roman church is held to be a heretic."[114] The latter formula Gregory attributed to Saint Ambrose; but so pointed a statement of the Roman primacy is not found in Ambrose's writings. It is worth noting that in the *Actus Mediolani* of Peter Damian, where such a statement of the primacy of Rome is certainly to be found, there is great emphasis on the *auctoritas* of Saint Ambrose in conjunction with the *privilegium Romanae ecclesiae*. In dealing with the Ambrosian church of Milan, Damian diplomatically referred to the authority of the father from whom that church derived its traditions. Gregory VII's inclusion of the name of Ambrose in his formulation of the *privilegium Romanae ecclesiae* may, therefore, be an indication that the *Actus Mediolani* was his actual source.[115] Certainly, Peter Damian's insistence on the Roman primacy and

---

[111] *Registrum* (n. 9 above) 1.27 (44). Cf. 1.15 (23-25); 1.28 (45-46); 1.43 (65-67); 3.9 (261-263).

[112] *Ibid.* 1.25, 26 (41-44: Herlembald); 3.15 (276-277: Wifred); 4.7 (305: Henry, Arderic and Wifred).

[113] Peter Damian, *Opusculum V* (PL 145.90C). Cf. *Registrum* 2.55a, c. 1 (202).

[114] Peter Damian, *Opusculum V* (PL 145.91CD). Cf. *Registrum* 2.55a, c. 26 (207); 7.24 (504-505).

[115] The common source of Peter Damian and Gregory VII may have been Ambrose, *De excessu Satyri* 1.47, PL 16.1362 (suggested by Erdmann [n. 33 above] 26 n., apropos of the similar formulation in the letter of Odo of Ostia).

that of Gregory VII sprang from the same preoccupation with ecclesiastical discipline. The obstacles which impeded the papal reform of the Church — such obstacles as Damian encountered in the conduct of the archbishop of Milan and the bishop of Florence in the 1050s and 1060s and as Gregory VII encountered in the attitude of the German bishops in the early 1070s — could be removed only by magnifying the pretensions of the Roman see, by subjecting all other ecclesiastical jurisdictions to the universal authority of Rome and by presenting the failure to obey papal commands as an aberration from the faith.

From the beginning of his pontificate, Gregory VII sought to undermine the independent position of the bishoprics of Western Christendom; and his progress can be traced in a series of episcopal protests composed during the 1070s, complaining of the aggression of the Roman Church. The case of the archbishopric of Ravenna, for example, reveals that this aggression was operative already in the first year of Gregory's pontificate. Archbishop Wibert of Ravenna in 1073 demanded an oath of fealty from the city of Imola in Emilia; whereupon some of the citizens complained to Gregory VII. The pope immediately commanded Count Guido of Imola to intervene in order to prevent the extortion of an oath from the citizens. "Our colleague, Wibert, archbishop of Ravenna, strives to subject [the inhabitants of Imola] to his sway," wrote Gregory, "and to force them to swear oaths of fealty to him against the honor of Saint Peter, to whom they have sworn fealty." [116] However, according to a centuries-old tradition, frequently confirmed, Imola was recognized as a possession of the church of Ravenna; [117] and Gregory VII's intervention in 1073 was an unjustified encroachment upon the archbishop's jurisdiction. The quarrel between Ravenna and Rome which predated the Investiture Contest — the failure of Archbishop Wibert to attend the Roman synod of Lent 1075 and his subsequent suspension and excommunication in 1078 [118] — must be attributed to the aggression of Rome. This aggression immediately provoked in Ravenna a defensive propaganda in the form, not of polemical treatises, [119] but of a series of forged diplomas. Spurious privileges in the names of Valentinian III, Pope Gregory I and Charlemagne extended the metropolitan jurisdiction of Ravenna at the expense of Roman claims. [120] The forged privilege of Gregory I gives the archbishop of Ravenna the right of investiture in the metropolitan diocese of Emilia and in sixteen other bishoprics and denies the right of the papacy to interfere in the succession to these bishoprics. [121] The forged privilege of Charlemagne places under Ravennese jurisdic-

[116] *Registrum* (n. 9 above) 1.10 (16).

[117] Cf. O. Köhncke, *Wibert von Ravenna (Papst Clemens III.)* (Leipzig 1888) 23.

[118] *Registrum* (n. 9 above) 5.14a (369).

[119] The Ravennese polemical treatises of Wido of Ferrara (*De scismate Hildebrandi,* MGH Libelli de lite 1.529-567) and Wibert of Ravenna (his first encyclical, not extant) belong to the later period (1085-1086) of crisis in the Gregorian ranks. The famous *Defensio Heinrici IV regis* of Petrus Crassus cannot with certainty be attributed to the Ravennese ambience. (The provenance of this work is discussed in my forthcoming study of the polemical literature of the Investiture Contest.)

[120] Cf. K. Brandi, "Ravenna und Rom," *Archiv für Urkundenforschung* 9 (1926) 15ff.

[121] P. Kehr, *Italia Pontificia* 5 (Berlin 1911) 32 (no. 62).

tion eight bishoprics lying adjacent to the Exarchate which traditionally belonged to the jurisdiction of Rome.[122] These forgeries bear witness to the determination of Wibert of Ravenna to exalt the status of his archbishopric, a policy with which he persevered even after he had become Henry IV's antipope: the confirmation of the privileges of the church of Ravenna which he issued in 1086 as "Pope Clement III" specifically refers to the spurious diplomas of Saint Gregory and Charlemagne.[123]

The background to the pretensions advanced in these Ravennese forgeries was the assault on the traditional privileges of the church of Saint Apollinaris of Ravenna (contemporaneous with the assault on the Ambrosian church of Milan) which Gregory VII had launched to vindicate the claims of the apostolic see. The Roman church, according to Gregory VII's propaganda, was "the prince and universal mother of all the churches and peoples"[124] — an echo of the ancient tradition that the West had been evangelized solely from Rome and by Rome.[125] From this tradition Gregory VII drew the conclusion that Rome was the unique repository of ecclesiastical authority and that no other church — not even a church of such dignified antiquity as Ravenna — possessed any authority independent of that transmitted by the *princeps omnium ecclesiarum et gentium:* "Whatever dignity or honor [the church of Ravenna] has held through Saint Apollinaris was conceded by the gift of the [apostolic] see."[126] When the archbishop of Ravenna failed to recognize his duty of subjection and obedience to Rome, Gregory VII preached rebellion to "all the citizens of Ravenna, great and small, who love Saint Peter and his son, Saint Apollinaris, martyr and bishop":

> You know very well how faithfully and how humbly the church of
> Ravenna always clung to Saint Peter and how she showed obedience in
> all things to her mother, the holy Roman church. But you have seen and
> felt, through your sufferings, how he who is now called bishop of the
> church of Ravenna has ruined by his tyrannical depredations a church
> which was once as abundant in wealth as it was in piety, and corrupted it
> by the example of his impious life . . . . Wherefore we command you all
> by the authority of Saint Peter, prince of the apostles, henceforward to
> show him none of the obedience due to a bishop.[127]

Finally, in 1080, the authority of Rome over Ravenna was to be demonstrated by substituting for the excommunicate and schismatic Wibert, Gregory's own candidate, ordained by the pope as "catholic" anti-archbishop. Gregory's letter introducing the anti-archbishop to the clergy and people of Ravenna characteristically evokes the legend that Saint Peter had sent Saint Apollinaris as a missionary to the Ravennese:

[122] Cf. K. Jordan, "Ravennater Fälschungen aus den Anfängen des Investiturstreites," *Archiv für Urkundenforschung* 15 (1938) 445-446.

[123] Kehr (n. 121 above) 5.56 (no. 187).

[124] *Registrum* (n. 9 above) 1.64 (93); 6.13 (416). Cf. *Registrum* 7.6 (465-467); 9.2 (569-572).

[125] Cf. P. Battifol, *Cathedra Petri* (Paris 1938) 47.

[126] *Registrum* (n. 9 above) 8.13 (533).

[127] *Ibid.* 6.10 (411-412).

"Be zealous in giving aid and counsel to our brother R[ichard], archbishop of Ravenna, whom Ravenna has very recently received from the Roman church, after being for a long time under the control of intruders — just as long ago Ravenna deserved to receive Apollinaris from Saint Peter." [128]

Simultaneous with this papal campaign to subdue the church of Ravenna was Gregory VII's attempt to intervene in the question of the primacy of the church in France. Traditionally, preeminence in the French church belonged to the archbishop of Sens (known since the ninth century as "primate of *Gallia*") and to the archbishop of Reims (the key figure both in the making of the king of the Franks and in the ecclesiastical politics of the kingdom). [129] Gregory VII challenged this tradition by raising up rivals to Sens and Reims among the other French archbishoprics, in particular exalting the status of the archbishopric of Lyons. On 20 April 1079 the pope issued a privilege which conferred on the archbishopric of Lyons primacy over the four ecclesiastical provinces of Lyons, Rouen, Tours and Sens. [130] The papal letter informing the metropolitans of these provinces of their new subjection contains a long definition of "primate" taken from the *Collectio Isidori Mercatoris*. [131] This letter reads superficially like a defense of the Pseudo-Isidorean order of the Church; but in fact it struck a shrewd blow against the established claims of the archsee of Sens and the status quo in the French church. The archbishops of Lyons who were the beneficiaries of this papal privilege during Gregory VII's lifetime were, firstly, Gebuin (1077–1082), the papal candidate whose election to the archbishopric had been secured by the papal legate, Hugh of Die, at the council of Autun; [132] and, secondly, that zealous papal agent, Hugh of Die himself. The rival primacy which Gregory VII had created in the French church was, therefore, conferred on trusted Gregorians. Equally indicative of Gregory's attitude towards the French episcopate is the case of Archbishop Warmund of Vienne (1076–1081), a former monk of Cluny and a close associate of Abbot Hugh of Cluny, and an earnest reformer whom the pope was to use as his legate in Flanders. [133] In his zeal for reform, Warmund interfered in the affairs of the archbishopric of Reims, deposing and then reinstating a number of priests (probably in 1077). When the archbishop of Reims complained to the pope that Warmund was "pretending that he was a Roman legate, which he was not," [134] Gregory seems not to have restrained or censured Warmund. He simply referred the case of Reims to Hugh of Die and to Abbot Hugh of Cluny, commanding the archbishop of Reims to show obedience to them. [135]

[128] *Ibid.* 8.14 (535).

[129] Cf. A. Fliche, "La primatie des Gaules depuis l'époque carolingienne jusqu 'à la fin de la querelle des investitures (876-1121)," *Revue historique* 173 (1934) 329-342.

[130] *Registrum* (n. 9 above) 6.34 (447-449).

[131] *Ibid.* 6.35 (451-452).

[132] Hugh of Flavigny (n. 37 above) 415-416; Hugh of Die, letter to Gregory VII, PL 148.744.

[133] On Warmund's relations with the papacy and with Cluny, see *Registrum* (n. 9 above) 4.16 (320-321); 6.27 (439); 6.28 (440-441); *Epistolae Vagantes* (n. 39 above) no. 38 (96); Cowdrey (n. 38 above) 54-55, 171.

[134] Hugh of Flavigny (n. 37 above) 419.

[135] *Registrum* (n. 9 above) 6.2 (394); 6.3 (395).

Three letters of protest issued in the name of Archbishop Manasses I of Reims (1069—1080) are extant, itemizing the various encroachments upon the traditional rights of the church of Reims which the pope had condoned. The first letter (composed in 1077) appeals to the pope against the sentence of excommunication pronounced upon Manasses by Hugh of Die at the council of Autun.[136] This sentence Gregory VII found to be excessively severe and he therefore restored Manasses to his see at the Lenten synod of 1078, in return for an oath of obedience. The archbishop was required to swear on the body of Saint Peter, that "if it pleases the lord Pope Gregory or his successor that I should answer charges before his legate, I shall perform this in full."[137] Manasses's second letter (probably of 1078) complained of the interference of other churchmen in the affairs of his archdiocese, and of the disobedience of members of his cathedral chapter;[138] and these complaints were answered by Gregory with a sharp reminder of the archbishop's obligation to obey any man, whatever his rank, whom the pope had invested with his own authority.[139] Manasses's third letter (of 1079) was a reply to the summons of Hugh of Die to submit his conduct as archbishop to the judgment of a council at Lyons. Manasses presented his grounds for disobeying this summons, the principal reason being that the pope had originally appointed Abbot Hugh of Cluny to judge his case, and that Manasses did not wish to be denied his proper judge.[140] Nevertheless, Hugh of Die deposed Manasses at the council of Lyons in 1080; Gregory confirmed the deposition,[141] and by the end of the year he was commanding the clergy and people of Reims to "resist [Manasses] by all means, that he may be torn from your midst and consigned to Satan for the destruction of his flesh."[142]

Archbishop Manasses of Reims was the most illustrious victim of Gregory VII's preoccupation with the primacy question in France, and a victim also of that Gregorian ecclesiological principle stated in *sententia* 4 of the *Dictatus papae,* "That [the pope's] legate, even if he is of inferior rank, takes precedence over all bishops in a council and he can pronounce sentence of deposition against them."[143] Manasses's ruin was accomplished by an alliance between the indefatigable papal legate, Hugh of Die, and a pro-papal faction within the archdiocese, and in particular within the cathedral chapter of Reims. The archbishop's principal opponents were the provost of Reims, Manasses (afterwards Archbishop Manasses II of Reims) and the chancellor and master of the schools, Bruno (the founder of the Carthusian order), who had

---

[136] Manasses's letter is found in the letter collection of Hanover, Niedersächsische Landesbibliothek MS XI.671, ed. Erdmann (n. 33 above) 178-182.

[137] *Registrum* (n. 9 above) 5.17 (378-379).

[138] The letter is preserved in the Chronicle of Hugh of Flavigny (n. 37 above) 419-420.

[139] *Registrum* 6.2 (392).

[140] *Apologia Manassae archiepiscopi Remensis,* ed. J. Mabillon and M. Germain, *Museum italicum seu Collectio veterum scriptorum ex bibliothecis italicis* 1.2 (Paris 1687) 119-127. A reaction to this letter is found in *Registrum* (n. 9 above) 7.12 (475-477).

[141] *Registrum* 7.20 (496).

[142] *Ibid.* 8.17 (539).

[143] *Ibid.* 2.55a, c. 4 (203).

made contact with Hugh of Die before the council of Autun.[144] At this council, canons of Reims accused their archbishop of simony;[145] and it is as a worldly, simoniac prelate, hostile to reform, that Manasses I is presented in pro-papal sources.[146] However, in the letters of Manasses and in the replies of Gregory VII, the issues which divided the archbishop and the pope can be seen to be, not those of simony and the moral reform of the Church, but those of ecclesiastical jurisdiction. Manasses complained of the conspiracy into which "the subjects of our church" had entered against him in 1077.[147] Here was an appeal to the Pseudo-Isidorean rule (as stated in the decretals of Zephyrinus, Fabian and Stephen I) which imposed the gravest penalties on clerks who conspired against their bishop.[148] Manasses asserted the metropolitan privileges of his see, which ancient tradition upheld, and condemned the meddling of other bishops in his archdiocese, which canon law forbade.[149] The principal object of Manasses I throughout his pontificate was not so much to hinder reform, as to preserve undiminished the traditions of the church of Reims as they had existed in the age of Isidorus Mercator and of the great Archbishop Hincmar.[150] The function of the Roman church, according to the ecclesiological assumptions of Manasses, was to protect the privileges of the other churches and to punish infringements of them.[151] The reaction of Gregory VII to Manasses's defense of the *privilegium* of Reims provides a striking illustration of the pope's attitude towards the traditional structure of the Church:

> As to what you say concerning a privilege, we briefly reply that certain things can be granted in privileges according to the case, the person, the time and the place, which again for the same circumstances may lawfully be altered, if a greater necessity or utility demands it. For privileges must not infringe the authority of the holy fathers, but provide for the utility of holy Church.[152]

[144] For the legate's relations with the archbishop's opponents, see Hugh of Die, letter to Gregory VII, PL 148.745. For Manasses's strictures on his opponents, see his letter of 1077, ed. Erdmann (n. 33 above) 179; his letter of 1078, Hugh of Flavigny (n. 37 above) 420; and *Apologia Manassae* (n. 140 above) 121.

[145] Hugh of Flavigny 415.

[146] E.g., Guibert of Nogent, *De vita sua* 1.11, ed. G. Bourgin (Paris 1907) 30. This is the view of Manasses I which is accepted by A. Fliche, *La réforme grégorienne et la reconquête chrétienne*, Histoire de l'église 8 (Paris 1940) 100. See also J. R. Williams, "Archbishop Manasses I of Rheims and Pope Gregory VII," *American Historical Review* 54 (1949).

[147] Letter of 1077, Erdmann (n. 33 above) 179.

[148] E.g., *Epistola Zephyrini* c. 3, 4; *Epistola Fabiani* c. 21; *Epistola Stephani* c. 21 (ed. Hinschius [n. 22 above] 131, 165, 186); cited in *Collectio in LXXIV titulos* (n. 31 above) 66-68; Anselm (n. 31 above) 3.58, 7.150; Gratian, *Decretum* C.3 q.9 c.13; C.11 q.1 c.31; C.3 q.4 c.8.

[149] Letter of 1078, Hugh of Flavigny (n. 37 above) 419-420. For the canon law on this subject, see the Pseudo-Isidorean materials collected under the title "Ut unusquisque suis contentus sit terminis" in *Collectio in LXXIV titulos* 119-121.

[150] Cf. H. Gaul, *Manasses I., Erzbischof von Reims* (Essen 1940) 40-42.

[151] Letter of 1078, Hugh of Flavigny (n. 37 above) 419.

[152] *Registrum* (n. 9 above) 6.2 (393).

Mere *privilegia* must yield to "the authority of the holy fathers," of which the pope was the principal guardian and interpreter.[153] The established pattern of ecclesiastical governance must occasionally be amended to meet the *necessitas* of the reform movement.[154] In the confrontation between Manasses and Gregory VII can be discerned two utterly opposite conceptions of the organization of the Church. Manasses conceived of the Church as a rigid hierarchy of jealously guarded privileges. Gregory's was a more dynamic conception, of an ecclesiastical structure which must be remodelled according to the needs of a regenerated Christian society: "For it seems to us far better to reestablish divine justice by means of new counsels than to allow the souls of men to perish along with the laws which they have neglected."[155]

A similar conflict of opinions concerning ecclesiastical authority and the ancient jurisdictional privileges of bishoprics was responsible for Gregory VII's uneasy relations with the German church in the first three years of his pontificate. The conflict is already apparent in the correspondence between Gregory and Archbishop Siegfried of Mainz in 1073-1074. Siegfried wrote to the pope in 1073 concerning the long dispute between his suffragans, the Bohemian bishops of Prague and Olomouc, which had broken out at the end of the pontificate of Gregory's predecessor, Pope Alexander II.[156] Bishop Jaromir of Prague laid claim to certain rights which Bishop John of Olomouc vigorously defended, supported by Jaromir's brother, Duke Vratislav of Bohemia, the founder of the bishopric of Olomouc. The bishop of Olomouc and his ally, Duke Vratislav, had appealed to Alexander II, whose intervention had resulted in the suspension of Jaromir of Prague from his episcopal office.[157] Siegfried of Mainz considered that Alexander II's action was prejudicial to his own rights as metropolitan; and he therefore wrote to the new pope, Gregory VII, that the case of the Bohemian bishoprics should be submitted to the judgment of the archbishop of Mainz. Siegfried did not doubt that the jurisdiction of the apostolic see extended throughout Christendom. He wrote indeed in the most exalted terms of *imperatrix Roma,* "the head of the churches," and described himself as "taken into

---

[153] For the pope as interpreter of the *sanctorum patrum auctoritas*, see, for example, *Registrum* 3.10: "He who does not refuse obedience to God, does not scorn to observe our counsels, which follow the statutes of the holy fathers" (265); and *Epistolae Vagantes* (n. 39 above) no. 14: ". . . not what we teach, but what divine authority teaches and decides, what the harmonious voice of the holy fathers judges" (40).

[154] On the concept of *necessitas* in the thought of Gregory VII, see *Registrum* (n. 9 above) 2.55a, c.7 (203); and Hofmann (n. 85 above) 76 ff.

[155] *Registrum* 2.45 (184).

[156] Siegfried's letter is preserved in the *Codex Udalrici,* ed. P. Jaffé, Bibliotheca rerum germanicarum 5 (Berlin 1869) 85 ff. G. B. Borino, "Le lettere di Gregorio VII e di Sigifrido di Magonza che si scambiarono fino al principio del 1075," *Studi Gregoriani* 6 (Rome 1959-1961) 265 ff., argues that the text in the *Codex Udalrici* is a conflation of letters written by Siegfried on two separate occasions.

[157] Cosmas of Prague, *Cronica Boemorum,* MGH Scriptores rerum germanicarum, nova series 2 (1923) 120.

service under the key-bearing hand of so great a pontiff." [158] Nevertheless, Siegfried claimed the rights which "the decrees of the canons" guaranteed to a metropolitan. He cited in his letter to Gregory VII the Pseudo-Isidorean principle (reiterated in Burchard's *Decretum* and in the "Collection in Seventy-four Titles") that a bishop must be judged in the first instance by his own metropolitan, and that if the case proved too difficult to decide, it should be referred to Rome. [159] Siegfried of Mainz believed — like Manasses of Reims — that the role of Rome was to guarantee to the churches of Christendom their traditional rights; and so he requested of Gregory VII "the privilege of grace which the Holy See has always allotted to the church of Mainz, as a pious mother to a favorite daughter." The archbishop of Mainz was made sharply aware that his notions of ecclesiastical authority were behind the times. "It is evident how little your advisers understand or pay attention to the rights of apostolic authority," wrote Gregory VII in reply. "You are not to image that you, or indeed any of the patriarchs or primates, can take the liberty of retracting apostolic judgments . . . . With God's help and by Saint Peter's authority, we shall contrive to settle the dispute justly." [160] *Necessitas* and *utilitas* — considerations which recked nothing of the privileges of metropolitans — had demanded that the pope should intervene in the case of the Bohemian archbishoprics; and thereafter no inferior authority could meddle in it.

Similar instances of papal intervention in the affairs of German bishoprics in 1074 and 1075 provoked the protest literature which survives in the late eleventh-century Hildesheim letter collection. [161] The Hildesheim collection contains the complaints of German bishops about Gregory VII's disregard of the dignity of their office: the pope has treated them as mere subordinates who have no independent voice even in the government of their own dioceses; and he has given credence to malicious charges brought against them by tale-bearing inferiors. This is the theme of a letter of Archbishop Udo of Trier, directed to Gregory early in 1075, concerning the case of Bishop Pibo of Toul, which the pope had commanded Udo to investigate. [162] A clerk of Toul had come to Rome and denounced his bishop to the pope as a simoniac; whereupon Gregory had written to the archbishop of Trier, demanding that a full inquiry be made and the clerks of Toul be questioned about the conduct of their bishop "or rather ex-bishop," "a wolf" who has obtained the place of a pastor. [163] Upon investigating the case, Udo of Trier and his colleagues found the bishop of Toul

---

[158] See Siegfried's letters to Gregory VII (n. 156 above) 85ff., and the earlier letters to Alexander II, *ibid.* 61, 63ff.

[159] Burchard (n. 69 above) 1.149-183; *Collectio in LXXIV titulos* (n. 31 above) 62-65 (52-54).

[160] *Registrum* (n. 9 above) 1.60 (87-89).

[161] The Hildesheim collection is found in the composite sixteenth-century codex, Hanover, Niedersächsische Landesbibliothek MS XI.671, and is edited by Erdmann (n. 33 above) 15ff., and discussed by him (n. 54 above) 200ff.

[162] *Hildesheimer Briefe* no. 17, ed. Erdmann 39-41.

[163] *Registrum* (n. 9 above) 2.10 (140-142). On this case, see Erdmann (n. 54 above) 252ff.

to be innocent. Udo's letter to the pope recording this judgment is highly critical of Gregory's handling of the case:

> Your letter was read out in the presence of more than twenty bishops and it was unanimously said by them all that a new and most unacceptable custom was being introduced into the Church; that an intolerable burden was imposed on us; that to force subjects to threaten their bishops in the name of obedience and under threat of anathema, to extort information about their private conduct, was to arm sons against fathers and to destroy reverence and piety; that to use loaded words like "ex-bishop" and "wolf" when the case was still undecided, was not in keeping with apostolic moderation; and that even if the bishop had been deserving of such terms, considerations of public decency — not to say ecclesiastical piety — should have prevented their use.[164]

Once again, Gregory VII's method of insuring the purity of the Church was condemned as a *nova et minima probanda consuetudo* which violated the Pseudo-Isidorean principle that inferior members of the clergy must not bring accusations and conspire against their superior. The complaint of Archbishop Liemar of Bremen, who had fallen foul of the papal legates and been suspended from his office in 1074, accurately summarizes the picture of Gregory VII which is presented by the protest literature of the Hildesheim collection: "The dangerous man (*periculosus homo*) wishes to order bishops about as if they were his bailiffs; and if they do not perform all his demands, they are to come to Rome or they are suspended without judgment."[165]

The accumulated resentments of the German episcopate during the first three years of Gregory VII's pontificate are reflected in the letter of the bishops assembled at the synod of Worms in 1076, renouncing their obedience to the pope. Like all the other episcopal protests of the 1070s, the decree of Worms emphasizes the pope's usurpation of the jurisdictional rights of the episcopate: "If an offence on the part of any of our diocesans (or even the bare rumor of an offence) comes to your notice, you claim that henceforward none of us has the power of binding or loosing in his case, and that this power belongs to you alone or to him whom you specially delegate." (Here there is an echo of the particular grievance of Archbishop Siegfried of Mainz in 1073-1074; and it is worth remarking that certain pro-papal sources attribute to Siegfried a leading role in the formulation of the bishops' charges at Worms.)[166] The pope was accused of "usurping a new and improper power, so as to destroy the proper rights of a whole brotherhood."[167] In thus referring to the episcopate as *universa fraternitas,* the decree of Worms gives a valuable insight into

---

[164] *Hildesheimer Briefe* no. 17 (n. 33 above) 39.

[165] *Ibid.* no. 15 (34).

[166] Donizo of Canossa, *Vita Mathildis comitissae,* MGH Scriptores 12.377; Paul of Bernried c. 66 (n. 33 above) 1.510.

[167] Erdmann (n. 1 above) 65-68.

the ecclesiological assumptions of Gregory VII's opponents. The bishops assembled at Worms in January 1076 conceived of the ecclesiastical hierarchy, including the apostolic see, as a fraternity of bishops who must show mutual respect for each other's traditional rights. This was the conception which Liemar of Bremen expressed in a letter of 1074 to his colleagues of Hildesheim and Halberstadt: "You will say, we are your brothers; divine law commands that whenever conflict and disputes arise between bishops, the neighboring bishops should meet and, through their reasonable mediation, put an end to disputes." [168] The mediation of the *fraternitas* of bishops, rather than the exclusive intervention of papal authority, was the appropriate means of solving the problems of the Church. The same vision of ecclesiastical harmony is found in a work composed about 1075 by a scholar who was later to be a staunch defender of the cause of Henry IV: the "Life of Bishop Theoderic of Metz" by Sigebert of Gembloux. Bishop Theoderic lived during the reign of Otto I, when "peace was restored to the churches and the integrity of religion was renewed by famous bishops and wise men"; [169] and Sigebert's biography is a celebration of the virtues of the Lotharingian episcopate in this Ottonian golden age. Theoderic of Metz and his colleagues constituted "an order of fellow-workers for good, excellent commanders and comrades-in-arms in the camp of the Lord God of Sabaoth." [170] The ideal expressed by Sigebert and by the other opponents of Gregory VII, of the Church as a brotherhood of bishops, reechoes the language of Archbishop Hincmar of Reims in the ninth century. In Hincmar's terminology, the bishops constitute a *collegium,* entrusted with the care of a Church whose unity derives from the unity of action of her pastors: the episcopate forms a single *chorus* receiving its joint authority from Saint Peter. [171]

On the eve of the Investiture Contest, therefore, there existed simultaneously in Western Christendom two sharply dissimilar theories of the structure of the Church. The opposition between the "pre-Gregorian" idea of the Church as a rigid hierarchy of inviolable jurisdictions and the idea of a papally oriented Church capable of radical reorganization, was at the heart of the conflict between Gregory VII and his episcopal opponents. From the letters in which this conflict can be traced, it is evident that the main point at issue was not "reform" — that is, the long-established movement against simony and clerical marriage which Gregory sought to accelerate by his Lenten synod of 1074. Gregory VII's episcopal critics did not oppose the eradication of these abuses; but they vigorously objected to the violent and precipitate manner in which the pope conducted his moral campaign. The cautious attitude of Siegfried of Mainz, who perceived that "it required no small effort . . . to

[168] *Hildesheimer Briefe* no. 16 (n. 33 above) 38.

[169] Sigebert, *Vita Deoderici episcopi Mettensis* c. 17, PL 160.700C. On the date of this work, see the indications given by Sigebert in his *De scriptoribus ecclesiasticis* c. 171, PL 160.587A.

[170] Sigebert, *Vita Deoderici* c. 17 (701A).

[171] Hincmar, letter to Pope Nicholas I (864), MGH Epistolae 8.1 (1939) 149; sermon on the consecration of Hermintruda, PL 125.815; *De coercendo et exstirpendo raptu viduarum, ibid.* 1017. Cf. Congar (n. 94 above) 166-177.

reform an aging world"[172] does not mark him out as an opponent of reform; for the great reformer Saint Peter Damian had also expressed the opinion that the world was now too old for new doctrine.[173] Gregory VII, however, was prepared "to reestablish divine justice by means of new counsels";[174] and experience soon taught the bishops that these *nova consilia* involved an assault on the traditional, Pseudo-Isidorean *ordo* of the Church. The time-honored privileges which Siegfried of Mainz, Liemar of Bremen and Manasses of Reims defended, seemed to Gregory VII to be merely the irrelevant incrustations of custom; and "any custom, however long-established and well-known, must give place to truth."[175] *Veritas* often meant for Gregory VII not what was written in the "canonical decrees," the Pseudo-Isidorean principles cited by bishops in their protests to Rome, but what the *utilitas* and *necessitas* of reforming politics dictated. "Reform" sometimes demanded that the pope accept accusations made by an obscure clerk against his superior, or that he encourage the laity of a diocese to put pressure on their bishop or to take action against delinquent priests. Such *nova consilia* naturally threatened discipline in the dioceses and created insecurity among the bishops. In January 1076 Gregory's *nova consilia* drove the imperial episcopate into rebellion, and subsequently insured that after 1080 Henry IV could always number many bishops — including some distinguished reformers[176] — among his supporters. Nearly twenty years after Gregory VII's death, the pro-Henrician clergy of Liège, with Sigebert of Gembloux as their spokesman, proclaimed their allegiance to the Church in these terms: "We adhere to our bishop, our archbishop, our provincial and comprovincial synod, according to ancient tradition . . . . We utterly oppose those legates who leave the side of the Roman bishop to run to and fro, filling their pockets."[177] There was no doubt in the mind of Sigebert that the party which guaranteed the survival of the traditional Catholic hierarchy was the party of the emperor.

School of History
Trinity College
Dublin 2, Republic of Ireland

[172] Lampert a.1074 (n. 71 above) 199.

[173] Peter Damian, *Liber Gratissimus* c. 29, MGH Libelli de lite 1. 58.

[174] *Registrum* (n. 9 above) 2.45 (184).

[175] *Epistolae Vagantes* (n. 39 above) no. 67 (150). The attribution of this fragment to Gregory VII is defended by G. B. Ladner, "Two Gregorian Letters: On the Sources and Nature of Gregory VII's Reform Ideology," *Studi Gregoriani* 5 (1956) 225-242.

[176] Cf. J. Fleckenstein, "Heinrich IV. und der deutsche Episkopat in den Anfängen des Investiturstreites," *Adel und Kirche: Festschrift Gerd Tellenbach* (Freiburg 1968) 221-236.

[177] Sigebert, *Epistola Leodicensium adversus Paschalem papam,* MGH Libelli de lite 2.459.

THE EARLY "ARS DICTAMINIS" AS RESPONSE TO A CHANGING SOCIETY

●

by William D. Patt

Although medieval epistolography has interested modern historians for over 125 years, the study of medieval letter-writing and letter collections has not advanced much beyond the beginning stages.[1] This is a regrettable situation, because the *ars dictaminis* was vitally important in medieval affairs. Broadly speaking, the medieval term *ars dictaminis* applies to all forms of Latin composition, and includes both

This article is a revised version of the paper read at the Tenth Annual Conference of the Medieval Association of the Pacific on 26 February 1977. I wish to express my gratitude to Professors Robert L. Benson and Richard H. Rouse, University of California, Los Angeles, for their guidance in its preparation and presentation. While their suggestions and corrections have been invaluable, any remaining errors are, of course, my own responsibility.

[1] Among the early studies worthy of mention is that of Wilhelm Wattenbach, "Iter Austriacum 1853," *Archiv für Kunde österreichischer Geschichts-Quellen* 14 (1855) 1-94. The long appendix, "Über Briefsteller des Mittelalters" (29-94) offers an overview which, though dated in matters of detail, can still be read with profit. When compared with the most recent studies, it not only shows how little progress has been made in the field, but also includes many dictaminal texts unavailable elsewhere. Since then, a large bibliography has accumulated. For the more important literature up to 1929, see Charles Homer Haskins's articles, "The Life of Medieval Students as Illustrated by their Letters," *Studies in Medieval Culture* (Oxford 1929) 1-35, and "The Early *Artes dictandi* in Italy," *ibid.* 170-192. For literature appearing between 1929 and 1970, see James J. Murphy, *Medieval Rhetoric: A Select Bibliography,* Toronto Medieval Bibliographies 3 (Toronto 1971) which, though not exhaustive, is useful. It may be supplemented from Hans Martin Schaller, "Die Kanzlei Kaiser Friedrichs II.: Ihr Personal und ihr Sprachstil," *Archiv für Diplomatik* 4 (1958) 264-327 (esp. on the relationship between *ars dictaminis* and diplomatics); J. Meisenzahl, "Die Bedeutung des Bernhard von Meung für das mittelalterliche Notariats- und Schulwesen, seine Urkundenlehre und deren Überlieferung im Rahmen seines Gesamtwerkes," Ph.D. diss. (Wurzburg 1960); the introduction to Giles Constable, *The Letters of Peter the Venerable,* 2 vols. (Cambridge, Mass 1967) 2.1-44 (tends to emphasize the relationship between *ars dictaminis* and authentic letters); and Hélène Wieruszowski's numerous articles concerning *ars dictaminis,* collected in her *Politics and Culture in Medieval Spain and Italy,* Edizioni di Storia e Letteratura, Raccolta di Studi e Testi 121 (Rome 1971) (mostly concerned with the period after 1200). For bibliography after 1970, see L. Génicot, *Les actes publiques,* Typologie des sources du moyen âge occidental 3 (Turnhout 1972); Carol Dana Lanham, *Salutatio Formulas in Latin Letters to 1200: Syntax, Style, Theory,* Münchner Beiträge zur Mediävistik und Renaissance-Forschung 22 (Munich 1975); Tore Janson, *Prose Rhythm in Medieval Latin from the 9th to the 13th Century,* Acta Universitatis Stockholmiensis, Studia latina Stockholmiensia 20 (Stockholm 1975); Ernstpeter Ruhe, *De amasio ad amasiam,* Beiträge zur romanischen Philologie des Mittelalters 10 (Munich 1975); and Giles Constable, *Letters and Letter-Collections,* Typologie des sources du moyen âge occidental 17 (Turnhout 1976).

prose and poetry within its scope.[2] In actuality, however, its most important aspect was the teaching and practice of letter-writing. One can distinguish at least two main reasons for this utilitarian tendency. First, letter-writing was one of the most common forms of composition practiced in the Middle Ages. Secondly, the *ars dictaminis* offered one of the few opportunities for a career in administration, government, and politics. The seats of power, the ecclesiastical and secular chanceries and courts, were accessible to those with training in law, theology, or *ars dictaminis*. Because the *ars dictaminis* was so indispensable, it was taught in cathedral and monastic schools, and later in the universities, all over Europe.

The technique of letter-writing taught by the *ars dictaminis* had little in common with the modern notion of letters.[3] To the Middle Ages, a letter was not a spontaneous and natural expression of thought or sentiment, but rather, a matter of rigid convention. Letters were supposed to be written according to definite rules, which over the course of time became increasingly formalized. There were rules for addressing superiors, inferiors and equals, rules which divided a letter into parts, rules for ordering those parts, and so on. It was with these rules that the *ars dictaminis* was primarily (but by no means exclusively) concerned.

Furthermore, letters performed a role in the Middle Ages very different from their role today. They were almost never private, but usually semipublic in nature. A letter was meant to be read or heard by many people: the clergy of a particular church or area, the citizens of a town, a learned circle. Letters were always painstakingly composed, and worded with utmost care. This self-consciousness is a characteristic worthy of particular note when one is dealing with the product of a chancery. A letter composed in the name of an emperor, a pope, or a king is not merely a medium for transmitting news, commands, requests, and the like. It is also a statement of ideology, whether that part of the message is set forth explicitly, or is concealed between the lines.[4]

---

[2] *Ars dictaminis* (also *ars dictandi*) is the medieval term for Latin composition, both prose and metric. The term has also been used in a narrow sense to denote a technical manual for teaching Latin composition, especially letter-writing, beginning in the late eleventh or early twelfth century. It derives from the Latin verb *dicto, dictare,* the intensive form of *dico, dicere,* "to speak." Since the ancients seldom composed in their own hand, but rather dictated to a scribe, *dictare* quite early became synonymous with "to write" or "to compose." The noun form, *dictamen, dictaminis,* denotes the product of *ars dictaminis* (sometimes the plural form, *dictamina, dictaminum,* appears in the singular sense of "composition"), and may be applied as a generic term for any form of medieval Latin composition. Also, it is interchangeable with the term *ars dictaminis* in most contexts. For the etymology of *dictare* and *dictamen,* with examples of usage dating from Late Antiquity through the twelfth century, see Wattenbach (n. 1 above) 29-33. For an analysis of St. Bernard's use of *dictare,* see Dom J. Leclercq, "Saint Bernard et ses secrétaires," in *Recueil d'études sur saint Bernard et ses écrits,* Edizioni di Storia e Letteratura, 3 vols. (Rome 1962) 1.3-25. The *dictator* practiced *ars dictaminis* as a profession; this term may denote a teacher of Latin composition, as well as one who composed Latin professionally, such as a notary.

[3] On medieval letters generally, their composition and collection, see the lucid accounts by Constable (n. 1 above).

[4] Concerning the dissemination of propaganda, especially through the circulation of letters, see Carl Erdmann, "Die Anfänge der staatlichen Propaganda im Investiturstreit," *Historische*

In addition, the letter collection quite early became an independent literary form. Letters were often composed and collected mainly for the sake of their stylistic qualities, with regard for factual or doctrinal content a secondary consideration. The letter format was also considered appropriate for other types of literature. Much of the polemic of the Investiture Controversy, for example, was composed in the form of letters. Finally, public and private documents were drawn up in a format resembling letters, making a knowledge of *ars dictaminis* mandatory (but also lucrative) for notaries. In short, letters were the primary medium of medieval communication, administration, and propaganda.[5]

It is disappointing, then, that the study of such an important subject has advanced so little over the years. In particular, the question of the origins of the *ars dictaminis,* while receiving much of the attention devoted to the subject overall, has not been adequately answered to date. Indeed, the inquiry has been misled, because "origins" has traditionally been understood to imply a sudden springing from some discrete, distinguishable starting point, rather than in the more appropriate sense of a gradual evolutionary process. As a result, the question has itself necessarily been formulated in a way which misleads. Obviously, if asked, "Who invented the *ars dictaminis,* and where?" one will try to answer with the name of a person and a place. Cast in this form, the question does not accurately reflect the usual process of gradual cultural

---

Zeitschrift 154 (1936) 503-512. An appreciation of the letter's potential as a vehicle for ideological and propagandistic statements may be gained from Heinrich Fichtenau, *Arenga: Spätantike und Mittelalter im Spiegel von Urkundenformeln,* Mitteilungen des Instituts für österreichische Geschichtsforschung, Ergbd. 18 (1957). Although Fichtenau's analysis is based on official documents, the relationship between such instruments and letters was extremely close during the Middle Ages. They were, after all, composed in the same general format, by the same chancery personnel, with the same awareness of the ideological content of formulas and phrases. See also Heinrich Fichtenau, "Monarchische Propaganda in Urkunden," *Bulletino dell' Archivio paleografico italiano* n.s. 2-3 (1956-1957) 299-318; and Peter Classen, "Kaiserreskript und Königsurkunde: Diplomatische Studien zum römischen-germanischen Kontinuitätsproblem," *Archiv für Diplomatik* 1 (1955) 1-87 and 2 (1956) 1-115 (now being reprinted).

[5] The value of *authentic* letters as historical documents has long been recognized. See Bernhard Schmeidler, "Über Briefsammlungen des früheren Mittelalters in Deutschland und ihre kritische Verwertung," *Vetenskaps-Societeten i Lund: Årsbok 1926,* 5-27; Carl Erdmann, *Studien zur Briefliteratur Deutschlands im elften Jahrhundert,* MGH Schriften 1 (Leipzig 1938); *idem,* "Die Briefe Meinhards von Bamberg," *Neues Archiv* 49 (1932) 332-431; J. Leclercq, "Le genre épistolaire au moyen âge," *Revue du moyen-âge latin* 2 (1946) 63-70; and Constable's discussions (n. 1 above).

The *ars dictaminis* can also yield valuable information to historians. For example, virtually all model letter-collections include at least some which involve actual historical personages and situations. These were intended to display the master's virtuosity, and at the same time introduce the student to the political ambience which he would encounter in the world of chancery and court. While these openly fictitious compositions are notoriously unreliable concerning dates, places, and events (from the absurd situations which occur in some, one may even infer a deliberately literary or satiric intent), they may at the same time provide valuable expressions of contemporary opinion or even propaganda concerning burning issues. Also, the *ars dictaminis* may illuminate contemporary social theory of reality, such as the hierarchical structure of medieval society; see Giles Constable, "The Structure of Medieval Society According to the *Dictatores* of the Twelfth Century," in *Law, Church and Society: Essays in Honor of Stephan Kuttner,* ed. Kenneth Pennington and Robert Somerville (Philadelphia 1977) 253-267.

change in the Middle Ages. Rather, one should ask, "From what sources did this develop, and by what process?"

The problem began with the nineteenth-century pioneers in the study of the *ars dictaminis*. Since few manuscript collections were as yet adequately cataloged, their attempts at an overview were necessarily based on fragmentary evidence. They perceived the *ars dictaminis* as emerging suddenly in the late eleventh century, spontaneously springing, Minerva-like, from the mind of a single creator, Alberic of Montecassino (died about 1105).[6] Responsibility for the identification of Alberic of Montecassino as the "father of the *ars dictaminis*" belongs largely to a German scholar, Ludwig Rockinger, who presented his theory in 1861.[7] In a twelfth-century south German manuscript, now in the Munich Staatsbibliothek, Rockinger found two dictaminal treatises clearly identifiable as Alberic's work.[8] These two were accompanied by another, entitled *The Rules of Composition* (*Rationes dictandi*), which he likewise attributed to Alberic, but solely on the basis of their juxtaposition within the same manuscript.[9] Unlike the other two treatises, the *Rationes dictandi* presented a mature, comprehensive theory of letter-writing technique, rendering substantial support to Rockinger's thesis.

[6] Benedictine monk, papal supporter in the Investiture Controversy, opponent of Berengar of Tours, hagiographer, scholar, and teacher, Alberic of Montecassino was among the leading figures of the cultural flowering at Montecassino under Abbot Desiderius in the last quarter of the eleventh century. For a summary of scholarship concerning Alberic up to 1960, see the article by A. Lentini, "Alberico," in the *Dizionario biografico degli Italiani* 1 (Rome 1960) 643-645. For the literature appearing since, see Herbert Bloch, "Montecassino's Teachers and Library in the High Middle Ages," *La Scuola nell' Occidente latino dell'alto Medioevo,* Settimane di studio del Centro Italiano di Studi sull'Alto Medioevo 19 (Spoleto 1972) pt. 2. 563-605, esp. 587-599.

[7] Ludwig Rockinger, "Über die *Ars dictandi* und die *Summa dictaminum* in Italien, vorzugsweise in der Lombardei, vom Ausgange des eilften bis in die zweite Hälfte des dreizehnten Jahrhunderts," *Sitzungsberichte der kgl. bayer. Akademie der Wissenschaften, phil.-hist. Klasse* 1 (1861) 98-151.

[8] The manuscript, Munich, Bayerische Staatsbibliothek Clm 14784, originally belonged to Sankt Emmeram (Regensburg). Alberic's *Dictaminum radii* appears on fols. 44-59, under the rubric *Flores rhetorici*; edited by D. M. Inguanez and H. M. Willard, *Alberici Casinensis Flores rhetorici,* Miscellanea Cassinese 14 (1938), but see the emendations and corrections (including the title) by Harald Hagendahl, "Le manuel de rhétorique d'Albericus Casinensis," *Classica et medievalia* 17 (1956) 63-70. The other work, Alberic's *Breuiarium de dictamine,* appears on fols. 67-104v; edition by Peter C. Groll, "Das *Enchiridion de prosis et de rithmis* des Alberich von Montecassion und die *Anonymi Ars dictandi,*" Ph. D. diss. (Freiburg/Br. 1963).

[9] This key dictaminal treatise, actually written about 1140 by an anonymous author, appears in Clm 14784, fols. 2-43v. It consists of two books: the first presents an elementary course in composition and letter-writing, the second a more advanced course. Unlike most earlier dictaminal manuals, it gives detailed, comprehensive explanations of doctrine, rather than scant summaries intended to stimulate the student's recollection of oral classroom instruction. It is a landmark text, not only because, with the appearance of the *Rationes dictandi,* the *ars dictandi* achieved identity, but also because it remained a source, directly or indirectly, for many important treatises of the following decades. See Haskins, "Early *Artes*" (n. 1 above) 181-182, and more recently, the review of James J. Murphy's translation of Book 1, in *Three Medieval Rhetorical Arts,* ed. Murphy (Berkeley 1971) 5-25, by Traugott Lawler, *Speculum* 48 (1973) 388-394. Certain points appearing in Book 1 are discussed by Aldo Scaglione, *The Classical Theory of Composition from its Origins to the Present* (Chapel Hill 1972) 99-100, 114-116.

Subsequently, in 1863, Rockinger published a two-volume collection of dictaminal texts including, under Alberic's name, a portion of the *Rationes dictandi,* along
with a portion of one of the other texts from the same Munich manuscript.[10] Soon
thereafter, however, it was noticed that an example in the *Rationes dictandi* made
reference to an invasion of Benevento by King Roger II of Apulia, and his alliance
with the burghers of Ancona. Since these events had occurred in 1137, long after
Alberic's death, Alberic could not possibly have composed the *Rationes dictandi,* and
Rockinger's view on this point was rendered untenable.[11] Nevertheless, Alberic's
genuine works were, and remain today, the oldest known treatises (except the few
produced in Antiquity) which deal at least partially with letter-writing theory. And
so, this revelation left the case for his primacy intact. In this way, the traditional
formulation of the question of origins became established. Rockinger had asked,
"Who invented the *ars dictaminis*?" and had advanced the name of a candidate.

The corollary naturally followed that, if Alberic had invented the *ars dictaminis,* it
began in a single center: Montecassino, where he had been educated and spent most
of his life. The fragmentary manuscript evidence seemed to indicate that, afterward,
the center of dictaminal studies passed from one place to the next, like the baton in a
relay race. According to this traditional view, it shifted from Montecassino: first to
northern Italy, especially Bologna, in the second decade of the twelfth century; then,
after 1150, across the Alps to the Loire region of France, especially Orléans; next,
back to Bologna around 1200, and so on.[12]

Rockinger's thesis found wide, though not universal, acceptance. Given his
formulation of the question of origins, only one major objection could be raised:
Alberic's dictaminal works dealt only marginally with letters. In fact, they were

[10] Ludwig Rockinger, *Briefsteller und Formelbücher des eilften bis vierzehnten Jahrhunderts,*
Quellen und Erörterungen zur bayerischen und deutschen Geschichte 9 (Munich 1863); repr. in 2
vols. (New York 1961). Book 1 of the *Rationes dictandi,* and a few excerpts from Book 2, are
printed, 3-28. Immediately following, 29-46, are excerpts from Alberic's *Breuiarium de dictamine.* In general, Rockinger's work remains indispensable today; but his texts, attributions, and
dating must be used with great caution.

[11] The decisive passage appears in *ibid.* 25, lines 16ff. See the discussion on this point in Adolf
Bütow, "Die Entwicklung der mittelalterlichen Briefsteller bis zur Mitte des 12. Jahrhunderts,
mit besonderer Berücksichtigung der Theorieen der *Ars dictandi,*" Ph.D. diss. (Greifswald 1908)
17-18, with bibliography. This conclusion was accepted by C. H. Haskins, "Albericus Casinensis,"
in *Casinensia,* 2 vols. (Montecassino 1929) 1.115-124, esp. 117, and "Early *Artes*" (n. 1 above)
172, 181-182, but missed by another influential scholar, Louis J. Paetow, *The Arts Course at
Medieval Universities, with Special Reference to Grammar and Rhetoric* (Urbana 1910) 72-73,
who continued to ascribe the *Rationes dictandi* to Alberic, and drew erroneous inferences from
this assumption. A. Lentini, "Note su Alberico Cassinese maestro di retorica," *Studi medievali* 18
(1952) 121-137, has tried unconvincingly to revive the claim of Alberic's authorship. The
question has at last been laid to rest by Bloch (n. 6 above) 587-588, esp. n. 76. Bloch reprints the
critical passage, an example of how to intermesh the parts of a multiple narrative with the parts
of the ensuing multiple petition.

[12] The classic statement of this view is Haskins's, "Early *Artes*" (n. 1 above) 186-192, and his
The Renaissance of the Twelfth Century (Cambridge, Mass. 1927) 140-143. Cf. Hélène
Wieruszowski, "Rhetoric and the Classics in Italian Education of the Thirteenth Century,"
Politics and Culture (n. 1 above) 589-627, esp. 593 n. 1.

devoted largely to technical aspects of rhetoric and composition in general, such as tropes and figures for ornamentation, and to grammar. In this, it could be argued, he more closely resembled his eleventh-century colleagues in the field of rhetoric, such as Onulf of Speyer and Anselm of Besate, than the fully fledged *dictatores* of the following century.

In the 1950s and early 1960s, the German medievalist Franz-Josef Schmale seized upon this doubt. Without revising the traditional formulation of the question, he nonetheless advanced a revisionist candidate for originator of the *ars dictaminis,* Albert Samaritani.[13]

Albert's manual, entitled *Composition Lessons* (*Precepta dictaminum*), was written between 1111 and 1118, making it the oldest known dictaminal treatise (after Alberic of Montecassino's works); and he is the first known *dictator* to be associated with Bologna. In contrast with Alberic of Montecassino, Albert Samaritani focused sharply on letter-writing technique, and presented less rhetorical and grammatical theory. Schmale concluded, therefore, that Albert had made a distinct break with the past. He had invented a new literary genre, whereas Alberic of Montecassino ought merely to be considered the last representative of the ancient rhetorical tradition, in the line of Cicero, Quintilian, and the compilers and commentators of late Antiquity and the Carolingian period.[14]

The close similarity between Albert's manual and other early Bolognese dictaminal treatises forced Schmale to carry his thesis to an extreme. He insisted that all of Albert's contemporaries, as well as all the *dictatores* of the subsequent generation, depended on Albert as their ultimate source. In addition, Schmale indicated Bologna as the birthplace of the *ars dictaminis,* and the center from which all knowledge of dictaminal theory emanated, thereby eliminating Montecassino as a step in the sequence of transmission.[15]

Since its introduction, acceptance of Schmale's thesis has ranged from cautious acknowledgement of plausibility to enthusiastic agreement.[16] The partisans of Alberic of Montecassino have by no means been driven from the field, however. On

---

[13] Franz-Josef Schmale, "Die Bologneser Schule der *Ars dictandi,*" *Deutsches Archiv* 13 (1957) 16-34; *Adalbertus Samaritanus Precepta dictaminum,* ed. Schmale, MGH Quellen zur Geistesgeschichte des Mittelalters 3 (Weimar 1961). First to call attention to Albert Samaritani and publish a portion of his work was H. Krabbo, "Der Reinhardsbrunner Briefsteller aus dem 12. Jahrhundert," *Neues Archiv* 32 (1907) 51-81, 717-719.

[14] Schmale, *Adalbertus* 1-4, and "Bologneser Schule" 16 n. 1.

[15] Schmale, "Bologneser Schule" 33, and *Adalbertus* 17-20.

[16] While cautiously maintaining a place for Alberic of Montecassino within the dictaminal tradition, Schaller (n. 1 above) 267-268 says that Albert Samaritani "scheint eine besonders wichtige Rolle gespielt zu haben . . . und darf wohl der Begründer nicht nur der Stilschule von Bologna, sondern der *Ars dictandi* überhaupt genannt werden." Full acceptance has been accorded Schmale's thesis by Hélène Wieruszowski, "A Twelfth-Century *Ars dictaminis* in the Barberini Collection of the Vatican Library," *Politics and Culture* (n. 1 above) 334 esp. n. 4. Others also expressing some degree of acceptance include Giuseppe Vecchi, *Il magistero delle "Artes" latine a Bologna nel medioevo,* Pubblicazzioni della facoltà di magistero Università di Bologna 2 (1958) 11; Scaglione (n. 9 above) 100 n. 5; Ruhe (n. 1 above) 63-68; Janson (n. 1 above) 77; and others (see Bloch [n. 6 above] 593 n. 92).

the contrary, the claim on his behalf has been defended with renewed vigor in recent years.[17] But the basic assumptions of the discussion, that the *ars dictaminis* originated with one inventor and then became the nearly exclusive possession of one center followed in turn by another, have remained unchanged.

Throughout the course of the discussion, there have been many who have wisely chosen to reserve judgment pending further evidence. For example, Charles Homer Haskins wrote in 1929, "The question of Alberic's predecessors and contemporaries still requires investigation."[18] More recently, Paul Oskar Kristeller called attention to letters composed in a style obedient to the rules of *dictamen,* but long before those rules are known to have been written down. He concluded, "The origin of such characteristic theories as the six parts of the letter must be traced back beyond the earliest extant writers on *dictamen.*"[19]

But there is abundant evidence to demonstrate that the *ars dictaminis* arose out of a Europe-wide school tradition which had been undergoing a centuries-long process of development. Manifestations of this tradition appear in the letter-writing doctrine which obviously lies behind the composition of letters antedating all known dictaminal treatises. The same doctrine later appeared in Alberic of Montecassino's works, adapted to the needs of his time, then emerged after a generation in Albert Samaritani's *Precepta dictaminum,* further adapted to changing conditions, finally achieving identity around 1140 in the *Rationes dictandi.* This means that the *ars dictaminis* was not a localized product which spread to the rest of Europe from individual centers which successively dominated the field, but rather a cultural development which occurred more or less simultaneously in Italy, France, Germany, and perhaps other parts of Europe as well.

The following arguments, while directed against Albert Samaritani and Alberic of Montecassino respectively, are not limited to them alone. Any attempt to seek the origins of the *ars dictaminis* in a single inventor would be undermined by the same evidence.

If Albert Samaritani had invented the *ars dictaminis,* one might expect him to have monopolized the field, at least in the beginning. Or, if he were simply the first to systematize the rules of *dictamen,* no manuals should have preexisted his own. In fact, neither of these is the case. Not only were contemporaries teaching and practicing *ars dictaminis,* but, more important, there were predecessors as well who

[17] Bloch (n. 6 above) 593-594 flatly states, "Alberic's works were truly landmarks in the history of education; he is the first representative of the *ars dictaminis,*" and follows up with a vigorous critique of Schmale's thesis (cf. also the objection raised against Schmale's thesis by Lanham [n. 1 above] 97). James J. Murphy, "Alberic of Monte Cassino: Father of the Medieval *Ars dictaminis,*" *The American Benedictine Review* 22 (1971) 129-146, is as unequivocal in his support of Alberic's primacy as his title suggests.

[18] Haskins, "Early *Artes*" (n. 1 above) 171 n. 2.

[19] Paul Oskar Kristeller, *Renaissance Philosophy and the Medieval Tradition,* Wimmer Lecture 15 (Latrobe, Pa. 1966) 89 n. 19, cited by Constable, *Letters and Letter-Collections* (n. 1 above) 31. Constable (34-35) writes, "Although *dictamen* now [sc. the eleventh and twelfth centuries] emerged for the first time as a discipline with clearly formulated rules, it had roots deep in the past . . . ." Cf. Erdmann's similar conclusions, n. 45 below.

taught, and wrote treatises on, Latin composition and letter-writing. This is clear from the evidence provided by two of Albert's contemporaries, Henry Francigena and Hugh of Bologna.

Henry Francigena wrote a dictaminal manual, vividly entitled *The Golden Gem* (*Aurea gemma,*)), which appeared immediately after Albert Samaritani's manual.[20] The names of actual persons and references to actual events in the appended collection of model letters allow it to be dated between 1121 and 1124. Pavia is frequently mentioned in these letters, and Pavia is also named in the prologue as the place where Henry wrote the *Aurea gemma.* It is reasonable, therefore, to assume that he taught *dictamen* there as well.[21] The prologue gives two indications of numerous *dictatores* practicing and teaching *ars dictaminis* at this time, and not only at Bologna. First, there is a warning to students to reject the "nonsense and maunderings" uttered by unnamed rivals under the guise of sound teaching, and to ignore their malicious and envious attacks.[22] A passage follows alluding to the earlier dictaminal manuals which Henry used as sources in the composition of his own treatise. "I shall write down," he says, "the rules of prose composition, not only out of the modest equipment of my own mind, but also by bringing together the ideas (*sententie*) of diverse others."[23]

The evidence provided by the other contemporary, Hugh of Bologna, is similar. As a Bolognese priest and canon, Hugh no doubt taught *dictamen* at the cathedral school. To supplement his oral instruction, he wrote a manual simply entitled *The Rules of Prose Composition* (*Rationes dictandi prosaice*).[24] Salutations and model

---

[20] See Meisenzahl (n. 1 above) 40-41 for earlier literature citing Henry Francigena. The letter-collection has been edited by Botho Odebrecht, "Die Briefmuster des Henricus Francigena," *Archiv für Urkundenforschung* 14 (1936) 231-261. The theoretical portion remains unedited except for the prologue (included as an appendix by Ernst H. Kantorowicz, "Anonymi *Aurea gemma,*" *Medievalia et humanistica* 1 [1943] 56-57). The analyses of Bütow (n. 11 above) 30-43 and passim, and Haskins, "Early *Artes*" (n. 1 above) 178-180, are based on erroneous assumptions about the manuscript evidence (see n. 32 below), and should be used with caution. Specific aspects of the theoretical portion (with brief excerpts) are discussed by Carl Erdmann, "Leonitas: Zur mittelalterlichen Lehre von Cursus, Rhythmus, and Reim," *Corona quernea: Festgabe Karl Strecker*, MGH Schriften 6 (1941) 15-28, esp. 22ff., and Lanham (n. 1 above) 101-105. The *Aurea gemma* circulated widely during the twelfth and thirteenth centuries. So far, seventeen manuscripts preserving all or part of it have been identified. For the manuscripts, see Haskins, "Early *Artes*" 178; Odebrecht 233-234; Erdmann, "Leonitas" 22; Schmale, "Bologneser Schule" (n. 13 above) 30 n. 39; Meisenzahl 122-123; and Peter von Moos, *Hildebert von Lavardin, 1056-1133,* Pariser historische Studien 3 (Stuttgart 1965) 335-336.

[21] Henry Francigena, *Aurea gemma,* prologue (ed. Kantorowicz): "Legat igitur studiosus dictator hunc libellum qui *Aurea gemma* intitulatur, quem Henricus Francigena ad utilitatem desiderancium dictare Papie composuit." Concerning the places mentioned in the letter collection, Odebrecht 235 says, "Bei weitem am häufigsten tritt Pavia auf."

[22] Francigena: "Quibus nostre Muse liber placuerit, deinceps ad aliorum nugas et musitationes, que pocius eos impediunt quam expediunt, recurrere nullatenus adtemptent. Si uero liuor [sit] edax illorum, qui nichil fructus in se uidentes facibus inuidie et acerbitatis odio accensi temerario ausu meum librum mordere, rodere, lacerare presumpserint: uos queso eis rebelles estote ut decet."

[23] *Ibid.*: "Scribam ... raciones dictandi prosaice, non tantum ex armariolo nostri ingenii, uerum etiam diuersorum sentencias in unum colligendo."

[24] Hugh of Bologna's *Rationes dictandi prosaice* appears in Rockinger (n. 10 above) 53-94. Little is known about Hugh or his career. See Bütow (n. 11 above) 44-46 and passim, and

letters included in it place its composition between the years 1119 and 1124, or about the same time as Henry Francigena's *Aurea gemma*. His prologue also contains two statements pertinent to this argument. Like Henry Francigena, Hugh denounces his rivals and recommends that their works be avoided. But unlike his colleague from Pavia, he mentions two of them by name. One is a certain Aginulf, about whom nothing is known beyond his typically Lombard name. The other is Albert Samaritani.[25] Also like Henry, Hugh of Bologna makes no claim to originality, but rather indicates that he has compiled his manual in the same way. "I have gladly brought it about," he informs the official to whom it is dedicated, "for yours as well as for the common benefit of all, that out of the works of many I should bring together into one corpus the rules of prose composition."[26]

At this point, someone may object that these statements are mere *topoi*, simply the employment of two of the commonest of rhetorical commonplaces: the adversary *topos* (the convention of an imaginary rival), and the humility *topos* (an expression of affected modesty). Such devices had been used since Antiquity to arouse the interest and sympathy of audiences, and accordingly, perhaps, ought not to be taken literally.[27]

Still, *topoi* should not be flatly rejected simply because they are commonplaces. Even *topoi* can yield valuable information. Here, the question arises: why should the obscure author of a dull dictaminal treatise expect the invocation of an adversary to excite the interest of his audience? Such an expectation makes sense only in the context of a school situation. It tells us that there had to have been other teachers and students of *dictamen*, anxious to relieve the tedium of everyday, who would be aroused by the prospect of a good fight.

Moreover, while expressing a conventional idea or sentiment, a *topos* may reflect a true factual situation. Whether or not Hugh of Bologna or Henry Francigena actually felt the humility which they expressed is unimportant. However, they both disclaim originality by subscribing to a method of compilation in common use during this period, the method of excerpting texts used by florilegists.[28] In a procedure metaphorically compared to picking flowers, one culled *sententie* — the word used by Henry Francigena — that is, maxims from authoritative sources, and gathered these *flores* (literally, "flowers") into collections which, completing the metaphor,

---

Haskins, "Early *Artes*" (n. 1 above) 180. Haskins lists four manuscripts, and Schmale, "Bologneser Schule" (n. 13 above) 29 n. 37 calls attention to another.

[25] Rockinger (n. 10 above) 53-54.

[26] *Ibid.*; "Feci itaque non inuitus, ut tum tua tum conmuni omnium utilitate rationes dictandi prosaice ex multorum gestis in unum corpus colligerem."

[27] The standard discussion of *topoi* is by Ernst Robert Curtius, *European Literature and the Latin Middle Ages*, trans. Willard R. Trask, Bollingen Series 36 (New York 1953) 79-105. See also E. R. Curtius, "Beiträge zur Topik der mittellateinischen Literatur", *Corona quernea* (n. 20 above) 1-14; Gertrud Simon, "Untersuchungen zur Topik der Widmungsbriefe mittelalterlicher Geschichtsschreiber bis zum Ende des 12. Jahrhunderts," *Archiv für Diplomatik* 4 (1958) 52-119 and 5-6 (1959-1960) 73-153; and Walter Veit, "Toposforschung: Ein Forschungsbericht," *Deutsche Vierteljahrsschrift für Literaturwissenschaft und Geistesgeschichte* 37 (1963) 120-163.

[28] For bibliography concerning medieval *florilegia*, see n. 29 below, and Richard H. Rouse, "The *A* Text of Seneca's Tragedies in the Thirteenth Century," *Revue d'histoire des textes* 1 (1971) 98-112.

were called *florilegia* ("bouquets"). One might then simply list these excerpts one after another. One such collection, the *Florilegium Angelicum,* probably composed at Orléans in the third quarter of the twelfth century, was compiled as a dictaminal aid, to provide a handy source of maxims for the embellishment of compositions. [29] Or else, one might produce a treatise by weaving the *flores* one has culled into a coherent structure, as in the ethical *florilegium* entitled *Moralium dogma philoso-phorum.* [30] If necessary, one could alter the wording of an excerpt in order to adapt it to a particular context, or for the sake of rhetorical elegance, [31] and perhaps cement it all together with a few comments of one's own.

This method of culling and combining various sources produced many more dictaminal treatises in the next decades. To name a few: the anonymous treatise, also called *Aurea gemma* (but not the same as Henry Francigena's), written in the 1130s, and preserved in two manuscripts, Oxford, Bodleian Library MS Laud misc. 569, and Leipzig, University Library MS 350; [32] the widely circulated manual of Bernard of Bologna, which first appeared in 1144-1145; [33] and what is perhaps the most

---

[29] The anonymous compiler states his intention explicitly in the dedicatory epistle with which he prefaces the collection: "Defloraui tamen flosculos digniores et candidiores manipulos tuis oculis presentaui. Patet ibi tam philosophorum quam diuinorum numerosa facundia et profundi sensus uenustissimis sermonibus uestiuntur. Et hoc multum credidi illi tue singulari excellentie conuenire ut semper ad manum habeas unde possis et personis et locis et temporibus aptare sermones." His training and skill as a *dictator* (of which this letter is an intentional display) is manifested in his consistent use of the *cursus.* See R. H. and M. A. Rouse, "The *Florilegium Angelicum*: Its Origin, Content, and Influence," in *Medieval Learning and Literature: Essays Presented to Richard William Hunt*, ed. J.J.G. Alexander and M. T. Gibson (Oxford 1976) 66-114 (includes an edition of the dedicatory epistle, 94-95); André Goddu and R. H. Rouse, "Gerald of Wales and the *Florilegium Angelicum*," *Speculum* 52 (1977) 488-521; and R. H. Rouse, "*Florilegia* and Latin Classical Authors in Twelfth- and Thirteenth-Century France," *Imitation and Adaptation: The Classical Tradition in the Middle Ages*, ed. D. M. Kratz (Columbus, Ohio, forthcoming).

[30] The *Moralium* is edited by J. Holmberg, *Das Moralium dogma philosophorum des Guillaume de Conches* (Uppsala 1929). The bibliography concerning the *Moralium* and its authorship is given in M.-Th. d'Alverny, *Alain de Lille: Textes inédits* (Paris 1965) 65.

[31] Detailed instructions for such rewording are given in the *Rationes dictandi, Liber secundus*, Clm 14784 (n. 8 above) fol. 21v line 14 - fol. 23 line 10, under the rubric *ueneratio sententiarum.* See Goddu and Rouse (n. 29 above) 490f.

[32] Appropriation of Henry Francigena's colorful title, as well as other borrowings in this similar but distinct treatise originally caused scholars much confusion. Bütow (n. 11 above) 30-43 and passim incorrectly ascribed the *Aurea gemma* in the Leipzig manuscript to Henry Francigena. He was followed in this by Haskins, "Early *Artes*" (n. 1 above) 178-180, who called attention to the Oxford manuscript. Odebrecht (n. 20 above) 233 noted that the Leipzig-Oxford *Aurea gemma* was *not* the work of Henry Francigena (however, since his primary interest was in the letter-collection, he did not carry this observation further). The problem was resolved by E. H. Kantorowicz (n. 20 above) 46 who concluded, "The [Leipzig-Oxford] manual is a later compila-tion which drew on the works of both Albert [Samaritani] and Francigena. Exactly this is exposed in plain words by the anonymous author . . . . He declares to have called his work *Aurea gemma* 'eo quod *ex fontibus doctorum* quasi ex auro et gemma sit compositus et informatus.' "

[33] Concerning this manual, see Ch.-V. Langlois, "Maître Bernard," *Bibliothèque de l'École des chartes* 54 (1883) 225-250 (outdated in most particulars, but the starting point for most subsequent discussions); Hermann Kalbfuss, "Eine bologneser Ars dictandi des XII. Jahrhunderts," *Quellen und Forschungen aus italienischen Archiven und Bibliotheken* 16 (1914)

illustrative example, the *Flores dictandi* of Albert de San Martino of Asti, written about 1150.[34] The very title, literally *Flowers of Composition,* alludes directly to the flower-picking metaphor. It opens with a concise statement of the method: "Here begin the *Flores dictandi* which Albert de San Martino of Asti culled from many places and, adding a few things himself, rendered into one."[35]

Both Hugh of Bologna and Henry Francigena offer further indications of a long-established dictaminal teaching tradition, and these cannot be slighted as *topoi.* Toward the end of his prologue, Hugh defends the still considerable reputation of Alberic of Montecassino, of whom he says, "Although he did not write amply about every kind of composition, he is justly believed to excel all others in letter-writing and composing privileges."[36] The "others" (*ceteri*) are unnamed, but the reference is clearly to other *dictatores* who had been writing on the subject at least since Alberic's time, perhaps earlier.

Within the body of his treatise, Henry Francigena, too, alludes directly to teachers of *dictamen* from the previous generation. First, he invokes the memory of his late teacher, a certain Master Anselm. In the context of a fundamental rule of dictaminal etiquette, the "law of salutations," he says, "I learned from my teacher, Master Anselm of blessed memory, this general rule, that in the salutation, the name of the higher ranking person comes first."[37] Further on, there is another reference to teachers of the past, again in the context of a doctrinal point from the common school tradition. In reference to the divisions of *dictamen,* he says, "From what has been handed down by our teachers, we know that there are two principal types of *dictamen,* namely, prose on the one hand, and metric on the other."[38]

Ironically, Albert Samaritani himself provides evidence that he worked in an already established school environment where *dictamen* had been taught for some

---

1-35 (includes the edition of numerous model letters); C. H. Haskins, "An Italian Master Bernard," *Essays in History presented to Reginald Lane Poole* (Oxford 1927) 211-216 (summarized in "Early *Artes*) [n. 1 above] 182-183; Haskins lists and describes eleven manuscripts); Edmond Faral, "Le manuscrit 511 du 'Hunterian Museum' de Glascow," *Studi medievali* n.s. 9 (1936) 80-88; Bjarne Berulfsen, "Et Blad av en *Summa dictaminum*," *Avhandlinger Utgitt av det Norske Videnskaps-Akademi i Oslo* 2: *Hist. -filos. Klasse.* no. 3 (1953); Mirella Brini Savorelli, "Il 'Dictamen' di Bernardo Silvestre," *Rivista critica di storia della filosofia* 20.3 (1965) 182-230; Bernardus Bononiensis, *Multiplices epistole que diuersis et uariis negotiis utiliter possunt accomodari*, ed. Virgilio Pini, Biblioteca di "Quadrivium" (Bologna 1969); *idem, Liber artis omnigenum dictaminum*, ed. Pini, Biblioteca di "Quadrivium" (Bologna 1970); and V. Pini, "Il codice 45 di Savignano sul Rubicone," *Quadrivium* 9 (1970). After two years of searching, I conclude that the latter two items are unavailable in North America.

[34] Haskins, "Early *Artes*" (n. 1 above) 184.

[35] *Ibid.*: "Incipiunt flores dictandi quos Albertus Astensis de Sancto Martino ex multis locis collegit et nonnullis insertis in unum redegit."

[36] Rockinger (n. 10 above) 55: "Etsi plene per singula dictaminis documenta non scriberet, in epistolis tamen scribendis et dictandis priuilegiis non iniuria ceteris creditur excellere."

[37] Henry Francigena, *Aurea gemma*, Paris, Bibliothèque Nationale MS n.a.l. 610 fol. 29: "Generalem enim regulam hanc a magistro beate recordationis Anselmo audiuimus, ut in salutatione semper dignior persona preponatur." This Magister Anselm is not further identified.

[38] *Ibid.* fol. 33: "Duo quidem genera dictaminum principalia nostris a magistris tradita nouimus, scilicet unum prosaicum, alterum metricum."

time. In the third prologue of his *Precepta dictaminum,* Albert calls attention to the
existence of rivals (and thereby, of a school environment) by anticipating their envy
and hatred. No doubt, he counted Hugh of Bologna among these enemies.[39] For,
whereas Hugh was a partisan of Alberic of Montecassino, Albert Samaritani was quite
the opposite. Albert attacked Alberic of Montecassino repeatedly, warning his
students to avoid the "harsh, perplexing, incomprehensible composition of Alberic
the Monk, which only the Sphinx could understand."[40] Further along, Albert writes,
"In what follows . . . one should not expect those inanities which Alberic concocted
in his book on composition, and which certain fools are spreading abroad."[41] By his
ridicule, Albert confirms Hugh of Bologna's indication that Alberic of Montecassino's
books were still popular texts for teaching *ars dictaminis,* and that there were other
teachers of *dictamen,* who were currently using them.

It is also ironic that, despite these repeated condemnations, many of Albert
Samaritani's teachings are similar to Alberic of Montecassino's. For example, both
call for the avoidance of excessive prolixity, which induces boredom, and excessive
brevity, which produces obscurity.[42] In addition, Albert's doctrine is almost wholly
compatible with that of his contemporaries, Hugh of Bologna and Henry Francigena.
In many instances, in fact, their teaching is exactly parallel. For example, all three
divide *dictamen* into two principal types, prose and metric; all three describe a
society divided into three ranks: upper, lower, and middle; and all three include a
statement of the "law of salutations": in the salutation, the superior must be named
before an inferior.[43] How is such uniformity to be explained?

As pointed out previously, Schmale founded his thesis on an erroneous premise,
the exclusion of Alberic of Montecassino from the dictaminal tradition. Alberic
could then be considered a non-dictaminal source, one of many on which Albert
Samaritani allegedly drew in creating the *ars dictaminis.* For example, no one would
consider Papias's dictionary, another possible source used by Albert, to be a dictaminal work. Conveniently, the treatises of Henry Francigena and Hugh of Bologna
are both a few years later than Albert's. Therefore, Schmale was content to explain
the many similarities among them as borrowings from Albert's manual.[44]

In view of the evidence presented thus far, however, his explanation is unsatisfactory. And on the same evidence, the whole traditional view of the transmission of

[39] Albert Samaritani, *Precepta dictaminum,* prologue 3 (ed. Kantorowicz [n. 20 above] 55):
"Quedam pro capacitate ingenii sub breuitate perstrinximus et compendiosa traditione sociis
nostris tradere dignum duximus, quod, licet emulorum mordeatur inuidia, sapientium tamen
iudicabitur dignum censura."

[40] Schmale, *Adalbertus* (n. 13 above) 51: "Spernat [sc. cupidus dictator] aspera et spinosa
dictamina Alberici monachi insolubilia, nisi Sphingi monstro familiaria."

[41] *Ibid.* 58: "Non eas nenias debere inquiri, quas Alberico in libro dictaminum finxit et
quidam nugigeruli per latum spargunt."

[42] *Ibid.* 50. In n. 2 Schmale cites the corresponding passage from Alberic's *Dictaminum radii*
(Inguanez and Willard, [n. 8 above] 54).

[43] Similarities among the early Italian dictaminal manuals are pointed out by Bütow (n. 11
above) 47-73, and Schmale, "Bologneser Schule" (n. 13 above) 29-32.

[44] Schmale, *Adalbertus* (n. 13 above) 11, 17.

the *ars dictaminis* from center to center comes into question. For this same consistency of letter-writing doctrine is not limited to northern Italy, nor to the time and place where Albert's alleged influence might have been felt. For example, in the mid-eleventh century, there was a keen interest in *ars dictaminis* in such southern German monastic and cathedral schools as Bamberg, Speyer, Tegernsee, Regensburg, and others. South German letter-writers were already composing in a style and format consistent with dictaminal rules, a generation and more before those rules were known to have been written down.[45] And at least one southern German treatise on rhetorical colors and their application to composition, Onulf of Speyer's *Colores rhetorici,* survives from this same period. While it does not deal specifically with letter-writing, its subject matter and didactic purpose are similar to Alberic of Montecassino's *later* work.[46]

Parallels can be found in other parts of Europe. In Italy, for example, Peter Damiani (died 1072) wrote letters according to the rules which would emerge in the dictaminal manuals half a century later,[47] and around the mid-eleventh century, Anselm of Besate wrote a rhetorical treatise entitled *De materia artis* (now lost).[48] In France, somewhat later but decades before any dictaminal treatise is known to have appeared there, Hildebert of LeMans (died 1133) composed letters which reveal his awareness of the rules of *dictamen,* and which would be considered paragons of stylistic excellence by subsequent generations.[49] His contemporary and compatriot,

[45] Erdmann, *Briefliteratur* (n. 5 above) 73-86. Concerning the doctrine of dividing letters into parts (usually five), Erdmann wrote, "Diese Lehre . . . ist im Kerne älter als die Briefkunst-Traktate" (80).

[46] Wilhelm Wattenbach, ed., "Magister Onulf von Speier," *Sitzungsberichte der kgl. preuss. Akademie der Wissenschaften, phil.-hist. Klasse* 20 (Berlin 1894) 361-386; Luitpold Wallach, "Onulf of Speyer: A Humanist of the Eleventh Century," *Medievalia et humanistica* 6 (1950) 35-56; Carl Erdmann, "Onulf von Speier und Amarcius," *Forschungen zur politischen Ideenwelt des Frühmittelalters* (Berlin 1951) 124-134. Concerning Onulf's intention, Wallach says, "He wrote the *Colores* for a young teacher of oblates who taught the field of *auctores,* pagan authors, Latin prose-writing, and imitative Latin poetry . . . in a monastic school" (45-46). The similarity of subject matter is noted by Inguanez and Willard (n. 8 above) 12: "L'opera di Alberico non differisce, in modo assoluto, da quella del suo contemporaneo Onulfo di Spira, o dal trattato un poco piu recente di Marbodio di Rennes." On the other hand, Onulf certainly included letters within the scope of his treatise. See Erdmann, "Onulf" 125 n. 6.

[47] Kurt Reindel, "Petrus Damiani und seine Korrespondenten" *Studi Gregoriani* 10 (1975) 210: "Wir wissen, dass das Mittelalter *artes dictandi* gekannt hat, Vorschriften über die richtige Abfassung von Briefen, Vorschriften, die selbstverständlich auch Daminani bekannt waren." Fridolin Dressler had drawn a similar conclusion in an earlier study, *Petrus Damiani: Leben und Werk, Studia Anselmiana* 34 (Rome 1954) 190. The letters and other works of Peter Damiani are printed in PL 144 and 145. Reindel is preparing a critical edition of Peter Damiani's letters for MGH.

[48] See Cinzio Violante, "Anselmo da Besate," *Dizionario biografico degli Italiani* 3 (Rome 1961) 407-409, with extensive bibliography.

[49] See von Moos (n. 20 above). In his analysis of Hildebert's letter-writing style (77ff.), von Moos points out that Hildebert could adhere strictly to dictaminal rules if the situation required, but frequently refused to be bound by them. Similarly, St. Bernard and Peter the Venerable were aware of the rules of *dictamen,* but likewise rejected their use. See Constable, *Peter the Venerable* (n. 1 above) 32, 35.

Marbod of Rennes (died 1123), in addition to letters, wrote a treatise in verse on the use of rhetorical colors in composition, called *De ornamentis uerborum.*[50]

This remarkable and widespread doctrinal consistency, and the similarities among Albert Samaritani and his contemporaries can be explained in the same way. The *dictatores* who wrote and taught in Albert's generation indeed drew upon a common school tradition. However, "school" in this context is not to be understood in the narrow sense which Schmale intended. It does not mean the followers of a single teacher, such as Albert Samaritani, nor does it mean the teaching associated with any circumscribed location, such as "the Bolognese school." Here, "school" means a body of doctrine within which there is widespread consensus: the oral and written teaching, common to all of Europe, which was received, adapted to prevailing conditions, then passed on by each succeeding generation. What Albert and his contemporaries received, they in turn adapted to their own needs. Some precepts were eliminated, some were added; some matters were expanded and elaborated, such as the discussion of *captatio beniuolentie;* and there was an effort to limit the discussion of other matters, such as ornamentation. By this process of change and adaptation, the dictaminal tradition had achieved an identity by the second quarter of the twelfth century.

The final, physical evidence against Albert Samaritani consists of two fragments of dictaminal treatises which appear to be older than Albert's *Precepta dictaminum.* One, now at Munich, may be as early as the eleventh century. It includes a discussion of the parts of a letter, standard fare in later dictaminal manuals.[51] The other, now in the British Library, includes salutations from the time of Pope Paschal II (1099-1118).[52] One may reasonably hope for further and similar discoveries yet to be made.

Similar arguments can be ranged against the modern partisans of Alberic of Montecassino. However, Schmale's attempt to exclude Alberic from the direct line in the development of the *ars dictaminis* has already been rejected. Alberic *did* deal specifically with letters.[53] Moreover, although Alberic devoted a greater amount of attention to grammatical and rhetorical matters, his epistolary doctrine was compatible with the teaching of the northern Italian *dictatores* of the next generations. They kept his memory and his texts alive, using them for teaching and as sources for writing their own dictaminal manuals.

To be sure, the highly rhetorical, mannered style recommended by Alberic was better suited to the polemic literature of the Investiture Controversy, to which he contributed, than to the mundane transactions of day-to-day administration in the burgeoning chanceries of Europe. In the late eleventh and early twelfth centuries, the growth of government at all levels brought on an increasing demand for larger

[50] Marbod's *De ornamentis uerborum* is printed in PL 171.1687-1692. For literature concerning Marbod of Rennes, see von Moos (n. 20 above) passim.

[51] Haskins, "Early *Artes*" (n. 1 above) 171 n. 2.

[52] *Ibid.* 176 n. 5.

[53] See the analysis in Lanham (n. 1 above) 94-97.

numbers of trained personnel.[54] They did not need the eloquence of Cicero, just a reasonable degree of competence, especially in letter-writing.

Accordingly, the *ars dictaminis* became more practical, and the focus on letter-writing sharpened. It became increasingly marked by a bareness and simplicity of style, adapted strictly to business, with the emphasis on utility. This process of adaptation also entailed limiting the amount of grammatical and rhetorical material presented to the student, so that a reasonable degree of proficiency could be acquired quickly. This permitted the growing personnel requirements of the chanceries to be met in less time. One did not need the literary talent of John of Salisbury to master the *ars dictaminis* of the northern Italian manuals. On the contrary, Henry Francigena claimed to have written his treatise so that even "dolts" (*minus intelligentes*) could profit from it.[55] One needed only commit its precepts to memory and recall them whenever a letter was to be written. This advantage over the laborious, time-consuming traditional method of learning composition, described by several who underwent it, seems to have been precisely the appeal of the theoretical treatises.

The fact that Alberic of Montecassino's works remain the oldest known dictaminal treatises does not constitute proof that they were the first ones. While anticipating the discovery of still earlier manuals than his, one can easily show that the rules of *dictamen* had been known for some time. The prevailing interest in *ars dictaminis* in the southern German schools, for example, has already been noted. Alberic himself also gives hints, such as his employment of the adversary *topos,* which shows that he functioned in a school situation with other teachers of *dictamen.*[56]

Therefore the history of medieval instruction in letter-writing does not begin with Alberic of Montecassino. The "golden age of medieval letter-writing" had begun toward the end of the tenth century. Soon, everywhere, increasing numbers of letters were being composed, gathered into collections, and used for study. This proliferation has been described by Professor Constable in these apt terms: "For the following two centuries, at least a few letters have survived from almost every literary figure of note, and from many of no note at all!"[57] Most of these letters were composed in accordance with the rules of *dictamen,* as these rules were later set down in theoretical treatises, indicating that the rules of *dictamen* were widely known in Europe at least from the end of the tenth century. Therefore, it follows that *ars dictaminis* was being taught before Alberic of Montecassino arrived on the scene.

[54] Discussed by R. W. Southern, *The Making of the Middle Ages* (New Haven 1953) 80ff.

[55] Henry Francigena, *Aurea gemma*, prologue (ed. Kantorowicz [n. 20 above]): "Leviter enim et compendiose hoc in volumine dictaminis eciam minus intelligentes aliquem fructum percipere possunt."

[56] Inguanez and Willard (n. 8 above) 33: "Hic Albericus euolat, hic palmam sperat; hic aduersarius sileat, obmutescat, miretur, obstupeat."

[57] Constable, *Letters and Letter-Collections* (n. 1 above) 31.

Having reviewed the evidence, we may now return to the original argument: that the traditional formulation of the question of dictaminal origins reflects a fundamental misunderstanding of the medieval intellectual process. A far more accurate reflection of the gradual medieval process of adaptation and change will result if the question is reformulated as follows: From what sources did the *ars dictaminis* derive, by what process, and in what stages did it develop?

Social factors influencing this developmental process, such as the vital importance of letter-writing in medieval society, the accelerating growth of government at all levels, and the cosmopolitan nature of interest in *ars dictaminis,* have been emphasized through much of this discussion. The remainder will focus on a consideration of some of the intellectual and cultural traditions which contributed elements to the make-up of the *ars dictaminis* — the epistolary tradition of Antiquity and the earlier medieval past, the study of grammar (including literature), the study of law, and the study of rhetoric.

Before any known technical manuals were written, *ars dictaminis* was taught using letter collections and formularies. Recently, Dr. Carol Dana Lanham has produced a brief but illuminating glimpse of how this method was employed from the early Middle Ages up through the eleventh century.[58] She has pointed out that many collections were expressly intended for school instruction in reading and composition, not as formularies for the use of notaries, as has often been assumed. For example, the *Formulae Marculfi,* from about 700, was intended for this purpose.[59] The Worms letter collection, dating from the late eleventh century, also seems to have been assembled for teaching, as were many others during the intervening centuries.[60]

In another recent article, I. S. Robinson of Dublin has shown how interest in *ars dictaminis* motivated the preservation of much of the surviving literature of the Investiture Controversy.[61] Beginning in the second quarter of the twelfth century, this work of copying was carried out in those same southern German monastic and cathedral schools, where enthusiasm for *ars dictaminis* continued from the previous century. It was not the discussions of cold issues, nor the obsolete theology, nor a desire to preserve the history of the Investiture Controversy which excited interest in those polemic tracts and pamphlets. Rather, they were valued as elegant stylistic models. Gathered into collections, they served as texts for the study of *ars dictaminis.*

Interestingly, to these same south German masters and scribes is due the preservation of many of the earliest dictaminal treatises, notably the works of Alberic of Montecassino. It must be added, therefore, that the teaching of *dictamen* using letter

[58] Lanham (n. 1 above) 89-93.

[59] *Ibid.* 91: "The preface to [the *Formulae Marculfi*] expressly declares it to have been compiled not for notaries but *ad exercenda initia puerorum* (p. 10.24)."

[60] *Ibid.* 91-93. The Worms letter collection is edited by Walther Bulst, *Die ältere Wormser Briefsammlung,* MGH Briefe der deutschen Kaiserzeit 3 (Weimar 1949).

[61] I. S. Robinson, "The *Colores rhetorici* in the Investiture Contest," *Traditio* 32 (1976) 209-238.

collections as model texts for students did not disappear with the introduction of theoretical treatises. Rather, it continued through the twelfth and thirteenth centuries and beyond, even in Italy. Such, for example, was the purpose of the Italian collection from about 1145, published by Mme. Wieruszowski from a manuscript in the Vatican Library.[62] The English *dictator,* Peter of Blois, a student in the mid-twelfth century, tells of learning *dictamen* by this method himself. "It was very valuable to me," he writes, "to be compelled in adolescence to learn by heart and repeat the urbane and elegant letters of Bishop Hildebert of LeMans."[63]

The large amount of grammatical doctrine included in most theoretical treatises suggests the study of Latin grammar as another source from which the *ars dictaminis* developed. Charles Thurot, a pioneer in the study of medieval Latin grammar, included excerpts from the works of several dictaminal authors in his classic monograph.[64] One of them, a certain Paul the Camaldolite (perhaps from the last quarter of the twelfth century), wrote a grammar as well as a dictaminal treatise.[65] More recent historians of the *ars dictaminis,* however, have tended to exaggerate the proportion of material devoted specifically to letter-writing, and overlook the significant grammatical element.[66] Actually, granted the sharpened focus on letters, dictaminal treatises still presented a course in surprisingly elementary Latin composition. Indeed, most of what the *ars dictaminis* taught about composition is learned nowadays in Latin II.[67]

It is not hard to explain the inclusion of so much grammar. Until around 1200, the standard texts used for teaching Latin grammar were the ancient authorities, Donatus and Priscian.[68] Whatever their virtues, these texts lacked an adequate discussion of composition. Therefore, they had to be supplemented. This supplement was at first provided in the form of glosses and commentaries. Later, matters of syntax were discussed in dictaminal treatises as well. It seems likely, therefore, that the roots of the *ars dictaminis* go back in part to such commentaries, especially on those chapters of the revered texts most nearly approaching the problems of

[62] Wieruszowski (n. 16 above) 382-393.

[63] Cited by R. W. Southern, "Peter of Blois: A Twelfth-Century Humanist?" in his *Medieval Humanism and Other Studies* (Oxford 1970) 117.

[64] Charles Thurot, *Notices et extraits de divers manuscrits latins pour servir à l'histoire des doctrines grammaticales au moyen âge, Notice et extraits* 22 (Paris 1868; repr. Frankfurt-am-Main 1964).

[65] Paris, Bibliothèque Nationale MS lat. 7517 is a manuscript of Paul the Camaldolite's collected works. It contains a grammatical commentary on Priscian and Donatus, a treatise on verse composition, a manual of prosody, a dictaminal treatise, and a treatise on canon law cast in the form of a model letter-collection. In his prologue, Paul claims to be the author of each of these. However, Bloch (n. 6 above) 585-587 has pointed out that the manual of prosody cannot be his. Bloch also provides some bibliography, n. 71a.

[66] Bütow's comment (n. 11 above) 47 typifies this view: "Ausscheiden aber wollen wir bei unserer Betrachtung alle specifisch grammatischen und stilistischen Anweisungen, da sie mit der *ars dictandi* im engeren Sinne unmittelbar nichts zu tun haben."

[67] For example, see the discussion of transitive, intransitive, "retransitive," and "reciprocal" constructions from an early northern Italian manual, in the Appendix below.

[68] For literature concerning medieval Latin grammar, see Murphy (n. 1 above) 42-54.

composition: Books 17 and 18 of Priscian's *Institutiones grammaticae,* which circulated separately from the rest under the title *De constructionibus,* or *Priscian minor;* and the third book of Donatus's *Ars maior,* which likewise enjoyed a separate circulation, under the title *Barbarismus.*[69]

The *Barbarismus* is basically a rhetorical text — a handbook on incorrect usages (*uitia* such as barbarisms and solecisms), and rhetorical figures. Along with other similar manuals, it was useful in fulfilling another of the grammarian's traditional tasks, the explication of the *auctores* (revered authors of authoritative texts, both classical and patristic). After acquiring the rudiments of Latin grammar, the student polished his reading and writing skills through the study and imitation of great literary models. The grammarian provided guidance, beginning with a discussion of the author, his works, his purpose in writing the work about to be read, and the division of knowledge (*philosophia*) to which it belonged. Then, as the reading progressed, he helped his students comprehend the more difficult, rhetorically embellished passages. For this, he needed a mastery of the rhetorical lore presented in the *Barbarismus* and similar texts. This didactic method, inherited from Antiquity, engendered a large body of literature, generically called *accessus ad auctores* (introductions to the authors), or simply *accessus* literature.[70] Significantly, almost all dictaminal treatises also include at least some discussion of incorrect usages and rhetorical figures. Alberic of Montecassino even devoted a separate treatise to the subject, entitled *De barbarismo et solecismo, tropis et schematibus.* The reading and imitation of the *auctores* is also an often recommended pathway to the improvement of style in composition.[71] To this extent, then, the domain of the grammarian, the ancient *rhetor,* and the medieval *dictator* overlapped. The *ars dictaminis* and the medieval *accessus* literature thereby appear to have roots in a common teaching tradition.

The teaching of grammar had a further aspect bearing on the *ars dictaminis*: the teaching of poetry. Another traditional office of the grammarian, it was performed by teachers of *dictamen* during the Middle Ages. Treatises on prose composition commonly refer to poetry as one of the principal types of *dictamen,* and frequently hold out the author's promise of a separate treatise devoted to it. And in fact, one

[69] Priscian, *Institutiones grammaticae,* ed. Martin Herz, *Grammatici latini* 3 (Leipzig 1859) 1-384; Aelius Donatus, *Ars grammatica,* ed. Heinrich Keil, *Grammatici latini* 4 (Leipzig 1864) 367-402 (the *Barbarismus* begins at 392). I am grateful to Professor Bengt T. M. Löfstedt, University of California, Los Angeles, for suggesting this hypothesis.

[70] For bibliography concerning *accessus* literature, see: *Accessus ad auctores, Bernard d'Utrecht, Conrad d'Hirsau, 'Dialogus super auctores,'* ed. R. B. C. Huygens (Leiden 1970); Günter Glauche, *Schullektüre im Mittelalter: Entstehung und Wandlungen des Lektürekanons bis 1200 nach den Quellen dargestellt,* Münchner Beiträge zur Mediävistik und Renaissance-Forschung 5 (1970); and Leslie G. Whitbread, "Conrad of Hirsau as Literary Critic," *Speculum* 47 (1972) 234-245.

[71] See, for example, the repeated exhortations of Albert Samaritani, Schmale, *Adalbertus* (n. 13 above) 50-51, 58-59. Cf. the famous description of Bernard of Chartres's method in John of Salisbury's *Metalogicon,* 1.24, ed. C. C. J. Webb (Oxford 1929) 56.

can cite numerous poetical treatises by authors of prose manuals.[72] In addition, many famous letter-writers were also renowned poets.

Historians have long assumed that a close relationship existed between the *ars dictaminis* and the study of law.[73] The most obvious connection lies in the fact that certain types of legal documents were drawn up in letter format. A notary, therefore, needed at least some legal training.

Moreover, legal studies began as a form of textual exegesis, which was, as already pointed out, a task that pertained to grammarians.[74] The study of Roman law involved explication of texts such as the *Corpus iuris ciuilis,* while canon lawyers sought to interpret and harmonize the opinions of the Fathers, the decisions of councils, and the decretal letters of the popes. In this context, then, it is significant that in the early revival of Roman jurisprudence, Irnerius had been a grammarian, and that he is reported to have written a *Formularius tabellionum,* a manual (unfortunately now lost) for the drafting of documents.[75]

Indeed, prior to the revival of legal studies in the eleventh century, law was considered closely bound up with rhetoric.[76] And ancient rhetoric, after all, was

[72] See, for example, Hugh of Bologna's brief outline of the three types of poetry, concluded with the promise of a fuller discussion elsewhere, Rockinger (n. 10 above) 54-55. Cf. the anonymous *Tractatus de dictamine,* Berlin, Deutsche Staatsbibliothek, MS 181 (Phillipps 1732) fol. 57 (see Appendix): "De quibus omnibus [sc. species metricae] in eo opere quod de metrica arte facere intendimus, Deo nobis uitam tribuente, tractabimus." Alberic of Montecassino wrote a discussion of accented poetry called *Consideratio rithmorum* or *De rithmis* (see Block [n. 6 above] 590 n. 81). A manual of poetry which follows the *Rationes dictandi* in Clm 14874 is perhaps by the same anonymous author (even if not, this juxtaposition still shows that the teaching of prose and the teaching of poetry were closely related in the mind of the manuscript's producer). Bernard of Bologna promised a discussion of poetry, and may have composed the poetical treatises which follow his prose-writing manual in some manuscripts (see Faral [n. 33 above] 80-88). In addition to a grammar and prose dictaminal treatise, a book on the art of poetry appears under the name of Paul the Camaldolite in B. N. MS lat. 7517 (but see n. 65 above).

[73] But often for the wrong reasons. The *ars dictaminis* was considered the companion of law because all knowledge of both was perceived as emanating from the same centers: Bologna, and later Orléans. For example, Haskins (n. 12 above) 141: "It was natural that *dictamen* should be closely associated with legal teaching after the full establishment of law as an independent subject of professional study, and that it should flourish most at the greatest of medieval law schools." And Paetow (n. 11 above) 72: "The growing *ars dictaminis* soon became the handmaid of law and the hand-books of *dictamen* gave an increasing amount of space to the rules for drawing up legal papers and even to the elementary principles of law . . . . It is not surprising, therefore, to find that the *ars dictaminis* originated in Italy and that it reached its fullest development at Bologna." That Bologna was an important center of both legal and dictaminal studies cannot be denied. However, dictaminal training could be obtained at any competent school in Europe, whether or not law was taught there.

[74] Philippe Delhaye, "L'enseignement de la philosophie morale au XIIe siècle," *Medieval Studies* 11 (1949) 91, describes the early legists as "utilisant le schème de l'*accessus ad auctores.* "

[75] See Horst Fuhrmann, "Das Reformpapsttum und die Rechtswissenschaft," in *Investiturstreit und Reichsverfassung,* ed. Josef Fleckenstein, Vorträge und Forschungen herausgegeben vom Konstanzer Arbeitskreis für mittelalterliche Geschichte 17 (1973) 181-182 and 193-195.

[76] R. R. Bolgar, *The Classical Heritage and Its Beneficiaries* (Cambridge 1958) 143: "By the beginning of the eleventh century, the Italian teachers of rhetoric were accustomed to include in

forensic rhetoric. To what extent oratory was practiced in the Middle Ages remains an open question.[77] In any case, both law and rhetoric had a common concern with persuasion: through elegant speech, through verisimilitude, through flattery. All of these were concerns of the *ars dictaminis* as well. Flattery figures especially prominently in the dictaminal manuals, which devote a considerable amount of attention to the etiquette of the salutation, and to the *captatio beniuolentie* (winning the good will of the audience). One should not exaggerate the extent and importance of these relationships, since the earliest dictaminal treatises contain virtually no legal doctrine. Still, one may expect to find that legal and dictaminal studies have at least some roots in common.

Finally, the *ars dictaminis* is firmly rooted in the rhetorical tradition. Although the similarity between an oration and a letter may not be immediately obvious, it becomes clear if one remembers that medieval letters were intended to be read aloud, often to an audience. The textbooks of ancient rhetoric, especially Cicero's *De inuentione* and the pseudo-Ciceronian *Rhetorica ad Herennium,* the two standard rhetorical texts of the Middle Ages, had a strong influence on the development of the *ars dictaminis. Dictatores* paraphrased and often cited them verbatim in their treatises, and used them as texts for oral instruction as well.[78]

Indeed, some historians have equated medieval rhetoric with the *ars dictaminis.*[79]

---

their courses a considerable amount of each legal information." Southern, *Medieval Humanism* (n. 63 above) 108: "Bologna had been a school of rhetoric before it became a school of law. The two subjects flourished side by side, and the distinction between them was by no means clear in the mid-twelfth century." Harald Zimmerman, "Römische und kanonische Rechtskenntnis und Rechtsschulung im fruheren Mittelalter," *La scuola nell'occidente latino dell' alto Medioevo,* Settimane di studio del Centro Italiano di studi sull' alto Medioevo 19 (Spoleto 1972) 780: "In dem für das frühmittelalterliche Unterrichtswesen normativen Fächerkatalog der *Artes liberales,* der das gesamte, einer schulischen Tradition für würdig erachtete Wissen enthielt, war auch die Jurisprudenz beheimatet. Sie hatte hier ihren Ort innerhalb der Disziplin der Rhetorik" Frederick Behrends, ed., *The Letters and Poems of Fulbert of Chartres,* Oxford Medieval Texts (1976) xxx-xxxi: "Yet the study of rhetoric was not as narrow as might be thought, for among other matters it included what we should call legal reasoning – indeed, rhetorical theory had developed from judicial oratory. Thus Fulbert's knowledge of how to apply the law to individual cases was probably acquired from the rhetorical manuals."

[77] Curtius, *European Literature* (n. 27 above) 76, pronounced oratory extinct, citing a passage from Wibald of Corvey (d. 1158) to that effect. Haskins (n. 12 above) 138-139, expressed a similar opinion (see n. 79 below). There is evidence, however, to suggest that the spoken word, including oratory, was considerably more important in medieval culture than previously assumed. For example, Fichtenau, *Arenga* (n. 4 above) 16-17, cites a report by Galbert of Bruges (*Passio Karoli comitis,* c. 1, MGH Scriptores 12. 562) about untrained lay persons engaging in forensic oratory, and displaying greater natural skill than their literate and schooled adversaries. Another example appears in Otto of Freising, *Gesta Friderici I. imperatoris* 2.29 (ed. 3 G. Waitz, MGH Scriptores in usum scholarum 135-136), in which a delegation from the Roman commune delivers a long-winded oration "Italico more."

[78] For example, see the extensive borrowings in the anonymous treatise edited by Franz-Josef Schmale in "Die *Precepta prosaici dictaminis secundum Tullium* und die Konstanzer Briefsammlung," Ph.D. diss. (Bonn 1950).

[79] Haskins (n. 12 above) 138: "Ancient rhetoric was concerned with oratory, medieval rhetoric chiefly with letter-writing." Curtius, *European Literature* (n. 27 above) 76: "Rhetoric became an art of letter-writing"

It is noteworthy, however, that during the twelfth century, at least, theoretical rhetoric was studied apart from *ars dictaminis* in the schools of northern France, and perhaps elsewhere. For example, Thierry of Chartres wrote a commentary on Cicero's *De inuentione* which is not a dictaminal work in any sense.[80] Therefore, a certain distinction should be drawn between applied or practical rhetoric (that is, the *ars dictaminis*) on one hand, and antiquarian theoretical studies (such as Thierry's) on the other. The relationship between them is not yet clear, because the investigation of theoretical rhetoric, while progressing, is even less far advanced than the study of *ars dictaminis*. They seem to have been closely related through common roots and mutual influence.

No new source materials have been introduced in the presentation of this study. Rather, it has been based on the same manuscript evidence that has, for the most part, been available since before the turn of the century. What I have suggested is a new evaluation of the old evidence, a different questioning of long-available sources. The result, however, is a much revised picture of the early *ars dictaminis*. The *ars dictaminis* is no longer seen as the gift of a Promethean genius, but as a cultural development emerging out of a long, gradual process of change through adaptation to changing needs. The florilegial character of dictaminal treatises has been pointed out, demonstrating the process by which each succeeding generation borrowed from its predecessors. Then, evidence can be brought in which shows the *ars dictaminis* developing more or less simultaneously all over Europe, not springing up and emanating from a single center such as Montecassino or Bologna. It also becomes clear that the *ars dictaminis* was not a distinct and separate discipline, but one closely related to several others, especially grammar. Having once perceived all this, one can begin to investigate in depth the possible cultural and intellectual sources from which the *ars dictaminis* evolved. A number of possibilities have been suggested, and perhaps there are others.

APPENDIX

The anonymous *Tractatus de dictamine*, a manual composed in northern Italy in the 1130s, has been transmitted in two twelfth-century manuscripts, each containing a

---

[80] An edition of Thierry's commentary is in preparation by Karin M. Fredborg. Excerpts appear in her article, "The Commentary of Thierry of Chartres on Cicero's *De inuentione*," *Cahiers de l'Institut du moyen-âge grec et latin, Université de Copenhague* 7 (1971) 1-36, and in the literature she cites. For examples of similar twelfth-century rhetorical commentaries, see Fredborg, "The Commentaries on Cicero's *De inuentione* and *Rhetorica ad Herennium* by William of Champeaux," *ibid.* 17 (1976) 1-39; *idem*, "Petrus Helias on Rhetoric," *ibid.* 13 (1974) 31-41; Harry Caplan, "A Medieval Commentary on the *Rhetorica ad Herennium*," in *Of Eloquence: Studies in Ancient and Medieval Rhetoric*, ed. Anne King and Helen North (Ithaca 1970) 247-270; and M. Dickey, "Some Commentaries on the *De inuentione* and *Ad Herennium* of the Eleventh and Early Twelfth Centuries," *Medieval and Renaissance Studies* 6 (1968) 1-41.

different version of the text. The version found in Copenhagen, Hafniensis Gl. kgl. S. 3543, fols. 19-22v (= H), gives a more satisfactory text, but is mutilated by the loss of a folio midway through the treatise. The other version, in Berlin, Deutsche Staatsbibliothek MS 181 (Phillipps 1732), fols. 56v-61v (= B) is complete but corrupt (it is, incidentally, the earliest known northern Italian dictaminal treatise to appear in France). The following excerpt is from the fuller text of H, corrected from B where necessary.

Bibliography: Valentin Rose, *Die Handschriften-Verzeichnisse der lateinischen Handschriften zu Berlin,* 12. Band (1893) 409ff.; E. Jørgensen, *Catalogus codicum latinorum medii aeui Bibliothecae Regiae Hafniensis* (Copenhagen 1923) 300; Walther Holzmann, "Eine oberitalienische *Ars dictandi* und die Briefsammlung des Prior Peter von St Jean in Sens," *Neues Archiv* 46 (1925) 34-52; C. H. Haskins, "An Early Bolognese Formulary," *Mélanges Henri Pirenne,* 2 vols. (Brussels 1926) 1.201-210; Giles Constable, "The Letter from Peter of St. John to Hato of Troyes," *Petrus Venerabilis 1156-1956: Studies and Texts Commemorating the Eighth Centenary of his Death, Studia Anselmiana* 40, ed. Constable and James Kritzeck (Rome 1956) 38-52; Schmale, "Bologneser Schule" (n. 13 above); *idem, Adalbertus Samaritanus* (n. 13 above); and Constable, "Structure of Medieval Society" (n. 5 above).

After some general considerations (etymologies of *prosa, metrum,* and *epistola,* the hierarchical structure of society and its consequences for letter-writing, the parts of a letter), the author discusses rhetorical colors. He calls them *positiones,* and limits their number to seven ("Modi positionum sunt vii quibus dictamen ornatur uelut pictura diuersibus coloribus coloratur: similitudo, comparatio, conditio, absolutio, resolutio, repetitio, conuersio.") He then proceeds to his next topic:

Constructio autem est alia transitiua, alia intransitiua, aut retransitiua, aut reciproca. Transitiua est quando facit transitum ab agente persona in patientem, aut^a a numero singulari in pluralem, ut: 'Iohannes docet discipulos suos.' Ecce enim una persona est Iohannes, altera discipuli, et is singularis numeri, illi uero pluralis. Intransitiua est que fit sine transitu personarum et numeri. Nominatiuus enim et uocatiuus intransitiue iunguntur uerbis suis. Unius enim persone et unius numeri debent esse, ut: 'Iohannes docet.' Est nominatiuus intellectus in ipso uerbo etsi non ponatur, et cuiuscumque numeri est nominatiuus, eiusdem est et uerbum, nisi forte sint duo nominatiui singulares qui exigunt uerbum unum plurale, ut: 'Virgilius et Cicero scripserunt,' uel nisi sit collectiuum nomen, quod in singulari numero significat multitudinem, ut: 'Populus manducant, cohors laudantur.' Retransitiua est quando una persona facit transitum actionis in aliam et illa rursus in tertiam, ut: 'Hera mea iussit me orare te ut si ames se, uenias ad se, ait enim se cupere uidere te.' Ecce enim hera est una persona que facit transitionem in aliam, id est ancillam, et illa rursus in tertiam, id est in Pamphilum, et iccirco dicitur 'retransitiua' quia primo fit transitio, deinceps retransitio. Reciproca est cum passio redit in agentem, id est cum

eadem persona et agit et patitur uel a se uel ab alia. A se, ut: 'Ego amo me ipsum,'
uel: 'Amat uxorem suam amantem se.' Ab alia, ut: 'Iohannes amat se ipsum' uel:
'Iohannes orat te ut misearis sui,' uel: 'Pauper rogat te ut des sibi panem.'

[a]aut B: ut H

1034 Calle Las Trancas
Thousand Oaks, California 91360, U.S.A.

THE FOUNDATION OF THE CONFRATERNITY OF TARRAGONA BY ARCHBISHOP OLEGUER BONESTRUGA, 1126–1129

•

by Lawrence J. McCrank

The role of confraternities in twelfth-century socio-economic and religious history is considerable, yet little has been done to depict the early development of these influential lay and clerical brotherhoods.[1] During the Iberian Reconquista the activity of confraternities or *cofradías* was especially important in frontier areas where the more elaborate organization, mature institutions and explicit canonical constitution of the diocesan Church had yet to become firmly established. There *cofradías* have been linked to the development of 1) the reformed monastic orders, their *familiares* and patronage systems; 2) the great Hispanic military orders and introduction of their international counterparts to the peninsula; 3) both trade

I would like to express my gratitude to the following who read this paper in draft and provided helpful criticism: Professors C. J. Bishko of the University of Virginia, Thomas Bisson of the University of California, Berkeley, and Robert I. Burns, S.J., of the University of California, Los Angeles. For an expanded discussion, see my initial investigation, "Restoration and Reconquest in Medieval Catalonia: The Church and Principality of Tarragona, 971-1177," Ph.D. diss. (University of Virginia 1974), vols. 1-2. After the initial full citation for each, the following abbreviations are employed in the notes: AHDE, *Anuario de historia del derecho español*; AST, *Analecta sacra Tarraconensia*; BRAH, *Boletín de la Real academia de la historia*; DHGE. *Dictionnaire d'histoire et géographic ecclésiastique*; EEMCA, *Estudios de Edad Media de la Corona de Aragón*; ES, *España sagrada*; VL, *Viage literario*.

This paper was read before the American Academy of Research Historians of Medieval Spain, meeting with the American Historical Association, Washington, D.C., 28-30 December 1976.

[1] The bibliography of confraternities is voluminous, but most titles are badly outdated and require revision. Although there is no satisfactory general treatment of the subject, consult Joseph Duhr, "La Confrérie dans la vie de l'église," *Revue d'histoire de l'église* 32 (1939) 437-465; *idem*, "Confréries," *Dictionnaire de spiritualité, ascétique et mystique, doctrine et histoire* 2.2 (Paris 1953) cols. 1469-1479; Henri Leclercq, "Confréries," *Dictionnaire d'archéologie chrétienne et de liturgie* 3.2 (Paris 1948) 2553-2560; H. Durand, "Confréries," *Dictionnaire du droit canonique* 4, cols. 128-176; Georg Schrieber, "Religiöse Verbände in mittelalterlicher Wertung," *Historisches Jahrbuch* 69 (1949) 184-359; *idem*, *Wallfahrt und Volkstum in Geschichte und Leben* (Berlin 1934); E. Benz, "Christliche Brüderschaften," *Zeitschrift für Religions und Geistesgeschichte* 14 (1961) 297-392; S. de Angelis, *De fidelium associationibus* 1 (Naples 1959) 2-7; Gabriel Le Bras, "Les confréries chrétiennes: Problèmes et propositions," *Études de sociologie religieuse* 2 (Paris 1956) 423-462; *idem*, "Confréries," in *Histoire de l'église* 12: *Institutions ecclésiastiques de la chrétienté médiévale*, ed. Augustin Fliche and Victor Martin (Paris 1965) pt. 1.414-420.

and craft guilds; and 4) the late medieval municipal *hermandades*.[2] In territory recently retaken from the Moors confraternities were often the primary social-service organizations, operating to advance Christian boundaries by providing for settlers behind the battle lines. Thus they appear throughout the twelfth and thirteenth centuries at Ávila, Toledo, Álava, Tudela, Barbastro, Valencia and other sites where *confrères* took on military obligations in addition to rebuilding their cities, social work and charities, and reconstruction of churches.[3] In non-canonical usage, all such labors were collectively sublimated under the rubric *restauratio*, the expressed purpose for which a confraternity was founded at Tarragona during the Catalan drive in the early twelfth century toward Muslim Lérida and Tortosa.

In this illustrative case of the involvement of confraternities in the Reconquista, it should be noted that a Christian "restoration" meant *ipso facto* the propagation of reconquest. In twelfth-century Hispanic ecclesiological usage *restauratio* meant much more than rebuilding a church edifice; it also envisioned the aim of reviving

[2] Cf. A. Guzmán, *Tratado del origen de la confraternidad* (Madrid 1730); Mascaró Bofarull y de Sartario, ed., *Colección de documentos inéditos de ACA* 40-41; *Gremios y cofradías de la antigua Corona de Aragón* (Barcelona 1876); R. Ruiz Jusué, "Las cartas de hermandad de España," *Anuario de historia del derecho español* 18 (1938) 387-463; José Mariá Font Rius, "Cofradías," *Diccionario de la historia de España*, ed. Germán Bleiberg (Madrid 1952; rev. ed. 1968) 1.862-863. For the nexus between *familiares* and *confratres* in Iberian monastic history, see Justo Pérez de Urbel, *Los monjes españoles en la Edad Media* (Madrid 1933-1934) 2.552-553; José Orlandis, "*Tradito corporis et animae*: Laicos y monasterios en la Alta Edad Media española," *Estudios sobre institutiones monásticos medievales* (Pamplona 1971 [1954]) 219-378, esp. 309, 371. Individual monasteries and the orders collectively used lay fraternalism for protection and partonage, and these arrangements could have widespread political, although not necessarily feudal, implications as in the case of Cluniac influence in Spain. Cf. Herbert E. J. Cowdrey, "Unions and Confraternity with Cluny," *Journal of Ecclesiastical History* 16 (1965) 152-162; and esp. Charles J. Bishko, "Fernando I y los orígenes de la alianza castellano-leonesa con Cluny," *Cuadernos de historia de España* 47-48 (1971 [1968]) 31-125; 49-50 (1972) [1969]) 50-116, esp. pt. 2 pp. 57-69, 81-96. For the military-monastic connection with *cofradías*, see Joseph O'Callaghan, "The Affiliation of the Order of Calatrava with the Order of Cîteaux," *Analecta sacri ordinis Cisterciensis* 15 (1959) 161-193; 16 (1960) 3-59, 255-292; Derek Lomax, *La Orden de Santiago (1170-1275)* (Madrid 1965) 1-5; Francisco Layna Serrano, "La histórica cofradía de 'La Caballador' en Atienza (Guadalajara)," *Hispania* 2 (1942) 483-556; Eloy Benito Ruano, *Hermandades en Asturias durante la Edad Media* (Oviedo 1972). For the importance of non-military confraternities in the development of guilds (which could assume military obligations) see Antonio Rumeu de Armas, *Historia de la previsión social en España: Cofradías, gremios, hermandades, montepíos* (Madrid 1944), especially chap. 5 for the medieval background.

[3] Cf. Lomax 1-5; R. I. Burns, *The Crusader Kingdom of Valencia: Reconstruction on a Thirteenth-century Frontier* (Cambridge, Mass. 1967) 1.126-127, 2.429-430; Francisco A. Roca Traver, *Interpretación de la cofradía valenciana: La real cofradía de San Jaime*, Consejo superior de investigaciones científicas, Escuela de estudios medievales, secc. de Valencia, Estudios medievales 2.2 (Valencia 1957) 37-83; Pedro Longás, "Estatutos de la Cofradía de Santa Cristina en Tudela (Navarra) a fines del siglo XII," *Revista internacional de sociología* 1 (1943) 209-217; Gonzalo Martínez Díez, "La Cofradía de Arriaga," *Àlava medieval* 2 (Vitoria 1974) 5-84. For confraternal construction activities under special *operarii*, see Le Bras, "Confréries" (n. 1 above) 417-418; S. Schröcker, *Die Kirchenpflegschaft* (Paderborn 1934) 34-40; Maurice Clément, "Recherches sur les paroisses et les fabriques au commencement du XIIIe siècle," *Mélanges d'archélogie et d'histoire de l'École française de Rome* 15 (1895) 387-418; John Moorman, *Church Life in England in the Thirteenth Century* (Cambridge 1946) 141-142.

the Church with its rights, territory and welfare system where it had once flourished in Romano-Visigothic Hispania and had disappeared after the Muslim intrusion.[4] In the quest for Tarragona neither the processes nor the ideologies of restoration and reconquest appear distinct: both entailed the imposition of a Christian regime on lands held for centuries by the Muslims.

The see of Tarragona had been the ancient ecclesiastical capital of northeastern Spain until its conquest in 714 by the Muslims, and although the Christians under the comital house of Barcelona had tried unsuccessfully to retake this strategic and symbolic site, at the opening of the twelfth century Tarragona city still lay beyond the Catalan occupation zone.[5] The surviving bishoprics of Tarraconensis during the interim of Muslim dominance over half of their old province were governed under the *tutela* of the neighboring metropolitans of Narbonne, except for a brief revival of the sub-Pyrenean metropolitanate at Vich under Archbishop Atto (971).[6] The archiepiscopal authority of Tarragona was again restored canonically under Archbishop Berenguer Seniofred de Lluçanès (1089-1099), also bishop of Vich, but the Catalans were never able to establish their metropolitan in his superior see.[7] The

---

[4] The word *restaurare* "no abunda en la Edad Media, lo cual sugiere se emplearía solo en ambientes eclesiásticos, como consecuencia, sobre todo su frequente uso en relación con iglesias durante la Reconquista": Juan Corominas, *Diccionario crítico etimológico de la lengua castellana* (Bern 1954) 3.1099. The strictly secular usage (i.e., an artistic replica) did not resume in Spain until the sixteenth century: A. M. Alcover, *Diccionari Catalá-Valencia-Balear* (Palma 1959) 9.428-429,. Cf. Gerhard B. Ladner, *The Idea of Reform: Its Impact on Christian Thought and Action in the Age of the Fathers* (Cambridge, Mass. 1959) 45-46, 239-283, and bibliography. The close association between restoration and conquest ideologies was discussed further in L. J. McCrank, "Restoration by God and Sword: Origins of the Crusade for Tarragona (1058)," read before the Medieval Association of the Pacific at Stanford University, 24 Feb. 1973; see also *idem*, "La restauración eclesiástica y la reconquista catalana del siglo once: Ramón Berenguer I y la Sede de Tarragona," *Analecta sacra Tarraconensia* (1977), forthcoming.

[5] For background concerning this region's reconquest, see Ferran Soldevila, *Història de Catalunya* (Barcelona 1934-1935; ed. 3, 1962) 1.87-146; Santiago Sobrequés, *Els grans comtes de Barcelona* (Barcelona 1961; ed. 2, 1970) 55-203; Emilio Morera y Llauradó, *Tarragona cristiana: Historia del arzobispado de Tarragona y del territorio de su provincia (Cataluña la Nueva)* (Tarragona 1897-1899) vols. 1-2, esp. 1.325-455; and the summaries of Joseph Iglésies i Fort, *La conquesta de Tortosa* (Barcelona 1961); *idem, La Reconquesta a les Valls de l'Anoià i el Gaià* (Barcelona 1963); *idem, La restauració de Tarragona* (Barcelona 1963); Josep Lladonosa Pujol, *La conquesta de la ciudad de Lléida* (Barcelona 1961).

[6] A. Lambert, "Atto de Vich," *Dictionnaire d'histoire et géographie ecclésiastique* (Paris 1912-) 5.191-195; Jaime Villanueva, *Viage literario a las iglesias de España* (Madrid 1803-1853) 6.153-156; Josef Blanch, *Arxiepiscopologi de la santa església metropolitana i primada de Tarragona*, ed. J. Icart (Tarragona 1965 [1951]) 1.68-69; Juan Luis de Moncada, *Episcopologio de Vich, escrito a mediados del siglo XVII*, ed. Jaime Collel (Vich 1891-1894) 1.350-365; and the related documents, Augustin Millares Carlo, ed., *Documentos pontificios en papiro de archivos catalans* (Madrid 1918) 115-180; Demetrio Mansilla Reoyo, *La documentación pontificia hasta Inocencio III (965-1216)* (Rome 1955) 1.1-2, no. 1; PL 135.983. For the strong Catalan-papal relations throughout the restoration era, see Paul Kehr, *Das Papsttum und der katalanische Prinzipat bis zur Vereinigung mit Aragón* (Berlin 1926).

[7] Cf. S. Ruiz, "Berenguer Seniofred, archevèque de Tarragone," DHGE 8.382; Moncada (n.6 above) 1.374-375; Enrique Flórez, *España sagrada, teatro geográfica-histórico de la iglesia de España* (Madrid 1747-[1897]) 28.153-178; Pius B. Gams, *Die Kirchengeschichte von Spanien*

Murābiṭ invasion caused the collapse of the great comital offensive of the 1090s, leaving the frontier zone much as it had been a half-century earlier under Ramón Berenguer I when the restoration movement had first gained impetus from prevailing reform attitudes of the generation of Catalan churchmen then coming into power. It is in connection with renewal of comital efforts to reconquer Tarragona and a crusade against the *ṭawā'if* kingdoms of Lérida and Tortosa, beginning in 1114 with campaigns to end Muslim naval supremacy over the western Mediterranean, that the metropolitanate was again revived on 8 March 1118 with Oleguer Bonestruga (1118-1137), then bishop of Barcelona, whose struggle to secure his new ecclesiastical capital led to the creation of the confraternity of Tarragona.[8]

There were ample precedents in both southern France and Catalonia for creating a confraternity to aid Oleguer's restorative efforts. These two regions were especially open to ideological exchange while the Catalan house of Cerdaña-Besalú controlled the metropolitanate of Narbonne (Archbishop Wilfred of Cerdaña, 1018-1079), which in turn governed the *Tarraconensis*; and when the political connections between the house of Barcelona and those of Carcassonne, Limousin, Montpellier and Narbonne were being solidified by a series of regencies and dynastic marriages.[9]

(Ratisbon 1863-1873; repr. Graz 1956) 3.1.186-188. The only specialized treatment of Archbishop Berenguer's career (which I have not been able to examine) is by Antonio Pladvall i Font, "Berenguer Seniofred de Lluçà, obispo de Lluçà, obispo de Vich y arzobispo de Tarragona (1076-1099)," Ph.D. diss. (Louvain 1963); cf. *idem*, "La verdadera filaciò de Berenguer Seniofred de Lluçà, primer arquebisbe de Tarragona del segle XI, conegut fins ara per Berenguer de Rosanes," *Boletín arqueológico de Tarragona* 66 (1966) 71-81.

[8] There is no critical biography of this influential churchman; the present essay is part of such a study now in preparation. Most modern accounts are based on the unreliable hagiography produced at the time of the archbishop's canonization, and these in turn are predicated on the *Vitae sancti Ollegarii* (preserved in fourteenth-century MSS of Barcelona, both of which are based on a single mid-twelfth-century, non-extant original). Flórez, Fita, Beer, Soldevila and others all attribute the earlier composition to Master Renald the Grammarian of Barcelona, a contemporary of Oleguer. See *Vitae sancti Ollegarii*, ed. Enrique Flórez, ES 29.472-499, appendices 21-22 (which Flórez entitles simply the *Vita* and *Vita altera* respectively, and which for greater clarity will be referred to hereafter as the *Vita prima* and *Vita secunda*). Cf. Fidel Fita, "Renallo gramático y la conquista de Mallorca por el conde de Barcelona D. Ramón Berenguer III," *Boletín de la Real academia de historia* 40 (1902) 50-90; *idem*, "Patrología latina: Renallo gramático," BRAH 49 (1901) 336-347; Rudolf Beer, "El Maestro Renallo, escritor del siglo XII," BRAH 10 (1887) 373-379. For Oleguer's life, see Antonio García Caralps, *Historia de S. Oleguer, arçobispo de Tarragona y obispo de Barcelona* (Barcelona 1617); AS March 1.482-489; Jodí Canadell, "Sant Oleguer, bisbe be Barcelona i arquebisbe de Tarragona (6 de Març)," *La paraula cristina* 6 (1927) 125-131; Sebastian Puig y Puig, "San Olegario," *Episcopologio de la sede barcinonense* (Barcelona 1929) 133-153; "Sant Oleguer," *Diccionari biogràfic catalans*, ed. Alberti (Barcelona 1966) 3.357-359.

[9] For background concerning the religious milieu in southern France at this time, see Élie Griffe, *Histoire religieuse des anciens pays de l'Aude* (Paris 1933); Elizabeth Magnou-Nortier, *La société laïque et l'Église dans la province ecclésiastique de Narbonne de la fin du VIIIᵉ à la fin du XIᵉ siècle* (Toulouse 1974) 447-518, 550-564; earlier religio-cultural intercourse between the Narbonensis and the Tarraconensis is discussed by Archibald Lewis, *The Development of Southern French and Catalan Society (718-1050)* (Austin, Texas 1965) 136-154, 242-260, 315-336; and the effect of mid-eleventh-century secular and ecclesiastical dominance by the southern French houses over Catalan political life on the formation of a restoration party is treated in McCrank (n. 4 above) "La restauración."

Whereas most of the earlier religious confraternities of the Narbonensis were Benedictine-related prayer associations which provided burial and intercession for their deceased members (laymen and clergy), others in Toulouse, Montpellier and Avignon were civic organizations, more socially oriented, which in addition to charities cared for their cities' defenses, the upkeep of bridges, and occasionally in times of crisis fielded large armies.[10] However, these latter more secular confraternities developed after Oleguer's time, and information about southern French confraternalism in the early twelfth century is almost nonexistent. Moreover, although the presence of confraternities in southern France seems important in view of Oleguer's strong connections with the region's nobility and long residence in Avignon, there are other more visible precedents for his actions in Catalonia itself where documentation for eleventh- and twelfth-century confraternities attests still broader objectives to meet exigencies of a prevailing frontier environment.

Because the foundation charter for the confraternity of Ivorra in Urgel, purporting to date from A.D. 1010 or 1011, is now known to be a forgery, perhaps the oldest *cofradía* in northeastern Spain was established in 1035 at San Pedro de la Portella, followed by others at Frontanya and Lillet shortly thereafter, and still another at Urgel around the turn of the century.[11] That of La Portella is especially significant because it fostered the reconstruction of churches in the march of Ausona just north of the diocese of Tarragona, and its members were bound by rules organizing themselves whenever they met into a semi-monastic community associated with a core of resident Benedictine monks at San Pedro's.[12] As indicated by their subscriptions to this confraternity's foundation charter, both archbishops Berenger and Oleguer joined this latter *cofradía* — at least as honorary *confrères*. Also, Oleguer's archiepiscopal predecessor from Vich had in 1092 met with the papel legate Gualter of Albano and the saintly bishop Otto of Urgel to found another confraternity in the

---

[10] The later case of the conventional non-military confraternity converting itself quickly into a recruitment organization at Toulouse is well known; this confraternity fielded an army of 5000 for the Albigensian Crusade. For a ready example of the customary provision of burial by confraternities connected with monasteries, see the *Libri confraternitatum*, ed. P. Piper, MGH Antiquitates (Berlin 1884) 1-14; confraternal burial customs of the nobility in southern France and northern Spain are treated by Léopold Delisle, "Des monuments paléographiques concernant l'usage de prier des morts," *Bibliothèque de l'École des chartes* 3 (1903) 361-412; José Orlandis, "Sobre la elección de sepultura en la España medieval," *Anuario de historia del derecho español* 20 (1950) 5-20. Cf. D. Pansier, "Histoire de l'ordre des Frères du Pont-d'Avignon," *Annales d'Avignon et du comtat Venaissin* 9 (1920-1921) 7-25.

[11] See the short introduction to the history of Catalan confraternities by José Rius Serra, "La confraría de Santa Eulalia del Campo," *Miscelànea de Rius Serra* 1 (San Cugat 1965) esp. 54-55, repr. from *Estudis Franciscans* 38 (1926) 174-186; cf. "Confratres," *Glossarium mediae latinitatis Catalonie* (Barcelona 1969) fasc. 5.640-641. For the forged constitution of Ivorra, see Paul Kehr, *Papsturkunden in Spanien* 1: *Katalanien: Urkunden und Register* (Berlin 1926) 246-249, no. 3. For other Catalan confraternities, cf. ES 28.198, 245-246, 303-304, app. 22; VL 6.338-339, app. 17; Archivo de la Catedral de Barcelona (ACB), MS *Libri antiquitatum* 1, fol. 27, no. 50 (Puig [n.8 above] 400-401, no. 58); J. Rius Serra, ed., *Cartulario de "Sant Cugat" del Vallés* (Barcelona 1945-1947) 3.134-135, no. 952; José Balari y Jovany, *Orígenes históricos de Cataluña*, ed. 2 (San Cugat 1964) 2.541.

[12] VL 8.259-260, app. 23.

latter's diocese, this time to rebuild the church of Santa María de Gualter "which for so long was possessed by the pagans and was inaccessible to the faithful of Christ." [13] During this site's dedication to the Virgin, the churchmen invoked the aid of Saint Michael's heavenly host, so that holy war and the ideology of ecclesiastical restoration do not appear unrelated to confraternalism in the Tarraconensis. Finally, Archbishop Berenger in the 1090s seems to have experimented with an organization closely resembling a military confraternity for the recovery of Tarragona. Charters at Vich from his episcopate demonstrate that, without naming their organization a confraternity as such, knights under the archbishop's direction banded together in three frontier castles where they lived communally, fasting, and contributing their services and large monetary donations for campaigns against the Muslims, vowing "to restore the church of Tarragona and that same city" as an act of penitence "for redemption from all their sins." [14] Archbishop Oleguer could not have been unfamiliar with these precedents or other confraternal models related to his work with the Augustinian Congregation of Saint Rufus of Avignon and the reform of the cathedral chapters in the Tarraconensis. [15] Moreover, as indicated by his subscription to its foundation charter, Oleguer was also *confrère* at Gualter, and he would also have been familiar with the option of a military confraternity; in early 1122 he attended the council of Montearagón to confirm Alfonso I of Aragón's foundation of the military *cofradía* of Belchite. [16]

Oleguer had been working for the cause of crusade in northeastern Spain since his abbatiate at Saint Rufus of Avignon when in 1113 he was instrumental in the formation of the Catalan-Provençal-Italian alliance against the Balearic pirates. [17] After

[13] Kehr (n. 11 above) 193-196, no. 29: "Volumus vestram, karissimi, fraternitatem deprecari, ut ecclesia . . . que non diu a paganorum possessione semota et a Christi fidelibus est incepta. . . ."

[14] Archivo de la Catedral de Vich, *Episcopologio*, nos. 75, 82 (formerly Armario de las antigüedades, caj. 6, no. 1452); VL 6.326-329, app. 39, nos. 1-2: "Omnibus provintiae Terragonensis principibus per paenitentiam in redemtione omnium peccatorum suorum mandaverit restaurationem eiusdem urbis et ecclesiae Terragonensis." Cf. Moncada (n. 6 above) 1.359-360; Kehr (n. 6 above) 47-49.

[15] Oleguer became active in the Augustinian reform of the Catalan chapters under Bishop Bertran of Barcelona, also a former abbot of St. Rufus of Avignon; after 1095 Oleguer served as prior of St. Adrian de Bésos near Barcelona, before his own election ca. 1113 to the abbacy of St. Rufus. He headed the Congregation until 1118, which is significant because throughout this period chapters were regarded simply as specialized confraternities, as indicated by the interchange of the terms in the local documents (*Glossarium Cat.* [n. 11 above] 5.640-641).

[16] Cf. Peter Rassow, "La Cofradía de Belchite," AHDE 3 (1926) 200-226; Antonio Ubieto Arteta, "La creación de la cofradía militar de Belchite," *Estudios de la Edad Media de la Corona de Aragón* 5 (1952) 427-434.

[17] In the chronicle wrongly attributed to Llorenzo Verones, the abbot of St. Rufus who in 1113 met with the Pisan consuls and Catalan nobles to arrange for the Mallorcan venture is called Nigelarius (or Nogelarius instead of Olegarius), but Oleguer's abbatiate at Avignon can be dated before 1114, so that the real chronicler Enric (the deacon of Archbishop Pietro of Pisa) seems to confuse his name. Cf. *Gesta triumphalia per Pisanos, facta de captione Hierusalem et civitatis Mayoricarum*, ed. L. A. Muratori, *Rerum italicarum scriptores* (Milan 1723-1751) 4.112-115; Carlo Calisse, ed., *Fonti per la storia d'Italia* 29: *Liber Maiolichinus de gestis Pisanorum illustribus* (Rome 1904) 48-49, 137; M. Bouquet, ed., *Recueil des historiens des Gaules et de la France*, ed. 2 (Paris 1899-1933; repr. 1968) 12.349-355; ES 29.258; Morera (n. 5 above) 1.376-378; Sobrequés (n. 5 above) 176-177.

Bishop Guillem of Barcelona's death at the siege of Palma in April 1115, Oleguer in 1116 had been elected his successor. At that time Paschal II promised Count Ramón Berenguer III, Oleguer's benefactor and suzerain, to promote a crusade against Tortosa, and in his bull of confirmation on 21 March 1118 granting Oleguer the pallium as the new archbishop of Tarragona (while retaining the see of Barcelona in plurality), Gelasius II granted him future ecclesiastical jurisdiction over Muslim Tortosa in anticipation of Tarragona's recovery and the rapid advance of the reconquest.[18] Calixtus II finally proclaimed a crusade in Spain at the council of Toulouse in 1119, and at the Lateran Council of 1123 Oleguer was appointed legate *a latere* in charge of crusade activities in New Catalonia.[19] In this capacity he endeavored to aid the count, continuing his diplomatic efforts to enlist southern French forces into Barcelona's service, and especially to secure Tarragona city behind the military front.

In accordance with the arrangements of 23 January 1118 for the see's canonical restoration, the lordship of Tarragona had been given to the Church, so that it was the archbishop's special task to direct this region's resettlement and his city's reconstruction while comital forces struck deeper into Léridan and Tortosan territory.[20] This was no small charge, for the area surrounding Tarragona's plain was a great *despoblado*, described in eleventh-century charters as a "vast and horrible" place where "no human lived nor sheep grazed."[21] Orderic Vitalis in reference to the events of 1129 reports that Oleguer's Tarragona was in ruins with its once proud walls

[18] Bull of 1116: Archivo de la Corona de Aragón (ACA), Canc. real, no. 12; Francisco J. Miquel Rosell, *Regesta de letras pontificias del Archivo de la Corona de Aragón* (Madrid 1948) 23-24, no. 12; PL 153.407; Mansilla (n. 6 above) 69-70, no. 50; Bull of 1118: ES 25.221-223, app. 16. See also the *Vita prima* 7-8 (ES 29.476-477, app. 21); *Vita secunda* 8 (ES 29.497-498, app. 22). Note that Gelasius II was John of Gaeta, an Augustinian who had lived at St. Rufus under Oleguer's abbacy and who as cardinal-deacon had worked closely with Paschal II and Cardinal Boson in the negotiations of 1116-1117, so that the papacy had a longstanding and continuous personal interest in Tarragona's restoration. It is significant, as subsequently argued, that the confraternity of Tarragona enjoyed papal sponsorship and protection, and was promoted at a legatine council.

[19] The *acta* of the council of Toulouse are lost, but the *Chronicon Maliacense* (ES 25.120) affirms that "Tolosae fuit concilium in quo confirmata est via de Hispania." It was after this that Oleguer began calling himself the *dispensator* or rector of Tarragona as well as metropolitan. Cf. Karl Hefele and Henri Leclercq, *Histoire des conciles d'après les documents originaux*, rev. ed. (Paris 1907-1952) 5.340. For the concern of the Church Universal over the crusade in Spain, note esp. Canon 10 of the Lateran Council which tries to enforce vows of crusaders for service in either Spain or the Holy Land: Giovanni Mansi, *Sacrorum conciliorum nova et amplissima collectio* (Leipzig 1903-1927) 21.217; PL 163.1305; cf. Hefele and Leclercq 5.1.635; James Brundage, *Medieval Canon Law and the Crusader* (Madison, Wis. 1969) 129-130. For the bull of Calixtus II appointing Oleguer his legate at this council, see ACB (n. 11 above) *Libri antiquitatum* 1, fol. 21, no. 25; cf. Josep Mas, *Notes historiques del bisbat de Barcelona* 10: *Rúbrica dels "Liber antiquitatum" de Seu de Barcelona* (Barcelona 1914) 285, no. 1306; PL *loc. cit.*; Mansilla (n. 6 above) 79-80, no. 62.

[20] Charter of 1118: ACA Ramón Berenguer III, no. 202 (with a copy of 1273 by P. Carbonell); Archivo de la Catedral de Tarragona (ACT) MS 335, *Llibre de Vilaseca*, fol. 28 (sixteenth-century copy of non-extant ancient MS, ACT, sign. 9, fol. 17, no. 16); ed. José María Font Rius, *Cartas de población y franquicia de Cataluña* (Madrid 1969) 1.82-84, no. 49.

[21] Federico Udina Martorell, *El "Llibre blanch" de Santes Creus* (Barcelona 1947) xxiv-xxxix, 11-12, no. 9 (referring to Forés in the northern Conca de Barberá); 19, no. 16 (referring to Puig d'Anguera just north of Tarragona's Alto Campo).

breached in several places; it was overgrown with beeches and other tall trees which were rooted even within the remains of the city's ancient cathedral.[22] In spite of the usual dating of the Christian occupation of the city in 1118 upon the initial grant, the site was not firmly within Christian hands until after 1122-1124 when comital forces made significant advances toward the Ebro valley. However, Tarragona's safety was seriously jeopardized when the crusaders met disastrous defeat at Corbins upon attempting an expedition into the heartland of the *tawā'if* kingdom of Lérida.[23] The city had no resident defense force until 1130-1131, its territory was not subjugated until 1153-1155, Muslim revolts and *razzias* continued into the 1170s, and the port suffered its last naval raid as late as 1188, long after Oleguer's episcopate. Nevertheless, it was Oleguer who initiated Tarragona's reconstruction as his contemporary biographer Renald affirms. However, the archbishop could not have been present to direct this work until after 30 June 1125 when after considerable activity in southern and central France his return to Barcelona is documented by charters in its cathedral cartulary, the *Libri antiquitatum*.[24] Thereafter Oleguer's presence in Catalonia can be determined, but only intermittently at Barcelona, when he may have been spending more time on the Tarragona project. It was at this juncture, 1126-1128, that several factors combined, compelling the archbishop to found a confraternity for support of his see's total restoration.

[22] Ordericus Vitalis, *Historiae ecclesiasticae libri tredecim*, ed. August Le Prévost (Paris 1835-1855) lib. 12, cap. 21 (PL 188.924-927); trans. Thomas Forrester, *The Ecclesiastical History of England and Normandy* (London 1854) 4.113-114.

[23] The battle of Corbins is dated variously between 1124 and 1126, but the *Chronicon Dertusense I* (VL 5.237, app. 10) places it in 1124, the most likely date in terms of Oleguer's proclamation of the crusade in 1123 and Aragonese encroachments upon Lérida in that same year which prompted the Catalans into action. Cf. Gerónimo Zurita, *Anales de la Corona de Aragón* (Zaragoza 1610-1621), ed. Angel Canellas López (Madrid 1966-1967) 48, 133, 138-145; José María Lacarra, ed., *Documentos para el estudio de la reconquista y repoblación del valle del Ebro*, in EEMCA (Zaragoza 1946) 2.35, no. 29. Note also Ramón Berenguer III's premature donation in 1123 of Lérida's mosque to the monks of Solsonna: F. J. Miquel Rosell, *Liber feudorum maior* (Barcelona 1945) 1.196, no. 186. The unfortified coastal towns as far north as Elna were subjected to Muslim naval raids in 1135 (VL 6.228) and Lérida-Tortosa did not fall until 1148-1149; this chronological framework illumines the precarious position of the Catalans in the 1120s at Tarragona.

[24] The *Vitae* do not clearly indicate Oleguer's itinerary and omit several important events, so that they cannot be trusted altogether for dating the archbishop's work at Tarragona; they ignore Oleguer's attendance at the councils of Toulouse and Reims (1119 and 1120 respectively) and simply generalize about his activities thereafter. Charters of the *Libri antiquitatum* indicate his presence in the vicinity of Barcelona throughout 1121, his return to Catalonia from the Lateran Council of 1123 by August 12, and local activity to July 1124; his whereabouts thereafter are unknown until 1126 when he was again in southern France, and supposedly in late 1126-early 1127 Oleguer was in the Holy Land. The *Vita secunda* provides the only definite date (being emphatic that Oleguer returned from his pilgrimage in 1127) but this juncture is inexplicable in terms of his required presence in Catalonia during the preparations for the new *hueste*, and he may have instead made his pilgrimage during the lull of reconquest activities following Corbins. Renald implies that the archbishop cut short his stay in Antioch because of concern for Tarragona: "Rediit Barchinonam patronus, ad metropolim metropolitanus, laetata est Barchino, diu spectata et desiderata praesentia patris. Gavisa est Tarrachona de optato reditu metropolitani." Cf. *Vita prima* 11 (ES 29.478-479, app. 21); *Vita secunda* 8 (ES 29.498, app. 22); ACB (n. 11 above) *Lib. antiq.* 1, fols. 80, 118, 285; IV, fols. 55, 195 (Mas [n. 19 above] 286-295, 300, nos. 1309, 1311, 1318, 1320, 1326, 1338).

According to the *Vitae sancti Ollegarii*, "in order to rebuild Tarragona, which for such a long time had remained deserted, the saintly metropolitan labored with great anxiety, bringing together urban dwellers, colonists, defenders and knights from everywhere, and, as he was able to, he conferred benefices regularly."[25] The *Vita secunda* affirms that "at long last he began to rebuild Tarragona city and its temples," and likewise charters of 1126-1127 in the area's monastic and cathedral cartularies testify to Oleguer's building program in Barcelona's diocese, especially repair of churches destroyed by the Muslim invasions of 985–1003.[26] We know also that after late 1130 Oleguer was drawn into the papal-imperial conflict and spent increased time and energy in southern France at the exile papal court, so that the archbishop's greatest restoration efforts at Tarragona can be placed between 1126 and 1130.[27] Moreover, during 1126 and 1127 Oleguer participated in the preparations for another crusade against the Ebro kingdoms which still clung tenaciously to his newly constituted diocese. He first conducted negotiations with Guillaume V of Montpellier about compensation for the latter's knights who served Barcelona in 1124-1126, and secondly the archbishop helped to settle a quarrel between Guillaume and his son Bernard IV of Melgueil-Substantion in order to solidify the Christian alliance against the Muslims.[28] It was in July 1128 that Ramón Berenguer III, Roger of Sicily and Guillaume V of Montpellier launched their new offensive against Tortosa,

[25] "Ad reaedificandam Tarrachonam, quae multo tempore deserta fuerat, multa solicitudine sanctus elaborabat metropolitanus, undique habitores, colonos, defensores, milites congregabat, et beneficia prout poterat, assidue impendebat [*Vita prima* 11]."

[26] *Vita secunda* 8 (ES 29.498-499, app. 21): "Coepit dirutam Tarraconensem civitatem et templa reaedificare," and again, "et cum primum autem revertitur ad ambas ecclesias perficiendam Tarraconensem ecclesiam applicavit, multasque alias ecclesias reaedificans." These "other churches" included Sta. María de Toba, San Andrés de Palomar, and San Vicente de Valldoreix as well as the castle chapel at Sitges: cf. ACB (n. 11 above) *Lib. antiq.* 1, fols. 43, 51, nos. 90, 516; 2, fol. 47, no. 123; 4, fols. 66, 360, nos. 162, 183 (Mas [n. 19 above] 312, 322, nos. 1364, 1387); Puig (n. 8 above) 146-148, 413-414, no. 64.

[27] The former of these *termini* is established above (nn. 23-24), while the latter is indicated by Oleguer's involvement in the Church's international crisis with the empire and the schism of the early 1130s. After the council of Narbonne in 1129 and a brief sojourn at Barcelona, Oleguer left with another legate, Cardinal Humbert, for Castile-León (Council of San Zoilo, 4 Feb. 1130), and thereafter traveled to Innocent II's court and the council of Clermont (18 November 1130). He returned to Catalonia for the "cortes" of 1131, but we know nothing about his activities between then and 1134; his last direct involvement in reconstruction on the Tarragona frontier seems to have been in 1130 when he arranged for the initial fortification of Valls. Cf. Archivo histórico archidiocesano de Tarragona (AHAT), MS Mariano A. Mari, *Nominum et actorum archiepiscoporum Tarraconensium expositio chronológico-histórica tribus libris distributa* (1783) 2, fol. 404; Puig (n. 8 above) 147-153; Morera (n. 5 above) 1.393-394. For the occupation of Tarragona see Ordericus Vitalis (n. 22 above) 13, cap. 2 (PL 188.927) and a later charter of 1149 which refers to the original subjugation and colonization of Tarragona: Font Rius (n. 27 above) 119-121, no. 74. Tarragona city was effectively refortified by 1154 as the Muslim geographer al-Idrīsī testifies in his *Kitāb Nuzhat al-Mushtāk al-āfāk*, ed. and trans., Reinhardt Dozy and M. J. Goeje, *Description de l'Afrique et de l'Espagne* (Leiden 1866) 2.255; cf. R. Dozy, *Recherches sur l'histoire et la littérature de l'Espagne pendant le Moyen Âge*, ed. 3 (repr. New York 1968) 2.362.

[28] Barcelona's allies then also included Guillaume IX of Poitiers whose men also appear among Tarragona's first colonists: cf. Claude de Vic and Joseph Vaissète, *Histoire général de Languedoc*, rev. J. Molinier et al. (Toulouse 1872-1904) 3.667-668; Antoni Rovira i Virgili, *Història nacional de Catalunya* (Barcelona 1922-1937) 2.29-30.

and in order to take advantage of this unique opportunity Oleguer required capital forthwith to speed Tarragona's recovery. The comital donation of 1118, generous though it was, produced no immediate feudal revenues, tithes or first-fruits, and the count's reserves were being poured into the campaigns rather than into the arch-bishop's reconstruction at Tarragona. As Renald indicates, the city's resettlement could be encouraged by land grants, but the cost of local defense, import of supplies, and support of clergy for the nascent church must have put a severe strain on the archbishop's financial resources. The coffers of Barcelona's church were also drained by its own diocesan building projects, so that its clergy could not simultaneously carry by itself the burden of Tarragona's restoration. By late 1126 and early 1127 both the count and archbishop were searching for additional funds; while acting as a peacekeeper among allies, Oleguer on behalf of Ramón Berenguer III negotiated at this time an important treaty with Genoa to increase comital and ecclesiastical revenues from Barcelona's port.[29] Consequently, the situation by 1128 appears to have been critical, when the archbishop was in desperate need of extra-diocesan support for his undertaking at Tarragona. It was then that Oleguer formed his con-fraternity – a corporation of contributors to a special fund for the see's restoration.

The primary evidence for the *cofradía* of Tarragona is preserved in two documents from the archives of Ager, the original of which has long been misconstrued as being the only authentic foundation charter for this confraternity. One of these was dis-covered in the eighteenth century by Jaime Caresmar whose transcription was pub-lished in 1774 by Enrique Flórez (*España sagrada*, volume 28); the other was pub-lished nearly a half-century later, in 1821, by Jaime Villanueva (*Viage literario*, volume 6).[30] Upon close examination of both texts it becomes apparent that the former *pergamino* (MS 2342) is predicated on the latter (MS 960) and is a summary of what must be considered the more authoritative text published by Villanueva.

[29] This treaty is known in part from the business of the so-called "cortes" of Barcelona in 1131, when Oleguer insisted that the Church receive its proper share of the comital port revenues. The depositions of this assembly designate this share "ad opus ecclesie" (presumably for the church of Barcelona), but also "in potestate archiepiscopi et predictorum episcoporum," imply-ing that the funds were to be used at the supra-diocesan level. This arrangement was in accor-dance with a donation of 1100 by the citizens of Barcelona to the cathedral chapter of Santes Creus of a tithe of all the maritime revenues, a right which had fallen into disuse and was the basis for Oleguer's claim. Note that the other bishops present at this cortes were those of Gerona (who with Oleguer was negotiating settlements of local disputes in his see) and especially Ramón Gaufred of Vich, the foremost supporter of his archbishop's restoration program. This suggests the possibility that Oleguer and his colleague pressed the count for this money to aid the con-fraternity's building projects. Cf. ACB (n. 11 above) *Lib. antiq.* 1, fol. 27, no. 50; Puig (n. 8 above) 400-401, no. 58; Fidel Fita, "Cortes de Barcelona en 1131: Texto inédito," BRAH 4 (1884) 75-84; *Cortes de los antiguos reinos de Aragón y de Valencia y Principado de Cataluña* 1: *Cortes de Catalunya* (Madrid 1896-1922) pt. 1.51, no. 2.

[30] ES 28.303-304, app. 22; VL 6.338-339, app. 46. Villanueva (VL 6.338) misleadingly describes the document as "Narbonensis concilii decretum pro restaurando ecclesia Tarraco-nensis" as if it embodied the conciliar *acta* as such. Note that Jaime Caresmar was at this time writing his own polemic against Toletan primatial claims: *La Primacía de Tarragona*. ed. P. Martí, AST 22 (1922) 153-163, 187-190, 229-232; 23 (1923) 7-10, 37-42, 62-67, 80-84, 109-115, 137-145; 24 (1924) 161-169.

This preferred text relates how a confraternity for the restoration of Tarragona's church was founded at the legatine council of Narbonne, commonly dated in 1129.

The chronology of what transpired between 1126 and 1130 becomes very important in determining the nature of this confraternity, but unfortunately the date of the council of Narbonne is a matter of dispute. Flórez cited 1127, but as Villanueva subsequently demonstrated, such an early dating of the council was based on the faulty reading of the Ager documents by Caresmar.[31] The latter scholar inexplicably sent Flórez only the short version of the text in question, although he must have seen both *pergaminos* at Ager in order to advise his colleague that the council could have met in either 1127 or 1128. The problem is that the original to which Caresmar referred actually reads 1128, not 1127, while the authoritative text published by Villanueva places the council on Easter Sunday 1129, that is April 14.[32] In other words, the issue should have been whether this assembly convened in 1128 or 1129. Unfortunately Oleguer's itinerary cannot be determined precisely enough to resolve this problem, and both years fall within the chronological *termini post quem* and *ante quem* provided by episcopates of the subscribants.[33] Morera y Llauradó, the foremost *investigador* of Tarragona's history, in 1899 accepted Villanueva's date of 1129 based on the longer of the two Ager parchments, and most historians thereafter have accepted, rightly so, this latter date. The discrepancy is best explained by scribal error because the *pergamino* giving 1128 is based on that citing 1129; and the latter contains the numerals XXVIIII for 1129, so that the omission of a single stroke by the copyist seems plausible. Moreover, placing the council in 1129 is in keeping with Oleguer's arrangements for Tarragona's defense in the same year (on 14 March 1129) just before the council would have met, when the archbishop enfeoffed the secular lordship of Tarragona to the Norman Robert Burdet, giving him the title *princeps Tarraconensis* which in effect made him the archepiscopal *:idame* or *defensor*.[34] In short, it can safely be assumed that Villanueva's date of 14 April 1129 is correct.

---

[31] ES 28.199; VL 6.226, 338 n. 1. The erroneous dating is retained in such standard sources as Ulysses Chevalier, *Répertoire des sources historiques du Moyen Âge: Topo-bibliographie* (Paris 1905-1907) cols. 2073-2074, and Bouquet (n. 17 above) 14.230-231; from these it commonly passes into secondary accounts. Despite their attention to the nexus between the sees of Narbonne and Tarragona, this council is ignored by De Vic and Vaissète (n. 28 above) vols. 3-4; likewise, it is omitted from the standard conciliar collections and does not receive its deserved attention by Hefele and Leclercq (n. 19 above) 5.1.808; cf. Gams (n. 7 above) 3.1.87.

[32] The dating of Easter for the documents in question is based on the tables compiled by Jacinto Agustí y Casanovas, "Hemerología," *Manual de cronología española y universal*, ed. José Vives (Madrid 1953) 187.

[33] VL 6.338-339, no. 46; P. B. Gams, *Series episcoporum ecclesiae catholicae* (Graz 1957 [1873]) 33, 76-90, 517-583, 638. Bishop Beremond of Béziers was consecrated only in 1128; the accession of Raymond of Maguelonne is given as ca. 1130 but must have been 1129, i.e., before the council; Bishop Arnaud of Carcassonne died in 1130; these dates rule out the possibility of the council's convocation in 1127, but do not make possible a distinction between 1128 and 1129.

[34] Enfeoffment of 1129: ACA (n. 17 above) Canc. Reg. 3, fol. 6; eighteenth-century copies are included in the Archivo de la Real academia de historia (Madrid), Varios privilegios (Col.

Neither of the Ager *pergaminos* preserves the conciliar *acta* as such but they are summaries of the business at Narbonne prepared for or by Abbot Arnold of Ager for his community. According to his account, this council met under the presidency of Honorius III's legate Arnaud of Levezon, the archbishop of Narbonne (who joined Oleguer in subscribing the constitution of the *cofradía* of Gualter). Although Oleguer also had legatine status and was the more esteemed and older of the two metropolitans present, the presidency may have been decided simply because the assembly met at Narbonne, the most central location for the churchmen of both ecclesiastical provinces, Narbonensis and Tarraconensis. The two archbishops were joined by the bishops of Toulouse, Agde, Maguelone, Carcassonne, Béziers, Lodève, Elna, Gerona, Vich, Urgel and Zaragoza, along with the abbots of Saint-Saturnin of Toulouse, Lezat, Ager, Saint-Ponce de Thomières and La Grasse, "to consider in what manner Christianity, which had suffered so much oppression and so many deaths at the hands of the Saracens, might be nurtured; they joined in counsel with God in order to undertake the restoration of the see of Tarragona which was the capital of Hispania Citerior," after which they "constituted for the restoration of this church, therefore, a symbol (*symbolum*) which was called a confraternity (*confratrium*)."[35]

Not only did those present join this confraternity, but the clergy, canons and monks of both provinces were enrolled in its membership by their superiors who spoke "for themselves and their subjects." Laymen were also invited into the fellowship, with each member paying twelve *denarii* annually "if not more" to Archbishop Oleguer. Nobles were obviously expected to contribute more, those without position less: *si impotentes fuerint, quod eis placuerit.*[36] Whenever the confraternity's ordained clergy met together, a special Mass was to be offered for the membership; and when a brother died, each priest was to dedicate a Mass in his intention. Moreover, members could enroll deceased friends and relatives merely by paying their dues. Finally, the council fathers declared that all those engaged in communal religious life were under the protection of Saint Peter, and before adjourning they proclaimed the Peace and Truce of God.

There are several questions to be raised concerning this confraternal agreement. First, why did the archbishop of Tarragona delay until 1129 to seek extra-diocesan

---

Burriel), XXVIII, fol. 111; AHAT (n. 27 above) MSS M. Mari, *Nominum* 1, fols. 228-232; *idem, Thesaurus sanctae metropolitanae ecclesiae Tarraconensis* (1783), fols. 177-180; ed. Font Rius (n. 20 above) 1.87-89, no. 51; ES 25.224-226, app. 18; VL 19.212, app. 3; Pierre de Marca, *Marca hispanica sive limes hispanicus*, ed. Étienne Baluze (Paris 1699; repr. Barcelona 1974) 1261. Cf. "Robert Bordet," *Diccionari* (n. 8 above) 1.329-330; Morera (n. 5 above) 1.374-396, 435-437; Dozy (n. 27 above) 2.350-361; Joaquín Miret i Sans, "La familia de Robert Bordet, el restaurador de Tarragona," EEMCA 1 (Huesca 1920) 53-74; Marcelin Defourneaux, *Les français en Espagne aux XIe et XIIe siècles* (Paris 1949) 225-227.

[35] VL 6.338, no. 46: "Considerantes qualiter Christianitatem, quae tot oppressiones et mortes a sarracenis assidue patitur, sucurrerent; consilium cum Deo inierunt, ut Tarraconensem sedem quae existit citerioris Hispaniae caput, restaurare satagerent . . . constituerunt itaque ad honorem Dei, et fidelium animarum salutem, et restaurationem ipsius ecclesiae symbolum, quod quod confratrium vocarunt."

[36] *Ibid.*: the bishops acted "pro se et pro sibi subiectis" in taxing their clergy and fraternal laity twelve *denarii* "si non amplius."

backing when his need was critical by late 1127? Secondly, why did this particular confraternity require the support of such an august assembly, when most *cofradías* were formed locally at small synods held by two or three bishops and their diocesan clergy? Here the paucity of documentation is most frustrating, but a plausible explanation to both queries can be formulated on the basis of two scant references in the cartulary of San Cugat de Vallés, the powerful Benedictine abbey just north of Barcelona which played a decisive role in the defense and colonization of the Barcelonese march bordering the Tarragona frontier. The first is a charter of 28 March 1128, the last testament of Ramón Uch in which he bequeaths "to the archiepiscopal household and especially to the confraternity of Tarragona" one mule or its equivalent worth, thirty *morabatinos*, to be paid by his debtor, the seneschal Guillem Ramón Moncada. This was followed four days later by a second bequest from the priest Ramón Mir whose last testament is even more telling about the Tarragona situation before early 1129.[37] Both donors left the bulk of their bequests to San Cugat, thus explaining the survival of these wills in this cartulary, but the latter specified that a large portion of his wealth was to be used to ransom captives taken prisoner presumably in the war zone around Tarragona: "Moreover, for the redemption of its captives let it be ordered that ten *morabatinos* be given to the Church of Santa María de Tamarit; let twenty *morabatinos* be given to the wife of Pedro Bernard in the hope that she will be able to purchase his release; and if not, let my executors ransom one of my nephews; let eight *morabatinos* be given to the Tarragona confraternity; and let two women be ransomed at the price of a single *morabatino* each." Since no cartulary for the *cofradía* of Tarragona has survived, we are

---

[37] The Latin of both chapters is ungrammatical, and possible emendations of the texts allow alternative readings, especially of the later. The donation of 28 March was made "ad domus archiepiscopus et ad ipsa fraternitate de Terrachona." That of 1 April makes moneys available for the redemption of Christian captives of the Muslims according to the following terms: "De redempcione autem sui captivi iussit dare X moabetinos ecclesie s. Marie de Tamarit, XX moabetinos uxori Petri Bernardi, si exierit ad redempcionem; et si non exierit mei manumissores redimant unum de meis nepotibus; et VIII. Terraconensi confratrie et duabus feminis singulos moabetinos." The first is dated "V. kal. apr., a. XX regnante Ledovico rege" and the second "scilicet VII. kal. marcii. Late condiciones kal. aprilis" and is signed "Annus Domini MCXXVIII, Guielmi, iudicis." ACA (n. 18 above) Cart. Sant Cugat, F. 383, N. 1113; (copy of 1155) fol. 255v, n. 784; ed. Rius, *Cartulario* (n. 11 above) 3.84-85, nos. 892-893; cf. Mas (n. 19 above) 5.176. The use of both terms, *fraternitas* and *confratria*, indicates that the meaning here cannot be construed as anything but "confraternity." Although in the first quotation it might be assumed that the reference is to the cathedral canons of Tarragona and that the bequest was to be divided between the archiepiscopal and chapter *mensae*, such cannot be the case because there was no chapter at Tarragona until 1154. The second charter suggests that men from Tamarit, seven miles north of Tarragona and the main coastal castle between Barcelona and Oleguer's see, had been captured in 1127 or early 1128; in short, the campaign to secure Tarragona may have suffered a severe setback sometime after the Christian defeat at Corbins. Ramón Mir's will also implies that Tarragona's *confrères* engaged in the ransom trade, and is one of the earliest references to the appearance of charitable redemptionism in northeastern Spain. For the nexus between twelfth-century Catalan confraternalism and the subsequent rise of the Redemptionist and Mercedarian Orders see the introduction to James W. Brodman, "The Trinitarian and Mercedarian Orders: A Study of Religious Redemptionism in the Thirteenth Century," Ph.D. diss. (University of Virginia 1974) 103-106.

left with this meager testimony about its existence by spring, 1128. These donations not only imply that its members were already active in redemptionism, but indicate that special funds were being collected for the archbishop's disposal and that Oleguer had now established an archiepiscopal treasury apart from that of the church of Barcelona. Most important, of course, is that because of their authenticity and exact dating, the San Cugat charters attest the operation of a local confraternity related to Tarragona's restoration one year before the archbishop journeyed in the spring of 1129 to Narbonne. By testifying to the apparent adversities being encountered by Tarragona's *confrères*, these documents not only provide evidence for Oleguer's motives in seeking a wider base of support for his project, but they account for how the archbishop was able to proceed with the pre-1129 activities at Tarragona which Renald describes.

Because of the lack of documentation describing this initial organization, perhaps centered at Barcelona rather than Tarragona, one can only speculate about its nature on the basis of the known activities of other late-eleventh- and twelfth-century Hispanic *cofradías*. We may conjecture that such a local confraternity was not primarily military, but could have nevertheless supported men-at-arms for the projected *hueste* against Tortosa or at least to defend the frontier. The *Vitae sancti Ollegarii*, without mentioning a confraternity as such, attest that Oleguer contracted knights to protect Tarragona and was subsequently instrumental in Ramón Berenguer IV's introduction of the Knights Templars into New Catalonia immediately adjacent to the ecclesiastical seigniory of Tarragona.[38] The *cofradía* could have shared the dominant characteristics of the religious confraternities already established in Catalonia, combining the widespread idea of a prayer association with that of restoration as an act of charity. In addition to ransoming captives, it would have provided such incentives to membership as special indulgences, guaranteed burial, prayers of intercession for the dead, and provisions for the care of the deceased's widow and chil-

---

[38] *Vita secunda* 8 (ES 29.498-499, app. 22). See the charter usually dated 1132 for the Templars' establishment at Barberá "ad defensionem Christianitatis," and the confirmation in 1135 of their possessions in the Conca just above Tarragona's Alto Campo "in nostra marchia contra sarracenos": ACA (n. 17 above) Privilegia Templariorum, Reg. 310, f. 21; ACA, Ramón Berenguer IV, nos. 14, 27, 28; Bofarull, *Colleción* (n. 2 above) 4.18, 29, nos. 22, 26, Cf. J. Miret i Sans, *Les cases de Templers y Hospitalers en Catalunya* (Barcelona 1910); Alan J. Forey, *The Templars in the Corona de Aragón* (London 1973) 1-18; Balari (n. 11 above) 1.358-360. Forey (7-8, 15-18) revises the chronology established by Miret i Sans, but there are still several large questions left unanswered concerning confraternalism in New Catalonia and the introduction of the international orders to this region. The evidence, albeit circumstantial at this point, suggests the possibility that there may have been some continuity between the confraternity of Tarragona, the sources of recruitment for the Tarragona campaigns from 1090 to 1130, and the formation and patronage of the first Templar corps in this same area. One must take into account the testimony of the *Vita secunda* that Oleguer was instrumental in the establishment of the Templars around his church's *señorío* before 1137, which is corroborated by the *Gesta comitum Barcinonensium* 16, ed. L. Barrau-Dihigo and J. Massói Torrents (Barcelona 1925) 38. It is noteworthy, furthermore, that the initial Templar *cavellerias* were placed strategically around Tarragona's *termini*, never within them, and that the families of the same *proceres* of Tarragona who participated in the *huestes* against Tortosa and Lérida from 1092 and 1128 are represented in the subscriptions to the earliest Templar documents.

dren — all essential services to this society at war.[39] In turn, the *cofradía* would have pooled all contributions and dues into one central treasury to provide a host of special services to Tarragona's colonists, particularly initial provisions which, according to Renald, were costing the archbishop more than he could afford. Hospitals, hospices, orphanages, alms distribution, endowments for ransoms and other forms of aid may have been envisioned for the future, once the archbishop rebuilt his city and had a chance to establish there the institutions commonly administered by the Catalan bishops in their sees.[40]

Although the possible scope of this confraternity's activities and the circumstances surrounding its foundation seem clear enough, the exact time and place of its institution cannot be determined. However, its foundation must be dated between mid-1126 and 28 March-1 April 1128. This assumption forces a reconsideration of the business undertaken at Narbonne in spring 1129, but there is no reason to alter the previously agreed upon date for this council since both Ager *pergaminos* place it on Easter Sunday. Easter in 1128 fell on 22 April after the bequests to the

---

[39] See nn. 10-11 above; and note also the connection with the care for dependents and *familiares* of the Catalan monasteries, especially Poblet near the Tarragona frontier. Cf. Orlandis (n. 2 above) *loc. cit.*; L. J. McCrank, "The Frontier of the Spanish Reconquest and the Land Acquisitions of the Cistercians of Poblet, 1150-1276," *Analecta Cisterciensia* 29 (1973) 57-78; Agustí Altisent, *Història de Poblet* (Poblet 1974) 25-27, 95-100. The above speculation about the Tarragonese confraternity's activities is supported by a passage in the *Vita prima* 10 (ES 29.478) which lauds Oleguer's charitable accomplishments and attests that his suffragan bishops were aiding his Tarragona project. If the sequence of Renald can be trusted, the archbishop's greatest effort in establishing orphanages and alms distribution to the poor and widows was coordinated with his colonization of Tarragona, feeding its populace, and care for the city's defense. This passage pertains to ca. 1124-1126, before his pilgrimage to the Holy Land, and perhaps describes works accomplished through his confraternity: "Adjunxit quoque papa Gelasius ut tandiu teneret Barchinonensem episcopatum, donec Tarrachona, cum suis expensis suficienter adhibitis haberet clerum, et civilis habitationis, et defensionis militiae, et populi munimentum." Renald continues, "Erat quidem S. antistes promptus consilio, benevolus, et prudens ad solvendas quaestiones tam in sacramentis, quam in ceteris ecclesiae institutis, largus pauperibus, occultas orphanis et viduis distribuebat eleemosynas . . . . In archiepiscopatu tam laudabili dilectione, et clementi castigatione omnes fovebat, omnes erudiebat, adeo ut omnes tam pontifices, quam alii praelati suae subjectioni et obedientiae quodam admirandae caritatis et benevolentiae se gauderent obligari vinculo."

[40] The funds collected by the bishops may also have augmented the comital war chest since there were many precedents, dating back to 1010, for churchmen contributing large sums for specific campaigns. In this regard Oleguer may be seen as operating in a tradition, for the *hueste* against Mallorca in 1114 which he helped to organize was funded by the bishops of Barcelona, Gerona, Vich, Urgel and Elna, together with the abbots of Ripoll, Sant Cugat, Besalú, Sant Pau del Camp, Canigó, Serrateix and Meià. In addition, the comital house commonly relied on the church to colonize specified frontier areas; Sant Cugat was instrumental in the defense and reconstruction of the march of Barcelona (the Panadés), and New Catalonia was divided into domains for the archbishop of Tarragona, the Cistercians of Santes Creus and Poblet, the Premonstratensians of Bellpuig, and the Carthusians of Scala Dei, as well as the nobility. Cf. Pseudo-Boades, *Feyts d'armes de Cataluña* (Barcelona 1930-1948) 200-201; Rovira (n., 28 above) 3.20-24; Sobrequés (n. 5 above) 175-177. Consequently, in addition to financing the initial diocesan organization of the church at Tarragona, Oleguer's creation of a confraternity may be seen as an attempt to regularize and centralize the Catalan church's support of the Reconquest in New Catalonia.

conternity of Tarragona are dated in the cartulary of San Cugat, so that 14 April 1129 is indeed the only acceptable date for the council of Narbonne. Therefore the creation of the original confraternity of Oleguer before spring 1128 must be seen as an act, if not independent, at least in anticipation by one or more years, of the action taken at Narbonne.

What then did this council of 1129 constitute? Or did this assembly merely confirm the archbishop's prior foundation? These critical questions are as difficult to answer as those just discussed, mainly because of the absence of corroborating documentation and the perplexing omission in the Ager documents of any mention of an attempt by Oleguer to found a confraternity of Tarragona before coming to Narbonne. It is plausible that the council affirmed the previous formation of such a confraternity rather than creating it anew, since in effect the 1129 declaration of the Peace and Truce of God was also a confirmation rather than an original proclamation. However, Oleguer as legate and metropolitan hardly needed the consent of the Narbonensian clergy for his local confraternity, unless he had something greater in mind.[41] It is therefore most significant that the assembly of Narbonne was a legatine council, that it incorporated two provinces, and promoted the confraternity conjointly with the Peace and Truce of God as extending throughout both the Tarraconensis and the Narbonensis.

The all-comprehensive nature of this new development at Narbonne goes beyond the normal limits of southern French and Catalan confraternal organization known until this time. It seems likely that, if a rudimentary *cofradía* for Tarragona's restoration existed before Oleguer's mission to Narbonne, it was now being assimilated into a larger supra-diocesan confraternity being organized at the provincial level by the two legatine archbishops. The Ager *pergaminos* do not describe a confraternity in the usual sense of the term, but in this formative period such terminology was still imprecise. *Societas, caritas, fraternitas, communitas, confraternitas, confratria, confraternia* are all terms found in contemporary documents used synonomously with *symbolus* (which can also mean a profession of faith) or confraternity.[42] It was not until the

----

[41] Most confraternities were established at diocesan synods or small provincial councils, never by the founder alone, in order to gain legal recognition of the organization and generate support. There is, however, no record of such an assembly in the Tarraconensis between 1123 and Oleguer's journey to Narbonne in 1129. The often-cited council of Barcelona which the archbishop supposedly convened in 1126 upon close examination turns out to be the previously mentioned "cortes" of 1131; the source of this error is Mansi (n. 19 above) 21.341; Francisco Diago, *Historia de los victorissimos antiguos condes de Barcelona* (Barcelona 1603; repr. 1974) 2.177-180. See n. 29 above; cf. ES 28.197-198; Hefele and Leclercq (n. 19 above) 5.1.661.

[42] For the scriptural basis of the equivalents *caritas* and *fraternitas*, terms commonly interchanged in papal diplomas of the eleventh-twelfth centuries, see the Vulgate, Rom. 12.10; I Thes. 4.9; II Peter 1.7; Heb. 13.4. Likewise there was ample confusion of patristic terminology for confraternities (*fossores, spoudaei, apotactises*, etc.): cf. Duhr, "Confréries" (n. 1 above) 1469. For the medieval terms see the following: C. du Cange, *Glossarium ad scriptores mediae et infimae latinitatis*, ed. L. Favre (Niort 1883-1887; repr. Graz 1954) 2.501; 3.598-600; *Thesaurus linguae latinae* (Leipzig, 1900-   ) 3 (1912) cols. 459-462; 6 (1923) cols. 1253-1260; A. Forcellini and J. Furlanetto, *Lexicon totius latinitatis*, ed. 2 (Bonn 1940; repr. 1965) 1.538, 788; J. L. Niermeyer, *Mediae latinitatis lexicon minus* (Leiden [1960-]1976) 245; S. Pedica, "Confrater-

Lateran Councils of 1179 and 1215 that churchmen sought greater clarification of the types of confraternities possible by 1) enforcing distinctions between laymen and clergy in these mixed religious fellowships; 2) condemning those which were not officially sanctioned by the Church and especially brotherhoods with nefarious purposes; 3) forming a dichotomy between secular and religious confraternities; and 4) insuring episcopal control over both kinds.[43] In any case, the council fathers at Narbonne so amplified the *cofradía* of Tarragona that it no longer had the limited, local characteristics of the other Catalan and southern French lay or religious confraternities. Consequently, it is possible here to advance an emergent archconfraternity hypothesis: that is, the development of a supra-diocesan and even extra-provincial fellowship which possessed the power to aggregate, affiliate or simply assimilate other smaller confraternities.[44] The distinction between the *cofradía* of Tarragona before 1128 and that described subsequently in 1129 seems to have been one of rank and size, not nature or purpose. In short, the amplification which occurred in this case suggests that the canon lawyers who at the turn of the thirteenth century defined what an archconfraternity was, invented nothing new but merely reflected in their codes the reality of twelfth-century developments.

---

nitas (Arch-confraternitas)," *Dictionarium morale et canonicum,* ed. P. Palazzini (Rome 1962) 3.888-891; *Glossarium lat. Cat.* (n. 11 above) fasc. 5.640-641; Angelis (n. 1 above) 1.2-3. Note the examples of varying nomenclature cited by Orlandis (*Estudios* [n. 2 above] 53-54, 248, passim) such as the *Beccero de Leire* (doc. of 1101: "Colligimus namque te in societatem et fraternitatem nostram," and again, "Facimus pactum et convenientiam de confraternitate cum clericis et laicis"). Like the council fathers at Narbonne, Catalan churchmen elsewhere declare that *confratria* is a vulgar term for *caritas*: e.g., the charter of La Portella (1035), "si quis vero ad ipsam caritatem, quo vulgo fratrias vocant' ; and the doc. of 1100 for Urgel's *cofradía* "faciant et perogatur karitas quo vulgo dicitur fraterna." Consequently, one might reconsider the most apparent translation of Renald's passage describing Oleguer's character and activities during 1124-1126 (cf. n. 39 above), where there may be a play on the words *caritas* and *fraternitas*; here Renald maintains that the archbishop was so effective in his admonitions, encouragement and teaching that all bishops subject to him, as well as other prelates, "rejoiced in their obligations to his bond of admirable and benevolent *caritas* (charitable love, or confraternity?)." Note also the much later interesting attempt by Alfonso el Sabiò's lawyers to define confraternity (in 1262): "familiares son llamados, o cofradres, los que toman señan de habito de alguna Orden," here reflecting the canonical definition of the intervening years which limited the concept to the religious. Cf. *Las Siete Partidas* (Madrid 1807) part 1, tit. 13, no. 8.

[43] The reaction of bishops against non-episcopal controlled confraternities can be detected in the *acta* of the councils of Béziers (1119), Rouen (1189) and Cognac (1240), as well as in canons 9 and 57 of the Lateran Councils of 1179 and 1215 respectively: cf. Mansi (n. 19 above) 22.223, 1046; Orlandis (n. 2 above) 248.

[44] Most archconfraternities in France and Italy originated between 1204 and 1244 (Duhr, "Confréries" [n. 1 above] 1422) and Pedica (n. 42 above) 888 places this development "post saec. XIII." See the *Codex iuris canonici* (Vatican City 1948) 239, for canons 701-708 and esp. 720, where confraternities are defined simply as "associationes fidelium fidelium quae non solum ad exercitum alicuius operis pietatis aut caritatis erectae sunt, sed et in incrementum publici cultus"; and "sodalitia quae iure pollent alias eiusdem speciei associationis sibi aggregandi, archisodalitia, vel archiconfraternitates, vel piae uniones, congregationes, societates, primariae appellantur." Cf. Fintan Lombard, "Confraternities and Archconfraternities," *New Catholic Encyclopedia* (New York 1967) 3.154; E. Quinn *Archconfraternities, Archsodalities and Primary Unions* (Washington, D.C. 1962); A. Vermeersch and J. Creusen, *Epitome iuris canonici* (Rome 1928) 353-355.

This elaboration upon the original *cofradía* of Tarragona is remarkable not only in demonstrating Oleguer's resourcefulness, but also his collateral activities and leadership as a legate and comital diplomat. This churchman's rapport with the Narbonensian clergy can be appreciated by remembering that in the 1090s the archbishops of Narbonne had rigorously opposed the canonical restoration of an independent Catalan metropolitanate and only in 1108 formally relinquished their *tutela* over the Tarraconensis.[45] Archbishop Arnaud's full cooperation with Oleguer suggests the latter's achievement of a genuine rapprochement between the two provincial hierarchies, especially in view of the fact that the inclusion of the southern French confraternities in the new "archconfraternity" meant the flow of funds across the Pyrenees into Catalonia. The required membership inposed by the council fathers was in effect a universal clerical tax, one of the first of its kind. Finally, because such a geographical and numerical dilation represents a greater ecclesiastical unity between the two provinces than had existed previously, the confraternity's expansion may be seen as paralleling not only the spread of the Peace and Truce of God movement, but also the growing political union as the house of Barcelona obtained recognition of its claims to suzerainty over southern France.[46] Just as the extensions of Tarragona's metropolitan jurisdiction over Aragón and into Navarra preceded the union of Aragó-Catalonia through a political marriage arranged in 1136 with Oleguer's active support and consent, the trend towards better trans-Pyrenean ecclesiastical relations could not but favor Barcelona's expansionist political ambitions.[47] The archbishop's scheme for a greater clerical solidarity between the two provinces can be associated with his shrewd diplomacy and should never be divorced from the vested interests of his protector and chief patron, the count of Barcelona. Like the political and military alliance system that Oleguer helped to forge, the "archconfraternity" was a response to the critical needs of greater manpower and financial resources for the Catalan reconquest and restoration program.

Regretably, there is little evidence by which one may judge the success of Oleguer's confraternal efforts. All of the see's *archiepiscopologios* credit the archbishop with beginning the reconstruction of several churches at Tarragona, but these may merely reflect the adulation of the *Vitae sancti Ollegarii.*[48] The individual contributions of which there is record were not great, but even the small dues required

---

[45] For the opposition of Narbonne to Tarragona's restoration see the Narbonese forgery attributed to Stephen VI: Marca (n. 34 above) 368-369, 813-817, app. 44; PL 129.855-856. Cf. Kehr (n. 6 above) 46-48; Griffe (n. 9 above) 255-263.

[46] Soldevila (n. 5 above) 1.126-146, "L'enllaç amb Provença i la restauracio de Tarragona."

[47] For time implications of the union of Aragó-Cataluña for the future of the Norman principality of Tarragona, see McCrank (unnumbered n. above) 2.339-504. Note Archbishop Oleguer's presence in Aragón while the dynastic union was arranged, when he presided over a council at Zaragoza: *Vita prima* 14-15 (ES 29.481-482, app. 21); *Vita secunda* 8 (ES 29.498-499, app. 22).

[48] *Vitae, loc. cit.*, esp. *Vita secunda* 11. See nn. 27-31 above; cf. Luis Pons de Icart, *Archiepiscopologio de Tarragona*, ed. J. Sánchez Real (Tarragona 1954) chap. 26; ES 29.121-122; Mari, *Nominum* (n. 27 above) 2, fols. 401-404; Blanch (n. 6 above) 83-84; Morera (n. 5 above) 1.392.

could have accumulated to a sizable fund. In 1131 the archbishop's resources must have been further augmented when, according to Pons de Icart, Innocent II directed all of Tarragona's suffragans to make additional contributions to the re-establishment of their metropolitan see.[49] Some of the Catalan bishops, notable Ramón Gaufred of Vich, appear to have been very generous in their support. In an undated letter to this prelate Oleguer displayed high esteem for this younger *confrère*, and on 24 October 1128 he acknowledged Bishop Ramón's valuable assistance by ceding to him the church of San Salvador situated in the *arrabal* or suburbs of Tarragona, with its future tithes and those of the see of Tarragona which accrued to the lord-archbishop's fishing rights.[50] Oleguer made this donation stating that "we have found none of the bishops as single-minded as you, dearest brother, in the revival of the church and city of Tarragona; in fact, not only have you vowed to make available all of your goods and those of your church of Ausona (Vich), but also you have vowed both your own person, as best you could, in this work of restoration, and the encouragement of whatever others could do for this same purpose."[51] This is the first non-comital donation at Tarragona of which there is record; although it could have been intended as a grant *in futuro*, it implies that by late 1128 during the offensive against Tortosa some progress was being made in Tarragona's reconstruction with the support of the Catalan hierarchy. It further supports the contention that a nuclear *cofradía* was already laboring for Tarragona's restoration before the council of Narbonne.

In spite of such progress and the obvious benefits after 1129 of an enlarged confraternity as a financial cooperative for the restoration, there is no extant documentation for the *cofradía's* activities after 1129 nor adequate record of its continuation after Archbishop Oleguer's death on 6 March 1137. While the prelate in his last years became involved in papal politics, the city was defended by Robert Burdet's wife, Inés; and the Norman *princeps* recruited more followers from his homeland and Italy for the total subjugation of the Tarragona frontier.[52] The see did not obtain its first resident bishop until 1146 with the election of Bernard Tort, finally ending the vacancy in the metropolitan office from 1137 to 1144, after which there appears to have been an attempted revival of the former Tarragonese confraternity.[53] Archbishop

---

[49] ES 25.121-122; Luis Pons de Icart, *Libro de las grandezas y cosas memorables de la metropolitana insigne y famosa ciudad de Tarragona* (Lérida 1572; repr. 1883) 150; *idem* (n. 48 above) *loc. cit.*

[50] ES 28.304-305, app. 23; S. Baluze, *Miscellanearum libri VII,* ed. 2 (Lucca 1761-1764) 2.197.

[51] ES 28.199-200: "Quia in restitutione Tarraconensis ecclesiae et civitatis, neminem episcoporum tam unanimem, quam te, charissime frater, invenimus: Tu enim non solum omnia tua, et ecclesiae tuae Ausonensis, bona exponere, sed etiam te ipsum in hoc restaurationis opere pro posse tuo, et alios quoscumque poteris, ad hoc incitare devovisti." It is unclear whether *frater* here refers to Bishop Ramón as an episcopal colleague, a member of the Tarragonese confraternity, or both.

[52] Ordericus Vitalis (n. 22 above) 13 cap. 2 (PL 188.927).

[53] The reason for this vacancy is unclear; note that Abbot Gregory of Cuixà was elected Oleguer's successor at the legatine council of Gerona (26 Nov. 1143) and was confirmed in 1144 by Lucius III, but he died before assuming his office at Tarragona (ES 26.484-488, app. 51;

Pierre de Marca preserves in his *Marca Hispanica* (1688) a short reference to a provincial council at Tarragona under Archbishop Bernard which convened after June 1146; his reference is based on non-extant records from this see's archives.[54] No account effectively relates this council with that of Narbonne in 1129 or the restoration program, but the surviving notice describes this *cofradía's* institution in the exact terms of the aforementioned documents from Ager, especially that the organization was a *symbolus* "which is called a confraternity." This suggests the possibility that a copy of the original *acta* of 1129 survived at Tarragona to which Archbishop Bernard and his suffragans added their subscriptions, just as archbishops Oleguer and Berenguer had signed the earlier foundation charters of the *cofradías* of Gaulter and La Portella. The only new information provided by De Marca is that in 1146 the honorary membership of the confraternity of Tarragona now included Eugenius III and the celebrated abbot of Clairvaux, Saint Bernard.[55] This seems consistent both with Archbishop Bernard's known association with the spread of the Cistercian order into the Crown of Aragón at precisely this time, and with the traditional monastic character of Catalan confraternal organizations and their support of the Reconquista. However, in the scant information we possess lies a conspicuous absence of lay membership in this revived confraternity which is described solely as an organization of "bishops, abbots and other religious men," as well as a lack of participation by the Narbonensian clergy. It seems therefore that the confraternity in 1146 was a mere reflection of that envisioned in 1129 by Oleguer. It too was a temporary creation, this time for financial backing of the crusade against Lérida and Tortosa which were to fall shortly thereafter (1148-1149).[56] In spite of a building program at Tarragona,

---

Mansi [n. 19 above] 21.603-608; VL 13.137). The papal confirmation of 1144 (Kehr [n. 11 above] 320, no. 53; Mansilla [n. 6 above] 87-88, no. 71) remarks how widely acclaimed was the restoration work of archbishops Berenguer and Oleguer: "ad cuius profecto restitutionem predecessores nostri plurimum laborasse noscuntur," here also claiming papal support of the restoration to be well known.

[54] Cf. Marca (n. 34 above) bk. 4; Mansi (n. 19 above) 21.699-702; Philippe Labbé, *Sacrosancta concilia,* ed. P. Cossart (Paris 1671-1672) 10.1819 (rev. ed. N. Coleti [Paris 1759-1779] 12.1639); José Sáenz de Aguirre and G. Catalani, *Collectio maxima conciliorum Hispaniae et novi orbis* (Rome 1693-1694; ed. 2, 1753-1755) 5.61; Hefele and Leclercq (n. 19 above) 5.1.807-808; Gams (n. 7 above) 3.1.196.

[55] See n. 2 above. Note that shortly after this, in 1150-1151, negotiations were under way for the establishment of the White Monks at Poblet just north of the seigniory of Tarragona: cf. G. Gilbert, "La date de fondation du monastère de Poblet," *Cîteaux: Commentarii Cistercienses* 15 (1964) 52-66; Altisent (n. 39 above) 592-599; Jaime Santacana Tort, *El monasterio de Poblet (1151-1181)* (Barcelona 1974); Josep Finestres y de Monsalvo, *Historia del real monasterio de Poblet* (Cervera-Tarragona 1753-1765; repr. Barcelona 1947-1955) 2.45-47. It was Archbishop Bernard who in 1155 joined Prince Robert of Tarragona and Ramón Berenguer IV in donating to the monks of Poblet the grange of Doldellops, and who first extended archiepiscopal protection to this monastery.

[56] According to the Genoese chronicles and Catalan documents of this period, the Catalan-Genoese assault on Almería, Menorca and Ibiza began in August 1146 in accord with Eugenius III's proclamation of a crusade aimed primarily at Tortosa, and already in February 1146 Ramón Berenguer IV had begun the encroachments against the Muslim defenses in the *comarca* of Ciurana. Cf. Bofarull, *Colección* 4 (n. 2 above) nos. 1, 51, 128, 132; Morera (n. 5 above)

especially the construction of the see's impressive cathedral (which was begun in 1171) for which Tarragona's suffragans all contributed, there is no record of the confraternity's survival.[57]

We may conclude, consequently, that unlike other confraternities whose purposes were mainly convivial, charitable and helpful toward salvation, the interface between Islam and Christendom in Catalonia turned those on the frontier into means of consolidating as Christian the areas newly seized from the Muslims. In the absence of an organized church on the Catalan frontier, the brotherhood of Tarragona was founded originally to meet temporary needs related to the post-1126 reconstruction efforts of Archbishop Oleguer, the comital offensive of 1128, and the creation of the Norman principality of Tarragona in 1129. As the reconquest drove south, such *cofradías* tended to evaporate "behind the lines" because, as in the case at Tarragona, their functions were replaced by the diocesan and provincial organizations of the church as the see became firmly established. In retrospect, the confraternity of Tarragona with its elaboration into an "archconfraternity" seems to have been the personal creation of Oleguer Bonestruga; and despite a temporary revival under Archbishop Bernard, the organization died with Oleguer after having accomplished its original objective: financing the defense and full restoration of the primatial see of Tarragona.

College of Library and Information Services
University of Maryland
College Park, Maryland 20742, U.S.A.

1.339-424. Archbishop Bernard had a special interest in the success of the Tortosan venture because this see was placed under Tarragona's direct jurisdiction by papal privileges and this see had yet to be restored (1148-1153).

[57] Sanç Capdevila i Felipe, *La Seu de Tarragona: Notes historiques* (Barcelona 1935) 5-7; cf. Françisc Vicens, *La Catedral de Tarragona* (Barcelona 1970). For the post-restoration church's financial condition, the health of which can be attributed to Oleguer's long-range planning and establishment of an ecclesiastical *señorío,* see L. J. McCrank, "The Fiscal Anatomy of the Post-Restoration Church of Tarragona: An Audit of the *Rationes decimarum Hispaniae* (1279-1280)," *Hispania* (forthcoming). It is curious that although local confraternities continued to flourish, the only two supra-diocesan *confradías* in the Tarraconensis, those of Tarragona and Belchite, disappeared upon the death of Oleguer.

A TWELFTH-CENTURY CONCEPT OF THE NATURAL ORDER

•

by Richard C. Dales

Much of the intellectual history of the modern Western world depends upon its acceptance of a natural order. It is therefore of considerable importance in understanding a major ingredient of our own thought to investigate when and in what form this concept came into being in our culture. A naturalistic view of the universe — indeed the very idea of a cosmos — was part of medieval Europe's legacy from the ancient world. Still, none of the ancient systems of thought was able to view nature as operating without some sort of spiritual mover, without considering it as related to God through an ascending hierarchy of levels of being, or without considering matter itself to be alive. The only exception to this statement I can think of is atomism, the most popular form of which, Epicureanism, by substituting chance for Logos or Nous, virtually rejected the notion of a cosmos.

The crucial break with ancient patterns of thought on this subject was made by the Christian writers, both Greek and Latin, of the fourth and fifth centuries; and scattered statements in the writings of Saints Basil, Gregory of Nyssa, John Damascene, Jerome, and even Augustine, imply at least a de-animation of nature. But these men were for the most part interested in different sorts of things. Even though they considered that nature, as a creature of God, was good, it did not rank high in their order of priorities; and although the patristic writings contained the seeds of the twelfth-century views we are investigating, a new concept of the natural order was not fully and clearly worked out during the patristic period. This would not occur until a higher value was placed on the natural world itself. We must seek the origins of this naturalistic attitude among a relatively small group of Latin writers of the twelfth century.

I hope to establish in this article the fact that the view holding that nature is a self-sufficient, largely mechanical entity was worked out and consciously held by at least some twelfth-century writers, and that there was a progression from the rather confused notions of Adelard of Bath at the beginning of the century to the more

A more general study including the subject of this paper, entitled "Toward a Re-Interpretation of Twelfth-Century Science," was read at the West Coast Lazzaroni meeting at Harvey Mudd College, 20 Oct. 1973. An earlier version of this paper was read at the Conference on Medieval Studies at Western Michigan University, 4 May 1976. I am indebted to Nancy Siraisi, Paul Knoll, Robert Westman, Robert Benson, Amos Funkenstein and John Benton for their helpful suggestions.

developed and precise views of Urso of Calabria and John Blund at the end. I should be very surprised if more such texts do not exist awaiting our notice, but I believe the ones adduced in the article are sufficient to make the point.

I have used the word "naturalistic" to describe this attitude. Unfortunately, the words "nature" and "natural law" appear in the twelfth century with a variety of meanings,[1] often different from the variety of meanings which the same terms have today. Specifically, we are seeking evidence of the view which holds that the physical universe operates in a uniform and rational manner; that it is autonomous and self-sufficient, so that no cause outside it need be invoked to explain its workings; that its operations are largely mechanical; that it is intelligible; and that it is valuable and worth studying in its own right.

In order to maintain a clarity of focus, I have avoided the exceedingly complex question of twelfth-century concepts of nature in general. For this I refer the reader to note 1 above. I hope only to illuminate one small part of a very large topic. A naturalistic viewpoint was certainly not universally, perhaps not even widely, shared by twelfth-century thinkers. Magic and superstition were significant ingredients in the outlook of the time, and one need only glance at Lynn Thorndike's *History of Magic and Experimental Science* to become aware of the magical ideas which were held by the intelligentsia. And the currency of various animistic, emanationist and sacramental views was even greater. But I hope to show that included in the outburst of curiosity and creativity which characterized the early twelfth century were a new interest in the physical world and a new attitude toward it.

Adelard of Bath is often pointed to as the harbinger of a new attitude among Latin Christians,[2] and with good reason. Adelard considered himself a philosopher and as such primarily interested in the way nature works. His often-quoted reply to his "nephew's" contention that all effects should be ascribed immediately to "the wonderful will of God" deserves to be quoted again: "I take nothing away from God," says Adelard, "for whatever exists is from Him and because of Him. But the natural order does not exist confusedly and without rational arrangement, and human reason should be listened to concerning those things it treats of."[3] Although the content of Adelard's "science" is scraped together "confusedly and without rational arrangement" from the traditional authorities, his *Natural Questions* is unified by his insistence that the only standard of truth in philosophy is reason, since nature operates regularly and rationally. He speaks constantly of the excellence of Arabic science and its exclusive reliance on reason, and he cites and praises Aristotle

---

[1] See especially M.-D. Chenu, *Nature, Man, and Society in the Twelfth Century* (Chicago 1968) and Tullio Gregory, *Anima mundi: La philosophia di Guglielmo di Conches e la scuola di Chartres* (Florence 1955) 175-246. On the mechanical aspects of the twelfth-century views of nature, see Chenu 42-45.

[2] See especially A. C. Crombie, *Robert Grosseteste and the Origins of Experimental Science, 1100-1500* (Oxford 1953) 11-12, and Stanley Jaki, *Science and Creation* (New York 1974) 219.

[3] Adelard of Bath, *Die Quaestiones Naturales des Adelardus von Bath*, ed. Martin Müller, Beiträge zur Geschichte der Philosophie und Theologie des Mittelalters 31.2 (Münster i. W. 1934) 8.

as a great philosopher, although at the time he wrote the *Natural Questions* he knew neither the Arabs[4] nor Aristotle's natural philosophy.[5] He was grasping for an embodiment of his own ideal of nature and human reason, and he could not find it in any of his Latin sources. He ransacked the Latin scientific compendia for rational accounts of causality in nature. He denied the efficacy of magic in preventing water from running out of a tube as long as the hole at the top was stopped. And he argued for the intelligent animation of the planets because their motions are not "natural," (that is, they are not uniform and regular, but they sometimes move one way, sometimes another, and sometimes stand still), but do "observe a definite numerical law and constant order" in their motions.

But however much Adelard may have derided magic and lauded reason, he nevertheless retained many vestiges of magic and animism in his thought. His explanation of why the water did not run out of the "vessel of wonderful power" was that the four elements which make up the natural world "are joined together by natural love in such a way that no one of them wishes to exist without the others."[6] Adelard's own statement, intended ironically, is quite near the truth: "If it was magic, it was nature's rather than any power of the water carrier."[7] But his assertion that the planets and stars are living rational beings which give life to things on earth and that the *aplanon* is divine, although allowing for the animation of the heavenly bodies, is nevertheless severely qualified by him: "If the question is about an immortal rational animal, then the *aplanon* must be conceded to be a god. But if it is about the true God, who is the universal cause of all, unimaginable, immutable, infinite, it would be abominable to call the outermost sphere God in that sense."[8] Thus he departs sharply from his Platonic source and is brought up short by the implication that there may be gods other than God.

Adelard then is not a thinker who had achieved a purely naturalistic, rational and mechanistic view of the cosmos. But few people have enunciated so uncompromisingly as he the attitudes which should logically lead to such a view.

Many *hexamera* were composed during the twelfth century, and they were of many different types, illustrating the diversity and vigor of Latin thought during this period. These commentaries on the creation story of Genesis provided an excellent opportunity for the delineation and definition of nature if the author should be inclined to pursue this line of investigation. Two *hexamera* in particular are of interest in this connection, those of Peter Abelard and Thierry of Chartres.

Abelard is best known as a tradition-breaking, free-spirited rationalist, author of

---

[4] See the extremely full discussion of this in Brian Lawn, *The Salernitan Questions* (Oxford 1963) 20-25, and Theodore Silverstein, "How Arabic Science Reached the West in the Earlier Twelfth Century," *Atti della Accademia nazionale dei Lincei* (1972) 369, 285-286.

[5] In his edition of the *Natural Questions* (n. 3 above), Müller could not identify either of Adelard's citations of Aristotle, although, as Silverstein has pointed out (n. 4 above) 286, they go back to an Aristotelian source through unidentified intermediaries.

[6] Adelard (n. 3 above) 54.

[7] *Ibid.* 54.

[8] *Ibid.* 68.

Sic et non,[9] brilliant logician, inventor of novel heresies on the Trinity, and as ill-fated lover of Heloise and author of the *Historia calamitatum.*[10] But compared to similar works of some of his contemporaries, his *Hexameron*[11] is surprisingly conservative, being based largely on Augustine, and to a lesser extent on Jerome, Ambrose and Bede. To Abelard, the creation of heaven and earth means not the creation of the corporeal and incorporeal, but rather of the four elements. He does not present a carefully worked out scheme of how and why creation proceeded from this instant onward, nor is he dogmatic about whether things proceed naturally from this point on, or whether God was the continuing efficient cause throughout the process (*Formator* as well as *Creator*), although he leans toward the latter view. The six days are not to be considered as six periods of twenty-four hours, or any particular length of time, but rather as distinctions of God's works in bringing about the world. "Evening" means the creation of things in God's mind (that is, the Word), and "morning" refers to the bringing to light of God's intention through His works. The first day contains all of creation potentially. Plato's intelligible world, he said, is "the very same Reason by which God made the world."[12] But this Reason had to be completed (or perfected) in work. It was first hidden in the mind of God and "afterwards emerged through the produced work toward light."[13] And so, despite the emanationist tendencies of his sources in this place, Abelard posits an absolute beginning, a creation by God in which He first planned rationally in His own Mind what He was going to do, and then without any intermediaries He did it. The fullest reality of the created world then is in its concrete existence, not in the Divine Mind.

In his discussion of how some of the waters got above the firmament and why they stay there, Abelard takes issue with some unnamed contemporary (probably Thierry of Chartres) on the necessity of providing a naturalistic explanation for all the details of creation, and in the process he defines very clearly what he means by "nature" and what he considers to be the relationship of the natural world to God:

> Although we now seek out or assign a power of nature, or natural causes, in certain effects of things, we should in no way do the same with regard to that prior work of God in forming the world, when God's will alone had the efficacy of nature in creating or arranging those things. [We ought to assign natural causes] only after those things were completed in six days by God's work. From then on, we are accustomed to give consideration to the force of nature; that is, when these [natural] things have already been thus made ready so that their nature or preparation

[9] This work has recently been edited by Blanche B. Boyer and Richard McKeon, *Peter Abailard Sic et non* (Chicago 1975).

[10] See John F. Benton, "Fraud, Fiction and Borrowing in the Correspondence of Abelard and Heloise," *Pierre Abélard-Pierre le Vénérable*, Colloques internationaux du Centre national de la recherche scientifique 546 (Paris 1975) 471-511.

[11] An edition is being prepared by Mary F. Romig. All references to Abelard's *Hexameron* in this article are to PL 178.732-784.

[12] *Ibid.* 738.

[13] *Ibid.* 740.

might be sufficient to do anything at all without miracles. Whence, we acknowledge those things which are done through miracles to be done rather against or above nature than according to nature, since the prior preparation of things could never suffice for bringing them [that is, miraculous events] about unless God should confer a certain new power upon those very things, just as He also did during those six days when His will alone had the force of nature. . . . If indeed He should now act as He did then, we should assuredly say that these things were being done against nature, just as if the earth should produce plants spontaneously without any seed.[14] . . . Therefore, we call nature the power of things conferred upon them at the beginning which prepared them henceforth to give rise to anything, that is, sufficient to bring it about.[15]

We should note especially two groups of words in the above quotation. First is the "then" and "now" distinction. "Then," that is, during the six days of creation, God's will alone had the force of nature; but "now," that is, after the work of the six days was completed, nature operates by itself. This is emphasized by the second group of words: "praeparatio" — things were "made ready" at the beginning "to bring about their effects" — "ad aliquid nascendum [vel] efficiendum;" "ad quoscumque effectus inde processuros vel tanquam nascituros" — by being given a "vim sufficientem" — sufficient power to cause these effects. Thus the world of nature exists solely by God's creative act, and it has its properties solely because God bestowed them; but God saw to it that nature should have sufficient power to bring about its effects.

The *De sex dierum operibus* of Thierry of Chartres[16] is a startlingly daring and

---

[14] This may be a dig at Thierry, who considered that living beings came about *naturally* without seed through the operation of the vital heat on the appropriate mixture of the elements.

[15] "Ad quod primum respondeo nullatenus nos modo, cum in aliquibus rerum effectis vim naturae vel causas naturales requirimus vel assignamus, id nos facere secundum illam priorem Dei operationem in constitutione mundi, ubi sola Dei voluntas naturae efficiam habuit in illis tunc creandis vel disponendis, sed tantum ab illa operatione Dei sex diebus illa completa. Deinceps vim natura pensare solemus, tunc videlicet rebus ipsis iam ita praeparatis, ut ad quaelibet sine miraculis facienda illa eorum constitutio vel praeparatio sufficeret. Unde illa quae per miracula fiunt magis contra vel supra naturam quam secundum naturam fieri fatemur, cum ad illud scilicet faciendum nequaquam illa rerum praeparatio prior sufficere possit, nisi quandam vim novam rebus ipsis Deus conferret, sicut et in illis sex diebus faciebat, ubi sola eius voluntas vim naturae obtinebat in singulis efficiendis. Quae quidem si nunc quoque sicut tunc faceret, profecto contra naturam haec fieri diceremus: veluti si terra sponte sua sine seminario aliquo plantas produceret . . . . Naturam itaque dicimus vim rerum ex illa prima praeparatione illis collatam ad aliquid inde nascendum, hoc est efficiendum sufficientem"; PL 178.749.

Slightly later he says: "Sed sicut iam supra meminimus in illis operibus sex priorum dierum sola Dei voluntas vim naturae obtinuit, quando ipsa etiam natura creabatur, hoc est vis quaedam conferebatur illis rebus quae tunc fiebant. Unde ipsa post modum ad multiplicationem sui sufficeret vel ad quoscunque effectus inde processuros vel tanquam nascituros"; PL 178-749.

[16] The latest and best edition, which also gives references to all earlier editions, is by Nikolaus M. Häring, S.A.C., *Commentaries on Boethius by Thierry of Chartres and his School* (Toronto 1971) 555-575. All subsequent references to this work will be to chapters in Häring's edition, placed in parentheses after the quotation.

original work. His opening words, in which he states his intention "to explain the first part of Genesis literally and according to natural philosophy" were traditional enough; it was Thierry's understanding of the literal meaning which constituted his novelty.

He begins by adopting Aristotle's four causes as the framework for his discussion: the efficient cause is God; the formal cause is God's Wisdom (that is, the Son); the final cause is God's kindness or good will (*benignitas*, that is, the Holy Spirit); and the material cause is the four elements. "From these four causes," he says, "all corporeal substances have their subsistence" (3). Concerning the apparent contradiction between the scriptural texts: "Qui vivit in eternum creavit omnia simul" (Eccli. 18.1), and "sex diebus operatus est Dominus" (Exod. 20.11), Thierry says that the former refers to primordial matter, the latter to the distinction of forms. Primordial matter contained the four elements in a confused state in which each had some of the characteristics of the others; it did not precede the fully differentiated elements temporally, but only according to reason, as confusion naturally precedes articulation. By the term "heaven," Moses meant fire and air, and by the term "earth" he meant earth and water.

Once this initial creation of "heaven and earth" had been accomplished by God, according to His Wisdom and because of His good-heartedness, everything else occurred naturally. At this point fire, rather than God, becomes, "as it were, the artisan and efficient cause." "For fire only acts, and earth is only acted upon; the two elements in the middle both act and are acted upon," and they "act as an administrator or vehicle of the power of fire toward the other elements" (17). His universe was an interdependent unity; "concord had been perfectly assigned to each of the elements, both with respect to its own properties and in relation to all the others" (16). Thierry asserts that swiftness and slowness cannot exist apart from each other, because each depends upon the other. The rapid motion of light bodies surrounds and compresses slower bodies and makes them corpulent and solid. Reciprocally, fast-moving bodies must have something solid to "lean on." To illustrate this, he points out that a man, in walking, must push against unyielding earth, a finger cannot move without pressing against the palm, a stone cannot be thrown unless the thrower is supported by something solid (19, 20). Similarly, circular motion "leans against" an immobile center (20). Therefore, the motion of fire and air cannot exist without a center against which to lean. "That center is solid and bound round by motion. Therefore, their motion cannot exist unless it leans against some solid object" (21).

And finally, Thierry seems to assert that even the apparently miraculous has a natural explanation: "We affirm that, in one of the aforesaid ways and from the originating causes which He bestowed on the elements in the space of six days, He produced whatever He created and still creates" (16).

Probably about the middle of the century, a philosopher named Marius, working in a center where both Latin Neoplatonic works and Arabic materials were available, wrote an extensive work on the elements,[17] devoting the first half to the simple elements and the second to their interaction. Marius posits a beginning, a creation by God of prime matter, totally devoid of qualities, which God then differentiated into the four elements through pairs of elementary qualities and set in motion. Creation ceased at this point, and everything else occurred naturally through the mechanical interaction of the four elements.

Marius's work is remarkable in several ways. First is his utterly materialistic attitude toward nature. Growth, or any increase in volume, is possible only by the addition of increments of matter to a thing.[18] Qualities (since they have no independent existence) cannot act on bodies; only other bodies can.[19]

Secondly, he explicitly raises the question of the animation of the elements or qualities and rejects it. In one place he had said to his student that in winter heat recedes to the interior of the earth as if fleeing from its contrary, and that "every contrary tries to destroy its contrary." The student asks how one quality can so abhor another that it seeks to destroy it, "since a quality has no discretion, nor does it know what it ought to do?" Marius explains that this is just a manner of speaking, as when we say "that when sleep approaches, a man ceases to be awake, and the other way around." "Thus," he says, "it should be understood about heat and cold, moisture and dryness."[20] This is completely consistent with his treatment of the impossibility of empty space: after showing by experiments that two bodies cannot occupy the same place, he simply asserts that "you cannot empty a place of a given body without another body's immediately entering it."[21] There is no recourse to the love binding the elements together which we noted in Adelard.

Third is the lack of any magical attitudes in Marius's work, despite their plentiful presence in many of his sources. He may have used the Hermetic *De secretis naturae*[22] or, if not, some work very similar to it, which abounds in magical gem lore; still, Marius's treatment of gem formation is wholly naturalistic, holding that all stones are formed by nature by heat enclosed in the earth's interior.[23] And in his treatment of metals, although he used several alchemical works, he asserts that, like gems, metals are formed by the earth's heat operating on various kinds of sulphur and mercury. They differ from each other because of variation in the purity and proportions of the sulphur and mercury and in the intensity and duration of the heat to which they are subjected in the earth's interior.[24] He also denies that species can

---

[17] *Marius On the Elements: A Critical Edition and Translation*, ed. and trans. Richard C. Dales (Berkeley 1976). A preliminary study is Richard C. Dales, "Marius 'On the Elements' and the Twelfth-Century Science of Matter," *Viator* 3 (1972) 191-218.

[18] "Nullum corpus augmentatur nisi sibi aliud adiciatur"; Marius (n. 17 above) 103.

[19] "Qualitas enim nichil operatur, sed opera sunt quod qualitati subicitur"; *ibid*. 141.

[20] *Ibid*. 138-141.

[21] *Ibid*. 103.

[22] Paris, Bibliothèque Nationale, MS lat. 13951, fols. 1-31. See also Lawn (n. 4 above) 73.

[23] Marius (n. 17 above) 141.

[24] *Ibid*. 153-155.

be altered; only qualities can.[25]   And in his discussion of first matter, although one of his principal sources was "Ibn Ḥasdāy's Neoplatonist,"[26] he purges it of its magical and emanationist characteristics and presents a naturalistic account.[27]

Other aspects of Marius's work to which we must call attention are its thorough-going experimental approach, its preoccupation with process, and its attempt to provide a quantified scheme of chemical combinations.

Marius's outlook was similar to that of Abelard and Thierry, neither of whom could really comprehend (or at least sustain for long an understanding of) Augustine's teaching on the first creation, in that his mechanistic and naturalistic viewpoint significantly altered the meaning of his sources. It is certain that he used at least Calcidius, Macrobius, Eriugena, several of the translations, including the *Pantegni*, of Constantine the African, the now-lost Ibn Hasday's Neoplatonist, Algazel's *Meta-physics*, and Isaac Israeli's *De dietis* (and very probably some other Arabic works that I have not been able to discover). It is remarkable to what extent he ignored the magic and emanationism which many of these contain.

An anonymous south Italian physicist, no later than 1170, wrote a treatise on the elements[28] which depends heavily on Boethius and Calcidius, and to a lesser extent on Macrobius, Aristotle, Lucan and Virgil, but whose principal inspiration was the *Hexameron* of Thierry of Chartres. Still, it differs from this last-named work in several important respects. First, it is not tied to the scriptural text and can therefore avoid some of the inconveniences contained in the Genesis account of creation. Secondly, it is more restricted in its scope, being purely an essay on natural philosophy. The author makes this clear in a rather extensive introduction, in which, after saying what philosophy is, what its divisions are, what function it performs, and what its final purpose is, he arrives at his chosen topic, which is *physica*. "Physics," he tells us, quoting Aristotle's *Physics* 2.1 (192b), "is the natural motion of any element *ex se*, as fire has upward movement, heat and gleaming *ex se*. How and through what means these qualities of the elements work other effects in things is called physics. Now we shall tell how the qualities of the elements operate in the elements themselves or in other bodies by composition and resolution" (*Prooemium*, 51-57).

The entire ensuing treatise is strictly controlled by this definition. The author begins the treatise proper by repeating the Aristotelian definition of *physis* and asserting that the elements clearly qualify as natural bodies. He next establishes the qualities of the elements, borrowing much from Thierry but making some radical departures of his own. In the first place, he says that the elements are eternal, and he

---

[25] *Ibid*. 177.

[26] This work is lost but has been partially reconstructed by Alexander Altmann in A. Altmann and S. M. Stern, *Isaac Israeli* (Oxford 1958) Scripta Judaica 1.98-105. Marius cites it as Aristotle *On the Elements*. Amos Funkenstein has pointed out to me the similarity between this and the doctrine of Ibn Ezra.

[27] Marius (n. 17 above)

[28] Latin text in Richard C. Dales, "Anonymi *De elementis*: From a Twelfth-Century Collection of Scientific Works in British Museum MS Cotton Galba E. IV," *Isis* 56 (1965) 174-189.

quotes Thierry's statement that "unity precedes all otherness, and therefore also all mutability"[29] among his arguments. Borrowing from Plato[30] the notion that it is motion descending eternally from the Craftsman which creates the elements, he describes the construction of the world. First came the two extreme elements, fire and earth, fire resulting from swiftness, earth from slowness; then the two middle elements, water and air. The elements consist of tiny particles, or atoms, and swiftness or slowness of motion refer to the movements of the atoms, not to those of the elements as a whole. Two other important ideas are borrowed from Thierry: that the two higher elements act as the Artisan, while the two lower are acted upon, like matter; and that heaviness and lightness are mutually necessary, for the light (swift) elements make the heavy (slow) ones by compressing them, while the heavy ones provide a stable center against which the light ones lean. (He also borrows Thierry's example of a man's foot pushing against the earth.) The author then derives all the qualities of each of the elements from their proper motion and in the second section of his treatise rigorously applies his principles in explaining a number of meteorological phenomena and sense perception.

Although the author says in his *Prooemium* that the notions of all things (that is, the ten Aristotelian categories) exist eternally in the Divine Mind, he does not return to this idea nor does he integrate it into the rest of his treatise. In spite of what appears to be a retreat from the creationist position in positing the eternity of the elements and considering God as the continuing source of the world's motion ("Origo elementorum est motus, qui motus est ab eterno" [1.6]), his statement is perhaps not so radical as it sounds, and it is possible that we should understand "ab eterno" as "from that which is eternal." Anonymous was using Thierry's *Lectiones in Boethii librum de Trinitate* in this place, and Thierry's words throw some light on his meaning: "But mutability descends from immutability. Matter is mutability. Nevertheless, it is itself between something and nothing, as is said in Plato. From this, the error is clear of those who have said that matter is coeternal with God, for it descends from God, and God created it; that is, He is its cause and principle. Therefore it is clear that the eternal simplicity which is God is without matter."[31] Still, Anonymous is more extreme than Thierry, and there remains some ambiguity as to his exact meaning. Thierry's words are an excellent example of how a creationist standpoint can alter the understanding of a Platonic text. In any case, Anonymous maintains the self-sufficiency of the world of nature by following Thierry's lead concerning the role of fire (and to a lesser extent of air) in acting as the Artisan (that is, efficient and formal causes). The rigor and the detail with which he deduces both the qualities of the elements and the interaction of the elements in

[29] *De sex dierum operibus* 30; ed. Häring (n. 16 above) 568.

[30] *Timaeus*, 52E; *Timaeus a Calcidio translatus commentarioque instructus*, ed. J. H. Waszink (London 1962) 51.

[31] "Sed ab immutabilitate descendit mutabilitas. Materia vero est mutabilitas. Ipsa tamen inter aliquid et nihil est, sicut in Platone dicitur. Unde patet error eorum qui dixerunt quod materia coeterna esset deo. Ipsa enim a deo descendit et deus eam creavit, i.e., eius causa et principium est. Patet igitur simplicitas eterna que deus est esse sine materia"; ed. Häring (n. 16 above) 163.

observed phenomena from his first principle (that is, that motion makes the elements) are clear advances over Thierry's treatment, and the resulting view of nature is more completely mechanistic.

It is likely that the anonymous author of *De elementis* was a southern Italian, although he cannot be more precisely identified, and it is clear that he was also intimately familiar with the works of Thierry of Chartres. A more ambitious result of the interaction of northern French and southern Italian intellectual currents is the *De commixtionibus elementorum* of Urso of Calabria,[32] the major work of the most renowned teacher of Europe's leading medical school in the late twelfth and early thirteenth centuries. Most of Urso's sources were those common to the Salernitan milieu – Alphanus's *Premnon physicon*, Constantine's *Pantegni*, Plato's *Timaeus* with Calcidius's commentary, Martianus Capella's *De nuptiis*, and fragments of Galen and Aristotle – but they also included William of Conches's *Dragmaticon*, from which he borrowed the distinction between the elements themselves and the *elementata*.[33]

Urso was no theologian, and there are several unbridged gaps between his Platonic source and his own thought. He begins his account of the physical world, following Plato-Calcidius, saying that the principle of all corporeal things is threefold: the Craftsman, matter and form. "The Craftsman was the effective extrinsic principle, without motion, from which things receive their origin causally; matter was the intrinsic principle, with motion, from which things derive their being simply and indeterminately; form was the formal principle, from which specified being was bestowed on things."[34]

But Urso then confuses matters by saying that "in the beginning God created from nothing a certain crude and primary matter, the source of all bodies, which the philosophers have called silva or hyle."[35] He follows Calcidius quite closely in his description of hyle, emphasizing its pure potency, its status between something and nothing, its lack of contrariety or anything that would enable it to generate the corporeal world by itself. Form is given it "by the command of [God's] creative power."[36] Hyle is then "clothed, as it were, by the utterly simple application of substantial and accidental forms, coming from without." This enabled it to pass "from potency to act into those simple, sensual and discrete things, upon which by His power alone it depended, namely the four elements, which were composite in

[32] *Urso von Salerno: De commixtionibus elementorum libellus*, ed. Wolfgang Stürner (Stuttgart 1976).

[33] Since the pure elements never actually exist but are always mixed together, the simplest actually existing constituents of bodies are the primary mixtures, or *elementata*. See Theodore Silverstein, "Elementatum: Its Appearance among the Twelfth-Century Cosmogonists," *Mediaeval Studies* 16 (1954) 156-162.

[34] "Opifex effectivum principium extrinsecus sine motu, a quo suam res causaliter traxere originem, materia intrinsecus fuit principium et cum motu, a quo res contrahunt simpliciter esse et indeterminate. Forma formale fuit principium, ex quo rebus specificatum esse est indutum"; Urso (n. 32 above) 39.

[35] "In principio enim creavit deus ex nichilo quandam rudem et primeriam materiam omnium corporum genitricem, quam silvam vel ylem appellaverunt philosophi"; *ibid*. 39-40.

[36] "Sue potestatis creantis imperio . . ."; *ibid*. 43.

that they were bodies and had quantity, quality, place and time, but were simple in that they had an identity of all their parts."[37]

Urso's scheme of the elements is quite complicated. The elements never existed in their pure state (that is, possessing identity of parts) but immediately mixed with each other, bringing into being the *elementata*, which they preceded only by nature, not temporally.[38] Each element has one essential and several accidental qualities. Fire is substantially hot; accidentally it is dry, light, mobile, subtle, sharp, rare, pure, bright, attractive, dissolutive, penetrating, burning, red, and has upward movement (*de centro*). Air is substantially wet; accidentally it is hot, light, mobile, subtle, obtuse, warming (*fovens*), mild (*lene*), nourishing, rare, blue (*indi coloris*), and has upward movement. Water is substantially cold; accidentally it is wet, heavy, mobile, obtuse, soft, liquid, flowing, thick, white, and has downward movement (*ad centrum*). Earth is substantially dry; accidentally it is cold, heavy, immobile, dense, obtuse, dark, rough, hard, attractive, constrictive, black, and has downward movement.[39] The *elementata* are divided into four main groups named after the element predominating in each mixture, and the main groups are subsequently subdivided into three species each, the higher, middle and lower of each kind. Everything else happens as a result of the interaction of the elements: "Ex quibus, elementata alia plura et varia generata sunt per varium elementorum commixtionis modum secundum quod de uno elemento magis vel minus vel tantundem quam de suo contrario venit in commixtione."[40] From this point on, the word "form" is taken to mean "commixtio elementorum unde proveniret in rebus tam multiplex genus et dissonum."[41] And, just as the *elementata* draw their being from the elements themselves with respect to their substance, so from the innate properties of the elements they have their specified being with respect to form.[42]

The remainder of the book is a naturalistic and materialistic account of the physical world seen as the interaction of the elements and their properties. It treats the effects of the elements, the operations of the natural powers, different kinds of mixtures of the elements, and the effects caused by the different mixtures. Urso is much more thorough and subtle than either Marius or the anonymous author of *De elementis*, but his attitude toward the natural world is the same.

Let us end our inquiry, as we began it, with an English scholar, this time John

---

[37] "Quasi simplicissima advenientium substantialem accidentialiumque applicatione formarum induta in ea simpla, sensualia et discreta actu prodiit, quibus sola potestate innitebatur, scilicet in quatuor elementa, que cum essent corpora, erant quanta, qualia, localia, temporalia composita; simpla, partium omnium habentia identitatem"; *ibid.* 43-44. I am indebted to my colleague, David Wiesen, for helping me make sense of the very difficult passage of which the above quotation is a part.

[38] "Elementa . . . natura precessissent elementata, non tamen tempore"; *ibid.* 44.

[39] *Ibid.* 54.

[40] *Ibid.* 46.

[41] *Ibid.* 49.

[42] "Sicut autem ex ipsis elementis elementata suum esse contrahunt secundum substantiam, ita ex qualitatibus ab ipsis proprietatibus elementorum innatis habent specificatum esse secundum formam"; *ibid.* 50.

Blund, and with the same question we discussed in connection with Adelard, namely the intelligent animation of the heavenly bodies. This particular issue provides a good gauge of the shift in attitude during the century that elapsed between Adelard and Blund, both of whom may be considered representatives of the *avant garde* of their days, because the celestial spheres were the part of the natural order most resistant to being de-animated, and an impressive array of authorities, including Plato, Aristotle, Avicenna and Averroes, had held that they were ensouled.

John Blund, an English master who studied and taught at Oxford and Paris from about 1200 to 1232 (d. 1248), was a scholar of considerable importance in his day; but only one work from his pen survives, a *Tractatus de anima*,[43] which he composed during the early years of the thirteenth century. In this work he defines a soul as a thing, whatever it may be, which moves a body in a manner other than what would result from the nature of the body itself, and he then discusses the question of whether the motions of the heavens are natural or voluntary. He is fully aware of his departure from the great *auctores*, and he states the prevailing view with precision:

> There are many who say that the higher bodies are moved by a soul, saying that they have this on the authority of Avicenna and others. They say that from the intelligence's knowing itself, insofar as this is possible, the soul of the heaven and the perfection of the heaven flows into it. This soul apprehends the First Cause, which is the Highest Good, by imagination, and by a motion aflame with great desire it is moved to acquire for itself that which is the Highest Good, and thus it is moved by the First Cause as a lover is moved by its beloved. For, as Algazel and Avicenna say, as a beloved moves its lover, and as desire for knowledge of a question moves a student and inclines him to acquire it, thus Pure Goodness, most greatly desired and imagined by the soul of heaven, moves the soul of the heaven to acquire that Pure Goodness for itself, so that it might enjoy it and be assimilated to it.[44]

But in his *solutio* to the question, Blund is explicit: "We say that the firmament and other heavenly bodies are moved by nature, not by a soul. For lower bodies are ruled by the motions of higher bodies, and when the lower ones are completely perfected the higher ones will cease from motion, and a natural rest will exist in them.[45]

Blund's world view is greatly influenced by that of Aristotle, but there is a crucial difference. That difference has to do with the distance between God and the world and is expressed by Blund's denial of the animation of the heavenly spheres. He accepts the Aristotelian view that the motion of the heavens exists for the sake of the perfection of the lower world, and he says that when that perfection is accomplished the heavens will rest. But their motion is part of their nature — in fact it is the

---

[43] *Johannes Blund Tractatus de anima*, ed. D. A. Callus and R. W. Hunt, Auctores britannici medii aevi 2 (London 1970).

[44] Blund 13.

[45] *Ibid.* 10.

essence of their nature. The forms of the heavenly bodies are totally immanent in matter and are not connected through a hierarchy of intelligences to God Himself, as they were in both Neoplatonic and Aristotelian thought. The Ideas may have existed in the Divine Mind (I know of no twelfth-century author who denies this), and they are the Thoughts according to which God created the world, but they are not ontologically connected with the forms that operate in nature. These latter are as contingent and as natural as the matter they determine and move.

Throughout these twelfth-century writings on nature, one is aware of the constant interaction between the basically Neoplatonic sources – especially Boethius, Augustine, Calcidius and Eriugena – used by most of the Latin writers, with their emphasis on emanation and the immanence of God in the world, along with the considerable degree of animism they permit, and the transcendent-creationist tradition of Christian thought. Although their language sometimes has an emanationist tinge, the thought of all the writers we have investigated was dominated by an awareness of the gulf between Creator and creature. Nature to them was a regular system of behaviors, but unlike the ancient Greek view it was not made up of self-regulating quasi-divine forces. It was created out of nothing and given its characteristics by its Creator. These characteristics contained everything that was necessary for its operation, so that it was a self-sufficient system. It was good because it was created by a good God out of His love. It exhibited rationality because its Creator was rational. But it was a system of mechanisms, not of intelligences, angels, demons and magical powers. Thus these Latin authors could read Arabic and Greek works of the most diverse types but strip them of their animistic and magical qualities as they pillaged them. This process was facilitated by the ambiguity and inconsistency in the use of terms in these sources.

Stanley Jaki, in a recent book, has claimed that "science owes its only viable birth to a faith, according to which the world is a created entity, that is contingent in every respect of its existence on the creative act of God, and that its existence has an absolute origin in time, majestically called 'in the beginning.' "[46] Jaki undoubtedly claims too much. Certainly there was no necessary causal relationship between Judeo-Christian creationism and the view of nature we are studying: even such a thinker as William of Conches, similar as he was in many ways to Thierry of Chartres, did not arrive at it; the most popular works among the twelfth-century translations were replete with magic and animism; and throughout the thirteenth century a certain amount of animism was general in the theory of matter, and most thinkers accepted the intelligences or angels as movers of the heavenly spheres. Our claim, somewhat more modest than Jaki's, is that, during the twelfth century in Latin Europe, those aspects of Judeo-Christian thought which emphasized the idea of creation out of nothing and the distance between God and the world, in certain contexts and with certain men, had the effect of eliminating all semi-divine entities from the realm of nature. Thus nature tended to become a mechanistic entity,

---

[46] Jaki (n. 2 above) 356.

running according to the characteristics with which it had been endowed and powered by the forces which it had been given "in the beginning." This view has the ironic consequence that, for the most part, God can be eliminated from scientific considerations, and nature can be considered strictly in terms of itself. Thus the basis for the modern atheistic view of nature was laid in the twelfth century.

By 1200, much remained to be done before the modern concept could emerge full-fledged. During the twelfth and thirteenth centuries, this view of nature would undergo assaults from Arabic superstition, Neoplatonic emanationism, Manichean contempt for the world, the Augustinian view that God is the only efficient cause of every effect, and a revived Greek animism in the form of Aristotelianism. But it survived all of these.[47] The writers of the twelfth century provided the basic ingredient of the scientific outlook of the modern world: they made clear what kind of thing it was that a natural philosopher investigated.

Department of History
University of Southern California
Los Angeles, California 90007, U.S.A.

[47] I am aware that I have not demonstrated this. I am currently working on a study of the de-animation of the heavens in the thirteenth and fourteenth centuries, and I hope ultimately to be able to document the continuity between twelfth-century thought and that of the early modern period.

THE PERFORMING SELF IN TWELFTH-CENTURY CULTURE

•

by Martin Stevens

In recent times, critics have used the term "performing self" as a way of identifying the artist whose work is centrally concerned with the act of his own creation. Using as his principal models the works of Frost, Hemingway, and Mailer, Richard Poirier in the title essay of his book *The Performing Self* observes that all three of these writers "treat any occasion as a 'scene' or a stage for dramatizing the self as performer," that for each "performance is an exercise of Power," which "presumes to compete with reality itself for control of the minds exposed to it."[1] In essence, Poirier sees the performing self as struggling with "language and literary shape" to gain self-awareness, the writer as realizing all along that *he* is "part of what needs to be clarified."[2] Although Poirier never directly claims that the performing self is exclusively a mode of the modern consciousness, he does imply that the stance of self performance and self creation is one of the hallmarks of contemporary technique. His context is American literature and his historical range extends back to Herman Melville, though he occasionally alludes as well to poets of the seventeenth century, notably Andrew Marvell. Disregarding the political implications that Poirier sees in the performing self, I would like to suggest that this figure is, in fact, not at all the creation of our time but that it already existed in the Middle Ages and particularly that its use is associated with the Renaissance of the Twelfth Century. I hope to demonstrate that, indeed, the performing self is one of the most important stylistic innovations of that fruitful time in the art of narration both in literature and in the visual arts. It is to these roots that we can eventually trace such noted performing selves as the created first-person characters of Gottfried, Dante, Chaucer, and even Rembrandt.

I

It is important at the outset of this paper to distinguish between the first-person narrator-persona and what I am calling the performing self. The term "persona" has

[1] Richard Poirier, *The Performing Self* (New York 1971) 86-87.
[2] *Ibid.* 11.

for some time been in vogue among literary critics to describe "the fallible first person singular"[3] who serves as storyteller and who is what Leo Spitzer has called the poetic and empirical "I" in medieval authors.[4] The Pilgrim Dante or the Pilgrim Chaucer are good examples of the type from the Middle Ages, while Lemuel Gulliver can serve as an example from a later time. The problem with the use of "persona" as a descriptive term for these literary characters is that it suggests fully-drawn characters who have an existence outside of and almost independent from their literary creators. Historically, a persona was first a mask used by a player, a term that eventually became generalized to refer to the character behind the mask. This metonymic usage of the term still occurs in the phrase *dramatis personae,* which of course singles out the people in a play as sentient beings who, for the time of the play — at least in an age of realism — have an existence of their own. For those who deny the applicability of the canons of realism to Chaucer or other writers of the Middle Ages,[5] this usage, whether it be *dramatis personae*[6] or just "persona," is objectionable. While, as I have said elsewhere, it may have been necessary for a time to separate the Poet Chaucer from the literary persona known as the Pilgrim Chaucer because critics like John M. Manly wanted to make real historical personages out of the Canterbury Pilgrims,[7] I believe we have now reached the point where the two — that is, the Poet and the Pilgrim — have achieved separate identities, and that way of seeing them is surely as wrong as the one that the persona was invented to correct.[8] The point is that neither the Pilgrim Dante nor the Pilgrim Chaucer are autonomous, free-standing figures. Yet sometimes I feel that criticism has moved to the position in which any views we may wish to form of the poet are invalid if they are based on what we learn from his persona. It is in such a situation that the term persona becomes a hindrance rather than an aid, for we do learn much about Dante and Chaucer as well as other artists from their fictional spokesmen. The fact remains that our biographical information, especially about a medieval artist's character (and, after all, that is what we are really interested in), usually rests not upon historical records but precisely on what he tells us about himself in his role as performer.[9] I would like, therefore, to suggest that we use the term "performing self" as a replacement for persona. What we witness in all medieval works of art containing a self-representation of the artist is a facet of the man as performer of his craft. He plays a role much of the time but he is also himself, since he is poet and actor or

---

[3] See, for example, E. Talbot Donaldson, "Chaucer the Pilgrim," *PMLA* 69 (1954); repr. in *Chaucer Criticism* 1, ed. Richard Schoeck and Jerome Taylor (Notre Dame 1960) 9.

[4] Leo Spitzer, "Note on the Poetic and Empirical 'I' in Medieval Authors," *Traditio* 4 (1946) 414-422.

[5] See Martin Stevens, "Chaucer and Modernism: An Essay in Criticism," in *Chaucer at Albany,* ed. R. H. Robbins (New York 1975) 193-216.

[6] G. L. Kittredge considered the pilgrims in the *Canterbury Tales* "dramatis personae"; see *Chaucer and his Poetry* (Cambridge, Mass. 1915) 155.

[7] See John M. Manly, *Chapters on Chaucer* (New York 1926).

[8] See Stevens (n. 5 above) 210-212.

[9] Donald Howard makes this point in his valuable discussion of "Chaucer, the Man," *PMLA* 80 (1965), repr. in A. C. Cawley's *Chaucer's Mind and Art* (Edinburgh 1969) 31-45.

painter and subject at once. In this respect, the term "performing self" is an especially apt way of speaking about the medieval artist, for he was, indeed, a performer or craftsman, and his immediate role before a living audience can never be totally separated from his less intimate relationship with the general reader. When William IX of Aquitaine begins one of his lyrics by addressing his companions, and exclaims,

> Farai un vers de dreyt nien:
> non er de mi ni d'autra gen
> (I will make a verse of exactly nothing:
> there'll be nothing in it about me or anyone else)[10]

we know instantly that the poem is concerned with the dialectic between performance and text. It must be read, first of all, as an address to those companions, as a performance in self-profession. Our reading is conditioned by our understanding of that performance; there is added humor in our perception that the poem is indeed very much about William and that his primary audience knows that fact.

An additional word must be said about the relationship of the medieval and the modern performing self. I disagree with Leo Spitzer's view on the matter, namely, "that in the Middle Ages, the 'poetic I' had more freedom and more breadth than it has today . . . [because it] dealt not with the individual but with mankind."[11] To the contrary, when the so-called poetic "I" is a performing self, it is invariably concerned with the individual, and it very much resembles the modern personae of such writers as Norman Mailer and Vladimir Nabokov. I would insist that it is precisely in the artist's struggle as performing self with "language and literary shape," to borrow Poirier's phrase once more, that we find a close artistic affinity between the medieval and modern periods. I wish, therfore, to suggest that the first-person figure of the artist who emerges in the autobiographical and prefatory writings of early twelfth-century authors and who later inhabits such widely divergent works of art as romances, chronicles, lyrics, plays, manuscript illuminations, sketches, sculptures, and portraits is the beginning of an important new artistic vantage point. I should emphasize that I do not claim the performing self as an invention of the twelfth century; a more primitive type certainly existed earlier, and the first person voice of classical literature surely helped give rise to the figure. What I am claiming is that the figure gains a fully-realized identity in the twelfth century, and that the mode of the artist speaking *qua* artist is a signal departure in the literature and art of Western civilization.

Before looking more closely at the rise of the performing self in the twelfth century, I would like briefly to examine two illustrations of the type from later periods of medieval literature to demonstrate their artistic function. First let us take Gottfried von Strassburg as we encounter him in the *Tristan*. What we realize right

---

[10] Frederick Golden, ed., *Lyrics of the Troubadours and Trouveres* (Garden City, N. Y. 1973) 24-25.

[11] Spitzer (n. 4 above) 415.

from the start is that Gottfried is the central character of his own fiction, and Tristan, the hero as artist (or poet of love) as W. T. H. Jackson has so perceptively shown,[12] becomes a surrogate for his creator. At various crucial moments in the narrative, Gottfried interposes comments of his own (usually misnamed "digressions" by the critics) which focus on the craft of writing or on his own limitations as observer and commentator. Take, for example, the passage describing Tristan's investiture, a point at which Gottfried writes his celebrated literary excursus. In effect, the passage is one of the finer moments of untrustworthy self-deprecation in medieval literature, for Gottfried tells us that his language simply will not do justice to the splendor and significance of the scene while creating just the opposite impression:

> For during my lifetime and earlier, poets have spoken with such elo-
> quence of worldly pomp and magnificent trappings that had I at my
> command twelve times my inspiration, and were it possible for me to
> carry twelve tongues in my one mouth, of which each could speak as I
> can, I should not know how to begin to describe magnificence so well
> that it had not been done better before. Knightly pomp, I declare, has
> been so variously portrayed and has been so overdone that I can say
> nothing about it that would give pleasure to anyone.[13]

There follows a long excursus of literary criticism discussing the styles of such contemporary men of letters as Hartman von Aue, Wolfram von Eschenbach, Bligger von Steinach, Heinrich von Veldeke and Walter von der Vogelweide. What is remark-able about this passage is that one of the highest moments in the career of the romance hero – his investiture as a knight – a moment treated reverentially in the convention of romance, here gives way to artistic introspection. As Jackson has pointed out, Gottfried has in effect given his hero "invisible clothes," so that the *edele herzen* for whom the poem is intended will recognize the special quality, the literary dimension which elevates Tristan above the mere knight of chivalry.[14] In the process, Gottfried, of course, highlights himself. At all climactic moments we are reminded of the poet and his struggle to create his unique vision. In this passage, as in the other so-called digressions, we are thus brought face to face with the performing self.

Geoffrey Chaucer will provide my second example. To my knowledge there is no work of the Middle Ages which gives a fuller insight into literature as performance than *The Canterbury Tales*. The whole of the work, as I read it, is concerned with storytelling generally and with Chaucer as literary critic specifically. It ranks among the very few works that create their own audience, and thus for once and in a limited sense allow us to see the medieval reader/listener as something other than a fiction of

---

[12] W. T. H. Jackson, "Tristan the Artist in Gottfried's Poem," *PMLA* 77 (1962) 364-372.

[13] *Gottfried von Strassburg's Tristan*, trans. A. T. Hatto, (Baltimore 1960) 104-105.

[14] W. T. H. Jackson, "The Literary Views of Gottfried von Strassburg," *PMLA* 85 (1970) 1000-1001.

the modern critic, as Robert O. Payne and Father Ong have in recent times separately and persuasively argued.[15] Harry Baillie is the perfect embodiment of the medieval "Common Reader," and through such stratagems as the so-called "Marriage Controversy," we get audience response as a generative device of Chaucer's fiction. At the center of this fiction stands Chaucer himself, speaking behind his mask or being spoken about by fictive narrators. What we are never allowed to forget is that Chaucer, rather than Harry Baillie, is the real impressario of the Canterbury journey; and he reminds us of his centrality to his fiction by emerging on several important occasions either as storyteller or as his own "auctorite." The tale of "Sir Thopas," while not attributed to Chaucer by name (except in the rubrics), is told by the performing self. Here Chaucer emerges, *in medias res*, from the anonymity within the group of twenty-nine, and subtly shows that the main concern of *The Canterbury Tales* is, indeed, with literary topics and perceptions. What the Common Reader rejects with the statement, "Thy drasty rymyng is nat worth a toord," is in reality a tour-de-force critique of the most popular middle-class mode of medieval narrative literature, the metrical romance. Thus, ironically, Chaucer manipulates his own audience to reject what traditionally it likes best. "Sir Thopas" is therefore the most direct warning we have from Chaucer as performing self that we must read all the tales as something more than the fictions of their literary tellers. It is for this reason that "Sir Thopas" stands at the critical center of *The Canterbury Tales.* At the periphery, in turn, the self-performer appears in another guise. I speak of the reference to Chaucer by the Man of Law in his introduction:

> But nathelees, certeyn,
> I kan right now no thrifty tale seyn
> That Chaucer, thogh he kan but lewedly
> On metres and on rymyng craftily,
> Hath seyd hem in swich Englissh as he kan
> Of olde tyme, as knoweth many a man;
> And if he have noght seyd hem, leve brother,
> In o book, he hath seyd hem in another.   (2.45-52)[16]

This single reference by Chaucer to himself *in propria persona*, followed by the Man of Law's rehearsal of Chaucer's bibliography, is a deft touch of self-advertisement.

And the humorous self-reference, here as elsewhere, serves to highlight Chaucer as a "man of gret auctorite" in the realm of literature. Surely we are meant to remember this allusion as the Man of Law, who confesses that he is "right now of tales desolaat" (2.131), plods wearily through his exhausting tale of Constance. What the passage does is once more to bring the author in the forefront. Here as elsewhere in *The Canterbury Tales,* we are concerned with the performing self.

[15] See Robert O. Payne, "The Historical Criticism We Need," *Chaucer at Albany* (n. 5 above) 180-183, and Walter J. Ong, "The Writer's Audience is Always a Fiction," *PMLA* 90 (1975) 9-21.
[16] Quotation from F. N. Robinson, ed., *The Works of Geoffrey Chaucer*, ed. 2 (Boston 1957).

II

The intellectual source for this style of self-allusion and incorporation lies in the twelfth century. As Ernst Robert Curtius has observed, it is in this century that "we find unadulterated pride of authorship."[17] For the first time in the literature of the Middle Ages, artists either insist on making themselves known by name or on including themselves by first-person reference in their works. Authors begin their works with personal allusions, and artists either name themselves in signatures or make portraits of themselves, even in the holiest of contexts. It is this age which brings to fruition autobiographical writing and the letter as a rhetorical form (as R. W. Southern tells us, "nearly all important writers kept copies of their own letters").[18] Colin Morris points out that autobiography

> was almost unknown in the ancient world. Classical self-expression did not take this form until the *Confessions* of Saint Augustine, which deserve to be called the first autobiography, if by that word we understand an account of the author's life written to illuminate the development of his beliefs and character. For a long time Augustine had no successors, except for some brief accounts written by monks of their conversion to the monastic life (that by Odo of Cluny was incorporated, still in the first person, into John of Salerno's life of him), and for the reminiscences of Ratherius of Verona in the tenth century. From the late eleventh century there is a great increase in the autobiographical content of books on a wide variety of subjects.[19]

Examples abound, as for instance, Abbot Suger's account of his political activities and his recollections of his design of Saint Denis; or Aelred of Rievaulx's personal remembrances of his friends; or Otloh of Saint Emmeram's *De doctrina spirituali* and *De tentationibus suis* which brood upon questions about the value of classical literature and about the reliability of Holy Scripture. One of the more remarkable autobiographical books of the Middle Ages is the volume of memoirs of Abbot Guibert of Nogent, completed about 1116. This very frank and personal account, often focusing on the frailties of its writer, is cast very much in the form of Augustine's *Confessions,* which must have been a spiritual source if not a direct model for Guibert. It begins as a book of personal confession and a prayer to God for his patience:

> To Thy Majesty, O God, I acknowledge my endless wanderings from Thy Paths, my turning back so oft to the bosom of Thy eternal mercy, prompted by Thee in spite of all. The wickedness I did in childhood and in youth, I acknowledge, wickedness that yet springs up in ripened age,

[17] E. R. Curtius, *European Literature and the Latin Middle Ages*, trans. Willard Trask (New York 1963) 517.

[18] R. W. Southern, *Medieval Humanism and Other Studies* (New York 1970) 87.

[19] Colin Morris, *The Discovery of the Individual, 1050-1200* (New York 1972) 79.

my ingrained love of crookedness, that in a body sluggish and worn yet lives on.[20]

One such wickedness, clearly, was Guibert's love of learning and his pride of authorship. He tells us how, in his youth, he steeped his "mind unduly in the study of verse-making, so as to put aside for such worthless vanities the serious things of the divine pages."[21] He read Ovid and the *Bucolics* of Virgil, aimed at "the airs and graces of a love poem in a critical treatise," and even wrote a series of letters.[22] He took great joy on one occasion to write out a sermon based on the Book of Wisdom at the request of his abbot, Garnier of St. Germer de Fly. Later, however, the abbot was annoyed by his writings and even forbade him to compose his commentary on the book of Genesis, which Guibert nevertheless continued in secret. There is, thus, in the very existence of the *Memoirs* a reminder of Guibert's self-confessed sin of "frivolous writing," as well as the vanity of authorship for which he berates himself repeatedly. The quest of identity and the power of self-revelation are simply too large to be contained within the prescribed pieties of the day.

But autobiography is a step removed from the full emergence of the performing self. I am arguing that the author appeared *in propria persona* as a first phase in the evolution that led to his absorption in works of fiction. Seen from this perspective, autobiography is one such preliminary form; the auctorial preface (or sometimes dedication) is another. It is once more in the twelfth century that the personal preface becomes popular. Indeed, virtually every major work, whether fictional or philosophical, begins with the author's allusion to himself and his book. Bernardus Silvestris's *Cosmographia* furnishes a useful and uncomplicated example of the type:

> To Thierry, doctor most renowned for true eminence in learning, Bernardus Silvestris offers his work. For some time, I confess, I have been debating with my innermost self, whether to submit my little work for friendly hearing or destroy it utterly without waiting for judgment. For since a treatise on the totality of the universe is difficult by its very nature, and this the composition of a dull wit as well, it fears to be heard and perused by a perceptive judge .... I have decided that a work so imperfect should not declare the name of its author until such time as it shall have received from your judgment the verdict of publication or suppression. Your discernment, then, will decide whether it ought to appear openly and come into the hands of all. If meanwhile it is presented for your consideration, it is submitted for judgment and correction, not for approval.[23]

This opening passage is marked by the topos of humility, which we have come to associate with the dedicatory epistle; the "dull wit" of Bernardus is incapable of

---

[20] *The Autobiography of Guibert, Abbot of Nogent-sous-Coucy*, trans. C. C. Swinton Bland (London 1925) 5.

[21] *Ibid.* 67.

[22] *Ibid.* 67

[23] From the translation by Winthrop Wetherbee, *The Cosmographia of Bernardus Silvestris* (New York 1973) 65.

grappling, as he tells us, with "the totality of the universe." In the treatise itself, we never again encounter the person of the author; nevertheless, our reading of it is shaped by the personality we meet in the preface — it becomes an informing presence for all that follows in the way of speculative comment about the megacosmos and the microcosmos. We are, moreover, assured by the preface that the work carries the implicit approval of Thierry of Chartres, "the foremost philosopher of all Europe,"[24] for, as Bernardus tells us, he will suppress publication and refrain from naming himself as author if Thierry does not approve of the work. Bernardus does name himself; the treatise was published; and so the ethical proof gives it substance as a work worthy of the reader's attention. It is thus that the authorship of Bernardus obtrudes in an otherwise impersonal work.

When we come to the *De amore* by Andreas Capellanus, we alight upon a much more difficult auctorial presence, revealed in part by the preface and in part by interspersed direct address to the putative reader throughout the work. The *De amore* is allegedly a handbook on love addressed to a certain Walter, who remains otherwise unidentified for posterity. He is there as a naive reader who lends directness and perhaps cause for irony to the pages that are dedicated to his welfare. Andreas's preface is straightforward enough: as a result of his friend Walter's continual urgings, he will teach him in the treatise that follows "the way in which a state of love between two lovers may be kept unharmed and likewise how those who do not love may get rid of the darts of Venus that are fixed in their hearts."[25] We know nothing more about Andreas than the fact that he writes in the first person (mostly in the form of the royal "we"), wherein he represents himself as a voice of experience and compassion desirous of imparting good counsel to his friend who has been pierced by Cupid's arrow. The voice is persistent; it emerges over and over again in the pages that follow. What is most significant about Andreas's presence is the "double lesson" (*duplicem sententiam*) that he imparts. Unlike the preface, which promises the anatomy of worldly love, the conclusion — as well as the last main chapter on "The Rejection of Love" — urges Walter to forsake the vanities of the world and to devote himself to the Bridegroom who "cometh to celebrate the greater nuptials." Andreas, in effect, tells Walter that he should disregard his earlier teachings:

> If you wish to practice the system, you will obtain, as a careful reading of this little book will show you, all the delights of the flesh in fullest measure; but the grace of God, the companionship of the good, and the friendship of praiseworthy men you will with good reason be deprived of. (p. 211)

One is put in mind here of Chaucer's *Troilus* which similarly departs from its readership posing as a "litel bok" with a double lesson. The divided message of the

---

[24] According to Clarembald of Arras in a prefatory letter to Thierry's *De sex dierum operibus*; see Wetherbee 144 n. 1.

[25] From the translation by John Jay Parry, *The Art of Courtly Love* (New York 1959) 27.

author thus brings into question the whole meaning of his writing. Are we to read the introduction and all that follows in the first two books ironically, as D. W. Robertson has suggested?[26] If so, Walter becomes an innocent in mind as well as body, and Andreas emerges as a humorous sophisticate and prototype of the unreliable narrator. This is not the place to adjudicate the elusive problem of Andreas's intent, but one nevertheless cannot disregard the questions that he raises for the reader with the double vision that he brings to his treatise. The effect is that Andreas himself is as much the focus of his book as his lessons on love. By raising the double perspective, he becomes omnipresent even in those passages —and there are many — which lack the first-person reference. He is, then, a far more complicated first-person author than any we have thus far encountered in the twelfth century, though yet not a true performing self.

III

As we move into the domain of fiction, the auctorial preface becomes even more distinct as a literary device. This is so because the author exists, at least in early works, on a different plane from his fictive setting. He is the voice of reality, the device that links the present with the past, the "here" with the "there." To examine the incipient performing self in the fiction of the twelfth century, I want to focus on two examples of the type: Geoffrey of Monmouth and Chrétien de Troyes. I do not claim that these two writers are necessarily models for their time, but they do illustrate, each in his own way, the new personality that infuses the world of fiction. Both make self-references and both, at least occasionally, reappear in the midst of the narrative with first-person observations.

Geoffrey of Monmouth has been called a great "faker of history" and his most famous work, the *Historia regum Britanniae*, "one of the world's most brazen and successful frauds."[27] The reason for this playful disparagement (for "fraud" must here be read as a synonym for "fiction") rests in the uncertainty over Geoffrey's veracity in the citation of the source for his *magnum opus*. Three times in his work he cites his own name, Gaufridus Monemutensis, and begs indulgence from his patrons, Robert, earl of Gloucester, and Alexander, bishop of Lincoln.[28] The first of these occurs in the prefatory dedication to Robert where he reveals that Walter, archdeacon of Oxford, presented him

> with a certain very ancient book written in the British language. This
> book, attractively composed to form a consecutive and orderly narrative,
> set out all the deeds of these men, from Brutus, the first King of the

---

[26] See the brilliant chapter on "Some Medieval Doctrines of Love" in D. W. Robertson, *A Preface to Chaucer* (Princeton 1962) 391-448.

[27] Roger Sherman Loomis, *The Development of Arthurian Romance* (New York 1963) 38, 35.

[28] See the translation by Lewis Thorpe, *The History of the Kings of Britain* (Baltimore 1966) 51-52, 170-171, and 257-258.

Britons, down to Cadwallader, the son of Cadwallo. At Walter's request I
have taken the trouble to translate the book into Latin, although, indeed,
I have been content with my own expressions and my own homely style
and I have gathered no gaudy flowers of speech in other men's gardens.
(p. 51)

There is great doubt that Walter's book ever existed, and the question of Geoffrey's
real sources is one of the great unsolved mysteries in literary history. Some go so far
as to say that the alleged book of Walter was really a first draft of the *Historia*
written by Geoffrey himself.[29] The doubts extend as far back as the twelfth century
itself, when Geoffrey's first known critic, William Newburgh, made the following
disparaging comment:

It is quite clear that everything this man wrote about Arthur and his
successors, or indeed about his predecessors from Vortigern onwards, was
made up, partly by himself and partly by others, either from an inordi-
nate love of lying, or for the sake of pleasing the Britons.[30]

But William notwithstanding, the next three centuries read Geoffrey's book as
history, and so for the time, at least, the authenticity of the self-professed chronicler
prevailed.

In striking his literary pose, Geoffrey succeeded so well that he has become
inextricably entwined with his own fiction. His *History,* which begins with the
mythical Brutus, thus extends from the twelfth century before Christ, as tradition
has it, not to Cadwallader of the seventh century after Christ, with which the
narrative ends, but to the very time of Geoffrey himself. As purveyor of the mythic
history, he is the intruder of the present who gives definition to the past. The book
thus rounds out human history for twelve centuries before and after Christ. Like
Chaucer who depended on a spurious Lollius to tell the history of Troy, Geoffrey
disclaims his authorship and poses simply as translator. But his presence is unforget-
table, and there are times, as during the description of the Whitsun feast at Arthur's
court, when he forgets his fictional role and intrudes as author: "If I were to describe
everything, I should make this story far too long" (p. 229). So, too, we cannot forget
the claim he makes in his preface that he "has gathered no gaudy flowers" when he
allows Arthur to deliver a speech "with Ciceronian eloquence" (p. 233). The
Historia regum Britanniae gains much of its interest from the many games that
Geoffrey plays with his reader. The act of writing mythic history is in itself part of
its subject matter.

---

[29] Robert A. Caldwell, "The Use of Sources in the Variant and Vulgate Versions of the
Historia regum Brittanniae and the Question of the Order of the Versions," *Bulletin biblio-
graphique de la Societé internationale arthurienne* 9 (1957) 123-124.

[30] R. Howlett, ed., *Historia rerum Anglicarum* in *Chronicles of the Reigns of Stephen, Henry
II and Richard I,* Rolls Series (London 1884-1885) *Proemium*, i, ii, Translation by Thorpe (n. 28
above).

Chrétien de Troyes begins four of his five extant romances by mentioning his name. He also frequently intersperses comments in the first person within his tales. In the prefaces, he tells us a good deal about himself and his interests in storytelling. We know, for example, that he writes for two patrons, Countess Marie de Champagne, whom he mentions at the beginning of the *Lancelot* as having commanded him to write the story and who provided him with the *matiere* and the *sens,* and Count Philip of Flanders, "the worthiest man in the empire of Rome" (p. 8), to whom he dedicates the *Perceval.*[31] By referring specifically to Count Philip's generosity ("only they know his largess who receive it" p. 8), Chrétien implies that he sought material reward from his patron and that, therefore, he was a professional writer.[32] The one note that rings loudly throughout his personal allusions is his pride in authorship; not only does he write to please his patrons, but he wants to improve upon the narrative craft of those who earn a living by mutilating and spoiling stories "in the presence of kings and counts" (*Erec,* p. 1). He venerates the past, and poses always as one who recounts his tales with great fidelity to his sources: his source for the *Cligés,* for example, is a book in the library of Saint Peter at Beauvais; it is described as "very old," a fact that "adds to its authority" (p. 91). This insistence upon fidelity leads him to intersperse comments showing him as controlled by his narrative, as for example in the scene describing the coronation of Erec when Chrétien tells us: "So it is a mad enterprise I undertake in wishing to describe it. But since I *must make the effort, come what may,* I shall not fail to relate a part of it, as best I may" (p. 87; italics mine).

What is perhaps most interesting to this study about Chrétien's references to his role as author is the implicit analogy that he draws between the craft of writing and knight errantry, between himself and his literary subjects, between learning and chivalry. At the beginning of the *Cligés* he is quite explicit on the latter correspondence:

> Our books have informed us that the pre-eminence in chivalry and learning once belonged to Greece. Then chivalry passed to Rome, together with that highest learning which now has come to France. (p. 91)

The equation of chivalry and learning makes clear that Chrétien is writing as much about himself as he is about the world of Arthur and his knights. Let me demonstrate my point by taking a closer look at the preface of the *Lancelot.* Here he speaks no longer simply as author but virtually as the knight who will perform errantry for his lady. The countess Marie thus becomes the informing spirit of the romance, and

---

[31] All citations from the *Erec, Cligés, Lancelot* and *Yvain* are to the translation by W. W. Comfort, *Chrétien de Troyes: Arthurian Romances* (London 1965); citations from the *Perceval* are to the translation by Roger Sherman Loomis and Laura Hibbard Loomis, *Medieval Romances* (New York 1957).

[32] We are reminded by Curtius that the rewards of authorship in the twelfth century are sparse. One poet writes: "How many poems have I written for prelates, and received empty words as my only reward. A buffoon is prized more highly than such as we" (n. 17 above) 472.

Chrétien, by telling the story she commands of him, does service for her much as Lancelot will for Guinevere. He begins as follows:

> Since my lady of Champagne wishes me to undertake to write a romance, I shall very gladly do so, being so devoted to her service as to do anything in the world for her, without any intention of flattery. But if one were to introduce any flattery upon such an occasion, he might say, and I would subscribe to it, that this lady surpasses all others who are alive . . . I will say . . . that her command has more to do with this work than any thought or pains that I may expend upon it. (p. 270)

Interestingly, there may even be an organic significance to Chrétien's self-reference by name in the preface of the *Lancelot*. As Bruce Finnie has shown, "in *Lancelot* . . . the hero's name is not given until the middle of the romance."[33] The first half constitutes a search for Guinevere in which the hero is known only as the "Knight of the Cart," a name that Chrétien himself uses as the title of his story in his preface. It is Guinevere who bestows his name upon him when she calls it out during the fight between Lancelot and Meleagant. At this point, then, Lancelot sheds his false, shameful identity and becomes the honorable and renowned protector of the queen. If we carry the Lancelot/Chrétien analogy into this context of names, we can only conclude that the writer is, in fact, superior to the knight of his story, for he has his identity from the very outset.

The romance of *Yvain* is generally thought to have followed that of the *Lancelot*.[34] This is the only one of Chrétien's tales that does not begin with a reference to his name. But it does begin with storytelling by the knights themselves. Calogrenant, who is identified as "a very comely knight" (p. 180), embarks upon a tale of his shame. He is interrupted by the intemperate Kay, who accuses the storyteller of acting superior to the other knights because he was the only one who jumped to his feet when Guinevere joined the circle. The queen then commands Calogrenant to "begin the tale anew" (p. 181), to which he replies, with obvious displeasure at Kay's loutish interruption: "Surely, lady, it is a very unwelcome command you lay upon me. Rather than tell any more of my tale today, I would have one eye plucked out, if I did not fear your displeasure." Then, in the resonances of Chrétien himself, he excoriates those who hear only with their ears, who lack understanding, who fail to let the word be carried to the heart. He finishes his remark as follows:

> Now, whoever will heed my words, must surrender to me his heart and ears, for I am not going to speak of a dream, an idle tale, or lie, with

---

[33] Bruce Finnie, "The Structural Function of Names in the Works of Chrétien de Troyes," *Names* 20 (1972) 93.

[34] It is interesting to note that the three romances of Chrétien's which begin in the court of Arthur – *Erec, Lancelot,* and *Yvain* – start with the celebration of a religious feast. The order of the tales may thus be established by the liturgical sequence of the feasts. *Erec* begins on Easter Day; *Lancelot* on the Feast of the Ascension; and *Yvain* at Pentecost.

which many another has regaled you, but rather shall I speak of what I
saw. (p. 182)

The tale of *Yvain* is thus generated by an internal storyteller. Chrétien has faded into
the background but he has clearly transferred his voice to Calogrenant, a storyteller
with a sense of mission who, in refusing to let Kay "mutilate and spoil" his story "in
the presence of kings," echoes the sentiments of Chrétien himself. In the tale of
Yvain, then, storytelling itself becomes part of knight errantry, and Chrétien
approaches a narrative voice not unlike that of Gottfried von Strassburg in the
Tristan.

IV

The analogue to literary self-reference in the visual arts is, of course, the artist's
self-representation in whatever medium or form he chooses. In the works of the
twelfth century, especially by monastic artists, we encounter frequent self-
representations and signatures. They appear in drawings, sketches, miniatures, reliefs
on church walls, sarcophagi, manuscript illuminations, carvings on choir stalls,
stained glass, and sculpture. Examples abound. There are numerous attempts at
self-portraiture by manuscript painters within their own illuminations, frequently
accompanied by inscriptions to make sure that the figure within the capital or in the
margin is recognized by the reader. The famous self-representation labelled *Hugo
pictor* in a marginal sketch of an Anglo-Norman *Commentary on Isaiah* by Saint
Jerome, dated about 1100, is regarded by some scholars as the first attempt of a
manuscript painter at self-portraiture (see fig. 1).[35] Hugo here shows himself holding
a pen, dipped into an inkhorn, in one hand while holding a knife to sharpen his quill
in the other. To his right is a representation of a book he is illustrating, and the
whole scene is accompanied by the inscription: "Imago pictoris et illuminatoris huius
operis." Here, clearly, the artist intrudes upon the content of his own work,
momentarily diverting attention from his decorations to himself. A similar and even
more direct self-reference is found in the miniature at the end of the famous
Canterbury Psalter (dated ca. 1150) where a monk named Eadwine, apparently the
supervisor of his workshop, calls himself the "prince of writers" — a reference to his
skill as illuminator (see fig. 2). I call this portrait more direct because it appears as a
regular miniature in the manuscript rather than as a marginal addition. As such it
becomes part of the illustrative scheme of the psalter proper, and it stands climacti-
cally at its end to call special attention to its maker. Beginning in the twelfth
century, one also frequently finds self-portraits of illuminators within capitals, as is
the case in the Passion of Saint Martin picturing the monk who calls himself Rufilus
(see fig. 3). In this self-representation, there is a noticeable effort at realism with the

[35] Andrew Martindale, *The Rise of the Artist in the Middle Ages and Early Renaissance* (New
York 1972) 12.

monk showing himself at work ornamenting the descender of the very capital *R* on which he is presently at work. Such illuminations add a strong personal quality to the splendid ornamental work of the manuscript painter in the twelfth century. They also give evidence of the new humanism wherein the abstract and impersonal are brought into touch with the subjective. It is in such ways that medieval art begins to advertise itself and to humanize and even contemporize its subjects.

Of special note is the humor contained in the new self-referential style. Just as the performing self in literature is, at his best, a caricature of his maker with the humor mockingly directed at the self (the obtuse Dante or the inept Chaucer), so is the artist's self-reference most interesting when it develops a comic perspective upon its maker. A fine example of such humor is in a drawing found unaccountably and surprisingly in a text of Augustine's *De civitate Dei* (see fig. 4). Here we see the artist, identified as Hildebert, throwing an object in exasperation at a mouse which is feasting on his lunch. To his side, the manuscript on which he is working rests on a stand and an apprentice named Everwinus is patiently painting a rinceau in the foregound. An intimate sketch of this sort, while totally unconnected to the serious content of the work in which it appears, nevertheless does much to depict not only the setting in which the artist does his work but the mood in which that work is accomplished. Above all, it depicts an impulsive joy in creativity; the artist simply bursts out of the constraints placed upon him, even if only for a vignette, and represents himself at play while at work.

A different kind of humor, wherein, however, the artist still depicts himself as victim, occurs in various renderings of miracles. Of special interest is the sequence in which the artist portrays the devil as an ugly grotesque who, then, suddenly appears in "life" to attack the artist in revenge. Usually, the Virgin Mary, whom the artist had depicted reverentially, comes to the rescue and, in her traditional role as Empress of Hell, defeats the devil. In a thirteenth-century manuscript of the *Cántigas* of Alfonso X, we thus see the devil destroying the scaffold on which the artist had painted his unflattering portrait (see fig. 5). By intervention of the Holy Virgin, however, the artist adheres to his painting and is saved from a fall, while the devil flees and a crowd gives thanks to Mary for having performed her miracle. What is especially interesting in such scenes is the intermixture of "reality" and depiction. The image of the devil is identical with his appearance putatively in the flesh. The artist, by taking part in the scene, is thus not only given dramatic prominence but he is, by implication, as "real" in his setting as the devil. Almost literally, then, the artist "adheres" to his work, and the boundaries between the worlds of myth and reality (on several planes) are obscured.

The sculptor and architect, much as the painter, frequently appear as figures in their own work. An early example occurs on a twelfth-century tomb in Saint Vincent of Avila, where the sculptor is shown working with his chisel on one of three sarcophagi in a setting that very much resembles the tomb on which the scene is depicted (see figs. 6 and 7). Another even more direct self-reference occurs on a capital in the Liebfrauenkirche at Maastricht where we see the Virgin Mary accepting a capital, much like the one on which the depiction occurs, from the sculptor who is identified above the scene as Heimon (see fig. 8). The master mason, conventionally depicted as wearing the skull cap which identifies his trade, is similarly shown in a presentation scene on the tympanum of the door leading into the Saint Gallus Chapel of the Basel Münster (see fig. 9). Here the mason holds a replica of the doorway that he has made for presentation to Christ and thus stands in the center of his own creation as a visual token of his artistic achievement.

While examples of such self-portraits could be multiplied, let it suffice here to refer to one more instance of a dramatic self-inclusion by the artist from a later work, to demonstrate how fully he could become incorporated in the design of his own work. In what is otherwise a fairly typical Last Judgment scene on the main portal of the west facade of the Frauenkirche at Rottweil, we see the architect with his masonry hammer stepping out of his grave in accompaniment of two bishops, holding their mitres, to be led as the first of the saved into heaven, which characteristically is represented as a Gothic cathedral (see figs. 10 and 11). This comic self-representation of the artist accentuates the special place he has reserved for himself in his created universe, and it emphasizes once more the merging of the profane and the sacred to which the new style of self-inclusion inevitably led.

While this is not the place to enlarge upon the significance of the self-referential in the art of the later Middle Ages and the Renaissance, we can, I believe, conclude that the emergence of the artist in his own work during the twelfth century was a revolutionary event. It leads eventually to the art of self-portraiture, to donor scenes, and to other commonplaces in which mythic subject matter is refracted by the vision of the contemporary. Two recent books, Virgina Wylie Egbert's *The Medieval Artist at Work* (Princeton 1967) and Kurt Gerstenberg's *Die deutschen Baumeisterbildnisse des Mittelalters* (Berlin 1966), provide ample documentation to justify the conclusion that self-representation in the visual arts is a new and important development of the twelfth century which leads to what can only be called a new style in the art of western Europe.

V

It remains yet to make a preliminary inquiry into the reasons for the remarkable upsurge of the artist's self-representation as a cultural phenomenon of the twelfth century. As is true of most new directions in the history of a culture, this stylistic departure was not sudden, and I am sure that any explanation of its causes will be inadequate. Nor will it be possible to establish direct or singular influences on a movement as diversified in character and widespread in its applications. Nevertheless, there are some reasonably plausible possibilities that may offer an initial explanation.

Certainly one of the developments responsible for the performing artist if not the performing self was the sudden rise in the early twelfth century of a cultivated society which expressed itself in the vernacular. As Erich Auerbach has pointed out in his important study, *Literary Language and Its Public in Late Latin Antiquity and in the Middle Ages*, between the years 600 and 1100 there was in all measurable terms no cultivated society in Europe.[36] Giving credit to the monastic reforms of the tenth century for an atmosphere in which new ideas and intellectual conflict could take place, Auerbach sees the rise of a "high society" that expressed itself in the vernacular, replacing the languages of antiquity "which served no longer as a means of expression but only as models and prototypes" for the emerging art and thought of the times. But, because the vernacular was still a relatively unused instrument for written communication, "none of what was written down in a vernacular language before the end of the twelfth century was addressed to readers, and even in the second half of the twelfth century readers in the vernacular were very rare; those who were sufficiently educated to read with ease read Latin."[37] In effect, this meant that the vernacular literature, including many of the texts to which I have made reference, were essentially intended for readers but presented to listeners, and their only mode of conveyance was therefore oral performance. It was inevitable under these circumstances that the writer and speaker identified himself with those he was addressing and, further, that he would in the course of time make remarks about his role as artist to his audience. The really important point to note is that the twelfth century is an unusual, perhaps unique, time in the history of authorship. It was a time in which performance was a necessary part of literary life, a time when non-dramatic literature was written for a listening audience, and when the author was, of necessity, a public figure. Self-consciousness is easily bred under such circumstances. In our age of television, as McLuhan has shown us, such self-consciousness surfaces again; however, the present-day creative artist is customarily represented by the media as a celebrity apart from his works. In the twelfth century he incorporated himself in his works, and thus created the public presence that differentiated him from his predecessors and that helped to initiate the mode of the performing self.

But the circumstances of authorship were only one reason for the emergence of the performing self. We must realize that the tendency of the artist to speak *in propria persona* and eventually to put himself at the center of his creation are acts of human identification with and control over the works of the mind. In this attempt, the artist expressed a dominant concern of his time — a renewal of interest in human causes and in nature as an earthly reality of which man was an integral part. He thus partook of the movement that Chenu has called the "desacralizing of nature."[38] The autobiography, the self-portrait of the sculptor, the romance in which the author identifies himself — all these assert that art is man-made and that the realm of the imagination is the outgrowth and even the territory of a particular human sensibility. In the most general terms, then, the new mode of self-representation was a develop-

---

[36] Erich Auerbach, *Literary Language and its Public in Late Latin Antiquity and in the Middle Ages*, trans. Ralph Mannheim, Bolinger Series 74 (New York 1965) 262.
    [37] *Ibid*. 284.
    [38] M. D. Chenu, *Nature, Man, and Society in the Twelfth Century*, ed. and trans. Jerome Taylor and Lester K. Little (Chicago 1968) 14.

ment of the so-called Twelfth Century Renaissance, a period that Southern sees as the beginning of "one of the great ages of humanism in the history of Europe, perhaps the greatest of all."[39] It was, in fact, the product of that humanism in both of its senses: the popular, or what Southern calls the "scientific," according to which "man ... understands himself as the main part, the key-stone, of nature"; and the "literary," which maintains that a renewed study of the ancient classics inculcated a deeper understanding of human qualities and concerns.[40] In the latter sense, the cosmology of Plato's *Timaeus*, which stood as a model for Chartrian thought, led to the perception of the universe as a unified whole, which stood as "the copy to an ideal exemplar."[41] According to this view, "the ultimate object of cosmological study is the orientation toward human life," and it becomes the function of poetry to bring "the subjective and the philosophical together."[42] This attitude toward the literary unquestionably elevated the place of the artist and allowed him new freedom in self-definition. He thus emerges as a palpable figure from the shadows of anonymity in the heroic past. It might even be said that in its literary contexts this new subjectivity is the really essential difference between the perspectives of epic and romance.

There is yet another aspect of literary humanism, the stylistic influence of Boethius's *De consolatione*, that may have contributed to the emergence of the performing self in the vernacular literature of the twelfth century. The overwhelming presence of Boethius in the culture of the twelfth century is a widely acknowledged fact. While I would not argue that the *Consolation of Philosophy* was necessarily a direct source of inspiration, it was so widely known and so much part of the literary heritage of the age that it cannot be disregarded as a potential shaping force on the literary consciousness of the age. As a Platonic dialogue between the author and Lady Philosophy, it contains a first-person character. The Boethius of the *Consolation* is, in fact, a prototype for the impercipient narrator whom we encounter later in Dante and Chaucer. As one who is brought from ignorance to knowledge by the wisdom of Lady Philosophy, he is, from one point of view, a fictional character; for the "real" Boethius knew from the start what his literary counterpart gradually comes to learn. Characterizing himself as an apt student, Boethius is nevertheless frequently perplexed by his mistress's fine logic, as, for example, in the following instance: " 'You are playing with me,' I said, 'by weaving a labyrinthine argument from which I cannot escape. You seem to begin where you ended and to end where you began.' "[43] Here, as elsewhere, Boethius playfully disfigures himself, and the Platonic dialogue becomes a dramatic fiction and a potential model for the self-referential mode of twelfth-century art.

[39] Southern (n. 18 above) 31.

[40] *Ibid.* 30, 32.

[41] Winthrop Wetherbee, *Platonism and Poetry in the Twelfth Century: The Literary Influence of the School of Chartres* (Princeton 1972) 30.

[42] *Ibid.* 143.

[43] From the translation by R. H. Green, *The Consolation of Philosophy* (Indianapolis ca. 1962) 72.

Still a further possible source — one intimately allied to the "scientific" humanism of the age — was the depiction of the Creator as artist and the artist as creator. God is frequently pictured as architect, circumscribing the world with a large compass.[44] He stands in the same relation to his handiwork as the artist to his work of creation. The concept of the poet as creator is, of course, an old one, as the Anglo-Saxon word *scop* sufficiently demonstrates. But the idea becomes graphic in the twelfth and thirteenth centuries, and the equation is pressed home analogically by the foremost thinkers of the age.[45] Here, for example, is a statement from Hugh of Saint Victor developing the point:

> This entire perceptible world is a book written by the finger of God, that is created by divine power, and individual creatures are as figures within it, not invented by Human will . . . but instituted by divine authority to make manifest the invisible things of God.[46]

Here God is clearly seen as author; the obverse of the writer perceived as creator logically follows. When, therefore, we encounter the artist in his own person, we are entitled to see him as the inspiring force, the "maker," of his works. The concept of "creation" was of central concern to Chartrian humanism and to the twelfth century at large. For an age that equated the macrocosm and the microcosm, it takes only a slight leap of the imagination to see the artist as analogue to Creator building his own universe. And that is manifestly what the artist's self-representation did for the work he informs.

But if there were good theoretical reasons for the rise of the self-referential in the art of the twelfth century, there were equally good practical reasons. While this is not the place to examine in any detail the social conditions that spurred the rise of the artist in the period, we must nevertheless bear them in mind. Surely, to some extent, the writer's self-reference is in part the effect both of his uncertain patronage and the conditions of oral performance which governed the dissemination of his art. As G. G. Coulton tells us in his enlightening chapter on medieval "Literary Life," the man of letters "was often a hanger-on about the household of great men."[47] He therefore was forced to advertise himself, and Coulton is no doubt right in suggesting that the first-person prologue served that purpose.[48] It also served to get the listening audience's attention and to forestall interruption and questioning. In a similar manner, the rise of autobiographical reference can no doubt be partially attributed to

---

[44] See especially John Block Friedman, "The Architect's Compass in Creation Miniatures of the Later Middle Ages," *Traditio* 30 (1974) 419-429. The idea of God as artist is also recognized by Kurt Gerstenberg: "In mittelalterlichen Handschriften, in Moralbibeln und Weltchroniken des 13. Jahrhunderts erscheint der Schöpfer aller Dinge als der Weltbaumeister, ausgestattet mit einem Riesenzirkel, so dasz sie in der Tat nichts anderes sind als lebendige Steine in seinem Weltenbau"; see *Die deutschen Baumeisterbildnisse des Mittelalters* (Berlin 1966) 8.

[45] See Curtius (n. 17 above) 319-326.

[46] Hugh of St. Victor *Eruditionis didascalicae*, 7.4 (PL 176.814).

[47] G. G. Coulton, *Medieval Panorama: The English Scene from Conquest to Reformation* (New York 1955) 580.

[48] *Ibid.* 577.

the trouvere and the troubadour who traditionally recited his verse as first-person poet-performer and who inspired a style of lyric poetry that was to sweep all over Europe.

The visual artist must similarly have been influenced by the conditions of his professional life. Art historians generally agree that "before the fifteenth century there is no evidence for any of the *mystique* which has since grown up around the Great Artist."[49] And yet, what we know about the conditions of the artist's life is precious little. One must, therefore, agree with Andrew Martindale's view that "it would be misleading . . . to suppose that medieval artists were essentially different creatures from those of the Renaissance."[50] Although personal prominence seems to have been rarely achieved by the artist in the twelfth century, concern with reputation (especially in the form of inscriptions and self-portraits) occurs especially among monastic manuscript painters and architects and sculptors. For the monastery, of course, the production of manuscripts was not only an important labor but it quickly became a source of institutional pride. We know well enough from the treatise *De diversis artibus* by Theophilus, a practicing monastic artist of the twelfth century, that artistic endeavor was a labor pleasing to God and necessary for the welfare of the monastery. Yet, while Theophilus upholds the Benedictine tradition against the artist's ambition for personal fame, he nevertheless leaves us a document of self-profession, no matter how humble his declarations to the contrary.[51] We also know that accomplished monastic artists were in short supply and were therefore much sought after. The praise heaped upon such fine artists as Master Hugo of Bury Saint Edmunds by the Bury chronicler is sufficient proof that really outstanding craftsmen were a source of institutional pride.[52] Small wonder, then, that artists began to identify with their works in the form of personal inscriptions and self-portraiture.

The same observations apply to architects, sculptors, and other artisans engaged in the proliferating art of church-building during the late twelfth and early thirteenth centuries. Here, however, an added fact must be taken into account, that of patronage. With the advent of the great cathedrals, much medieval art came to be supported by the rising bourgeoisie, who, as part of the price for their support, insisted on becoming the subject of the artist's work. Thus, to cite one example, the sculptors themselves became donors of a stained-glass signature window in the ambulatory of Chartres Cathedral featuring a scene of their craft (see fig. 12). As a result of such incorporation of donors in cathedral art, there developed a great admixture of sacred history and the present-day world in the art of the Middle Ages.[53] The same principle was at work in the production of mystery plays, in which

---

[49] Martindale (n. 35 above) 9.

[50] *Ibid.* 106.

[51] Theophilus, *The Various Arts*, trans. C. R. Dodwell (London 1961).

[52] Martindale (n. 35 above) 70.

[53] For a development of this point, see Henry Kraus, *The Living Theatre of Medieval Art* (Bloomington 1967) 91, and the chapter on "The New Classes as Donors and Subjects" 63-99.

the craftsmen, like the Carpenters presenting the Crucifixion, drew on their skills to depict Biblical scenes. This process, called "the rationalization of the mystery" by Otto Pächt,[54] yields a similar effect to that of the artist's self-incorporation in his work. It is a reaching out for contemporary representation in subject matter that is otherwise remote in setting, and it leads to a new interpretation of traditional subject matter within a frame of reference that is immediate and alive.

I have tried to show in this paper that the rise of the artist as a subject of his own work is a signal development of the twelfth century. It must rank as one of the important artistic innovations of medieval culture, and in the area of stylistics it stands as a significant contribution to the history of Western art down to our own day.

Office of the Dean of Humanities
Herbert H. Lehman College
City University of New York
Bronx, New York 10468, U.S.A.

[54] Otto Pächt, *The Rise of Pictorial Narrative in Twelfth-Century England* (Oxford 1962) 41.

FIG. 1. Oxford, Bodleian Library, MS Bodl. 717, fol. 287v.

FIG. 2. Cambridge, Trinity College, MS
R.171.1, fol. 238v.

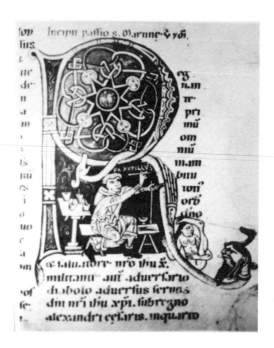

FIG. 3. Formerely in Sigmaringen, Hof-
bibliothek, MS 9, fol. 244.

FIG. 4. Prague, University Library, MS
Kap.A.xxi, fol. 133.

FIG. 5. Escorial, Biblioteca Real, MS
T.i.i., fol. 109.

FIG. 6. Avila, Church of San Vincente, tomb
of Vincent, Cristeta, and Sabina.

FIG. 7. Upper left-hand corner of fig. 6.

FIG. 8. Maastricht, Liebfrauenkirche.

FIG. 9. Basel, Munster, St. Gallus
Chapel, tympanum.

FIG. 10. Rottweil, Frauenkirche.

FIG. 11. Lower left-hand corner of fig. 10.

FIG. 12. Chartres, Cathedral of Notre
Dame, north apse window.

THE INDIAN TRADITION IN WESTERN MEDIEVAL INTELLECTUAL HISTORY

•

by Thomas Hahn

Among all the interests of medieval people, Indians scarcely hold a leading place. Yet the medieval West did turn its attention to India and the East, and it absorbed from this interest a number of cultural features like the fiddle bow, the stirrup, the blowgun, the iconography of the water buffalo, and perhaps some devotional practices.[1] But the Indians played a still more visible role in western consciousness: for many medieval writers the Brahmans — or Gymnosophists — stood as a symbol of natural goodness; they embodied the possibility, or even the certainty, of salvation without Revelation and outside the institutional Church. From the fourth century on, Western writers showed progressively greater favor towards the Indians, and by the twelfth century a coherent image had materialized. The Indians appear as a simple, upright people who please God, and invite Christian imitation, through their strict adherence to the laws of nature. From the twelfth to the fourteenth century Westerners reproduced this portrait often enough for us to be sure that it is a conventional view. This idealization of the Indians clearly reflects Christian values, and it does not provide very much reliable information about Eastern life. Yet it is the made-up character of this tradition that gives it a claim on our attention, for its invention tells us a great deal about the frame of mind of the medieval West.[2]

The Brahmans, often confused or conflated with the Gymnosophists, were introduced to the West through the first-hand accounts of India written by those who accompanied Alexander the Great on his expedition (327-325 B.C.). The Alexander historians included soldiers like Nearchos and Aristobulos, who wrote fairly straightforward accounts, and Onescritos, who inclined more to romance; those attached to Alexander's own party, such as Chares his chamberlain, and Eumenes his

---

[1] See Lynn White, jr., "Indic Elements in the Iconography of Petrarch's *Trionfo della Morte*," *Speculum* 49 (1974) 201-222; *idem,* "Tibet, India, and Malaya as Sources of Western Medieval Technology," *American Historical Review* 65 (1960) 515-526. I should like to acknowledge here the great help Professor White has given me, both through his writings and his personal criticisms.

[2] For a full account of the factors that seriously modified this tradition in early modern Europe, see Francis Jennings, *The Invasion of America: Indians, Colonialism, and the Cant of Conquest* (Chapel Hill 1975) and, on the survival and modifications of the "Indian tradition" in particular, Thomas Hahn, "Indians East and West: Primitivism and Savagery in English Discovery Narratives of the Sixteenth Century," *The Journal of Medieval and Renaissance Studies* 8 (1978), forthcoming.

secretary, who took a more personal, anecdotal viewpoint; and Callisthenes, Aristotle's nephew, the official historian.[3] These accounts were quickly refashioned by those who had stayed at home, like Cleitarchus, author of the popular or "vulgate" tradition, and by Megasthenes, who had done some traveling of his own. In turn, these narratives were reinterpreted by a number of writers around the time of the birth of Christ — Ptolemy, Diodorus Siculus, and Strabo — and then later, in the second century, by Arrian. Obviously, this welter of treatments presented ample opportunity for the growth — and disappearance — of many oral and written traditions, and even to late Antique historians, many of the early writers were little more than names: Strabo, for example, complained of the scanty and contradictory information with which he had to deal.[4]

Medieval acquaintance with the Brahmans, then, depended upon whatever information passed through the hands of these writers. A survey of the circulation of these texts among English writers will offer some notion of their diffusion during the Middle Ages. Orosius, relying upon Justinus's *Epitome* of Pompeius Trogus, included some material in his *Historia adversus paganos* (fifth century A.D.), which influenced a number of Anglo-Latin writings and the Middle English romance *Alexander A.*[5] Quintus Curtius Rufus produced the *Gesta Alexandri Magni* (first century B.C.), which Walter of Chatillon used as the principal source for his *Alexandreis* (1180). However, Pseudo-Callisthenes (so called by Isaac Casaubon in the sixteenth century) produced the definitive literary omnibus in his now-lost Alexander romance around A.D. 300.[6] Within twenty or thirty years Julius Valerius brought out a Latin version, *Res gestae Alexandri Macedonis*, and this, in an abridged version (the *Zacher Epitome*, before the ninth century) was the chief source for the fourteenth-century romance of *Kyng Alisaunder.*[7] However, the most influential of the translations from

---

[3] See L. A. Pearson, *The Lost Histories of Alexander the Great* (London 1960); J. W. M'Crindle, *The Invasion of India by Alexander the Great* (Westminster 1896). For medieval knowledge of India, one must consult George Cary's exhaustive work, *The Medieval Alexander* (Cambridge 1956); a brief and more intelligible study is D. J. A. Ross, *Alexander Historiatus*, Warburg Institute Surveys 1 (London 1963).

[4] Strabo, *Geography* 15.1, sections 1-10, 57, 68; ed. H. L. Jones, Loeb Library, 8 vols. (Cambridge, Mass. 1930) 7.2-15, 95, 119.

[5] Cary treats the historical material and its limited influence (n. 3 above) 16-17, 68-70, and he furnishes information on *Alexander A,* 48. All dates given in parentheses are intended as guides to the time when a writer flourished or a text enjoyed currency, and they should therefore be taken as approximate.

[6] Pseudo-Callisthenes, and the interpolations that occur in the text, are the chief sources for the romantic tradition of Alexander. For editions and bibliography, see Cary (n. 3 above) 9-16, and his entire discussion of medieval Alexander materials, 9-70. Complete bibliographical information on texts would have overburdened this survey, and so I have merely provided references to Cary or Ross. The precise relations between the early texts and the successive revisions merit detailed study, and I have begun work on this problem from the perspective of the Western image of the Indians during the Middle Ages.

[7] Julius Valerius translated the a-recension of Pseudo-Callisthenes; see Cary (n. 3 above) 27-37, for information on Julius, the epitomes of the *Res gestae* and their influence. For the English romance, see *Kyng Alisaunder,* ed. G. V. Smithers, Early English Text Society (EETS) 227, 237 (London 1952, 1957). Smithers discusses the sources, 237.28ff.

Greek to Latin appeared more than six hundred years after Julius Valerius, when Archbishop Leo of Naples assembled a new digest of Alexander stories. The earliest copy of Leo's work includes a version of Pseudo-Callisthenes containing expanded sections on the Brahmans and India, together with the *Commonitorium Palladii* (early fourth century), *Dindimus de Bragmanibus* (?fourth century), a redaction of the *Epistola Alexandri . . . ad Aristotelem . . . de situ Indiae* (early tenth century or before), and the *Collatio Alexandri cum Dindimo* (revised version, ?tenth century), a fictional exchange of letters between the world conqueror and the leader of the Brahmans. English writers translated the *Epistola Alexandri* and an affiliated work, the *Epistola de mirabilibus Indiae,* as early as the eleventh century.[8] Some time in this same century, an anonymous author managed to draw all of these strains, and some elements from Orosius, into a fairly unified whole, called the *Book of Battles* (*Historia de preliis* I[1]); before the middle of the twelfth century this was revised, and the resulting text provided the basis for the alliterative poems *Alexander and Dindimus* (*Alexander B*) and *Alexander A* (both ca. 1340-1370). A third recension of the *Book of Battles* (*Historia* I[3]) was revised by an English writer after 1150 (*Historia* I[3a]), and the *Prose Life* of Alexander (the "Thornton Alexander," before 1440) and the *Alexander C* (*The Wars of Alexander,* first half of the fifteenth century) follow this version, of which no Latin text apparently survives.[9] There also

---

[8] The *Epistola Alexandri* derives from Pseudo-Callisthenes (3.17), and was translated by Julius Valerius (ca. A.D. 320), and then translated again into Latin as a fuller version. It enjoyed wide popularity throughout the Middle Ages, and may have been a source for the *Epistola de mirabilibus.* The *Epistola Alexandri* was translated into Old English ca. 1000; see *Three Old English Prose Texts,* ed. S. Rypins, EETS 161 (Oxford 1921) for Latin and Old English texts. Worcester Cathedral Library MS 172, fols. 136-146v, contains a Middle English prose translation of the *Epistola,* though the *Manual of Writings in Middle English* 1 (New Haven 1967) and the revised *Cambridge Bibliography* do not mention it. See Cary (n. 3 above) 15, and in particular, Thomas Hahn, "The ME *Letter* of Alexander to Aristotle: Introduction, Text, Sources, Commentary," *Mediaeval Studies* 42 (1980), forthcoming. For more information on the "Indian tractates," see nn. 24-30 below.

[9] Leo's original translation of the δ-recension of Pseudo-Callisthenes has not come down to us; it survives only in two differing recensions. All of the interpolated versions (each designated "I") derive from Leo, and Cary (n. 3 above) provides bibliographical information on these, 38-61. Two very recent editions may be noted here: *Die Historia de preliis Alexandri Magni, Rezension J[3],* ed. Karl Steffens, Beiträge zur klassichen Philologie 73 (Meisenheim am Glan 1975); and for a convenient parallel text of I[1], I[2], and I[3] together with a recension of Leo, see *Die Historia de preliis . . . Synoptische Edition,* ed. Hermann-Josef Bergmeister, Beiträge zur klassichen Philologie 65 (Meisenheim am Glan 1975). Unfortunately, this parallel-text edition stops short of the Brahman episode. Friedrich Pfister's edition, *Der Alexanderroman des Archipresbyters Leo,* Sammlung mittellateinischer Texte 6 (Heidelberg 1913), contains an excellent introduction, of great help in surveying the history of the Brahmans in the West; and see Pfister's essays, "Das Nachleben der Überlieferung von Alexander und die Brahmanen," *Hermes* 76 (1941) 143-160, and "Die Brahmanen in der Alexandersage," *Berliner philologische Wochenschrift* (1921) 569-575. G. L. Hamilton, "A New Redaction of the *Historia de preliis* and the Date of Redaction J[3]," *Speculum* 2 (1927) 113-146, attempts to reconstruct the source of the *Prose Life.* For bibliographical information on *Alexander and Dindimus,* the *Prose Life,* and *The Wars of Alexander,* see Cary 49, 56-57. F. P. Magoun, *The Gests of King Alexander of Macedon* (Cambridge, Mass. 1929) offers further information and bibliography on the English versions and their sources.

exists a fifteenth-century English version of the first rendition of the *Epistola Alexandri* (*Epistola* I), as well as other Latin, Scottish, and Irish treatments of the matter of India.[10]

Merely establishing the lines of transmission for the five versions of the Alexander legend in medieval England has given some indication of the proliferation of this material, and so it should not be surprising that many authors show a knowledge of the Brahmans and take it upon themselves to comment on these wise men of India. Philo the Jew (A.D. 50) alludes to the order of Gymnosophists who, through ethical and natural philosophy, make their lives an example of virtue; these good heathens, Philo says, because of their ardent righteousness, deserve as much praise as Abraham.[11] Other writers, like Plutarch (A.D. 120) and Philostratus (early third century), mention the asceticism of the Brahmans, but traces of ethnocentrism limit their approval. Apuleius (A.D. 160-170) is more favorably impressed with their customs and philosophical aspirations, and Porphyry (A.D. 305), citing the Indians as an example of continence, points out that the Brahmans are really a part of the group of holy wise men whom the Greeks usually call Gymnosophists.[12] The acquaintance that these writers show with Indian material predates the convenient miscellanies of the fourth and fifth centuries, and some of the early Christian writers exhibit a similar anecdotal familiarity. Clement of Alexandria (ca. 215), for example, starts from the premise that philosophy is the common possession of all nations, having come to the Egyptians, the Assyrians, the Greeks, and so on, from the Barbarians — "Ἰνδῶν τε οἱ γυμνοσοφισταὶ ἄλλοι τε φιλόσοφοι βάρβαροι."[13] He goes on to quote Megasthenes on the sources of these philosophers: "Ἅπαντα μέν τοι τὰ περὶ φύσεως εἰρημένα παρὰ τοῖς ἀρχαίοις λέγεται καὶ παρὰ τοῖς ἔξω τῆς Ἑλλάδος φιλοσοφοῦσι · τὰ μὲν παρ' Ἰνδοῖς ὑπὸ τῶν Βραχμάνων, τὰ δὲ ἐν τῇ Συρίᾳ ὑπὸ τῶν καλουμένων Ἰουδαίων:" Through the study of nature, the Brahmans possess the outlines of Greek philosophy, which Clement, because of his gnostic penchant, considered a divine gift to mankind. Clement manifests a somewhat lower opinion of their natural philosophy elsewhere, however, and he names the Brahmans as an instance of vain asceticism: "Οἱ δὲ διὰ τὸ μῖσος τὸ πρὸς τὴν σάρκα τῆς κατὰ γαμον συναλλαγῆς καὶ τῆς τῶν καθηκόντων βρωμάτων μεταλήψεως ἀχαρίστως ἀπαλλάττεσθαι ποθοῦντες ἀμαθεῖς τε καὶ ἄθεοι ἀλόγως ἐγκρατευόμενοι, καθάπερ τὰ πλεῖστα τῶν ἄλλων ἐθνῶν. Βραχμᾶναι . . . ."[14] Evidently, the Brahmans might

---

[10] See Cary (n. 3 above) 22, 35, 37, 52, 60, and 68-70; n. 8 above contains more information on the Middle English *Letter*.

[11] Περὶ τοῦ πάντα σπουδαῖον ἐλεύθερον εἶναι 14 (*Philo*, ed. F. H. Colson, Loeb Library, 12 vols. [Cambridge, Mass. 1941]) 9.62-66; for the comment on Abraham, see Περὶ Ἀβράαμ 33-34 (6.88-92).

[12] See Plutarch, *Life of Alexander* 8.65; Philostratus, *The Life of Apollonius* 3.15-16; Apuleius, *Florida*; Porphyry, *On Abstinence* 4. All these texts are contained in Sir Edward Bysshe, *Palladius de Gentibus Indiae* (London 1665; repr. 1668). Bysshe participated in the revival of sorts that the medieval "Indian tradition" enjoyed in the later seventeenth century. For further remarks on the possible philosophical connections of the Brahmans with the West, see A.H. Armstrong, "plotinus and India," *Classical Quarterly* 30 (1936) 22-28.

[13] Clement of Alexandria, *Stromatum* 1.15 (PG 8.777). For the next quotation see PG 8.781.

[14] *Stromatum* 3.7 (PG 8.1164).

answer for a remarkable example, either good or bad depending upon the author's need, and Clement later reverses himself again, and adverts to the courage and spirituality of the Indians against Alexander the Great.[15] The third-century *Recognitiones*, associated with Clement of Rome (d. A.D. 97), also regard the Brahmans favorably: "Sunt similiter et apud Bactros in regionibus Indorum immensae multitudines Bragmanorum, qui et ipsi ex traditione majorum, moribus legibusque concordibus, neque homicidium neque adulterium committunt, neque simulacra colunt neque animantia edere in usu habent, numquam inebriantur, numquam malitiose aliquid gerunt, sed Deum semper timent."[16]

Saint Hippolytus (A.D. 236) included the Brahmans among the "heretics" whose doctrine he chose to correct in the *Philosophumena* ("Refutation of All Heresies"), and his detailed treatment suggests that he, like Plotinus, may have had some first-hand acquaintance with Indian ideas; whatever the truth of this, the significant fact is that though Hippolytus allows the Brahmans some truth in their beliefs, he considers them, like other heretics, outside the fold of the elect.[17] Tertullian (A.D. 220), who himself wrote some works in Greek, and was familiar with the earlier Brahman material, in one passage scorns the "naturalness" and primitivism of the Indians; he protests that Christians do help to uphold the state and are every bit as civilized as non-Christians, "neque enim Brachmanae aut Indorum gymnosophistae sumus, sylvicolae et exules vitae."[18] Thus, the hostility towards the Brahmans as non-Christians grows among the apologists of the early Church, and Prudentius (A.D. 410), in his poem on the origin of sin, picks on the Indians as the symbol of vain knowledge: "Hinc gerit Herculeam vilis sapientia clavam,/ ostentatque suos vicatim gymnosophistas."[19] This apologetical defensiveness, and enmity towards the Brahmans in particular, culminates in the writings of Saint Augustine (A.D. 432), who takes the role of *advocatus diaboli* in the issue of Indian salvation: "Et Indorum Gymnosophistae, qui nudi perhibentur philosophari in solitudinibus Indiae, cives ejus mundi sunt, et a generando se cohibent. Non est enim hoc bonum nisi cum fit secundum fidem summi boni, qui Deus est."[20] The outlook for the Brahmans had suffered a distinct change from the ambivalence of Clement of Alexandria, and, if the use that Saint Augustine makes of his knowledge of them were representative of the Fathers, the Indian holy men might have looked for a harsh time of it during the Middle Ages.

However, during Augustine's lifetime — that century of translations from the Indian sources into Latin — there appear signs of alternative attitudes among the Western Fathers. Saint Ambrose, for example, in a letter to Simplicianus, compares

---

[15] *Stromatum* 4.7 (PG 8.1263).

[16] The *Recognitiones* survive only in a Latin translation of the original. See PG 1.1410.

[17] See PG 16.3052. Jean Filliozat uses the text of Hippolytus as a basis for interesting speculation about the possibility of extensive contact between East and West in the first Christian centuries: "La doctrine des Brahmanes d'après saint Hippolyte," *Revue de l'histoire des religions* 130 (1945) 59-91.

[18] Tertullian, *Apologeticus* 42.1 (PL 1.490-491).

[19] Prudentius, *Hamartigenia* 402-403 (PL 59.1040).

[20] Augustine, *De civitate Dei* 15.20 (PL 41.463).

himself to the Indians: "Non enim de contemptu mortis libros philosophorum depromo, aut gymnosophistos Indorum, quorum prae caeteris Calani laudatur responsum Alexandro, cum juberet sequi."[21] Another of the great Fathers, Saint Jerome, thinks the Brahmans an apposite model for a Christian virgin's behavior: "Alioqui, quod Indaica superstitio ex parte facit in rejectione quorumdam animalium atque escarum, quod et Indorum Brachmani et Aegyptiorum Gymnosophistae in polentae et orizae, et pomorum solo observant cibo, cur virgo Christi non faciat in toto? Si tanti vitrum, quare non majoris sit pretii margaritum?"[22] Jerome's comparison, superficially unfavorable to Christians, is fundamentally a criticism of non-Christian life, though on the other hand it does prove the prevalence of the Brahmans' reputation for good works during the patristic age.[23]

More graphic and compelling evidence of an increasing esteem and good will towards the Brahmans is the appearance of a number of unconnected fictional treatises that chose to exalt the lives of the Brahmans above all the rest of the bulky mass of Alexander material. This focus upon the Indian holy men is the most notable and systematic attempt to separate out and emphasize one part of the Alexander legends against the remainder, although other more general expansions, like the later *Epistola Alexandri* and its derivative, the *Epistola de mirabilibus*, also evince a continuing special interest in India, rather than in Alexander's other exploits. Two of the Indian tractates derive from the Pseudo-Callisthenes textual tradition: Bishop Palladius of Helenopolis in Bithynia (ca. 365-425), whom Saint Jerome accused of Origenism (holding that all human beings, Christian and non-Christian alike, would be saved), interpolated an essay upon the Brahmans into the Greek account of Alexander (Pseudo-Callisthenes 3.7-16); this was thought important enough to be translated into Latin twice, and the earlier rendition, apparently made soon after the original composition in Greek, was traditionally ascribed to Saint Ambrose (3.7-10).[24] Though it has been suggested that Palladius drew upon a first-hand account of the Brahmans, his work in fact shows little truly historical knowledge of India beyond a reading of Arrian, and apparently it was Palladius's intention to write a fictionalized account of the Indians as virtuous heathen; Palladius takes an explicitly Christian viewpoint, but his presentation of the material bespeaks a

[21] Ambrose, *Epistola* 37 (PL 16.1138). Compare the statement of Ambrose with that of Philo (n. 11 above). Calanus, a gymnosophist mentioned in the histories of Alexander's invasion, often exchanged roles with Dindimus in later accounts of the Indians.

[22] Jerome, *Epistola* 107.8 (PL 22.874); Migne prints "Iudaica" for "Indaica", but critical editions have firmly established the latter reading.

[23] Jerome seems to have Matt. 13.46 in mind; cf. his *Epistola* 125. He thus underscores the difference between the infidelity of the Brahmans ("vitrum") and the pearl of faith, which through Christ's mediation sanctifies the deeds of Christians.

[24] The *Commonitorium Palladii* was first translated into Latin, perhaps in the fifth century, in the version attributed to Ambrose (PL 17.1067-1084), and then again in the tenth century by Archbishop Leo, in his text of the *Historia de preliis*. See Cary (n. 3 above) 12-16 for bibliography, and for a transcription of the Vatican Library text and English translations, see *The Brahman Episode: St. Ambrose's Version of the Colloquy* . . . ed. S. V Yankowski (privately printed: Ansbach 1962).

universalistic outlook associated with Origenism.[25]   Succeeding redactions heighten
the piety and holiness of the Brahmans, and these elements carry over into the
Pseudo-Ambrosian version; this latter text, in fact, elaborates upon this structure,
adds a number of details from other writers, and is the most fictionalized of all the
versions of this text — it departs from the Greek original frequently in order to
amplify the narrative of the Brahmans' habits.[26]   A supplementary Latin translation
of Palladius (Pseudo-Callisthenes 3.11-12), *Dindimus de Bragmanibus*, provided
further information on the holy Indian philosophers, but this seems to have exercised
little influence except as a part of the *Book of Battles.*[27]

Still another work, the *Collatio Alexandri cum Dindimo*, written between the
fourth and sixth centuries, endeavored to offer a detailed description of the
Brahmans' customs and beliefs.[28]   The *Collatio* took the form of a series of letters
exchanged between the king of the Macedonians and the king of the Brahmans, and
it seems to be a totally imaginative work, relying upon the historians and Pseudo-
Callisthenes only for its general subject, and espousing a favorable view of the Indians
that had by this time become almost traditional. In its original form the work
apparently attempted to rebut the Cynic and Christian accusers of the conqueror;
consequently, traces of the *Apologeticus* of Tertullian and the writings of other
Christian apologists may be found in the letters of Dindimus. Dindimus had already
appeared as an implicitly Christian spokesman in the Palladian essay attributed to
Ambrose, and that work so strongly established his character that a revision of the
original defense of Alexander was undertaken, in the manner of Pseudo-Ambrose. As
a result, Dindimus became more thoroughly and openly Christian. The *Collatio*
portrayed the Brahmans as "in fact instinctive Christians, the true type of Noble
Savage, exhibiting in their untutored lives all the traits of the saint and philosopher."[29]   These letters enjoyed an immense popularity throughout the Middle Ages,
and they helped to endow Dindimus and the Brahmans with an existence apart from
the Alexander legends, and to infuse them with an individuality, a special character

[25] P. R. Coleman-Norton, "The Authorship of the *Epistola de Indicis gentibus et de Bragmanibus*," *Classical Philology* 21 (1926) 154-160, argues that Palladius himself may have made a
journey to the East (see Armstrong on Plotinus [n. 12 above] and Filliozat on Hippolytus [n. 17
above]). Less provocative but more substantial is J. Duncan M. Derrett, "Palladius: *De vita
Bragmanorum narratio, alias Palladii de gentibus Indiae et Bragmanibus commonitorii necnon
Arriana opusculi versio ornatior*," *Classica et Mediaevalia* 21 (1960) 64-135.

[26] See André Wilmart, "Les textes latins de la lettre de Palladius sur les moeurs des
Brahmanes," *Revue bénédictine* 45 (1933) 29-42.

[27] This tract is also based on an interpolation in Pseudo-Callisthenes (3.11-12), but this was
apparently not inserted by Palladius, though it is sometimes attributed to him. Leo evidently
translated a version in his *Historia,* for it appears in the I[1] redaction, and the second version is
known as *Anonymus de Bragmanibus,* printed by Bysshe (n. 12 above).

[28] The *Collatio* exists in three versions, one associated with Julius Valerius, one with Archbishop Leo's translation, and a final redaction that appears in the *Historia* I[1]. For the complex
links between the versions, see Cary (n. 3 above) 13-14, and Edm. Liénard *"Collatio Alexandri
et Dindimi,"* *Revue belge de philologie et d'histoire* 15 (1936) 819-838.

[29] See George Boas, *Essays on Primitivism and Related Ideas in the Middle Ages* (New York
1966 [1948]) 147. Boas may overstate the case just a bit because of his special perspective.

as virtuous heathens in every way like, not to say better than, Christians. In almost every derivative of the *Collatio*, the personality and the role of Dindimus are expanded (at the expense of Alexander), and his Christian nature becomes more and more pronounced.[30] The eras of Apologetics and of the Fathers, then, predictably devised the first anti-Indian propaganda, but this same age provided the texts that were the foundations upon which the legends and dispositions favorable to the Brahmans grew.

The rationale for the early condemnation of the Brahmans is not far to seek: it stems from the assurance, widespread during the first Christian centuries, that all the world had heard the Word. In his letter to the Thessalonians, Saint Paul, the Apostle of the Gentiles, had written: "A vobis enim diffamatus est sermo Domini, non solum in Macedonia, et in Achaia, sed et in omni loco fides vestra, quae est ad Deum, profecta est ita ut non sit nobis necesse quidquam loqui" (1 Thess. 1.8).[31] In the division of the apostolic labors, Saint Thomas was traditionally credited with the conversion of India. The *Acts* of Thomas — one of the five principal Acts, and among the longest and most popular apocrypha — rehearse Thomas's extensive missionary activities in India, undertaken through the personal intervention of Jesus. Just before his martyrdom, Thomas proclaims to God and to the world: "I have planted thy vine in the earth; it hath sent down its roots into the depth and its growth is spread out in the height, and the fruits of it are stretched forth upon the earth and they that are worthy of thee are made glad by them, whom also thou hast gained."[32] The apocryphal accounts of Mary's assumption often spirit Thomas back from his conversion work in India to the Blessed Virgin's side, and other early apocryphal histories include accounts of Thomas's evangelization of the Indians.[33] This non-canonical literature had an important effect upon vernacular traditions, as Anglo-Saxon remarks upon India attest. The Peterborough version of the *Chronicle* (an. 883) records the mission of two of King Alfred's emissaries to the shrine of Saint Thomas in India, indicating that this historian, at least, had no doubts about India's inclusion in the Christian world.[34] And Cynewulf's *Fates of the Apostles*, a poem

---

[30] See George Cary, "A Note on the Mediaeval History of the *Collatio Alexandri cum Dindimo,*" *Classica et Mediaevalia* 15 (1954) 124-219.

[31] See also Rom. 1.8; Col. 1.6, 23; 1 Tim. 3.16, and other texts that illustrate this common idea.

[32] *The Apocryphal New Testament,* trans. M. R. James, rev. ed (Oxford 1969 [1953]) 428.

[33] For narratives of Mary's assumption, see *Apocryphal New Testament,* 204, 217-28; for accounts of the missionary work of Thomas, see 24, 268.

[34] See *Two of the Saxon Chronicles Parallel,* ed. Charles Plummer (Oxford 1892) 79: "þy ilcan geare laedde Sighelm & Æðelstan þa ælmessan to Rome þe Ælfred cing gehet þider. & eac on Indea to sēe Thome. & to sēe Bartholomee." William of Malmesbury gives a variation of this account in *Gesta regum anglorum* (2): "Ad Sanctum Thomam in India multa munera misit. Legatus in hoc missus Sigelinus, Scireburnensis episcopus, cum magna prosperitate, quod quivis hoc seculo miretur. Indiam penetravit; inde rediens, exoticos splendores gemmarum, et liquores aromatum, quorum illa humas ferax est, reportavit" (PL 179.1082). William marks a watershed in the Western image of India, for he brings together two traditions: on the one hand, he seems to consider it a part of Christendom, a place perfectly suited for a visit from an English bishop; on the other, he shows the influence of the new romantic outlook (perhaps he had been reading the Old English *Epistola Alexandri* or the *Wonders of the East*), for he also makes India a strange and remote place, markedly different from Christendom.

that takes as its subject the conversion of the entire world, also credits Thomas (and Bartholomew) with the conversion of India:

> Swylce Thomas eac   þriste gene ðe
> on Indea   oðre daelas,
> þaer manegum wear   mod onlihted
> hige onhyrded   þurh his halig word.[35]

Even apart from the Thomas legends, however, certainty about the evangelization of India ran strong: Eusebius (ca. 340), the "Father of Church History," established Christianity in India for the many writers to whom he was the chief authority; for he recounts that Pantaenus of Alexandria had won many souls in India, and had also discovered that a Christian community, founded by the apostle Bartholomew, already existed there.[36] Likewise Saint Jerome chooses the particular example of India to illustrate just how far the Gospel had spread: "Ubi tunc totius orbis homines ab India usque ad Britanniam, a rigida septentrionis plaga usque ad fevores Atlantici Oceani, tam innumerabiles populi et tantarum gentium multitudines . . . . Nunc vero passionem Christi et resurrectionem eius cunctarum gentium et voces et litterae sonant . . . haec Indus, Persa, Gothus, Aegyptius philosophantur . . . et totius mundi una vox Christus est."[37] And in another letter, he chooses a figure involving India to demonstrate how thoroughly Christianity has pervaded the world: "De India, Perside et Aethiopia monachorum quotidie turbas suscipimus."[38] Saint Jerome seems here to exaggerate, or to have confused India with some part of Africa or even with some parts of Persia or Ethiopia, which he classes with India; but whatever the historical facts, they do not undercut Jerome's conviction of Christianity's universality.[39]

Saint Jerome's pronouncements bespeak an extremely patterned, abstract view of world history and geography, conformable in all ways to the standard outlines of providential history; and this outlook finds its counterpart in the schematized maps of the earlier Middle Ages. These *mappae mundi* did not try to convey fact about the land masses or the oceans of the physical world, but instead they took up spiritual geography, indicating the *real*, spiritual significance of the waters and continents. "Box and V" maps, for example, often bear no legends other than the names of Noah's three sons, Japheth, Shem, and Ham, who, according to the biblical histories of Saint Augustine, Saint Isidore, and others, divided the settlement of the world among themselves: obviously neither "cartographer" nor reader supposed that such a chart might be a guide for world travel.[40] Similarly, "T and O" maps, another popular convention, place greater importance upon geometrical than upon

---

[35] See *The Vercelli Book*, ed. G. P. Krapp, Anglo-Saxon Poetic Records 2 (New York 1932), 51-54. I have quoted lines 50-53 of the poem.

[36] See Eusebius, *The History of the Church* 5:10, PG 20.453-456; trans. G. A. Williamson (Harmondsworth, England 1965), 213. See also Jerome, *Epistola* 71 (PL 22.667).

[37] Jerome, *Epistola* 60.4 (PL 22.591-592).

[38] Jerome, *Epistola* 107.2 (PL 22.870).

[39] See John Kirtland Wright, *The Geographical Lore of the Time of the Crusades* (New York 1965 [1925]) 272-281, 303, 466 n.

[40] See Wright 64-69, 247ff. See also Denys Hay, "The Concept of Christendom," *The Dawn of European Civilization*, ed. D. Talbot Rice (London 1965) 341.

geographical accuracy, though these usually do exhibit the names of the three major continents, rather than merely three biblical personages. The maps associated with the Apocalypse Commentary of the Spanish monk Beatus of Liebana (eighth century) furnish more detail, but this is because they conform to a notion of salvation history, which, if different, is no less diagrammatic and abstract than those that inspired the "Box and V" and "T and O" *mappae mundi*. The Beatus maps record the *divisio apostolorum*, the dispersion of Christ's disciples to all the ends of the earth, and so in effect they attest the Christianization of the world. Saint Thomas remains the Apostle of India, which appears regularly at the limits of the world, though the map makers sometimes vary in placing India at the far right (which seems naturally Eastern) rather than at the very top of the diagram, which is the formal East.[41] The Beatus maps present a pictorial explanation of Saint Jerome's use of India as a symbol of world conversion, for it was literally at the farthest reaches of the earth.

One of the fairly consistent features especially of the later Beatus maps is the juxtaposition of India and the Garden of Eden, and it was perhaps this conjunction, along with the extreme cartographical remoteness of India, that encouraged enthusiasm for the wonders and marvels described in the *Epistola Alexandri* and the *Epistola de mirabilibus*. Later maps, such as the Hereford map (1313), not only evince a greater geographical accuracy (in consonance with the keen attentiveness to nature of the later Middle Ages), but they also show an expanding capacity for the exotic, romantic aspects of the world at large. This same taste for the literature of travel — a craving that looks forward to the later thirst for exploration itself — was embodied in the Vézelay tympanum portraying Christ and the apostles, and the diverse human nations, especially the marvelous peoples of India, awaiting conversion.[42] This fascination with far-off fantasies and prodigies might be deemed a new credulousness; surely, though, it marks a widening of the world view beyond the old diagrammatic schema, a new receptiveness, a perception and a willing acceptance of human diversity. Despite high hopes and heartening reports, travelers and military expeditions had not made contact with Christian allies in India; and the more realistic geographical perspective of the period, while it confirmed India's remoteness, dispelled the notion that India was within the tightening boundaries of Christendom.[43] Now Europeans reveal a disposition to acknowledge India's dissimilarity and separateness, and in the later Middle Ages India's isolation becomes proverbial. In fact, an "India topos" occurs among Latin writers as early as Virgil,

[41] See Hay 332-333 for reproductions of these maps, and Hay's commentary, 341-343. See also Wright (n. 39 above) illustrations at 69, 123; on the latter map, India appears at the top.

[42] For the Hereford map, see Wright (n. 39 above) 276-277. The tympanum at Vézelay is described by Henri Focillon, *The Art of the West*, ed. J. Bony, trans. D. King, ed. 2 (New York 1969) and plates 120, 121; for a more detailed description, see Adolf Katzenellenbogen, "The Central Tympanum at Vézelay: Its Encyclopedic Meaning and Its Relation to the First Crusade," *The Art Bulletin* 26 (1944) 141-151.

[43] Denys Hay, *Europe: The Emergence of an Idea* (New York 1965 [1957]) offers a general treatment of the concept of Christendom in relation to the new geographical ideas which were taking hold.

whereby India becomes a designation for the remotest regions of the world, and it seems probable that Saint Jerome, in the allusions quoted above, also had this conventional synecdoche in mind.[44] The vernacular literatures continue to use this figure occasionally, but it attains exceptional prominence in English literature of the fourteenth and early fifteenth centuries, when more than twenty-five different instances may be observed.[45] Most of these occurrences serve to emphasize a superlative, as in the *Seven Sages of Rome* (1.2274): "Thar es none swilk fra hethin to Ynde," or the Chaucerian *Romaunt of the Rose* (622-624), "for swetter place/ To pleyen ynne he may not fynde,/ Although he soughte oon intyl Ynde."

But India is not merely a land of Cockaigne. Although the contrasts with the Christian world ordinarily center on India's distantness, they often imply as well a superiority on the part of the Indians. Dante gives us another fourteenth-century example of the transformation of the Indians' image from the suggestion of mere isolation, first to blameless ignorance of Christianity, and then even to transcendence of European culture.[46] In *Paradiso* 29 he uses "a li Spani e a l'Indi" (101) to signify the western and eastern limits of the world.[47] Earlier in the *Paradiso*, in Canto Nineteen, Dante had introduced a passage based upon this same trope: here, in the Heaven of Jupiter, the Eagle of Divine Justice says to Dante:

> ché tu dicevi: "Un uom nasce a la riva
> de l'Indo, e quivi non è chi ragioni
> de Cristo né chi legga né chi scriva;
> e tutti suoi voleri e atti buoni
> sono, quanto ragione umana vede,

[44] Ernst Robert Curtius, *European Literature and the Latin Middle Ages,* trans. W. R. Trask (New York 1963 [1953]) 160-161, mentions this topos and gives five examples, from the *Aeneid* (6.794), Fortunatus, Boethius, the *Chronicle of Novalesa,* and *Aymeri de Narbonne.* Another Latin example, which balances the later popularity of this topos in the vernacular, occurs in a letter written by a merchant associated with the Riccardi, bankers to the popes. In the letter (dated to 1 November 1301; Public Record Office E101/601/5, page 37) "India" clearly signifies the ends of the earth; the author fears that the pope "will take from us all we have even if we could escape to India . . . . May God help us." I am grateful to my colleague, Professor R. W. Kaeuper, who called this passage to my attention.

[45] See B. J. and H. W. Whiting, *Proverbs, Sentences, and Proverbial Phrases from English Writings Mainly before 1500* (Cambridge, Mass. 1968) C63, D160, I135, L427, and O52. G. L. Kittredge, "The Authorship of the English *Romaunt of the Rose,*" *Harvard Studies and Notes in Philology and Literature* 1 (1892) 21-22, provides three examples beyond those Whiting mentions (I would like to thank Ms. Jeanne Carriere for calling my attention to this article.) For other examples, see *Morte Arthure,* ed. Edmond Brock, EETS 8 (Oxford 1871) 573; Bradwardine, *De causa dei,* ed. H. Savile (London 1618) 225. For biblical authority, see Esther 1.1 – "Assuerus qui regnavit ab India usque Aethiopiam." Ælfric translated this line in his version of Esther, so that he furnishes the first example of the "India topos" in the vernacular.

[46] I have discussed Dante's use of the "Indian tradition" in a forthcoming essay, Thomas Hahn, "I gentili e 'un uom nasce a la riva del'Indo,' " *L'Alighieri* 18 (1977). Dante also mentions India because of its hot climate (*Inferno* 14.32, *Purgatorio* 26.21) and its remarkable trees (*Purgatorio* 32.41), but these references do not seem to have any direct bearing on the question of non-Christian salvation.

[47] All quotations from Dante are taken from *The Divine Comedy,* ed. Charles S. Singleton, 6 vols. (Princeton 1970-1975).

> sanza peccato in vita o in sermoni.
> Muore non battezzato e sanza fede:
> ov' è questa guistizia che 'l condanna?
> ov' è la colpa sua, se ei non crede?" (19.70-78)

The Eagle perceives that Dante has been seeking the solution to this question since the beginning of his journey, when he asked Virgil about the salvation of the just pagans in Limbo; it is quite significant, however, that the Eagle formulates the proposition in just this way, choosing as his single, representative example of the virtuous heathen an Indian. The use of the phrase "good . . . insofar as human reason determines" (73-74) also helps to define the context of this problem; for Dante here echoes, no doubt consciously, the long succession of canon lawyers, theologians, philosophers, and literary writers who bound reason and nature together, and attempted to describe the prospects of salvation for a human being who used only his natural, human reason in his struggle to know God.[48] Dante, through the reply of the Eagle, takes a thoroughly moderate stance in this familiar discussion:

> Or tu chi se', che vuo' sedere a scranna,
> per giudicar di lungi mille miglia
> con la veduta corta d'una spanna? (19.79-81)

In effect, the Eagle has taken the conventional synecdoche and extended the metaphor, so that the immense distance of India now symbolizes the unbridgeable gap between divine and human understanding.

The Eagle goes on to assure Dante that the fate of virtuous non-Christians accords with God's perfect justice, and then explains:

> Ma vedi: molti gridan "Cristo, Cristo!"
> che saranno in giudicio assai men prope
> a lui, che tal che non conosce Cristo;
> e tai Cristian dannerà l' Etiòpe,
> quando si partiranno i due collegi,
> l'uno in etterno ricco e l'altro inòpe. (19.106-111)

Here Dante dramatizes the contrast between the good pagan who, by the light of reason alone, leads a faultless life consonant with God's will and commandments, and the reprehensible Christian, who has not made good use of his access to God's revealed truth. The Indians and other virtuous heathen living in a kind of utopia and observing naturally God's eternal precepts, provide a foil for the blameworthy or apathetic Christians; and though the Eagle had previously maintained an ambiguity about their fate, the advance of the heathen to eternal treasure, which the Eagle mentions, seems to indicate a full and definite solution to the problem.[49]

---

[48] All the late medieval redefinitions of nature, reason, conscience, and righteousness generally bolstered the links between these terms; Huguccio of Pisa's statement is typical: "Ius ergo naturale dicitur ratio, scilicet naturalis vis animi ex quo homo discernit inter bonum et malum, eligendo bonum et detestando malum" (text in Odon Lottin, *Le droit naturel chez saint Thomas d'Aquin et ses prédécesseurs,* ed. 2 [Bruges 1931] app. 5).

[49] Dante raises the question again when he introduces Trajan and Ripheus in the following Canto (20); a full discussion appears in Hahn (n. 46 above).

It was not only the remoteness of the Indians, however, that urged the candidacy of the Brahmans for virtuous heathen *par excellence*; their reputation began a period of steady growth in the Carolingian Renaissance, and an impulse towards the study of ethnology in the later Middle Ages also favored them. Albertus Magnus, in his *Liber cosmographicus*, maintained that the torrid zone in which they lived did not hamper the Indians' wisdom, for the works of astronomy and philosophy that they had passed on to the West evidenced their great learning.[50] Moreover, John of Spain had translated Mohammed ben Musa al-Kharizmi's treatise upon Arabic figures under the title "De numero Indorum," and thus the Indian philosophers were associated with many of the advances in mathematics and the other sciences that marked the later Middle Ages.[51] The first reference to the special fame of the Brahmans for the practice of virtue as well as wisdom occurs in lines attributed to Alcuin of York, describing the *Collatio Alexandri cum Dindimo*: "Gens Bragmana quidem, miris quae moribus extat,/ Hic legitur, lector mente fidem videat."[52] Another Englishman, John of Salisbury, in the twelfth century presents the Brahmans as ascetics, spurning wealth and all intercourse with the world, adding no affectation to nature and holding all goods in common; at the conclusion of their letter to Alexander, they protest, "Quem enim locum haberet uindicta, ubi nulla fit iniustitia?" And this so moves Alexander that he leaves them in peace.[53] Ratramnus, in the ninth century, had mentioned the Brahmans' belief in Buddha's birth from a maiden as a parallel to the Virgin Birth of Christ.[54]

There is a clear tendency among later medieval authors, however, to single out one of the Brahmans, their leader Dindimus, for particular praise. Abelard seems the first, and in some ways the most conspicuous of these writers: in his *Introduction to Theology*, Abelard writes:

> Juvat autem et Didimi regis Bragmanorum inferre testimonium, ut in quatuor regum auctoritate nostrae assertio fidei praemineat. Duorum quidem Judaeorum, et duorum gentilium, David scilicet et Salomonis, Nabuchodonosor et Didimi sintque hi quatuor reges quasi quatuor rotae nobilis quadrigae summi regis, per quas videlicet fides quatuor evangelistarum de sancta Trinitate per universum deferatur mundum . . . [cap. 23]. Ait itaque Didimus in prima ad Alexandrum epistola, ait, inquam, sic: "Inter caetera religionis vel fidei suae gentis insignia, non suscipit Deus sacra sanguinea; cultum diligit incruentum. . . . Nam verbum Deus est, mundum creavit, hoc regit atque alit omnia, hoc nos veneramur, hoc diligimus, ex hoc spiritum trahimus, si quidem Deus ipse spiritus atque

---

[50] Clarence J. Glacken, *Traces on the Rhodian Shore* (Berkeley 1967) 262-275, treats medieval environmental ideas, especially the view of Albertus Magnus; in addition, see A. P. Newton, *Travel and Travelers in the Middle Ages* (New York 1926) 11.

[51] See G. G. Neill Wright, *The Writing of Arabic Numerals* (London 1952) 37ff.

[52] PL 101.1375. Cary (n. 3 above) 14, 92, and 280, notes this as the first reference to the *Collatio*.

[53] John of Salisbury, *Policraticus*, ed. C. C. J. Webb (Oxford 1909) 1.270-271.

[54] See Ratramnus, *De eo quod Christus ex Virgine natus est* (PL 121.87). Ratramnus mentions this example, but makes no explicit judgment on the Brahmans' moral stature.

mens est atque ideo non terrenis divitiis nec largitate munifica, sed religiosis operibus et gratiorum actione placatur . . . ." Quantae autem religionis seu abstinentiae populus Brachmanorum fuerit, ut illis Deus supra universas nationes fidei sacrae intelligentiam inspirare deberet, epistolae ipsae Didimi ad Alexandrum continent. Quibus quidem epistolis, si fides exhibenda sit, nulla hominum vita quantumcunque religiosorum innocentiae atque abstinentiae Brachmanorum aequiparanda videtur.[55]

Abelard's opinions warrant quotation at such length because they illustrate the unshakable establishment of the holiness and sanctification of the Brahmans, according to the thought of one of the most notable if controversial theologians of the later Middle Ages. Abelard's conclusions were by no means moderate, or even orthodox, but they stood as a precedent and a provocation for all succeeding thinkers. We may rest assured that Abelard's canonization of Dindimus and the Brahmans remained a challenging proposition for later writers, for he took care to include the assertion in other passages of his work; in his *Christian Theology*, he affirmed: "Haec quidem, ni fallor, illa est ara misericordiae, cui a supplicibus non immolabatur, nisi illud Brachmanorum sacrificium, hoc est orationes et lacrymae." In this work, he also averred that the Indians had an understanding of the Trinity, a statement echoed in the *Sic et Non*: "Quod philosophi quoque Trinitatem seu Verbum Dei crediderint, et non."[56] Abelard consistently maintained that the virtuous heathen would be saved, and that indeed they were the proto-Christians: "Ne quis, post legem etiam datam usque ad adventum Christi, de salute fidelium gentilium desperet, si sine perceptione sacramentorum sobrie ac juste vixerunt: inter quos quidem philosophi tam vita quam doctrina claruisse noscantur."[57] Abelard's attempt to open wide the church door to the virtuous heathen had the momentous effect of forcing this issue, which in discussions of many of the most vital and pressing questions was frequently just below the surface, upon the consciousness of the intellectuals of the later Middle Ages, and of furnishing models of argument and method for the legitimization of non-Christian salvation. Even more crucial, however, is Abelard's elevation of Dindimus and the Brahmans to the foremost place among those who passed a virtuous life without Christ or Revelation, and his effort to usher them into the Church before all others.

[55] Peter Abelard, *Introductio ad theologiam* 1.22-23 (PL 178.1032-1033). Abelard also quotes St. Jerome's comment on Pantaenus's evangelization of India (see n. 36 above).

[56] Peter Abelard, *Theologia christiana* 3 (PL 178.1225). In Book 1 of this work, Abelard had repeated in full the assertion quoted above from the *Introductio* (1164). The passage from *Sic et Non* appears at 1385 (number 25).

[57] Abelard *Theologia christiana* 2 (PL 178.1174). Almost all of Book 2 touches upon the issue of non-Christian knowledge of salvific truths (see 1064ff.). For still another discussion, see Peter Abelard, *Epitome theologiae christianae,* 1712ff. Louis Caperan clarifies the historical context of Abelard's opinions in *Le problème du salut des infidèles,* ed. 2 (Toulouse 1934) 173-177. This is the most detailed and helpful study of non-Christian salvation from the perspective of historical theology.

Abelard's ardent partisanship on the side of the philosophers and pagans, like his flamboyance and zeal in other matters, put many of his contemporaries off, but his concerns in this case were much more symptomatic of his age than they were eccentric. We may again compare his ideas with those of his more moderate and younger contemporary, Hugh of Saint-Victor, in order to see just how they conform to the general interests of the period. Hugh in fact reveals a similar solicitude for the situation of good pagans; in his treatise on the sacraments, he reflects on the problem of precisely what knowledge non-Christians must possess in order to merit salvation, and his solution is that God demands only that the individual recognize the unity of the Creator, and that he realize that God, through his goodness and mercy, would bring man to happiness.[58] Hugh considered this knowledge the equivalent of a veiled understanding of the Christian faith and, though he refused to go along with Abelard and call the philosophers Christians, he did say that those who adhered to such general notions were, at bottom, one with the Christian Church. A dialogue by one of Hugh's disciples, *Questiones in epistolas S. Pauli*, illustrates the scope and the urgency of this topic at the time. Here, the nonplussed master maintains a Hugonian outlook while he deals with a remarkable variety of propositions, including some of Abelard's and some more Pelagian than Abelard's, submitted by his disciples.[59] The response to the final question, whether the philosophers knew the Trinity through natural reason, concludes the dialogue: the master somewhat ambiguously affirms the doctrinal knowledge of the pagans, but then adds that grace must have had some part in the attainment of such understanding. The Master of the Sentences, Peter Lombard, also thought the question of heathen salvation topical enough to include it in his work, and his view resembles that of Hugh. The Lombard concludes that the majority of people before Christ (the "simplices") understood the Christian truths only "in mysterio," that is, according to a vague perception that did not really distinguish individual dogmas; and for those without Revelation, this availed for salvation.[60] The inclusion of this case in the *Sentences* insured that later thinkers would have to grapple with this same issue that perplexed the foremost twelfth-century writers, and these successors unreluctantly continued and advanced the patterns set by Hugh and the Lombard, and influenced by Abelard.

This heritage of attentiveness and generosity, bequeathed especially to Dindimus and the Brahmans, owed a good deal to two other dialogues by Hugh of Saint-Victor – his *Epitome of Philosophy* and his book *On the Science of Grammar*.[61] In both of these colloquies, the chief interlocutor is the philosopher Dindimus. Whether Hugh had come under the sway of Abelard, or had been reading Dindimus's own

[58] See *De sacramentis* 1.10.6-9 (PL 176.335-344). The most important points, especially concerning pre-Christian salvation, occur at 339-341.

[59] See *Questiones in epistolas sancti Pauli* 38-40 (PL 175.440-441).

[60] See Peter Lombard, *Libri quattuor sententiarum* 3, d. 25 (PL 192.809-810).

[61] See Hugh of St-Victor, *Epitome Dindimi in philosophiam,* ed. Roger Baron, *Traditio* 11 (1955) 91-148. The *Epitome* is also included in Hugh, *Opera propaedeutica,* ed. R. Baron (Notre Dame 1966).

"correspondence" or one of the other Indian tractates, his intention in creating these pedagogical roles for the chief Brahman seems transparent: both works deal with subjects that fall exclusively into the province of reason. Earlier, in the *Didascalicon*, Hugh had differentiated between sacred and profane knowledge, and he has the non-Christian Dindimus deal with matters that belong to the latter category in his dialogues. In the *Epitome*, the Brahman defines philosophy as "studium querende sapientie, et diligens investigatio ueri."[62] This fervent pursuit of beneficial, valid knowledge might be undertaken by any human being, and was as helpful to pagans as to Christians. Similarly, grammar, the first of the seven liberal arts, included the study of philology and classical texts as well as the technical rules of language; and the discussions of grammar and of the other liberal arts by Alan of Lille in the *De planctu naturae* and the *Anticlaudianus*, and by Thierry of Chartres in his *Hepatateuchon* demonstrate how advantageous and edifying twelfth-century authors considered them. Hugh, in the *Didascalicon*, himself says that the arts may make a reader perfect, and elsewhere suggests that this natural knowledge, properly ordered, leads to divine understanding.[63] Hugh chose to name his fictional counterpart "Dindimus" because he wished to draw upon all of those associations that the Brahman would call forth; Hugh must have conceived of Dindimus therefore as the model of rectitude and devotion to the truth, the symbol of what a human person might achieve without Revelation or any special divine aid. Such a conception on Hugh's part says much for the growth of Dindimus's reputation before the mid-twelfth century, and Hugh's dramatization of the Indian philosopher did not hamper his fame. Thierry apparently pays tribute to Hugh's choice in his *Heptateuchon*, and in the *Anticlaudianus,* Alan wrote, "Partes grammatice dissutas cogit in unum/ Dindimus et propriis describit singula formis."[64] These allusions from the later twelfth century confirm Hugh's tendency to see the Brahmans in the most favorable light possible, indeed as the embodiment of the possibility, and the reality, of non-Christian salvation.

Later writers were satisfied to accept and to enhance the tradition of the Brahmans' exemplary goodness. Geoffrey of Viterbo incorporated the correspondence of Dindimus into his *Pantheon* (ca. 1185); however, he modified the collection of five letters by assigning a sixth fictional missive to the king of the Brahmans, so that he might have the last word in rebuttal of Alexander's paganism. Geoffrey repeatedly has the Indian philosopher employ paraphrases and quotations from the Bible in his castigation of the boastful Macedonian king, and in this way the poet demonstrates the less-than-veiled understanding of the Brahmans and their adherence

---

[62] Hugh, *Opera,* 189.

[63] See Hugh of St-Victor, *Didascalicon* 3.4 (PL 176.768-769); *De sacramentis,* "Prologus" (PL 176.183-185).

[64] *The "Anticlaudian"...,* trans. W. H. Cornog (Philadelphia 1935) makes Dindimus into a mountain that alludes to Thierry; for a critical edition, see *Anticlaudianus,* ed. R. Bossuat (Paris 1955) 89, lines 498-499. Bossuat prefers "Didimus" (from two manuscripts only) and interprets this as an allusion to the ancient grammarian mentioned by Priscian. However, even in this variant spelling (the same spelling used by Abelard), the reference to the chief of the Brahmans seems clear. Bossuat corrects Cornog in his index, s.v. "Dindimus" (216).

to divine truths. As in Abelard, so here the chief of the Brahmans is an authority on the proper worship and prayer to God, and Geoffrey has him end his first letter by invoking the Golden Rule for Alexander's edification.[65] In attributing the Golden Rule to the Brahmans (a passage not found in the *Collatio*), Geoffrey reflects the new definition of the natural law established in theology by Hugh of Saint-Victor and in canon law by Gratian; the text implies that the Brahmans' righteousness derives from their observance of the law of nature.[66] In the last letter, which Geoffrey invented, the Indian philosopher ends the exchange by again striking the note of his own holiness, his trust in God, and his hope for his own salvation:

> Sola mihi cura sit ad illa venire futura
> Quando Dei pura fiet manifesta figura,
> Qua veniente, meum credo videre Deum.[67]

James of Vitry (thirteenth century) also presented the Dindimus-Alexander correspondence, but his version completely eliminated the replies of Alexander, enabling Dindimus to present the case for his virtue without any adversary. James himself comments upon the Indian's exposition: "Ex his patet quam religiose et secundum legem naturae vixissent isti Brachmani qui nec legem Mosaicam nec legem evangelii audierant."[68] James makes explicit the connection between the godliness of the Brahmans and the law of nature, as well as their separation from the guidance of the Old and New Testaments. Thomas of Cantimpré (ca. 1250) reveals influence of this same perspective in his book on the extraordinary peoples of the East; in his Latin text, he refers to

> Homines praeterea alii sunt valde mirabiles, ultra Gangem fluvium habitantes, quos Bragmanos appellamus; quos mirabilis religio, innocentia, mores et vita mirifice decorant. Hii etiam, antequam Christus veniret in carne, de eius coeternitate cum Patre aperte scripserunt. Nam quidam Dindimus, didascalus ipsorum Bragmanorum, rogatus ab Alexandro Macedone mirabilem epistolam scripsit ad eundem Alexandrum de vita et sanctis moribus Bragmanorum et de cultu unius Dei et de coeternitate Filii cum Patre.[69]

---

[65] For Geoffrey of Viterbo, see Lucienne Meyer, *Les légendes des matières de Rome, de France et de Bretagne dans la "Pantheon" de Godefroi de Viterbe* (Paris 1933) 82-97; Meyer provides long quotations and a close comparison of Geoffrey's treatment with his sources.

[66] For Hugh's discussion, see *De sacramentis* 1.2.7 (PL 176.347); for Gratian, see the first distinction of his *Decretum* (PL 187.29). The connections between personal righteousness and the legal and theological concepts of natural law in the later Middle Ages are implicit in the texts that Dom Lottin provides in his appendixes (n. 49 above).

[67]*Pantheon* 11, quoted by Meyer (n. 65 above) 96, from the edition of Pistorius-Struve (Regensburg 1726). I have relied upon Meyer for the accuracy of this quotation, since I have been unable to check this edition.

[68] Cary (n. 3 above) 280 refers to Jacques de Vitry, *Historia Hierosolymitana: Gesta Dei per Francos* (Hanover 1611). I have not examined this edition.

[69] Thomas of Cantimpré, *Liber de monstruosis hominibus orientis aus Thomas de Cantimpré: De natura rerum,* ed. Alfons Hilka (Breslau 1911) 27. Hilka prints the Latin text at the foot of each page.

The use of "didascalus" for "teacher" and the conviction that the virtuous Indians understood the One God in Three Persons suggest that Thomas had been reading Abelard's or Hugh's remarks on the situation of good non-Christians, and they attest the vitality of these views in the thirteenth century. Thomas also translated the work into Old French, and here he was just as generous in his estimate of the Brahmans' knowledge:

> Brangmanos sont apiele cil,
> Si ne metent mie a escil
> Leur travail, car opinion
> Ont ferme et bone par raison,
> Car un Diu aourent ensanle
> Pour çou que verités lor sanle
> Que plussour s'acordent envis,
> Si los aporte lor avis
> Que de celui Diu naisteroit
> Uns hom qui sans pecié seroit,
> Par coi li mons seroit lavés
> De peché dont estoit ordés
>
>   . . .
>
> Ensi a[u]ourent celui Diu
> Et le tienent cescun a siu.
> Noble entendement ont icil
> Qui ne sont precciét en escil,
> U il travaillent nuit et jor
> Por venir a la Diu amor;
> Car bien sevent que tos jors faut
> Li aise, et li airs qui ne faut
> Chiet si sovent u on ne dote;
> Que mout sovent vone en desroute
> Les bieles fietes et les gius
> C'on voit sovent en plusors lius;
> Ce sevent cil que vos devis,
> Qui es chius font torner lor vis.[70]

The Brahmans possess a perception of some of the essential Christian mysteries, an ardent devotion to God, and desire for their own salvation: Thomas has here interpreted the Indians for his reader in such a way that none could overlook their high morality or holiness, which they had attained before the Incarnation, but which surpassed most examples of Christian virtue. Doubtless, almost everyone appreciated their unambiguous goodness, their paganism or remoteness from Christianity, and almost all who read Thomas aright would have conceded that these, at least, represented one example of salvation outside the Church.

A similar portrayal occurs in James of Cessolis's essay on the game of chess, and the *Renart le Contrefait* (ca. 1340) transforms the substance of Dindimus's letters

---

[70] Hilka 27-28, lines 157-186.

into a general attack on idolatry. The chronicler Martin of Poland, like James of Vitry, presents only the arguments of Dindimus, so that his righteousness and spiritual advice remain unchallenged.[71] Vincent of Beauvais apportions six sections in the historical segment of his encyclopedia to an "Epilogus de pace Bragmanorum cum Alexandro." Here Alexander at least receives a chance to reply, but to no avail; the Brahmans follow the "ratio naturae" — the law of nature — and live in expectation of their life in the next world.[72] The *Speculum morale*, apparently written by one of Vincent's associates, demonstrates that the Indians' reputation for goodness was strong enough to turn several narratives, originally unconnected with their history, to their advantage. Here Dindimus asks Alexander the questions that are customarily attributed to an anonymous Gymnosophist; and in other sections of the work, as well as in other works, Dindimus is confused with or substituted for another moral philosopher and example of virtue, Diogenes.[73] Likewise, Humbert of Romans praises the Brahmans for censuring Alexander's vain, worldly ambition, retelling in their name an anecdote usually associated with the Gymnosophists.[74] A final thirteenth-century author who may be mentioned as showing special consideration to the Brahmans is the Englishman Robert Grosseteste. In the "Prooemium" to his *Hexaemeron*, he makes a particular effort to discuss the Brahmans and their land "quam acceperunt a deo in hereditatem." Grosseteste apparently thought the Indians important enough to merit a new translation from Palladius, and his description of them, as well as his decision to describe them at the outset of his work, signifies his favorable attitude towards them.[75]

In the fourteenth century the Indians achieved the height of their fame as the best of the good pagans — in the proverbial allusions mentioned above, in Dante, and in a number of other Latin and vernacular works. Most striking among these are two English books, the alliterative romance *Alexander and Dindimus* and *Mandeville's Travels*. The detailed portraits in these works leave no doubt that the Brahmans'

---

[71] See Cary (n. 3 above) 280-281 for comment and editions.

[72] See Vincent of Beauvais, *Speculum historiale* 4.66-71 (Douai 1624) 135-137. This is the "Epilogus de pace Bragmanorum cum Alexandro."

[73] See *Speculum morale* (Douai 1624) 514 (Dindimus) and 569-570 (first Diogenes, and then the virtue of the Brahmans at length). Cary's comment on the shaping of the legendary material deserves notice: "In the medieval Alexander tradition there were three philosophers among whom the best things were normally divided: Aristotle, Diogenes, and Dindimus" (n. 3 above) 147. See also 148, and 297-298.

[74] Cary 298 quotes Humbert's "Exemplum de Alexandro" (*Maxima bibliotheca veterum patrum* 25 [Lyons 1677] 566, col. 1): "Ideo Bragmani Alexandro . . . petent[es] immortalitatem . . . bene responderunt dicentes: 'Tu mortalis cum sis, quare tot mala faciendo discurris?' quasi dicere deberent: 'Recogitatio mortis te deberet facere cessare a malis.' " The request for immortality frequently figures in the exchanges between Alexander and the Indians.

[75] Grosseteste's "Prooemium" has not been printed in its entirety; an excerpt is included in Richard C. Dales and Servus Gieben, O.F.M., "The 'Prooemium' to Robert Grosseteste's *Hexaemeron*," *Speculum* 43 (1968) 459. These two scholars conclude that Grosseteste made his own translation from the Greek, but see J. T. Muckle, "Robert Grosseteste's Use of Greek Sources in his *Hexaemeron*," *Mediaevalia et Humanistica* 3 (1945) 33-48. If, as Muckle contends, Grosseteste could not read Greek, perhaps he had a translation produced for the *Hexaemeron* by one of his associates.

goodness rests upon their natural understanding and behavior, and that they are safe
from hell.[76] Other descriptions endorse this assertion in shorter compass: The
Eulogium historiarum of Thomas of Malmesbury presents a chronicle of events up to
1366 that includes an account of the happy life of the Indians.[77] Thomas shows
himself a Brahman sympathizer by re-ordering the correspondence between Alexander and Dindimus: Dindimus not only sends three letters to Alexander's two, but
he has the first and last word in the dispute besides. Ranulf Higden included an
elaborate description of the Indian utopia in his *Polychronicon*; John of Trevisa
translated this to English in the 1390s, and an anonymous fifteenth-century author
produced another translation, so that the *Polychronicon* exerted continuous influence on English literature into the Renaissance.[78] In the *Confessio Amantis* John
Gower demonstrates the literary use to be made of Dindimus, for he singles the
Indian out as a spokesman for truth, against the false religion of the Greeks.[79]

One other fourteenth-century tribute may be noted – Philippe de Mézières's
Epistre au roi Richart (1395), which combines political, literary, religious, and
historical views of the Brahmans. Philippe, former chancellor of Cyprus, petitioned
Richard II to help secure international peace: he based his appeal on practical
issues – political alliances through marriage, economic and military benefits, a
resolution of the Great Schism – and on more abstract and spiritual considerations.
His last, conclusive argument draws upon an allegory of two gardens – "la paix"
("tres delicieux") and "la guerre" ("horribel et perilleux"). He describes first "le
vergier delitable" – a place filled with nourishing and delightful vegetation, free from
inclement weather and all ill health:

> Tous les fruis du vergier estoient communs aus habitans, a chascun selonc
> sa necessite, et ceste parole, c'est assavoir "propre" et "mien," estoient
> banis du vergier. Les habitans du dit vergier en si grant joye vivoient l'un
> avec l'autre, qu'il leur sembloit qu'il n'en veillissoient point. Toute
> tyrannie et crueuse seignourie estoient banies du vergier, et toutes foiz il
> y avoit un seigneur et roy ou dit vergier qui representoit la seignourie et
> la chose publique des dessusdiz habitans.[80]

[76] The self-conscious modification of the "Indian tradition" in *Alexander and Dindimus* and
Mandeville's Travels, and the relation of such treatments to characteristic outlooks of fourteenth-
century England are discussed at length in Thomas Hahn, "God's Friends: Virtuous Heathen in
Later Medieval Thought and English Literature," Ph.D. diss. (UCLA 1974).

[77] Thomas of Malmesbury, *Eulogium (historiarum sive temporis),* ed Frank Scott Hayden,
Rolls Series 9.1 (London 1858). Hayden discusses the connection of the *Eulogium* with Higden
in his introduction (lxxviii); the account of Dindimus and the Indians appears in Book 3.122-126
(pp. 428-434).

[78] *Polychronicon Ranulphi Higden . . .,* ed. J. R. Lumby, Rolls Series 41.3 (London 1871)
455ff. For the literary use of historians in the Renaissance see H. A. Kelly, *Divine Providence in
the England of Shakespeare's History Plays* (Cambridge, Mass. 1970). John Taylor's *The
Universal Chronicle of Ranulf Higden* (Oxford 1966) discusses Higden's general influence; for
particular connections with More, see Hahn (n. 2 above).

[79] See Gower, *Confessio Amantis,* in the *English Works of John Gower,* ed. G. C. Macaulay,
Early English Text Society, Extra Series 81, 82 (London 1900, 1901) 5.1453-1496.

[80] Philippe de Mézières, *Letter to King Richard II,* ed. G. W. Coopland (Liverpool 1975) 127.
Coopland also includes his translation of the letter.

This passage deserves quotation at such length because it demonstrates how conventional the Indians and their attributes had become. By calling up these associations, Philippe evidently meant to put Richard and others in his audience in mind of Dindimus and the Brahmans, who live a virtuous and simple life according to natural reason. Philippe makes his allusion explicit when he describes the setting of "la paix":

> Es dis murs, dedens et dehors, estoient figures, en painture solempnelle et permanable, les temps dores de ce monde, c'est assavoir la gracieuse policie des Bargamains et de leur roy, esquelz convoitise, orgueil et luxure, du tout en tout estoient banies. Il vivoient en commun et estoient content de cavernes, sans edifier maisons. Il ne faisoient aucune mension ne d'or ne d'argent ne de pierres precieuses. . . . Leur roy n'estoit point empesche de faire justice. Quel merveille, car il ne mesfaisoient riens l'un a l'autre. Le roy‾ Alixandre visita les dessus dis Bargamains, et pour ce qu'il n'y trova n'or ne argent ne seignorie tirannique, il ne fist con es des dis Bargamains.[81]

Philippe uses the Indians as models for Richard's understanding of the ideals of international Christianity, and, as in *Mandeville's Travels,* their charitable and "natural" behavior contrasts with the misguided and self-destructive strife that marks the Christians. Philippe's resort to this set of traits in this context demonstrates the uniformity of the Indian racial stereotype during the later Middle Ages, and the consistency of the literary understanding of the "Indian tradition" as a vehicle for satire and gentle self-criticism.

Among all the possible interpretations that might be put on the matter of India, only this idea of the Indians as virtuous non-Christians consistently reoccurs; and it would be very hard to cite an unfavorable notice of the Brahmans to parallel Saint Augustine's at any time after the Carolingian Renaissance. The elements in this Western image of the good Indians include wisdom through natural philosophy, holiness through simple and devout behavior, and an appealing "otherness" that complements belief in the "universal" and familiar religious truths of Western Christianity; ordinarily this otherness and sameness co-exist, for the Indians' exoticism is closely bound up with their virtue and their hope for salvation, and these

---

[81] *Ibid.* 128. Coopland apparently did not understand this allusion as a part of the "Indian tradition," for he translates without comment except for a reference to another of Philippe's works, *Le Songe du Vieil Pelerin,* also ed. G. W. Coopland, 2 vols. (Cambridge 1969) 224-227. Philippe's treatment of the Indians on this fictional pilgrimage is strikingly analogous to the outlook in *Mandeville's Travels,* and it adds one more instance of self-conscious resort to the "Indian tradition." That he did intend these passages as conventional allusions appears the more certain because Philippe's diplomatic activities had put him in touch with a Genoese merchant who had lived in India for fifty years (see *Songe* 1.118-119). We may note also that Philippe twice uses the "India topos" in the *Songe:* in Book 1 he says that when the Hospitallers were in the Holy Land, "la gent Mahommet faisoit si grand desroy, qu'ilz voulassent bien qu'ilz fussent en Ynde la Majeur, et que jamais n'oyssent parler de leur retour." In Book 2, he writes of the French ship of state, "qui veist les grans, soutilz et precieux edifices, des ornemens des palaiz et chasteaux de la nef, il se puet bien dire que jusques a la mer d'Inde n'ara telle carraque" (*Songe* 1.258 and 545-546).

characteristics make them outstanding models for Christian imitation. This image is a composite, but the elements recur with sufficient constancy for us to recognize a unified tradition of thought about these virtuous Indians, and what is more, we can see that medieval writers recognized it as well.

Department of English
University of Rochester
Rochester, New York 14627, U.S.A.

NEW LIGHT ON THE TRANSMISSION OF DONATUS'S "COMMENTUM TERENTII"

•

by M. D. Reeve and R. H. Rouse

Much of Donatus's commentary on Terence survives only in fifteenth-century manuscripts, and next to nothing is known about its medieval circulation. Very welcome, therefore, was Margarethe Billerbeck's discovery that in borrowing from a passage of *Eunuchus* Hugo Primas, otherwise Hugh of Orléans, puts to his own use Donatus's comments on 936 and 939.[1] We now report explicit citations taken a century later from what may well have been the same manuscript.

Sometime in the middle years of the thirteenth century a lexicographer working in and about Orléans made extensive notes from ancient Latin authors in the margins of his books, most notably in his copy of Papias's dictionary, now Bern Burgerbibliothek MS 276.[2] He drew on a number of little-known works, among the rarest of which is the commentary of Donatus on Terence. In the margins of Bernensis 276 are over fifty extracts from the commentary.

Bernensis 276 is an early thirteenth-century volume containing the dictionaries of Papias and Huguccio. In the late fourteenth century it belonged to John of Guignecourt, chancellor of the University of Paris 1386-1389,[3] and in the mid-sixteenth to Pierre Daniel, who left his signature on fols. 2, 496 ("Ex lib. Petri Danielis Aurelii 1565") and his annotations beside numerous references to little-known ancient texts in which he was interested; one of these provides the key to where he acquired the book. On fol. 176v the annotator adds an example of the word *pistrinum* from "Plautus in Aulularia." Daniel spotted this as a quotation from the Pseudo-Plautine *Querolus*, of which he prepared the first printed edition in 1564; and he added next to it "Plautus in Querolo." In the preface to the edition he says "Eiusdem [i.e. Queroli] fit mentio in vetustissimo libro glossarum, quem mihi una cum hac comoedia suppeditavit amplissima fani Benedicti Floriacensis ad Ligerem

---

[1] M. Billerbeck, "Spuren von Donats Terenzkommentar bei Hugo Primas," *Rivista di filologia e di istruzione classica (Riv. fil.)* 103 (1975) 430-434.

[2] Regarding the annotations see R. H. Rouse, "Florilegia and Latin Classical Authors in Twelfth- and Thirteenth-Century France," in *Imitation and Adaptation: The Classical Tradition in the Middle Ages,* ed. D. M. Kratz (Columbus, Ohio), forthcoming.

[3] Fol. 2, "Ad usum fratris Johannis de Guignicuria pro conventu Belvacensi." Regarding Guignecourt see H. Denifle and E. Chatelain, *Cartularium universitatis Parisiensis* 3 (Paris 1894) 84, 344, 380, 388, 397, 417, 481, nos. 1527, 1533, 1552, 1558, 1609, 1656.

bibliotheca." The manuscript of the *Querolus* is doubtless Leiden, Bibliotheek der Rijksuniversiteit MS Voss. lat. Q 83 (s. ix), which bears Daniel's signature; and the "liber glossarum" with a mention of the *Querolus* can only be Bernensis 276. The *Querolus* is not cited in the great *Liber glossarum;*[4] and the description "vetustissimus," seemingly inappropriate to Bernensis 276, is notoriously flexible. The volume was not, however, written at Fleury; nor was it at Fleury in the thirteenth century, for it came there only after it had been in the hands of John of Guignecourt. It passed with Daniel's books to the library of Jacques Bongars, and thence to the Burgerbibliothek, Bern.

Bernensis 276 is one of five manuscripts annotated by the same thirteenth-century scholar. The others are: Bernensis C 219 pt. I fols. 1-8v, s. x-xi (J. Bongars), Cicero's *Topica;* Bernensis 291, s. xiii[1] (J. Bongars), Isidore's *Etymologiae* and Bede's *De orthographia;* Paris, Bibliothèque Nationale MS lat. 8213, s. xii[2] (D. Lambin), Horace; and Vatican Library MS Pal. lat. 1514, s. xi-xiv (Fugger Library), Cicero's *Tusculan Disputations.* One can tell from the manuscripts that he owned and the authors that he cites approximately where and when the annotator worked. Among the numerous authors and texts cited in the margins of these five books there are a number whose transmission is closely associated with the Loire if not Orléans, and in particular with two twelfth-century *florilegia,* the *Florilegium Angelicum* and the *Florilegium Gallicum,* and with a thirteenth-century private library, that of Richard de Fournival, which have been shown to have been formed wholly or (in Fournival's case) at least in part at Orléans.[5] The key to the group is the *Florilegium Angelicum,* a collection of extracts from ancient and patristic letters and orations for use in the composition of letters.[6] Working in the third quarter of the twelfth century, its author drew on the ninth-century collection of texts assembled by Heiric of Auxerre, now Vatican Library MS lat. 4929, for his extracts from Censorinus's *De die natali* and the *Querolus.* Vatican lat. 4929 was in Orléans from the late eleventh century if not before; it contains a list of parishes paying tithes to the cathedral – as well as a gloss from Tibullus (1.7.12) which refers to the Loire..The author of the *Florilegium Angelicum* also drew on Bernensis 136 for his text of the younger Pliny's letters; and this manuscript, as well as that containing the oldest extracts from the *Florilegium Angelicum,* Bernensis 633, belonged in the sixteenth century to the Orléans jurist Pierre Daniel. Among the rarer texts in the *Florilegium Angelicum,* the annotator of Bernensis 276 cites the *De die natali* and the *Querolus,* as well as offering at least nineteen citations from Pliny's letters and twenty-three from Ennodius, both of them texts that were used in the schools of the *ars dictaminis* in Orléans. The *Florilegium Gallicum,* the oldest manuscript of which, Paris, Bibliothèque Nationale MS lat. 7647

---

[4] J. Mountford, *Quotations from Classical Authors in Medieval Latin Glossaries,* Cornell Studies in Classical Philology 21 (Ithaca 1925).

[5] The origin of these collections summarized here is dealt with in detail in Rouse (n. 2 above).

[6] Regarding the *Florilegium Angelicum* see R. H. and M. A. Rouse, "The *Florilegium Angelicum:* Its Origin, Content and Influence," in *Medieval Learning and Literature: Essays presented to R. W. Hunt,* ed. J. J. G. Alexander and M. T. Gibson (Oxford 1976) 66-114.

(s. xii²), again belonged to Daniel, also drew on Vatican lat. 4929 for its text of the *Querolus.*[7] Among the rarer authors contained in the *Florilegium Gallicum* are Tibullus, Petronius and Calpurnius. The annotator of Bernensis 276 cites Tibullus twice, Petronius's *Satyricon* three times, and Calpurnius twice. The ancestor of all surviving manuscripts of Tibullus was owned by Richard de Fournival, and is item 115 in the *Biblionomia* or catalog of his library.[8] Among the rarer texts represented in his library were Propertius (Leiden MS Voss. lat. 0 38) and the oldest surviving manuscript of Plato's *Phaedo* in Latin translation (Paris, B. N. MS lat. 16581 fols. 94-162). The annotator of Bernensis 276 provides two lines from Propertius and at least thirteen citations from the *Phaedo.* The only medieval extracts from Propertius were once in Paris, B. N. MS lat. 15155, s. xiii, which was sold in the early fourteenth century by Henri François of Orléans to a Rouen master. The appearance of Censorinus, the *Querolus,* the letters of Pliny and Ennodius, as well as Petronius, Calpurnius, Tibullus, Propertius and Plato's *Phaedo* in these works ties them together and indicates that they have to a large degree drawn on the same collection of books.

The background exhibited by the authors and works cited in Bernensis 276 fits well with the references to Orléans and nearby libraries in the manuscripts owned by the annotator. His manuscript of Horace, Paris, B. N. lat. 8213, ends with a twenty-line oration written by Master R. of Orléans; and for its text of Horace it is a descendant of a manuscript from nearby Fleury, now Paris, B. N. lat. 7973, s. ix.[9] There is a *nota* mark beside *Liger* in the annotator's copy of Isidore, Bernensis 291 fol. 70. In addition there is the Bongars, and hence possible Daniel and Orléans, background for this manuscript, as there is also for Bernensis C 219. The annotator has indicated several times in Bernensis 276 where he found manuscripts of one author or another. Particularly interesting among these is a long note on fol. 63 in which he attempts to sort out the different men named Donatus and what they wrote.

> Donatiste heretici a Donato quondam Affro dicti]
>> Fuit Donatus Afer hereticus. Item Sanctus Donatus. Item Donatus grammaticus Romanus. Item ille de quo sic loquitur antiquum commentum Romani Donati armarii Sancte Crucis Aurelianensis IX: 'igitur duplex littera, ut ait vetus Donatus grammaticus Troianus, non fuit apud veteres.' Similiter dicit de eo Virgilius Asianus in libro epythomes. Iste est qui fecit commentum Virgilii quod est apud Sanctam Κολῦβαμ σενοῦ: 'Tiberii Claudii Donati ad Tiberium Claudium Donatianum filium suum. Incipit liber interpretationum

---

[7] Regarding the *Florilegium Gallicum* see J. Hamacher, *Florilegium Gallicum: Prolegomena und Edition der Exzerpte von Petron bis Cicero, De oratore* (Frankfurt 1975).

[8] Concerning Fournival see R. H. Rouse, "Manuscripts of Richard de Fournival," *Revue d'histoire des textes* 3 (1973) 253-269. The *Biblionomia* is edited by L. Delisle, *Le cabinet des manuscrits...* 2 (Paris 1874) 518-535.

[9] O. Keller and A. Holder, *Q. Horatii Flacci Opera* 1 (Leipzig 1899) lxxiv. The oration was published from this manuscript by Holder in *Neues Archiv der Gesellschaft für ältere deutsche Geschichtskunde* 1 (1876) 416.

> librorum Eneidos Virgilii. Illos qui Mantuani vatis michi carmina tradiderunt.' [At the head of the list but written last:] Item Donatus praetorius, de quo dicit Donatus in libro epythomes.[10]

The annotator apparently saw a commentary on Donatus at the cathedral of Sainte Croix in Orléans,[11] and knew of a manuscript of Ti. Claudius Donatus on Virgil at Saint Columba's in Sens.[12] On fol. 94v he notes that Helenus is referred to in the Pseudo-Boethian *De disciplina scholarium,* which he has seen in a manuscript at nearby Fleury:

> Helenus auctor Grecorum] . . . Iste fuit grammaticus de quo loquitur Boetius in libro *de scolastica disciplina.* Is liber est apud Sanctum Benedictum Floriacensem in arhca [sic] Boetii quam b . . . [?] alios transtulit [?]

Lastly, he refers again to the cathedral of Sainte Croix on fols. 119 and 123v:

> *Lentus* id est plenus, Remigius in commento Martiani circa principium, luculentus id est lucis lentus id est plenus ςικ εςτ ω λιβρω ςκη κρυκις αυρελ

> Littera dicitur quasi legit iter [sic ut vid.], ut dicit . . . [liber ? volumen ?] Sancte Crucis Aurelianensis[13]

The sense of these notes would suggest that the annotator was not a member of any of the institutions to which he refers but that he had access to them. He might well have been a master at Saint Aignan or Saint Euverte in Orléans, both of which were closely attached to the cathedral. To judge from the nature and number of his notes, he appears to have been an active lexicographer and should be identifiable. He knew the Greek alphabet and recopied Greek words in Papias into the margins, occasionally transliterating Latin names, such as "Columbam Senon." above, in Greek letters. The authors to whom he refers provide some indication of his date. He knows the standard trivium authors of the late twelfth and early thirteenth centuries,

[10] "Donatus in libro epythomes" must be a mistake for "Virgilius in libro epythomes"; cf. *Virgilii Maronis grammatici opera,* ed. J. Huemer (Leipzig 1886) 73.14-15. Daniel found this passage in two manuscripts, one of which, Bernensis 123, omits *praetorius.* Variants make it unlikely that his other manuscript was any of those known to Huemer or to Th. Stangl, *Virgiliana* (Munich 1891) 48. Like the annotator's it read *Donatus,* not *Donatius;* perhaps it was the same manuscript. If it survives, it is most likely to be among the Reginenses.

[11] We have not been able to identify the commentary on Donatus containing this passage. It was probably the source of the note on *littera* that we cite below; cf. H. Keil, *Grammatici latini* 4 (Leipzig 1864) 421.2-4 (Servius on Donatus's *Ars maior*) and 5 (Leipzig 1868) 98.15-16 (Pompeius on the same), and H. Hagen, *Anecdota Helvetica* (Leipzig 1870) 221.17-19 (anon. on the same).

[12] The beginning of this commentary is preserved in Florence, Biblioteca Medicea Laurenziana MS 45.15 (s. viii-ix), Vatican Library MS Reg. 1484 (s. ix), and a handful of fifteenth-century manuscripts. None of these gives the *incipit* in quite the same form as the annotator, and the Reginensis further differs in reading *post illos.*

[13] We are grateful to Mr. Bruce McMenomy for referring us to the note on fol. 119, and to Dr. Ch. von Steiger for examining the texts of these notes.

Peter Riga, Alexander of Villedieu, Huguccio and Eberhard of Bethune. The latest works to which he refers are Aristotle's *Ethics* in the translation from the Arabic made after 1250, glosses on the *Ethics* by Adam Marsh (fl. 1226-1258), and William Brito's dictionary, compiled between 1249 and 1272. With the exception of these three there is no indication that he knew any works from the second half of the century. It seems safe, thus, to place him in the third quarter of the thirteenth century.

Four medieval manuscripts of Donatus's commentary on Terence are known to have existed besides that at Orléans, and two of them survive. The older of these, Paris, B. N. MS lat. 7920, s. xi (A), is said by Wessner and others to have been written at Fleury. Although the hand is perfectly acceptable for the Loire, there is no evidence to tie it to Fleury save the fact that it was owned by Pierre Daniel in the sixteenth century.[14] The manuscript contains only the commentaries on the *Andria* and the *Adelphoe* to 1.1.40, where it ends in the middle of a page — a partial text rather than a fragment. The other medieval manuscript survives in two fragments in Vatican MS Reg. lat. 1595 fols. 1-20, s. xiii(B); nothing is known about its origin.[15] Two other medieval manuscripts were discovered in the fifteenth century, one at Mainz by Giovanni Aurispa in 1433 and the other in the cathedral library of Chartres by Jean Jouffroy in the late 1440s.[16] They were both transcribed, and both subsequently perished. Lost manuscripts owned by R. Stephanus and Cujas also seem from their readings to have been medieval.[17]

Whether the forty or so manuscripts produced in Italy in the fifteenth century all derive from the Maguntinus and the Carnotensis is not settled, and none of them derives indisputably from one rather than the other, because the earliest date in any

[14]Fleury recedes from view if it came to Daniel from the jurist Antonius Contius [Le Conte] of Bourges, as it almost certainly did; see P. Wessner, ed., *Aeli Donati Commentum Terentii,* 3 vols. (Leipzig 1902-1908) 1.ix, xvi-xvii. Professor Jean Vezin of the École des hautes études, Paris, has very kindly given us his opinion of the script: "L'écriture de ce MS est tout à fait du XIe siècle, mais n'évoque à mon esprit rien de Fleury. Tout au plus peut-on dire, avec beaucoup de prudence, que ce livre a pu être copié dans la région de la Loire entendue dans un sens extrèmement large: de Chartres à l'Auvergne et de Nantes à Auxerre." Contius also owned Paris, B.N MS lat 16689 (s. xi) of Horace, which passed by way of Richelieu to the Sorbonne; see Delisle (n. 8 above) 377, and Keller and Holder (n. 9 above) lxxx.

[15]The last part of the Reginensis, a composite manuscript, bears the signature of P. Daniel. The first part belonged to A. Petau.

[16]R. Sabbadini, *Le scoperte dei codici latini e greci ne' secoli XIV e XV* 1 (Florence 1905) 194 nn. 52-53; *idem, Carteggio de Giovanni Aurispa* (Rome 1931) 119 nn.3-4; A. Franceschini, *Giovanni Aurispa e la sua biblioteca*, Medioevo e umanesimo 25 (Padua 1976) 55, 108, 117, 126, 163, 168.

[17]See Wessner (n. 14 above) 1.xv-xvii, and the works there cited. Perhaps more information about the Cuiacianus could be extracted from the two surviving sources, Lindenbrog's edition and Gronovius's copy of Pithoeus's collation (Leid. 759 c. 16). Stephanus's manuscript also needs further investigation. The lost Hulsianus, though rightly classed among the *meliores* by Wessner 1.xvii, was certainly not medieval, because its omission in *Hecyra* associates it with two undistinguished fifteenth-century manuscripts. I have made an abortive attempt to trace it beyond *Bibliotheca Hulsiana* (The Hague 1730) 1.323 no. 4981 (in fol.) "Donati commentarius in Terentium. MS. characteribus supra fidem nitidis exaratum in pergameno, mar." (M.D.R.).

is 1459. Furthermore, their relationships change several times in the course of the commentary. As we do not wish to immerse ourselves more deeply in these problems than the task of providing an apparatus for the citations in Bernensis 276 demands, we must content ourselves with referring to the work done by Sabbadini, Wessner, and Zwierlein,[18] and promising to justify our innovations elsewhere. These, then, are the witnesses that we shall cite:

A = Paris, B. N. MS lat. 7920

B = Vatican MS Reg. lat. 1595

K = Vatican MS Chig. H VII 240[19]

Θ = the source throughout the commentary of Oxford, Bodleian Library MS Canon. class. lat. 95 (C); where C is the only descendant of Θ whose readings are known to us, we cite it instead, and where Vatican MS lat. 2905 (T) differs from C, we cite them separately

Δ = the source in *Eunuchus* and *Hec.* 3.5.8 — *Phorm.* fin. of Rome, Corsiniana MS 43 E 28 and a few allies

Λ = the hybrid and interpolated source from which most of the manuscripts derive for most of the time

M⁴ = the Greek added later to Cesena, Malatestiana MS S. 22.5

It is commonly thought, and we agree, that Θ was either Decembrio's copy of the Maguntinus or the Maguntinus itself. At least between *Andr.* 1.1.1 and *Ad.* 1.1.40, where A breaks off, its close relative K almost certainly derives from the Carnotensis. Possibly Δ either derived from or was Aurispa's copy of the Maguntinus. Λ we ignore where A Θ or B Θ are on hand.

We now set out the notes in Bernensis 276. Some of them paraphrase (for example, nos. 12, 45), others merely indicate that Donatus says something relevant (for example nos. 11, 58), others comment not on a usage of Terence's expounded by Donatus but on a usage of Donatus's own (nos. 8, 57), and three we have failed to pin down (nos. 16, 17, 25); but wherever the annotator's wording may shed light on the tradition, we give the text of Donatus and any variants that could be significant. We resolve all the annotator's abbreviations except ·|· for *id est*.

(1) fol. 6   item adprime ·|· admirabiliter secundum Donatum in commento Andrie Therentii (1.60.21-22)

---

[18] Sabbadini's contributions appeared in *Museo italiano di antichità classica* 3 (1890) 381-468; *Studi italiani di filologia classica* (SIFC) 2 (1894) 1-134, 3 (1895) 249-363, 5 (1897) 289-327, 11 (1903) 185-201; *Riv. fil.* 39 (1911) 541-3. Many of them are reprinted or summarized in his *Storia e critica di testi latini* (Catania 1914), itself reprinted in *Medioevo e umanesimo* 11 (Padua 1971) 153-181. See also P. Wessner, "Die Überlieferung von 'Aeli Donati commentum Terentii' " *Rheinisches Museum* 52 (1897) 69-98, and edition (n. 14 above); M. Warren, "On Five New Manuscripts of the Commentary of Donatus to Terence," *Harvard Studies in Classical Philology* (HSCP) 17 (1906) 31-42; C. H. Beeson, "The Text Tradition of Donatus' Commentary on Terence," *Classical Philology* 17 (1922) 283-305; O. Zwierlein, *Der Terenzkommentar des Donat im codex Chigianus H VII 240* (Berlin 1970); and M. D. Reeve, "The Textual Tradition of Donatus's Commentary on Terence," forthcoming in *Hermes* (but already out of date).

[19] Professor Zwierlein very kindly allowed us to consult his collation.

(2) fol. 17   Donatus dicit quod *ain* ·|· aisne est verbum perconctativum ·|· interrogativum. hoc dicit in commento Andrie. Probus vero querebat an esset una pars orationis

> 1.242.3-6 AIN TANDEM . . . quaerit Probus 'ain' quae pars orationis sit et an una sit. est autem 'ain' quasi aisne . . . ergo 'ain' percontativum verbum est

> > *an una* Θ : *ain unde* AK: *ain unum* B

(3) fol. 23v   *axioma* multi dicunt anxioma, et sic legitur in commento Donati in Andriam Therentii (1.55.13-56.1)

> *AΞIΩMA* A: *AΞIO . . .*/ *AΞIOAAA* K: *auziono/auzioma* T: ?/*auroma* C: ἀξίωμα M[4]

(4) fol. 26v   *bonus* ·|· plenus secundum Donatum in commento Eunuchi Therentii (1.339.1)

(5) *ibid.*   item *bonus* ·|· magnus vel multus secundum Donatum in commento Eunuchi (1.292.10)

(6) *ibid.*   *bonus* . . . Donatus dicit in commento Phormionis Therentii quod ad animum transfertur quod est corporis ut mag^m' [= magnus ?]

> 2.476.12-13 . . . ad animum transtulit quod est corporis   *corporis* ΔΛ: *corporum* Θ

(7) fol. 43v   *cocus* dicit tamen Donatus in commento Adelphorum quod coquus dicebant antiqui (2.92.3-4)

(8) fol. 44   *colligo* ·|· sillogizo secundum Donatum in commento Echyre Therentii (2.244.15)

(9) fol. 46v   Donatus in commento Andrie: condicio est cum uno certamen certam legem continens (1.66.12-13)

> *cum uno* Θ : om. AK   *certamen* Θ : om. AK   *in se continens* codd.

(10) fol. 47   conflictatio est contactus corporum invicem et collisus. hoc dicit Donatus in commento Andrie (1.69.17-18)

> *tactus invicem corporum* codd.   *collisus* AK: *collis* Θ

(11) fol. 58   quid sit designator dicit Donatus in Adelphe commento, ut notatum est ·|· capitulo S (2.24.24-25.1; cf. no. 54)

(12) fol. 64v   *echinus* aliter dicitur iste pisciculus remora quia navem detinet et remoratur, ut dicit Donatus in commento Eunuchi Therentii

> 1.334.1-2 REMORATVS EST a remora pisciculo, qui ἐχεναΐς vocatur, remoratio et moraratus dicitur

> > *ethinais* BC: *echinais* T: *et ethinais* vel sim. Δ: deest K

(13) *ibid.*   idem dicit in commento Andrie ut puto

1.217.14-16 'remorer' retardem, retineam: a remora, pisce minutissimo
qui navem retinet; nam Graece ἐχεναίς vocatur
EXEINAIC ABK: lac. Θ: ἐχῖνος M⁴

(14) fol. 71   *epytheta* . . . Donatus in commento Eunuchi: epitheta adduntur causa
discretionis, proprietatis, et ornatus. exempla ponit

1.341.14-16   ἐπίθετα autem tribus de causis nominibus adduntur:
discretionis, proprietatis, ornatus. discretionis, ut . . .
epitheta ΔΛ: . . . *et* T: *ut* C: lac. K   *ornatus* KΘΛ: *et ornatus* Δ

(15) fol. 77   *facio* ·|· probo, ostendo, intelligo. hoc dicit Donatus in commento
Echyre Therentii (2.247.7-8)²⁰

(16) *ibid.*   item idem in eodem facio ·|· mitto (?)

(17) fol. 81v   *fingo* ·|· facio et m⁰ [=?] secundum Donatum in commento Andrie
(?)

(18) fol. 87   *funus* est pompa exequiarum dicta a funibus. Donatus in commento
Andrie Therentii

1.72.15-16 *dictum a funalibus* codd.

(19) fol. 98   *honestus* ·|· pulcher secundum Donatum in commento Eunuchi
(1.375.10)

(20) fol. 102v   integrasco . . . idem Donatus in commento Therentii

1.205.19-21 HOC MALVM INTEGRASCIT integratur, quod ad integrum
redit . . .
lemma et *quod* om. B: hab. AKΘ

(21) fol. 107v   Donatus in commento Eunuchi Therentii *intercipit* ·|· totum capit.
sic Plautus in Aulularia (1.283.14-15)

(22) fol. 108   Therentius in Andria interminatus ·|· minatus secundum Donatum
in commento Andrie

1.169.3 *pro minatus* AB Θ: *pronuntiatus* K

(23) fol. 110   ira dicitur ab eo is quod cito it secundum Donatum in Adelphis
Therentii

2.155.20-21 . . . ira ab eo quod est ire dicitur, quod a se eat qui irascitur
et furit

(24) fol. 111v   *item* ·|· similiter. Donatus in commento Andrie (1.69.1)

²⁰The annotator has misunderstood the syntax of "alii 'faciunt' probant, ostendunt
intelligunt."

(25) fol. 135v   honor ·|· honestas secundum Donatum in commento Eunuchi Therentii (?)

(26) fol. 136   *methaphora* . . . Donatus dicit in Adelphis quod quoniam et postquam sunt reciproca (2.9.3-4)

(27) fol. 139v   *modus* ·|· arbitrium, voluntas. Donatus in commento Andrie Therentii

>   1.82.16-17 'meo modo' mea voluntate, meo arbitrio   *voluntate*
>   Stephanus: *voluptate* codd. (*-nt-* DL)

(28) *ibid.*   *modus* ·|· moderatio et regimen. Donatus in commento Andrie (1.70.5)

(29) fol. 159   . . . unde Mulciber a multando quasi Multiber, ut dicit Donatus in commento super Adelphis Therentii

>   2.25.22 *a multando quasi Multiber* CΛ: *quasi Multiber a multitudo* K

(30) fol. 166v   item *plus satis* et *plerique omnes,* super quibus bene loquitur Donatus in principio commenti Andrie Therentii (1.58.12-59.13)

(31) fol. 172   *peryfrasis* . . . simile huic dicit Donatus in commento Therentii: 'consuetudinis imago est vituperare presentia' (2.365.10-11)

(32) fol. 178   *plerique* componitur cum omnes ut dicatur plerique omnes secundum Donatum in commento Andrie Therentii (= no. 30)

(33) fol. 185   *presente* ·|· coram vel presentibus mihi vendidit. super hoc loquitur Donatus in commento Therentii (2.434.15-18 ?)

(34-35) fol. 194v   *qui* ·|· utinam, *qui* ·|· quomodo. hoc dicit Donatus in commento Phormionis Therentii (2.383.2, 384.21)

(36) *ibid.*   idem in commento Echyre *qui* ·|· unde (2.251.26)

(37) fol. 196v   *quinimmo* ·|· quare non. Donatus in commento Andrie

>   1.131.1-2 QVIN TV HOC AVDI 'quin' modo pro immo, alias quare non
>   *immo* ABK: *omnino* Θ

(38) *ibid.*   idem *quin* ·|· quare non in commento Adelphorum

>   2.54.19 *quare non* KC: *nunc quare* Λ

(39) *ibid.*   *quin* Donatus in commento Phormionis Therentii *quin* ·|· cur non

>   2.404.6 *cur non* ΔΛ: *cur* Θ

(40) *ibid.*   idem in commento Echyre *quin* ·|· qui non

>   2.206.7 QVIN qui non. ITA PARET hoc verbum . . .   *quin qui non
>   paret* K: *quin ita non paret* CΛ[21]

---

[21] Wessner wrongly ascribes to C *quin ita qui paret.* It may be that the annotator is referring to another passage altogether, 2.234.26 *QVIN quae non.*

(41) fol 199v   item *regina* ·|· dives, ut dicit Donatus in commento Eunuchi Therentii (1.301.6, 302.2-4)

(42) fol 203   *remoratur* dicitur a remora pisciculo, qui sui adherentia navem detinet, qui aliter dicitur echinus. hoc dicit Donatus in commento Phor (!) Eunuchi prout notavi supra capitulo E (= no. 12)

(43) fol. 203v   *res* veritas secundum Therentium in Adelphis, et sic exponit Donatus eius commentator (2.146.13-14)

(44) *ibid.*   *res* pecunia et consuetudo secundum Donatum in commento Adelphorum (2.158.4-9)[22]

(45) fol. 204   . . . nam equitas est remissa iusticia secundum Donatum in commento Therentii (2.19.6-8)

(46) *ibid.*   *retulit* profuit; et producit re sillabam. Donatus in commento Andrie

> 1.169.8 *profuit vel interfuit* codd. (*vel* om. B)

(47) fol. 204v   *rex* dives secundum Donatum in commento Eunuchi (1.302.3-4 ?)

(48) *ibid.*   *rex* Donatus in commento Phormionis Therentii: rex alias regnator, alias dominus, alias dives significat (2.432.11-12)

(49) *ibid.*   item regina ·|· dives secundum Donatum in commento Eunuchi Therentii (= no. 41)

(50) fol. 212v   scirpus quid sit ostendit Donatus in commento Andrie Therentii (1.255.3-4)

(51) fol. 214v   Donatus in commento Andrie *sedulo* simpliciter et ex animo et sine dolo

> 1.204.7-8 AT FACIO SEDVLO id est ex animo et sine dolo; 1.81.11-12 'sedulo' . . . id est simpliciter

(52) fol. 215v   Donatus in commento comedie Therentii que dicitur Adelphe vocat macrologiam senilem (2.21.17)

(53) fol. 218   . . . vocatur enim iusticia a Donato in commento Adelphe Therentii vel ius quod idem est. remissa vero dicitur equitas ab ipso Donato (= no. 45)

(54) fol. 220   *signo* hinc designo, de quo sic dicit Donatus in commento comedie Therentii que dicitur Adelphe: 'designare est novam rem facere in utramque partem, et bonam et malam; nam et designatores dicti qui ludis funebribus presunt, credo ob eam causam quod in ipsis ludis multa fiant nova et spectanda'

> 2.24.23-7 *novam rem* C: *rem novam* KΛ   *ludis funebribus praesunt* KΛ: *ludum funeribus praesumit* C   *in* om. codd.   *et spectanda* Λ: *expectanda* K C

---

[22] The annotator has made a gloss of the lemma *MITTO REM CONSVETVDINEM IPSORVM.* Does this indicate how the lemmata were written in his manuscript?

(55) fol. 220v *silicernium* bene exponit Donatus in commento Adelph. (2.122.4-8)

(56) fol. 227 *stat* . . . super hoc loquitur Donatus in commento Andrie Therentii (1.208.4-9 ?)

(57) fol. 232 *summa* ·|· finis. Donatus in commento Andrie (1.81.20-21)

(58) fol. 232v *superbia* . . . Donatus in commento Andrie Therentii: 'summum indicium securitatis est superbia'

> 1.235.8-9 *iudicium* et *superia* B: recte AK Θ

(59) fol. 247v *verbena* super hoc bene dicit Donatus in commento Andrie Therentii (1.215.8-15).

As Dr. Billerbeck did not discuss the text of the passages used by Hugo Primas, we give the variants there too:

> 1.467.3 . . . eleganter et morose cumque multo fastidio . . .
> *morose cumque* Λ: *more secum quae* C: *in ore secum quae* K: *more senum* Δ

> 11-12 apparet et sordidum esse quia sit ater et durum utique qui ex iure hesterno sit comedendus
> *esse* . . . *utique* Wessner: *sed qui si taceret durum uterque* K: *eis et quia si taceret durum utrique* C: *ei sed qui si taceret durum uterque* (vel *veterque*) Δ: *eis et quasi acer ut durus veterque* Λ

In order of occurrence in the commentary the passages concerned are as follows (we give only the page):

Andria 1.55, 58, 60, 66, 69, 69, 70, 72, 81, 81, 82, 131, 169, 169, 204, 205, 208, 215, 217, 235, 242, 255

Eunuchus 1.283, 292, 301, 302, 334, 339, 341, 375

Adelphoe 2.9, 19, 21, 24, 25, 49, 54, 92, 122, 146, 155, 158

Hecyra 2.206, 244, 247, 251

Phormio 2.365, 383, 384, 404, 432, 434, 476.

It is an open question whether any significance should be attached to the vacant stretches of *Eunuchus* (1.376-497) and *Hecyra* (2.252-342), which are twice as long as any other. If, as seems likely, Hugo Primas had the same manuscript in front of him, the former is cut by 30 pages. It happens that some fifteenth-century manuscripts omit part of the latter (2.271-319), nor does any passage fall within the section of Phormio omitted by Θ (2.409-412). Even with these gaps, however, the manuscript used by the annotator would have been much fuller than our oldest manuscripts, A and B. That it was not A is shown by its contents; that it was not the manuscript that B formed part of is shown by errors in B (see below). There is no way of telling whether it put *Adelphi* after *Andria* like AK or after *Eunuchus* like Θ.

Not surprisingly the manuscript seems to have been superior to those now extant. In at least two places where they agree in error it apparently had the truth (nos. 27, 40),[23] and only once does it agree in error with any of them (no. 3);[24] meanwhile there is no shortage of errors in AK (nos. 2, 9), B (nos. 2, 20), Θ (nos. 6, 14, 37, 39), or Δ (no. 12, 1.467.3). On the other hand, beyond establishing the antiquity of a dittography found in Θ (no. 9) it brings no startling vindication of any reading that has hitherto rested on doubtful authority. We have no verdict to deliver on the discrepancies in nos. 9, 10, 18 (though *dicta* can hardly be right), 23, 37, 46, and 51 (?). In short, the main lesson to be learnt from the citations is that in the region of France to which A appertains, the Loire Valley, a tradition different from that of AK and in some respects better was still represented in the thirteenth century. Further conclusions must wait upon a clarification of the stemma.

To this picture, such as it is, should be added the medieval references to the commentary.[25] The modern editors of Terence assume that it was available to Carolingian monastic scholars, because it is quoted in the scholia that appear in a number of ninth- and tenth-century manuscripts of Terence.[26] In casting doubt on the Terence lemmata found in the surviving manuscripts of Donatus's commentary, Lindsay stated that the commentary was actively used in Carolingian schools and influenced by contemporary manuscripts of Terence;[27] these views were repeated by Jones and Morey in their study of the illustrated manuscripts of Terence.[28] Yet, while Terence was widely known in the ninth century, there is little evidence to suggest that the Donatus commentary was, at least to judge from the lack of traces it has left in the form of manuscript fragments, mention in booklists and the like. The scholia attached to manuscripts of Terence, moreover, are said to represent the commentary not only in the form that has come down to us but also in a fuller form or in other abridgements.[29] The present form could not have been written in Antiquity,[30] and Lindsay thought it post-Carolingian.

---

[23] In No. 27 the manuscripts present are AK Θ, but the error is trivial; in no. 40 they are CKΛ. That reduces the importance of the two passages.

[24] We assume that *an-* and *au-* have the same origin.

[25] Papias cites in his dictionary "*Decrevit* Apud Donatum in Andria Ter. (1.3.14) decernere est de magnis rebus certam proferre sententiam. Idem in Ecyra (1.2.73) decreverim statuerim et defixerim"; cf. Sabbadini, SIFC 2 (1894) 39, verified in the 1476 edition of Papias. The same texts are cited by Johannes Balbus in the *Catholicon*. We shall not deal with them here because they represent an Italian tradition.

[26] W. M. Lindsay, "Notes on the Text of Terence," *Classical Quarterly* (CQ) 19 (1925) 28-36; *idem,* "Gleanings from Glossaries and Scholia," CQ 20 (1926) 103-105; *idem,* "The Donatus Extracts in the Codex Victorianus (D) of Terence," CQ 21 (1927) 188-194.

[27] See for example Lindsay, "Notes" 28: "When Donatus' *Commentum Terenti* (or scraps of it, with adventitious matter) was made available for monastery schools in Charlemagne's time (and later), any Terence text that was handy was used to provide a peg on which to hang the scholium."

[28] L. W. Jones and C. R. Morey, *The Miniatures of the Manuscripts of Terence* 1 (Princeton 1931) 17-19.

[29] Traces of the full commentary or other abridgements are found in the scholia to Vatican Library MS lat. 3226, s. iv-v, edited by J. F. Mountford, *The Scholia Bembina* (Liverpool 1934),

We have on the one hand the glosses, and on the other hand no trace of any manuscript of the commentary. The simplest explanation is the traditional one, that the glosses from Donatus do not derive directly from a manuscript of the commentary used by some annotator of the ninth or tenth century, but rather were copied en bloc from earlier glossed manuscripts of Terence. This appears to have happened in Florence, Biblioteca Medicea Laurenziana MS 38.24, in which the scholia are all written by one hand and seem to be a unit. The commentary may have been known only as glosses to a text until the late eighth or ninth century, at which time portions of it were formed, perhaps at an insular center of learning,[31] into the present independent volume, which survived while the late antique glossed manuscripts of Terence perished.[32] This would explain the absence of any traces of independent codices of Donatus. Whatever the form in which the commentary came to the ninth century, codex or gloss, it is likely that the Donatus lore in the old Terence manuscripts had been in gloss form for a very long time.[33]

---

and most recently discussed by J. E. G. Zetzel, HSCP 79 (1975) 339-353, and in Florence, Bibl. Med. Laur. MS 38.24 (codex Victorianus D), s. x, studied by Lindsay (n. 26 above). Remains of our version appear in late tenth- or early eleventh-century scholia to Paris B.N. MS lat. 7899, s. ix (P), which belonged to St. Denis in the thirteenth century; in Vatican Library MS lat. 3868, written at Corbie in the second quarter of the ninth century; and in Florence, Bibl. Riccardiana MS 528, s. xi. Each of these manuscripts is discussed by Wessner (n. 14 above) 1.xxxvii-xl. On P see also R. Kauer, *Wiener Studien* 33 (1911) 144-154, 323-335, and P. Wessner, *Berliner philologische Wochenschrift* 41 (1921) 428-432, 449-455.

[30] E. Löfstedt, "Die Bembinusscholien und Donatus," *Eranos* 12 (1912) 43-63.

[31] See Beeson (n. 18 above). Beeson shows no knowledge of Warren's article on the Chigianus (cf. n. 18 above) and Beeson's article in turn escaped both Zwierlein and me (M.D.R.). I am in complete agreement with Beeson about the desirability of keeping within the narrowest limits possible the number of medieval manuscripts that came to light in the fifteenth century; but I do not feel competent to judge his arguments about errors due to insular script, and so I will comment here only on three other points. (1) On 286-287 Beeson refers to Sabbadini for evidence of a manuscript in France that contained three plays and points out that Paris, B.N. lat. 7921 (s. xv) fits this description. In *Carteggio* (n. 16 above) 119 n. 4, however, Sabbadini identified the French manuscript with the Carnotensis, and B.N. lat. 7921, whether or not written in a French hand, is an unimportant offshoot of a well marked Italian family (it also breaks off at the end of a gathering). (2) On 301-303 Beeson suggests that the *defectus* of the Carnotensis in *Phormio* was not a gap but the mixture of versions in 2.3. Valla's words are "non integra quinta ἐκυρᾶ, item cum defectu in sexta, quae dicitur Φορμίων," and I do not believe that they will bear this interpretation. On *defectus* see Silvia Rizzo, *Il lessico filologico degli umanisti* (Rome 1973) 236-237. (3) On 299-301 Beeson derives T and C independently from the Maguntinus. If he is right, my attempt to derive the *deteriores* from a different copy of the Maguntinus up to *Ad.* 2.3 must be abandoned; but again I do not feel competent to judge, and in any case I now have other reasons for abandoning it.

[32] A suggestion of this kind was first made by F. Umpfenbach, *Hermes* 2 (1867) 337. Cf. also Wessner (n. 14 above) 1.xlvi; H. T. Karsten, *Mnemosyne* 32 (1904) 211-214; G. Jachmann, *Die Geschichte des Terenztextes im Altertum* (Basel 1924) 122 n. 70; Zetzel (n. 29 above) 340, 353. Later the process was reversed at least once: the commentary is added in the margins of a fifteenth-century manuscript of Terence, British Library MS Add. 11906.

[33] In addition, as Wessner notes (n. 14 above) 1.vii, the title "Donatus in Terentium" appears in a grammatical treatise found in Bernensis 83 fols. 1-17v, 63-74, as one of a series of titles to demonstrate this use of the preposition *in* – "Servius in Virgilium, Pompeius in Donatum, Donatus in Terentium." The treatise has since been shown to be the work of Gottschalk of

Lupus of Ferrières refers to the commentary in a letter to Pope Benedict III (A.D. 855-858). Having asked for "a manuscript of venerable antiquity which contains the commentaries of Saint Jerome on Jeremiah" to copy, he goes on to say: "We also request Cicero *De oratore* and the twelve books of Quintilian's *Institutiones oratoriae* . . . . We have parts of each of these authors, but we wish to obtain with your help their entire works. Equally earnest is our demand for the commentary of Donatus on Terence."[34] This was interpreted by Beeson to mean that Lupus had a copy of Donatus but one which was deficient.[35] It is surely more likely that by not including Donatus with the *De oratore* and the *Institutiones,* which he goes out of his way to say that he has, Lupus indicates that he does not have the Donatus and, what is more, that he did not know of a copy in the Loire houses with which he was so familiar — Tours, Fleury, Micy, Orléans, Auxerre. We do not know if Benedict sent him a manuscript. It seems rather doubtful, considering Benedict's short time in office. That Lupus did nevertheless acquire a manuscript of the commentary is suggested by the fact that it circulates in the Loire Valley, namely in A of the eleventh century and in the Carnotensis. If all the manuscripts descend from an insular archetype, it would seem likely, as Beeson has suggested, that Lupus acquired his manuscript of the commentary from some German insular center, perhaps the same one which produced the codex form of the text and perhaps also the same one which supplied the Mainz codex.

Whatever the identity of the annotator's manuscript, it may well be the one quoted by Nicholas of Clemanges at the end of the fourteenth century, in letters written to the Avignonese bibliophile Cardinal Galeotto Tarlatti Pietramala (d. 1396-1397) and to Nicholas of Baya.[36] Clemanges knew the Orléans libraries, having found there Bernensis 136, the contents of which he transferred into his great collection of Cicero's orations, Paris, B. N. MS lat. 14759.[37] He cites only two passages from Donatus, but both are interesting. At 1.8.17, if the printed text of his letter can be trusted, he found *Terentio non similem dices quempiam.* where all the extant manuscripts have *dicens* and Θ omits *non.* At 2.410.25-26 he may have taken it upon himself to supply *monet* before *tum,* but more important, the citation falls in the middle of a short passage omitted by Θ and commonly assumed to have been missing from the Maguntinus.

Orbais and to have been composed in Hautvillers near Rheims ca. 850-855; see C. Lambot, "Opuscules grammaticaux de Gottschalk," *Revue bénédictine* 44 (1932) 120-124, and for the passage in question his edition, *Oeuvres théologiques et grammaticales de Godescalc d'Orbais,* Spicilegium Sacrum Lovaniense 20 (Louvain 1945) 365. The passage is too slight to make anything of.

[34] *Loup de Ferrières, Correspondance,* ed. L. Levillain, 2 (Paris 1935), ep. 100: "Petimus etiam Tullium De oratore et XII libros Institutionum oratoriarum Quintiliani, qui uno nec ingenti volumine continentur; quorum utriusque auctorum partes habemus, verum plenitudinem per vos desideramus obtinere. Pari intentione Donati commentum in Terentio flagitamus."

[35] Beeson (n. 18 above) 284-285.

[36] R. Sabbadini, *Riv. fil.* 39 (1911) 541-543.

[37] Rouse and Rouse (n. 6 above).

The only other manuscript that may antedate the discoveries at Mainz and Chartres, Milan, Biblioteca Ambrosiana MS L 53 sup. fols. 92-99, s. xv[1] (S), written in a French hand, contains the introduction to the commentary.[38] Sabbadini states that it is part of the manuscript used by Clemanges,[39] but there is no known connection between the two. S belonged to Francesco Pizolpasso, archbishop of Milan,[40] who acquired it, Sabbadini suggests, while he was bishop of Aquis in Gascony, 1422-1423. Surely, however, the archbishop, who traveled extensively, could have acquired it at any time before his death in 1443; and Sabbadini did not actually show that it cannot derive from the Maguntinus, which went through his hands in 1436.

The medieval references to Donatus on Terence corroborate the conclusions that we have drawn from the examination of the manuscripts, namely, that it owes its survival in large part to the medieval scholars and libraries of north central France and, in particular, the Loire Valley, where it was better known than has hitherto been assumed.

Exeter College
Oxford OX1 3DP, England

Department of History
University of California
Los Angeles, California 90024, U.S.A.

---

[38] R. Sabbadini, SIFC 11 (1903) 185-199, where the Ambrosianus is fully collated with Wessner and E. Franceschini, *Studi e note de filologia latina medievale* (Milan 1938) 57-58, 177ff. The watermark, *Mont*, is similar to Briquet 11678-11715 and 11851-11888.

[39] "In quel codice del Pizolpasso noi possediamo un frammento del testo scoperto dal Clemangis," Sabbadini (n. 36 above) 543; "un frammento del Donato scoperto dal Clemangis si conserva nel cod. Ambrosiano L 53 sup.," Sabbadini, *Storia e critica* (n. 18 above) 154.

[40] Regarding Pizolpasso's library see A. Paredi, *La biblioteca del Pizolpasso* (Milan 1961). The manuscript is no. 79 in the inventory of 1443 (p. 82) and is discussed on 127-128. See also G. D. Jack, "Francesco Pizolpasso, c. 1380-1443," B. Litt. diss. (Oxford 1958).

NARRATIVE ANOMALIES IN "LA CHANÇUN DE WILLAME"

•

by John D. Niles

In an article published in *Romania* in 1915, Maurice Wilmotte records his dismay when faced with the task of criticizing a work "qui, à côté de beautés réelles et fortes, montre une absence complète d'ordonnance et de goût, abonde en lacunes, en répétitions et en contradictions, semble, enfin, avoir été écrite − et surtout transcrite − à la diable."[1] The work in question is *La Chançun de Willame*. Ever since the *editio princeps* of this poem was issued in 1903 in an elegant though inaccurate private printing,[2] the work has presented a scholarly problem. That this brilliant and at times offensive *chanson de geste* is no hoax, as at first was suggested,[3] has long been acknowledged. Still, generations of scholars who have turned their attention to the poem which is preserved in a unique Anglo-Norman version in British Library MS Add. 38,663 have been unable to discover a great deal of unity and coherence to the text as it stands. Apart from the matter of possible lacunae, repetitions, and instances of lack of taste, the poem generally has been thought to be a compilation of two separate stories which were joined together rather crudely. The poem's ablest editors are in agreement with a number of distinguished critics that the manuscript text represents a conflation of a "true" or "primitive" *Chançun de Willame* (G¹) and a later addition to this story, a *Chanson de Rainouart* (G²). The first of these has received high praise as the Old French epic poem whose artistic quality is most nearly comparable to that of *La Chanson de Roland*. The second has had few admirers. In 1964, Jeanne Wathelet-Willem was able to declare that the duality of the work is "aujourd'hui presque unanimement admise."[4]

Any reader of the poem will be familiar with the way in which its action falls into two broad movements, one tragic and one comic. The first movement tells of

[1] Maurice Wilmotte, "La *Chanson de Roland* et la 'Chançun de Willame,' " *Romania* 44 (1915-1917) 55.

[2] The anonymous Chiswick Press edition − *La Chançun de Willame* (London 1903) − is attributed to the owner of the manuscript at the time, George Dunn. All textual references in the present study are to the two-volume edition by Duncan McMillan, *La Chanson de Guillaume* (Paris 1949-1950).

[3] Emile Tron, *Trouvaille ou pastiche? Doutes exprimés au sujet de la* "Chançun de Willame" (Bari 1909), 16 pp. Jean Acher composed a detailed response to Tron: "A propos d'un doute sur le livre de Chiswick," *Revue des langues romanes* 55 (1912) 60-76.

[4] Jeanne Wathelet-Willem, "A propos de la technique formulaire dans les plus anciennes chansons de geste," *Mélanges de linguistique romane et de philologie médiévale offerts à M. Maurice Delbouille* (Gembloux 1964) 2.727.

Vivien's heroic resistance against an overwhelming Saracen army at Archamp, and of the vain efforts of Vivien's uncle Willame to rescue him. The second movement tells of the burlesque adventures of the kitchen-boy Reneward at or near the same battlefield of Archamp. Granted this broadly twofold structure, the proposed surgical division of the text into two halves is a procedure attended by certain difficulties. Usually, major surgical operations are advised only *in extremis*. If the patient is rugged, a wise physician may wish to withhold action until the need for surgery is proved beyond a doubt. In the case of *La Chançun de Willame*, I would suggest, doubt still exists. A consideration of the poem's structure and unity from a different point of view, the point of view of oral poetics, may cause one to question the certainty of the diagnosis set forth by most scholars. If the proposals set forth in the present essay are accepted, the song yet may be saved from the knives of its critics, and the manuscript text may emerge whole from the controversy which has surrounded it for the past seventy years.

If a surgical operation is called for, the critical question is: Where shall we wield the knife? The fact that the surgeons are not in agreement on this point does not bode well for the operation. Hermann Suchier considered lines 1-927 to constitute the "oldest kernel" of the song.[5] Raymond Weeks considered line 2648 to mark the beginning of the appended *Chanson de Rainouart*.[6] In recent years, most scholars have followed Franz Rechnitz in considering line 1980 to mark the beginning of G^2.[7] When such formidable scholars as Suchier, Weeks, Rechnitz, Bruno Valtorta, Duncan McMillan, Jean Frappier, Jean Rychner, and Jeanne Wathelet-Willem are in agreement that the poem is to be divided, though the precise point of division may be a matter of dispute, to offer a dissenting opinion would seem as foolhardy an act of resistance as Vivien's lone self-sacrifice at Archamp. Still, the matter is not so simple. At line 1980, Willame is still in the midst of the battlefield at Archamp. Of all his great army of Franks, only he and his nephew Gui survive. Although he has killed the Saracen king Deramed, he still is confronted by an immense hostile army, an army which is on French soil. Not yet has he found Vivien, whose mangled body lies where Saracens have hidden it. As yet there has been no return to Willame's castle, no

[5] Hermann Suchier, "Vivien," *Zeitschrift für romanische Philologie* 29 (1905) 648. Suchier's critical edition of the poem *La Chançun de Willame: Französisches Volksepos des XI. Jahrhunderts* (Halle 1901) consists of lines 1-1980.

[6] Raymond Weeks, "Études sur *Aliscans*," *Romania* 34 (1905) 241. Weeks also postulates two earlier divisions, A and B, but does not specify where B begins.

[7] Franz Rechnitz, "Der Refrain in der unter dem Namen *La Chançun de Willame* veröffentlichten Handschrift," *Zeitschrift für romanische Philologie* 32 (1908) 184; Bruno Valtorta, "*La Chanson de Willieme*," *Studi Romanzi* 28 (1939) 19-140; McMillan (n. 2 above) 2.127-130; Jean Frappier, *Les Chansons de geste du cycle de Guillaume d'Orange* 1: *La Chanson de Guillaume, Aliscans, La Chevalerie Vivien* (Paris 1955) 131, 141-148, 203-205, and 210; Jean Rychner, "Sur la *Chanson de Guillaume*," *Romania* 76 (1955) 28-38 and *idem, La Chanson de geste: Essai sur l'art épique des jongleurs*, Société de Publications romanes et françaises 53 (Geneva 1955) 46-47 and 159-164; Jeanne Wathelet-Willem, "*La Chançun de Willame*: Le problème de l'unité du MS British Museum Add. 38663," *Le Moyen Age* 58 (1952) 363-377 and *idem, Recherches sur la Chanson de Guillaume*, Bibiliothèque de la Faculté de philosophie et lettres de l'Université de Liège 210 (Liège 1975) 1.393-453.

celebrations of the victory, no lamentations of the loss. In such circumstances, the narrator's declaration in line 1980 — "Ore out vencu sa bataille Willame" — is a cry which rings a bit hollow if taken as an ending to the poem.

Why then do scholars wish to declare an end to the "true" poem at line 1980, in the absence of any significant division in the manuscript at this point? The chief reason is that in the ensuing part of the narrative, there occur three rather striking anomalies. (1) In line 2212, Willame is said to return straight to his castle at Orange ("dreit a Orenge"). Previously, the same castle was situated not at Orange but at Barcelona (see lines 932-933: "A Barzelune la le dirrad al cunte Willame./ Li quons Willame ert a Barzelune"). (2) When Willame arrives at his castle, his wife Guibourc fails to recognize him and refuses to let him in, as he is clad in Saracen arms ("paenes armes li pendent al costez," 2232). Previously, nothing has been said about his wearing any arms other than his own. (3) Most important, in lines 2031-2052 Vivien recovers himself sufficiently to open his eyes, to speak, and to receive the sacrament, even though some 1100 lines and some few days previously he had been killed definitively by the Saracens (see lines 913-928).

Given the assumption that the poem preserved in British Library MS Add. 38,663 is the product of self-conscious literary craftsmanship, there seems to be no way out of the difficulties posed by these three anomalies other than by a theory of multiple authorship and scribal *remaniement*. The assumption which leads to this conclusion is not inevitable, however. In recent years Jean Rychner has proposed a different way of reading this and other *chansons de geste*: not as the work of learned clerics, but as the products of traditional, oral composition, composition like that of skilled singers who have been recorded in our own day in the Balkans.[8] Improving markedly on Rychner's methodology, Joseph J. Duggan has made an exhaustive, computer-aided study of the diction of ten early *chansons de geste* and has built a strong case for their oral nature.[9] In particular, he has shown that, under a strict and consistent definition of the formula, the formulaic density of *La Chançun de Willame* (thirty-one percent) is about twice that of Old French poems known to have been composed pen in hand (fifteen to seventeen percent). While the question of the oral or written nature of any individual *chanson de geste* is not likely to be resolved by formula count alone,[10] still, at the very least Duggan's research justifies the *hypothesis* that

[8] Rychner 9-25. Previously Albert Lord had maintained the oral provenience of at least some versions of *La Chanson de Roland* in "The Singer of Tales," Ph.D. diss. (Harvard 1949); for a later statement of his conclusions see his book *The Singer of Tales* (Cambridge, Mass. 1960) 202-206.

[9] Joseph J. Duggan, *The Song of Roland: Formulaic Style and Poetic Craft*, Publications of the Center for Medieval and Renaissance Studies, UCLA, 6 (Berkeley 1973) 16-30.

[10] For example, Rudy S. Spraycar, "*La Chanson de Roland*: An Oral Poem?" *Olifant* 4 (1976) 63-74, points out that at least one South Slavic poem known to be of written provenience is composed in a highly formulaic style, while Larry D. Benson, "The Literary Character of Anglo-Saxon Formulaic Poetry," *PMLA* 81 (1966) 334-341, demonstrates that blind formula-count is not enough to distinguish Anglo-Saxon poems which are clearly literary from Anglo-Saxon poems which have been thought to be oral. Clearly, formula-count is no touchstone for determining the oral style, for any author may manipulate formulas. In determining the

La Chançun de Willame was composed by a skilled singer and only later was recorded in writing. And used with caution, a shrewd hypothesis may be a useful instrument of discovery. In the case of *La Chançun de Willame*, the hypothesis of the poem's oral mode of creation and delivery is able to account not only for the formulaic density of the work but for its ragged meter and confused geography as well. According to Wathelet-Willem (*Recherches* 1.69), 47.6% of the poem's verses are hypermetric. Any collector of oral literature is familiar with the difficulty of obtaining metrically smooth texts, whether these texts are taken down by dictation to a scribe or by modern recording apparatus. Albert Lord has found that only when songs are taken down by an active and intelligent scribe, a scribe who repeatedly stops the singer to request a good metrical line, does the recording of songs from oral tradition result in metrically smooth texts.[11] As for the poem's geography, a Europe in which Bordeaux is a single night's journey from Barcelona or from Orange scarcely seems to be the Europe known to lettered clerks. Such geography might well reflect the hazy conceptions of an unlettered singer, however, particularly a singer composing in far-away Norman England. In addition, though judgments here must remain dangerously subjective, the oral hypothesis seems to be in accord with the poem's ethos. A poem as crude as *La Chançun de Willame* scarcely seems to have been composed for the cloister, though it may have been sung there. Its mixture of the sublime and the obscene is what one might expect of a song sung for the entertainment of a group of barons at a time before these barons had fallen under the spell of the new ethos of chivalry. Unless my judgment is at fault, the poem was composed by a man who knew war at first hand, a man like Willame's own jongleur (see lines 1258-1274) or like the legendary Taillefer; and it seems fair to suppose that the text came to be written down because someone with a scribe at his disposal thought the song of value.

There seems to be no reason to dismiss the oral hypothesis out of hand, therefore. I would suggest that, given this hypothesis, several of the striking anomalies of the poem are easily explained. In oral story poetry, the main criterion for a song's success is its immediate aesthetic effect. Minor discrepancies of name and of number tend to go unnoticed, at the same time as both the poet and his audience concentrate their attention on the immediate action. When a singer of tales sings before a live audience, the story's the thing. He may forget certain details and may confuse others, but his performance still may be a success as long as the basic story continues to capture attention.[12] At one point in *La Chançun de Willame*, the poet suffers

---

provenience of a given work, one needs to know not only *if* the author used formulas, but *how* the author used formulas, and whether the author integrated formulas into complex sets of *formulaic systems,* as I argue in an article titled "Formula and Formulaic System in *Beowulf*" scheduled to appear in a new journal to be called *Proteus.*

[11] Lord, *Singer of Tales* (n. 8 above) 125-128.

[12] See Albert B. Lord, "Homer and Huso II: Narrative Inconsistencies in Homer and Oral Poetry," *Transactions of the American Philological Association* 69 (1938) 439-445; David Gunn, "Narrative Inconsistency and the Oral Dictated Text in Homeric Epic," *American Journal of Philology* 91 (1970) 192-203; Michael D. Cherniss, "*Beowulf*: Oral Presentation and the Criterion

momentary confusion as he relates how Willame is attacked by Deramed and a company of fifteen other Saracen kings:

> ... Deramé li salt d'un aguait,
> Od lui quinze reis que jo nomer vus sai:
> Encas de Egipte e li reis Ostramai,
> Butifer li prouz e li forz Garmais,
> Turlen de Dosturges e sis nief Alfais,
> Nubles de Inde e Ander li Persans,
> Aristragot, Cabuel e Morans,
> Clamador e Salvains e Varians,
> E li reis de Nubie e li guerreres Tornas.   (1707-1715)

(Deramed leaps on him from an ambush. With him are fifteen kings whose names I can tell you: Encas of Egypt and King Ostramai; Butifer the bold and the mighty Garmais; Turlen of Dosturges and his nephew Alfais; Nubles of India and Ander the Persian; Aristragot, Cabuel, and Morans; Clamador, Salvains, and Varians; and the king of Nubia and the warrior Tornas.)

As a matter of fact, how many kings in addition to Deramed are named? Most auditors would never know, but a reader is able to count not fifteen but sixteen. Such an error is not likely to have been introduced by a scribe, but a thoughtless scribe might have perpetuated it. Somewhat later, the poet attempts a similar catalog again. Willame is fleeing toward Orange, and fifteen Saracen kings are in hot pursuit:

> Sur li corent Sarazin e Escler,
> Tels quinze reis qui ben vus sai nomer;
> Reis Mathamar e uns reis d'Aver,
> E Bassumet e li reis Defamé,
> Soldan d'Alfrike e li forz Eaduel,
> E Aelran e sun fiz Aelred,
> Li reis Sacealme, Alfamé e Desturbed,
> E Golias e Andafle e Wanibled.
> Tuz quinze le ferent en sun escu boclé,
> Pur un petit ne l'unt acraventé.   (2056-2065)

(Saracens and Slavs rush upon him; there are fifteen kings whose names I well can tell you; King Mathamar and a king of the Avars; Bassumet and King Defamé; Soldan of Africa and the mighty Eaduel; Aëlran and his son Aëlred; King Sacealme, Alfamé, and Desturbed; Golias and Andofle and Wanibled. All fifteen smite him on his embossed shield, they almost smash him to the ground.)

In this case the reader is able to count not fifteen kings but fourteen. During performance before an audience, of course, such a passage is likely to have been a

of Immediate Rhetorical Effect," *Genre* 3 (1970) 214-228; and William F. Hansen, "The Conference Sequence: Patterned Narration and Narrative Inconsistency in the *Odyssey*," *University of California Publications in Classical Philology* 8 (1972) 22ff.

sheer cascade of sound. The author of the *Willame* was a talented poet, and his skills may have been comparable to those of the finer South Slavic singers who have been recorded in our own time, concerning one of whom, Avdo Međedović, Albert Lord has written: "His singing ran ahead of his fingers on the instrument; thoughts and words rushed to his mind for expression, and there were times when he simply ran the bow slowly back and forth over the strings while he poured forth the tale in what seemed to be prose of lightning-like rapidity but was actually verse."[13] What mattered to the *Willame* poet and to his audience was not the precise number of kings, of course, but the blur of exotic names and the sense of a man's fighting against overwhelming odds.

The poet's naming of Orange instead of Barcelona (or Barcelona instead of Orange) may be accounted for in similar fashion. The poet simply seems not to have been concerned whether Willame's castle was located at one point or the other. His mind was on other things; the precise location of the castle is not as important as the fact that the hero returns home, pursued by Saracens, to face his own shame and possible humiliation for having lost an entire army of Franks. After a lapse of 1300 lines, the miraculous transposition of Willame's castle from Barcelona to Orange is an event which might never have been noticed by a live audience, just as (to judge from personal experience) it might not be noticed on a first reading even by a modern scholar who is reading the story for pleasure. Errors of the kind are common in oral poetry. In a song which Milman Parry and Albert Lord recorded in 1934 from the lips of the Serbian tavern-keeper and poet Đemail Zogić, for example, there occurs a similar error, and neither Zogić nor his audience seems to have been disturbed by the mistake. The first six hundred lines of the song concern a spirited attempt to rescue a certain maid named Emina. After the singer pauses to catch his breath and then resumes the tale, the same maid is named not Emina but Fatima. The singer offers no explanation for the change, which Lord corrects in his published transcription.[14]

The second anomaly, Willame's unexplained acquisition of Saracen arms, seems to be the result of similar forgetfulness on the part of the singer. The singer rightly has Guibourc fail to recognize Willame when the hero arrives at Orange clad in Saracen arms. He rightly has Willame seek to evade capture by speaking in Saracen tongues, a means of escape which is inexplicable unless Willame were disguised at the time (lines 2169-2172). But somewhat previously, the singer failed to prepare the way for these later scenes in that he forgot to say how the hero came to don Saracen arms. The account should have come in the neighborhood of lines 2151-2161. At this point in the action, Willame has unhorsed the Saracen emir Alderufe and has traded his own horse for Alderufe's. To prepare the way for the later scenes, he should have taken Alderufe's arms at the same time. The author of *Aliscans* made no such error. In his later version of the same song, the poet has the hero don the arms of Alderufe's counterpart Aerofle (lines 1365-1373), and the later scene in which the hero arrives

[13] *Serbo-Croatian Heroic Songs*, collected by Milman Parry, 3: *The Wedding of Smailagić Meho*, by Avdo Međedović, ed. Albert B. Lord (Cambridge, Mass. 1974) 10-11.

[14] Parry, *Serbo-Croatian Heroic Songs* 1: *Novi Pazar: English Translations*, ed. Albert B. Lord (Cambridge, Mass. 1954) 408 n. 22.

home unrecognized is well motivated.[15] To judge from *Aliscans*, the hero's donning of captured armor was a traditional and familiar theme in the tale. If so, the members of the audience would have had no trouble perfecting the action of *La Chançun de Willame* in their own minds. Conceivably, of course, the motif of the hero's donning captured arms was omitted from the text through scribal oversight. In the absence of textual evidence indicating a breakdown in the song's written transmission, however, it seems simpler to postulate a lapse on the part of the singer. Again, lapses of the kind are well attested in oral poetry. In the same song by Ðemail Zogić to which I already have referred, the singer commits an error concerning which Lord writes as follows:

> One of the most glaring inconsistencies ... within my experience of Yugoslav oral song occurs in Ðemail Zogić's song of the rescue of Alibey's children by Bojicić Alija. ... The young hero has neither a horse nor armor with which to undertake his mission, and his mother borrows them from his uncle, Rustembey. Later in the poem there is a recognition scene in which Alija is recognized because he is wearing the armor of Mandusić Vuk, whom he [once] overcame in single combat. Zogić has not made the necessary adjustment in the theme of recognition so that it would agree with the theme of the poor hero who borrows his armor.[16]

In the Serbocroatian song, the hero is recognized because he appears wearing the armor of his uncle Rustembey. In *La Chançun de Willame*, the hero is not recognized because he is wearing captured Saracen arms, even though the poet has said nothing about his having changed his own arms for captured ones. The two errors are comparable, and they are paralleled elsewhere in South Slavic oral poetry[17] as well as in *La Chançun de Willame*.[18] Each error is accountable in terms of the singer's oral verse-making technique, a technique which forces the composer-performer to concentrate on one narrative event at a time even at the expense of narrative consistency. To account for Willame's Saracen disguise, one need not postulate a lacuna in the written text, as do Paul Meyer, Weeks, and McMillan.[19] One need not fall back upon the theory that a literary *remanieur* excised all mention of Alderufe's arms. One simply may acknowledge that we are dealing with a work of sung literature, and that the singer made an error.

* * *

The third anomaly presents a greater problem. What are we to make of Vivien's miraculous recovery? It would be convenient to say that the oral hypothesis alone

[15] E. Wienbeck et al., eds., *Aliscans* (Halle 1903).
[16] Lord, *Singer of Tales* (n. 8 above) 94-95.
[17] See Lord (n. 12 above) 441-442.
[18] In lines 1541-1561, when Guibourc arms the young hero Gui, much is made of the fact that his arms are small to suit his small stature. Yet in lines 2358-2362 she recalls that she gave Gui the arms of illustrious warriors.
[19] Paul Meyer, "La Chançun de Willame," *Romania* 32 (1903) 613; Weeks (n. 6 above) 247; and McMillan (n. 2 above) 2.144-147.

could account for this anomaly, but such is not the case. Here there can be no question of forgetfulness or confusion on the part of the singer. The incident is in no way comparable to that in Book 13 of the *Iliad*, in which a certain warrior named Pylamenes appears even though the poet had killed him in Book 5. The death of Vivien at Archamp is no casual adventure, one among many. It is the very heart of the first part of the poem. Vivien's death is presented in a scene seldom rivalled elsewhere in Old French epic poetry for its dramatic intensity. After his last companion has been cut down at his side, the young Vivien staggers through the field of battle alone. His bowels are trailing between his feet, and he holds them in with his left hand as best he can. Only by leaning on his sword is he able to stand upright. At this point, after the last syllable of a prayer has left his lips, a Saracen rides by and delivers a blow which scatters Vivien's brains to the grass and knocks the man to his knees. Other Saracens rush from all directions to cut him down: "tut le detrenchent contreval al graver" (line 925). The Saracens drag the body away and hide it beneath a tree, "for they do not wish that Christians find it" (line 928). After a scene as vivid as this, one is astonished to find that after a lapse of a number of days, the same Vivien opens his eyes and speaks. This later scene is no bit of foolery; it too is told in deadly earnest. As if the first death scene had not been sufficient, the poet presents us with a second:

> A la funtaine dunt li duit sunt mult cler,
> Desuz la foille d'un grant oliver,
> Ad bers Willame quons Vivien trové.
> Par mi le cors out quinze plaies tels,
> De la menur fust morz uns amirelz.
> Dunc le regrette dulcement e suef:
> "Vivien, sire, mar fustes unques ber,
> Tun vasselage que Deus t'aveit doné!
> N'ad uncore gueres que tu fus adubé,
> Que tu plevis e juras Dampnedeu
> Que ne fuereies de bataille champel,
> Puis covenant ne volsis mentir Deu.
> Pur ço iés ore mort, ocis e afolé.
> Dites, bel sire, purriez vus parler
> E reconuistre le cors altisme Deu?
> Si tu ço creez, qu'il fu en croiz penez,
> En m'almonere ai del pain sacré,
> Del demeine que de sa main saignat Deus;
> Se de vus le col en aveit passé,
> Mar crendreies achaisun de malfé."
> Al quons revint e sen e volenté,
> Ovri les oilz, si ad sun uncle esgardé.
> De bele boche començat a parler:
> "Ohi, bel sire," dist Vivien le ber,
> Iço conuis ben que veirs e vifs est Deu."   (2011-2035)

(By the spring whose waters run so clear, beneath the shade of a great olive tree, the noble Willame found Count Vivien. His body was pierced by fifteen wounds, of the least of which an emir would have died. Then he laments him sweetly and tenderly: "Vivien, my lord, would that you had never been so brave! Would that the Lord had never made you such a knight! It is not long since you were dubbed a knight, when you swore a solemn oath to the Lord God that you would not flee from the field of battle. Then you did not wish to betray your pledge to God. For this you are dead, utterly slain. Speak, my fair lord: can you speak and recognize the Body of the most high God? If you believe that He was crucified on the Cross, in my wallet I have a piece of consecrated bread of the very kind which the Lord blessed with His own hand. Once it has passed your throat you need not fear the devil's accusations." The Count came to his senses, he opened his eyes and gazed at his uncle. His fair lips began to speak: "*Ohi*, fair lord," said the noble Vivien, "now I know well that God is true and living.")

That Vivien is indeed dead there can be no question. Despite McMillan's understanding that the hero has been only "grièvement blessé," [20] Frappier undoubtedly is correct in concluding that the second death scene is in "contradiction totale" with the first.[21] Realistically, there is no way that Vivien could have survived the prior attack, especially after lying for days without food or water. The poet calls attention to Vivien's fifteen wounds, any one of which would have been sufficient to kill an emir (lines 2014-2015). Willame laments unequivocally that his nephew is "mort, ocis" (line 2023). Given the fact of Vivien's death, there is only one way to account for his later recovery, and that is by viewing this recovery not as an example of narrative inconsistency but as a genuine miracle, as Barbara Levy Silver has argued convincingly.[22] Still, the question remains: how are we to account for the presence of such a miracle in the work?

Vivien's miraculous recovery will cease to appear so puzzling, I believe, once one reads this part of *La Chançun de Willame* against the background of a pattern of narrative development very familiar in the realm of folk literature. As yet, the structural analysis of European folk literature is a discipline still in its infancy. All the same, a great deal has been accomplished in the present century to reduce this

---

[20] McMillan 2.13. McMillan's judgment may possibly be influenced by the corresponding scene in *Aliscans* (lines 693-887), in which Vivien is discovered still living after having fallen earlier the same day.

[21] Frappier (n. 7 above) 143 n. Wathelet-Willem, *Recherches* (n. 7 above) 1.320 n. 188, concludes that Vivien is imagined to have been lying "dans une sorte de coma." She finds the first "death" scene hard to reconcile with the second: "On se trouve en présence d'une scène remaniée." See further Jean Frappier, "Le caractère et la mort de Vivien dans la Chanson de Guillaume," in *Colloquios de Roncesvalles 1955* (Saragossa 1956) 229-243, and Jeanne Wathelet-Willem, "Sur deux passages de la chanson de Guillaume," *Le Moyen Age* 65 (1959) 33-40.

[22] B. L. Silver, "The Death of Vivien in *La Chançun de Willame*," *Neuphilologische Mitteilungen* 71 (1970) 306-311. Silver calls attention to a number of details in the scene of Vivien's recovery which are reminiscent of details accompanying miraculous events in saints' legends.

immense and overwhelmingly complex body of literature to a finite number of reiterated motifs, tale-types, and abstract patterns of narrative development. Of particular interest to the present discussion is the achievement of Vladimir Propp in his celebrated study *The Morphology of the Folktale*.[23] By taking a ruthlessly functional approach to the problem of form, Propp was able to show that the action of almost any traditional wondertale can be accounted for in terms of a single scheme of thirty-one abstract narrative events (or *functions*). Not all these functions will occur in a given tale, and some may be repeated several times; but with minor exceptions, the functions which occur will occur in a predictable sequence.

Propp's conclusions are based on the empirical analysis of one hundred Russian folktales of the nineteenth century. Since most if not all of these folktales are examples of international tale-types, however, Propp's *Morphology* is the closest thing we have to a morphology of the European folktale in general. In addition, since many of these tale-types are of some antiquity, Propp's conclusions have been of interest to medievalists and to classicists as well as to folklorists. Previous research has demonstrated the usefulness of Propp's methods and conclusions to the analysis of works which are not themselves folktales, though they may have a folktale base: the *Odyssey, Beowulf*, and certain Middle English romances, for example.[24] In a separate study,[25] I have pointed out the usefulness of bringing comparative folktale morphology to bear on the question of the structure of *Le Pèlerinage de Charlemagne*. If I am not mistaken, Propp's *Morphology* provides a key which will help to unlock the puzzle of the revival of Vivien as well.

There is no need to summarize the whole of Propp's morphological scheme. The relevant part is the sequence of functions designated **G-H-I-J-K-↓-Pr-O-M-N-Q**. Here occur events which tend to be at the heart of a tale. In paraphrasing the sequence, I shall rely on the French translation[26] of Propp's *Morfológija skázki*, as, unlike the current English translation,[27] it is based on the revised (1969) Russian edition.

[23] V. Propp, *Morfológija skázki* ed. 2 (Moscow 1969; ed. 1, Leningrad 1928).

[24] See Phillip Damon, "Dilation and Displacement in the *Odyssey*," *Pacific Coast Philology* 5 (1970) 19-23; Thomas Alan Shippey, "The Fairy-Tale Structure of *Beowulf*," *Notes and Queries* 16 (1969) 2-21; Daniel R. Barnes, "Folktale Morphology and the Structure of *Beowulf*," *Speculum* 45 (1970) 416-434; Bruce A. Rosenberg, "Morphology of the Middle English Romance," *Journal of Popular Culture* 1 (1967) 63-77; and Shirley Marchalonis, "*Sir Gowther*: The Process of a Romance," *Chaucer Review* 6 (1971) 26-28. In a paper titled "Folklore Methodology and Medieval Literature" presented in mimeographed form for the Seminar in Folklore and Literature at the annual meeting of the Modern Language Association of America, San Francisco, 28 December 1975, Rosenberg also pointed out the dangers of blind applications of Propp's *Morphology* to archaic literature and to genres other than the folktale. See further his study "Folktale Morphology and the Structure of *Beowulf*," *Journal of the Folklore Institute* 11 (1975) 199-209. While I share certain of Rosenberg's reservations, the accuracy with which the scheme identified by Propp accounts for the plot structure of parts of certain archaic works still seems to me so striking as to call for attention.

[25] J. D. Niles, "On the Logic of *Le Pèlerinage de Charlemagne*," forthcoming in *Neuphilologische Mitteilungen*.

[26] *Morphologie du conte*, trans. Marguerite Derrida et al. (Paris 1970). The parts of Propp's scheme which I shall be paraphrasing may be found on pages 63-77; the corresponding pages in the English translation are 51-62.

[27] *Morphology of the Folktale*, ed. Louis A. Wagner, intro. Alan Dundes, ed. 2 (Austin 1968).

After a number of preliminary functions which need not concern us, the sequence begins as the hero journeys to a kingdom other than his own (**G**: *déplacement dans l'espace entre deux royaumes*). Here, in that class of tales which features a physical combat, he battles against an antagonist (**H**: *combat*), he is wounded or marked (**I**: *marque*), and he defeats the antagonist (**J**: *victoire*). An original misfortune or lack is now eliminated in any of a number of ways: an object of quest may be found, or a person may be released from a spell, or a prisoner may be released, and so on (**K**: *réparation*). The hero now returns home (↓: *retour*), often pursued by the same or by new antagonists (**Pr**: *poursuite*). The tale may end shortly after his rescue from pursuit, or it may continue in several ways. In one favorite sequence, the hero arrives home but is unrecognized, frequently because he is disguised (**O**: *arrivée incognito*). He is posed a special task (**M**: *tâche difficile*), and he accomplishes the task readily (**N**: *tâche accomplie*). Either now or after showing additional proof of his identity, he is recognized and is welcomed home (**Q**: *reconnaissance*).

Leaving aside its ornamental details, the central part of *La Chançun de Willame* (lines 1505-2328) consists of a sequence of events which closely resembles this part of Propp's scheme. After a good deal of preliminary action, Willame sets out for the second time from his home castle to the battlefield at Archamp. In Propp's terms, we could call this event **G**: *déplacement dans l'espace entre deux royaumes*. Here he battles fiercely against the Saracen king Deramed (**H**: *combat*). Willame is cut off from his comrades, is knocked to the ground, and is wounded in the throat (**I**: *marque*). His nephew Gui comes to his rescue, and together the two Franks succeed in killing Deramed (**J**: *victoire*; see line 1980, "Ore out vencu sa bataille Willame"). Willame now finds the body of Vivien, and Vivien briefly revives. Let us provisionally call this event **X**. Soon thereafter, a new Saracen onslaught forces Willame to flee to his home castle, chased by the pagans (↓: *retour*, and **Pr**: *poursuite*). When he arrives, his wife Guibourc fails to recognize him because he is wearing Saracen arms (**O**: *arrivée incognito*). To test his identity, she sets him the task of rescuing singlehanded a group of Christian captives from a passing host of 7000 pagans (**M**: *tâche difficile*). He accomplishes the task (**N**: *tâche accomplie*); and when he then unhelms and reveals his features — it is not clear why he did not do this at first — she recognizes him and welcomes him home (**Q**: *reconnaissance*).

This portion of the poem therefore resembles very closely a pattern of narrative development which Propp has identified as one of the commonest sequences encountered in folktales: **G-H-I-J . . . X . . . ↓-Pr-O-M-N-Q**. The event which is of interest to us — event **X**, Vivien's miraculous recovery — occurs at the point when one would expect some realization of Propp's function **K**: *réparation*. And in fact, this is exactly what occurs. As a special subgroup of function **K**, in Propp's *Morphology*, we encounter the situation whereby a dead person revives (**K**[9]: *le mort ressuscite*). In other words, Vivien's recovery occurs right on schedule, as it were. Study of Propp's morphological scheme could not have predicted that Vivien was to come back to life, but it could predict that if Vivien *were* to come back to life, he would do so at this very moment. In other words, when one considers *La Chançun de Willame* within the broad context of traditional, oral storytelling, the miracle of Vivien's recovery no longer seems anomalous and there is no need to explain it away.

We may conclude that, at this point in its action, the Old French epic poem appears to approach closely to the logic of the wondertale. A familiar folklore motif — the revival of a person thought dead[28] — seems here to have been realized in Christian, heroic terms, terms appropriate to the world of the *chansons de geste*. In its *narrative function*, the consecrated bread which Willame offers Vivien appears to be roughly equivalent to the magic object or gesture (for example, life-giving waters) which raises a folktale hero from the dead or which breaks an enchantment. In its nature, of course, the bread scarcely is to be confused with analogous objects in fairy tales. The bread is the Eucharist. Holy as the ordinary Eucharist may be, this bread is yet more powerful: it is bread of the same kind which the Lord blessed with His own hand ("del demeine que de sa main saignat Deus," 2028). How Willame obtained it, we are not told. The point is that he has it, and that it works. We may conclude that the author of *La Chançun de Willame* pleased himself and his audience (and at the same time baffled modern critics) by shaping his tale in accord with a common folktale pattern, a pattern which he realizes in sacral terms.

What then of the critics' postulated *Chanson de Rainouart* (G2)? In reviewing the central action of the work, we have seen no point at which one might say, "The authentic and primitive poem ends here." Certainly line 1980 is not such a point, for this line falls before the climax of this part of the poem, Vivien's recovery, nor has Willame yet returned home. Up until line 2328, the action constitutes a seamless whole. Once he has returned to his home castle, Willame is grief-stricken at the thought of his losses at Archamp. He takes Guibourc's advice and rides to the court of the emperor Louis at Laon. The reinforcements which Louis gives him include the "ash-boy" hero Reneward (*gaite-tison*, or male Cinderella), and from this point on, Reneward steals the stage. The poem's first great narrative move, which concerns chiefly Vivien and Willame and which draws to a close in the neighborhood of line 2328, dovetails neatly into the second great narrative move, which concerns chiefly Reneward and Willame and which continues to the end of the poem. To seek to divide the work more strictly into two halves, G1 and G2, would be artificial. The poem is one, though its action falls into two broad movements.

Still, one is not surprised that critics have felt uncomfortable with Reneward, this massive buffoon who would seem more at home in the pages of Rabelais than in a self-respecting *chanson de geste*. Several attempts have been made to account for the indignity of Reneward by discovering evidence of a change of authorship between G1 and G2. McMillan calls attention to what he considers a changing structure of the laisse, a changing use of the refrain, and a deterioration in meter between G1 and G2, as well as to certain changes in formulaic diction. Frappier, drawing on the work of Valtorta, cites in addition the loose and repetitive structure of G2 and the fact that only in G2 are persons described physically. Wathelet-Willem cites numerous minute

---

[28] See Stith Thompson, *Motif-Index of Folk Literature*, ed. 2, 2 (Bloomington 1956) motifs E0-E199 ("Resuscitation").

stylistic changes between G1 and G2.[29] Particularly offensive to some critics is the change of tone which results when Reneward steals the stage from Willame.

Each of these comments must be weighed on its merits. Still, if I am not mistaken, certain changes of tone and of texture are practically inevitable in a long narrative work. Such changes may be especially noticeable when a new and striking personage comes on the scene. We should not expect a homogeneous work. Given almost any medieval poem of comparable length on which to exercise their ingenuity, most scholars would be able to find minute changes or discrepancies which could be construed as indicating multiple authorship. I would not claim that the changes cited by McMillan, Valtorta, Frappier, and Wathelet-Willem are illusory. I would suggest, however, that many of them are accountable within the theoretical framework which is advanced in this paper. Certain of the changes cited — the loosening structure of the laisse, the diminishing use of the refrain, the deterioration in meter, and a general increase in formlessness — are just the sorts of changes which one would expect to find in a long poem recorded from oral tradition. Many collectors of oral literature have experienced difficulty in obtaining long texts which do not decline in quality toward the end. There are several reasons why this is so. First, singers often have perfected only the first part of a song, the part which they have sung most often and which tends to attract the audience's most alert attention. The end of a song they may have sung less often, or less carefully. As a result, a song's beginning may be highly effective and stable, whereas the latter part may deteriorate and may vary from performance to performance. Second, the human lungs, lips, hand, and mind have powers which are limited, as anyone may verify who has spent long hours continuously singing or writing. It is physically tiring for a singer to perform a long song at a speed slow enough for oral dictation, just as it is physically tiring for a scribe to record the song by hand. Instrumental interludes may be frequent at first, but may become more rare as the song progresses (hence, very possibly, the widespread tendency for laisse length to increase as a song continues). The mind which once was alert becomes dulled and easily distracted; errors creep in, and the song which had begun famously proceeds to a mediocre close. As the Chadwicks remark about the Tartar epic songs recorded by Radlov, for example, "the weariness of the singer, and the consequent lapses of memory and flagging narrative are constantly brought home to us as we draw towards the close of Radlov's poems, which offer a striking contrast to their brilliant opening scenes."[30] Other putative evidence for the poem's bipartite nature is no more convincing: for example, the fact that the prelude (lines 1-11) omits all mention of Reneward or of the final defeat of the Saracens. Such omissions are found commonly in oral literature, in the prelude to the *Odyssey*, for example, in which much is made of the eating of the cattle of Helios but no mention is made of Telemachos, or Penelope, or the Contest of the Bow.

---

[29] McMillan (n. 2 above) 2.127-130; Frappier (n. 7 above) 203-205; Valtorta (n. 7 above) 40-70; Wathelet-Willem, *Recherches* (n. 7 above) 1.395-453.

[30] Hektor Munro Chadwick and Nora Kershaw Chadwick, *The Growth of Literature* 3 (Cambridge 1940) 183.

Enough has been said, I believe, to cast doubt on the right of literary critics to condemn Reneward offhand to the particular spot of hell reserved for literary imposters. Although no great admirer of Reneward, Joseph Bédier put the matter well: "Dante l'a placé dans son Paradis aux côtés de Guillaume [*Paradiso* 18:28-48]; ne soyons pas plus sévères que Dante ni plus délicats."[31]

The application of new methods of analysis to the text of *La Chançun de Willame* thus has yielded interesting results, results which are at variance with the judgment of all but a few scholars who have concerned themselves with the question of the poem's unity.[32] First, by drawing on oral poetic theory and the experience of field collectors of oral literature, I have tried to show that several of the poem's anomalies are accounted for easily, given the hypothesis that the work derives from oral tradition. By reverse token, the presence of striking anomalies in the work could be taken as corroborating the oral hypothesis. Second, by drawing on comparative folktale morphology, I have shown that Vivien's recovery falls into place when one views the poem against the background of a narrative pattern absolutely basic in the realm of European folk literature. Since the remaining evidence which has been thought to indicate the poem's multiple authorship carries comparatively little weight, no longer does there seem to be a need for theories of scribal compilation or *remaniement* of the text. In physics, if two theories can account for the same phenomena, the simpler one is to be preferred. In case of the poem which is preserved in British Library MS Add. 38,663, a theory which can account for the facts of the poem by postulating a single author and a single performance is to be preferred to a theory which postulates two or more authors and any number of *remaniements*. In other words, if my diagnosis is correct, the critics may put away their knives.

Department of English
University of California
Berkeley, California 94720, U.S.A.

[31] Joseph Bédier, *Les légendes épiques*, ed. 3, 1 (Paris 1926) 96.

[32] Defenders of the poem's unity include J. Salverda de Grave, "Observations sur le texte de la *Chanson de Guillaume*," *Neophilologus* 1 (1915-1916) 1-18 and 181-192; Wilmotte (n. 1 above) 84-85 and passim; and Alfred Adler, "Rainouart and the Composition of the *Chanson de Guillaume*," *Modern Philology* 49 (1951-52) 160-171. Silver (n. 22 above) and Duggan (n. 9 above) implicitly accept the poem's unity.

"OF HEIGH OR LOUGH ESTAT": MEDIEVAL FABULISTS
AS SOCIAL CRITICS

●

by Arnold Clayton Henderson

Perhaps not every bishop enjoys being likened to a snail or an ox, but those who
lived in England in the thirteenth century had opportunities enough to get used to it.
While Odo of Cheriton sprinkled ecclesiastics of all degrees throughout his collection
of fables, Marie de France laid out lessons for secular lords or commoners in her
somewhat earlier collection, and the Hebrew fabulist Berechiah flayed the rich. These
writers begin something new. In the moralizations of their collections, social terms

The following abbreviations and short references are used in the course of this article:

Aes, Aesopica. Ben Edwin Perry, *Aesopica: A Series of Texts Relating to Aesop* . . . 1: *Greek and
Latin Texts* (Urbana 1952). The same *Aes* numbers are used in Perry's *Babrius* . . . (see
below), containing an appendix of English translations and summaries of medieval texts in
Aesopica.

Augustana. Second-century fables with later additions, all in *Aesopica* (see above).

Avianus. In J. Wight Duff and Arnold M. Duff, *Minor Latin Poets* (Cambridge, Mass. 1961). Ca.
A.D. 400.

Babrius. Greek fables in Ben Edwin Perry, *Babrius and Phaedrus* (Cambridge, Mass. 1965). First
cent. A.D.

Ber, Berechiah. Berechiah ben Natronai, ha-Nakdan, Hebrew fables (12th cent.) in *Mischle
schualim, die Fuchsfabeln des Berekhja ben Natronaj,* ed. Lazarus Goldschmidt (Berlin 1921).
I use the translation by Moses Hadas, *Fables of a Jewish Aesop* (New York 1967).

Bidpai. Indian fables with derivatives in many languages, indexed and summarized in Chauvin
(below).

Bozon. Nicole Bozon (13th-cent. French fables written in England), cited by chapter no. in *Les
contes moralisés* (n. 45 below). Medieval Latin trans. in Hervieux (below) 4.256-263.

Bromyard. John Bromyard (14th-cent. sermons); see n. 3 below (Owst).

Chauvin. Victor C. Chauvin, *Bibliographie des ouvrages arabes ou relatifs aux Arabes publiés dans
l'Europe chrétienne de 1810 à 1885,* 12 vols. (Liège 1892-1922). Index and French summaries of Arabic fables.

Dukes. Leopold Dukes, *Rabbinische Blumenlese* (Leipzig 1844). Contains Hebrew fables.

*Ecbasis captivi. Ecbasis cuiusdam captivi per tropologiam: Escape of a Certain Captive told in a
Figurative Manner,* trans. Edwin H. Zeydel (Chapel Hill 1964).

Fabulae. See Odo of Cheriton, below.

Fabulae rhythmicae. Thirteenth-century fables in Hervieux (below) 2.714-757.

FR. *Fabulae rhythmicae* (above).

Guillaume le Clerc. *Le Bestiaire: Das Thierbuch,* ed. Robert Reinsch (Wiesbaden 1967 [1892]).
A rhymed bestiary in French, A.D. 1210/11.

Henryson. *The Poems and Fables of Robert Henryson,* ed. H. Harvey Wood, ed. 2 (Edinburgh
1958).

Hervieux. Léopold Hervieux, *Les fabulistes latins,* ed. 2, 5 vols. (Paris 1899).

Isopet(s). A series of French fable collections, all ed. Bastin (n. 35 below).

such as rich and poor or *seignur* and *serf* frequently replace the moral terms — strong and weak, malicious and innocent — of the ordinary Romulus or its English derivative, the Romulus of Nilant. These social fabulists could be put into a broad picture of the rise in social criticism in the age of the *Roman de Renart,* Walter Map, and *exempla.* In a narrower perspective, their collections could be arranged for study according to definite textual borrowings from one another, particularly where they

John of Sheppey. English 14th-cent. fables (Latin) in Hervieux (above) 4.417-450.

JS. John of Sheppey (above).

Jacques de Vitry. *The Exempla . . . of Jacques de Vitry,* ed. Thomas Frederick Crane (London 1890). His sermons (13th cent.) include fables.

Kalilah. Arabic tales (from Indian) summarized in Chauvin (above); medieval Latin trans. (Kalila et Dimna) in Hervieux (above), vol. 5.

Lydgate. John Lydgate, *Isopes Fabules* in *The Minor Poems of John Lydgate,* ed. Henry Noble MacCracken, pt. 2: Secular poems, Early English Text Society (London 1934; repr. 1961).

M. Marie de France, n. 2 below.

Map. Walter Map, *De nugis curialium,* ed. Montague Rhodes James (Oxford 1914) and trans. Frederick Tupper and Marbury Bladen Ogle, *Master Walter Map's Book De Nugis curialium (Courtiers' Trifles)* (London 1924).

Mishnah. See Talmud, below.

O. Odo of Cheriton (below).

Odo of Cheriton. There are two collections (13th cent.) in Hervieux (above): *Fabulae* (0), Odo's own collection, Hervieux 4.173-246 (additions 248-255, some by Odo); and *Parabolae* (0*Parabolae*) extracted by Hervieux from Odo's sermons, Hervieux 4.265-343.

Ordinary Romulus. See Romulus (below).

NB. See Bozon, above.

Neckam. Alexander Neckam, fables (start of 13th cent.?) in Hervieux (above) 2.392-416.

P. Phaedrus (below).

Parabolae. See Odo of Cheriton (above).

Perotti. Fables copied after medieval times, apparently from lost MSS of Phaedrus; in *Babrius* (above).

Phaedrus. First-century Latin fables in *Babrius* (above).

R. The Ordinary Romulus (see Romulus, below).

Renart. Roman de Renart (below).

RN. Romulus of Nilant (see Romulus, below).

Robert's Romulus. See Romulus (below).

Roman de Renart. The basic edition is Ernest Martin, ed., *Le roman de Renart* (Strasbourg 1882).

Romulus. Several medieval fable collections attributed to Romulus are printed in Hervieux (above), vol. 2. The Ordinary Romulus: 2.195-233.

 Robert's Romulus (Romulus Roberti, Romuli anglici nonnullis exortae fabulae): 2.549-563; MSS of 14th cent., uncertain relationship to Marie and Trier.

 Romulus of Nilant (Romulus Nilanti): 2.513-548; by 11th cent., ancestor of versions made in England.

 Romulus of Trier (also called "LBG fables" from the location of MSS or, by Hervieux, Romulus Anglici cunctis): 2.564-652; of problematic date and relationship to Marie and to Robert's Romulus.

Sanhedrin. A division of the Talmud: see n. 13 below.

T. Romulus of Trier, see Romulus (above).

Talmud. References come principally from the Babylonian Talmud, n. 13 below, and are by section number within each book (Aboth, Abodah Zarah, Sanhedrin, etc.), but see also n. 24 for minor tractates.

Theobaldus. *Physiologus: A Metrical Bestiary of Twelve Chapters by Bishop Theobald,* ed. and trans. Alan Wood Rendell (London 1928); also ed. Richard Morris, *An Old English Miscellany Containing a Bestiary . . .* (London 1872) 201-209.

share the special stories of the "Anglo-Latin" tradition.[1] Both perspectives are worth taking, but I intend in this paper to work on an intermediate scale, grouping together and surveying those collections of fables which, whether direct borrowing can be proved or not, share a new richness and specificity of social applications.

Some grouping of the many medieval collections of animal fables is needed if we are to find our way among them, and groups formed on stylistic or thematic principles can further the literary studies that are of late succeeding the older philological studies. When we deal with, say, Robert Henryson — one of the few medieval fabulists currently receiving literary attention — we should set him against not only the two or three collections he directly echoes, and not only against the whole undifferentiated mass of the fable tradition, but also against those currents of style and theme within which and against which he works. Social criticism is such a current. Space lacks here for tracing it through its later manifestations in the French *Isopets* and in the English fables of Lydgate and Henryson. We can, however, clear the way for studies of these and other individual authors by sketching the first flowering of the satirical spirit in Marie, Berechiah, and Odo, and tracing it out into the peripheral *Fabulae rhythmicae*, Romulus of Trier, Nicole Bozon, and John of Sheppey. The constant focus will be not the plots of fables but the applications (moralizations), and the fables chosen will be those in collections, not those scattered in other works. Which applications in a given author are distinctive and which borrowed? What perspectives and social concerns are special to an author? From what strata of society do our authors come? Where do these origins foster particular allegiances, and where do these fabulists adopt perspectives universal enough to allow scrutiny of their own classes?

Of Marie de France's nearly thirty fables with specific social applications (out of a collection of 102), most deal with lay figures, particularly the dynamically contrasting pair, the *seignur* and his people (*sa gent*).[2] With her writings now dated in the late

---

TMI. Stith Thompson, *Motif-Index of Folk-Literature,* 6 vols. (Bloomington 1955-1958).

Trier. Romulus of Trier, see Romulus (above).

Walter. Fables attributed to Walter the Englishman in Hervieux (above), 2.316-382.

[1] For *exempla* collections showing social criticism, see Frederic C. Tubach, *Index exemplorum,* FF Communications 204 (Helsinki 1969), esp. 521-523. For the Anglo-Latin tradition and the suggestion that England was its center, see Joseph Jacobs, *The Fables of Aesop,* 2 vols. (London 1889) 1.178-180. Broad-based source studies of the tradition include Léopold Hervieux, *Les fabulistes latins,* ed. 2, 5 vols. (Paris 1899); Karl Warnke, "Die Quellen des Esope der Marie de France," in *Forschungen zur romanischen Philologie: Festgabe für Hermann Suchier* (Halle 1900) 161-284; Philip Warner Harry, *A Comparative Study of the Aesopic Fable in Nicole Bozon,* University Studies of the University of Cincinnati, ser. 2, 1.2 (Cincinnati 1905). Forthcoming volumes of Ben Edwin Perry, *Aesopica* (Urbana 1952-) promise new materials. For moralizations and literary effects in the social fabulists, see Arnold C. Henderson, "Moralized Beasts: The Development of Medieval Fable and Bestiary, Particularly from the Twelfth through the Fifteenth Centuries in England and France," Ph.D. diss. (U. of California, Berkeley 1973).

[2] *Die Fabeln der Marie de France,* ed. Karl Warnke, Bibliotheca normannica 6 (Halle 1898). Marie deals primarily with rich and poor, courts and government (nos. 2, 4, 6, 7, 10, 11 [both versions], 14, 16, 18, 19, 23, 27, 29, 34, 36, 38, 46, 56, 62, 84, 88). She also treats miscellaneous themes that could be called social (8, 15, 43, 47, 49, 85, 101), and her fables on women deal implicitly with social roles (21, 44, 45, 72, 95, plus references in 50 and in the version of 1 found in some MSS).

twelfth century and with her self-acknowledged model, the English fables of "Alfred," no longer extant, she must stand as the pioneer among our social fabulists. She and Berechiah ben Natronai share the ordinarily early trait of calling the beasts by generic names rather than the personal names of the soon-to-be-popular *Roman de Renart*.[3] Marie is a pivotal figure, influential and innovative, yet in some respects old-fashioned. Stylistically, she is one step from the older Latin tradition: her colloquial vigor and brief dialogues foreshadow what would develop under Renardian influence into the *Isopet* of Lyon and Henryson's *Morall Fabillis*. Her repertory of fables, while introducing the new "Alfredian" themes, will be enlarged by the Romulus of Trier, Berechiah, Odo, and others. Her applications newly define the world in feudal terms, but it is still the world of laymen.

There is no need here to document afresh the ways Marie adapts the moralizations of this first extant vernacular collection to her new feudal and aristocratic audience. H. R. Jauss has shown how the moral terms of the older tradition, as represented by the Romulus of Nilant, become Marie's social terms. Her *riche* translates such varied terms as *potens, dives, melior, cupidus* and *reprobus*; her *povre* translates *impotens, miser, inferior, inutilis,* and *innocens.*[4] It may be worth reminding ourselves, however, of what is still old in Marie. Such generalized moral terms as *felun* (M3, M8, etc.) remain alongside newer social terminology.[5] The two modes differ subtly in their effect on the audience's experience of the fables as they are read. One naturally identifies with morally neutral terms such as *riche* or *povre, seneschal* or *seignur,* whichever happen to fit one's image of one's role in life. Yet no one is inclined to see himself or herself in a *felun hom* or a *fol*. Moral terms thus encourage us to see the fable through the eyes of the better characters, the victims, not the oppressors, or else to regard the whole action from a dispassionate observer's position. This is the mode of two-thirds of Marie's collection. In the other third, with more socially defined applications, the detached stance is still possible, but one may also occasionally be pricked by rebukes to the faults proper to one's own class. This is particularly likely to occur when the audience for the fables is the same as the group most directly rebuked.

Determining the audience Marie had in mind for particular fables is complicated

---

[3] While names such as Renart and Isengrim may be old, the post-*roman* vogue for them begins about 1210/1211 in Guillaume le Clerc, *Le bestiaire,* ed. Robert Reinsch (Leipzig 1892; repr. Wiesbaden 1967) vv. 1308f., 1342, 1731. Odo of Cheriton, however, is the earliest I know to use them in a fable collection (*Parabolae* 150 and *Fabulae* 19, 22, 23a, 30a, 39, and 43: Hervieux 4 [n. 1 above]). His coupling of personal and generic names (e.g., "Ysemgrino, id est Lupo," 23a, cf. 39, 43) implies that the audience was not yet fully familiar with the new names. Later collections using Renardian names include Robert's Romulus 6, 21; Nicole Bozon 4; *Isopet* of Lyon; *Isopet* I and II (1, 8, 22, 26) of Paris; *Isopet* of Chartres 24; *Le chastoiement d'un père à son fils*; and John Bromyard's sermons. (For Bromyard see Gerald Robert Owst, *Literature and Pulpit in Medieval England* [Cambridge 1933].) By the time of *Isopet* III of Paris, *Regnart* has itself become a mere generic name. The absence of Renardian names, of course, proves nothing, and John of Sheppey will do without them in the fourteenth century.

[4] Hans Robert Jauss, *Untersuchungen zur Mittelalterlichen Tierdichtung* (Tubingen 1959) 49.

[5] Marie in Warnke (n. 2 above): I cite fables throughout by initials (author or title) plus fable or chapter (not page) number; see list before n. 1 above.

by the realization that one need not be present to have a moral made at one's expense, and that one may find one's own faults in a fable nominally directed to others. Giving a moral "for" a category of persons is merely the mechanism used in fables to discuss those persons, not proof that any such are in the audience. The old view that Marie was simply the champion of the poor against the rich has been much modified by E. A. Francis, who points out that in many cases the *povre* are expected to do things, such as choosing masters wisely (M19, M46), which seem more appropriate to the weaker nobles than to serfs, servants, and the desperately poor.[6] A recent computer study of medieval French records has shown an unsuspectedly large class of people for whom wealth and title do not go together.[7] Titled (perhaps as a reward for military service), they are respectable, yet they live a material life indistinguishable from that of ordinary people, rarely leave their names in court records more than once or twice, and might consider *povre* all too apt. The fundamental processes of fable literature depend on relative, not absolute terms: the conflict of a powerful beast with a weak one suggests by analogy a lesson for any pair of persons, one of whom is more powerful in some respect than the other. Those who are weak with respect to the mightiest barons may be strong with respect to others. We need not fix the relative terms *riche* and *povre* to particular classes at all, and we need not expect the same class to be meant whenever the same word occurs. There is no difficulty in taking Marie's unfavorable references to the poor (by a variety of terms) to include the lowest of the common folk. Her favorable references, too, may spread over both the lesser nobles and the still lower bondsmen that the poorest of the nobles would scorn. Marie's *serfs* whispering in the fields (foolishly overdoing the caution their weak position demands, M41) are really serfs, and the object of her ridicule. In the fable of the flea who rides a camel and apologizes for giving trouble the camel never felt (M38), the contrast of beasts implies an immense contrast in social class, and *povre gent* could reasonably extend to poor commoner as well as poor noble.[8] Marie seems on the side of the poor (*povre*) in the fable of the fox who lost its cub to a marauding eagle and had no way to make its pleas for mercy heard except to threaten burning the eagle's unreachable nest (M10). Her urging that the poor (*povre*) must combine an implicit threat with their pleas for mercy before the proud rich (*riche orguillus*) will listen, need not seem too unmedieval an exhortation to the masses even if we allow *povre* to mean what its literal sense would convey. Such a reading would not violate the structural contrast between eagle and earth-bound fox that other fabulists — Phaedrus, the ordinary Romulus, Walter of England, and later the *Isopets* — translate into human society as a contest of the

---

[6] E. A. Francis, "Marie de France et son temps," *Romania* 72 (1951) 78-99, esp. 82.

[7] Theodore Evergates, "The Aristocracy of Champagne in the Mid-Thirteenth Century: A Quantitative Description," *Journal of Interdisciplinary History* 5 (1974) 1-18. For similar findings in the Forez district of France, see Edouard Perroy, "Social Mobility among the French *Noblesse* in the Later Middle Ages," *Past & Present* 21 (1962) 25-38. Presumably England would not fundamentally differ even some decades earlier.

[8] Jauss (n. 4 above) 49f. admits to difficulty fitting this use of *povre* to his general finding that Marie reserves *povre* for classes above the poorest, leaving *vilein* for the rural classes.

powerful or lofty in station with their inferiors. Their terms are only less precisely economic than hers. The fable's structure implies any pair of greater and lesser, whether nobles and lesser nobles, nobles and commons, or — as we will see in the *Fabulae rhythmicae* (FR 1.12) — great prelates and their subordinates. In Marie as in the others, the potentially revolutionary exhortation to the weak to issue threats is less a genuine exhortation to an audience of the weak than a vivid way of describing the way the world goes: the rich or powerful are too often unmerciful unless they see mercy in their interest. Anyone could take heed from such a fable, perhaps most of all the great *seignur* who would shun such evil exemplars of his class.

If fables were read aloud at court, their audience must have included not only the person who commissioned them but also his inferiors and occasionally superiors, even the servants moving in and out. Marie has a fable for grumbling servants (*serjant* M84), the fable of the oxen complaining of the indignity of having to haul dung until they are reminded that they created it. What is framed as a moral "for" servants becomes, in the hearing of the rest of the audience, a jest at their expense. The *cunte Willalme* to whom Marie dedicated her fables did not stop listening, or, if he was reading to himself, did not turn the page when confronted with fables giving either friendly or unfriendly advice to a class other than his own; he made of it what he could. Before a courtly or mixed audience, telling the poor to beware choosing evil masters — even if in historical fact they have little option — is in effect hinting to the master to beware evil behavior.

The scorn that Marie betrays for ignorant or ungrateful poor — *vilein, serf* (M41), *nunsachanz* (M41, M43), *la fole gent* (M35, M86), *li fols pueples* (M43), and perhaps *povre* (M38) — is compatible enough with a genuine concern that rich and noble should behave themselves properly toward them. That old fable known to the Egyptians, the Belly and the Members, provides Marie with an opportunity for a lesson in a central medieval political tenet, that lord (*li sire*) and free vassal (*frans huem*) are mutually dependent (M27). Marie is best seen neither as the champion of the poorest classes, nor as the conscious speaker for any particular class interest, whether upper or lower nobility, but as one attempting to be the conscience of society. Commissioned by the wealthy and presumably herself born to the privileged classes, she defines the world in their terms and shares their automatic contempt for those faults peculiar to *vileins,* servants, and the ill-educated. Yet she takes advantage of her welcome among the upper classes to remind them of the duties their social role entails.

The stance of independent moralist is one of long standing in the tradition of fable collections, formerly achieved by making the applications so universal as not to seem partisan. One may be a fool in any class. In anchoring their fables more and more to recognizable social situations, fabulists from Marie onward allowed new tensions into their work. They to some degree sacrificed lofty impartiality in defense of a never-quite-defined innocence threatened by an equally indefinite wickedness, exchanging it for a more dynamic interplay of personal emotions. Marie, in stepping from behind the impartial fog of the older generalized applications, sometimes betrays her class prejudices: mockery of the superstitious *vilein,* a readiness to discount the grumbling *serjant*'s perhaps genuine complaints in comparison to his forgetfulness of his own flaws. But she also, and in many more instances, sets herself against the excesses of a ruling class whose avowed moral principles are no different from her own. Thus her balance is a dynamic one that consists not merely in relating the evils of the world to a set of principles on which all agree, but in choosing sides from moment to moment as now the *seignur,* now the vassal, violates the ideal order. Had she not named names so openly, her aristocratic prejudices might not have shown, but she would also have had less occasion to make the faults of those around her real enough to be matters of passion.

* * *

Since Marie's feudal terminology is part of her characteristic modification of the older Romulus tradition, one naturally wonders what became of it in any collection suggested as derivative from her. The Romulus of Trier (along with the closely-related Robert's Romulus) is usually held to derive from Marie, but in any case has some special relation to her as well as common membership in our group of fabulists.[9] In Marie, *seignur* is a word with feudal connotations, though it may simply denote the master of animals (M15=T16; M20=T21) or the husband of a woman (M72=T115). Trier's usual equivalent, *dominus,* fits the master of animals naturally enough, as does replacing *sire* as a form of address by *domine mi* (M93=T72). But *dominus* lacks the feudal aura in other cases (M6=T8; M18=T19; M29=T77; M84=T63), most significantly in M27 (=T34+T75), the fable of the Belly and the Members, where Marie's reciprocal and feudal dependence of *frans huem* and *sun seignur* or *sire* becomes Trier's *servus* and *dominus.* The feudal connotation of *seignur* as protector is present, but in a non-feudal term, in Trier's *tutandum* (M19=T20). In several cases Trier avoids any equivalent term at all (M23=T27; M62=T52; M65=T55; M95=T74; M88 [*sire*]=T66). *Seignur* can also become merely a rich man, *dives* (M7=T9; M15=T16). The terms would be as at home in the Roman Empire as in medieval feudalism. The same fate befalls other specialized feudal terms for the noble class: *vescunte* vanishes into *tyranni* (M2=T2), *chevalier* disappears (M100=T131), one *bachelers* disappears (M83=T126) while another who figures as a lover becomes merely *amator* (M45=T37). *Seneschal* is replaced by an office common to Antiquity and feudalism alike, *iudex* (M62=T52).

Perhaps more striking is the fate of those at the other end of the social scale, the *vilein.* He may, in Marie, sometimes be merely a servant (M53=T43), where Trier's *servus* is an appropriate equivalent, but in nearly every case Marie uses *vilein* for the special figure of rural feudal society who is translated as *rusticus* in Marie's Latin

---

[9] Texts in Hervieux (n. 1 above) 2.549-563 (Robert's Romulus) and 2.564-652 (Romulus of Trier), discussion 1.763-800. See also Ed. Mall, "Zur Geschichte der mittelalterlichen Fabellitter-atur und insbesondere des Esope der Marie de France," *Zeitschrift für romanische Philologie* 9 (1885, Halle 1886) 161-203; Warnke (n. 2 above) xlviii-lx and (n. 1 above) 161-284.

headings. Trier only occasionally so translates the term (M72=T115; M84=T63). The *vilein* that Marie also calls *bergiers* (shepherd) in her version of the widespread Thief and Dog is her rustic addition to Phaedrian tradition. (Berechiah seems the only fabulist to share the rustic character.) Since Marie's shepherd is also the dog's master (*seignur*), Trier gets by with *dominus* (M20=T21) as in the old tradition. Marie's *vilein* usually, as here, figures in the plot, not the moralization: the figure is a stock character for jokes which could as well have been told of someone else. Thus *vilein* may simply be replaced in Trier by *homo* (M37=T85; M45=T37; M52=T42; M55=T45; M83=T126; M94=T73; M95=T74) or, especially in marital stories, by *maritus* (M44=T36) or *vir* (M45=T37; M94=T73; M95=T74). Marie's *vilein* may also be identified in Trier by a term based on his role in the plot, as a seller (*venditor* M47=T38). One fable shifts about within the whole set of terms: a *vilein* who is also his wife's *seignur* is identified successively as *homo, vir,* and *rusticus* (M72=T115). Only once in Trier is he an *agricola* (M54-T44), and only once the term we perhaps were expecting, *villanus* (M57=T47). Most striking, perhaps, among these changes are those in three fables where there are few if any analogues in collections before Marie. Her *vilein* pregnant with a beetle becomes a *fur* (thief) (M43=T35) just as if the scorn heaped by nobles on the stock-comic *vilein* had already shifted the term to its coming status as insult, and Trier had recognized this by translating a rural insult by one that could be urban. Marie's two whispering *serfs* become *latrones* (servants or brigands) (M41=T113), with emphasis on their being up to no good rather than on the timidity Marie's plot had suggested. The *vilein* with a talking bird actually becomes the opposite of a rural figure, an *urbanus* (M56=T46), again with the satire intensified.

Did the author of the Romulus of Trier deliberately remove Marie's feudal aura? The effect is to return the collection to the pre-feudal largely urban world of ancient fable, but I do not see the point of such an effort. Certainly the author does not consistently restore a pagan atmosphere, since he or she preserves the few religious terms Marie had. Her *reclus* or *eremita* is Trier's *heremita* (M53=T43), her *prestre* or *presbyter* is *presbiter* (M81=T124), and her *evesques* is *episcopus* (M101=T132). I cannot help feeling that these indefinite or urban settings are too much at home in the world of the antique Phaedrus and the early medieval Romulus to be a late re-creation of that world, and that it is Marie's *vilein* who is the new medieval intruder. Indeed, in matters of arrangement, names of characters, and details of action, Trier sometimes seems older in motif than in age of manuscript. In any case, Marie's special feudalizing of fable stands out more clearly against the Romulus of Trier's presentation of what seem to be her new plots in an older largely urban and non-feudal setting.

* * *

The conflict of rich and powerful with poor and weak remains the major social theme in medieval fabulists from Marie onward. In her contemporary, the Hebrew fabulist Berechiah ben Natronai, ha-Nakdan, it is nearly the only explicitly social theme, and he gives it a special intensity all his own. He does, to be sure, have one fable against the pride of those who boast of their various professions (Ber94) and four on lawcourts,[10] but most of his nearly thirty socially-explicit fables treat either oppression of the poor or, less often, the foolishness and pride of the poor putting on upper-class airs.[11]

Giving Berechiah a local habitation and a date has proved one of the more confusing tasks of medieval scholarship, but Hermann Gollancz seems to have cleared away the mistaken hypotheses as well as can be done in the absence of direct life-records. Berechiah, according to Gollancz in 1902, composed his major ethical treatises, *The Compendium* and *The Maṣref,* "in or near Lunel in the South of France ... between 1160 and 1170."[12] He would be an older contemporary of Marie's, probably born near the start of the century, adapting Adelard of Bath's *Quaestiones naturales* before 1161, and finishing his career with the fables. In his collection, as in Marie's, the names for the beasts give no sign that he wrote late enough to know or be interested in alluding to the *Roman de Renart*. The suggestion that Berechiah's title, *Mishle Shualim* (Fox Fables) constitutes an allusion to the

---

[10]*Fables of a Jewish Aesop,* trans. Moses Hadas (New York 1967) nos. 3, 63, 84, 101. Ber63, a dispute between cock and hen over where the cock is to repay a loan of wheat, each hoping any grain spilled in the measuring will fall on his or her own floor, reflects the peculiarly medieval system of dividing justice as a kind of property right, with numbers of lords or ecclesiastics gaining income from fines. Paris, for example, had about two dozen districts, and "jurisdiction over a street could be split several ways and might be sliced down to a single house or even part of one" (Henry Kraus, *The Living Theatre of Medieval Art* [Bloomington 1967] 20).

[11]Berechiah's fables on rich and poor follow, with all analogues in collections sometimes called sources (P, R, RN, M, T), key others where these fail, and none only where none is known. Note that no collection accounts for all. Further comparison shows most analogues to concern plot, not social content. In this, Berechiah is independent of even the socially-conscious M and T (if indeed they antedate him). 1 (P R RN M14 T15); 3 (P R RN M2 T2); 5 (P R RN M5 T5); 8 (P R RN M7 T9); 11 (P R RN M10 T12); 12 (P R RN M11 T7); 15 (R RN M16 T17); 24 (P R RN M18 T19); 32; 33 (Avianus 11); 38 (R RN); 39 (*Aesopica* 434); 42 (R RN M49 T32 and an early Jewish proverb, Leopold Dukes, *Rabbinische Blumenlese* [Leipzig 1844] no. 493); 59 (variant of Avianus 31, Babrius 112, cf. Dukes no. 565, eastern versions with camel and scorpion, and Jacobs [n. 1 above] 1.114); 61 (P R RN M26 T33); 65 (P R RN M35 T83); 66 (Petrus Alphonsi *Disciplina clericalis* 4); 69 (combines the European lion's share in which the strongest seizes all, with the Arab motif of granting it to the oldest, Victor Chauvin, *Bibliographie des ouvrages arabes,* 12 vols. [Liège 1892-1922] 8.73 no. 40); 73 (R RN M38 T86); 76 (P R RN M6 T7); 79 (P R RN M28 T76); 87 (vaguely like Chauvin 2.114 n. *Anwari*); 90 (only somewhat like Babrius 84, Ber73, *Aes*724 and Chauvin 3.30 *Lokman*); 91; 95 (Babrius 30, Avianus 23, *Aes*307); 96 (I know no analogues but the proverb is in Dukes no. 252 [misnumbered as 251] and *Talmud Aboth* chap. 4 *mishnah* 15, and *Sanhedrin* 37a); 100 (I know no analogues among fable collections, but it presumably comes, as do others, from general story collections); 101 (cf. *Aes*427); 107; 110; 111 (contains motifs of spilled poison, Chauvin 2.122, and a creature's refusal of a man's apology, Chauvin 2.102 no. 62 *Kalilah,* and Ber22). I wish to thank Doris Sommer, Livingston College of Rutgers, for verifying Hadas's translation of "rich" as an economic term at crucial points in the Hebrew.

[12] Hermann Gollancz, *The Ethical Treatises of Berachya son of Rabbi Natronai ha-Nakdan* ... (London 1902) xxxvif. Gollancz sums up all earlier scholars, notably Steinschneider and Jacobs, but add Joseph Jacobs in *Jewish Encyclopedia* (New York 1901-1906) vol. 3 s.v. Berechiah.

Renart cycle will not work for dating: *Mishle Shualim* was, from Talmudic times, the ordinary Jewish title for fables with animals as characters, just as *Aesop* or *Isopet* became the ordinary Christian vernacular term.[13] Berechiah shares with Marie and the Romulus of Trier so many fables special to the Anglo-Latin tradition that they must surely be closely related.[14] Yet over half Berechiah's collection is not found in Marie at all, and social applications occur in the two collections at different points, often where Marie lacks the fable. Thus in social content as in arrangement, inclusiveness, and style, Berechiah is without parallel.

Berechiah treats the rich perhaps more harshly than Marie does. He will be matched only centuries later by Henryson. Berechiah's fable of the camel-riding flea who apologizes for being a burden (though the camel felt nothing) is common in European collections, yet I know of no other where the camel, instead of simply disdaining the flea's insignificance, becomes aggressive toward it, earning the fabulist's scorn. For Berechiah, camel and flea are rich and poor, and, as Hadas translates, "hatred of the poor is inscribed in the heart of the rich" (p. 134).[15] Berechiah brings in God — rare in fables — to add solemnity to the anti-rich fable of the thrifty ants raided by mice but finding vengeance through the aid of the cats (Ber110). God, Berechiah informs us in a verse addition to his rhymed-prose fables, "impoverishes the rich and the poor he enriches" (p. 209). In the next fable, a spider driven from his home in the palace returns with massed armies of insects and kills the humans, a parable "for the poor and needy, upon whom the rich take no mercy. . . . But the poor . . . shrewdly take vegeance" (Ber111, p. 211).

An agressive champion of the underdog, Berechiah contrives to express sympathy for the honest poor even while directing a fable against those other poor whose poverty is due to idleness (Ber87). He lacks Marie's condescension toward the poorest. His two fables against the boasting of ignoble persons conceivably imply hereditary limits to one's ability to rise in society. But Berechiah focusses on the boasting, not on the attempt to rise; and if he does accept limits, the concept is fostered by the very shape of these particular fables.[16] More Berechiah's own is that

---

[13] That the title alluded to the *Roman de Renart* was W. T. H. Jackson's suggestion in Hadas (n. 10 above) x, but see *Talmud, Sanhedrin* 38b, 39a in *The Babylonian Talmud Translated into English*, ed. Isidore Epstein (London 1935) 4.5.246 and n.; cf. Jacobs (n. 1 above) 1.120, *Jewish Encyclopedia* (n. 12 above), and Dukes (n. 11 above) 7, 11.

[14] Warnke considers Marie the original of both Berechiah and Trier, but note that he worked before Gollancz (n. 12 above) placed Berechiah in the last quarter of the twelfth century (n. 2 above) xlviii-lx, lxviii-lxxx. Goldschmidt in 1921, while not closing the issue, inclines toward Berechiah's priority: *Mischle Schualim: Die Fuchsfabeln des Berekhja ben Natronaj*, ed. Lazarus Goldschmidt (Berlin 1921) viii.

[15] Most fabulists apply the fable to those too insignificant either to help or hinder, e.g., Romulus 4.18, RN3.9, *Fabulae rhythmicae* 2.29, Neckam 36, *Isopet* II of Paris 35. Marie and the Romulus of Trier implicitly side with the great: Marie's poor are foolish in apologizing for taking favors the rich scarcely noticed giving (M38), and Trier calls the great capable of aiding others without feeling the burden (T86). Perhaps only the *Isopet* of Chartres 33 approaches Berechiah's favor toward the poor, not championing them, but warning them to avoid contests with the great.

[16] Ber65, of the ass hunting with the lion and uttering a bray that would frighten anyone unaware of its parentage, has roughly the same moral throughout the Romulus tradition. Ber66,

deep sadness with which he sides with the oppressed in several fresh moralizations and in his original proem on the theme of the world-upside-down.

A particular mark of Berechiah's attitude is that he seems to distinguish the ruler from the class of the rich and powerful. While Marie does reserve the term *prince,* she allows *seignur* to blur together with the rich as a single ruling class defined neither exclusively politically nor exclusively economically. Berechiah isolates the ruler as such, the equivalent of both *prince* and *seignur,* treating him with respectful uneasiness rather than the blistering attack accorded the rich. We may see here the effect of Berechiah's being a Jew. The Christian hierarchy of power was closed: Jews could become rich, but never lords. When baron and burgher rampaged, English Jews were thankful enough to be declared the personal property of the royal family. Humiliating it might be, but it was a protection. As money-lenders they earned the king's favor and the barons' hatred, for in effect they sopped up the barons' money in interest payments, then transferred it to the king as the gifts he demanded of his servants.[17] Criticism of the rich could apply to Jew or Christian; criticism of the ruler touched too close to their protector. Even were a Jewish fabulist to see a point in seeking applications outside the world of Jews, here would be a ground to tread softly.

Berechiah's special theme of the ruler's favor toward a subject emerges from the, real power relationships, seen most clearly in the English system, where royal control was more centralized than on the Continent.[18] From among the wealthy of the Jewish communities, the monarch chose those who would serve him in collecting the special gifts demanded from time to time of the Jews. At the head of all Jews, at least for the purposes of collecting these "gifts," was the arch-presbyter – a salaried secular official perhaps nominated by the Jewish community or taking his position almost by hereditary right, but remaining only at the king's pleasure. The few prominent individuals and families rising to great wealth from the predominantly poor Jewish masses held sway only until such time as the king, become more needy than usual or suspecting "his" Jew of holding out on him, would choose to drain his protégé and leave him in poverty. Such a fate befell the most prominent Jew of England, Aaron of York, in 1243.[19] Though France established such a centralized system with a single chief rabbi only in the fourteenth century, the twelfth-century synods of French Jews were much concerned with another aspect of the situation: keeping Christian lords or king from interfering in Jewish legal disputes.[20] Jews with powerful Christian friends, it seems, were not above appealing

---

of the mule who speaks only of a noble horse-uncle, not of his parents, is unknown in Romulus but probably circulated among Jews. It is found among the stories of the converted Jew, Petrus Alphonsi, *Disciplina clericalis,* ed. Alfons Hilka and Werner Söderhjelm (Heidelberg 1911) ex. 4. Berechiah gives both fables his usual personal tone, even naming himself (Ber66), but the boasting of the ignoble is not a characteristic concern of his.

[17] Michael Adler, *Jews of Medieval England* (London 1939) 101f., 127.

[18] Salo Wittmayer Baron, *A Social and Religious History of the Jews,* ed. 2 (New York 1958) 5.63.

[19] Adler (N. 17 above) 144f. (for Aaron) and 139 (arch-presbyter).

[20] Baron (n. 18 above) 5.63, 70.

to them to influence or overturn decisions of the Jewish legal system, and the king
sometimes intervened without any appeal from one of the parties. Thus favored
individuals, like Berechiah's man who was given an elephant (Ber107), could suddenly rise without merit and oppress their fellows with impunity. The Jews of Lunel,
the apparent center of Berechiah's activities, though receiving unusually fair treatment from the local lords, must often have recalled that loss of this favor could also
destroy them – as indeed it finally did in 1319.[21] Small wonder that Berechiah
would be fond of the saying that "the king is likened to a fire, in which thou hast no
hope; in storm thou hast need of it, but if thou draw nigh it will burn thee" (Ber24,
Hadas p. 53). In the fable of the dog who accuses the sheep (Ber7=M4), Berechiah
transforms the usual judge into the ruler, a good person who sometimes hearkens to
false witnesses. In the fable of the wolf's vow not to eat meat (Ber36=M50),
Berechiah is unique in having the king impose this vow.[22] The rather strange Eastern
fable of the hunter and the elephant (Ber107) would not seem, from the plot, to
have much to do with a king. A hunter, unable to trap an elephant, appeals to the
people about, who capture the elephant and present it to him. He thereupon has the
means to terrify and plunder the countryside, finally regaining rectitude by the
puzzling restitution of half his thefts. But Berechiah contrives to bring the king into
the moralization. This hunter is like a man suddenly granted the favor of the king
and thereby given the power to harm his neighbors. "When," as Hadas translates,
"the word of the king touches him so that his fortune waxes strong upon him and
raises him ever higher, as when the master of the elephant was enlarged, he must keep
his hand from rapine and theft and from the deeds he had wrought, as did that man
with his booty" (p. 203). The concept of the king's favor is even less organic to the
fable of the frightened hares who would flee their homes until they find that the
frogs are even more terrified than they (Ber38=M22). Berechiah admonishes those
who would thus wander seeking "a refuge" that they "abide until the storm shall
pass from thy tent and the spirit of the ruler favor thee" (p. 74f.). The fable of the
lean lion and the fat dog (Ber61=M26), wherein the lion prefers free poverty to
luxury bound to another's table, is told for "the man whom the king delighteth to
honor" (p. 109). While the concept of the ruler's favor may go back to the biblical
phrases out of which Berechiah weaves his Hebrew text, it is tempting to see in its
unusual prominence here, even in fables whose structure gives little excuse for it, a
recognition of the realities of the Jewish position vis-à-vis their "protector."

Berechiah's fables are, of course, intended for Jewish audiences, and rather
learned ones at that, since Hebrew was a learned rather than a vernacular language
with Jews throughout the Middle Ages.[23] But Berechiah's specifically Jewish touches
are light. The wolf who seeks to learn the alphabet (Ber113=M81=Aes688) naturally

---

[21] *The Jewish Encyclopedia* (n. 12 above) 8.280.

[22] Only Berechiah and Henryson have the vow imposed by any authority figure at all (a
wolf-confessor in H4). This is one of a handful of parallels suggesting tenuous links between
Henryson and a Hebrew fabulist whom he surely never read.

[23] Baron (n. 18 above) 7.8.

begins with aleph, beth, gimel, though, like his Christian analogue, he adds them up
to say only "sheep." I detect in him no explicit references to religious ritual, no
Jewish equivalent to the *pater noster* of Odo's analogous wolf fable (022), no cat
posing as bishop (M101=NB50=T132=*Aes*692), no Lenten occasion or father-
confessor to inspire the wolf's vow to abstain from flesh (Ber36=M50=*Aes*655=
Henryson4). Thus in the social world portrayed there is little explicit Judaizing,
especially in contrast to the Christianizing and feudalizing so characteristic of the
Roman de Renart, some of whose stories occur here, whether by direct borrowing or
not. The wolf, for example, is drawn up from the well by a family (Ber117), not by
monks as in the *Roman* (*branche* 4). In Berechiah no wolf seeks to become a rabbi,
as Ysengrin had sought to become a monk. Where humans and animals mingle, the
humans are peasants, merchants, lords, or kings, but never rabbis or cantors, still less
monks, priests, or papal legates. In Berechiah, religion, though present enough in its
moral aspect, is absent in its social aspect. The pervading Jewishness of his fables
comes, not from his including figures of Jewish society, but from his complex verbal
web of Old Testament echoes.

In the absence, however, of explicit references to religion or to particular social
customs, an audience may still bring its own special interpretations to neutral items,
even to items that are the same in both Christian and Jewish tellings of a fable. A
medieval Jewish author might count on a Jewish audience to experience in a special
way the fable of the beast with no heart. A boar (Ber105) or stag (M70) is
summoned before King Lion. Refusing at first, it finally appears and is killed. The
fox, ordered to ready the carcass for his master, steals the heart, explaining to the
outraged lion that any creature who would willingly respond to such a dangerous
summons (or return to such a dangerous place, depending on the version) surely had
no heart in the first place. The explanation makes sense ultimately through a
not-necessarily Jewish belief in the heart as the seat of some relevant mental
quality – Nicole Bozon's fox, for example, explains that "Remembraunce vient hors
de queor" (NB142, p. 177). But Jewish law gave a disturbing significance to a beast
with the heart cut out. It seems that the Jews' heathen neighbors, in sacrificing to
their gods, first cut the heart out and offered that. The Jews naturally held unclean
any beast used in heathen sacrifice; suspicion extended to any beast even cut at the
heart under unknown circumstances. In the Talmud is a prohibition against writing
the Talmud's text on parchment made from a skin so cut.[24] Where the Christian lion
is outraged that his property has been tampered with, the Jewish lion suffers both an
outrage to property rights and also a ritual polluting of the carcass intended to be
offered to the king. With the offense doubled, the lion's fury has more weight, the
fox's impudence more audacity, and the fable a deeper resonance.

I know nothing to preclude Berechiah's adding more specifically Jewish touches

---

[24]*Abodah Zarah* 29b in *Babylonian Talmud* (n. 13 above) 4.7 (*Seder Nezikin*) 145 and n. 11;
Sefer Torah, trans. Israel W. Slotki, in *The Minor Tractates of the Talmud,* ed. A. Cohen (London
1965) 2.631 n. 4. For the fable itself in Jewish collections, see Moses Gaster, *The Exempla of the
Rabbis* (London 1924) 105, 229 (no. 244).

than he did. He chose not to. The world of fable collections had traditionally been a generalized world — that is part of the reason fables travel so well from culture to culture, from the Bidpai of Buddhist India to the *Kalilah* of Arabs and Jews and the Aesop and Romulus of Christian Europe. Berechiah had already not only gone "further than any of his predecessors in spelling out the moralistic purpose of his collection," as Baron puts it, but he had spelled out that purpose in a specific way, bringing passionate observation to the relations of rich and poor, ruler and ruled, in a real society.[25] Berechiah presumably saw no point in further limiting his characters and applications.

* * *

Odo of Cheriton (d. 1246/7) brings the church massively into fables, concentrating on just that element of the medieval world wholly missing in Berechiah and largely avoided, especially as a subject for rebuke, in Marie. This English preacher not only scattered a few true animal fables among his sermon-*exempla* (*Parabolae*), but also brought together a collection of *Fabulae* standing on their own with self-contained moralizations. He brings to fable collections the omnivorousness of the *exemplum* tradition, where scraps of bestiaries, proverbs, and anecdotes are as acceptable as the doings of talking animals and the few other subjects sanctified by traditional inclusion. But even in the fables that he shares with Marie and others, Odo sets himself off by his special thoroughness and originality in developing moral applications. We might expect the heir to a great lord to follow Marie's lead in fitting fables to aristocratic lay society, but Odo's interests led him to the church: a theological education in Paris and preaching probably there, then in Spain (sometime between 1220 and 1224), and especially in England, leaving others to run much of his inherited estate.[26] Where Marie begins the systematic application of fables to lay society, Odo is, among medieval writers of fables in collections, the master critic of ecclesiastical society.

Odo's chief theme is the conflict of overbearing greater officials with their underlings — who in turn have vices of their own: ambition, envy, and petty oppression of still weaker clerics and laymen. Odo frequently points his morals toward a short list of specific groups, often including regular, secular, and lay together as if determined to miss no one (Olc, 8, 25).[27] One fable (052) includes so many orders that it is difficult to imagine any but a clerical audience for it.

Since the older assertion that Odo was a monk has now been abandoned, one might ask under what circumstances a preacher would not only point his moralizations toward abuses among both secular and regular clergy, but so often point them toward internal conflicts. It happens that slightly over half of English thirteenth-

---

[25] Baron (n. 18 above) 7.189f.

[26] Albert C. Friend, "Master Odo of Cheriton," *Speculum* 23 (1948) 641-658.

[27] Hervieux (n. 1 above) 4: numbers preceded by O are Odo's *Fabulae* (Hervieux 4.173-246), by O*Parabolae* are fables excerpted from sermons (Hervieux 4.265-343).

century cathedrals originated as monastic churches, so that when a bishop was to be named by vote of the local chapter — as in the moralization of Odo's first fable — the persons voting were, in about half the cases, monks, and in the other half, canons. Odo's church of Saint Martin's, Cheriton, would be quite near two of the monastic cathedrals, Canterbury and Rochester.[28] At Rochester he himself was to be buried. One of his fables — joke is a more accurate term — turns on the distinction between orders: a cat becomes a monk, thus lulling the suspicions of the mouse, who approaches too near where the cat is at table with the other monks, and who is caught. "What will become of your vows if you eat me," protests the mouse, "are you not a monk?" "When I wish to be a monk," replies the cat, "I'm a monk; when I wish otherwise, I'm a canon" (*"quando uolo, sum monachus; quando uolo, sum canonicus"*). He eats the mouse (O15=*Aes*592). Odo makes the old fables in which birds or trees select their rulers (O1c;O1=*Aes*262) include bishops, abbots, and lay rulers alike among those selected, with monks and congregations without pastors among those doing the selecting. The qualified people often shun such honors, leaving the electors in danger of choosing among those who would accept the post as an opportunity for oppression, not service. The lesser clergy, both regular and secular, have their own vices, particularly ingratitude (O4a) and ambition. In the Fable of the Inflated Frog (O62, *De rana inflata*), lesser monks and clerics puff themselves up like frogs imitating the great ox-like *episcopi, abbates, archidiaconi*. Unqualified persons thrust themselves upward into offices we might at first associate with the secular clergy only — *sacerdotes, archidiaconi, episcopi* — in the fable of the ass who seeks the master's favor through jumping up like a lap-dog (O69). But it was perfectly possible for a monk to aspire to such offices, and one of Odo's direct followers among fabulists, John of Sheppey, would become monk-bishop of near-by Rochester in 1353.[29] We do not know if Odo preached at one of these monastic cathedrals with its mixed audience of monks, secular clerics on the bishop's staff, and varying numbers of laymen. With such an audience, however, his fables would fit the church's advice that preachers should rebuke the vices, not of clerics before lay audiences or laymen before clerical audiences, but the vices of those who have come to hear.[30]

As one leafs through the fables of Odo, clerical abuses and difficulties flow past almost as if one were instead perusing such a modern study as John R. H. Moorman's *Church Life in England in the Thirteenth Century* (Cambridge, 1945). There are the

[28] John R. H. Moorman lists cathedrals according to the membership of their chapters in *Church Life in England in the Thirteenth Century* (Cambridge 1945) 160.

[29] *Dictionary of National Biography* s.v. Sheppey. Moorman 51 shows that at some point or other in the Middle Ages, practically every male order had a member functioning as the person in charge of a parish, and for the thirteenth century we have such records of several canons, a few monks, and apparently one Dominican friar.

[30] Gerald Robert Owst, *Preaching in Medieval England* (Cambridge 1926) 224, 251-253. Since both the church at Cheriton and the cathedral at Canterbury were dedicated to St. Martin, the presence in Odo's *Fabulae* 7 and *Parabolae* 61 of a joke about a certain bird of St. Martin would be equally appropriate for either place.

priests — *prelati ignorantes* — who devote themselves to barns and livestock, calling
forth Odo's rebuke (029) as they would soon call forth Grosseteste's or Pecham's. [31]
There are simony, usury, and the various fiscal dodges used by rectors who would
rather live comfortably than save themselves or their parishioners (016). [32] The
struggle for benefices is the subject of Odo's fable 55 and Moorman's chapters 5 and
12. To the hordes who sought to shine in the courts of king and lord, whether they
be *monachi, scolares, clerici,* or *layci,* Odo offers the fable of the ass who sought to
ingratiate himself with the lion by his singing, but whose bray was not appreciated
(068). The clutter of possessions and throngs of dependents in the *familiae* or
households of bishops and rich laymen come under fire in 048. [33] There are rebukes
to those low in status, monks who, poor but dishonest, enter the monastery only to
fill their bellies (050). There are rebukes, too, to those rather higher, prelates and
bishops who, in their capacities as judges, pounce on poor defendants like spiders on
flies, but slip quickly out of the way when the rich, like great bees or wasps, rumble
their threats (048b). Several fables deal with a subject also found in the *Fabulae
rhythmicae,* but not usually in fable collections, the oppression visited on the lesser
members of the ecclesiastical hierarchy by the bishop and other officials. Certain of
these take an amusing serial form: the rat eats the cheese and the cat eats both cheese
and rat: so the chaplains (*capellani*) devour those of their parish (*parochia*) until the
archdeacon (*archidiaconus*) comes to devour both (021). The dog eats the meat, but
the crow picks the bones he leaves: so a whole series of officials devour the poor
chaplain and cleric, and another series of officials pick what bones are left
("Cardinales, legati, episcopi, archidiaconi deuorant capellanos et pauperes clericos.
Postera ueniunt garciferi et nuncii, et deuorant si aliquid circa ossa sacerdotum
remanet"; 021a). The series is both ecclesiastical and lay in 053, by which time the
victims of so many oppressors seem ready to fight back — in 054a — but, alas for the
clerics and monks who would protest against their bishops, priors, or abbots, it is the
fable of the belling of the cat, and none dares attach the bell by lodging a formal
protest.

This first appearance of the Belling of the Cat in an English collection gives it an
application within ecclesiastical politics. [34] Later, during the fourteenth century,
Langland's *Piers Plowman* will again turn the fable to political contexts, this time lay.
Between these two points, the satire slackens as *Isopet* I turns to a more general
application and Nicole Bozon retains Odo's ecclesiastical setting only in a rubric, yet

---

[31] Cf. Moorman (n. 28 above) chaps. 3 and 8.

[32] On the church's particularly strict rejection of simony, see Moorman (n. 28 above) 6, on
clerical incomes chaps. 9 and 10, and on the many forbidden ways the lesser clergy eked out a
little extra — selling wine, cheating on taxes, and many more — see chap. 11.

[33] Moorman's picture of the plight of bishops, saddled with forty or more men and constantly
on the move because no single manorhouse could long support the whole *familia,* makes a pair of
the most amusing chapters (13 and 14) in *Church Life* (n. 28 above).

[34] Odo's 54a is, according to Perry (n. 1 above) 1.xi, perhaps the first appearance of the
Belling of the Cat (*Aes*613) in Latin collections. Chauvin (n. 11 above) 2.109f., no. 74 cites a
similar motif in the Arabic *Kalilah.*

even here the gathering of mice is described in words (*parliament* or *concilium*) which could have political senses to link Langland and Odo.[35] Langland's *conseille* (B Prol. 148) recalls the Latin *concilium* of Odo and Walter the Englishman, but Langland applies his fable to king, courtiers, and burghers: a lay application as explicit as Odo's ecclesiastical one.

When Odo does move outside church matters, it is often only a partial move, showing the poor oppressed by something of a cartel of rich man, bishop, and occasionally king (08, 9, 48b). But sometimes, as so often in Marie, the conflict is seen in the purely lay terms of rich and poor (*diuites, pauperes*: 023, 24). Such justice and protection as the poor can expect from authorities in answer to their appeals is satirized in the fable in which the doves complain to the bird called the Grand Duke (*Dux*) that a hawk has carried off one of their number (02=*Aes*588). The Duke reassures them with a resounding *Cloc!* but depredations continue, and by the third occasion the doves begin to realize that *Cloc* will never keep the hawk from the dovecot. Yet on occasion the rich are themselves seen as victims to avaricious flatterers who beg gifts of land or cash until the poor rich man, like the King of Aragon, has given away his strength and remains helpless (066=*Aes*621). Among the flatterers in this fable are a goodly number of church figures, *Hospitalarii, Templarii, monachi, canonici,* all promising the rich man-peacock that they will say masses for his soul in return for the gift of a few of his many feathers. It took praiseworthy detachment in Odo, as a member of the clergy, to treat the church's collecting of gifts quite so broadly.

Among recurring figures in Odo's lay applications is the bailiff, a chief middleman between high and low whose hands would actually commit the extortions directed by his masters as well as a few of his own (040, 42b). Advocates are rebuked in 039, and in 075 we have a rare instance in which Odo rebukes the body of laymen together. He charges that they manage to right their souls by communion at Easter and Pentecost, but backslide for all the time between. This reference to infrequent communion-confession and to the great backsliding between may have been up-to-the-minute: it was a concern of the Fourth Lateran Council of 1215.[36]

But if Odo must be credited for the extent and precision of his social concerns, are we to grant him also full originality, or did his social applications come to him from the same sources that gave him his plots? Marie de France and Berechiah ben Natronai may both have preceded Odo, and both are rich in social applications. Whatever Berechiah's exact date, his elaborate embellishments immediately rule out his fables as a source — besides, Odo would have to have read Hebrew. But Marie's

---

[35] Odo and Latin texts of Walter the Englishman (found in MSS of *Isopet* I of Paris) use *consilium* or *concilium* (Hervieux [n. 1 above] 2.368f., 4.225), while cognates of *parliament* occur in *Isopet* I (ed. Julia Bastin, *Recueil général des Isopets,* 2 vols. [Paris 1929-1930] 2.324f., no. 62) and in Nicole Bozon, chap. 121 (*Les contes moralisés,* ed. Lucy Toulmin Smith and Paul Meyer [Paris 1889] 144; Hervieux 4.260). *Isopet* I has *concile* in the heading.

[36] On Fourth Lateran's role in promoting confession and confessional literature, see M. Dominica Legge, *Anglo-Norman Literature and its Background* (London 1963) chap. 9. On the ordinary thirteenth-century practice of only annual communion, see Moorman (n. 28 above) 87.

manuscripts were circulating in England, and one naturally asks if perhaps Odo simply lifted social applications from her. The case, however, appears lost the moment that we start to count fables: only the minority of Odo's social fables appear in Marie at all. For that matter, many appear in no extant European collection before him: he either invented them, took them from a lost or unpublished collection, assembled them from fables scattered among various authors, or elevated into fables a variety of proverbs, anecdotes, bestiary chapters, or oral tales.[37] Less than a dozen of Odo's fables with social applications are analogues to fables in Marie, and here the applications themselves regularly differ. The closest correspondences involve the oppression of poor by rich in The Wolf and the Lamb Drinking (M2=024=Phaedrus 1.1) and The Wolf and the Crane (M7=06=Phaedrus 1.8). The two versions of the fable of the crow in borrowed feathers belong to separate textual families: Odo's crow (03=Babrius 72) wears feathers from a variety of birds, while Marie's wears the peacock's feathers only (M67=Phaedrus 1.3).[38] Thus their agreement in applying the fable to those who love worldy goods seems not a case of borrowing, particulary since Odo develops this application differently, listing the beasts who provide us with the wool, leather, and so on for our fine clothes.

Most often, a moral to the lay world in Marie fits the ecclesiastical world in Odo. Odo's Town Mouse and Country Mouse (016=M9=Romulus 1.12) not only adds to the plot a cat and omits a visit by town to country mouse, but fits the moral to usurious and simoniac rectors. Odo's Frog and Mouse (021b=M3=Romulus 1.3) lacks Marie's distinctive elements of the mouse's mill and the final escape of the mouse (traits which help to show Lydgate's debt to Marie), and his moral to rectors who lead their parish to the devil is quite his own among the many medieval versions, so far as I know. Marie's ass who tries to win his master's favor by leaping up like a lap-dog (069=M15=Romulus 1.16) represents unworthy persons generally, while Odo (and *Fabulae rhythmicae* 1.16) specifies ambitious misfits in the church. Odo does

[37] I find none of the following animal fables of Odo's in Marie at all, and all seem to me social in their applications. Many are of uncertain origin, and I list selected key analogues or index numbers in Perry's *Aesopica* and *Babrius and Phaedrus* or Stith Thompson's *Motif-index* (TMI). One might draw a different line between social and more broadly moral applications, but adding or subtracting a few numbers would clearly still leave Odo with many social fables or animal exempla wholly missing in Marie: 01=*Aes*262=Judges 9.8; 02=*Aes*588; 04a; 08=*Aes*576=Romulus 4.7; 09; 010=TMI B751.3, cf. bestiaries; 011=*Aes*590, cf. M80; 015=*Aes*592; 015a cf. Theobaldus's bestiary; 015b; 021=*Aes*594; 021a; 023=*Aes*596; 023a=TMI B275.1.3.1; 025=*Aes*597, cf. *Roman de Renart*; 026=*Aes*188=Augustana; 028a=TMI U122; 029=*Aes*599; 033=*Aes*600; 040=*Aes*606; 041=TMI U144; 042a; 042b; 043=*Aes*607; 048; 048a; 048b; 050=*Aes*611; 051=*Aes*451=Nikephoros Basilakis; 052; 053; 054=*Aes*612; 054a=*Aes*613; 055=*Aes*614; 059=*Aes*617=Phaedrus 4.20=Babrius 143; 062=P 1.24=Babrius 28; 066=*Aes*621; 067=*Aes*622; 067a; 068; 074=*Aes*625, cf. *Roman de Renart;* 075 cf. P 4.25, Jacques de Vitry 189, ed. Crane. At least one of the *Parabolae* might belong here also, *Parabolae* 150=Jacques de Vitry 174=*Roman de Renart,* cf. Babrius 86, while others of the *Parabolae* resemble the *Fabulae* above. Hervieux's excerpts do not allow a judgment of what the *Parabolae* signified in the original sermons.

[38] For the history of these motifs, see H. D. Austin, "The Origin and Greek Versions of the Strange-Feathers Fable," in *Studies in Honor of A. Marshall Elliott* (Baltimore [1911?]) 1.305-327.

not continue Marie's new moral about courts in the fable of the lying man and the truthful man at the court of the ape-king, but instead refers to flatterers of prelates (027a=M34=Phaedrus 4.13). Furthermore, his plot resembles Phaedrus's more than Marie's in lacking her new motif of the king whose ape mimics him, and in opening instead with the question whether truth or falsehood is more profitable. Marie and Odo both have a wolf who tries to learn something but can say only sheep instead, but Marie's wolf seeks to learn his ABC's and Odo's his *pater noster* (M81=*Aes*688; 022=*Aes*595). What Odo's wolf learns fits his desire to become a monk and Odo's consequent moral to monks (*Fabulae* 22) or to religious generally (*Parabolae* 13). Marie has nothing of this unless we take item 65b in Warnke's edition as a missing or cancelled part of this fable. There, Odo would have found that wolves remain wolves, though taught to be priests. Yet if he took this hint, he scarcely needed it: the fable appeared in an ecclesiastical context in a papal bull of 1096.[39]

For a few of Odo's social fables shared by Marie, the fables are rare enough that their mere presence in both suggests some kinship. The fable of the cat with one trick and the fox with many (M98=039=*Aes*605) is not only a rare one they share, but in both the fox brags of having a sackful of tricks, and the cat calls out to him – as the fable's punchline – to open his sack. Yet even in such an apparently close analogue, Odo not only adds Renardian names but replaces Marie's general application to true and false men with a specific attack on advocates with their many tricks. The uncommon fable of the hawk who raises the owl's (or buzzard's) young among its own, but finds that the intruder befouls the nest (M79=04=*Aes*644), varies in plot and characters in the two, but is recognizably the same fable, with even a rough French equivalent (vv. 29-31) to an English expression Odo uses. Yet Odo's ecclesiastical moral could not come from Marie: the devil's chicks get into the nest of the church only to foul it, that is, unfit persons enter orders only to envy and accuse their associates. Both fabulists have variants of the fable of birds choosing their king wherein a gentle bird is nominated or elected before the final fierce one, though the birds and the outcomes differ (M46; Olc). Odo characteristically refers his version to the election of kings, bishops, and abbots; Marie mentions lay rulers only.

Perhaps Marie counts as more of a pioneer than Odo: she not only precedes him in introducing new fables and in adapting to her society the moralizations of old ones, but she does it in a language and versification new to fable literature. Odo faced fewer formal problems than she. Latin prose had already been used for fable collections and sermon *exempla* alike. French verse had not. This left Odo only one major problem as he combined the two genres into his *Fabulae*: how to incorporate within the format of self-contained fables something of the range and depth of analysis possible when the stories occurred within the larger didactic structure of a sermon.[40] But in developing the moralizations he needed, he produced the first fable collection applied in any significant degree to the ecclesiastical world. His applica-

---

[39] Warnke (n. 1 above) 238.

[40] Even this may have been partly solved for him if, as Friend suggests, he heard of Caesarius of Heisterbach's (or other) collections of *exempla* (Friend [n. 26 above] 647).

tions are new and numerous and set him off even more than Marie's new moralizations set her off from the long-standing tradition of broadly moral applications.

* * *

Odo's fables were in turn a direct source for two fabulists of very different stations in life. Nicole Bozon was a poor Franciscan; John of Sheppey, whose fables are often abridgments of Odo's, was a Benedictine monk who rose to become bishop of Rochester (1353) and treasurer of England (1356-1358).[41] We might expect that such different figures, in taking up Odo's fables, would, if they changed his social applications at all, change them in ways reflecting their different stations or aspirations.

John's bare-bones collection omits much detail, but about a third of his seventy-three fables have topical applications, either in a rubric or in a brief concluding moralization. In a few cases, as one might have expected, the future bishop of Rochester either removes Odo's rebukes to bishops or dilutes them by adding priests alongside them.[42] He ends his collection with three fables on the church hierarchy, in the first and last of which he adds bishops, which Odo did not have.[43] In these John reminds bishops of responsibilities rather than blaming them: it is those whom bishops appoint who are inclined to oppress others, though a bishop commits wrong in absenting himself and giving scope for an underling's wickedness. Thus John ends his collection with a picture of the bishop, his eyes fixed on God, leading the more worldly to salvation. Whether or not yet appointed bishop, John shows unusual interest in the job in ending with this testimonial of what he believes a bishop should be.

With themes other than the bishop, the church is somewhat less present in John's social applications than in Odo's, and may be evoked in more general terms, such as *prelatus* (JS18=O1c=M46) or *omne genus regularium* (JS22=O52), where Odo named specific offices and orders.[44] The net effect of John of Sheppey's changes in the

---

[41] Charles Lethbridge Kingsford in *Dictionary of National Biography*. John's fables, like his sermons, were likely completed before his elevation to the bishopric. One MS of Odo's fables (British Library, MS Harl. 219) also contains an odd item so exactly fitting John of Sheppey's career, a list of the offices in the granting of the treasurer of England, that I like to imagine that it belonged to him. It lacks, however, too many of his borrowings from Odo to be his source. See Hervieux (n. 1 above) 4.63f. for this MS and 4.161-170 for John.

[42] JS19=048b (spider, fly, wasp); JS45=048a (snail retracting horns); JS63=048 (snail carrying house).

[43] JS71=023a (sheep entrusted to wolf); JS72=021=Aes594 (cheese, mouse, cat); JS73=010, cf. bestiaries (eagle, young, sun).

[44] JS1=024 (wolf and lamb drinking; poor and rich [0] or powerful [JS])=P 1.1; JS5 cf. 020 cf. Aes149, M11 (lion's share, carnivorous beasts: Odo's lesson of Adam and Eve is not social, John's of the powerful is marginally so); JS17=01=Aes262 (trees elect ruler: John omits monks); JS18=01c=M46 (birds elect ruler: Odo's kings, bishops, and abbots become John's prelates); JS20=050=Aes611 (fox and chickens: both treat monks, Odo more fully); JS21=051 (fox and sheep); JS22=052 (white sheep, black sheep, ass and goat: John omits Odo's list of religious orders); JS24=02=Aes588 (hawk, doves, and eagle or owl: John restricts the lesson to judges);

applications of Odo's fables is not so much a protection of bishops and monks, though that happens incidentally, but a watering-down of the social satire to fit the new abbreviated format.

Nicole Bozon, an English Franciscan who probably wrote toward the end of the thirteenth century, compiled fables, proverbs, scriptural passages, and *exempla* of various sorts, grouping them according to theme so that he or another preacher could elaborate on them at will.[45] With such a format and such a purpose, he does not need, as Odo did, to make each combination of fable and moralization complete and self-contained within the collection of *Fabulae*. Occasionally a single sentence may stand as a reminder to an entire fable, and its position with others under a heading is enough to suggest the sort of moralization it might bear. At other times, however, Nicole elaborates fables for drama and verve as well as moral point, producing bouncy little fragments fit for a beast epic. His French dialogue has life enough to draw an audience used to *Renart,* and his catchy proverbs are sometimes given in English as familiar asides to his audience. His verve, like his social stance, is a double inheritance from the preacherly dash of Odo of Cheriton and the more elegant stylistics of Marie de France.[46]

Between the influence of Marie's more generally moral applications and the need to group his materials under broad headings, Nicole somewhat favors the older style of moral themes over Odo's newer social ones, while remaining firmly within the group of social fabulists. He retains, with variations, some of the purely moral or general applications that Odo already had (NB8=070=M13; NB21=058; NB53a=064; NB75=063=M73; NB128=019), and he sometimes dilutes the social applications that he does retain from Odo. Thus the cloister and the clergy may drop out (NB15=011=M80; NB124=015a, though here Nicole follows Odo's *Parabolae* 156 in place of the *Fabulae*). Usury, which Odo often associates with the clergy, regularly vanishes (NB46=074; NB120=033; NB145=0*Parabolae* 150). Odo's rebukes to the clergy remain, but diluted, in NB17=04=M79 and in two items from Nicole's chapter 121, the Snail Retracting its Horns (=048a) and The Belling of the Cat (=054a). Odo's remarks on the lay conflict of rich and poor fare better than his ecclesiastical applications, though the difference is not great. Nicole omits the theme once (NB55=023) and retains it twice (NB49=024=M2; NB72=06=M7). As it is Marie's major theme, her general influence may be suspected even where Odo was also a model. When Nicole drops Odo's application to advocates, he diverges from both

---

JS25=040=Romulus 3.5=*Aes*606 (crow, pigeon, and its young: baillif, poor and rich [0] or masters [JS]); JS26=053 (sledge and ox: John deletes ecclesiastics); JS29=042b (ants and pigs: John adds the church); JS31=069=Romulus 1.16 (ass and lap-dog: John *de inuidia*; Odo those seeking church offices). John also adds JS64 cf. bestiaries (ape and its two young: the rich).

[45] I cite Bozon's fables by chapter number from *Les contes moralisés de Nicole Bozon,* ed. Lucy Toulmin Smith and Paul Meyer, Société des anciens textes français (Paris 1889). For revised biographical data see Sister M. Amelia Klenke, O.P., "Nicholas Bozon," *Modern Language Notes* 69 (1954) 256-260.

[46] We know that Nicole was well acquainted with Marie's collection and — though he uses them somewhat less — with Odo's *Fabulae* and at least some of the *Parabolae*. See Harry (n. 1 above) 64-71.

Odo and Marie (NB116=039=M98). The general impression left by comparing Nicole's applications to Odo's (in those fables where Odo furnishes an analogue) fits with what we would expect from the difference in their languages. Odo's Latin fables treat ecclesiastical concerns for ecclesiastical audiences; Nicole's Anglo-French fables include ecclesiastical matters in a lower proportion to suit his audiences of laymen.

Nicole's concern with the lay world most marks those fables where Odo supplied no analogue, and Nicole follows Marie, his own invention, or other sources. His most common social theme is the oppressive noble, *les grantz seignours* (NB56; NB23=M29; NB50=M101). Nicole sometimes joins prelates to Marie's lay lords and masters (NB129=M16; NB34 and 121=M40). Like Marie, Nicole would keep servants in their place, though he speaks with less of her aristocratic scorn (NB130 *serfs*=M84 *malvais serjant*). Most distinctively different from Marie are Nicole's application of the fable of the cock and the gem to those more irked by a short sermon than by seven days' labor (NB26=M1), and his application of the fable of the lion's share to unscrupulous executors of inherited estates (NB131=M11).

Since Nicole echoes either Odo or Marie so often in his plots, the freedom with which he shifts about in the moralizations that he gives to those plots underlines what seems to be a law of medieval fables, that one might freely vary the application or "meaning" of an old fable one was retelling so long as each application worked sensibly with the inherent structure of the fable itself. If the plot shows a big beast oppressing a weaker one, then the pattern is maintained as much by an application to great prelates and poor rectors as by applications to the rich and the poor, or simply the strong and the weak. Odo of Cheriton's two English followers, the monk and statesman John of Sheppey and the poor friar Nicole Bozon, freely vary his applications within this broad similarity, just as they freely expand or contract the dialogue and narrative detail of the plots whose outlines they take from him or from analogues to him.

Given this freedom, what is remarkable is the broad similarity of social attitudes among the three fabulists of different branches of the church, differing social status, and differing personal ambitions. All are willing to attack cleric and layman alike, all are particularly sensitive to the abuse of power by great lords and great prelates. Each varies the balance among these themes more for the concerns of their different audiences and for the different functions their collections are to fill, than out of the prejudices of their social classes or religious stations. One may find hints of the author's situation in the way he sees the world, but the wandering mendicant, the learned and aristocratic Paris-trained preacher, and the equally learned but probably more worldly and ambitious future treasurer of England all seem to be attempting, at least, to stand aside from life to view it impartially, but with passion. Their ideal is that of Chaucer's Parson, to "snybben sharply" any obstinate person, whether "of heigh or lough estat."

* * *

Sometime within Odo's century was set down another Latin collection not directly deriving from him yet sharing a few touches of his ecclesiastical topicality. These

Fabulae rhythmicae of the thirteenth century generally stick close to the eleventh-century Romulus of Nilant, the grand-daddy of English Romulean collections, including Marie's.[47] Thus by textual affinities and social applications both, this humble little unsigned Latin versification, diverging not too far or too often from its Latin prose model, earns a place in our social group. The current of social criticism spreads beyond the great names and personal stylists.

No other collection so conservative in its selections and general handling ventures into ecclesiastical criticism. In the fable of the ass who tries to flatter the master as a lap-dog does by leaping up on him (FR1.16=069), Odo and the *Fabulae rhythmicae* depart from all other fabulists even within the socially-conscious group. Both apply the fable specifically to unqualified persons seeking advancement within the church, to fools who would be bishop ("stultus in cathedra prima uult locari" FR) or other official ("sacerdotes, archidiaconi, episcopi" 0). Most other fabulists apply the fable to servants (RN1.16) or to unworthy persons generally (M15, etc.) seeking unspecified offices or honors. *Isopet* I (no. 17) specifies an ecclesiastical office only in the course of making a broader philosophical statement against breaking from one's nature-ordained role to aspire to become "pape, roy ou duc."[48] Thus Odo and the *Fabulae rhythmicae* share a satirical bite and ecclesiastic relevance paralleled nowhere else. Which came first is not certain, and little in the wording suggests direct borrowing: they both, however, use *paterfamilias* for the beasts' owner where other Latin versions use *dominus* or *herus*. In another fable, that of the wolf and lamb drinking (FR1.2=024), both fabulists have a new reference to the poor (*pauperes*). Since, of Odo's fifty or more animal fables with social applications, less than a handful even roughly share applications with their analogues in the *Fabulae rhythmicae,* the one or two closest parallels prove no general acquaintance between collections. Ordinarily, the *Fabulae rhythmicae* stick even closer than Marie does to the general moral terms of the Romulus of Nilant. What new social terms they introduce often occur where Odo lacks the fable entirely, but the several small changes add up to something like his spirit.[49] The *Fabulae rhythmicae,* then,

---

[47] Hervieux (n. 2 above) prints the Romulus Nilanti, 2.513-548, and the *Fabulae rhythmicae,* 2.714-757; he discusses them, 1.708-718, 808-815. FR was the collection edited by Thomas Write for the Percy Society in *Early English Poetry, Ballads, and Popular Literature of the Middle Ages* 8 (London 1843).

[48] Bastin (n. 35 above) 2.231.

[49] The social term *pauperes* appears in the fable of dog, sheep, and bread (FR1.4) where RN1.4 spoke of *innocentes et miseres* and M4 had *povres* (Odo lacks the fable). FR adds *diuites* to 1.5 (dog and reflection=RN1.5=M5=061) and *magistratus* and *principatus* to 1.15 (aged lion scorned by beasts cf. RN1.15 *omnes potentes,* M14 *seignur;* 0 lacks). FR's two versions of the lion's share (1.6, 7=RN1.6, 7=M11) do not so much change the application as add new immediacy by the authorial touch of saying that we (*nos*) brothers (*fratres*) should avoid the company of the powerful, and further by calling the moral of 1.7 applicable in our own time: *Temporibus nostris plures hac fraude ruerunt.* 020 is less social than theological here, but other versions have terms as social as those of FR: *riche* and *povre* (M11), *grans satrapes* and *seigneur* (*Isopet* I of Paris 6). In one fable at least, a social term (*pauperes*) was already present in the ordinary Romulus (3.17) and others before FR used one (*indigentes* 2.19, fox and ape; O lacks); the opposite to the poor in this fable was *diuites* in RN2.19, but a moral term in FR (*auarus*) and M28 (*aver hume*). FR2.20 (lion reigning) is barely social in referring to the lion's subjects

represent a tentative social initiative largely independent of the greater pioneers Marie and Odo.

The church enters as early as the prologue; and Hervieux, thinking primarily of the new Christian piety of this recasting of the traditional prologue, believed that the *Fabulae rhythmicae*'s main originality lay in its "esprit religieux."[50] But this tone appears principally in the opening homage to the Trinity and (closing the collection) in an allusion to God as director of the heavens (FR2.34). More prominent throughout the collection is the author's sympathy for the weak inside or outside the church hierarchy. In FR 1.12, an eagle carries off a fox's cub and, feeling secure in its high nest, refuses to return it — until the fox threatens to set the tree on fire. This old fable had always dealt with the strong and the weak in some form. Some named them rich and poor (M10=T12=Berll=Walter 13 appendix, Hervieux 2.355). But only the *Fabulae rhythmicae* specify *prelati* oppressing their subordinates (*subditi sui*). These may one day rise to higher positions, just as the fox on the ground may find a way to avenge her unheeded pleas. Presumably these harsh prelates were once themselves among the lesser clergy, the ambitious scramblers rebuked in 1.16. The thirteenth-century excess of clergy over financially-viable ecclesiastical posts must often have thrown subsidiary clergy into struggles for preferment, with the prize not necessarily to the best qualified.[51] The religious setting of these two fables, together with the potentially religious term *synodus* chosen for a gathering of hares (FR2.7), makes it plausible that when our fabulist addresses the readers as *fratres* and groups himself with them under the pronoun *nos* (FR1.6), he is not merely using a familiar form of address (one his fox uses in 2.32), but revealing himself as part of a religious order. He would then join Odo, John, and Nicole Bozon as a maker of fable collections critical of the church while himself a cleric.

The oppression of weak by strong, with the countertheme of the weak's occasional triumph through wit, has apparently always and in many cultures informed fables and animal tales generally, witness the *Roman de Renart*. It is tempting to ascribe the moral stance of fables to an origin among the oppressed, or at least to continuing circulation among them: Phaedrus and Aesop were slaves centuries before Uncle Remus and the black slaves of America who were so fond of wit's triumph over force. Yet Phaedrus and Aesop, like other slaves of the ancient world, may have been highly literate foreign captives put to intellectual work; besides, they were freed. Demetrius of Phalerum was a head of state, though in exile. The American slaves told their stories from a stock learned in more-or-less free Africa, where the

---

(*subiecti*): RN2.20 already had the concept in other terms, and Marie developed the point by pairing the *seignur* and *sa gent* (M29; O lacks). FR's moral for the fable of the crow on the sheep's back (FR2.31) is no more social in terminology than other versions (e.g., Perotti 26; RN3.11; M40; O lacks), but an interjected alas (*heu*) makes us sense that the fabulist is moved by some relevance to his own times. I sense in the apparently unique final line to this fable ("Militis arma tamen gerit hec gens heu! simulata") an allusion to roving soldiers who, returning perhaps from war or crusade, turn their arms against helpless citizens; it was a common medieval problem.

[50] Hervieux (n. 1 above) 1.809.

[51] Moorman (n. 28 above) 52-58.

West African storytellers (*griots*) were professionals in the service of leading families.[52] Berechiah and rabbinical fabulists experienced the Jew's oppression in Christian Europe, but in their own society they were, even if poor, men of authority and learning. Marie seems from her dedications to have had noble connections. Clerics are known to be responsible for much of medieval beast epic. The *Ecbasis captivi* is a work of the cloister and for the cloister. For the *Roman de Renart* we know of *le prêtre de la Croix-en-Brie,* and John Flinn considers the authors "pour la plupart des clercs."[53] Among medieval fabulists, too, we know of churchmen at all levels: Jacques de Vitry (bishop, cardinal), Walter of England (archbishop of Palermo), Alexander Neckam (abbot of Cirencester), Odo of Cheriton, Nicole Bozon (Franciscan), John of Sheppey (Benedictine, bishop, treasurer of England), John Bromyard (Dominican), and John Lydgate (Benedictine). Robert Henryson, as schoolmaster at a monastery school, was an employee of monks though probably not himself one. The anonymous author of the *Isopet* of Chartres seems to reveal himself in his epilogue as a student, presumably of divinity, taking two weeks out from his Aristotle. More authors of animal tales and fables share a common intellectual status than a humble social position. Certainly once fable becomes written literature, particularly in verse, its authors must be among the educated of their society.

Yet the medieval intellectual, if he did not happen to be the king's half-brother (Alexander Neckam) or an important official (Jacques de Vitry), might well consider himself or herself, while perhaps not allied to the serfs, at least cut off from the center of power. There were too many lesser clergy for all to ingratiate themselves into power even where they wished it. What from one perspective seems a privileged class, from another is a class often standing aside from society in either frustration or simple detachment. The intellectual seeking a fantasy-triumph over the man of action may create it through literature valuing wit over strength: the *Renart* cycle; the *fabliaux,* with their clever clerks and extortionist millers; or the more pessimistic world of fable. There, brute power prevails, wit wrings no mercy from the wolf, and yet sympathy goes to the victim. In the largest sense, perhaps all literature says one thing, that the works of the human mind outvalue the wealth and power of the world: the message is implicit in the very act of spending the time to write literature at all. Fabulists may choose moral terms to embody this opposition — pride and humility, aggression and innocence — or they may choose economic or social terms — rich and poor, *seignur* and *sa gent*.

The late twelfth century saw Renart leap to popularity as an embodiment of both

---

[52] For a picture of one *griot,* see Birago Diop, *Tales of Amadou Koumba,* trans. and foreword by Dorothy S. Blair (London 1966). At least one eminent folklorist would de-emphasize the protest content of Br'er Rabbit: "A number of critics regard Rabbit in United States Negro folktales as the symbol of the crafty, underdog slave or black man, unaware that American Negroes possess a considerable body of overt protest tales. Local and universal symbolisms may infuse the same tale, but a full interpretation should consider both sets of symbols"; Richard M. Dorson, *African Folklore* (Bloomington 1972) 38.

[53] John Flinn, *Le roman de Renart dans la littérature française et dans les littératures étrangères au moyen âge* (Paris 1963) 10, 34.

halves of the opposition: as relatively small beast he triumphs wittily over brute wolf and bear, but as relatively large carnivore he is tripped up by titmouse and rooster or fooled into a well-bottom by his own lusts. In the same period, a line of social fabulists rose to give new immediacy to fable's inherent opposition of powerful and innocent, challenging audiences of aristocrats, clerics, or ordinary laymen to perceive social situations morally. Such vital, even joyous literature could not be powered solely by a passive sympathy or regret for victims: deep down these writers affirm values actively, whether embodying those values in the triumphs of witty characters or in the affecting defeats of innocent ones. Standing slightly aside from a world they perceived so intensely, and building on a deep affirmation, these fabulists preserved a comic vitalism even while seeing with fresh precision fable's typically pessimistic world of born victims and of oppressors scarcely to be eluded.

Department of English
Livingston College
Rutgers University
New Brunswick, New Jersey 08903, U.S.A.

MAGISTERIUM AND LICENSE: CORPORATE AUTONOMY AGAINST PAPAL AUTHORITY IN THE MEDIEVAL UNIVERSITY OF PARIS

•

by Alan E. Bernstein

Local conflicts, if they occur in the right place, sometimes herald more general oppositions.[1] In the thirteenth-century University of Paris, the secular masters' defense of the magisterium against the papally sponsored mendicants is an example. When the distinction between the magisterium and the license to teach is understood as the principle by which professors of the university sought to control membership in the guild of teachers and hence to protect the corporation's autonomy, the history of the university in the thirteenth century breaks down into two phases.

At the beginning of the century, the masters began to consolidate their organization into a guild for the purpose of regulating their profession independently. Their efforts opposed the interests of the chancellor, who claimed jurisdiction over students and teachers in Paris with the right to fine, excommunicate, and jail them, as well as exclusive power to grant the license to teach.[2] In the conflict that naturally developed, the teachers' staunchest allies were popes Innocent III, Honorius III, and Gregory IX. In the first phase, the popes supported university autonomy.

In the second phase, the popes insisted that the mendicants be admitted to the professors' corporation against the will of its members, and this policy led the Parisian teachers to ask by what authority the pope could impose his will on a recognized corporation. As a result of this reassessment, some seculars came to see the king of France as a more dependable defender of their interests than the pope. This tentative shift of allegiance constituted a kind of proto-Gallican experiment, one that makes it possible to identify in the 1290s a climate of emotion not dissimilar from one that would be much stronger in French history, beginning about a century later.

[1] I wish to thank Professors Paul Oskar Kristeller, John H. Mundy, Gavin Langmuir, Howard Kaminsky, and Richard H. Rouse for the help and encouragement they gave me in producing this study.

[2] H. Rashdall, *The Universities of Europe in the Middle Ages*, ed. F. M. Powicke and A. B. Emden, 3 vols. (London 1935) 1.304-305. Especially illustrative of the extent of the chancellor's claims is *Chartularium universitatis Parisiensis*, ed. H. Denifle & E. Chatelain, 4 vols. (Paris 1889-1897) 1.102-104, no. 45 (hereafter cited as *Chart.*).

To describe the teachers' perception of their autonomy and the institution through which it was protected, it is necessary to consider briefly the twelfth-century cathedral school and the exclusive jurisdiction over education and the teacher's license that popes had earlier conceded to episcopal authority. Gregory VII, greatest of the eleventh century's reforming popes, who sought to remove the Church from lay control and consolidate it under papal direction, made education the responsibility of each bishop, ordering in 1079 that "all bishops should cause the discipline of letters to be taught in their churches."[3] Thus the diocesan schools, which became the institutional antecedents of the early universities, had themselves received formative impetus from papal efforts to promote education in Latin Christendom. Gregory's legislation naturally obtained uneven results, but within the next century schools such as those at Laon, Reims, Orléans, Paris, and Chartres in northern France, and Winchester, London, York, and Lincoln in England became the most advanced educational institutions in Europe, at least for the study of philosophy, literature, and theology. These schools were usually administered either by the bishop himself or by a subordinate official in the cathedral chapter, such as the archdeacon or chancellor (as at Paris). In other chapters a canon might be promoted to the office of *scholasticus, magister scholarum,* or *caput scholae.* Because education was an episcopal responsibility, the chancellor or schoolmaster had a monopoly over instruction in the diocese.[4] Following Rashdall, Philippe Delhaye cites papal confirmations of the chancellor's exclusive rights dated 1139 and 1169.[5] However, not all schoolmasters were episcopal functionaries. Some directed schools in monasteries or collegiate churches exempted by papal privilege from episcopal jurisdiction. The school of the canons regular of Sainte-Geneviève in Paris is an important exception of this type.[6] The rule nonetheless holds that to teach in the district of a particular schoolmaster, one needed his permission, or license.

It was Alexander III who issued the first general legislation concerning the license. In his pronouncements of the 1170s, he forbade the chancellor to demand any fee for granting it, but gave no indication how the candidate's competence was to be determined.[7] Should the chancellor make the decision alone, or should the opinion of other teachers be taken into account? This silence is especially surprising because

---

[3] "Ut omnes episcopi artes litterarum in suis ecclesiis docere faciant." J. D. Mansi et al., *Sacrorum conciliorum nova et amplissima collectio . . .,* 53 vols. (Florence, etc. 1759-1927) 20.50. Quoted in P. Delhaye, "L'organization des écoles au XIIe siècle," *Traditio* 5 (1947) 240.

[4] All these terms are synonymous, varying only by local custom. I shall use "schoolmaster" to refer generically to this office in any diocese, and "chancellor" to refer specifically to the bishop's delegate in Paris. The terms "professor," "master," and "doctor" are also synonymous. Students were called "scholars." and student teachers "bachelors." As will be seen below, there is a significant difference between a "licentiate" and a master.

[5] Delhaye (n. 3 above) 254; Rashdall (n. 2 above) 1.281.

[6] H. Denifle, *Die Entstehung der Universitäten des Mittelalters bis 1400* (Berlin 1885, repr. Graz 1956) 655-694.

[7] *Corpus juris canonici* X. 5, 5, 1 and 3; ed. E. Friedberg, 2 vols. (Leipzig 1879) 2.769. See also G. Post, "Alexander III, the *Licentia docendi,* and the Rise of the Universities," in *Anniversary Essays in Medieval History by Students of Charles Homer Haskins* (Boston 1929) 255-277.

it was precisely in the late twelfth century that the masters must have begun to initiate newly licensed teachers into their number. Later sources tell us that the honor of admission into the guild of masters was called the *magisterium* and it was awarded in a ceremony called "inception."

The introduction of a formal admission procedure marks the first emergence of the masters teaching in Paris from a mere coterie of similarly employed men into at least a primitive formal association, guild, or corporation. It is precisely upon this process of incorporation that Rashdall bases his history of the University of Paris, thus laying the foundation for an interpretation that has justifiably supported successive contributions ever since.[8] Rashdall's contention is that as the masters perceived their common interests more clearly, they followed the example already established by many communes, guilds, and religious confraternities, and modeled their association after the pattern of a corporation as described in Roman Law. He traces the university's evolution toward the full status of a corporation having the privileges of a collective legal person: the right to make its own bylaws, elect its own officers, have a seal, and be represented at law.[9] Throughout the history of the university, its members described their community in terms that derive from Justinian's *Corpus juris civilis: universitas, societas, collegium.*[10] The earliest term that we know to have been used to describe the Parisian teachers as a group is *consortium.*[11]

With the gradual evolution of the university into an autonomous corporation, the masters were increasingly able to review the men licensed by the chancellor and to control admission to their guild. The licentiate had to meet a series of requirements and examinations before he was accorded the magisterium. In the Faculty of Arts,

[8] Rashdall (n. 2 above) 1.5, 292-94, and 298ff.

[9] *Ibid.* 299-315. Rashdall's treatment is reviewed in detail by G. Post, "Parisian Masters as a Corporation, 1200-1246," *Speculum* 9 (1934) 421-445. Gabriel dissents from Rashdall's and Post's legal interpretation and places the "formation and consolidation of the Association of the Masters" much earlier, in the years 1140 to 1178; A. Gabriel, "The Conflict between the Chancellor and the University of Masters and Students at Paris during the Middle Ages," *Die Auseinandersetzungen an der Pariser Universität im XIII. Jahrhundert,* Miscellanea Mediaevalia 10 (Berlin 1976) 106-154, at 107. He refers to his *Garlandia: Studies in the History of the Mediaeval University* (Notre Dame 1969) 26, 39ff. where, however, there is no further documentation on this point. Note that Post 444 concludes by describing the period 1200-1215 as that in which the university developed into a legal corporation "fully recognized by the highest ecclesiastical authority." Other discussions may be found in G. Leff, *Paris and Oxford Universities in the Thirteenth and Fourteenth Centuries* (New York 1968) 17; J. Verger, *Les universités au moyen âge* (Paris 1973) 25-36; and A. B. Cobban, *The Medieval Universities* (London 1975) 81-84.

[10] Digest, III, 4, 1, and *Chart.* (n. 2 above) 1.293 no. 256. Cf. Rashdall (n. 2 above) 1.164 and n. 1, where he cites Code, III, tit. XIII. For a more thorough discussion of the *universitas* in Roman law, see R. E. Korneman, "Leges collegiorum" in A. F. von Pauly, *Real-Enzyklopädie der klassischen Altertumswissenschaft,* ed. G. Wissowa (Stuttgart 1894-1903) 4.415ff.

[11] T. Walsingham, *Gesta abbatum monasterii Sancti Albani,* ed. Riley, Rerum britannicarum medii aevi scriptores 28, vol. 4.1 (London 1867) 217, where it is said of John, abbot of St. Albans, 1195-1214, "Hic, in juventute scholarum Parisiensium frequentator assiduus, ad electorum consortium magistrorum meruit attingere." Also cited, along with other examples, in *Chart.* (n. 2 above) 1.ix.

after the chancellor's examination and the granting of the license, candidates for the magisterium had to wait from six months to as much as three years, depending on the period in question.[12] Much later, after the reform instituted by Urban V's two legates in 1366, licentiates in arts were not allowed to apply for the magisterium until they had returned to the schools and studied Aristotle's *Ethics* and *On Meteors*.[13] On the evening before his inaugural lecture, the candidate had to take part in the "vespers," a final, formal disputation.[14]

In the Faculty of Theology, the vespers were succeeded on the next day by the *aulica* in the bishop's hall (*aula*) and then, on the next regular day of classes by the *resumptio*, in which the candidate replied to points raised in the earlier debates.[15] Technically the magisterium was awarded in the *aulica*, for it was here that the beret was conferred,[16] but it should be stressed that progress through these disputations was not automatic. In 1387 a Dominican friar named Juan de Monzon asserted in his vespers that it was against the faith to say the Virgin Mary had not contracted original sin. When he defended this view in his *resumptio*, he was attacked by the Faculty of Theology and never gained admission to the university.[17]

This example from the late fourteenth century is not inappropriate, because most of the detailed information about procedure in these ceremonies comes from documents of that period. A description of the conferral of the magisterium that survives from late fourteenth-century Paris clearly expresses the distinction between the license and the magisterium. Prior to his vespers, the candidate for the magisterium is called the *licentiatus vesperiandus*. Later, as he takes his seat for the *aulica*, he is called *magister novus aulandus*, and when he is done, the *aulatus magister*. The ceremony which changes him from a *licentiatus* to a *magister* is described as follows:

> The lord chancellor or his substitute first receives an oath from the man about to incept that he will provide faithful testimony about the bachelors to be licensed in the future. Next, he and the candidate's sponsor (called the "magister aulator") put on their own berets and then place another upon the head of the new master while one of them says, "I place the magisterial beret upon your head in the name of the Father, and of the Son, and of the Holy Ghost, amen." At once, each of the masters [in attendance] places upon his own head a beret from among

---

[12] Rashdall (n. 2 above) 1.461 and n. 2.

[13] *Chart.* (n.2 above) 3.145 no. 1319.

[14] Rashdall, 1. 461. For more detail see L. J. Paetow, *The Arts Course at Medieval Universities* (Urbana 1910) and, although largely outdated, C. Thurot, *De l'organisation de l'enseignement dans l'Université de Paris au moyen âge* (Paris 1850).

[15] P. Glorieux, "L'enseignement au moyen âge: Techniques et méthodes en usage à la Faculté de Théologie de Paris au XIIIe s.," *Archives d'histoire doctrinale et littéraire du Moyen Age* (AHDLMA) 35 (1968) 65-186, esp. 99 and 141-147.

[16] *Chart.* (n. 2 above) 2.693.

[17] *Chart.* 3, nos. 1557-1583. The title "magister" was applied to Monzon, however, because he had received his beret in the aulica. For other men who encountered difficulties in their "actes de maîtrise," see Glorieux (n. 15 above) 169-174, esp. items 101, 103, 123, and 127.

those distributed by the bedel. Then the chancellor gives him permission to incept (*licentiam incipiendi*) in the name of the Father, and of the Son, and of the Holy Ghost. With a blessing, the new master immediately begins his brief *principium* in praise of holy Scripture.[18]

This rite of passage from licentiate to master clearly shows the succession of the two stages and makes it impossible, I believe, to treat the award of the license and the magisterium as if they were the same.[19] The tendency to equate these honors may stem from misinterpretation of the expression *licentia incipiendi*. If this were the same as the *licentia docendi* previously awarded by the chancellor, then the distinction between the *licentiatus vesperiandus* and the *magister novus aulandus* would make no sense. The phrase therefore refers to inception; but it may not be taken to indicate that the chancellor gives the *incipiendus* the authority to participate in magisterial acts only then, during the *aulica*, for that authority was already conferred upon the graduate along with the license. In awarding the license the chancellor was considered to have given "permission (*licentiam*) to dispute, lecture and preach, and to exercise all the acts that pertain to a master in the theological faculty."[20] Yet the license is only an ecclesiastical authorization to perform these acts, not the masters' acceptance of the individuals so authorized. Those who leave the licensing ceremony are called *licentiati*.[21] Those who leave the *aulica* are masters.

The title of master, the magisterium, therefore, is conferred in the *aulica* with the joint imposition of the beret (*birretatio*) by the chancellor and the new master's sponsor and with the other masters of his faculty in attendance. The chancellor's participation in the *birretatio* survived lamely as a symbolic consequence (Rashdall calls it "a curious relic") of his earlier position, before the formation of the masters' guild, as sole director of the cathedral school.[22]

The distinct character of the two ceremonies may be further supported with reference to the academic calendar. Licenses were granted around All Saints Day of alternate years, a season called the Jubilee.[23] Bachelors were allowed until Saint Catherine's day, November 25, to prove that they had met all the requirements for the license.[24] The chancellor then had to make his decision, based on the testimony of regent masters and taking his own opinion into account, within three months.[25] Thus a license requested in the course of November would have to be granted in the

---

[18] *Chart.* 2.693. This description comes from a Bolognese manuscript, but Denifle has adjusted it to Paris usage by collating the Italian text against a similar description referring to Paris found in Vienna, Nationalbibliothek, MS lat. 4929, fols. 261v ff. It is assumed that by the time these customary rituals were described in writing, they were very old.

[19] As does Glorieux (n. 15 above) 98-99.

[20] *Chart.* (n. 2 above) 2.683, quoted by Glorieux 99.

[21] *Ibid.*

[22] Rashdall (n. 2 above) 1.486.

[23] *Ibid.* 480.

[24] Glorieux (n. 15 above) 98, citing *Chart.* (n. 2 above) 2.701 no. 49.

[25] As provided in *Parens scientiarum*; see below at n. 51.

course of February. But the dated vespers and *aulicae* that we have were given mostly in March or April.[26]

The license and the magisterium, therefore, were two different things. The license represented a permission to teach granted by ecclesiastical authority. It certified satisfactory completion of a course of studies. It was granted by the chancellor in the name of the bishop, ultimately representing the pope, and it always preceded the magisterium. The latter term signified membership in the guild of masters and implied both the masters' approval of the inceptor and the newcomer's acceptance under oath of the bylaws, jurisdiction, and officers of the corporation.[27] The license alone was no guarantee of eventual membership in the professors' guild at Paris and without the magisterium a teaching career there would be very difficult. Although the masters could not actually prevent a licentiate from lecturing, they could boycott him and threaten his students with eventual exclusion from the guild. The control that the masters gradually obtained over the admission of members to the teaching corps at Paris depended upon the magisterium's not being just a routine complement to the license. Even the early use of the term *consortium* referred specifically to a body of "chosen masters."[28] Clearly the magisterial honor would be debased if popes or chancellors could compel the professors to accept an outsider who had not observed the requirements outlined above or who would not swear loyalty to the guild. Because the professors' ability to control admission to their group depended upon its status as a guild or corporation, it is necessary to consider briefly the nature of a corporation at that time.

The Church of the early thirteenth century has been characterized as "a federation of semi-autonomous units, a union of innumerable greater or lesser corporate bodies."[29] In Roman law, the corporation was considered comparable to a state (*ad exemplum rei publica*),[30] but imperial jurists also anticipated the paradigm preferred by the canonists — that of a body, whose internal structure was analyzed through an analogy to the relationship of head and members.[31] This frame of reference for intra-

---

[26] Glorieux (n. 15 above) 142-144. In other passages, Glorieux distinguishes clearly between the two honors, as at 169.

[27] Gradually, this oath came to be exacted even earlier than the master's inception, at the point when a student became a bachelor and began his career as a student teacher. Although the teaching by bachelors *cursorie* and that by doctors *ordinarie* were carefully distinguished, the concept of the teaching profession here is the same as in the primitive university: no one shall actually lecture, even as a student teacher, unless he has accepted the authority of the corporation of masters, or at least of the masters in his faculty. For the oaths sworn by bachelors about to "determine," see *Chart*. (n. 2 above) 1 nos. 201 and 501.

[28] See n. 11 above, and Rashdall (n. 2 above) 1.305-306.

[29] B. Tierney, *Foundations of the Conciliar Theory* (Cambridge 1955) 97.

[30] *Corpus juris civilis*, D. 3. 4. 1.: "Quibus autem permissum est corpus habere collegii societatisve [read: sodaliciive, Cohn], sive cuiusque alterius eorum nomine proprium est ad exemplum rei publicae habere res communes, arcam communem, et actorem sive syndicum, per quem tanquam in republica, quod communiter agi fierique oporteat, agatur fiat." Here the metaphor of the body is juxtaposed with the simile of the republic, which is used twice.

[31] A. Ehrhardt, "Das Corpus Christi und die Korporationen im spätrömischen Recht," *Zeitschrift der Savigny-Stiftung für Rechtsgeschichte: Romanistische Abteilung* 70 (1953),

corporational disputes anthropomorphizes the more abstract relationship of the parts to the whole, with one part, the head, given primacy. The organic conception of the corporation led many thinkers to view the Church itself as a corporate body, and to superimpose the concomitant legal constructions upon the theological metaphors that, since Saint Paul, had portrayed the community of Christians as a single body. Hostiensis, a product of the law schools of Bologna, who taught in Paris around 1239 and probably began his influential *Summa* there,[32] played an important role in applying the theory of ecclesiastical corporations to the whole Church.[33]

Because of the university's own structure, corporation law was no mere theoretical abstraction for professors of the Parisian *studium*. When they conceived of the Church as a corporate body, their experience within an analogous constitution tempted them into certain simplified formulas when dealing with questions of ecclesiastical politics. Their alma mater was itself a federation of collegiate bodies — nations, faculties, and colleges — and masters were well schooled in both guiding the evolution and enduring the stress of conflicting collective interests. The disputation itself and the concomitant literary genre of the *quaestio* provided yet another occasion for university men to experience the conflict between parts and wholes that should theoretically be in equilibrium. It is no accident, therefore, that university members tended to portray the *studium* as a microcosm of the whole Church, and to project the premises of corporation theory onto a wide variety of problems.

The trend toward corporate cohesion within the body of teachers at Paris became identifiable as a threat to the chancellor of Paris very early in the thirteenth century. The date of about 1210 may be taken as a *terminus ante quem* for the institution of the inception and boycott, because it was about then that the chancellor began to resist it. He sought to neutralize the masters' new veto power by demanding an oath of obedience from each new licentiate, so that, if necessary, he could compel the acceptance of all whom he licensed. The implications of the oath exacted by the chancellor were clear to the masters and they appealed to papal authority, the source of the initiative that had established the cathedral schools.[34] In 1213 Innocent III forced representatives of the university and the chancellor to work out a compromise. This settlement provided the first opening for the masters to act as advisers to the chancellor. Here it was stipulated that, when a candidate seeking the license in either theology, law (Roman law was not prohibited at Paris until 1219), or medicine is recommended by a majority of the masters of his faculty, the chancellor may not deny him the license. At the same time, the chancellor remains free to license men not recommended by the masters.[35] This provision, I think, was intended less to

---

299-347; 71 (1954), 25-40. Medieval developments of this theme are traced by Otto Gierke, *Das deutsche Genossenschaftsrecht*, 4 vols. (Berlin, 1868-1913) 3.517 n. 7, 546-550.

[32] C. Lefebvre, "Hostiensis," in *Dictionnaire du droit canonique*, ed. R. Naz, 7 vols. (Paris 1935-1965) 5.1211-1227, esp. 1212, 1216.

[33] Tierney (n. 29 above) 147.

[34] Rashdall (n. 2 above) 1.308.

[35] *Chart.* (n. 2 above) 1.75-76 no. 16; and similarly, but with minor exceptions, for law and medicine.

preserve the chancellor's freedom than to reserve the possibility of his awarding the license to men designated by the pope without interference from the professors. It also shows, as Denifle suggests, that even at this early stage in university history, the chancellor could act as a representative of papal authority; that he was no longer a mere diocesan official.[36]

The first instance of direct papal intervention in these licensing procedures was to support the masters. In 1218, Honorius III wrote to three Parisian masters of theology, authorizing them to examine a certain Matthew of Scotland and, if they found him worthy, so to advise the chancellor, who could then no longer delay in licensing him.[37] It is clear that in this case the three masters had petitioned the pope on Matthew's behalf. But later, as a consequence of the quarrel over the mendicants, to be discussed below, the popes dispensed with examination by the masters and both the chancellor and the masters were forced to accept papal protégés. Examples become more frequent toward the end of the century. In 1288, Nicholas IV had to be very insistent to obtain a license for John de Murro, O.F.M., and he was aided in his efforts by the death of the reluctant Parisian chancellor, Nicholas of Nonacuria.[38] In his struggle with Philip IV, Boniface VIII suspended the right to confer the license anywhere in France.[39] Consequently, his successor, Benedict XI, had to confer the license personally upon two candidates and authorized Chancellor Simon to license two more, Boniface VIII's prohibition notwithstanding.[40] On 18 April 1304, Benedict restored normal operations.[41] Under John XXII and his successors, the licenses granted at special papal request became so numerous that masters who, by contrast, had earned their degrees within the Parisian system came to refer to the papally sponsored ones as *licentia bullata*.[42] The pact of 1213, therefore, provided two paths to the license: first, through normal academic procedures and the recommendations of the masters; second, through the chancellor's direct grant of the license to "men of his own choice" at papal "request." The position of the chancellor as a papal delegate was thus established as a convenient focus for influence from Rome.

In the Faculty of Arts, the situation was different because the number of masters was so great. The compromise of 1213 stipulated that a majority of a panel of six masters, three named by the Faculty of Arts and three by the chancellor, should be empowered to make binding recommendations to the chancellor.[43] Thus the

---

[36] Denifle (n. 6 above) 686-687.

[37] *Chart.* (n. 2 above) 1.85 no. 27.

[38] *Chart.* 2 nos. 548, 550, 551.

[39] *Ibid.* no. 636.

[40] *Ibid.* nos. 639, 640, 643.

[41] *Ibid.* no. 645.

[42] E. Delaruelle et al., *L'église au temps du Grand Schisme et de la crise conciliaire (1378-1449)*, vol. 14 of *Histoire de l'église*, ed. A. Fliche and V. Martin (Paris 1962-1964) pt. 2.471-473. Note, however, that this practice did not await the outbreak of the Great Schism. For the pontificate of John XXII, many examples may be found in *Chart.* 2, beginning with no. 748.

[43] *Chart.* (n. 2 above) 1.76 no. 16.

chancellor's control over candidates nominated by masters became only indirect, for his discretionary power extended only to the appointment of his three examiners, who still had to be masters of arts. Nor was there any guarantee that those licensed either on the recommendation of the panel or at the chancellor's personal initiative would be allowed to incept. Thus the terms elaborated in 1213 cut deeply into the chancellor's control of the license.

The last document emanating from the appeal of 1212 was handed down by the papal legate Robert of Courzon in 1215. His decision was later referred to as *Servus crucis* after its opening words. Courzon implicitly recognized the masters' association by distinguishing clearly between inception and the license when he said, "Let no one licensed by the chancellor or another incept if he gave him money, swore an oath, or made some other agreement."[44]

For the Faculty of Arts, Courzon specified that the candidate was to be tested publicly and "examined according to the form . . . contained in the peace [of 1213] between the chancellor and the scholars." For the Faculty of Theology, the statement is more vague, saying that only those men may solemnly lecture or preach in Paris who are of proven morals and learning.[45] Presumably, the proving was to be done in the old style, in front of the chancellor. Thus, in the superior faculties, the masters of theology, law, and medicine lost their two-year-old power to compel acceptance of recommended candidates.

The next important development is difficult to date. To escape the chancellor's fee and oath of obedience, many masters began to move their classes from the Ile de la Cité, where Notre-Dame stands, to the left bank of the Seine, where they placed themselves under the jurisdiction of the independent congregation of canons regular of Sainte-Geneviève. The chancellor countered by requiring those who sought the license to swear to teach only between the two bridges linking the Ile de la Cité to the right and left banks of the Seine, that is, within his jurisdiction. The masters appealed to the pope and, in 1227, Gregory IX confirmed the abbot of Sainte-Geneviève's immunity from episcopal authority and supported his right to license masters of theology, canon law, and arts.[46] By 1255 the abbot had appointed a chancellor of Saint-Geneviève who swore an oath before the Faculty of Arts promising to examine candidates in good faith.[47] As it turned out, candidates in arts were the only ones to frequent the chancellor of Sainte-Geneviève, but they did it in such great numbers that he was nicknamed "Chancellor of Arts."[48]

In 1229, the Parisian provost's men suppressed a carnival riot with tactics that resulted in the death of several students. When satisfaction was denied, the members of the university left Paris en masse until 1231, an action known as the Great

[44] *Ibid.* 79 no. 20: "Nullus incipiat licentiatus a cancellario vel ab alio data ei pecunia vel fide prestita, vel alia conventione habita."

[45] *Ibid.* 78-79.

[46] *Ibid.* 111 no. 55.

[47] *Ibid.* 299 no. 260; Rashdall (n. 2 above) 1.340-341.

[48] Rashdall 1.341.

Dispersion.[49]   Gregory IX used this occasion to reconsider the nature of the university and how it should be run. The result of his reflections is the bull of 13 April 1231, *Parens scientiarum*. Here there is a significant change. Although no mention is made of the testing mechanism in the Faculty of Arts[50] or of the compromise of 1213, the chancellor was forced to swear that he would grant the license only to worthy candidates following consultation with the masters. Thus, although the superior faculties could no longer actually dictate their choices to him, the chancellor was obliged to align his standards more closely with theirs. For the Faculty of Medicine, Gregory merely reiterated what he had said for arts, that the chancellor must "consult the masters." But for theology and canon law, he prescribed a complex and thorough investigation into the candidates' "morals, knowledge, and eloquence, as well as their plans and potential for advancement." The pope further directed that "within three months of the request for the license, [the chancellor] must take testimony not only from all the masters of theology present in the city, but also from other honest and literate men from whom the truth may be known" concerning the qualifications named above, and "when the investigation is finished, in the light of what in good faith seems decent and expedient, the chancellor may grant or deny the requested license according to his own conscience." To assure the validity of the consultation, Gregory provided that henceforth, when a new master incepted, he would have to swear publicly that he would provide honest testimony concerning petitioners for the license. In turn, the chancellor should promise not to reveal any detrimental testimony.[51] Although unfavorable reports were to be kept secret, it is hard to imagine that laudatory statements about a candidate refused by the chancellor would not quickly become known to all. It seems that, in reality, under the system established by *Parens scientiarum* the chancellor could only exceptionally refuse a candidate recommended by a large plurality of masters. After 1231, therefore, the chancellor retained relatively little of the discretionary power he had enjoyed at the turn of the century.

Parens scientiarum ends the first phase of university history, a period characterized by the masters' efforts to escape from the chancellor's jurisdiction by asserting their corporate rights and, through their legal representative at Rome, appealing to the superior authority of the pope.

At mid-century, the dispute over the introduction of the mendicant orders into the university was to modify this relationship considerably. For now the popes were seen as misguided champions of the deeply distrusted friars, while the professors and chancellor, as well as other influential prelates from northern France, joined forces

---

[49] *Ibid.* 334-338, and P. Kibre, *Scholarly Privileges in the Middle Ages* (Cambridge, Mass. 1962) 92-94.

[50] This had been stabilized by Robert of Courzon. Furthermore, once the abbot of Ste-Geneviève could confer the license, many candidates, especially in arts, never dealt with the chancellor of Notre-Dame. Gregory IX's silence on this subject may be explained by a desire to see what the further consequences of his 1227 decision would be.

[51] *Chart.* (n. 2 above) 1.137 no. 79.

against them. Until the arrival at the Parisian *studium* of the Dominicans in 1217 and the Franciscans in 1220, teaching at the University of Paris had been a monopoly of the secular clergy. It would be hard to overestimate the emotion felt by the professors when confronted by rival teachers belonging to the new orders. For the mendicant mentality fostered a radical reassessment of the clerical mission, founded on such sweeping self-abnegation that a friar could actually deny he had a will of his own, on the grounds that he had nothing of "his own." The seculars considered the mendicant conception of poverty a threat to their idea of the Church and the religious life. Nonetheless, the popes encouraged the mendicants.

As both papal support and popular acceptance of their mission increased, the mendicants began to hear confession, assign penance, and assume other sacramental functions of the parish clergy — activities interpreted by bishops and priests as an invasion of their own special area of competence. Thus the university masters were not alone in their opposition to the friars, and, on this issue, professors and chancellors were able to make common cause.

In 1229 the bishop of Paris, William of Auvergne, over the head of his chancellor, gave the license in theology to Roland of Cremona, *lector* at the Dominican *studium* in Paris. Roland was then succeeded by another Dominican, Hugh of Saint-Cher. Next, Roland's teacher, John of Saint-Giles, already a master in the Faculty of Theology, joined the Dominican order and kept his chair. Then another master, Alexander of Hales, was converted to the Order of Friars Minor. By 1231, three chairs out of twelve belonged to mendicants. One sign that boded ill for the future was the promotion of these men during the university's Great Dispersion. Their behavior aroused the suspicion that they had deliberately remained in Paris to take advantage of the seculars' absence.[52]

As time passed and William of Auvergne died, suspicion of the friars remained unallayed. In 1250, Innocent IV learned that the chancellor of Paris, Aimery of Veire, was cooperating with the masters and exploiting a technicality to withhold the license from mendicants. One consequence of the friars' renunciation of will was their refusal to petition for the license to teach. Pointing to *Parens scientiarum*, Aimery was able to show that Gregory IX had referred to the "requested license," and he maintained that because the friars would not request the license, he could not award it to them. Innocent IV undercut this excuse, saying that "the act of petitioning makes no one more worthy of having the license," and therefore the chancellor henceforth is to license those whom he finds worthy according to the formula of Gregory IX, even when the scholar does not actually seek the honor.[53]

In 1252, when the mendicants again refused to support a university-ordered

---

[52] Rashdall (n. 2 above) 1.370-376. See also the discussions of this first phase of the masters' conflict with the mendicants in Leff (n. 9 above) 34-47, Kibre (n. 49 above) 103-117, Verger (n. 9 above) 83-91, Cobban (n. 9 above) 90-94, and P. R. McKeon, "The Status of the University of Paris as *Parens scientiarum*: An Episode in the Development of its Autonomy," *Speculum* 39 (1964) 651-675. A new, magisterial book has been devoted entirely to this subject: M.-M. Dufeil, *Guillaume de Saint-Amour et la polémique universitaire parisienne, 1250-1259* (Paris 1972).

[53] *Chart.* (n. 2 above) 1.219 no. 191 and n. 2.

dispersion, the seculars resolved that thereafter no one could be admitted to the
magisterium nor any bachelor begin his student teaching unless he had sworn to
observe all the university's statutes, including the rule that duly voted boycotts be
honored by all.[54] When the Dominican masters refused to swear the oath, they were
excluded from the university.[55] Lawsuits followed. Although the university's
proctor at Rome, William of Saint-Amour, was able to win an initial victory from
Innocent IV (*Etsi animarum*, 10 May 1254) just before the latter's death,[56] the new
pope, Alexander IV, who had been cardinal protector of the Franciscans, reversed his
predecessor's judgment immediately after taking office. In *Quasi lignum vitae*, issued
14 April 1255, Alexander spelled out the papal conception of the magisterium, a
conception deeply antithetical to that of the masters.

Alexander annulled the legislation against the friars and, *de potestatis plenitudine*,
ordered the masters to reinstate the Dominican professors into their *consortium*.[57]
Next, he ordered the chancellor to offer the magisterial title as an enticement to
naturally gifted students.[58] The pope then restated the position that the chancellor
should grant the license to men whom he finds worthy on the basis of the
investigation prescribed in *Parens scientiarum*.[59] Thus, in two consecutive sentences,
Alexander used the terms "magisterium" and "licentia" in analogous positions, as if
they were synonymous. It is clear that Alexander knew that he was advancing
beyond the earlier distinction between the license and the magisterium. He explicitly
declared that the chancellor should consider not only the terms of *Parens scientiarum*
as regards licensing, but that he should also consider diligently the condition and
needs of the whole Church and, on the basis of this broader view, stimulate good
students with the title of master.[60] For the sake of a kind of "raison d'église,"
therefore, Alexander was prepared to disregard the professors' autonomous control

[54] *Ibid.* 243 no. 219.

[55] *Ibid.* 255 no. 230.

[56] *Ibid.* 267-270 no. 240.

[57] *Ibid.* 279-285 no. 247, at 284: "Predictos insuper Predicatorum Ordinis fratres theologice
facultatis magistros ad magistrorum consorcium ipsosque ac auditores eorum ad Universitatis
collegium de nostre potestatis plenitudine restituentes omnino et decernentes, ad eadem
consorcium et collegium a vobis in dulcedinis ubere sine difficultate qualibet admittendos."

[58] *Ibid.* 283: "Et hiis, quos . . . viderit ad magisterium promovendos, sic faveat, quod capacem
sensum a natura sortiti ad profectum scientie proposito studiosis magistralis tituli premio
provocentur."

[59] *Ibid.* 283: "Nolumus ex hoc viam aliquem vel plures habendi precludi, si cancellarius
omnibus que considerari debent inspectis . . . licenciam eis viderit . . . concedendam."

[60] *Ibid.*: "Ipse [cancellarius] tamen circa licenciandos . . . non solum ea, que attendenda in
constitutione ipsius G[regorii] exprimuntur, verum etiam statum et necessitatem ecclesie
generalis et populorum salutem diligenter attendat," etc. as in n. 57 above. Cf. McKeon (n. 52
above) 658 who, in treating *Quasi lignum vitae*, stresses Alexander's provision that future
boycotts must be approved by a two-thirds majority in each faculty. The mendicants in the
Faculty of Theology, comprising more than a third of its members, would therefore have a veto
over the university's exercise of the right to suspend lectures assured in *Parens scientiarum*
(*Chart.* 1.138 no. 79). However crippling this consequence, it seems to me to derive from the
more fundamental loss of the control over membership, since only members vote on boycotts.
Cf. Rashdall (n. 2 above) 1.383; Leff (n. 9 above) 42; Dufeil (n. 52 above) 154-156.

of the magisterium. When he reinstated the two Dominicans to their chairs, he effectively overrode the masters' traditional review of licentiates and awarded the magisterium directly. He ordered his deputy, in the future, to do the same.

To resist Alexander's imposition of unwanted members upon the corporation, the masters symbolically dissolved the university.[61] More important than this dramatic gesture, they sought allies outside the *studium*. Their strategy was not only to defend the autonomy of their own corporation, but also to take on the role of spokesman for all seculars who felt their rights imperiled by the pope's support of the mendicants. The most articulate opponent of Alexander IV and the friars was William of Saint-Amour, whose writings illustrate the rationale of seculars both inside and outside the university. His discussion is noteworthy for its assumptions about the inviolability of parts in a corporate whole.

In his appeal for support from the offended prelates of France, William of Saint-Amour stressed the separateness of each distinct jurisdiction within the Church, whether bishopric, parish, or corporation. Just as the pope acts unjustly in imposing the friars upon the university, William argued, so he errs in allowing them to preach at will in dioceses and parishes without the permission of bishop or priest:

> We do not wish to dispute about the power of the lord pope or of the bishops, but nonetheless, according to both divine and human law, there may be only one priest in a church, otherwise the church would be not a bride but a harlot (C.21 q.2 c.4), nor should there be many heads in one church, lest it be made a monster (X. 1. 31. 14.). Moreover, since the office of preacher is chief in the rule of churches (X. 5. 7. 12.), if the lord pope grants to some people the power to preach everywhere, it must be understood to mean, "where they are invited to do so," because even bishops ought not to approach ecclesiastical matters outside their own diocese unless they have been so invited (C.9 q.2 c.9)[62]

Thus for William the Church is a honeycomb of particularisms, each with very firm boundaries that cannot be breached without violence.

The question is how to determine who is an outsider. Can a papal license to preach in someone else's parish or diocese remove the stigma? The answer for William lies in understanding the correct distribution of functions within the Church. These were laid down by Christ himself, when he chose the twelve apostles, who prefigure the bishops, and the seventy-two disciples, who were succeeded by the parish priests. Later, "helpers" were instituted to aid the others. And these have been established and are regulated by fixed procedures. But if the lord pope were to allow an infinite and undetermined number of men, unknown to himself and not elected, to preach,

[61] *Chart.* (n. 2 above) 1.293 no. 256: "Attendentes etiam quod societas non per violentiam solet, sed per amicitiam copulari; considerantes nichilominus quod secundum juris normam in communionem aut societatem nemo compelli potest vel detineri invitus: a predictis collegio et consortio, sicut nobis a jure conceditur, . . . discessimus."

[62] *De periculis novissimorum temporum*, ed. M. Bierbaum, in *Bettelorden und Weltgeistlichkeit an der Universität Paris* (Münster i.W. 1920) 10-11.

hear confessions, and enjoin penances (which functions constitute for the most part the cure of souls), it is unlikely that he would understand these men to be general apostles or helpers able to operate anywhere in the Church uninvited or unwanted by the regularly constituted prelates. And this is because Christ, whose vicar he is and whom he should therefore imitate, only sent out certain persons chosen individually by him, that is, the twelve apostles and seventy-two disciples.[63] Thus, William argued, the precincts of the Church were firmly established and the proper personnel was sent by Christ himself to administer to the spiritual needs of residents within each district. No pope, therefore, can legitimately send newcomers to do the same work because this would trespass over an inviolable boundary and usurp a function already delegated by Christ. In a corporate body, the head can not intervene in affairs proper to one member. Even a secular ruler knows better than to do this, for, says William, quoting Roman law, "a prince does not wish to prejudice the jurisdiction of another by his mandates (X. 1. 8. 5; 1. 31. 12; D 16. 43. lex 8) lest, God forbid, injustice might seem to arise from the very place where rights are born (C. 8. 4. lex 6; X. 5. 1. 24)."[64] Local or corporate self-determination is therefore the ideal that William opposed to the universal authority invoked by Alexander IV.[65]

But the locality need not always be as restricted as a parish or diocese, as William's reference to a prince suggests. Indeed, as the controversy with the mendicants wore on through the thirteenth century, the university masters and prelates of northern France (archbishop of Reims, bishops of Bourges and Amiens) worked more and more closely together. Two years after Clement IV issued *Quidam temere sentientes* in 1265, freeing friars from the need to seek the permission of the parish priest before preaching in his parish, a council at Reims declared its opposition and Master Gérard d'Abbeville was its spokesman. After Martin IV's *Ad fructus uberes* of 1282, which gave sole supervision of the friars' pastoral work to the heads of the mendicant orders, Masters Henry of Ghent and Godfrey of Fountains cooperated with William of Mâcon, bishop of Amiens, to seek its reversal.[66] Secular resentment of *Ad fructus uberes* continued in northern France until 1290, when Benedict Gaetani came to Paris as a legate of Nicholas IV. Approached by William of Mâcon to consider a revocation of the objectionable bull, the future Boniface VIII delivered the most resounding insult to the masters in a half-century of litigation over the friars. The legate quashed all the acts of the French synods that had opposed *Ad fructus uberes* and forbade any further discussion of the bull. Further, he suspended Henry of Ghent from teaching because the professor had dared to question the decision. Then, when delegates of the four faculties sought to have this punishment

[63] *Collectiones catholicae et canonicae scripturae*, in Guillaume de St-Amour, *Opera* (Constance 1632) 144ff., quoted in Y. M.-J. Congar, "Aspects ecclésiologiques de la querelle entre mendiants et séculiers . . .," ADHLMA 35 (1960) 54 n. 34a.

[64] *De periculis* 10.

[65] As observed by McKeon (n. 52 above) 665.

[66] D. L. Douie, *The Conflict Between the Seculars and the Mendicants at the University of Paris in the Thirteenth Century*, Aquinas Society of London, Aquinas Paper 23 (London 1954) 17-30.

mitigated, Benedict denounced the university and praised the mendicants as the only sound member of the Church.[67]

As pope, Boniface modified his position. In his bull of 1300, *Super cathedram*, he granted the seculars concessions they had long sought. Mendicants could preach in the streets only when it did not conflict with the parish priest's sermon and in churches only with the priest's permission. Only those friars could hear confession and assign penances who had been chosen by their order and licensed by the bishop of each diocese. Absolution of the most serious sins — incest, rape, murder, sodomy, and so on — was reserved to the bishop and could no longer be dealt with by friars. When people desired to be buried on the grounds of a friary, the mendicants would give one-quarter of the customary payment to the parish.[68]

But Boniface did not recover the loyalty of the French clergy with these moves, however welcome they were. The community of dissident prelates emerging in northern France could hardly help feeling that a king of France might be a more reliable defender than the pope. Moreover, by the turn of the century Philip IV had begun to incorporate the French clergy into the realm, by consulting its members in embryonic representative assemblies, taxing them, and seeking their approval of actions aimed against Boniface VIII. Generally, the French clergy and the University of Paris worked together in support of the king in the historic conflict between Philip IV and Boniface VIII.[69] Although Philip had to exert pressure to obtain university concurrence in the condemnation of the Templars, when Boniface excommunicated adherents of the king, three faculties out of four supported the king's effort to try the pope before a general council.[70]

The last half of the thirteenth century and the first decade of the fourteenth, therefore, saw the prelates and professors of northern France forming an increasingly coherent coalition against the universal authority of popes defending the ecumenical mendicant orders. The fundamental premise that underlay their position was a belief in the distinctness and inviolability of the discrete parts of a whole, or, in less

---

[67] P. Glorieux, "Prélats français contre religieux mendiants," *Revue d'histoire de l'église de France* 11 (1925) 309-331; 471-495, esp. 491ff. The cardinal's words, as recorded by a contemporary, may be found in C.-J. Hefele, *Histoire des conciles*, ed. H. Leclercq, 6.2 (Paris 1915) 1478-1480.

[68] *Corpus juris canonici, Constitutiones Clementis papae V*, 3. 7. 2.; ed. Friedberg (n. 7 above) 2.1162-1164.

[69] K. Schleyer, *Anfänge des Gallikanismus im 13. Jht.: Der Widerstand des französischen Klerus gegen die Privilegierung der Bettelorden*, Historische Studien 314 (Berline 1937) 56ff.; Rashdall (n. 2 above) 1.395; Leff (n. 9 above) 48.

[70] *Chart.* (n. 2 above) 2.101-102 no. 634; Rashdall 1.412. There is a lack of studies on the University of Paris during the reign of Philip IV. Not even the documentation in the *Chartularium* of the university is complete. To fill the gap, one must refer to the classic works on the king's encounter with Boniface VIII: P. Dupuy, *Histoire du différend d'entre le pape Boniface VIII et Philippes le Bel, roy de France* (Paris 1655; repr. Phoenix, Ariz. 1963); H. Finke, *Aus den Tagen Bonifaz VIII: Funde und Forschungen* (Münster 1902); G. Digard, *Phillippe le Bel et le Saint-Siège de 1285 à 1304*, 2 vols. (Paris 1936); and J. Strayer, "Consent to Taxation under Philip the Fair," in J. Strayer & C. Taylor, *Studies in Early French Taxation*, Harvard Historical Monographs 12 (Cambridge, Mass. 1939).

abstract terms, the autonomy of local administrative districts. They portrayed their opponents as intruders upon their territory or usurpers of their rights. As the thirteenth century came to a close, however, and the French monarchs established a more widespread and reliable civil order, there developed a new loyalty to another sub-ecumenical entity, the French or Gallican church. Benefiting from the attitude toward the monarch fostered by Roman law, illustrated earlier in the quotations used by William of Saint-Amour, and increasingly desirous of turning the wealth of the clergy to his own ends, a king like Philip IV could pose as a defender of the local rights of the French clergy against the demands of Roman popes. Even though the king made demands too, French prelates were inclined to look to him for protection against a Roman see that, over the last half-century, had seemed to violate their rights and contravene their interests consistently. The new loyalty, called Galli-canism, may be defined, therefore, as the consciousness of a viable, particular, French church, united in defense of local rights, and protected by the king of France.[71]

To recapitulate, it may be stated that the cumulative constitutional effect of papal judgments concerning the University of Paris during the first half of the thirteenth century, as enshrined in *Parens scientiarum*, gave the masters considerable control over the selection of teachers at the chancellor's expense. In the second half of the century, however, these gains were undercut by the very agency that had awarded them. Alexander IV's *Quasi lignum vitae* made such deep inroads that the seculars considered it more a "lignum mortis."[72] In defending the mendicants, the popes buttressed the independent approach to the license and compelled the Faculty of Theology to award the magisterium to friars. In opposition, the masters appealed beyond the Latin Quarter to the interests of the northern French clergy. If the pope could impose his conception of the magisterium, appointing masters against the will of the university, they argued, he could override episcopal control of the diocese or the priest's rights in the parish. In common defense of corporate particularism, the masters and northern French prelates together learned to take a more independent look at papal claims and the theories describing the authority of a corporation's head over its members.

The tensions whose origins in France can be seen in the period described here, although relaxed somewhat after the reign of Philip IV, never disappeared com-pletely,[73] and re-emerged in the subtractions of obedience during the Great Schism and in the period of the concordats that followed the Council of Constance.[74]

---

[71] Cf. V. Martin, *Les origines du Gallicanisme*, 2 vols. (Paris 1939) 1.31. Martin (34) maintains that the invocation of Gallican liberties around 1300 was against the lay aristocracy; "aucun souci de se défendre contre le pape."

[72] *Chart.* (n. 2 above) 1.292 no. 256.

[73] One example of Gallican thought in this "suspended" phase is studied in my forthcoming book, *Pierre d'Ailly and the Blanchard Affair: University and Chancellor of Paris at the Beginning of the Great Schism.*

[74] See H. Kaminsky, "The Politics of France's Subtraction of Obedience from Pope Benedict XIII, 27 July 1398," *Proceedings of the American Philosophical Society* 115 no. 5 (1971) 366-397 and, more generally, Delaruelle et al. (n. 42 above).

Although full-fledged Gallicanism could not exist without explicit reference to protection from the French king, some premises underlying the particularist idea of a French church can be traced back to the university masters' defense of their corporate interests against an assertion of expanding papal authority.

Department of History
Stanford University
Stanford, California 94305, U.S.A.

ARISTOTLE AND THE FRENCH MONARCHY, 1260–1303

•

by Thomas Renna

Aristotle championed the supremacy of law. Europeans in the later Middle Ages welcomed the rediscovery of Aristotle's *Politics* (1260) because they saw in the work a natural-law support for the *de facto* tendency towards consitutional political communities. Aristotle's ideas of law and citizens were useful antidotes to the absolutist doctrines inherent in the revised Roman law and papally-centered canon law.

Such at least was the prevailing opinion among twentieth-century historians of medieval political theory until about the 1950s.[1] Although more qualified, variants of this simplistic view continue to appear in scholarly writings.[2] Since Aristotle was summoned in defense of constitutional forms of government between the twelfth and nineteenth centuries, it is alleged, surely he must have been so interpreted by thinkers immediately after 1260 when the *Politics* was translated into Latin. But the difficulty with this approach is that it ignores the obvious fact that in France — perhaps the region where Aristotle's *Politics* was most widely read between 1260 and 1320 — the *Politics* was used to bolster monarchy. To assume that French royalists who referred to Aristotle felt threatened by the allegedly "democratic" tendency in the *Politics* is to read history backwards. They experienced no such crisis of conscience.

The historian of French political though must first determine which problems the thirteenth-century authors themselves tried to solve;[3] he cannot look for guides

---

This article is a revision of a paper read at the Ohio Conference on Medieval Studies II, 17 October 1975, at John Carroll University. The writer wishes to thank the American Philosophical Society, the National Endowment for the Humanities, and Saginaw Valley State College for providing him with grants used in research for this study.

[1] The most influential, but now seriously outdated, of these modern surveys are R. W. and A. J. Carlyle, *A History of Medieval Political Theory in the West* 5 and 6 (London 1928, 1936), and C. H. McIlwain, *The Growth of Political Thought in the West* (New York 1932). The errors of the Carlyles are repeated in most surveys of Western political thought. See, e.g., G. Sabine, *A History of Political Theory,* ed. 3 (New York 1961), chaps. 13-15.

[2] Among recent scholars, Walter Ullmann is perhaps the ablest defender of the traditional view of Aristotle's influence in late medieval Europe. See esp. his *The Individual and Society in the Middle Ages* (Baltimore 1966); *A History of Political Thought: The Middle Ages* (Baltimore 1965); *Principles of Government and Politics in the Middle Ages* (London 1961).

[3] See the intelligent remarks of J. Dunbabin in "Aristotle in the Schools," in *Trends in Medieval Political Thought,* ed. B. Smalley (Oxford 1965) 65-85; see also Smalley's introduction.

among, say, fifteenth-century commentaries on the *Politics* to help him comprehend the intentions of pre-fifteenth-century commentators. Historians[4] have too readily assumed that the *Politics* contains a consistent, clear "thesis," a thesis which was presumably evident to thirteenth-century authors. These historians then evaluated Aristotelian writers such as John of Paris according to this *a priori* norm. John of Paris is dubbed a "true" Aristotelian insofar as he conforms to this contrived absolute.

This ahistorical methodology — the interpretation of texts on the basis of a pre-conceived thesis in the *Politics* — may dispose us to forget that thirteenth-century authors had no interest in the historical Aristotle. They made no effort to analyze the *Politics* as a product of fourth-century Greece. French writers did not believe their monarchist readings of the *Politics* were distortions of Aristotle's original intention. Further, historians have often exaggerated the importance of church-state conflicts in French political theory, 1260-1303. By focusing on two-power theories and Philip the Fair's publicists we may have oversimplified the process by which Aristotle was transposed into a monarchist.

As a concrete test case of how Aristotle was absorbed into French political theory, 1260-1303, this essay will examine a single question posed by Aristotle: "Is it better to be ruled by the Best Man or by the Best Laws?"[5] It will be argued that this question became increasingly royalized in the hands of French thinkers. This test question would seem a particularly revealing one because of its uncompromising and blunt nature. It would seem that any respondent to the *questio* would be forced to declare himself either a radical monarchist or a radical constitutionalist.

THOMAS AQUINAS

Aquinas scholarship in the past twenty-five years has generally stressed the monarchist direction of Thomas's political theory[6] — a welcome corrective to the traditional emphasis on his supposed tendencies toward representative or even democratic forms of government.[7] His notion of mixed monarchy is now seen as less inconsistent with the strong king outlined in the *De regimine principum* than had formerly been believed. Whatever the truth, it must be admitted that Thomas's idea of monarchy remains ambiguous and incomplete.

---

[4] Such as Ullman; see n. 2 above.

[5] Aristotle, *Politics* 3.15.

[6] Typical of the more recent approach is J. B. Morrall, *Political Thought in Medieval Times* (New York 1962 [1958]) 77-79; Dunbabin (n. 3 above). Modern scholars are reluctant to comment on the practical implications of Aquinas's theory of monarchy because the theory itself is so abstract. When historians attempt to present Aquinas's concept of kingship in strictly theoretical terms, the result is of little use in understanding Aquinas's suggestions in the context of thirteenth-century Europe; cf. T. Gilby, *The Political Thought of Thomas Aquinas* (Chicago 1958) 284-300.

[7] See, e.g., W. Parsons, "St. Thomas Aquinas and Popular Sovereignty," *Thought* 16 (1941) 473-492.

At any rate, Aquinas greatly influenced the French Aristotelians in their approach to the *Politics*. As much as any thirteenth-century thinker, Aquinas provided the French monarchists with a political vocabulary and some ideological weapons. He left them a three-fold legacy. First, Aquinas dignified the concept of kingship by giving philosophical proof in favor of its superiority — supported by no less an authority than Aristotle. Monarchy is the best form of government because it contains the most unity. Since monarchy is "natural," it is inherently good, irrespective of ecclesiastical sanction.[8]

Second, Aquinas gave respectability to certain functions of government. The prince leads his subjects to virtue both directly (by his laws) and indirectly (by his justice).[9] Aquinas implied that in an emergency the prince can dispense with the letter of the law, and rule uninhibited for the common good. This ill-formed idea of emergency power would later provide the basis of the monarchical theory expounded by Philip the Fair's publicists.[10]

Third, Aquinas showed how to place the king under the law. The king is subject to the law when the law is considered a "directive force" (or moral norm). But the king is above the law when it is considered a "coercive force."[11] In other words, the king is morally obliged to obey the law, but no one has the right to compel him to do so. Thus, Aquinas in effect suggested that it was possible — even desirable — for a *civitas* or *regnum* to be ruled by the best man *and* the best laws. This distinction between the directive and coercive laws was useful for French propagandists (for example, Philip the Fair's publicists) who wanted to portray their king as a dutiful servant of the law.

Although Aquinas never treated the best man-best laws question directly,[12] it seems safe to infer that for him the two terms were not mutually exclusive. In the *De regimine* Aquinas stresses the best-man tradition; in his other writings, he is more concerned with the benefits of rule by law.[13] Had he responded at length to the

---

[8] *De regimine principum* (Turin 1948) 1.3; 2.3. It is possible that Thomas's idea of kingship was influenced by St. Louis, although this has never been proved.

[9] *De regimine* 2.1-4.

[10] *Summa theologiae*, (hereafter ST) 1-2 qq. 95-97. See below, pp. 319-322.

[11] ST 1-2, 96, art. 5.

[12] In his *Commentary on the Politics*, Aquinas did not go beyond Book 3.6: the best-man-best-laws *questio* is in *Politics* 3.15. See A. O'Rahilly, "Notes on St. Thomas," *Irish Ecclesiastical Record* 30 (1927) 614-622. My own study of Aquinas's commentary has convinced me that extreme caution must be used in drawing conclusions about Aquinas's monarchical thought on the basis of this work; the few nuances which appear in Aquinas's text are minor. Aquinas states that he wants merely to explain Aristotle's thought, not his own. Hence, his commentary is a near-literal paraphrase of the *Politics* — although commentaries after Aquinas are often less literal. I find nothing in Aquinas's commentary to suggest that he favored mixed rule, or any other kind of rule. But F. E. Cranz sees a preference for mixed government; see "Aristotelianism in Medieval Political Theory: A Study of the Reception of the Politics," Ph.D. diss. (Harvard 1940) 139-141; this is otherwise an excellent dissertation. See also H. Dondaine, "Le *Super Politicum* de saint Thomas," *Revue des sciences philosophiques et théologiques* 48 (1964) 585-602; C. Martin, *The Commentaries on the Politics of Aristotle in the Late 13th and Early 14th Centuries* (Oxford 1949) chap. 2.

[13] See esp. ST 1-2, 90-97.

best-man *questio* it is perhaps likely he would have given the *cives* a larger role in legislation than contemporary French theorists would have liked.

In any case, Aquinas's kingship was unsatisfactory. Thomas's monarch was predicated upon the man of exceptional virtue. But what if the king were a child, a heretic, or a madman? To say that the best man was the *ideal* to which princes should aspire would in effect make *de facto* monarchy a second-best form of government; actual monarchy was at best an imitation of the perfect way. French theorists asked: How are royal subjects to prevent the king from lapsing into tyranny? Aquinas's reply was of no help, given the Dominican's propensity to remove constitutional restraints on the king.[14] For their propaganda, the French royalists needed a king who was strong enough to be effective, yet not so strong as to threaten privileges. They required a notion of authoritarian monarchy which was not entirely dependent on the man of heroic virtue. It was all too easy for a critic of royal policy to point out the shortcomings of any particular king. They had to appease the secular and religious clergy, nobles, and townsmen who jealously guarded their privileges. The argument that the king was below the law as a directive force might have impressed some university intellectuals, but such an idea was ill-suited to win the hearts and minds of hard-nosed prelates.

In short, the French polemicists had to neutralize the traditional charge of tyranny, while at the same time not tie their king to an impossibly high degree of moral behavior. The French sought a way to retain the Aristotelian-Thomist concept of the common good, a concept linked less to the individual who happened to be then sitting on the throne than to the institution of monarchy. Finally, Aquinas said little about royal-ecclesiastical relations.[15] He did not sharply define the king's jurisdictional rights vis-à-vis the French clergy and the pope. He left loopholes through which prelates could claim the right to intervene in the temporal and spiritual affairs of the secular *regnum*. He was not, after all, an apologist for the French monarchy, but a theologian who speculated on the abstract notion of kingship. Aquinas left it to polemicists to apply his lofty principles to specific circumstances.

EGIDIUS ROMANUS

Shortly after the death of King Philip III Egidius Romanus wrote his *De regimine principum* (ca. 1280) for the use of young Philip IV. Well schooled in Thomistic

---

[14] While Aquinas's ideal of kingship could hardly be termed absolutist, it was too authoritarian for use in French propaganda. The French had no use for the tyrannicide theories of either Aquinas or John of Salisbury, cautious though these theories might be. See M. A. and R. H. Rouse, "John of Salisbury and the Doctrine of Tyrannicide," *Speculum* 42 (1967) 693-709.

[15] While modern explanations of Aquinas's two-power theory can be clever, his two-power ideas were too general and too brief to be of use for French royalists. Whatever his two-power theory might have meant if put into practice in St. Louis's France, there seems little doubt that the tendency of Aquinas's thought is towards the trimming of clerical prerogatives in temporal matters. Contemporaries would have been struck by the extensive rights Aquinas granted the

philosophy, Egidius applied Aquinas's natural-law theories to the concept of monarchy. He appears ready to sanction the French king's steady encroachment upon local privileges. With Aquinas he defined kingship as the rule by one man of exceptional virtue for the sake of the common good.[16] The *regnum* is the best *principatus* because it is the most natural form of government, and because it brings the most peace and unity.

But, compared to Aquinas, Egidius's king is more clearly delineated, and is granted more extensive authority in temporals. To the question, "Is it better to be ruled by the best king or the best law,"[17] Egidius declares unequivocally for the best king.[18] Egidius cites Aristotle's argument on behalf of the best laws only to show the opposite: since human laws are general and imperfect, a virtuous king is needed to correct defects in the law, and to apply the law in concrete cases. The king is the *medium* between positive law and natural law. He is above positive law, but below natural law. It is better to be ruled by the best man when one is referring to positive law; it is better to be ruled by the best laws when one is referring to natural law.

With this clever shift of emphasis, Egidius here avoids Aristotle's objection that the best man can be corrupted. Egidius puts the burden of proof on the law which itself can be "corrupted," that is, the law is imperfect and too abstract. Since positive law is by definition universal, the king must have the authority to apply it to particular cases. Whereas Aquinas's "law as moral norm" could be interpreted as part of positive law, Egidius considers "law as directive norm" to be part of natural law.[19] Thus Egidius's king is more clearly above positive law.

But how to keep the king below natural law? How do subjects keep the best man from degenerating into tyranny? Egidius's answer: proper education of the monarch. By an enlightened education young princes will grow up with their gaze upon the Aristotelian ideal of the common good.[20]

---

monarch, even in spirituals (at least as pertains to "natural" virtue). See L. Boyle, "The *De regno* and the Two Powers," in *Essays in Honor of Anton Charles Pegis,* ed. J. R. O'Donnell (Toronto 1974) 737-747. It is not surprising that Thomas the Dominican would have narrowed the temporal scope of prelatial jurisdiction.

[16] See *De regimine* (Rome 1607) 1.2.12; 2.1.14; 3.1.5; 3.2.1-15, passim. See Cranz (n. 12 above) 233-253; C. Lohr, "Medieval Latin Aristotle Commentaries, Authors A-F," *Traditio* 23 (1967) 313-413, esp. 332-334.

[17] "Qualiter melius regitur civitas aut regnum, utrum melius regatur optimo rege, quam optima lege" (3.2.29). Note that Egidius says "best king," not "best man." Since the Carlyles erroneously believed that the "normal medieval tradition" was for the best laws, they mistakenly dubbed Egidius an exception who supported "absolute monarchy" (n. 1 above) 5.71. See H. Dosher, "The Concept of the Ideal Prince in French Political Thought 800-1760," Ph.D. diss. (Chapel Hill 1969) 200ff. Egidius obviously intended the king to uphold the best laws. Much of 3.2 is devoted to the need for good laws based on custom.

[18] "Melius est igitur regnum regi rege quam lege ut per legem corrigi possint legales defectus" (3.2.29).

[19] Egidius simply ignores Aquinas's subtle distinction between law as coercive force and law as moral norm. He states bluntly that the king is above positive law, with no mention of the *cives'* lack of authority to force him to obey the law. The king rules his kingdom as the living *recta ratio* which manifests natural law (3.2.29).

[20] The pedagogical intent is evident in the Mirror of Princes genre. Egidius's *De regimine* is part of this literary tradition, although this work is more pronouncedly Aristotelian. For

Egidius narrows *regimen regale* to a single dimension: royal rule (*regimen regale*) is the rule by one man who rules according to the laws he himself has made.[21] Indeed, Egidius seems to interpret Aristotle's best man-best laws *questio* as "Is it better to be ruled by the king who rules according to laws he has made, or by the king who rules according to the laws the citizens made?"[22] Thus, Egidius reduces Aristotle's famous question to a choice between two kinds of kings.

But Egidius left his French successors with three puzzles. First, he offered no guarantee that the king will not become a tyrant. A good education does not necessarily produce a good king. And what about the accident of a boy king? Surely every Christian must concede that even the best man — who of course cannot be morally perfect — is subject to base passions. Egidius made no promises that the best man, as an ideal of kingship, can be realized in practice.

Second, Egidius's king appears too powerful. In an attempt to mollify nervous subjects, Egidius assures them that the king cannot abuse his power because natural law guides the king's reason.[23] Hence, the king rules according to law, not will! But this kind of sophistry might appear great nonsense to most Frenchmen at the time. To be sure, Egidius cautions against hasty changes in customary law.[24] But he never clearly explains the king's relation to custom. Besides, Egidius permits no limitation of the royal legislative and executive functions. Monarchy works properly when the king's *intention* is correct. To meet the objection of tyranny Egidius responds with the familiar Aristotelian adage: the true king, unlike the tyrant, governs for the common good of his subjects.

Third, Egidius does not apply his theory of royal rule to church-state problems, an omission which makes his treatise curiously unrealistic.[25]

---

education, see Book 1; 3.2.1-29. Summaries of Egidius's *De regimine* are in L. Born, "The Perfect Prince: A Study in 13th- and 14th-Century Ideals," *Speculum* 3 (1928) 470-504; M. Bryne, "An Examination of the Political Theory of Giles of Rome," M. A. Thesis (St. Louis Univ. 1960); D. Bell, *L'idéal éthique de la royauté en France au moyen âge* (Geneva 1962).

[21] "Dicitur autem quis praeesse regali dominio, cum praeest secundum arbitrium et secundum leges, quas ipse instituit" (2.1.14). Egidius uses this restricted view of *regimen regale* throughout his *De regimine.* When he does mention other kinds of rule, he dismisses them as inferior to royal rule.

[22] Such an interpretation — the *questio* as referring to two types of monarchs — is consistent with Egidius's use of *regimen regale* throughout 3.2. Cf. 2.1.14. Clearly he prefers royal rule to a *regimen politicum* in which the king rules according to the laws the *cives* have made. Cf. the thirteenth-century French translation of the best-man passage in S. Molenaer, ed., *Li livres du gouvernement des rois* (New York 1899; repr. 1966) 352-55; 3.2.29 in the Rome 1607 ed. is 3.2.27 in the French version.

[23] 3.2.29, passim. If it be objected that Egidius could be expected to exaggerate kingly authority since he wrote his treatise for a king (Philip IV), I should add that a) the *De regimine* was a quasi-public form of writing, intended to be read by many, and b) the tract contains numerous limitations on royal power, however ineffectual these may be in practice.

[24] Esp. 3.2.16-31. In his discussion of the judiciary Egidius assumes that judges should be permitted a minimum amount of discretion.

[25] Egidius treats neither the king's rights in church affairs nor the church's rights in the secular kingdom. This omission is more noticeable in view of the abundant practical advice offered in his *De regimine.* While Aquinas in his *De regimine* focuses on the origin and function of kingship, the more earthly Egidius is by comparison concerned with the actual workings of the *regimen regale.*

PETER OF AUVERGNE

In his *quodlibet* on the best man-best laws Peter of Auvergne reconciles kingship and law in the formula: it is better for a *civitas* to be ruled by the best man *per se*. But men, even the most virtuous, are subject to passion. Therefore, it is better *per accidens* to be ruled by the best laws.[26]

At first reading, the above *quodlibet* would seem to stress a drawback of monarchy, namely, the king's propensity to succumb to passion. But in fact Peter of Auvergne's Commentary on the *Politics*, especially in Books 3 and 4, reveals a preference for one-man rule. Peter is particularly fascinated by Aristotle's fifth kind of constitutional king: the king of heroic virtue who rules according to his own will, and for the common good of his subjects.[27] Where he is not compelled by Aristotle's text to do otherwise, Peter assumes that *regnum* means Aristotle's absolute monarchy.[28]

Peter elaborates on Aristotle's definition of the two main classes of monarchy: a) the king rules according to laws, and performs specific duties, and b) the king preeminent in virtue rules according to his own will, and is supreme in all matters.[29] Whereas Peter's remarks on the first type — the political rule — are usually only paraphrases of Aristotle's text, his comments on the second type — absolute monarchy — are replete with clarifications and digressions.[30] Peter seems particularly struck by the immense benefits which allegedly flow from the "rule of reason," a

---

[26] Paris, Bibliothèque Nationale MS lat. 16089 (bk. 3, q.22) fol. 297rb; same *quodlibet*, with slight variations, also in Bologna, Univ. Library, MS 1625, fol. 10ra. Incipit: "Consequenter quaeritur utrum melius sit civitatem regi optimo viro vel legibus et arquitur quod legibus quia melius est eo regi civitatem . . . ."

[27] See Aquinas, *In libros politicorum expositio*, ed. R. Spiazzi (Turin 1951) 3, lectio 12, nos. 463, 486, 487, etc. Peter's commentary begins at bk. 3, lect. 7. See also G. M. Grech, ed., *The Commentary of Peter of Auvergne on Aristotle's Politics: The Inedited Part: Book III, less. I-VI* (Rome 1967). Whereas Aquinas's commentary is virtually a literal paraphrase of Aristotle's text, Peter's commentary sometimes interpolates quite freely — especially when the text concerns the topic of monarchy. In no. 323, Aristotle deals with the king as a "deum inter homines" in 4 lines; Peter's commentary (no. 463) on this brief passage runs 56 lines! See also C. Martin, "Some Medieval Commentaries on Aristotle's *Politics*," *History* 35-36 (1950-1951) 29-44.

[28] Peter's explanation of Aristotle is of course largely determined by the text he is commenting upon. The express purpose of a thirteenth-century commentary on Aristotle was to clarify the intention of Aristotle. Thus the historian can never be certain which, if any, of Peter's comments reflect the mind of Peter himself. It seems nevertheless safe to argue that those passages in Peter which deviate sharply from Aristotle's text mirror, at least in a general way, the convictions of the commentator.

[29] 3, lect. 14.

[30] I have found a large number of "monarchical" passages in Peter's commentary which are not found in Aristotle. Examples: Peter digresses to show why law is deficient in particulars, and thus must be directed by a prudent *optimus vir* (no. 490); Peter makes rule by law merely rule *per accidens* in the absence of a great man (nos. 507-520) — a misreading of Aristotle's text; Peter refers to *cives* as if they were royal subjects (no. 464, passim). Peter twists Aristotle's argument in favor of ostracizing the great man into an argument for having the great man remain in the *civitas*, provided he rule for the common good (no. 471).

situation best achieved when a man of exceptional virtue and political ability governs the state without restriction.[31]

When Peter comments on the advantages of the rule of the many, he minimizes the force of Aristotle's evident preference for this kind of rule. Peter implies that the rule of the many is better than the rule of one man only when the citizens are equal in virtue and political ability.[32] Thus, even in Aristotle's most "constitutional" passages, Peter implies that rule by law is a second-best solution for *cives* (equal in virtue) who cannot find the *optimus vir*.[33] The best kind of state is one in which the man of heroic virtue rules, whether or not the *cives* are equal in virtue. While Aristotle stresses the difficulty of locating and then tolerating the heroic man, Peter dwells on the advantages for the *cives,* should they find such an exceptional man. If the best man does become corrupt, it is the *cives'* fault for permitting this to happen. If the *cives* are so misguided as to expel the great man from the *civitas,* it is their misfortune, not his. Peter's *rex* is not a *civis,* and, therefore, is not bound by the laws — laws which are made only for the *cives.* The addition of a superman is usually an improvement on the *civitas* in which the many already rule — a distortion of Aristotle's own notion of the rule of the many.

Yet despite Peter of Auvergne's tendency to accept monarchical ideals, he does not resolve the dilemmas faced by Egidius Romanus. First, Peter offers no constitutional or legal way to prevent the king from lapsing into tyranny. Indeed, it seems probable that he *will* become a tyrant, given man's propensity to *passio.* Peter ignores any practical difficulties which may arise when the *cives* attempt to install the best man as king. In the best-man passages Peter does not even mention the necessity of a proper education for the monarch.

Second, Peter's ruler is nearly absolute. The king is "like a god" and released from the law. Indeed, the king is an *alternative* to rule by law. The only difference between the *rex* and the tyrant is that the former is virtuous and rules for the common good, while the latter is selfish and rules for his private good. Even more than Egidius, Peter makes the legitimacy of the monarchy depend on the virtue of the monarch. Peter upholds the *optimus vir* because the latter can best apply the universal norms contained in the law to concrete circumstances. Peter presents an impossible situation: the best form of government is the rule of the man of extraordinary virtue; but virtuous citizens will not tolerate one so superior to them.[34]

---

[31] 3, lect. 15, nos. 499, 513, 539.

[32] 3, lect. 15, nos. 509, 511, 515, 517, 518, 519, 520, 522.

[33] Nos. 520, 522, 525. Whereas Aristotle uses the argument for equality among the *cives* as a case against monarchy, Peter cleverly makes the same argument work in *favor* of monarchy. While Peter agrees with Aristotle that the absolute king should not rule equals, he adds that the unequal (i.e., higher in virtue and dignity) ruler would benefit the *cives.* If the *cives* are immoral they especially need a good leader. If they are virtuous they will probably find such a leader intolerable, and throw him out. Cranz (n. 12 above) 157 has Peter prefer limited monarchy in nos. 499, 525. But it seems to me that these passages, if anything, reveal Peter's prejudice for *principatus regalis.* Peter does not equate royal with despotic rule. Subjects in a royal rule, moreover, are *not* less virtuous than *cives* in a political rule. These passages must be read in context.

[34] The historian can never be sure which remarks of Peter reflect his own thinking. Peter presents no theory of monarchy, and his comments on monarchy and law contain inconsis-

Third, Peter offers no guidelines for relations between the temporal and spiritual powers. He does not say if the superman can intervene in church temporals, if the clergy can define virtue and the ends of the state, if the church can and should anoint the god-like man.

It should not be forgotten, however, that Peter's infatuation with the *optimus vir* does not lead to an abandonment of the principle that all persons (the ruler included) should obey the laws — even if only *per accidens*. Further, many citizens should *per accidens* participate in the legislative and executive functions of government; since most *cives* will not be so fortunate as to have the best man, they must settle for some kind of self-government.

Peter's contribution to the Aristotelian tradition of monarchy is his implication that monarchy is not necessarily tied to positive law and the citizenry. He has so exalted the concept of kingship — without reference to ecclesiastical checks — that any lessening of royal power would seem almost to destroy monarchy, and to deprive the people of the benefits which flow from one-man rule. Yet from the view of French royal propagandists, Peter of Auvergne's notion of kingship was of limited value because it was too abstract and speculative.

Close textual analysis of Peter's *quodlibet* and Commentary does not necessarily suggest that he had any first-hand acquaintance with Egidius's *De regimine principum* or Aquinas's political works. What is more significant historically than the precise textual transmissions of Aristotelian ideas is that Peter found these strongly monarchist concepts so attractive. Writing at about the same time as Egidius, Peter reflects the growing sentiment in favor of the policies of Louis IX and his successors. Louis's favoritism towards the friars notwithstanding, the climate of opinion at the University of Paris probably supported Louis IX's propensity to arbitrate disputes. Although Peter never alludes to contemporary events, he is one of numerous writers at the time who want to show that Saint Louis is not the anachronistic boor his critics make him out to be. It may well be that Peter wanted to present Louis as a thoroughly modern ruler in step with the latest Aristotelian fashions.

QUODLIBETA LITERATURE

Masters in the Paris faculties of philosophy and theology composed *questiones* on the *Politics* of Aristotle. Their solutions to the best man-best laws *quodlibet* are remarkably similar. The typical *determinatio* is: it is better to be ruled by the best man *per se*; but it is better to be ruled by the best laws *per accidens*. Ideally, the man of

---

tencies. Peter's digressions on absolute monarchy seem to have an Averroistic tone; he seems fascinated with the logic of his arguments, no matter how impractical they might be in thirteenth-century France. The philosophical, not political, advantages of kingship impressed Peter, particularly the possibility of the rule of universal reason. Whereas Egidius stressed the royal function (rule according to the common good), Peter stressed the king's personal virtue. But even though Peter's kingship is static and utopian, the point is that his experimentation with Aristotle's "absolutist" texts could easily encourage other thinkers to explore further the "monarchical" possibilities in the *Politics*.

preeminent goodness is effective in ensuring the rule of virtue, for his prudence can adapt reason to particular cases. But man (unlike laws which are universal and without passion) has appetite. Therefore, his judicial decisions are apt to be swayed by his emotions. Hence, in practice, it is better for the state to be ruled by the best laws *per accidens.*[35]

In these *quodlibeta, per se* might be translated "in itself." The more elusive *per accidens* might be rendered "because of other consequences"[36] or "indirectly." Included in this use of *per accidens* is also implied "in practice," that is, rule by the best laws is more feasible given the actual state of human affairs. In the *quodlibeta* the distinction between king and law is clearer than it is in Aquinas or Egidius. Similar to Peter of Auvergne, the *quodlibeta* present the *questio* primarily as a choice between king or law.[37] This readiness to accept a dualist answer – king *per se,* laws *per accidens* – may reflect an Averroist influence. The masters seem unconcerned with the usual Thomist attempts to make positive law conform to divine-natural law. They appear lukewarm to positive law as a possible guide for the ruler's actions. Their emphasis on the necessity for a prudent ruler to apply law to particular cases could easily lead to the notion of a king unrestrained by positive law.

[35] This (paraphrased) solution is virtually the same in every *quodlibet* that I have found to date. Typical incipit: "Utrum magis expediat civitatem regi optimo viro vel legibus," or some variant. *Quodlibeta* I have seen (authors are anonymous, unless specified otherwise): Milan, Bibl. Ambros., MS A 100 Inf., fol. 31 vb; Vatican MS lat. 982, fols. 110vb-111ra; Vat. MS lat. 2173, fol. 38ra-b (virtually the same as Vat. MS lat. 832, fols. 31vb-32ra); Paris, B.N. MS lat. 16089, fol. 75v (John Vath), and fol. 216rb-va (Egidius of Orleans); B.N. MS lat. 15106 (fol. 36ra-b); Bordeaux, MS 167, fol. 217ra-b (James of Viterbo; my microfilm copy of this *quodlibet* is illegible; listed in Glorieux, *Quodlibétique* [see below] 2.147); Peter of Auvergne's *quodlibet* n. 26 above); cf. Buridan's less monarchist solutions, *Quaestiones Buridani super octo Politicorum Aristotelis* (Paris 1530) bk. 3, q.4, fols. 34rb-35ra. Four of the above *quodlibeta* are printed in Cranz (n. 12 above) 332-347. It would be instructive for some industrious scholar to examine all the related *quodlibeta* (e.g., rule by many or one, hereditary or elective kingship, etc.). Some related *quodlibeta* include: Todi MS 98, fols. 26ra-29va; Vat. MS lat. 1086, fols. 217-220v; Tortosa, Bibl. capit. MS 244; Padua, Antoniana MS 662, fols. 187-209. Some *optimus vir* and related *quodlibeta* are listed in P. Glorieux, *La littérature quodlibétique de 1260 à 1320* (Paris 1925, 1935); *La faculté des arts et ses maîtres au XIIIe siècle* (Paris 1971). I am grateful to Dr. C. J. Ermatinger, Vatican Microfilm Librarian at St. Louis University, for his kind assistance during my visit to the Vatican Film Library in 1974. I also thank Fr. L. J. Daly of St. Louis University for his valuable suggestions on interpreting Aristotelian commentaries. Particularly helpful was Fr. Daly's explanation of the commentators' ahistorical approach to Aristotle. Should any reader know of best man-best laws *quodlibeta* other than the ones mentioned above, I would appreciate hearing about them.

[36] See L. J. Daly, "Medieval and Renaissance Commentaries on the *Politics* of Aristotle," *Duquesne Review* 13 (1968) 41-55, esp. 46.

[37] But the best man *per se*-best laws *per accidens* resolution does not necessarily mean that the presence of the best man precludes the rule of the best laws, and vice versa. Indeed, the *quodlibeta* authors could argue that they had discovered a way to reconcile king and law with their formula *per accidens.* At any rate, the *quodlibeta* offer no hint of how such a contrived solution might work in political reality. On the face of it, the *per se-per accidens* scheme – not found in this sense in Aquinas or Egidius – makes king and law harder to synthesize. It is not known if the *quodlibeta* represent an "Averroist" solution. But see Pierre Dubois's comment on Siger of Brabant in C. Langlois, ed., *De recuperatione* (Paris 1891) 121 chap. 132; in order to justify his rash proposals against the church Dubois not surprisingly appeals to the best laws. Cf. Marsilius of Padua, *Defensor pacis,* trans. A. Gewirth (New York 1956), discourse 1, chap. 11.

Basically the kingship implied in the solutions of the *quodlibeta* does not differ from the kingship of Aquinas and Egidius. The main point here is that the *quodlibeta* authors accept the ideal of kingship *per se*. But the masters have trapped French royalist writers into a logical corner. With their *per se-per accidens* solution it would seem that they have at last made it impossible to combine the best man with the best laws.

First, the *quodlibeta* authors appear to have given up hope in trying — philosophically — to prevent the good prince from falling into tyranny. They assume that tyranny will inevitably result from one-man rule.

Second, the sole justification for monarchy is the presence of the heroic man on the throne. There is little attempt to rationalize the idea of kingship; rather, the masters focus on the advantages of having a philosopher king.

Third, the ideal of kingship is diluted by the admission that, in practice, men must be ruled by the best laws. No French royalist could admit, at least in public, that kingship is something to be tolerated because of man's propensity to corruption. Moreover, no one could accept an ideal of kingship which might appear to exclude the rule of law.

Fourth, this philosophical solution is abstruse, and unrelated to the king's actual political problems in France. Propagandistically speaking, the solution is worthless.

To be fair to the professors, it must be noted that the *quodlibeta* were probably not propaganda intended for the king's use. The *questiones* usually read more like playful mental exercises. The nature of the *questio* genre precludes hard conclusions about the sincerity of the authors' solutions, and about the impact of their ideas on public opinion and the policies of the royal court. The historical significance of the *per se-per accidens* view of kingship lies in the manner in which the previous ideas of *regimen regale* were narrowed and simplified. The *quodlibeta* portray a crude notion of authoritarian kingship. 'Tis a pity, they seem to say, that we mortals cannot be blessed with the Perfect Prince. The striking similarity of their theories of kingship, at least in this *questio,* reveals how receptive the Paris philosophers were to authoritarian rule and, one may presume, to the actual policies of Louis IX and Philip III.

JOHN OF PARIS

The publicists of King Philip the Fair continued to develop a monarchical ideology. Of these royal apologists only John of Paris relied heavily on Aristotle for his theory of kingship, and made extensive use of *regimen regale*.[38]

Influenced by Aquinas, John of Paris attempted to apply Aristotelian ideas of monarchy to the relations between the temporal and spiritual powers. In the process

---

[38] Historians may have overstated the Aristotelian element in the other publicist writings. See T. Renna, "Kingship in the *Disputatio inter clericum et militem,*" *Speculum* 48 (1973) 675-693. (Even after Philip the Fair, Aristotle's influence on fourteenth-century French political ideas was minimal.) While John of Paris never stated the best laws-best man *questio* as such, it will be seen that his extensive use of the Aristotelian king and the *per se-per accidens* formula makes his solution directly applicable to the problem posed by the *questio.*

of working out his two-power theory John of Paris resolved the dilemmas found in Aquinas, Egidius Romanus, Peter of Auvergne, and the *quodlibeta.* By changing the perspective of the problem John instructed the French king on how to exploit Aristotelianism effectively to the needs of the crown. Far from treating the idea of kingship as an abstract intellectual problem, John summoned Aristotelian concepts of monarchy to serve a specific practical end: the deposition of Boniface VIII.

John's major contribution to the evolution of kingship was to liberate the king from the demands of exceptional virtue — a remarkable achievement in view of Aristotle's stress on the monarch's moral qualities. No longer is the king defined entirely in terms of his claim to preeminent goodness. John felt no need to defend the personal virtue of Philip the Fair. Instead, the Dominican theologian moved the discussion from the king's virtue to four other areas.

First, John focuses on the realm, not on the king as such.[39] John builds his monarchical ideal upon the allegedly urgent need to defend the kingdom. He simply assumes that the king will respond quickly and effectively to guard the French people and France from papal encroachments. Moreover, the realm is itself holy, a sort of *corpus mysticum.* France is the cradle of the Christian priesthood and the true faith. Thus, John changes the emphasis from the personal characteristics of the king to the characteristics of the thing to be defended. John's fervent national sentiment makes the reader feel treasonous if he does not rush to the defense of sweet France. No time to quibble about Philip the Fair's moral habits. John is less concerned about what the king *is,* than he is about what the king *does.* After taking the king's virtue for granted, John elaborates on why and how the endangered realm is to be protected.

Second, John sanctifies the royal family more than any given king. Since God has blessed the Capetian dynasty, there is no need to justify the holiness of one of its members, Philip the Fair.[40] John invokes Saint Louis as proof of the special grace God has granted the Capetians.

Third, John says less about the nature of kingship than about the problem the king has to solve. John defines kingship in terms of how best to depose a useless pope.[41] He in effect argues that royal rule is the best kind of rule because it is the most effective in purging evil from the church. In setting up his ecclesiology and a

---

[39] Much of what follows is from T. Renna, "The *Populus* in John of Paris' Theory of Monarchy," *Tijdschrift voor Rechtsgeschiedenis* 42 (1974) 243-268. This stress on the realm to be defended is typical of Philip the Fair's publicists. See T. Renna, "Royalist Political Thought in France 1285-1303," Ph.D diss. (Brown Univ. 1970). While Aquinas and Egidius were also aware of the defense of the realm argument, it is nowhere so pronounced as it is in John of Paris.

[40] Professor Joseph R. Strayer kindly pointed this out to me in a private conversation in 1974. I appreciate his valuable suggestion. See Strayer, "France: The Holy Land . . .," in *Action and Conviction in Early Modern Europe* ed. T. Rabb and J. Seigel (Princeton 1969) 3-16, and *idem*, "Defense of the Realm and Royal Power in France," *Studi di onore di Gino Luzzato* 1 (Milan 1949) 289-296. Cf. F. Bleienstein, ed., *Johannes Quidort von Paris* [critical ed. of *De potestate*] (Stuttgart 1969) chaps. 5, 21, 22. Further references in Renna, "John of Paris."

[41] See Renna, "John of Paris" 253-266. For summaries of John of Paris's complex two-power theory, see the references there in nn. 3, 4, 5.

legal structure which can remove a pope, John is forced to define the temporal power because his two-power theory rests on a series of parallels between the two powers. Thus John analyzes the legal mechanism within which the secular prince operates. For John, the abstract *questio,* whether it is better to be ruled by the best laws or the best man, becomes in effect: "It is better to be ruled by a *regimen regale* because this form of government is most compatible with the proper legal mechanism which governs (or should govern) relations between the two powers."

Fourth, John describes kingship primarily in terms of its emergency powers.[42] With this stress on the practical means with which a ruler deals with a temporary emergency, the issue of the king's personal virtue becomes irrelevant. The *rex,* who is normally bound by customary law, is temporarily released from the restraints of positive law in order that he can rectify the immediate disorder in either the realm or the church. In this instance the king acts as God's avenger. He is "defending" himself and his people from the unlawful intervention of a bad pope.

By this judicious use of the concept of casual jurisdiction John has retained the most monarchist tendencies of Aristotle's *Politics.* Within the idea of the royal extraordinary authority John combines the concepts of a) the king acting for the common good, b) *regimen regale* as the rule of one man acting according to his own will or according to the laws he himself has made, c) the rule of one man superior to all others in virtue, and d) the prince who is above positive law. John integrates these four aspects of kingship into his royal casual *potestas.*

John's theory of monarchy is well suited for propaganda. In normal circumstances the king must obey customary law. But he must at times assume the roles of *dominus* and intercessor in spiritual affairs whenever special conditions arise (for example, the realm is attacked, or the pope is a heretic). During such unusual occasions the ruler acts in the interest of the common good. When the king acts in his capacity as the "best man," John would have us believe he is not acting arbitrarily; rather, he is simply being carried along by a complex legal and moral structure which maintains harmony between the two powers.

John's *De potestate* was the most formidable tract from the royalist side during the controversy with Pope Boniface VIII because its two-power theory appeared the most even-handed. Instead of focusing on the personal character of either Boniface or Philip, he offered an ecclesiology in which the pope seemed to possess as much power as the king.[43] Just as the pope is circumscribed by other churchmen (the

---

[42] There is a parallel between John's functionary approach to kingship and his nonrealist doctrine of the Eucharist. He stresses the immediate practical effect of royal power, not the "divine" nature of the kingly office. So too, John's impanation theory of the Eucharist can be easily adapted to the clergy's pressing pastoral concerns. See J. H. Martin, "The Eucharistic Treatise of John Quidort of Paris," *Viator* 6 (1975) 195-240.

[43] If, however, John's two-power theory were to be put into practice in the Europe of 1302, the king's authority would have been considerably greater than that of the pope. Thus the pope's alleged right to induce the French *populus* to overthrow Philip the Fair was in fact impossible to exercise. So, too, the alleged checks the *populus* would have imposed on the king would be illusory in practice. See Renna, "John of Paris" (n. 39 above) 253-257, 264-268.

cardinals, or the bishops acting collectively), so too the king is supposedly curbed by his barons and *populus.*

Unlike the theories of previous Aristotelian writers, John's kingship is closely related to *de facto* political conditions.[44] John links his doctrine to war, papal intervention in French affairs, royal interference in the temporals and spirituals of the clergy. He accepts the Thomist-Aristotelian concept of a natural-law monarchy which does not derive its authority directly from the clergy; thus, he gives the secular realm its own reason for being, and a degree of autonomy from church authority. But John goes beyond this natural-law principle, and demonstrates how the naturalist state actually functions in the context of the earthly church. John of Paris synthesized the Aristotelian, natural-law monarchy with the hierarchical church. A Christian *regimen regale* was incorporated into an "Aristotelian" ecclesiology. Where Aquinas is universalist and abstract in his two-power theory, John is particular and concrete. John was not a commentator on Aquinas in the way the latter was a commentator on Aristotle. John reveals nothing of Peter of Auvergne's half-playful tendency to follow an argument to see where it will lead. The Dominican of Paris is a serious pragmatist who rummaged Aquinas's writings in search for usable texts.

Nowhere does John of Paris cite explicitly the *per se-per accidens* solution of Peter of Auvergne and the *quodlibeta.* Instead, John applies the *per se-per accidens* formula to his ecclesiological doctrine of direct and indirect powers.[45] In one passage, however, John does allude to the *regimen regale* as the best form of government *per se* – provided this government is not debased.[46] In the course of defending *regimen regale* as acceptable to God, John digresses into an analysis of mixed government which, he claims, was well suited to the Jews in their corrupted state. John implies that the Christian *regimen regale,* that is, modern France, is the natural completion of the earlier primitive government of the Jews.[47]

While John agrees that royal rule is the best form of government *per se,* his emphasis in this passage is different from that of Peter of Auvergne and the *quodlibeta.* First, Peter implied that a strong leader was required when the people

[44] The rhetorical form of John's *De potestate* is, to be sure, abstract and impersonal. He makes no overt reference to the Boniface VIII-Philip the Fair dispute; unlike Nogaret, he is not given to *ad hominem* attacks on Boniface. But his arguments bear so closely on the events of 1296-1302 that virtually every modern critic of the treatise has perceived it as a defense of Philip's side. Indeed, his entire two-power theory aims directly at the need to remove an erring pope. John's doctrine of secular monarchy is purposefully brief so as not to distract from his explanation of how kings act against the spiritual power. In Chapter 1 of his tract John paraphrases and simplifies Aquinas's description of kingship – carefully omitting the latter's reservations about overly strong kings. John says nothing about the psychological theories advanced in the *quodlibeta.*

[45] E.g., when a king commits a temporal offense, the barons can proceed directly against him. If they cannot correct the king, the barons may call in the church for assistance. The pope, as the church's representative, would in this case be acting *per accidens.* See Bleienstein (n. 40 above) 139. I should point out, however, that John of Paris's use of *per se* and *per accidens* throughout this discussion (chap. 13) is loose and inconsistent.

[46] Bleienstein (n. 40 above) 174f.

[47] See Renna, "John of Paris" (n. 39 above) 258-261.

were corrupt; therefore, a virtuous people presumably required a limited or even weak ruler. But John suggests that a limited ruler is needed when the subjects are corrupt;[48] if John were to be logically consistent, he would have to admit that a strong king is best when the people are virtuous!

Second, John does not say that the best man cannot be found. Nor does he say that the rule of the best man — if such a man is discovered, and then made king — will inevitably degenerate into tyranny. When John does admit that "perfect virtue is to be found in few men," he quickly adds, "particularly of that people, for the Jews were cruel and given to avarice, the very vices with which tyranny operates."[49] John shifts the burden of guilt (that is, the responsibility for permitting tyranny) to the people, and away from the ruler! When John's remarks on the best man are compared with the best-man solutions of the *quodlibeta* tradition, it becomes clear that John was determined to avoid the traditional solution (namely, that the best man will soon become corrupt). John wants to exploit the *quodlibeta* (royal rule is the best form of rule *per se*), but without the *quodlibeta* qualifications (the best man will succumb to passion). John simply leaves open the possibility of the appearance of a man of heroic virtue. He makes no mention of the need for education to ensure that the ruler will become and remain virtuous.

Third, John in this passage assumes that the king in a *regimen regale* is *ipso facto* the man of exceptional virtue. Such an assumption about royal rule is in fact consistent with John's use of this kind of rule throughout his treatise. In Chapter 1 John explains that *regimen regale* is indeed the best form of government. He takes it for granted that royal rule is perfectly suited for the kingdom of France.

Fourth, John does not mention the best laws in this passage. The only place in his tract where he discusses the rule of laws is in his definition of political rule.[50] But even here he makes no judgment as to the merit of political rule. Nor does he note its relevance for France.

But despite John's slight change of emphasis in his treatment of kingship, he does not break with the tradition established by his Aristotelian predecessors. While he certainly takes liberties with passages from Aquinas, John's idea of monarchy can be called Thomistic. What marks John's treatise is the practicality of his approach to royal rule. While Aquinas, Egidius, Peter, and the Paris masters experimented with an Aristotelian theory of kingship, only John of Paris developed a two-power theory which was designed for immediate application.

After the *De potestate*, no king need be anxious about the dissemination of current Aristotelian ideas about *cives*, natural-law communities, and rule by law. John of Paris wrote not for Boniface's allies, but for King Philip's supporters, both lay and cleric, who needed their consciences reassured. It was comforting to know

[48] Such a claim is in harmony with John of Paris's emphasis on the institution of monarchy, and not on the necessity for the king to be virtuous.

[49] Bleienstein (n. 40 above) 175. The translation of this passage is that of J. A. Watt (John of Paris, *On Royal and Papal Power* [Toronto 1971] 207).

[50] Bleienstein (n. 40 above) 161. In this passage John may have borrowed his definition of *regimen regale* from Egidius (2.1.14). See Renna, "John of Paris" (n. 39 above) 257-258.

that the Philosopher was on the royalist side. Those familiar with the work of John of Paris need not fear the rebuke: "Thou art not a Christian. Thou art an Aristotelian." For the historian of French politics the question of John of Paris's dependence on available Aristotelian-inspired texts is largely irrelevant. More to the point than the exact method of the dissemination of Aristotelian ideas are his responses to immediate crises in the French and Roman churches. John perceived Aristotelian concepts of kingship more through the eyes of Nogaret than of Aquinas. But whereas Nogaret the royal hatchetman saw in Aristotle only a call to quick political action, John the theologian-pastor saw a rationalization for a reformed papacy and a spiritualized French clergy.

The tendency among Aristotelian-inspired theorists in France, 1260-1303, was towards authoritarian monarchy. They knew nothing of "popularist" ideas in the *Politics*. Indeed, these writers enthusiastically embraced Aristotle's best man in order to strengthen royal power. In their search for a vigorous leader, they were attracted to the Aristotelian idea of the common good which seemed to justify a more centralized form of monarchical government. Royalists welcomed Aristotle's notions of the natural political community, citizen, and the law.

While the French at first used Aristotle to support further curtailments of local privilege, some Italians came to see in the *Politics* ways of increasing (civic) privilege vis-à-vis emperors and bishops. Historians should admit that Aristotle's impact on Western political thought from the thirteenth to the eighteenth centuries has been to reinforce *both* the "absolutist" and the "democratic" traditions. In late thirteenth-century France a variety of monarchical ideas interacted in subtle and complex ways. For French thinkers, there was no more a single "Aristotelian" view of monarchy than there was a single "Romanist" one. The habit of classifying political ideas as Aristotelian, civilian, or whatever, is modern, not medieval.

Department of History
Saginaw Valley State College
University Center, Michigan 48710, U.S.A.

RELIGIOUS CAREERS AND RELIGIOUS DEVOTION IN THIRTEENTH-CENTURY METZ

•

by Charles McCurry

The fervent spirituality associated with the mendicant orders is only one aspect of religion in medieval towns. Established institutions which experienced virtually no growth often changed to reflect the development of urban life in the thirteenth century. Urban growth, after all, took place in several spheres, including the religious; both devotion and access by the ambitious to established institutions played a role. The institutions created by past centuries' piety, as well as those created by urban piety in the thirteenth century, provided hundreds of places for those devoting their lives to religion. This paper considers the changes in the number and composition of certain churches during the century of Metz's greatest growth.

Describing spiritual devotion is far more difficult than counting institutions and analyzing memberships, even from the spotty surviving references. The information which is available concerns virtually only the oligarchy — those eligible to vote and to hold public office by their membership in one of the vaguely familial groupings in Metz known as *paraiges*, which took more definite form during the thirteenth and fourteenth centuries. The terms "elite" and "oligarchy", when used in this paper, refer to the members of the five *paraiges* and the notables of the *Commun*, which came to form a sixth *paraige* after 1300. In this period the *paraiges* were fairly accessible to newcomers, who could gain membership by marriage; the children of such marriages naturally inherited their mother's status. The term "bourgeois" is used in a general sense, referring to the citizens in general, including the elite as well as prosperous non-members and the rest of the population.

The urban society that is the object of this research left no written records directly expressing the citizens' spirituality; we can only make deductions from the institutions which their piety founded or favored. Surviving written evidence is virtually all business records, concerned in one way or another with questions of money: in the case of religious institutions, income, privileges, donations and the obligation of commemoration thereby imposed on them. Lists of donors and personnel do, however, illustrate certain aspects of urban religious culture.

An earlier version of this paper was presented at the annual meeting of the American Historical Association, Washington, D.C., December 1976.

I

Metz in the thirteenth century shared the general growth of the European economy.[1]
Long an important episcopal city, its commercial and financial influence extended
over a large region. Its citizens were never important figures in long-distance trade
but grew rich in regional trade, domination of the countryside, and the perilous
business of financing the local nobility. In Metz as in other cities in the western part
of the empire, people of such economic consequence were unlikely to remain
content with political subordination to their lord, the bishop. The citizens made
urban political institutions as bourgeois as the economy, having won effective
independence from the bishop in 1232.

Ecclesiastical institutions in the early thirteenth century were decidedly un-
bourgeois. The rural aristocracy provided their major support and most of their
members.[2] The cathedral chapter included fifty-eight canons; only five bourgeois
canons are known up to 1215, and their families were linked with the bishop's
familia or vassals. Similarly, bourgeois were only a small fraction of the benefactors
of those same churches. Nothing can be said about the citizens' spirituality as shown
in their involvement in the twenty-six parish churches, for which virtually no sources
survive from the thirteenth century. Citizens who sought religious expression in some
more monumental institution than a parish church could turn to institutions whose
public was the rural aristocracy. Urban culture was not yet developed enough to have
its own institutions. Given the improvement in the citizens' political and economic
standing in relation to the regional elite, it was to be expected that their weight
would come to be felt in existing religious institutions which were in or near the city.
By the same token, most of the enormous increase in the numbers of religious in
twelfth-century Europe had occurred in the countryside. The turn of the cities came
in the thirteenth century, when urban ecclesiastical society developed, creating new
institutions which were added to the citizens' domain.

Urban society expressed its formal devotion in two spheres. On the one hand, the
elite gradually acquired a position of dominance or importance in nearly all the old
chapters and abbeys of the city. On the other hand, members of the same elite, as
well as lesser citizens, flocked both to the mendicant foundations and to enthusiastic
groups whose bond was a common fervor, rather than a rule.

[1] The standard study of medieval Metz is Jean Schneider, *La ville de Metz aux XIIIe et XIVe
siècles* (Nancy 1950). Much of the material on which this paper is based is studied in greater
detail in Charles McCurry, "Bourgeois Society and Religion in Medieval Metz, ca. 1200-1378,"
Ph.D. diss. (Yale University 1978).
[2] Michel Parisse, *La noblesse lorraine*, 2 vols. (Paris 1976) is an important study and a rich
mine of information. M. Parisse describes a number of relationships between the urban and rural
elites, relationships which were particularly important in allowing bourgeois into the cathedral
chapter. Despite their occasional family ties, however, the two elites had more points of
difference than of similarity. The distinctive urban qualities of Metz's oligarchy were not
submerged in the ties with the vassals of neighboring princes, which after all had the function
(among others) of emphasizing the high standing of members of the city's oligarchy.

The significance of bourgeois memberships in older institutions is many-sided. On the most straightforward level, large numbers of the oligarchy adopted a religious vocation which had not previously attracted many of them. There may have been a growing number of children, beyond the elite's need for successors, who needed to be given careers. But genealogical studies to support such a view are lacking. Or simply in terms of who dominated society, the elite of the townspeople, as befitted a group whose regional importance had increased enormously, were sharing one more part of the wealth, that held by the Church. It is the latter view which the available evidence best supports. The names of bourgeois ecclesiastics are largely the names of the small group of families eligible to hold office. The coincidence of political power and access to wealthy, established institutions is clear. But there was no quid pro quo: The traditional churches failed to attract large gifts from the townspeople. The role of those churches was to be a reward for the powerful.

The rate of bourgeois access can best be demonstrated in the case of the cathedral, where family names were used fairly often from the early thirteenth century on. In the Benedictine monasteries, family names become common only toward the end of the century, when bourgeois membership was already considerable. Of eleven bourgeois who are mentioned as cathedral canons between 1215 and 1270, ten were related to mayors; five of those ten in fact were sons of mayors.[3] The eleventh belonged to a family of Lombards who had married into the city's office-holding elite. Clearly, then, only the most powerful urban families had access to the cathedral chapter in the years before 1270. The situation is reflected in papal provisions made during the period. In a flurry of provisions by Innocent IV, sons of bourgeois were provided not to the cathedral but to the chapter of Saint Sauveur, to which bourgeois gained access much more easily.[4] In fact, by 1271, when virtually only the relatives of mayors could become cathedral canons, Saint Sauveur's chapter of nineteen canons was overwhelmingly bourgeois, including a preponderance of canons from *paraige* families and a sprinkling of lesser families.[5]

By the end of the thirteenth century, the oligarchy were approaching the peak of their influence in the chapters and abbeys. The dean and two others of the eight dignitaries of the cathedral chapter were bourgeois, as were forty percent of the canons as a whole. The Benedictine monasteries may have been even more heavily bourgeois; toward the end of the century the abbot of Saint Vincent and most of the monks belonged to urban families. Detailed information about the monks is available only in the case of Saint Vincent, and only because of a necrology on a flyleaf of a Berlin manuscript.[6] Sources for the history of individuals in thirteenth-century Metz

---

[3] By "mayor," understand *maître échevin*, the chief magistrate of the city, elected for a one-year term by six ecclesiastical electors; in 1300 the electors were required henceforth to choose among candidates of each *paraige* and the *Commun* in rotation (Schneider 149-152).

[4] E. Berger, *Les registres d'Innocent IV*, 4 vols., Bibliothèque des Écoles françaises d'Athènes et de Rome, ser. 2, 1 (Paris 1884-1921) nos. 1677, 1678, 1682, 1683.

[5] The canons of Saint-Sauveur in 1271 are listed in Paris, Bibliothèque Nationale (hereafter abbreviated BN) MS lat. 10029, fol. 56.

[6] Berlin, Deutsche Staatsbibliothek Phillipps MS 1655, fol. 1.

are very poor, especially for clerics. (The fourteenth-century sources are much richer, given the love of wordiness and litigation, involvement of the record-minded papacy, and the monk's acquisition of personal incomes.)

The obvious question is what such a change in membership meant. The concern of this paper is with memberships as rewards to bourgeois achievers and with one particular achievement, that is, inclusion of a large and discrete social institution — the Church — in their hegemony. There is little information on the reaction of the rural nobility, and one cannot say whether the churches' state of near-total decay in the fourteenth century was due to the citizens' dominance. The internal evolution of the city's old churches is hard to assess; intellectual eminence was long gone, and bourgeois membership did not bring any infusion of new capital. As for the relations of the churches with the city government, there were two conflicts during the twilight of episcopal rule, in 1209 and 1227.[7] Thereafter all was generally peaceful until the fourteenth century, when concern in the face of a faltering, then crumbling economy turned the city's attention to ecclesiastical wealth and its uses.

Traditional forms of religious associations, then, did attract large numbers of citizens. The religious nature of such vocations can be assumed by definition only; more subtle levels and cases are elusive. Fervor, however, certainly cannot be assumed.

II

The situation which I have just described does not exemplify religious fervor, but that phenomenon was indeed evident in Metz — first in heretical, then in mendicant circles. The city is a good example both of the results of that spirituality and of its later subdued development. The sources, again, allow a description only of institutions created by the spirituality, not of individual expressions of piety.

The earliest known example of popular religious activity was a spectacular one. Waldensian preachers attracted a fervent following in 1199, and the bishop was stymied by the opposition of powerful citizens. A chronicler attributed their opposition not to piety but to anger against the bishop, who had forbidden the interment of a usurer in hallowed ground. Known only from chronicles and an exchange of letters between the bishop and Innocent III, the incident apparently involved a substantial sympathetic audience.[8] But such dissent from traditional ecclesiastical society was eventually channeled into orthodox forms, for heresy — social or religious — was not a characteristic of medieval Metz.

Those orthodox forms were, of course, the mendicant alternative to traditional religion, which appealed to a large bloc of citizens. A Dominican house was established by 1221, when a former mayor undertook to build a church which was not

[7] Schneider (n. 1 above) 106, 33.

[8] The incident, often discussed, is treated in detail by G. Voigt, "Bischof Bertram von Metz 1180-1212 (Fortsetzung)", *Jahrbuch der Gesellschaft für lothringische Geschichte und Altertumskunde* 5.1 (1893) 51-55.

completed, however, until a final fund drive in the 1280s. Two of the founder's sons joined the order, and he as well as another son (a mayor) and other leading citizens were buried there. The widow of an important banker built a more modest church for the Franciscans around 1235. These two were the only mendicant foundations in the first half of the century, and both were closely linked to the city's elite, receiving members and donations, and giving spiritual aid which included, by the end of the century, serving as testamentary executors and, as their enemies sometimes successfully argued, winking at usurers.[9]

The great expansion of religious activity came in the third quarter of the century. The Order of Mary Magdalene, Clares, Carmelites, Trinitarians, Augustinians, and Sack Friars all established houses between 1250 and 1270. Equally striking are the numbers of women who adopted various kinds of religious life not under the discipline of a rule. Enough information is available about beguines and about the Clares to show which classes of society were most attracted by such new forms.

The least formal of these groups will also be the most difficult to define. Common in medieval towns in northern Europe, beguines were most numerous in the Rhineland and the area of modern Belgium. They and their male counterparts, beghards (or occasionally beguins), were lay folk who lived according to a discipline which varied from one place to another but included a revocable vow of chastity and manual or charitable work, along with a deep mystical piety. Except in the case of the large beguinages of Belgium, statutes and narrative sources are extremely rare; the movement is best known, therefore, through those houses and becomes increasingly obscure as one's attention is turned toward smaller communities and populations.[10]

With the beguines of Metz, there is a basic problem of nomenclature. The word "beguine" appears in no source before 1290.[11] By 1250, however, there were three houses of "pucelles" (maidens), which are generally assumed to have been houses of beguines;[12] the identity of the individual members is unknown. There were also women designated "vaudoises" (Waldensians) in the sources, who have been generally assumed to be in fact Waldensians. Most probably they should instead be considered single beguines or members of small groups of beguines. It is difficult to believe, for example, that the *vaudoise* who was the domestic servant of a Benedictine abbot was called "the Waldensian," that society began to tolerate scores of defiantly named heretics from 1251 (when the name first occurs) into the fourteenth century, that sixty-four of sixty-seven female Waldensians were unmarried, or that Odeliate de Gorze "la vadoize" living in front of the Dominican convent in 1297 was a heretic,

---

[9] Schneider (n. 1 above) 37-38, 42, 269.

[10] Ernest W. McDonnell, *The Beguines and Beghards in Medieval Culture* (repr. New York 1969) is the standard work on the subject. Dayton Phillips, *Beguines in Medieval Strasbourg: A Study of the Social Aspect of Beguine Life* (Stanford 1941) is a study whose fine detail shows the full complexity of a vital and changing variety of urban religion; it has allowed recognition of similar phenomena with a very dissimilar name in Metz.

[11] The first occurrence is an entry in the roll of property transactions, Karl Wichmann, *Die Metzer Bannrollen des dreizehnten Jahrhunderts*, 4 vols., Quellen zur lothringischen Geschichte 5-8 (Metz-Leipzig 1908-1916) 2.308 no. 306.

[12] Schneider (n. 1 above) 44.

especially since ten years later a woman called "la beguine" lived in the same place.[13] In fact, a third of these much-maligned women lived in front of or behind various churches. There are two difficulties, however. One is that the men, "vaudois" (half as numerous as the women), fit no recognizably beghard patterns; but these male counterparts of the beguines have not been much studied. I would also be happier if somewhere else beguines were called Waldensians. So far I have found no other cases, although in the early thirteenth century, of course, beguines were commonly called various kinds of heretics.[14]

Contemporaries' identification of these beguines with the heretics of 1199 may well have resulted from elements common to the piety of both. In addition to questioning priestly authority, the Waldensians had translated parts of Scripture into the vernacular, translations which the ecclesiastical authorities burned. Beguines were devout laywomen who had much in common with the uneducated (in an academic sense) vernacular piety of the Waldensians. For townspeople whose outlook was limited to a region on the periphery of French-language civilization, it was easy to associate two kinds of piety with one name. That these women were orthodox in their devotion — no source except the name suggests otherwise — is a more important point than the question of labeling them beguines. Part of a general European phenomenon, they resemble both the beguines of Strasbourg and the recluses of Italy, who were as numerous as their like-named counterparts in Metz were scarce.[15]

These tentatively identified beguines seem to have been the most generally recruited category of religious, assuming that they may for our purposes be included among the religious. Even so, in the fourteenth century, a third of the beguines came from families of the oligarchy, although the very greatest families were only slightly represented. They owned modest amounts of property, and from the non-binding nature of their vocation may be considered women of considerable religious zeal.

The greatest insight into the results of the new spirituality in thirteenth-century Metz can be gained from studying the Clares. The sources, by the standards of Metz, are unusually rich: an obituary calendar of benefactors, a necrology of the nuns, and a few score documents.[16] The house was founded in August 1258 by Fulque de

[13] Metz, Archives de la Moselle (hereafter abbreviated Mos.), G.879 and G.977. The area was soon to become very popular with beguines, if it was not already. At least sixteen beguines, each in her own house, lived in the two streets around the Dominican convent in 1330 (Paris, BN MS fr. 11846, fols. 9v-11v, 19v, 20v). The same source, a *censier* bound with the cartulary of the cathedral chapter, mentions no beguines living near the Franciscans. That evidence, however, is far from conclusive; the chapter had far less property in that area, which figures only slightly in the *censier.*

[14] McDonnell (n. 10 above) 436-438; Herbert Grundmann, *Religiöse Bewegungen im Mittelalter,* ed. 2 (Hildesheim 1961) 377-389.

[15] This paragraph owes much to the comments made by Professors Marjorie Reeves, Thomas Bisson, and Robert Brentano when this paper was read at a meeting of the Committee on Medieval Studies, University of California, Berkeley, in May 1977.

[16] The obituary calendar is Nancy, Bibliothèque Municipale MS 1385; the necrology of nuns, Mos. H.4176; most of the individual documents are in Mos. H.4217 and Paris, BN, Collection de Lorraine 975.

Jurue, who settled the nuns in a house in the newer, northwest corner of the city. Two years later, an aristocratic lady, Anel de Vaux, gave the nuns her own house near the Franciscan convent and the cathedral. She soon gave her fortune to the convent to build a church and she herself became a Clare and the third abbess. A characteristic of the Clares' early history was the recruitment of upper-class women who brought large sums of money. The Clares differed in this respect from Benedictine and capitular foundations, whose entrants, bourgeois or not, in this period never gave large sums. The Clares' own situation changed in later years, when entrants rarely gave large gifts but the convent, in contrast to most of the non-mendicant foundations, received large gifts from laymen, a very tangible testimony of devotion. While only a third of the later beguines came from elite families, among the Clares of the first fifty years, the proportion was fifty percent. In the fourteenth century, the proportion rose to three-quarters. Some families provided a disproportionate number of nuns — ten families (leaving relations by marriage aside) provided over forty percent of the upper class nuns. The usual pattern, however, was clusters of nuns in two generations — mother, daughters, nieces — rather than the succession of three or four generations found in the cathedral. The large gifts, large representation of single families (a mother and her three daughters in one case), the social diversity, and the genuine personal poverty of the Clares in the thirteenth century make it clear that the successful appeal which they made to the city's women was far more a matter of religious devotion than was the case among the secular canons and Benedictine monks. No male order received a privilege like that which Alexander IV gave the nuns of Saint Mary Magdalene in 1255; they were too poor to provide a winter habit of lambskins as prescribed by the Order's statutes and received permission to use something less costly.[17]

The religious appeal to women is further evident in the number of informal communities of devout women who eventually found it prudent to adopt the regular life of an established order. Unlike the Clares, whose adoption of the Franciscan rule seems to have been immediate, other devout women gathered as unorganized houses of beguines. Of these four houses, the two earliest adopted rules. That first mentioned in 1243 became a house of Dominican nuns in 1271. The second, mentioned in 1250, adopted the Augustinian rule around 1290. Other beguines kept their original style;[18] adoption of a rule may have been an act of institutionalization which not all wished to imitate. In terms of social origins, both the mendicant nuns and the beguines who formed small communities generally belonged to elite families. The elite was devout but liked order.

The relatively good documentation for Clares and beguines should not be allowed to give the false impression that women of the oligarchy did not imitate the men's entry into the older institutions. Although no nun of the city's monasteries is known

[17] C. Bourel de la Roncière et al., *Les registres d'Alexandre IV*, Bibliothèque des Écoles françaises d'Athènes et de Rome, ser. 2, 15 (Paris 1895-1960) no. 789.

[18] Schneider (n. 1 above) 42, 44.

by family name until the last decade of the thirteenth century, the numbers of bourgeois nuns in Sainte Glossinde and Sainte Marie in the fourteenth century is a strong argument that wealthy citizens whose sons entered chapters and abbeys in the thirteenth century did not neglect to provide similarly for their daughters. In fact, a document probably unique for Metz, noteworthy both for specifying the gift made upon profession and for its early date, is the act of 1247 by which Dame Sebelie, daughter of the late Sire Luckin de Porsailli, "ait rendut" her daughter Suffiette to God and to the Cistercian monastery of Freistroff (eighteen miles northeast of Metz) to be a nun. Sebelie's unmentioned (presumably deceased) husband was probably a relative of the child's guardian, Faucon de la Fosse, canon of the cathedral.[19]

The question remains of the forms of devotion of citizens who did not belong to the political elite. At the end of the century, they could at least become beguines. Earlier, it had been less difficult to join the Clares, but by 1300 the family of one novice paid an entry fee of 10 l. and 5 l. more for robes and other necessities for the first year.[20] Other poorer orders may have been more accessible, but their records have not survived. For most people, the expression of devotion which survives in the archives is donations. Gifts of a shilling were duly noted; some differences appear among the orders, but the scant sources allow only a few tentative observations. The Augustinian and Trinitarian friars appear to have received fewer gifts from the upper classes,[21] who favored Dominican and Franciscan friars and nuns. An impression of the clientele of the Dominican friars is given in a list of thirteen bequests made in the five years around 1300.[22] Twelve of the thirteen donors were women, and eight of them came from elite families. These were, of course, the very people with leisure time to devote to religious inquiry and activity. The bequests ranged from 1 l. to 200 l. Of the forty friars in the convent, ten were mentioned by name as beneficiaries of nearly all the amounts bequeathed. One lady mentioned a friar as her confessor; another friar was designated by four women; he was more likely, then, a confessor than a relative. Dominican confessors were not forgotten by their charges, and such responsiveness was all the more enraging to the parish priests who drew up the list of bequests in question. This example of the common occurrence of strife between the mendicants and the local clergy should be tempered by an example of the smooth acceptance of the mendicants by other members of the city's clergy. A beguine in 1307 made her will in which most of her bequests were to her parish priest, two Cistercian monasteries, and for the windows and the fabric of her parish church. For other unspecified bequests, her executors (a widow and a beguine) were to take the advice of a Franciscan friar. She was to be buried in the Franciscan church.[23]

---

[19] Mos H.681 bis, p. 85 (cartulary of Freistroff).

[20] Paris, BN, Collection de Lorraine 975 no. 55.

[21] Paris, BN MS lat. 11025, fols. 19v-25r is a fragment of the cartulary of the Augustinians; scattered documents of the Trinitarians survive, notably in Paris, BN, Collection de Lorraine 971, and Nancy, Bibliothèque Municipale MS suppl. 1384.

[22] H. V. Sauerland, *Vatikanische Urkunden und Regesten zur Geschichte Lothringens,* Quellen zur lothringischen Geschichte 1-2 (Metz 1901-1905) 1.57-59.

[23] Mos H.681 bis, pp. 66-67.

III

The expressions of religiosity discussed here are only surface features — all that available evidence preserves, particularly in the thirteenth century. Then, as in succeeding centuries, a large part of the bourgeois elite entered the well-endowed older institutions without leaving any traces of devotion — quite often the contrary. The mendicant nuns appear to have begun with fervent devotion, but even they by the end of the century were well-born and well propertied. Religious life had taken on a settled, well-organized air among canons, nuns, and even friars despite their significantly different styles. The varying religious needs of the population, but especially of the urban privileged, were now met by a suitable variety of institutions. The life of the parish priests and chaplains remains unknown, as does much of the history of the non-elite groups from which they came. Even in its settled state, religion, like other institutions in this city which knew little social unrest, continued to attract popular support, as far as we can tell from the continuing flow of donations not to the cathedral or abbeys but to mendicants and parishes. The exceptional donors were those who made enormous gifts or who, seeking to establish a new standard of religious life, continued to found convents and hospitals. Similarly, parish churches appear in the fourteenth century to assume new importance as centers of religious life. But to an extremely devout citizen in 1370, it seemed that fervent religion in Metz was dead. Anxious to surround himself with piety, he turned to an order not already represented in Metz and invited Celestine monks to accept his foundation.[24] They in their turn attracted substantial numbers of the city's elite, always eager to welcome the religious ideal with the deadly embrace of their favor.

The religious institutions discussed here were characterized both by their recruitment from the upper classes and by their creation as or transformation into urban institutions. The latter is the more important quality. The wealthy had long been those with the means and the time for careers and interests in the Church. The striking aspect of the ecclesiastical development of Metz during a period of less than a century is the equipment of an urban community with an array of ecclesiastical conveniences which the citizens had lacked almost completely. The non-parochial churches in 1200 may have accommodated a dozen urban clerics; by 1300 they accommodated perhaps 250. Spectacular as was the growth of the population and wealth of Metz, the extent of the ecclesiastical change was proportionately an even greater urban achievement.

School of Law
University of California
Berkeley, California 94720, U.S.A.

[24] The *Chronique des Célestins* (Metz, Bibliothèque Municipale MS 833) is a lively narrative of the convent's foundation and its early years. The foundation deed is printed in Nicolas Tabouillot and Jean François, *Histoire de Metz par des religieux de la Congrégation de Saint-Vanne*, 6 vols. (Metz-Nancy 1769-1790) 4.261-265.

THE NETHERLANDS HERRING FISHERY IN THE LATE MIDDLE AGES: THE FALSE LEGEND OF WILLEM BEUKELS OF BIERVLIET

•

by Richard W. Unger

Since the fifteenth century, writers have been claiming that Willem Beukels of Biervliet invented a new way of processing herring so that the fish would keep for a long time. The story has taken various forms, but in most cases that citizen of a fishing village in northern Flanders, now in the province of Zeeland in the kingdom of the Netherlands, is credited with starting the great expansion in the Low Countries herring fishery. His invention around 1400 made it possible for herring to be stored for long periods and to be shipped over long distances. He, then, so the story goes, was responsible for the rise of the Dutch herring fishery in the sixteenth and seventeenth centuries and in turn in part responsible for the unprecedented economic prosperity of Holland in those years. Even the famous seventeenth-century Dutch poet, Jacob Cats, sang the praises of Beukels, naming him as the first to learn how to preserve herring.

The story is appealing for its simplicity. Problems arise almost immediately, however. It is difficult to establish when Beukels lived, what his occupation was and precisely what he did, if anything, that was revolutionary.[1] The pattern of change in the herring fishery in the fifteenth century is far from clear. Examination of custom, toll and shipping records along with reports on piracy show that technical innovation was far from instantaneous. But the greatest problem is the causal allegation which places the origin of Dutch success in the province of Flanders a century before the steady and impressive rise in total production of cured herring. Insisting on the

I am indebted to J. P. van de Voort of the Visserijmuseum, Vlaardingen, and Professor Lynn White, jr., for their comments on an earlier draft of this paper.

[1] See for example Robert Ergang, *Europe from the Renaissance to Waterloo*, ed. 2 (New York 1954) 289-290. G. Doorman, "Het haringkaken en Willem Beukels," *Tijdschrift voor Geschiedenis* 69 (1956) 371-372, gives a short bibliography of those who accepted the story in the sixteenth and seventeenth centuries and in the nineteenth and twentieth. Included in the list are the sixteenth-century Italian who lived in Antwerp, Ludovico Guicciardini, the seventeenth-century Dutch chroniclers, T. Velius, M. van Boxhorn, Joh. Potanus, M. Smallegange, among others, and the modern historian of the Flemish fishery, Roger Degryse. See also R. Degryse, "Oorsprong van het haringkaken in Vlaanderen," *Nederlandsche Historiebladen* 1 (1938) 204-205; H. Blink, "De Geschiedenis en Beteekenis der Nederlandsche Haringvisscherij," *Vragen van den Dag* 45 (1930) 985.

connection of Beukels to seventeenth-century Dutch prosperity unnecessarily obscures the technical change of the fourteenth and fifteenth centuries. Moreover it tends to minimize the importance of a complex process of innovation. It is not in an immediate contribution to the economy or to the nutrition of medieval Europeans that the significance of change in the herring fishery is to be found. Rather it is valuable as an illustration of technological change in a period when Europeans were finding innovation easier.

It will probably never be possible to isolate Willem Beukels's precise contribution. It is possible, however, to say a great deal about the development of the herring fishery especially in Flanders in the fourteenth and fifteenth centuries, its growth and the changes in technique used by Netherlands fishermen. The transformation was intimately connected to the commercial position of other suppliers in Europe and to the action and reaction of government to the pattern of supply. That process of transformation shows the incremental nature of technical innovation and the complex of forces which typically make technological change less than dramatic.

I

A chronicler writing in the sixteenth century claimed that Willem Beukels invented a new way of treating herring. The town of Ostend, in a declaration of 1483, also attributed the success with herring to the same man. The story, then, was obviously a popular one even in the fifteenth century, and the chronicler was probably just repeating an oral tradition. Other writers picked up the tale and repeated it in much the same form again and again over the centuries. There is little substantive difference in the accounts. In each instance Beukels is given credit for discovering *kaken* or curing herring, of finding the way to make *kaakharing* or *pekelharing*.

The method of curing is still in use. Immediately after the herring is caught it is slit open with a sharp cut from a short curved knife especially designed for the job. Then the gills, stomach, heart, liver, gall bladder and genitals are pulled out of the body cavity. That way the fish quickly loses its blood. It eliminates the parts of the fish most subject to rapid deterioration. The fish are then put directly into barrels where salt is placed above and below the layers of gutted fish. The remaining blood and the salt immediately form a brine. That cuts the fish off from the air which would cause it to rot. While in this brine the fish slowly change in color, odor and taste. The process of curing is aided by the enzyme, trypsin, of the pyloric caecae. Those appendices of the stomach are often missed by fishermen when they pull out the viscera. Leaving them in the fish speeds the process of curing and improves the quality of the final product. When the herring is brought to shore it is repacked; and a white brine, that is, one with no blood, is added. That improves the preservation of the fish and also makes it possible to fill the barrels and compensate for evaporation and shrinkage.[2] *Kaakharing*, then, was not just any herring in barrels, but herring specially treated and packed from the time it was caught. In that form it could last for some time, usually a year or more depending on the quality of the gutting and packing.

It is certain that Willem Beukels did not invent that method of curing herring. It was used in Europe well before 1300. Herring was treated in that way on shore in a number of places, most notably on the coast of southwestern Sweden in the then Danish province of Scania. Certainly by the mid-thirteenth century herring was caught there in the narrow waterway between the mainland and the Danish islands and landed on the small Skanör peninsula where they were prepared and packed. The fishermen were apparently Danish using open boats, 5000 to 7000 of them altogether, each with six to ten men. Merchants regulated the treating of the fish, bought them from the producers and then shipped them to markets throughout northern Europe. The herring were so numerous in the strait that ships, it was said, had trouble using their rudders. The fishery went on from August to November-but the catch was concentrated in September and October. Since there was a serious problem with the garbage from the work on the herring, there can be little question that they were gutted before being packed. It was illegal to treat fish in the boats. Fishermen had to bring them to shore directly after catching. The merchants could only operate from *vitten*, small plots along the shore granted to them or more precisely to their town.

From 1200 the preparation and sale of Scania herring was largely under the control of merchants from German Baltic ports and especially from Lübeck. It was those men from towns belonging to the Hanseatic League that handled the shipping of the Scania *tonharing* to markets in Germany and in western Europe. By the second half of the fourteenth century production was probably above 8000 lasts per year.[3] The Low Countries formed an important market for Hansa merchants. In fact Scania herring was a major item in their trade with Flanders, a western terminus of their trading network. By the late fourteenth century Hansards delivered some 1700 lasts of herring annually in Flanders.[4] From there other merchants moved the

[2] A. van Dijk, in *The Technology of Herring Utilization,* Report of the FAO Meeting (Bergen 1950) 225; A. F. M. G. Luijpen, *De Invloed van het Kaken op de Rijping van Gezouten Matjesharing* (Utrecht 1959) 15-17, 37-39.

[3] The last usually refers to a wagon-load of grain equal to about two English tons in weight. For herring, however, at least by the fifteenth century, the last was made up of 12 casks or *tonnen.* Each of those barrels contained between 800 and 1000 fish but generally about 900. A herring last was thus about 12,000 fish. If it took some 9 herring to make a kilogram the weight of the herring last would have been about 1300 kilograms, or less than the weight of a last of grain. The barrels added some weight but the increase was marginal. In the Dutch herring industry one last was equal to 17 casks on board ship and 14 casks repacked on shore. The estimate for the size of the Scania catch is open to question. For lower limit estimates which, however, show confusion about the size of a last see H. Henking, *Die Ostseefischerei: Handbuch der Seefischerei Nord-Europas* 53 (Stuttgart 1929) 8-9.

[4] G. W. Coopland, "A Glimpse of Late Fourteenth-Century Ships and Seamen from 'Le Songe de Vieil Pélerin' of Philippe de Mézières (1327-1405)," *The Mariner's Mirror* 48 (1962) 190-191;

preserved fish on to markets in the Low Countries, in Germany and in France. Herring appeared as a trade item in many parts of northern Europe throughout the later Middle Ages. Netherlands shippers often carried herring to England. In 1348 Holland and Zeeland shipmasters landed at least 198½ lasts of herring at the port of Yarmouth. Herring is often mentioned in the lists of cargoes landed in England in the fourteenth century.[5] The great majority of the herring was imported either for immediate consumption or to be treated. It is doubtful that much if any of it had already been cured. That was less true of the herring shipped to Germany. Shippers carried the product up the Rhine to the important market of Cologne and as far as Basel. Cologne merchants visited towns in the Low Countries to buy fish and bring it back themselves. From 1439 to 1441 about 375 lasts of herring went from the province of Holland alone to Germany and that did not include smoked herring, a popular product in the German market.[6] The figure for the late fourteenth century was undoubtedly lower and the figure for cured herring even lower than that. The greater the distance that the herring had to travel the more likely that it had been given a full curing treatment. Low Countries exports to France in the fourteenth century, then, were more usually simply reexports of Scania herring. Ports like Saint-Malo, Dieppe and Rouen were common destinations for Netherlanders shippers carrying herring. From there the fish were taken to Paris and to many other markets in the interior reaching Franche-Comté, Toulouse, the Dauphiné, the papal table at Avignon and even Spain. Whether by sea or overland and by river, herring also reached the Mediterranean. Herring was one of the typical products of the North which formed the basis for the commercial connection with southern Europe. Herring was therefore naturally in the cargoes of the northern European ships which invaded the Mediterranean in the sixteenth century.[7]

Doorman (n. 1 above) 378-379; J. Travis Jenkins, *The Herring and the Herring Fisheries* (London 1927) 57-64; Aksel E. Christensen, "La foire de Scanie," *Société Jean Bodin . . . Recueils* 5 (1953) 244-255; R. Degryse, "Schoense en Vlaamse Kaakharing in de 14de eeuw," *Bijdragen voor de Geschiedenis der Nederlanden* 12 (1957) 102-105; idem, *Vlaanderens Haringbedrijf in de Middeleeuwen* (Antwerp 1944) 93-96.

[5] H. J. Smit, *Bronnen tot de Geschiedenis van den Handel met England, Schotland en Ierland* 1: *1150-1485* (The Hague 1928) no. 444; Nelly J. M. Kerling, *Commercial Relations of Holland and Zeeland with England from the Late 13th Century to the Close of the Middle Ages* (Leiden 1954) 89-95.

[6] J. A. Van Houtte, "Die Beziehungen zwischen Köln und den Niederlanden vom Hochmittelalter bis zum Beginn des Industrie-Zeitalters," *Kölner Vorträge sur Sozial- und Wirtschaftsgeschichte* 1 (1969) 12; F. Ketner, *Handel en Scheepvaart van Amsterdam in de Vifftiende Eeuw* (Leiden 1946) 55, 67; W. S. Unger, *De Levenmiddelenvoorziening der Hollandsche Steden in de Middeleeuwen* (Amsterdam 1916) 140-142.

[7] Z. W. Sneller and W. S. Unger, eds., *Bronnen tot de Geschiedenis van den Handel met Frankrijk* 1: *753-1585* (The Hague 1930) nos. 33, 51, 52, 61, 52, 122; Henri Touchard, *Le commerce maritime breton à la fin du Moyen Age* (Paris 1967) 83, Michel Mollat, *Le commerce maritime normand à la fin du Moyen Age* (Paris 1952) 125, 313-317; Philippe Wolff, *Commerces et marchands de Toulouse (vers 1350-vers 1450)* (Paris 1954) 214; Fernand Braudel and Ruggiero Romano, *Navires et marchandises à l'entrée du port de Livourne (1577-1611)* (Paris 1951) 34-35, 50-51.

The quantities of herring shipped in the fourteenth century were small relative to the total volume of commerce. The figures were even less impressive the greater the distance from the centers of production. But what made the trade important was precisely that the herring could be moved over great distances. The curing process made it biologically possible for at least a part of the herring catch. The use of barrels for shipping the product made it economically feasible. Romans used barrels in some cases to carry wine and other commodities including fish. They learned to build them from Celts, and it was principally in northern Europe that barrels were the containers for shipment. Compared to jars, barrels are fifty percent more efficient, that is, in terms of the proportion of cargo space taken up by the container.[8] Cured herring entered commerce already packed in its relatively efficient container. The result was a good which could form the basis of long-range commercial connections, no matter how tenuous. A fleet of about a dozen of the largest deep sea trading vessels could have handled the total quantity of cured herring going from Scania to Flanders. But of course the number of ships carrying the product was much greater. Ships of lesser tonnage made the voyage and few if any made the trip loaded only with herring. In that trade and to a lesser degree in others cured herring was a commodity which could be counted on to find a market. It traveled well and could be stored for some time. Shippers then could use cured herring as the basis of a shipment and include more speculative items. That in turn over time could form the basis for further commercial connections. The trade between the Baltic and the Netherlands is only the best example.

The comital government of Flanders controlled the trade in herring from Scania. The German merchants had to bring the fish to a specified staple port. The fish arrived starting in October. No herring could be shipped from Scania until 9 October. The cargoes may have included some herring from Norway where a coastal fishery had long been established. In 1164 the pope had granted the inhabitants of the coast the privilege of fishing on feast days and Sundays if and when the fish came close to shore. Hansards landed their fish at the port of Damme or, after 1372 when the staple was moved, at Sluis in Flanders. They then repacked it before sending it on to customers either in that county or inland. After serious difficulties with the Flemish authorities which led to a boycott of the port of Bruges the Hansards in 1360 got the right to repack and repickle their herring in Flanders. There can be no question that Netherlands fishermen were fully familiar with this curing of herring on shore. Some towns got the right to have their own district on the Skanör peninsula. Fishermen from Kampen and Harderwijk, two towns in the northeast Netherlands, were operating there by the end of the twelfth century. In the second half of the fourteenth century men from towns in the province of Holland also became involved in the Scania fishery. Amsterdam, Enkhuizen, Wieringen and Brielle in 1350 joined their

[8] F. C. Lane, "Progrès technologiques et productivité dans les transports maritime à la fin du Moyen Age au debut des temps modernes," *Revue Historique* 251 (1974) 278-279; R. J. Forbes, "Food and Drink," in *A History of Technology* 2, ed. C. Singer et al. (Oxford 1956) 136.

two Netherlands predecessors in getting the right to have *vitten* at Skanör. At one
point eleven towns from the Low Countries had concessions in the Scania fishery.[9]

Netherlanders used the method very little if at all along their own coast. It was
not because they did not have a herring fishery. Coastal fishing for the *clupea
harengus* in the Low Countries dates from the Roman period and probably before.
Crews of four to seven men caught the fish, working from open boats. They would
go out in the evening and return the next morning with herring. The fishing was done
at night because then the herring came toward the surface to feed and fishermen
could see them more easily because of their luminous appearance. The fishermen sold
the catch as fresh or lightly salted herring. In the latter form it was taken by water or
wagon to nearby markets. The light salting could slow the deterioration of the fish
but could not stop it. Salt came from local salt pans. A Flemish writer said in 1125
that the herring was a little fish which could be easily salted to make it last for a long
time. He was apparently describing the coastal fishery. After 1150 that fishery
expanded in Flanders with the establishment of a series of new fishing villages along
the coast. Production could be large, a total catch of about 1000 lasts being reported
in 1321 for Calais alone. But the herring did not get the same treatment as that given
fish at Scania.[10] It was because of the time of the year. Herring was caught along the
Netherlands coast in November and December and up to as late as Candlemas,
2 February. This fish found a ready market in the large towns of Flanders in those
winter months as fresh herring, since supplies of fresh meat almost disappeared after
the slaughtering in early November. The herring found along the coast in that period
were full herring, that is, fully developed males and females. During December the
quality of the herring deteriorates as the fish spawn and their fat content falls. In
May through July the fish find their best food in the North Sea and in those months
their fat rises most rapidly. It goes down slowly through the winter.[11] The full
herring caught in the southern North Sea from the end of October to early December
is best suited to consumption as fresh fish or as smoked herring. Smoking was the
usual method of preserving the coastal catch if it was preserved at all. The *bokking*
was packed in barrels and shipped to Cologne and the Rhineland. In the thirteenth
and fourteenth centuries, given the kind of herring they caught and the nature of the
market, Netherlands fishermen had no reason to use the curing method along their
own shores.

Netherlanders did catch herring for curing, along the English coast off Norfolk
near the port of Yarmouth. Fish taken there through November was sold as full
herring. It received the same treatment as did the product of the Flemish coastal

---

[9] A. Beaujon, *The History of Dutch Sea Fisheries* (London 1884) 8-9; Nelly Gottschalk,
Fischereigewerbe und Fischhandel der niederlandschen Gebiete im Mittelalter (Bad Wörishafen
1927) 12-13; Degryse, *Haringbedrijf* (n. 4 above) 96-97; Henking (n. 3 above) 7-8; Jenkins (n. 4
above) 8-9.

[10] Doorman (n. 1 above) 376; G. Doorman, "Nogmaals: de middeleeuwse haringvisserij,"
Bijdragen voor de Geschiedenis der Nederlanden 14 (1960) 104-105; Degryse, *Haringbedrijf*
(n. 4 above) 10-27, 54-55. The 1321 figure was unusual. The normal catch was under 500 lasts.

[11] Luijpen (n. 2 above) 13-14.

fishery. By 1300, though, some of that herring was cured. That was especially done with fish taken earlier, in July or August. Yarmouth was the great market for all herring caught along the English coast by all fishermen. Fish was exported from there to other English towns and to the Continent. In 1295 King Edward I of England issued an order that fishermen from Holland, Zeeland and Friesland coming to fish off the coast near Yarmouth should not be molested or robbed by his subjects. It is likely that Netherlanders were visiting the "Deepwater" fishing bank off Norfolk in the eleventh century and that the 1295 order was just a repetition of earlier regulations. In any case the royal ruling apparently had little effect since it had to be reissued in 1327.[12] Fishing off England came a little earlier than the fishing off Flanders, so Netherlanders were able to extend their season. The equipment and personnel were the same, so there was no change in technique or increase in investment. Fishermen then could follow the herring as they moved south from late August until the beginning of the following February. The fish caught off the English coast were also of high quality, matching the best full herring of the Flemish coastal fishery. Englishmen handled the curing of that part of the catch which was to be preserved. All the work was done on shore. At the end of the fourteenth century some Netherlanders apparently were going ashore to do their own curing, since the English government complained about foreign fishermen clandestinely landing with casks and salt to treat their fish. But that was a late development and certainly exceptional. The Netherlanders typically caught the fish and sold them to English merchants who contracted to act as brokers. They arranged for supplies of food for the fishermen to be available on shore. They also handled the marketing of the catch. For this the brokers got a share of the revenue from sales, usually five percent. That practice and indeed the whole of the Norfolk fishery was well established by the thirteenth century.

II

In the fourteenth century there was a series of steps which moved the curing of herring from the shore to the fishing boats. In essence it was a problem of transportation. As Netherlanders fished further and further north along the English and then along the Scottish east coast they increased the distance to their markets in the Low Countries and France. Fishing further north had a number of advantages. It meant that the season could begin earlier, in June, so that fishermen could increase the returns from their investment and more than ever could specialize in their work.

[12] Eric Dardel, *La pêche harenguière en France* (Paris 1941) 23-29. R. Degryse and O. Mus, "De laatmiddeleeuwse Haringvisserij," *Bijdragen voor de Geschiedenis der Nederlanden* 21 (1966-1967), 82-87; R. Degryse, "De Vlaamse Haringvisserij in de XVe Eeuw," *Handelingen van de "Société d'Emulation" te Brugge* 88 (1951) 116 n. 3; Y. N. Ypma, *Geschiedenis van de Zuiderzeevisserij* (Amsterdam 1962) 14-15; G. Doorman, "De Haringvisserij in de Middeleeuwen," *Bijdragen voor de Geschiedenis der Nederlanden* 19 (1964-1965) 162-163; Smit (n. 5 above) nos. 238, 247, 268, 269, 274, 281, 300.

It meant catching large autumn spawning herring of that same high quality which was found off the coast of Norfolk, and with an even higher fat content. The advantages could only be exploited if a method could be found to preserve the catch during the long voyage home. The standard practice when fishing off Norfolk was to take the last catch home in the boat and sell it in the Low Countries. If the fishermen were operating on the Dogger Bank or off the coast of Scotland, as much as 400 kilometers from their home ports, and they wanted to do that, then they had to keep the fish from going bad for three or four days if the weather was good and longer if it was not.

The solution found and used by 1252 was a partial salting. The resulting product was called *korfharing*. The treatment may have been similar to that used on shore in the Flemish coastal fishery. The herring was lightly sprinkled with a layer of salt and packed loosely in hampers. There was no question of gutting the fish. Later, by the early fourteenth century, Flemish fishermen also sold a type of herring called *vivelo*. The term referred to Filey, a port on the Yorkshire coast, but it probably meant more than just that the fish were caught there. It indicated that the herring came from further north than was common before. So it may also suggest that some small improvement was made in the preservation method. Since the distances were greater and the fish could be preserved to some extent, it made sense to use a larger fishing vessel. The corver became the typical ship for that longer-range fishing. Corvers must have been seaworthy and capable of carrying a sizable crew because in wartime they found work as privateers. In fact the word came to be a generic term in Flemish for privateer. Moreover the vessels had to carry salt to the Yorkshire and Scottish coast for treating the fish, since local salt was too impure for the job. They landed their salt, then went out for herring, salting it lightly and then bringing it into ports like Scarborough. The fish was shipped from there to the Low Countries. Vessels late in the season would not bother with going into an English port but would go straight to the Continent. The brokers for those corvers were not English but Flemish, that is, from the home port of the fishermen. Clearly they expected to market some if not all of the catch. Small open boats with a capacity of two lasts or less were also used often in company with a larger corver.[13] No matter the type of vessel, the treating of herring on board, albeit in a simple manner, expanded the scope of the herring fishery.

It also increased the value of the catch. The salt content of the North Sea is greater than that of the Baltic because it is warmed by the Gulf Stream, warmer water having a higher degree of salinity. The salt content also rises toward the northern North Sea away from the outflow of rivers. The salt content of waters on the Dogger Bank is about twice that of the waters off Scania. The higher degree of salinity meant there was more plankton and thus more food for the herring. The

---

[13] Degryse, *Haringbedrijf* (n. 4 above) 90, 98, and "Schoense" (n. 4 above) 100-101; R. Degryse, "Van 'Buza' tot 'Buis': De Ontwikkeling van het Vlaamse Visservaartuig (12^e-16^e Eeuw)," *Ostendiana* (1972) 139-145; Degryse and Mus (n. 12 above) 88-97; Doorman (n. 12 above) 163-165, 168-169, and (n. 10 above) 106-110.

herring in the North Sea were bigger, from one-third to half again as large as those of the Baltic or from the Netherlands coast. They had more vertebrae and incidentally more of the trypsin needed to get the best curing.[14] The move into the open North Sea and further north allowed fisherman to increase the amount of food per fish caught, with at most a marginal increase in effort.

By 1300 Netherlands fishermen were certainly capable of handling large catches and taking them in deep waters. They had already developed the *vleet,* a type of large net which was a combination of smaller existing nets. Open boats in the coastal fishery would carry as many as forty nets, while for fishing in English waters the number went up to 75. These long drag nets had to be combined into one great one so that fishermen could handle them. The fishing boats grew in size to accommodate the larger net. Moreover already in the fourteenth century there were regulations fixing the minimum size of the holes in the net to prevent taking fish which were too small. The goal may also have been to protect the supply of fish.[15]

Despite the diffusion of the method of treating herring to much of northern Europe through the thirteenth century, curing was still done exclusively on shore. The critical change, the change most important to the long-term development of the herring fishery in the Low Countries, was the transfer of the *kaken* method from land to fishing vessels. The change meant that the major part of the work of preserving the fish was done on board and the ship was saved from making daily or almost daily visits to any coast. It is in fact that innovation and not the development of the curing method which was the decisive step of the fourteenth century and the one which created the potential for the long-term growth of the herring fishery in northwestern Europe.

Netherlanders at some time in the fourteenth century developed the ability to bring cured herring onto the market. Such fish, without the head, are mentioned in toll tariffs of 1377. In the third decade of the fourteenth century Flemings were delivering *kaecharicx* to Paris. Indeed the French word for cured herring, *caque-haring,* was the Flemish term which suggests that fish treated in that way first came to France from Flanders and in the early fourteenth century. If Netherlanders were able to supply cured herring by the 1330s then the questions are whether or not they did the job of preserving and, if they did, whether or not that work was done on board ship.

In the 1320s and 1330s Netherlands fishermen had trouble gaining access to the English coast where they had traditionally landed their catches. Even from 1270, because of diplomatic troubles among England, France and Flanders and also because of English wars with Scotland and France, Netherlands fishermen were subject to piratical attacks in the North Sea. In fact Edward I's order of 1295 was to stop just those attacks. Though there was some improvement after 1320, the outbreak of the 100 Years' War in 1337 led to another deterioration in conditions. In that year the

[14] Ypma (n. 12 above) 14-15; Jenkins (n. 4 above) 37-54.
[15] Degryse, *Haringbedrijf* (n. 4 above) 62 and (n. 13 above) 139.

town of Ghent, fearful of a shortage of fish, required that none of the catch be salted or preserved and that it all had to be delivered fresh. So certainly some salting methods were being used. Deprived of their market for herring in England and, more important, of access to the shore where the fish could be treated, Netherlands fishermen in the years from 1315 to 1330 may have turned to working on the herring on board their ships.[16]

The evidence for the adoption of curing on board at that early date is not convincing. It is impossible to say whether the cured herring shipped by the Flemings to Paris had been prepared on board or not. The threat of attacks by other fishermen, of being closed out of ports and troubles like those were a commonplace of the medieval fishery. There was little that was unique about the years around 1300. Fishermen did not need the excuse of a war or letters of marque to attack other fishermen. They always found it easy to shift to privateering when the opportunity presented itself. At any point through the thirteenth and fourteenth centuries the problem of piratical attacks and reprisals existed. The *korf* and *vivelo* methods served before the second and third decades of the fourteenth century for fish caught as far north as Yorkshire, so distance was not a critical consideration. And there are a number of letters of complaint surviving from those years addressed to the government of Flanders from fishermen detailing what they had lost to pirates. The inventories mention nets, ropes, trade goods, cash, salt; but none of them mentions casks on board.

It is probable that in the course of the fourteenth century Netherlands fishermen experimented with a full curing of herring on their ships. If they did cure and pickle the herring at sea, the quantities involved were small. The figures were low not only for the total European catch and for the total Netherlands catch but also in terms of the catch for each fishing boat. If fishermen did gut and pack herring it was a small proportion of what they took, perhaps the first and best fish. A larger proportion was lightly salted and then a proportion, often far and away the largest, was brought to port as fresh herring.[17] The fishermen did that because of the presence of adequate supplies of cured herring on the Netherlands market, that is, herring imported from Scania. In 1400 German merchants still imported the great majority of cured herring into the Netherlands. The fact that local fishermen had the technical capability to prepare cured fish was of little consequence. A series of changes in the legal and political circumstances of the Netherlands herring fishery in the last decade of the fourteenth century and in the first third of the fifteenth indicates that it was in precisely those years that, at least in Flanders if not the rest of the Low Countries, the production of cured herring became important to the fishery.

[16] R. Degryse, "La pêche et la marine dunkerquoises vers 1300," *Marine Academie van België: Mededelingen* 13 (1961) 22-23; *idem, Haringbedrijf* (n. 4 above) 34-48, 88-89; Doorman (n. 1 above) 374-376.

[17] Degryse (n. 12 above) 125-126; R. Degryse, "Het Avontuur van Meeus de Crooc, Stuurman van Lombardsijde (1403)," *Marine Academie van België: Mededelingen* 13 (1961) 33-41; Degryse and Mus (n. 12 above) 94-99, 103.

III

In 1395 for the first time Flemish fishermen delivered their cured herring at Sluis, the staple port for herring imports. Already presumably Hollanders and Zeelanders were treating some of their herring in the same way. In fact French merchants at that time were travelling to Zeeland to buy *kaakharing*. The Flemish government outlawed the landing and sale of herring which had been treated in any way. The prohibition included all types of preserved herring, not only cured herring but also *vivelo*, dried *korfharing* and even fresh herring placed in casks. The edict presumably dates from 1396. The duke of Burgundy, who was the count of Flanders, may have been inspired to act in that way by petitions made to him by the town government of Bruges. There were two reasons for the legislation. First, the Hanseatic League was never reluctant to use political and economic pressure to protect its markets. The Hansa merchants living at Bruges undoubtedly did not like the idea of having to face competition from locally produced cured herring which would damage their virtual monopoly in the county and through much of the region. Second and probably more important was the desire to protect the supplies of fresh herring for Flemish cities. If Netherlands fishermen had started to cure some of their catch, urban governments may have seen the potential for increases in that proportion. Cured herring would be for distant markets and that in the short run could only mean supply problems for local markets.

The government prohibition did not work. Protests from fishing villages along the coast pointed to the loss of sales of cured herring. Foreign and native merchants, they said, went to Zeeland outside the lands of the duke of Burgundy to buy the fish from Hollanders, Zeelanders and Englishmen. The duke in 1399 rescinded the earlier prohibition but clearly did so grudgingly. He allowed Biervliet fishermen to place herring in casks from 24 August to 21 September. The fish had to come from north of Harwich on the English coast. After the closing date all herring caught had to be either smoked or sold as fresh fish. The cured herring could only be landed at the town of Biervliet and had to pay a tax of one noble for each last. This was consistent with the government policy of establishing fixed ports for specific trades. It was also consistent with the policy of taxing any trade or industry that the government could. The grant was only for one year but it was renewed. It was still against the law to sell the cured herring in the interior of Flanders, so the product was for the export market.[18] That ruling was presumably to placate the Hansa merchants. So was the requirement that the casks of Flemish herring had to have a special mark or brand which would distinguish the fish from Scania herring. The grant was specifically for Biervliet and may have been first given by the lady of Biervliet, the duke's wife.

---

[18] Degryse (n. 1 above) 203-204, 207-208, 216-218. He gives a full transcription of the order of 5 August 1399. R. Degryse, "Het Begin van het Haringkaken te Biervliet (±1400)," *Handelingen van de "Société d'Emulation" te Brugge* 95 (1958) 72-74; Degryse and Mus (n. 12 above) 101-102.

Biervliet was at least for a short time the center of the production and the trade in Flemish cured herring. And that may be the origin of the notoriety given to Willem Beukels. The name is not uncommon in coastal Flanders and certainly there was more than one Willem Beukels who lived there in the fourteenth century. There is a difference in the reports, some writers giving the date of his death as 1347 and not the usual 1397. It may well be that the important man was a certain Willem Beukels who lived at Biervliet in the early fourteenth century and who at that time experimented with the curing method used at Scania. Conversely, the story may have originated with a Willem Beukel who is mentioned at Biervliet in 1392, or even with a Willem Beukel of Hughevliet, a nearby village closely associated with Biervliet, mentioned in 1388 and again in 1396. The last was a captain and probably an owner of fishing vessels who at times turned his hand to privateering. A Pieter Beukels was involved in salt boiling in the first half of the fifteenth century at Biervliet and he may well have been the son of Willem Beukel of Hughevliet. The two were associated with men later involved in landing cured herring at Biervliet. So it is possible that the late fourteenth-century Willem Beukel of Hughevliet was a promoter of the curing of herring at sea and that he was a man of enough stature to be able actively and effectively to lobby the government to change the law in favor of Biervliet. It is also possible that he made some change in the method of packing the fish on board, perhaps in the way the herring were placed in the cask.[19] But that, like so much surrounding the story, is conjecture. The most likely explanation is that the family assumed a coat of arms which included two of the small knives which were used in gutting herring. The legend may have grown out of that mark on the grave of one of the Beukels who lived in Biervliet and who was buried in the church there. As memories of events around 1400 faded it was not illogical to associate that family and then one Willem Beukels with the increase in curing of herring in the first half of the fifteenth century. If there was any change in technique around 1400 it certainly was not a major one. The transfer of curing to shipboard may well have been practiced and promoted by a Willem Beukels. His influence on that change, however, was certainly much less than that attributed to him by legend.

The legal and political battle over the sale of cured herring by Flemings continued through the first two decades of the fifteenth century. Once the grant had been made to Biervliet other ports wanted the right to receive cured herring. After being petitioned the government responded by granting such privileges but the fish still had to be sold at Biervliet. By 1412 four more ports were allowed to receive cured herring but in all cases it had to be exported and could not be sold for consumption in Flanders. In 1413 even that restriction was dropped, at least for the fishermen of the village of Nieuwpoort. The required landing port was moved in 1413 from

---

[19] Dardel (n. 12 above) 46; Degryse, "Schoense" (n. 4 above) 105-107; R. Degryse, "Willem Beukel en het Begin vat het Kaken: Een Antwoord," *Bijdragen voor de Geschiedenis der Nederlanden* 15 (1960) 215-220; Doorman (n. 1 above) 377, 383-385. The town of Ostend claims a citizen, one Jacob Kien, as the inventor of the process. Ouddorp on the island of Goeree in South Holland has its own candidate, one Jan Machiel Duffel.

Biervliet to Damme. In the last years of the 1410s the pressure mounted again to outlaw the landing of cured herring. In 1419 the town of Ghent prohibited the sale of any cured herring from Flanders, Holland and Zeeland in its markets. The reason given was the shortage of fresh fish. Ghent was joined by other large towns in Flanders, apparently convinced that they could get adequate supplies of cured herring from Scania or convinced that unless they acted there would be nothing but *kaakharing* available. The reaction from the fishing ports along the coast was strong and immediate. After delays a meeting was finally held in 1420 at which the towns withdrew their prohibition and Flemish fishermen immediately went back to curing herring and selling it in Flanders.

That finally swept away the remnants of restriction placed on the Flemish herring fishery in about 1396. It left the industry almost free to pursue the opportunities created by curing fish on board ship. And the new duke of Burgundy, Philip the Good, proved more interested in aiding the herring fishery than had his predecessor, John the Fearless. In 1424 Philip sharply reduced the duty charged on cured herring. A treaty negotiated with England in 1407 gave Flemish fishermen a guarantee of safety while working in English waters. In 1433 Holland and Zeeland were officially added to the possessions of the duke of Burgundy. That gave fishermen from those two northern provinces the same protection as Flemings, protection reaffirmed in a treaty with England of 1439. In Zeeland and Holland the herring fishery never had to face the political pressure of the Hansa. By the mid-fourteenth century governments there were trying to develop markets in the two provinces for cured fish. The presence of potential outlets for the product acted to increase the curing of herring on board ship. The port of Brielle by the early years of the fifteenth century, perhaps drawing on the experience of fishermen at Scania, had established itself as a center for the Dutch herring industry.[20] By the 1430s all Netherlands fishing ports were under the same government, one which enjoyed some power in international affairs. The dukes of Burgundy were less dependent on the Hanseatic League for the supply of all kinds of goods and of shipping services for their lands, once they had added Holland and Zeeland to their domains. The Dutch were already competing effectively with German traders. So the government, if not positively committed to the promotion of the curing of herring by Netherlands fishermen, at least was not going to impede those men from finding and using the most profitable techniques.

IV

Even in the first two decades of the fifteenth century the quantity of cured herring landed in Flanders could not compare with the imports of Scania *tonharing* of the

[20] Degryse, *Haringbedrijf* (n. 4 above) 49-51, 102-105, and (n. 1 above) 208-210, 218; Gottschalk (n. 9 above) 10-11; Doorman (n. 12 above) 171; S. Haak, "Brielle als vrije en bloeinde Handelsstad in de 15de eeuw," *Bijdragen voor Vanderlandsche Geschiedenis en Oudheidkunde,* ser. 4, 6 (1907) 35-36.

last years of the preceding century. Biervliet, the staple for all Flemish cured herring, received an annual average of less than forty-six lasts of herring from 1398 to 1408. The years were somewhat unusual since the area was devastated by a flood in 1404. The total value of the herring catch at Ostend rose some eight times from 1418 to 1467 and by the latter date volume was up to some 1600 lasts for that single port. The same kind of turnaround in the Netherlands fishery dating from the 1420s occurred in other ports. At Biervliet in 1426-1427 the annual average production of cured herring was 324 lasts. At Damme, then the staple port, the average annual landing of cured herring was 754 lasts in 1437 through 1441. About twenty-two percent of the total was brought there by fishermen from Holland and Zeeland. And those years were not especially good ones. There was a breakthrough some time in the second third of the fifteenth century when Netherlands production of cured herring replaced imports from Scania in the large Flanders market. The records of institutions confirm the shift away from traditional supplies. Netherlands cured herring was also exported, not just to inland markets in Brabant but also to Germany. Still the quantities were a far cry from the production totals of Scania in the fourteenth century. The towns of Flanders in 1423 after an investigation called for the promotion of putting herring in casks at sea because they felt production was not rising fast enough.[21] That was a sharp change from the attitude of just four years before.

The change in production methods and in government policy depended on related developments in technology and business methods. More important were certain specific and unique circumstances which made it commercially advantageous for fishermen to raise the proportion of their catch which they treated on board. Taking more herring further north and curing it, although technically feasible, was advisable only if ships and working capital could be found to make the voyages. It took time for Low Countries shipbuilders and fishermen and merchants to implement the necessary changes. The spread of the use of the large *vleet* net throughout the Netherlands did not take place until the second decade of the fifteenth century. It was in that same ten year period that shipbuilders produced the first herring buss. That ship type was probably a modification of the standard Scandinavian cargo ship of the thirteenth century. It was built to handle the heavy seas that herring fishermen met off the coast of Scotland and built to deal specifically with problems of using the big net. Men with more capital and with more extensive trading connections were drawn into the fishery and into the shore-based industry devoted to repacking and then distributing the fish. More money then could be advanced to crews for their longer voyages. The wealthier brokers were in a position to sell the product over a

[21] Degryse and Mus (n. 12 above) 105-106; Degryse (n. 18 above) 74-81; R. Degryse, "De Crisis in het Haringbedrijf te Oostende en te Damme van 1437 tot 1441," *Handelingen van de "Société d'Emulation" te Brugge* 102 (1965) 53-64; *idem*, "De Biervlietse Kaakharingproductie in de Jaren 1426 en 1427," *Marine Academie van België: Mededelingen* 13 (1961) 43-58; E. Vlietinck, *Het oude Oostende en zijne driejarige Belegering (1601-1604)* (Ostend 1897) 73; Ypma (n. 12 above) 37.

wider market.[22] The first signs of such changes in the organization of the industry date from the first half of the fifteenth century. The expansion of Low Countries production could only proceed as rapidly as constraints were removed, as rapidly as herring busses came into use and as investment increased.

While those developments in related technologies acted to remove restrictions, the commercial situation in the years around 1400 was a positive impetus to Netherlands fishermen to make more *kaakharing*. Their competitors, the merchants of the German Hansa, were periodically handicapped. There were short run problems of supply of cured herring from Scania. Production in Scania was always subject to variation, but in the late fourteenth and early fifteenth centuries the problems became more acute. The fishery there was always highly vulnerable both strategically and biologically. Supplies could be and were intermittently interrupted and each time that happened consumers were forced to seek a substitute. That meant using other types of fish or, increasingly, as knowledge of curing herring spread, looking for alternate sources of *kaakharing*.

Netherlands fishermen consistently exploited the opportunities created by the difficulties of the Scania fishery. Moreover, the Hansa merchants inadvertently helped them to do just that. The war between the Hanseatic League and Denmark which ended with the Treaty of Stralsund in 1370 forced the suspension of fishing in Scania in 1367 and 1368. The victory of the League was so complete that it then tried to eliminate all non-Hansa merchants from Scania. The League was not entirely successful. From 1388 to 1392 Hansards boycotted the Bruges market, so that none of their goods reached the Flemish staple of cured herring. In both cases a restrictive policy suddenly cut off supplies and drove more Netherlands merchants to take an interest in buying and marketing herring caught and cured on the North Sea. In 1393 fishing in Scania had to be suspended because of the activity of pirates. Presumably no cured herring was shipped to the Netherlands in that year and local fishermen were again put under pressure to supply the product. Since the herring was probably not edible for much more than a year it was impossible to stockpile it against such interruptions in supply. In any case it is doubtful that any merchant or government was in a position to finance such stockpiling. In 1410 the herring simply did not appear at Scania. There were other instances of such a sudden change in the spawning habits of the fish in the fifteenth century. There were poor catches reported in 1411, 1412, 1416 and 1425, for example.[23] By no means did the herring permanently disappear from the coast of Scania. It was not some shift in the Gulf Stream which led to the disappearance of the herring. Rather, coastal herring along the eastern side

[22] J. Ploeg, "Speurtoch naar Haringbuizen," *Mededelingen van de Nederlandse Vereniging voor Zeegeschiedenis* 25 (1972) 25-31; Theodorus Velius, *Chroniick van Hoorn* . . . (Hoorn 1648) 17; Degryse (n. 12 above) 121-127, and (n. 13 above) 146-150. He is correctly sceptical about giving an early fifteenth-century date for the full development of the herring buss.

[23] Gottschalk (n. 9 above) 11; Degryse, *Haringbedrijf* (n. 4 above) 99-100; Doorman (n. 1 above) 381-382; H. van der Wee, *The Growth of the Antwerp Market and the European Economy (Fourteenth-Sixteenth Centuries)* (The Hague 1963) 2.42-43, n. 76.

of the North Sea were subject to such sudden but short term changes in habits. They reappeared with the same irregularity.

The troubles with supply of Scania *tonharing* in the 1390s, the 1400s and the 1410s certainly affected government policy in Flanders. Indeed the laws seemed to change with the fortunes of imports from the North. In years when the Hansa merchants could not supply fish the government was defensive. It tried to prevent great increases in the output of domestic *kaakharing* for fear that it would add to their problems by generating a shortage of fresh herring. That had the political advantage of gaining the friendship of the Hansa merchants and increased the likelihood that, when supplies were available, those men would send them through Flemish ports. When there was enough cured herring for local markets and for those along the Rhine and in France the Flemish government lessened the restrictions on local producers but not enough to disturb their relations with the German traders. After about 1420 the interruptions led to a permanent change in government policy. The war between the towns of the Wendish coast, members of the Hanseatic League led by Lübeck, and Holland from 1437 to 1441 cut off supplies from Scania again. It was exactly in those years despite the activity of Dutch privateers and the generally high level of violence at sea that Netherlands fishermen proved themselves able to fill the vacuum left by a suspension of Scania supplies. It would be wrong to point to any single interruption or event which destroyed competition for Netherlands fishermen in preparing cured herring. A few years of peace in the first half of the fifteenth century which their principal competitors did not enjoy certainly helped. Earlier the change in the course of the river Yare and the silting of the harbor at Yarmouth from 1347 worked to the disadvantage of English fisherman and forced Netherlanders to look for alternate ports or simply to cure their herring at sea.[24] The fact that no other producer could consistently and reliably supply the Netherlands market graphically demonstrated again and again the advantages of curing herring on board. Each of the sudden collapses of supply gave Netherlands producers of cured herring windfall profits. Each time the gains led to increased production and to increased investment in equipment to raise production. Netherlands fishermen ranged over a wide area of the North Sea. Though there were good and bad years in the deep sea fishery a complete collapse of that catch is unheard of, unlike coastal fisheries. Netherlanders therefore always had a greater security of supply. Improvements in the safety of fishing vessels at sea through treaties or through arrangements for their protection along with the construction of ships of better quality all served to increase that advantage of the deep sea fishery. Each time that competitors had problems, Netherlands merchants were able to make inroads into new markets with herring produced by local fishermen, cured on board ship. And they could keep those markets as output rose. By the late fifteenth century even Hansa towns found themselves buying cured herring from Dutch fishermen.[25]

[24] Christensen (n. 4 above) 264-265; Degryse, "De Crisis" (n. 21 above) 62-63; Doorman (n. 12 above) 172; Jenkins (n. 4 above) 9-11.

[25] R. Degryse, "De Omvang van Vlaanderens Haring- en Zoutevisbedrijf op het Einde van het Frans-Bourgondisch Conflict (1482)," *Marine Academie van België: Mededelingen* 15 (1963) 45-47; Vlietinck (n. 21 above) 98; Ketner (n. 6 above) 18-19.

The prices of cured herring in the Netherlands reflected the sudden interruptions in the supply of fish from Scania. They also show the mechanism which existed for keeping the Flemish government informed of the situation in the herring market. The price data for the Low Countries around 1400 are scanty at best. The graph shows the pattern of price changes at Antwerp from 1387 to 1450. The figures reported are the three-year moving average of prices. While using such averages obscures the most violent fluctuations, at the same time it more clearly shows the trends over a long term, the kinds of changes which influenced investment decisions. Antwerp in those years was an increasingly important market for all goods, acting both as a center of consumption and a transshipment point for taking goods inland.[26] The Antwerp prices then are probably a good reflection of the general situation in the Netherlands.

In the 1390s the prices of cured or wet herring as they were called rose sharply at Antwerp. In 1395 the average price was at almost two and one-half times the level of 1386. The sudden jump can only be explained by a failure of imports of *tonharing* from Scania. With amounts like that being paid for a cask of cured herring it is not surprising that Flemish fishermen brought their own cured herring to the staple port for the first time in 1395. The high prices, and the greater concentration on curing the herring catch which followed from them, were probably the reasons for the government's acting so sharply to prevent the production and sale of preserved herring by Flemings. The grant by the duke of Burgundy in 1399 to allow limited production was only a small concession, since there had been a dramatic collapse in prices. The level was even below that of 1388 when the troubles with the Hanseatic League began. With the economic incentive for curing herring largely removed the destruction of the legal barrier was little more than symbolic. Prices began to rise again after a period of decline from 1404. That was the year of the flood which destroyed Hughevliet, badly damaged Biervliet and also disrupted salt production in the province of Zeeland. All that certainly limited the output of cured herring in the Low Countries. The flood may explain the small and slow rise in prices after 1404. But it was still what happened in the Sound that had the greatest and indeed the overwhelming influence on prices in Antwerp. The failure of the catch in Scania in 1410 sent the average price of *tonharing* up more than eighty-five percent from 1409 to 1413. After abating in 1414 and 1415 the rise became even more marked, reaching a maximum in 1419. The price then was more than three times that in the year before the flood, 1403. It was in 1419 that the Ghent city government took strenuous action to stop Flemish fishermen from preserving their herring. Undoubtedly those men made every effort to take advantage of the higher prices and cured higher proportions of their catch. It was a repetition of the situation in the mid-1390s. The sharp fall in prices from 1420 through 1422 explains the decision of Ghent and other towns to withdraw from their policy of restriction and indeed explains why they gave in relatively easily to petitions from the fishing villages in

---

[26] Van der Wee (n. 23 above) 1.227-280. This is the source for the data presented in the graph. Another price series from Antwerp appears in C. Verlinden et al., *Dokumenten voor de Geschiedenis van Prijzen en Lonen in Vlaanderen en Brabant* (Bruges 1959-1972) 2.2.731-737. The series begins in 1426 and is not such as to contradict conclusions drawn from the fuller series of van der Wee.

GRAPH: Herring prices at Antwerp, 1387-1450   3-year moving average in Brabant money of account

1420. Prices were already falling. The relative stability of prices but at a high level over the following decade undoubtedly contributed to the newfound government interest in promoting domestic production of cured herring and also to the interest of Netherlands fishermen in increasing their output of the product. The Wendish War in 1438-1441 led to another increase in the delivered price of herring at Antwerp. But the average annual increase in the worst years, 1440 through 1442, was only eleven percent. The rise was not anywhere near the scale of the increase during the Hansa boycott of Bruges from 1388 to 1392, though admittedly the latter was from a lower base. Indeed the fluctuations in prices were less and less extreme over the whole period. It seems that by the 1440s production in the coastal provinces of the Low Countries, in Friesland, Holland, Zeeland and belatedly in Flanders, was at such a level that it could offer an effective substitute for at least a significant part of the imported Scania *tonharing.*

V

The troubles in the last two decades of the fourteenth century, reflected in the high prices of Scania herring, created the necessary impetus for Low Countries fishermen to increase sharply their curing of fish on board ship. Moreover the problems gave governments the incentive to consider ways to promote that production. Once the sudden price increases had created the opportunities for profits from curing herring, then investment in the technique in the form of ships and casks and nets was created either from the profits themselves or from the wealth of merchants interested in getting part of those profits. The increase in curing also gave more fishermen a chance to learn how to use the method and become accustomed to gutting and packing fish on board. This learning-by-doing combined with the windfall profits created a compulsive sequence in which advance on one front made for opportunities for advance on another. Once started the process of adoption of the technique gathered momentum. By the middle of the fifteenth century that sequence along with the changes in prices had generated a new and sizable industry in the Low Countries producing a commodity which had formerly been imported.

The change to domestically produced cured herring did not imply any change in the volume shipped. With the general increase in population in Europe through the fifteenth century the demand for herring rose. But there is no indication that the transfer of curing from the shores of Scania to Netherlands fishing boats in the North Sea created any major shift in consumption. The trading patterns of the fourteenth century, then, remained the same. The Hansa ships which carried herring to the Low Countries did disappear. But they were partially replaced by Dutch ships carrying the same product in the opposite direction. That gave some small aid to the expanding Netherlands merchant marine. More important was the increase in the tonnage of the fishing fleet, a direct result of the change to deep sea fishing. Given the level of production there were probably at least 50 and as many as 200 herring busses operating from the Netherlands coast in the fifteenth century. In the off-season owners used those vessels to carry other cargo, thus increasing the available tonnage at Low Countries ports. Beyond the fishermen and sailors the domestic herring fishery also meant work for packers on shore and suppliers such as coopers and shipcarpenters among others. Still the quantity of herring produced was small. The trade in wine from Bordeaux to England suffered badly in the first half of the fifteenth century because of wars but still the annual average export of wine from Bordeaux from 1400 to 1440 was about 11,000 tons. That was eight to ten times the volume of herring cured on board ship by Netherlanders at that time.[27]

Netherlands production of cured herring in the fifteenth century rose to a point where it could replace imports of Scania *tonharing*. But it was not until the mid-sixteenth century that Netherlands output reached that of the Baltic fishery at its height. By 1580 the Netherlands herring fishery produced about 20,000 lasts annually, more than twice the figure for the fourteenth century Scania fishery. The annual average export of herring to the Baltic in the 1560s was about 2800 lasts, almost two-thirds more than the quantity traveling in the opposite direction in the late fourteenth century.[28] Netherlands fishermen and merchants reached and surpassed the record of the Scania fishery by tapping the growing market for food. They were able to take advantage of that potentially larger market for herring because of developments in their own fishery, the development of complementary techniques and the evolution of a legal and commercial framework for the industry at home and elsewhere in Europe.

No sudden breakthrough in herring production or trade was possible in the later Middle Ages because it was not a product for mass consumption. Even if all the cured herring brought from the Baltic in the late fourteenth century had been consumed in the three great Flemish towns of Ghent, Bruges and Ypres, at most each resident would have had one herring per day. The population of the Low Countries around 1400 was probably under 2,000,000; but even so, imports from Scania could only supply each person with about 12 fish each year.[29] Since there was extensive reexport of cured herring, that figure should be at least halved. There was good reason for the limited market for herring, despite the method of preservation and the relative ease of transportation. Herring unquestionably was and is a good source of protein. It compares favorably with other fish as a source of fat and vitamin D. In

[27] Margery K. James, "The Fluctuations of the Anglo-Gascon Wine Trade during the Fourteenth Century," in *Essays in Economic History* 2, ed. E. M. Carus-Wilson (New York 1962) 143-144; Yves Renouard, "Les transformations économiques et sociales," in *Histoire de Bordeaux* 3, ed. Charles Higounet (Bordeaux 1965) 423-424.

[28] H. A. H. Kranenburg, *De Zeevisscherij van Holland in den Tijd der Republiek* (Amsterdam 1946) 39-43; W. S. Unger, "De Sonttabellen," *Tijdschrift voor Geschiedenis* 41 (1926) 143-144.

[29] Population data are notoriously difficult to find and inaccurate at best. See David M. Nicholas, *Town and Countryside: Social, Economic and Political Tensions in Fourteenth-Century Flanders* (Bruges 1971) 234. The estimate for the three towns assumes that they all had a population at least as great as that of Ypres in 1412. That much is certainly true. See B. H. Slicher van Bath, "Historical Demography and the Social and Economic Development of the Netherlands," *Daedalus* 43 (1968) 609-610.

general the mineral content is high as is the calorific value per unit weight.[30] The problem at least in the first half of the fifteenth century was cost. In general consumers in Brabant paid less for fat, calories and even protein when it came in cheese, rye or wheat than when it came embodied in herring. Data for meat are not as complete but they suggest that in the third quarter of the fifteenth century herring was a cheaper source of calories and about equally as expensive a source of protein as meat. In famine years when grain prices skyrocketed to record levels then herring was a less expensive source of protein than rye. That was true in 1437 and 1438. Wheat was about as good a source of protein for the same expenditure as herring. But even in years of record grain prices herring was still a much more expensive source of calories. And in any case cheese was always a better buy, except in one year, 1438, when protein from cheese cost slightly more than protein from herring.

Ratios of the Cost of Calories, Protein and Fat from Cheese, Rye, Wheat and Meat Relative to the Cost of Calories, Protein and Fat from Herring in Brabant[31]

Food	Period	Calories	Protein	Fat
Cheese	1386-1450	.41	.57	.56
Rye	1392-1450	.16	.53	.04
Wheat	1427-1450	.29	.91	.03
Meat	1453-1474	1.84	.95	.04

The estimates are subject to sizable but unspecified error. Still it would be surprising if all errors were consistently one-sided. Even if the ratios are off by as much as fifty percent, the conclusion that herring was a relatively expensive source of nutrients is not in jeopardy. Cured herring was valuable in diversifying the diet of medieval Europeans. It was valuable as a source of protein at times when other sources were not available. It was valuable in satisfying religious prohibitions against the eating of meat. But, economically, consumers were wise to choose other foods. Grains were a significantly better source of nutrients for equal expenditures and in any case that was all the less well-off could afford.

The adoption of curing herring on board ship in the early fifteenth century did not mean a major change in nutrition for Europeans. Nor did it mean an immediate or massive change in employment or industrial practice in the Low Countries. Rather what the technical innovation did do was lay the basis for the long-term development of a large industry which depended on international trading connections both for

[30] Olav Notevarp, "Herring, the Raw Material," in The Technology of Herring Utilization (n. 2 above) 38-39; Charles Louis Anderson, "Preserved Pickled Herring," University of Washington Publications in Fisheries 1 (1925) 24.

[31] Prices are taken from van der Wee (n. 23 above) 1.175-176 (rye in Antwerp), 184 (wheat in Lier), 218-220 (cheese in Antwerp), 225 (meat in Malines), 279-281 (herring in Brabant). Relative food values are from B. K. Watt et al., Composition of Foods, rev. ed., Agriculture Handbook no. 8 (Washington 1963) table 1. Adjustments are made for the historic change in the specific gravity of grain following Lord Beveridge, "The Yield and Price of Corn in the Middle Ages," in Essays in Economic History 1, ed. E. M. Carus-Wilson (London 1954) 16-17.

supplies of raw materials and for sale of the finished product. The trading complex which emerged over time stretched throughout Europe. The innovation also made possible the more extensive use of a previously untapped resource, that is, fish in deep water. It also involved a shift in the source of supply of cured herring to western Europe from the Baltic. But most important the development in the Netherlands herring fishery offers a good example, despite some confusion, of the process of technical innovation in the later Middle Ages. In the face of the economic troubles of the fourteenth and fifteenth centuries Europeans produced a number of important changes in technology. The absolute and relative figures of output in this case as in many others tend to mask the importance of the qualitative change as well as to diminish the significance of the process of innovation itself.

The *kaken* method of preserving herring was well known and widely used in Europe before 1300. Its use on board ship probably began early in the fourteenth century. But it took the sudden and sharp falls in supply created both by political decisions and by the variations in the catch of the coastal fisheries to lead Flemish and all Low Countries fishermen to adopt extensively the curing method on board their herring boats. Apparently there was a Willem Beukels living at the time of that change in practice and apparently he was to some extent involved in promoting that change. His presence and the association of his family with the herring fishery at Biervliet explains the traditional association of his name with the adoption of the technique. It does not explain the concentration of so many writers on this one man or their insistence on his action as the reason for the success of the Dutch herring fishery in the first half of the seventeenth century. The adoption of any innovation depends on a great deal more than simply the presence of the invention. The survival of the legend of Willem Beukels of Biervliet serves only to obscure the complexity of that process. It also serves to misrepresent the intimate relationship in this case of the economy and government policy to technical change. The history of medieval technology is undoubtedly filled with many similar examples.

Department of History
University of British Columbia
Vancouver, British Columbia V6T 1W5, Canada

THE COMMUNITY OF LAW AND LETTERS: SOME NOTES ON THOMAS USK'S AUDIENCE

•

by May Newman Hallmundsson

Commenting upon *The Testament of Love*, Gervase Mathew, in his book entitled *The Court of Richard II*, presents the reader with a viewpoint concerning Thomas Usk, which on every account must be adjudged completely misleading. According to Mathew, the audience to whom the work was addressed was made up exclusively of members of the court circle. *The Testament*, he continues, "was intended to appeal to powerful patrons."[1]

At first glance, the statements seem plausible enough; after all, even the title of the piece promises its readers the kind of literature which was usually composed for a court audience. Moreover, due to the scholarship of Professors Bradley[2] and Skeat,[3] it is now common knowledge that Usk made extensive use of Chaucer's works, including the poet's contribution to court entertainment, that is, *Troilus and Criseyde* and *The House of Fame*.[4] Therefore, since both these pieces were written for a court audience, it is to be expected that Usk's *Testament of Love* would be similar in content and style. Yet, it is evident at once, if only from the twisted sentence structure of the prose in Book 1, that *The Testament* is anything *but* entertaining or courtly. For that matter, it is not even poetry!

The work is divided into three books, Book 1 deals with the political intrigues which landed Usk in prison. These grew out of the larger factional strife between those Londoners who supported Richard II and those who followed his uncle, the duke of Lancaster — a strife which eventually cost the king his crown. Overtaken by the changing fortunes of municipal politics, Usk, rather than perjure himself, preferred to reveal certain "secret dealings." But, in so doing, he incurred the wrath of many of his former friends. In prison, Heavenly Love appears to him. She comforts him, but warns that he must submit to the adversity which has overtaken him: the slanderous tales whispered by his past associates and the loss of position, wealth, and

---

[1] Gervase Mathew, *The Court of Richard II* (London 1968) 54ff.

[2] H. Bradley, "Thomas Usk and *The Testament of Love*," in his *Collected Papers* (London 1928). Cf. also his article in the DNB. Professor Bradley first identified the author's name in an article which appeared in *The Athenaeum* 1 (1897) 184, 215.

[3] W. W. Skeat, *The Complete Works of Geoffrey Chaucer* 7 (Oxford 1894-1897) viii-xxxi. An edition of *The Testament of Love* is included (1-145).

[4] Skeat's *Introduction* to the text includes a listing of parallel passages that occur in *The Testament*. More significantly, he shows the extent to which Usk drew upon Chaucer's translation of Boethius's *Consolation of Philosophy*.

so on. Book 2 discusses the mutability of the fortunes of men. Usk comes to an understanding of the meaning of true repentance, and, content with the promise of heavenly bliss, he praises the virtues of Margaret, that is, Holy Church or Divine Grace. Book 3 teaches that all joy can be obtained through faithful service in love, for charity (or love) toward one's fellow-man is a service to God. Such a service is a "testament," that is, a "witnessing" of the divine grace.[5]

If Usk was not addressing members of Richard's court, exactly whom did he have in mind? Usk had written his work while imprisoned in Newgate.[6] If he had had a "powerful patron," he might never have been there in the first place. Furthermore, if he was hoping to secure the help of such a person, it is very probable that he would have "named" him somewhere in *The Testament* itself. There is, however, no mention of a dedication, or any indication as to who "he," or "they," could be. The only one whom Usk actually hints at is Chaucer,[7] and certainly, during this period, Chaucer had troubles of his own. He had been deprived of his office as comptroller of the customs in 1385, possibly due to the fact that he was one of Sir Nicholas Brembre's associates.[8] In 1386, Philippa Chaucer died, and in the same year Chaucer was occupied with transferring his residence, evidently to Kent.[9] After that, he visited London only when his presence was required at meetings of Parliament.[10] During the second period of Usk's imprisonment, that is, 1387-1388, Chaucer was himself avoiding arrest, as various actions were brought against him to recover debts. Warrants were issued, but he was not to be found in London.[11] Besides, he was scarcely what one would call a "powerful patron."

It is true that other members of London's literary community, such as Chaucer, Clanvowe, Froissart, and Scogan were, in all likelihood, writing for a court audience. It is also true that they knew and were, in some way or another, personally involved with individual members of the court circle. Any attempts, however, to discover similar connections for Usk prove, in the end, to be unrewarding. There were, of course, two or three members of the court circle with whom Usk was acquainted, such as the young heir of Richard, lord of Ponynges,[12] Michael de la Pole, earl of

---

[5] See Skeat's note concerning the use of this word (n. 3 above) 7 p. xxviii.

[6] He was imprisoned twice, once in 1384 and again in 1387. As a result, there has been some problem regarding the date of composition. See R. Bressie, "The Date of Thomas Usk's Testament of Love," *Modern Philology* 26 (1928) 17-29.

[7] Cf. Book 3, chap. 4, lines 248-259, in which he speaks of the poet as Love's "owne trewe servaunt" and "the noble philosophical poet."

[8] Nicholas Brembre, a grocer by trade and several times mayor of London, was a member of the king's party. In 1385, Brembre was under investigation by members of Gloucester's committee.

[9] *Chaucer Life-Records*, ed. M. Crow and C. Olsen (Oxford 1966) 91-92; hereafter cited as LR.

[10] LR 364-367.

[11] LR 388-401.

[12] In 1387, the manor of Iffeld in Sussex was committed to Nicholas Extone until Robert Ponynges came of age. Among those who mainprised Extone was Thomas Usk (cf. *Fine Rolls Richard II, 1381-91* 10.199). Extone, fishmonger and friend of Brembre, had been an alderman in 1382, when Usk was a member of the opposing faction, i.e., the non-victualling party headed by Northampton. But by this date, i.e., 1387, Usk had already changed sides, and his former enemies

Suffolk, and Robert Vere, earl of Oxford.[13] But they could hardly have been interested in what Usk had to say, for Robert Ponynges was only eight years old in 1388, and the earls of both Suffolk and Oxford had fled the country.[14] On the other hand, there are indications that Usk would have had many associates in Chancery, especially among those concerned with the complex administration of its judicial department. Of the others, with whom Usk was indicted, there were six chief justices of the Common Bench, one sergeant-at-arms, one apprentice of the law, and one sheriff. Aside from these, Usk had dealings with, at least, two more sergeants-at-arms and one recorder.[15]

It seems appropriate to note here that the exhaustive investigations of Professor T. F. Tout have shown that, by the beginning of the fourteenth century, the Chancery was no longer merely an administrative body, but had developed as a court of law.[16] That is, in addition to issuing writs of summons[17] and writs of expenses,[18] the clerks of Chancery now began to "receive petitions" and to "present" them to the "triers of petitions," that is, the magnates and judges who, in turn, were authorized to consult ministers and sergeants-at-law, when they needed advice. Muriel Bowden has observed that during Chaucer's time a sergeant of the law was "one of a superior order of barristers . . . from whom were chosen all the Common Law judges . . . ."[19] Usually, the "triers of petitions" were assigned by the king. But by the time Usk was writing his *Testament*, this was no longer the case. Beginning in 1385, those men who tried petitions were nominated by a clerk of Parliament, and such a clerk *always* belonged to the Chancery.

This change in the procedure of appointing a "trier of petitions" has great bearing on the question which was posed at the outset, that is, if *The Testament of Love* was not addressed to the court circle, to whom was it meant to appeal? Obviously, Usk would have been concerned with reaching those who could give him immediate aid, inasmuch as Newgate prison was hardly the kind of place conducive to long periods of waiting.[20] If, indeed, he was to be helped, that help would have to come from

---

were now his friends. Extone also knew Ralph Strode, one of the two men to whom Chaucer had dedicated his *Troilus and Criseyde*. Strode served as common pleader during Extone's mayoralty (cf. *Letter-Book H* in the *Calendar of Letter-Books of the City of London*, ed. R. R. Sharpe [London, 1901-1907] 305-306). Another member of London's literary circle who was involved with the Ponynges family was Geoffrey Chaucer. (See LR 302.)

[13] Their names appear together with Usk's on the indictment (cf. *Close Rolls Richard II, 1385-89* 3.474; *Patent Rolls Richard II, 1385-89* 3.469, 546). Vere would have also known Chaucer, for he was the poet's superior in the royal household. When Chaucer petitioned to have a permanent deputy at the Customs, Vere intervened for him (LR 169).

[14] Pole went to Paris and Vere to Bruges, thereby escaping the punishment Usk suffered.

[15] See below.

[16] T. F. Tout, *Chapters in the Administrative History of England*, 6 vols. (Manchester 1935). One of the results was that the Chancery became increasingly involved in the treacherous politics which brought the century to a close.

[17] The purpose of a writ of summons was to bring Parliament together.

[18] Such a writ served as proof of a knight's or a burgher's wages.

[19] Muriel Bowden, *Commentary on the General Prologue to The Canterbury Tales* (New York 1948) 165.

[20] For the unwholesome conditions of Newgate prison two hundred years later, see John Stow, *A Survey of London* (Oxford 1908 [1603]) 1.36, 350; 2.355.

persons capable of seeing that his petition was "properly directed" and that his case was promptly reviewed. It is, therefore, quite likely that Usk was appealing to the clerks, lawyers, and judges of Chancery, and that *The Testament* was a "plea"[21] on the part of the accused to convince them of the justification of his actions.

Two questions now remain to be answered. First, are we able to identify some of the people connected with the Chancery, and, second, what, if any, was their relationship to other members of London's literary community?

Officially, Usk began his political career as a "scryveyn"[22] or private secretary to John de Northampton, mayor of London:[23]

> In my youth I was drawe to ben assentaunt and (in my mightes) helping
> to certain conjuracions and other grete maters of ruling of citizens. (Bk.
> 1, chap. 4, lines 53-55)

Prior to this, he appears to have served in the capacity of attorney,[24] main-

---

[21] That is, in the legal sense of the term.

[22] *6 Aug. 1384.* Appointment of Thomas Godlake and John Chirche to seize and bring to London, to be there imprisoned at the disposal of the mayor, William Essex, draper, Thomas Usk, "scryveyn," Robert Fraunceys, goldsmith, and John Lincolle, goldsmith; *Patent Rolls Richard II, 1381-85* 2.500. Godlake's father-in-law, John Gravesende, citizen and draper of London, had had dealings with Gower concerning his holdings in Kent (cf. John H. Fisher, *John Gower: Moral Philosopher and Friend of Chaucer* [New York 1964] 337 n. 71). William Essex, member of the Common Council, was acquainted with Strode and attended the meeting on 1 August 1376 at which the latter, as common sergeant, presented the city's plea to Parliament that it cease making slanderous accusations against the civic government. He also knew John Gower, having witnessed the 1367 transation (noted above) between the poet and John Gravesende, draper. Robert Fraunceys was master of the goldsmiths and a member of the Common Council. Like Essex, he was acquainted with Strode who, as common sergeant, had represented Fraunceys in a case of defamation (cf. *Plea and Memoranda Rolls* 2.228). It is also possible that he knew Chaucer, for as clerk of the works the poet received money from the Exchequer "per manus Roberti Calnelstede" for work executed by Fraunceys (LR [n. 9 above] 439). John Fraunceys, goldsmith and probable kinsman of Robert, endorsed a writ distraining Chaucer to account at the Exchequer in 1391 (LR 447-448, and cf. Sylvia Thrupp, *The Merchant Class of London* [Ann Arbor 1962] 342).

[23] John de Northampton, draper and head of the non-victualling party, was the favorite of London's poor. Upon assuming office in 1381, he devoted his attention to crushing the powerful victualling companies headed by Brembre, Philipot (Grocers), and Extone (Fishmongers). As a result, he kept the price of food in the city from soaring, and for a time he was even successful in suppressing the ubiquitous monopoly of the city magnates. However, in 1383, Brembre, with the additional help of the craft misteries, won re-election and thereupon proceeded to hound Northampton in the streets of London. Constantly surrounded by hundreds of his followers, Northampton incurred the suspicion of his successor, who lost no time in arresting him for sedition. Brought before the king at the council of Reading, Northampton denied all of Usk's accusations, including the implication that he had aligned himself with those at court, who were seeking to curtail the power of the monarch. He was sentenced to life imprisonment, although Robert Vere was able to secure his release in 1387. Northampton was not permitted to return to London until 1390, but five years later all privileges of the city were restored to him. He died in 1397. (It should be added that he also knew Strode, having served as alderman of London in 1375, when the latter was common pleader of the city; cf. *Letter-Book H* [n. 12 above] 305-306.)

[24] *11 July 1376.* John Mangell, mercer, Richard Notyngham, John Walton, Henry atte More and William Bateman were summoned to answer John Bere, haberdasher, who prosecuted by Thomas Usk, his attorney, in a plea of trespass; *Plea and Memoranda Rolls* 2.221.

perneur,[25] and witness[26] in various actions involving a diverse segment of the commonalty of London. There may also be some truth in the persistent belief that he was a member of the lay clergy, for in a document dated 1375 he is listed as a "clerk."[27] Evidently, Usk did not begin to travel in Chancery circles until 1384, and then only after he had "confessed" at the Council of Reading.[28] Indeed, it was this testimony that set off the chain of events which for many ended in banishment or on the gallows. Usk refers to the incident in his *Testament*:

> But now it greveth me to remembre these dyvers sentences, in janglinge of these shepy people; certes, me thinketh, they oughten to maken joye that a sothe may be knowe. For my trouthe and my conscience ben witnesse to me bothe, that this (knowinge sothe) have I sayed for no harme ne malice of tho persones, but only for trouthe of my sacrament in my ligeaunce, by which I was charged on my kinges behalfe. (Bk. 1, chap. 6, lines 160-166)

It is the opinion of Sharpe and Bradley that Usk was suborned by Nicholas Brembre,[29] and there is some reason to believe that such was the case. Usk himself tells us that

> me rought litel of any hate of the mighty senatours in thilke cite, ne of communes malice . . . . Now than tho persones that suche thinges have

---

[25] *14 May 1376.* Robert Markeby, skinner, attached to answer the Mayor, Aldermen, and Commonalty, as well as John Rote and other Wardens of the mistery of Skinners, for that [he] . . . had offered violence to the Masters of the said mistery . . . . A day named, and the said Robert mainprised by Ralph Coo, Thomas Usk, and William Depyng; *Letter-Book H* (n. 12 above) 29-30. The mayor referred to in the document was John Haddele, grocer, who held the office from 1376 to 1380. Together with Chaucer, he mainprised John de Ramsey, treasurer of Calais, and with Brembre, Philipot, and Waleworth was appointed treasurer of war under Richard II. Haddele also knew Strode, for the latter, as common pleader of London, tried various cases before him. See LR (n. 9 above) 277-278, and cf. *Letter-Book H* 72.

[26] *21 Nov. 1379.* William Waryn, executor of the will of Alice, widow of William Spicer of Devizes, proved the said will by the oaths of Thomas Usk and Thomas Farnham; *Plea and Memoranda Rolls* 2.257-258. *12 Sept. 1384.* Henry de Frowyk . . . to William de Middelton . . . Surrender and quitclaim . . . of a tenement in the parishes of Wyllesdon and Hendon with houses thereupon built, lands, meadows, rents etc. . . . Witnesses: John Bryan . . . Thomas Usk; *Close Rolls Richard II, 1381-85* 2.125. Usk's co-witness, John Bryan, fishmonger, served as alderman in 1377, 1380, and 1382. Besides Usk, Bryan knew Strode, having been appointed auditor in a case which the common pleader tried (cf. *Plea and Memoranda Rolls* 2.265).

[27] *13 Sept. 1375.* Release and quitclaim from Margaret Mitford of London to Thomas Usk, clerk, of all actions arising out of any claims up to the present day; *Plea and Memoranda Rolls* 2.204.

[28] Usk was arrested in August 1384, together with William Essex, Robert Fraunceys, and John Lincolle; on 18 August he was brought before the Council: *20 Aug. 1384.* To the mayor of London. Order to bring Thomas Usk "scryveyn" again to London, and to keep him in prison in safe custody as the mayor shall think best until further order for his deliverance; as lately the king commanded him to cause the said Thomas, then imprisoned in his custody, to come before the king and council at Redynge, to do what by advice of the council should be appointed; *Close Rolls Richard II, 1381-85* 2.476. Essex, Fraunceys, and Lincolle remained confined in Newgate prison, but Usk was released sometime before 24 September: *24 Sept. 1384.* Pardon to Thomas Usk, "scryvein," for all treasons, felonies and other offenses whereof he is indicted in the city of London; *Patent Rolls Richard II, 1381-85* 2.467 (cf. also *Patent Rolls Richard II, 1381-85* 2.470).

[29] See *Letter-Book H* (n. 12 above) xxxvii, and cf. DNB.

cast to redresse, for wrathe of my first medlinge shopen me to dwelle in
this pynsande prison, til Lachases my threed ne lenger wolde twyne. (Bk.
1, chap. 6, lines 60ff.)

But upon his release, men who formerly had been Usk's "enemies" suddenly became
his associates, while Brembre himself saw to it that his prime witness was properly
rewarded. Thus, between 1384 and 1387, Usk was appointed sergeant-at-arms and
under-sheriff of the county of Middlesex,[30] and the ambitious young "scryveyn"
from Newgate[31] now found himself a guest in the house of the mayor and in the
society of men who held high places in the Chancery.[32] Among them were one of
Richard's most trusted advisors, Robert Tresilian, the chief justice of the King's
Bench, and Robert Bealknap, chief justice of the Common Bench.

Tresilian, who is mentioned in Gower's *Cronica Tripertita*, had been appointed
justice in 1381, shortly before the suppression of the Peasants' Revolt, and in time to
sentence John Ball to death. But when Northampton was brought to trial, the chief
justice refused to be one of the presiding justices on the grounds that the jurisdiction
of the case belonged to the mayor.[33] He did, nevertheless, get to know Brembre's
chief witness, for, having consented to attend the proceedings, Tresilian was present
when Usk testified.

The chief justice, like his friend Brembre, had many friends who were interested
in literature. He knew Trevisa's patron, Thomas Berkeley, with whom he served as
justice of the peace in Gloucestershire.[34] He had also been associated with John de

---

[30] *2 Sept. 1387.* Letter of Privy Seal to the Mayor and Sheriffs of London bidding them
appoint Thomas Usk, the King's Sergeant-at-arms, to be Under-Sheriff of the county of Middlesex in the place of John Boterwyk, who was getting too old for work; *Letter-Book H* 316-317.
7 Oct. 1387. Letter of Privy Seal from the King to the Mayor, Aldermen, and Commons,
thanking them for their loyalty . . . . It was his [i.e., the king's] intention . . . to grant a pardon
to all who confessed their misdoings and prayed his favour . . . . He charges them to see that no
one troubles him with petitions to show greater favour to the traitors John Norhamptone, John
More, and Richard Norbury, but to learn particulars as to the property of these men, and
safeguard the same until further orders. He is gratified that, in accordance with his request, they
have appointed Thomas Usk to the office of Under-Sheriff of Middlesex, and promises that such
appointment shall not form a precedent to the prejudice of the City's franchise; *Letter-Book H*
317.

[31] It is somewhat ironical to imagine Usk as a child, playing in the shadow of the very prison
where he was later to spend the last days of his life.

[32] A number of them belonged to London's literary community. Brembre, for example, was
intimately acquainted with Strode, who, as noted earlier, was common pleader during this first
administration, i.e., 1377. Brembre continued to concern himself with the lawyer's welfare when
he returned to office (cf. *Letter-Book H* [n. 12 above] 89-90, 245, 287-288). Brembre was also a
long-time friend of Chaucer's, having been a collector of the wool customs in 1374-1375 and
1377-1378, when the poet was comptroller of wool and wool hides (LR [n. 9 above] 339).
Again, Brembre was a collector of customs on wine and all other merchandise from 1379 to
1386, during the period in which Chaucer served as comptroller of the petty customs (LR
153ff.).

[33] The mayor in question was, of course, his friend, Nicholas Brembre.

[34] On 20 March 1380, they were commissioned to array and equip the men of Gloucester (cf.
Patent Rolls Richard II, 1377-81 1.474). Together, they acted as justices of the peace on 26 May
1380 (*Patent Rolls Richard II, 1377-81* 1.513), 8 March 1382 (*Patent Rolls Richard II, 1381-85*
2.138), and 8 February 1385 (*Patent Rolls Richard II, 1381-85* 2.529).

Beauchamp, who was a friend of the Clanvowes and probably of Gower.[35] Moreover, Tresilian was acquainted with Chaucer, who testified before him during the Scrope-Grosvenor proceedings, and with whom he had been appointed justice of the peace in Kent in 1386.[36] (In this connection it is interesting to note that Tresilian's daughter married the probable owner of the ship called the "Maudeleyne," mentioned in the *General Prologue* to the *Canterbury Tales*.)[37]

Unfortunately, when Usk was indicted in 1387,[38] the chief justice was hardly in a position to review the case. Having appended his signature to the Nottingham Declaration,[39] Tresilian brought down upon his head the wrath of the lords appellant. He was convicted of treason on the morning of 19 February 1388, and hanged later the same day.

Another member of Chancery with whom Usk was acquainted was Robert Bealknap, the chief justice of the Common Bench.[40] During his career, Bealknap, like Tresilian, had met many men who belonged to the literary circle. In 1382, for example, he served on a commission[41] with Thomas de Brinton, the Benedictine monk whose sermons all London flocked to hear.[42] Others on that commission included William Septanus,[43] Arnold Savage,[44] John de Cobham,[45] and Thomas Colpepir[46] — all of whom were friends of Gower. In 1385, Bealknap and Chaucer

---

[35] Cf. Fisher (n. 22 above) 61.

[36] LR (n. 9 above) 361. One of the most celebrated cases of the fourteenth century was the suit between Sir Richard le Scrope and Sir Robert Grosvenor concerning the right to use a certain coat of arms. While this may appear trivial by modern standards, the fact that it involved the honor of two knights made it a matter of considerable consequence. The proceedings, which were held in the Court of Chivalry and not in a regular court of law, lasted for six years. Final judgment favored Scrope. For further discussion, see J. G. Nichols, "The Scrope-Grosvenor Controversy," *The Herald and Genealogist* 1 (1863) 385-400.

[37] See John Manly, *Some New Light on Chaucer* (New York 1926) 179.

[38] *28 Dec. 1387.* To the mayor and sheriffs of London. Order to cause Thomas Usk, taken and imprisoned in their custody it is said, to come before the king in chancery on Tuesday next, with the cause of his imprisonment, to give information etc.; *Close Rolls Richard II, 1385-89* 3.393.

[39] In this document, the judges pledged themselves to uphold Richard's power over the Parliament.

[40] He was appointed chief justice in 1374.

[41] Those whom Richard commissioned were empowered to keep the peace in Kent (cf. *Patent Rolls Richard II, 1381-85* 2.138).

[42] Brinton, who was the king's confessor, often preached at St. Paul's in London.

[43] Gower purchased a moiety of Aldington Manor from Septanus for 80 marks. The transaction, however, proved to be illegal, for Septanus was still a minor. For Gower's alleged role in this transaction, cf. Fisher (n. 22 above) 53ff.

[44] Sir Arnold Savage, who witnessed Gower's will, was a justice of the peace for Kent and one of Chaucer's acquaintances. Fisher (66) points out that Sir Arnold's daughter eventually married William Clifford, the son of Chaucer's friend, Lewis.

[45] John de Cobham, to whom Gower granted his manor of Kentwell in Suffolk, also knew Chaucer, having served with the poet as a justice of the peace and as a member of Parliament for the county of Kent. John's unique contribution to letters was that he founded Cobham College. For further information see LR (n. 9 above) 361, 366 n. 6; and Fisher (n. 22 above) 53.

[46] Thomas Colpepir was one of the knights who became involved in the "Septanus affair." Having known the elder William Septanus, Thomas took part in an inquisition post mortem, the purpose of which was "to find out . . . the true age of [the heir], who swore to . . . the incorrect age, and who counseled him [the heir] to commit the fraud" (Fisher 52-54, 314ff.).

were both appointed justices of the peace for Kent,[47] and in the following year the poet appeared before him as a mainperneur for Simon Manning, whose wife, Katherine, may have been Chaucer's sister.[48]

Had circumstances been different, Bealknap could have helped Usk secure another hearing. But, as it happened, the chief justice of the Common Bench signed the Nottingham Declaration and was, like Tresilian, forced to suffer the consequences. Bealknap was banished to Ireland and his property confiscated by the Crown.[49]

In addition to the aforementioned judges,[50] Usk was associated with others in Chancery, such as John Blake, an apprentice-at-law who had come up to Westminster from Cornwall. Apparently, Blake was well on his way to achieving a brilliant career, for he had caught the attention of Tresilian, who secured a place for him on the king's council.[51] Such a position would have made him a valuable person to know, especially if one was in need of legal aid. Unhappily, there was not much chance for anyone to benefit from Blake's newly acquired prominence. Sometime before 25 August 1387, he was summoned to Nottingham, at Tresilian's suggestion, to draw up a document which demanded that the royal prerogative be acknowledged above all others. More specifically, the document was to insist upon recognition by the lords and commons that they were to discuss only what the king presented to them, that the punishment of ministers could only be carried out with his permission, and, finally, that the king had the power to dissolve Parliament at his pleasure.

Blake, having rendered these principles into questions, submitted them to the

---

John Colpepir, his kinsman, was well known to Chaucer, for both had been justices of the peace, members of Parliament, and commissioners of walls and ditches for the county of Kent; cf. LR (n. 9 above) 340, 351, 362.

[47] LR 361. Bealknap was also one of the six judges before whom Chaucer testified in the Scrope-Grosvenor case.

[48] Simon Manning was brought to court for a plea of debt. The possibility that his wife, Katherine Manning, was Chaucer's sister is examined in LR 288-289.

[49] William de Wykeham, bishop of Winchester, was given Bealknap's house in the parish of St. Mary, London, as well as his manor of Crokes Eston in Southampton (cf. *Patent Rolls Richard II, 1385-89* 3.492, and *Fine Rolls Richard II, 1383-91* 10.242). Bealknap and Wykeham had been associated as early as 1362, when they served together in Chancery (cf. *Patent Rolls Edward III, 1361-64* 12.237-238). Wykeham, who was one of the wealthiest men in England, founded a school at Winchester and a college at Oxford "for the relief of poor scholars and the training of secular clergy"; see DNB.

[50] Among the remaining judges were John Holt and William Burgh. John Holt was one of Bealknap's subordinates, having been appointed judge of the Common Bench in 1383. Like Tresilian and Bealknap, John Holt signed the Nottingham Declaration, for which he was banished to Ireland.

William Burgh, justice of the Common Bench, may have been a kinsman of Simon Burgh, who is mentioned in the inquisition post mortem of William Septanus. According to the testimony given, Simon "caused himself to be retained with the said heir [William's son] as of his counsel and made the heir grant a yearly rent of £10 to him and his heirs out of the manor of Melton"; Fisher (n. 22 above) 315. In view of Gower's involvement with William Septanus the younger, it is quite probable that Simon knew the poet. Certainly, he was acquainted with Chaucer, for both of them were esquires in the king's household from 1368 to 1373 (LR [n. 9 above] 95, 98, 100). In 1378, Simon received a life annuity of ten marks at the same time as the poet's wife, Philippa.

[51] See Tout (n. 16 above) 5.423-424.

judges who were present[52] and on 14 September, as the propriety of the law demanded, witnessed their declared affirmation. It was a tragedy for Blake, as well as for Usk, that he did.[53]

The foregoing examination has tried to show the kind of audience for which *The Testament* was written. Admittedly, it has dealt with only those members of the legal profession whose circumstances made it impossible for them to act upon Usk's plea. Even so, it must be recognized that there were others like them, to whom Usk could appeal. The fact that he knew such well-known figures in Chancery points to the likelihood that this is where his associates were to be found.

The irony is not that these influential people were unable to come to Usk's aid (or, for that matter, even to their own), but that the actions of the Parliament of 1388 made all such acquaintanceships worthless. Its members, who were, indeed, "merciless," were determined to fashion a "Nottingham" document of their own; it was the king who now was made subordinate to the Parliament, which declared itself at once both legislator and judge. Of far greater importance was the restriction they imposed upon Richard's ministers to challenge the law of the land, for it denied to those accused the right of appeal. The significance of this new interdict must have been painfully apparent to Usk, for it meant that any re-examination of the trumped-up charges against him was completely out of the question.[54]

Usk's unhappy fate — "the fate of the literary man turned politician" — may have, as Professor Tout points out, "convinced . . . Chaucer of his wisdom in holding aloof from politics."[55] Certainly, it seems to have cautioned other members of the literary community to tread softly in the political arena.

Department of Engligh
Dyson College of Arts and Sciences
Pace University
Pace Plaza
New York, New York 10038, U.S.A.

[52] Bealknap, Tresilian, Holt, Burgh, Lokton, and Fulthorp attended the council.

[53] Blake was executed on 4 March 1388 — a few hours after Usk.

[54] According to *Letter-Book H* (n. 12 above) xlvii, he had had "himself appointed Under-Sheriff of Middlesex for illegal purposes."

[55] Tout (n. 16 above) 3.434.

PIERS PLOWMAN AND HOLYCHURCH

•

by Margaret Jennings, C.S.J.

Among the more persuasive efforts to explicate Langland's *Piers Plowman* is that which concentrates on the identification of the text's hero with the "Whole Christ," or what would, in medieval terms, be equivalent to the doctrine of the Mystical Body.[1] But Langland's work is, despite its patristic base, a poem, not a theological tractate, and critics should be periodically reminded that the Plowman can be viewed poetically, that is, not as walking dogma but as a *figura* of the reality which that dogma defines: the Church itself. Positing a figural identity for Piers corresponds with the thesis that the *Vision of William* was directed not only at churchmen who might be aware of dogmatic definitions but also at common folk who would hardly have been able to digest strictly theological fare.[2] In addition, such an approach accords with typological patterning in areas of medieval preaching and poetry and perhaps explains why critics have discerned the influence of typology on the poem without being able to supply for it a consistently convincing model.[3] For a figure is essentially tentative, pointing to something that is in need of constant interpretation, "which will indeed be fulfilled in the concrete future, but which is at all times present, fulfilled in God's providence which knows no difference of time."[4]

But to specify the figural identity of Piers, one needs to examine how the theoretical speculations of clerics were translated into the simple but powerful language of the ordinary member of the Mystical Body. Archbishop Thoresby's *Catechism* is an obvious starting point. It had presented an inclusive definition of "halikirk" as the "communyng and felawred of al cristenfolk,/ That communes togedir in the sacramentz"[5] and popular approval of such extra-prelatical expansion

[1] Sister Mary Clemente Davlin, "*Petrus, id est, Christus:* Piers the Plowman as 'the Whole Christ,' " *Chaucer Review* 6 (1972) 280-292.

[2] Raymond St. Jacques, "Langland's Christ-Knight and the Liturgy," *Revue de l'Université d'Ottawa* 37 (1967) 157.

[3] Elizabeth Salter and Derek Pearsall, eds., *Piers Plowman* (London 1967) 27, talk about figural meanings in the poem but identify Piers vaguely as "the operation of God through a man in the state of grace." Mary C. Schroeder, "*Piers Plowman:* The Tearing of the Pardon," *Philological Quarterly* 49 (1970) 11, discerns a typological pattern in the *Visio* but its application would end with Passus 7.

[4] Erich Auerbach, "Figura," in *Scenes from the Drama of European Literature*, trans. Ralph Manheim (New York 1959) 59.

[5] Thomas F. Simmons and Henry E. Nollott, eds., *Lay Folks Catechism,* Early English Text Society (EETS) o.s. 118 (London 1902) 11.

of the concept *ecclesia* is reflected in simple poetic statements like

> þere as gadryng of goode men ys
> is holy chyrche of flesche and bones[6]

and, more significantly, in pronouncements emanating from the medieval pulpit. There, the three parties comprising Holy Church — priests, knights, and laborers — are depicted as mutually dependent, yet the onus of sustaining the church falls on the last: "If the labourers were nought, both knightes and priestes must become acre men and herdis, and els they shuld for default of bodily sustenance deye." [7] Bromyard's *Summa predicantium* maintained that while knights might defend the church in the fashion of hands and clergy rule it after the manner of eyes, it fell to laborers to support it after the manner of feet.[8] The preaching emphasis on the importance of workers and on the idea that the Church should resemble Christ who had come to earth as a poor working man[9] practically dictated the manner in which Holychurch would be personified. In addition, allegorical interpreters found in the plowman an ecclesical image par excellence[10] while patristic exegesis inspired a specific name in its assertion that "Peter bears the figure of the church."[11] From numerous medieval sermons, then, emerge the familiar features of "our immortal Pieres the Plowman, he who by a stroke of poetic genius was one day himself to become the chosen prophet of the Gospel of Truth and Reconciliation"[12] — the figure of Holychurch.

The figural import of Plowman-as-Church is further signified in the development of the Dreamer. Fundamentally, Will can be seen as a device whereby the poet reveals the need of God's people for the guidance of the Church, that is, Piers Plowman. He is of tremendous value in explaining the appearance of Piers in the "Visio," for the Plowman's stance seems defined "by the souls he is guiding rather than by his own spiritual nature. The way Piers is seen and understood is determined by the degree of spiritual progress reached by other souls";[13] or, translated into figural terminology: "The more fully the figure is interpreted, the more closely it is integrated with the external plan of salvation, the more real it becomes."[14] In the poem's first section,

[6] J. Furnivall, ed., *Minor Poems of the Vernon Manuscript* 2, EETS o.s. 117 (London 1901) 721; Oxford, Bodleian Library MS Digby 102 counsels the loving of "holichirch" in the edition of J. Kail, *26 Political and Other Poems,* EETS o.s. 124 (London 1904) 103.

[7] From the "harangue" of Master Thomas of Wimbleton at St. Paul's Cross in 1388, cited in Gerald R. Owst, *Literature and Pulpit in Medieval England* (New York 1961) 450-451. Cf. London, British Library, MSS Harley 4894, fol. 189, and Add. 41321, fol. 65v.

[8] Johannes Bromyard, *Summa predicantium* (Basel 1484), "Accidia."

[9] Owst 572.

[10] The tradition is at least as early as Augustine who makes use of it "In Psalmos XXXVI," PL 36.358. Various glosses embellished the implications; see, for example, the *Biblia sacra in se continens glossam ordinariam cum expositione Lyrae litterale et morale* pt. 4 (Lyons 1520) on the text of Amos, chap. 9, and Hugh of St. Cher, *Opera omnia* pt. 5 (Venice 1732) fol. 190.

[11] "Petrus figuram gestat Ecclesiae," from *Sermo CI de scripturis Veteris et Novi Testamenti* in the supposititious sermons of St. Augustine, PL 39.1940.

[12] Owst (n. 7 above) 574.

[13] Edward Vasta, *The Spiritual Basis of Piers Plowman* (The Hague 1965) 137.

[14] Auerbach (n. 4 above) 71.

Truth and Love must be practical things concerned with digging and delving and garnering. "Work is honesty and that is practical truth. The harvest will bring food for all and that is practical love."[15] These are the things which Holy Church must do in order to be understood by Will, the representative but here spiritually dulled soul. As this representative soul grows spiritually he also grows in understanding of the knightly and prelatical as well as the laboring facets of the Plowman figure; and finally his desire for Piers — a true and loving church — is almost overwhelming, for Will himself is approaching the real life of charity. With this function of the Dreamer in mind, Piers can be seen throughout the poem as the forerunner, model, servant, source of inspiration, teacher, and example for other souls; but in his ideal form he is perfect from first appearance to last. When he remarks in B Passus 7 (lines 118-119) that he no longer will busy himself about his "bely-ioye" he is not thereby illustrating a lapse in spiritual perfection but rather seeking to produce by example a change of heart in other souls.[16] Since the Dreamer's search for truth seems a result of failures in both ecclesiastical and civil authority to cope with falsehood and evil, the poet must make an artistic attempt to harmonize the theory and practice of the Church — his age's supreme synthesis — in order to show that the theoretical ideal of charity could be actualized in his own time under the inspiration of a loving Church, figuratively expressed in the person of Piers Plowman.

While the literary equation of Piers with the figure Holychurch seems possible in the light of contemporary reference and older tradition, several problems remain. The most obvious is the actual appearance of a character entitled "Holychurch" in the initial passus. A brief consideration of her words and actions, however, will reveal no conflict with the position adopted in this paper. Though she lays down certain fundamental theological principles which may be taken as premises for exposition in the rest of the poem,[17] these principles exist in the realm of theory; and Holychurch's advanced reflections on the purposes of human life under the hand of God are quite beyond the province of a spiritually dull-witted Dreamer. In B 1.140-145, she specifically withholds the "better" mode of living because this "kynde knowyng" is obviously beyond Will's ken. Even when she emphasizes the role of the will in the accomplishment of God's designs and uses the *deus caritas* epistle as her sermon's basis, Lady Holychurch presents merely the theory of redemption — the theological aspects of the love of God. She does not, and apparently cannot, implement the Dreamer's quest for salvation and, therefore, does not fulfill the primary mission of the Church in the world: *Salus animarum suprema lex.* Though Piers's teaching embodies the same goal and essentially the same means as the Lady's, it has a very

[15] Nevill Coghill, "The Pardon of Piers Plowman," *Proceedings of the British Academy* 31 (1945) 15.

[16] Vasta (n.13 above) 137. Citations to the poem are taken from the edition of W. W. Skeat, *The Vision of William Concerning Piers the Plowman* (London 1961).

[17] D. W. Robertson and Bernard Huppé, *Piers Plowman and Scriptural Tradition* (Princeton 1951) 48. It is only in Passus 20 when the Dreamer can obey the precept "lerne to loue" that the import of her message is realized. Lady Holychurch's speech is analyzed at length in Ben H. Smith, *Traditional Imagery of Charity in Piers Plowman* (The Hague 1966) 39ff.

different character. In keeping with her role as Magistra, she deals only with the basic principles governing the way of perfection; in keeping with his role as God's "co-worker" in the salvation of mankind, Piers deals with the moral steps leading the soul to union with truth. It is up to Piers to encourage the soul and to make it persevere. His instruction strengthens its patience by enabling it to foresee the labor of the way, and its desire by showing it the final reward. Theoretically, the treasure of truth — charity — was explained by Holychurch in the *deus caritas* section of B Passus 1 (lines 86ff.); actually, this same message is the burden of Will's vision of the Tree of Charity which Piers guards in Passus 16. But in the latter passus, the abstract becomes concrete and Piers, as figural Church, endeavors to become all things to all men that all might be saved.

A second problem area could be the "family" of Piers in B Passus 6 (lines 80-83). But, given the state of spiritual deprivation manifest in him to whom the poem is admittedly addressed, Piers's "family" can be seen as obvious devices — in the manner of the Dreamer himself. "Dame Worche-whan-tyme-is" could easily have gotten her name from Saint John's counsel to "work while you have the light for night is coming in which no man can work" (John 9.4) — a verse that Hugh of Saint Cher glosses: "praesens vita dicitur dies et mors dicitur nox."[18] Thus Holychurch (Piers) is wedded to life in this world on the allegorical level, or literally, to the working out of salvation while "tyme" exists for each soul. The children's names emphasize the necessity for doing right and for obedience — the virtues, in common parlance, of which Lady Holychurch spoke so eloquently in Passus 1. Piers's will, which in the B version awards his soul to him who best deserves it, does allow allegorical interpretation, for the Holy Spirit is traditionally cited as the "soul of the Church." However, it is also probable here and in the discussion of charity in Passus 7 (lines 210ff.) that example, whereby the rest of mankind might benefit, is a primary concern.

Other problem areas, conversely, seem minimized by a figural reading. If Piers is a figure of the Church, then line 206 of B Passus 15: "Petrus, id est Christus" presents little difficulty. Since "petra, id est Christus" is almost a refrain in biblical commentaries,[19] the changed ending in "Petrus" can probably indicate both the apostle and the prelacy and stand for Christ in the visible history of the Church Militant just as "petra" stands for Christ in the scriptural text. The connection with charity comes obviously from John 21.5, where Peter's affirmation and Christ's commission join in propounding an example of fervent love as well as the special obligation to exercise charity's two great precepts.[20] Evidently, both scriptural and patristic references point ineluctably to an ecclesial definition, as does the name Piers (*Petrus* in Latin), because it is through Piers in this poem that Langland wishes to build his concept of a united and loving Church. The statement in line 206, growing as it does out of

---

[18] Hugh, pt. 6 (n. 10 above), fol. 345r.
[19] R. E. Kaske, "Patristic Exegesis: The Defense," in *Critical Approaches to Medieval Literature,* ed. Dorothy Bethurum (New York 1960) 41.
[20] *Ibid.* 42.

Will's question about whether clerks who keep Holy Church know charity, seems to show the necessity for a spontaneous, burning love as the requisite whereby one may become a figure of Christ himself. Ultimately it is implied that the great charity of Piers Plowman will enable him to carry on as earth's most potentially perfect figure of the Redeemer: Holychurch; he is the living counterpart of the C text's definition in 15, lines 125-129. There, in response to the direct question: "What is holychurche, frend?" Anima says briefly: "Charite." Piers knows that this charity involves life, love, and loyalty in one belief and one law, producing as it must a love knot of all Christians of one will, heart, and mind. Moreover, Anima's terse answer embodies the direction the poem has taken in its reformation of ecclesiastical society. In the final analysis, the root of each sin against one or more members of the Mystical Body as we have observed in the Lady Meed episode, on the half-acre, and throughout Christendom is lack of charity. Though faith is described as the binding force of the Church on earth, it is not the dynamic power of life in the Mystical Body. This vital principle is love, and Piers the Plowman – its exemplar and teacher – functions, then, as an ideal Church, not built with hands but by the *caritas unitatis*.[21]

A simple extension of the latter concept explains B Passus 16, line 104, where Piers is said to teach Christ the art of healing: "lered hym lechecrafte." Since Augustine had seen the Church as the unity of the faithful, Piers, as the figure Holychurch, is not limited just to the present age, although its corruptions are the chief target of Langland's zeal. According to medieval standards the Church existed as early as Abel's sacrifice – an oblation which indicated an interior belief or disposition to believe whenever revelation should declare the *plenitudo temporis*. Thus, Christ can learn from Piers how to plow the hearts of men and how to sow the seed of God's word because Piers represents in any age the community of believers, those faithful ministers of the diety who did his bidding and were in their own days agents for his healing, his preaching, and his miracles.[22]

Similar principles underlie the building of the Barn of Unity in B Passus 19, lines 314-330. There the narrator equates Unity with Holychurch "in English," but it is obvious that neither a physical building nor a hierarchical structure is intended. The components of the building are the cross, baptism, mercy, Christ's passion, and Holy Scripture. Surely it is not difficult to see here a reference to the external manifestations which should accompany Christian faith. For the fourteenth century, Langland seems to be saying, the Thomistic definition "ecclesia, id est fides"[23] needs support.

---

[21] This definition of the Church is generally attributed to Augustine "to whom we owe the characteristically Western ideal of the Church as a dynamic social power"; T. P. Dunning, *Piers Plowman: An Interpretation of the A-Text* (London 1937) 107. Augustine supports the statement "caritas ista non tenetur nisi in unitate ecclesiae" in several texts: *De unico baptismo* 15.25; *De ciuitate Dei* 18.51; *De unitate ecclesiae* 4.7, *De baptismo* 3.16.21 and in numerous sermons and epistles. For a complete listing see Geoffrey Grimshaw Willis, *Saint Augustine and the Donatist Controversy* (London 1950) 107-126.

[22] Robertson and Huppé (n. 17 above) 196.

[23] St. Thomas Aquinas, *Summa theologiae*, pt. 3, q. 8, 1.2378B. For commentary see Yves Congar, *The Mystery of the Church* (Baltimore 1960) 97-118.

As John of Torquemada explained it, men are brought into holy unity through faith and through some outward signs of faith — an observation which had been made also by Wyclif and which was to be expanded into an entire treatise by John Driedo in the early sixteenth century.[24] The barn of unity, then, should not be equated with the figure of the Church but with the concept of faith as the unifying and binding force within the Church. Certainly, faith's embodiment in a physical structure corresponds with Saint Paul's emphasis on the charity which should be exercised toward all men but especially toward those who are of the household of faith (Galatians 6.10). That this barn cannot comprise the whole Church as it is defined in *Piers Plowman* is equally evident; the perfect Church will be united in the faith, it is true, but it will live by virtue of charity which is first in the order of perfection: "For if I have faith so as to move mountains and do not have love, I am nothing" (1 Cor. 13.2).

A final scene requiring some degree of explication is that of Pentecostal visitation described in B Passus 19, lines 196ff. With a vivid depiction of the descent of the "spiritus paraclitus" Langland comments, "and thanne bigan Grace to go with Piers Plowman" (line 208). It is obvious that the poet wishes to make an explicit distinction between the apostle Peter and the plowman Piers. If Piers is the figure of Holychurch, then Grace goes with him because it is his duty to distribute this free gift of God to the other members of the Mystical Body; indeed, a little later in the passus, Grace — the sharing in God's divine life — makes this function imperative, since he instructs the witnesses concerning the designation of Piers as his manager: "My prowor and my plowman Piers shal ben on earthe,/ And for to tulye treuthe a teme shal he haue" (lines 252-256).

With the sacerdotal dispensations of Piers in this passus, the wheel of signification in Langland's poem has come full circle. As the Church according to the preaching canon was thought to be composed of laborers, knights, and clergy, so Piers has embodied all three states.[25] Since the greatest emphasis in religious sources is given to the lower classes where virtue, supposedly, has less chance of being choked by the weeds of worldly corruption, the largest portion of the text was devoted to the laboring plowman. But though the unlettered were numerically dominant in medieval society, knights and true clergy were also necessary for the perfect fulfillment of Christ's Church. Hence, in Passus 18, Christ's jousting is done in Piers's armor, "humana natura" — a reference to the knightly class which was to protect the flock in this world and/or a reference to that spiritual knighthood which would struggle against the world's evil.[26] Here, in Passus 19, Piers's functions are obviously those assigned, in the economy of salvation which is exhibited in the Church, to the priests,

---

[24] Theodore Foley, *The Doctrine of the Catholic Church in the Theology of John Driedo of Louvain* (Washington 1946) 9.

[25] The parable of the Vineyard offered a preacher the opportunity of discoursing on the three groups comprising Holy Church: the priests, knights, and laborers; see Harley MS 4894, fol. 189, and other sources compiled by Owst (n. 7 above) 450-451.

[26] Spiritual knighthood is treated extensively in Rosemond Tuve, *Allegorical Imagery* (Princeton 1966) 36, 43-45.

and on certain levels, to the prelates and to the pope. But the importance of humility and charity is again stressed by reason of the Plowman image which does not change even in the most exalted of those activities designated as Piers's. Perhaps because wealth had brought the venality into the Church which the poet deplored and hoped to amend, Piers remains the poor and loving laborer, generally lost to the fourteenth-century world but able to be discerned wherever Conscience can be stirred and so prompted to seek him. In knowing Piers as Holychurch, one finds the end of the poem far from the despairing and inconsequential interpretation which some critics have seen there. True, a state of warfare exists, but warfare is, according to the scriptures, the life of man in this world; more importantly, there is the possibility of renovation because Piers is being sought, because, at last, individual Christians realize their need for a unity of faith and love within Holychurch.

How different is the situation which confronts the reader at the end of B Passus 5, just before the initial appearance of the Plowman. Here, the insecurity of a Church with dogma, authority, and hierarchy but without a dynamic bond of love is exemplified as the newly-confessed pilgrims of Truth wander aimlessly — unsure of their road, destination, and purpose. Fortunately, Piers then makes his dramatic appearance and revitalizes their search. In this figure is embodied the "fundamental teaching of Holy Church that the beginning of the good life is labor and obedience and toward this figure the whole of the vision has been moving as the apex of the struggle against evil."[27] When the Plowman puts forth his head, his claim to know truth is not uttered as a boast; he knows Truth naturally, as a scholar knows his books. His credentials are a whole way of life and they are the same credentials established by Lady Holychurch at the outset of the poem in her colloquy with the Dreamer: conscience and natural understanding. The Truth will again be put forward for human comprehension; the Church, like its divine exemplar, will again minister to man's needs.

Piers is equally the Church at the end of the Visio where he receives the first of the two pardons granted to him. Literally an indulgence and allegorically God's covenant with man offered through the intermediacy of the Church, it is sent specifically to Piers; but it promises distributable benefits to many souls, because he is a figure for the institution which acts as mediator between God and man. The intercessory power of Piers is also pointed to in the gratitude of the merchants for their share in the pardon, and a consistent emphasis on true charity (which gives to all without stinting) is maintained. Though the Dreamer is still puzzled here about the meaning of Piers and the whole signification of his dream, he has learned the initial lesson of Christian living — doing well — a learning to be extended in B Passus 10, lines 186-187 when he is instructed that to find do-wel he must truly love, because do-better and do-best are both allied to charity, and do-best is its perfection. Gradually thereafter, the Dreamer discovers several details concerning the real nature of Piers. In Passus 11, he recognizes the need for learning the law of love as Christ

[27] Bernard Huppé, "The Authorship of the A and B Texts of *Piers Plowman*," *Speculum* 23 (1947) 600.

taught it, for in a poor man's clothing and in the guise of a pilgrim God has often been encountered among the needy. As the Dreamer comes to acknowledge the faults of the clergy and of the members of the Church Militant, he also comes to see the fallacies inherent in any mode of life that has as its end something other than the law of love. Even Learning, in Passus 13.125ff., comments that Piers has taken him to task and shrugged aside all the sciences except love. In this passus also the Dreamer is further prepared for the ultimate revelation of Piers-as-Church by Conscience's assurance that Piers will say nothing against the Holy Scripture and that he will show do-wel in practice (lines 132ff.).

In Passus 14, and in a manner similar to that in Passus 5, a final prelude to the unfolding of the character of Piers occurs. The deadly sins again parade, but this time it is their interior malice which is stressed, for Piers in Passus 15 by reason of his Christ-given authority is empowered to judge the confessions of the heart. Later, in 16, Piers is guardian of the tree of charity which is nourished by faith and productive of all the good men in times past and to come. But Piers, wishing to explain his custodianship, exposes the enemies of all Christian souls and, as has been the Church's duty throughout the ages, wages war against these enemies through the merit gained in the incarnation and redemptive sacrifice of Jesus Christ. Coupled with the function of teaching the world about the mysteries of the Godhead — especially that of the Trinity — is the undertaking by Piers-as-Church of the practical duties of charity, and hence he is seen by Will in the likeness of the Good Samaritan (B Passus 18, lines 10ff.). Piers's identification here with the Church is readily accepted by most commentators who miss the long preparation of the Dreamer for the final revelation. When Piers, in the Dreamer's eyes, is at last going out to "tuyle treuthe," that is, to tell truth with the aid of the theme of the Gospel and to till the soil of truth in human hearts with the aid of the team of lion, ox, eagle, and winged man,[28] Will is finally aware of the full meaning of the plowman figure. In retrospect now, both he and we can recognize that at the poem's core lies Langland's desire to effect in his day a more perfect version of Christ's Mystical Body, the Church, and that Piers Plowman is its consistent and efficient figure.

St. Joseph's College
245 Clinton Avenue
Brooklyn, New York 11205, U.S.A.

[28] Bernard Huppé, " 'Petrus, id est, Christus': Word Play in *Piers Plowman,* the B Text," *English Literary History* 17 (1950) 168.

CONTRIBUTIONS OF FOREIGNERS TO DUBROVNIK'S ECONOMIC GROWTH IN THE LATE MIDDLE AGES

•

by Bariša Krekić

I

Geographical position and circumstances of historical development made Dubrovnik (Ragusa) a city extremely attractive to foreigners in the late Middle Ages.

Geographically, Dubrovnik is situated in a most convenient place, from the point of view of both sea routes in the Adriatic and overland roads towards the Balkan hinterland. The eastern or Dalmatian coast of the Adriatic with its numerous bays and islands (which were used as shelters), mountains (which served as orientation points), favorable winds and currents, was the customary navigational route, in preference to the western or Italian coast, which is flat and offers none of these advantages. This became especially important during the time of the growing Venetian trade with Byzantium and the Levant, which resulted in large numbers of Venetian ships moving along the Dalmatian coast, going to and from the East. Dubrovnik was particularly favored, situated as it is at the end of the chain of islands. Ships plying down the coast from Venice before sailing into the open seas, put in to her harbor to refit and complement their crews. On the return journeys Dubrovnik was the first major Adriatic city that the ships visited. Thus it played a major role in the navigational patterns in the Adriatic area.[1]

At the same time, Dubrovnik was connected by several land routes to the central regions of Bosnia and Serbia in the Balkan hinterland. These connections became especially important after mining was started in those areas. In Serbia, in the middle of the thirteenth century, mining operations were begun by Saxon miners. Serbian mining progressed with great rapidity in the second half of the thirteenth and in the early fourteenth century. Then, in the first half of the fourteenth century mining began in Bosnia. Dubrovnik's merchants grasped immediately the magnitude of the opportunity offering itself to them. In the late twelfth century they had already established commercial links with both Balkan states and were now able to move quickly into the mining areas. There, they became the leading entrepreneurs and intermediaries for the export of Serbian and Bosnian minerals to the West. Thus

---

This paper was presented in the symposium on "Urban Societies in the Mediterranean World" at the Dumbarton Oaks Center for Byzantine Studies, Washington, D. C., in May 1976.

[1] J. Tadić, "Venezia e la costa orientale dell' Adriatico fino al secolo XV," in *Venezia e il Levante fino al secolo XV* 1 (Florence 1973) 690-691.

copper, iron, lead — but above all silver, sometimes mixed with gold — began to flow in large quantities from the Balkan hinterland to Dubrovnik and from there to the West, 'mainly through Venice. This trade reached enormous proportions, especially in the first half of the fifteenth century, with silver as the main commodity, and it brought to Dubrovnik immense wealth and prosperity.[2]

Aside from these geographical and economic factors, two other elements in Dubrovnik's historical development must be taken into consideration. One is its political stability and the other is its social peace in the city. Dubrovnik was a patrician city-state, with a constitution similar in many ways to that of Venice, under whose domination Dubrovnik was from 1205 to 1358. The city was governed by three councils, Major, Minor and the Senate (Rogati), consisting exclusively of men belonging to a limited group of families. Although this group closed its ranks only after 1330, for all practical purposes it was well defined and in charge of the affairs of the city already by the mid-thirteenth century. The system proved to be extremely stable and worked very smoothly not only during and after the Venetian domination, but for centuries thereafter.

It should be noted, however, that the Ragusan patricians, like the Venetian ones, were not a landed aristocracy drawing their income from large estates. They were merchants drawing their substance from commerce.[3] Thus, their policies and interests coincided with those of the only other group in the city which could have challenged the patrician power, that is to say, the non-noble merchants, shipowners and craftsmen. This convergence of interests contributed greatly to social peace in Dubrovnik. What unrest there was, as for example in 1400, was very minor and easily stemmed.[4] The Ragusan government, like those of the Italian communes, saw its state — as Robert Lopez put it so aptly — as "l'État comme une bonne affaire" — a government "of the merchants, by the merchants, for the merchants."[5]

Thus, geographical position, economic opportunity, political stability, and social peace attracted foreigners to Dubrovnik from the thirteenth century onward.

II

Who were these foreigners coming to Dubrovnik?

It is easier to divide them into three groups: Slavs, Italians and others. The bulk of foreigners coming to Dubrovnik was made up of the Balkan Slavs. The greatest influx of these Slavs was from an area not far from Dubrovnik which was very poor and barren, and whose population traditionally looked to the city to provide better

[2] J. Tadić, "Privreda Dubrovnika i srpske zemlje u prvoj polovini XV veka," *Zbornik Filosofskog fakulteta u Beogradu* 10.1 (1968) 527-528. B. Krekić, *Dubrovnik in the 14th and 15th Centuries: A City between East and West* (Norman, Okla. 1972) 20-22, 50-52.
[3] See I. Mahnken, *Dubrovački patricijat u XIV veku,* 2 vols. (Belgrade 1960), esp. 1.27.
[4] B. Krekić, "Prilozi unutrašnjoj istoriji Dubrovnika početkom XV veka," *Istoriski glasnik* 1-2 (1953) 63-70.
[5] R. Lopez, *Su e giù per la storia di Genova* (Genoa 1975) 28, 36.

opportunities. Some of these people came as merchants and craftsmen, many were engaged on ships, but most were quite simply a source of manpower for Dubrovnik.[6] Slavs also came from much more distant areas of the Balkan hinterland, from Serbia and Bosnia, especially when trade with those regions, due to the mining, became very lively in the fourteenth and fifteenth centuries. Finally, a number of Croatians from Dalmatia came to Dubrovnik by sea, mostly as seamen, captains, merchants and the like.

It is obvious that the Slavs were not an economically powerful element, or people who, because of their skills and expertise, could do much to contribute to or to influence Dubrovnik's development. However, their sheer numbers were of decisive importance for the whole future of the city, and it was because of their massive presence that they exerted such a strong impact on Dubrovnik's destiny. It is, of course, impossible to gauge the number of Slavs who either visited or settled down in Dubrovnik in the late Middle Ages. There is no doubt, however, that their number was overwhelming. By the mid-thirteenth century Dubrovnik had become a predominantly Slavic city. Statistics are, as we well know, a dangerous game to play when data is partial, but I would still like to use some numbers here, even if just to give an idea of the "ordre de grandeur." In the fourteenth century there were in Dubrovnik 583 servants recruited from among the hinterland Slavs. Of these, over 82 percent spent from between one and ten years in the city. Also, between 1321 and 1399, we find 205 apprentices from the nearby hinterland coming to Dubrovnik to learn various crafts. Many of these remained in the city permanently and others for long periods of time.[7]

More important are some further sets of numbers that we may use. It has been calculated (although these calculations are not quite satisfactory) that 225 persons were granted Ragusan citizenship in the course of the fourteenth century.[8] Of these, 174 (77.33 percent) were Slavs. Of these Slavs, eighty-three (47.7 percent) were from the hinterland and from the Serbian coastal areas south of Dubrovnik; fourteen (8.04 percent) were from Dalmatia; and seventy-seven (44.25 percent) were of unknown provenance. It should be pointed out that we are talking here only of those Slavs who had obtained citizenship; and — while constituting 77.33 percent of new citizens — they represented just a small percentage of the total number of Slavs in Dubrovnik (as we shall see later, to obtain citizenship was not an easy matter).

The second most numerous group of foreigners in Dubrovnik were the Italians, mostly from Venice and Apulia.[9] Again, we do not have an exact and full count of this group, but there are some numbers and some comparisons which can be used to

[6] D. Dinić-Knežević, "Prilog proučavanju migracija našeg stanovništva u Italiju tokom XIII i XIV veka," *Godišnjak Filozofskog fakulteta u Novom Sadu* 16.1 (1973) 39-62.

[7] D. Dinić-Knezević, "Migracije stanovništva iz bližeg zaledja u Dubrovnik u XIV veku," *Jugoslovenski istorijski časopis* 1-2 (1974) 19-40.

[8] Mahnken (n. 3 above) 1.91-96. See also J. Mijušković, "Dodeljivanje dubrovačkog gradjanstva u srednjem veku," *Glas Srpske akademije nauka i umetnosti* 246 (1961) 103 n. 69a.

[9] J. Lučić, "Gli stranieri a Ragusa nel Medio evo," *Bollettino dell'Atlante linguistico mediterraneo* 13-15 (1971-1973) 345-348.

show the importance of the Italian presence in Dubrovnik. Among the newly-made citizens of Dubrovnik in the fourteenth century, there were only sixteen Italians. [10] This is only 7.11 percent of the total number of naturalized Ragusans, but it constitutes 47.05 percent of all non-Slavic new citizens. The Venetians, because of their particular political position, maritime and economic power, were especially well represented in Dubrovnik, not only among the Italians, but among the foreigners in general. I have been able to establish the presence of close to six hundred Venetians in Dubrovnik between 1278 and 1400. [11] There is no doubt that the real numbers were far greater, but we can deal only with those who, for one reason or another, have left traces of their presence in the vast Ragusan archives.

But, even if we take into account only the Venetians who are mentioned in documents, interesting conclusions can be drawn, always bearing in mind that we are dealing with a city which, in the fourteenth century, probably had a population of about four thousand, and at its peak, towards the end of the fifteenth century, something like five to six thousand. [12] The Venetian presence in Dubrovnik was at its strongest between 1311 and 1350. The average annual record of Venetians in Dubrovnik in the decades between 1311 and 1350 varied from eleven to twenty-one persons, while it fell to between six and nine persons in the period from 1351 to 1400. This diminution should probably be ascribed, above all, to the change in the political climate unfavorable to Venice (the loss of Dalmatia and Dubrovnik in 1358, the war of 1378-1381 in the Adriatic, and so on), but, again, one should never forget that we are dealing with only a part of the whole.

The vast majority of Venetians appear in Ragusan documents only once. This is the case of 431 out of 597 persons (72.19 percent); but a number of Venetians returned to Dubrovnik several times through the years, and some lived in the city for quite protracted periods of time (Franciscus speciarius, 1311-1341; magister Fele Aldigheri, 1319-1345; Franciscus Scarpaçius, merchant, 1331-1348; Çaninus Salimbene, speciarius, 1373-1414, and so on). Sometimes whole families moved from Venice to Dubrovnik, or several generations of the same family were active there for long periods of time. In addition, members of many leading Venetian families lived in Dubrovnik, owned property, traded, and engaged in financial operations there. For example:

13 Contarini (1298-1398)	7 Condolmer (1313-1356)
11 Quirino (1285-1382)	6 Nigro (1319-1398)

[10] Mahnken (n. 3 above) 1.91-96.

[11] All calculations are based on extensive research in the Historical Archives of Dubrovnik.

[12] Krekić (n. 2 above) 54-55. Venice in the fourteenth century had about 120,000 inhabitants: F. C. Lane, *Venice, a Maritime Republic* (Baltimore 1973) 18-19; and Lopez (n. 5 above) puts the population of Genoa in the fifteenth century at about 100,000 inhabitants, D. Herlihy, *Pisa in the Early Renaissance: A Study of Urban Growth* (New Haven 1958) 36, estimates the population of Pisa toward the end of the thirteenth century at about 38,000, the population of Lucca at the same time at 40,000 (p. 43) and that of Florence at about 96,000 (pp. 43-44). See also D. Herlihy, *Pisa nel Duecento* (Pisa 1973) 74-75, where he thinks that Pisa and Lucca had populations of about 40,000 each and Florence 120,000 in the fourteenth century.

9 Bono (1283-1397)

9 Trivisano (1283-1388)

8 Bollani (1282-1320)

8 Vener (1281-1370)

7 Baldella (1291-1389)

6 Soranzo (1336-1378)

5 Aldighero (1319-1343)

5 Delfino (1282-1329)

5 Giorgio (1332-1367)

5 Giustinian (1319-1347)

Furthermore, individuals from other prominent Venetian families were present in Dubrovnik from time to time (four each: Barozzo, Loredan, Leon, Quintavalle; three each: Badoer, Gradonico, Morosini, Memmo, Sirano, Signolo, Zeno; two each: Bonvisino, Corner, Dandolo, Falier, Pollani, Valaresso; and so on).

By far the majority of Venetians coming to Dubrovnik were merchants, captains and shipowners, but one also finds craftsmen. There were, for example, eleven goldsmiths, eight shoemakers, five glassmakers from Murano, five carpenters and thirty-eight other craftsmen of various kinds among the Venetians in Dubrovnik between 1278 and 1400. In addition, highly skilled professionals came to Dubrovnik from Venice and its area; among them were nine doctors, eight pharmacists, three "protomagistri," three painters and others. Finally, the presence of a number of Venetian diplomats and officials was registered in Dubrovnik at this time (thirteen ambassadors), but these officers usually stayed very briefly in the city.

I have dwelt in more detail on the Venetians for two reasons: one, because we have much data on them and, two, because their presence was in many ways exceptionally important to Dubrovnik. One comparison will suffice to prove this point: during the fourteenth century we find 80 Greeks and Levantines in Dubrovnik, while the number of Venetians is 515 (1:6.4).

Another group of Italians which should be at least briefly mentioned were the Tuscans, especially representatives of the Florentine bankers from the great companies of Bardi, Peruzzi, Acciaiuoli and Buonaccorsi, in the first half of the fourteenth century;[13] and the merchants and craftsmen from Prato, who played a leading role in financing and organizing the local production of textiles in Dubrovnik in the first half of the fifteenth century.[14]

Apart from Italians, the Greeks and Levantines were certainly an important group of non-Slavic foreigners in Dubrovnik in the late Middle Ages, with more than two hundred and seventy of them there between 1268 and 1460.[15] Closer to the city itself, the Albanians made their presence felt in Dubrovnik; and a few Germans, most probably Saxon miners or their descendants from Serbia and Bosnia, are mentioned in the documents. The Jewish presence was small in numbers until the end of the fifteenth century, but some of the Jews in Dubrovnik were quite important because

[13] B. Krekić, "Four Florentine Commercial Companies in Dubrovnik (Ragusa) in the First Half of the Fourteenth Century," in *The Medieval City*, ed. H. A. Miskimin et al. (New Haven 1977) 25-41.

[14] M. Popović, "La penetrazione dei mercanti Pratesi a Dubrovnik (Ragusa) nella prima metà del XV secolo," *Archivio storico italiano* 117.4 (1959) 503-521.

[15] B. Krekić, *Dubrovnik (Raguse) et le Levant au Moyen Age* (Paris 1961) 135-144.

of their professional skills (six doctors).[16] Finally, one more group deserves mention: the Catalan merchants, who were the main importers of raw materials, such as wool needed by the textile manufacturers in fifteenth-century Dubrovnik.[17]

There are many interesting and even picturesque individuals who should not be forgotten when we speak of the foreigners in Dubrovnik, because of their importance and their contribution to the development and well-being of the city. I shall mention briefly just four. The Florentine Bencius del Buono, father of the famous Italian novelist Franco Sachetti, lived in Dubrovnik for at least twenty-four years from 1318 to 1341. (His son was most probably born in Dubrovnik between 1330 and 1335). During that period he became one of the leading merchants and financiers in the city. From Dubrovnik his activities embraced Venice, Florence, southern Italy, the Balkan hinterland, Dalmatia and the Serbian coastal areas. In Dubrovnik itself Bencius dealt very actively with the local people as well as with all kinds of foreigners, including representatives from the above-mentioned great Florentine bankers, prominent Venetians, and others. Bencius was granted Ragusan citizenship in 1329, but lost it later when he moved to Venice. Owing to his great wealth, Bencius was of great financial assistance to the Ragusan government on more than one occasion by granting huge loans to enable the city to meet its obligations, especially to the Serbian kings.[18]

Another notable foreigner is Francesco Baldella, an outstanding Venetian merchant and member of a Venetian family that had sent seven of its members to Dubrovnik during one hundred years, from 1291 to 1393. Francesco himself lived and worked in Dubrovnik for almost forty years, from 1350 to his death in 1389. He was a great businessman, active in many and varied business deals, credit operations, and so on, which englobed Dalmatia, Italy (especially Venice), and the Balkan hinterland. In spite of his long stay there and the great respect he enjoyed in Dubrovnik (as is witnessed by his being called "ser" in the documents), Baldella never became a Ragusan citizen, but remained a "habitator." It is for this reason that he was not spared being sent to jail, at the time when every Venetian in Dubrovnik was arrested during the "Guerra di Chioggia," which took place from 1378 to 1381, after Dubrovnik had joined the anti-Venetian coalition.[19] Baldella spent from September 1378 to March 1380 in jail, and was them temporarily released into the custody of his wife, who was a Florentine, because of poor health. Even his family was not allowed to live "in aliqua domo ad maritimam prope muros civitatis." However, after this sad episode, Francesco remained in Dubrovnik, and continued to work and prosper there until his death in 1389.

The third prominent foreigner I would like to mention here is Pietro Pantella,

[16] J. Tadić, *Jevreji u Dubrovniku do polovine XVII stoljeća* (Sarajevo 1937) 243-254. See also B. Krekić, "The Role of the Jews in Dubrovnik (Thirteenth-Sixteenth Centuries)," *Viator* 4 (1973) 260-261.

[17] M. Spremić, *Dubrovnik i Aragonci, 1442-1495* (Belgrade 1971).

[18] I. Voje, "Bencio del Buono," *Istorijski časopis* 18 (1971) 189-199. Krekić (n. 13 above) 37.

[19] B. Krekić, "Dubrovnik i rat oko Tenedosa (1378-1381)," *Zbornik radova Vizantološkog instituta Srpske akademije nauka i umetnosti* 5 (1958) 21-47.

from Piacenza, who lived in Dubrovnik from 1416 to his death in 1464. Pantella initiated and organized the textile production in Dubrovnik and became teacher to generations of local artisans. He branched out as a shipowner owning almost ten percent of the Ragusan merchant fleet between 1416 and 1440; he was involved in financial operations, and owned houses, land and property. Pantella was granted Ragusan citizenship in 1430 and was one of the richest and most influential men in mid-fifteenth-century Dubrovnik, with connections in Italy, Spain, Albania, the Balkans and the Levant.[20]

Finally, Johannes Sparterius (Exparter), from Saragossa in Spain, lived in Dubrovnik from 1439 until his death in 1469. He was the most important Catalan merchant in Dubrovnik and played a leading role in supplying wool to Dubrovnik's developing textile manufacture. Closely connected with Catalan merchants in the Levant, in Venice, southern Italy, Sicily, Spain and elsewhere, Sparterius invested large amounts of money in trade, in credit operations, and so on. From 1458 to 1469, he was the Catalan vice-consul in Dubrovnik ("vice-consul vassalorum et subditorum serenissimi domini Ferdinandi, regis Sicilie"). He was never granted Ragusan citizenship, because in 1449, Dubrovnik forbade its citizens to be consuls of foreign nations in Dubrovnik.[21]

III

The question we must now try to answer is this: what was the standing of all these foreigners in Dubrovnik?

Their position was regulated by local law and international treaties. The earliest local rules dealing with foreigners in Dubrovnik are to be found in the *Liber statutorum civitatis Ragusii* of 1272,[22] and in the *Liber statutorum doane* of 1277.[23] Later on, other regulations were issued as required by circumstances. In many instances, Ragusan law treated foreigners and Ragusans in the same way, but, of course, there were situations in which foreigners were singled out for special treatment. The *Liber statutorum*, for example, carefully explained which foreigners were supposed to pay the "arboraticum" for their ships and how high it should be.[24] Those who paid the "arboraticum" had also to pay the "sostaticum."[25] Foreigners holding goods belonging to Ragusans, if challenged in court, could not leave the city before clearing up the matter.[26] But Ragusans holding foreign property, while

[20] D. Dinić-Knežević, "Petar Pantela, trgovac i suknar u Dubrovniku," *God.Fil.fak. u Novom Sadu* 13.1 (1970) 87-144.

[21] Spremić (n. 17 above) 71-73.

[22] *Liber statutorum civitatis Ragusii,* ed. V. Bogišić and C. Jireček, Monumenta historico-juridica Slavorum Meridionalium (Zagreb 1904).

[23] *Dubrovački zakoni i uredbe,* ed. A. Solovjev and M. Peterković, Istorisko-pravni spomenici (Belgrade 1936) 385-447.

[24] *Liber statutorum* 11.

[25] *Ibid.* 23.

[26] *Ibid.* 65.

coming under similar rules, were allowed to leave provided they left a representative.[27] A foreigner visiting but not residing in Dubrovnik was forbidden to bear arms while in the city.[28]

In the customs laws of 1277, the selling of various goods (textiles, hides, and so on) to foreigners in Dubrovnik, who would then carry them away, was considered as the exporting of goods; and the Ragusan seller, not the foreign buyer, was liable for the customs fees.[29] If, however, a foreigner bought those goods from other than Ragusans, he was then exempt from customs.[30] On the other hand, when Ragusans exported from Dubrovnik foreign-owned goods, the customs taxes were supposed to be paid again by Ragusans.[31] No merchandise could be sold to foreigners for export without a previous report to the "doanerii" and payment of the customs fees.[32]

The well-being of Dubrovnik depended largely on the strength of its merchant fleet, Venetian limitations before 1358 notwithstanding (four ships up to 70 miliarii annually to Venice). Thus it is not surprising that the Ragusan government kept constant watch over its fleet and tried to restrict the role of foreigners. Already in the *Liber statutorum* of 1272 it was forbidden for Ragusans to hire (*naulicare*) foreign ships, with the exception of Venetian ones[33] (we shall return to this point later on). Also, Ragusans were not allowed to sell, donate or lease their ships to Slavs, who would then come to the Ragusan harbor with their merchandise, thus hurting the local merchants and seamen.[34] In 1313, it was decided that the Ragusans could not "vendere, donare, obligare, ad naulum aliquo modo vel ingenio dare lignum aliquod, quod possit poni ad remos alicui persone foresterie" without permission from the government.[35] In 1358, two more important provisions affecting the position and role of foreigners in the Ragusan merchant marine were made and written into the statutes: "ut marinareça Ragusii, que est amissa, possit reffici et recuperari," it was decided that no Ragusan could thereafter "habere partem nec dare partem de navigio alicui foresterio."[36] It was also legislated that a Ragusan who already shared the ownership of a ship with a foreigner, "teneatur . . . ponere super dicto navigio tot marinarios de habitatoribus Ragusii et tocius districtus ejus, quot partes habebit in ipso."[37] This protectionism of the Ragusan merchant fleet at a time when the breach with Venice had just taken place, was well justified in view of the events that followed, especially in the realm of Veneto-Ragusan competition.

[27] *Ibid.* 64. For Split see G. Novak, *Povijest Splita* 1 (Split 1957) 263-264.

[28] *Liber statutorum* (n. 22 above) 133.

[29] *Dubrovački zakoni* (n. 23 above) 402-403, 409.

[30] *Ibid.* 409.

[31] *Ibid.*

[32] *Ibid.* 414.

[33] *Liber statutorum* (n. 22 above) 163. For Venetian restrictions on their own citizens as far as foreign ships are concerned see Lane (n. 12 above) 378, 380.

[34] *Liber statutorum* 193.

[35] *Dubrovački zakoni* (n. 23 above) 36-37.

[36] Historijski arhiv u Dubrovniku (HAD), *Reformationes* XVII, fols. 81v-82. *Liber statutorum* 148-149.

[37] *Reformationes loc. cit.; Liber statutorum* 148.

The treatment of foreigners, however, was also a matter of international agreements and mutual arrangements. Thus it was decided in 1326 that all foreigners importing goods into Dubrovnik should pay "illam doanam que accipitur hominibus de Ragusio in eorum civitatibus et locis." Simultaneously, every Ragusan selling or buying goods to or from foreigners in Dubrovnik, was bound to give a list of these goods to the customs officials on the same day that the transaction was concluded. The same rule applied to foreigners buying or selling merchandise among themselves, should the value surpass ten hyperpers.[38] The scribes on board Ragusan ships bringing foreign-owned goods were supposed to hand a list of those goods to the customs officials before the merchandise was unloaded. Similarly, when taking on board foreign-owned goods the scribes were supposed to give a list to the "doanerii" before loading.[39]

In 1372 the position of foreigners in Dubrovnik deteriorated drastically as a result of the decision of the Ragusan Major Council prohibiting trade among foreigners in Dubrovnik and its territories, and forbidding trade between Ragusans and foreigners.[40] Such grave measures should most probably be linked to the antagonism existing between Dubrovnik and Venice, which had been simmering ever since 1358, and which sometime later exploded during the Chioggia war. Dubrovnik, which had trouble in persuading the Venetians to recognize the rights of the Ragusans — rights that Venice herself had granted them in 1358, as we shall see — probably tried by means of the general restrictions imposed in 1372 to obtain Venetian assent to its demands, or else to deprive the Venetian merchants in Dubrovnik of the special privileges that they still enjoyed. However, these Ragusan restrictions certainly did not last long, for they would have gravely damaged the local economy. There is no information as to when the restrictions were lifted or modified, but there is a new decree dating from 1385 as to the payment of customs by foreigners in Dubrovnik, which indicates that matters were back to normal.

Once again, in this decree, the reciprocity of treatment was emphasized. Indeed, the decision notes "quod . . . pro solutionibus doanarum forinsecorum persepe solent oriri litigia inter doanerios nostros et forinsecos mercatores." To avoid this it was decided that foreigners unloading and selling their merchandise in Dubrovnik, should pay three percent or more, depending on that which Ragusans were required to pay "in civitatibus et locis talium forinsecorum." Venetians, Dalmatians, Anconitans, Slavs and others with whom Dubrovnik had treaties and conventions were excluded from these rules. Foreigners unloading their goods in Dubrovnik, but re-expediting them without selling them in the city, were supposed to pay only one percent. However, should their goods be destined "a Corfino citra scilicet in Bulgariam, Sclauoniam, Gentam, Bosnam et regnum Hungarie et ad alia loca inter ista nominata posita" where Ragusans pay customs, then the foreigners would have to pay three

---

[38] *Reformationes* VIII, fols. 30-30v. *Dubrovački zakoni* (n. 23 above) 421. For reciprocity of treatment in Split see Novak (n. 27 above) 263.

[39] *Reformationes* VIII, fol. 46.

[40] *Dubrovački zakoni* (n. 23 above) 93.

percent in Dubrovnik, even if only for unloading.[41] Finally, in 1392, another regulation was made, according to which foreigners importing "panos vel frustaneos" in Dubrovnik would have to pay six percent customs fees and the buyer another six percent tax; but Venetians and others with whom Dubrovnik had treaties were exempted from this rule and would pay according to mutual conventions.[42]

The privileged position of the Venetians in Dubrovnik — which we have mentioned several times already — was a source of constant friction between the two cities. It was established most probably already at the time Dubrovnik recognized Venetian supremacy in 1205, but it is not referred to in the surviving Veneto-Ragusan treaties from the thirteenth century (1232, 1236, 1252).[43] The explicit statements concerning the special position of the Venetians are to be found first in the city statutes of 1272, and then in the customs laws of 1277. In the city statutes, the Venetians are never listed among strangers because they were to be treated as if they were Ragusans, or even superior to them. Therefore in the article listing the numerous foreigners bound to pay the "arboraticum," there is no mention of Venetians. More clearly, in the article prohibiting Ragusans from hiring foreign ships is added, "excepto quod navem Venetorum bene possit nauliçare."[44]

This privileged treatment accorded the Venetians can be understood even better in the *Liber statutorum doane*. In an article dealing with the slave trade in Dubrovnik, it was stated — among other things — that a Ragusan, or a foreigner, buying a slave in Dubrovnik from a Slav must pay a customs fee of four grossi "exceptis Venetis qui non solvunt."[45] A similar statement is to be found concerning the bird trade. Both Ragusans and foreigners exporting from Dubrovnik "austures, terciolos, falcones et sparauarios" were required to pay one grosso per bird, "exceptis hominibus de Veneciis qui nichil solvere teneantur."[46] Furthermore, every Ragusan exporting foreign-owned merchandise to a wide area on the Dalmatian and Albanian shores was supposed to pay the same fees that were charged to Ragusan-owned goods, but again, "exceptis hominibus de Veneciis pro quibus non solvat."[47] Ragusans importing their own or foreign-owned merchandise into the above-mentioned area were required to pay customs fees, the same exception being accorded Venetian-owned merchandise.[48] More exceptions were granted to Venetian merchants trading with Kotor in articles added between 1280 and 1282, and in 1305.[49]

It is clear that not only were the Venetians not considered foreigners in Dubrovnik, but their position was oftentimes more favorable than that of the

[41] *Reformationes* XXVI, fols. 123v-124; *Dubrovački zakoni* 423-424.

[42] *Reformationes* XXIX, fol. 133.

[43] S. Ljubić, *Listine o odnošajih izmedju Južnoga Slavenstva i Mletačke Republike* 1 (Zagreb 1868) 46-49, 53-55, 82-85.

[44] *Liber statutorum* (n. 22 above) 11, 163.

[45] *Dubrovački zakoni* (n. 23 above) 403.

[46] *Ibid.* 405.

[47] *Ibid.* 409.

[48] *Ibid.* 410.

[49] *Ibid.* 416, 419.

Ragusans themselves. There can be no doubt that Venetian privileges in Dubrovnik contrasted very sharply with the controls and limitations imposed on the Ragusans in Venice. Such a situation could only provoke resentment and dissatisfaction on the part of the Ragusans and create friction in the relations between the two city-states. However, Dubrovnik could not do much else but conform to Venetian wishes and orders in this matter, as long as the Venetians were its overlords.

There is, nevertheless, one instance in which the Ragusans insisted on treating Venetians as foreigners in their city, and they persisted in this attitude despite Venetian protests. In 1305 the Ragusans decided that foreigners should not be admitted as witnesses against Ragusans, nor should their depositions be accepted. The Venetian government reacted quickly and sharply to this decree. The Quarantia demanded that it be modified within fifteen days of the receipt of the Venetian letter in Dubrovnik, "in tantum . . . quod Veneti non intelligantur in ipso statuto nec sunt ad illam conditionem . . . sed sint ad conditionem Raguseorum." In the meantime, Ragusans were to be refused as witnesses against Venetians and their depositions were to be rejected in Venice herself, and in all her possessions.[50] In spite of Venetian pressure, Dubrovnik did not change her mind. It was only in 1325, when they were hard pressed for Venetian assistance against the Serbian menace, that the Ragusans expressed readiness to accept Venetian testimony in Ragusan courts. The Venetians actually used the Serbian danger to blackmail the Ragusans, in 1326, into accepting Venetian terms, under which the Venetians in Dubrovnik not only were readmitted as witnesses in local courts, but their privileged position in the city in general was reinforced.[51]

Sometimes, before permitting privileged treatment, the Ragusan authorities would demand written proof from Venice ("litteras dominationis ducalis") that a man was, indeed, a Venetian citizen.[52] But the Venetian impact on the Ragusan treatment of foreigners before 1358 went even beyond their own privileged position in the city. At the end of January 1340, the Venetian government expelled every Florentine from Venice and forbade trade with them. Similar orders were sent to Dubrovnik; and the local authorities conformed completely to the Venetian position, also prohibiting trade with the Florentines.[53] At the same time, the Venetians never tired

---

[50] Ljubić (n. 43 above) 1.211.

[51] B. Krekić, "O ratu Dubrovnika i Srbije 1327-1328," *Zbornik* (n. 19 above) 11 (1968) 195, 198.

[52] For example, HAD, *Diversa cancellariae* XII, fol. 307v, of 5 February 1351. Sometimes the Ragusans singled out the Venetians as a particular category of local residents. Thus, in September 1330 it was decided "quod nulla persona, tam civis, quam foresterius, vel de Veneciis, audeat . . . ire per civitatem post tercium sonum campane cum armis vel sine armis." *Reformationes* IX (n. 36 above) fol. 117.

[53] HAD, *Diversa notariae* VI, fol. 122. The Venetians had made an alliance with Florence against the Scaligers of Verona in 1336, but in 1339 a separate peace was arranged between Venice and Verona, which angered the Florentines. This might have led to frictions between Venice and Florence and to anti-Florentine measures in Venice, in 1340. See *Andree Danduli Venetorum Ducis Chronicon Venetum a Pontificatu Sancti Marci ad annum usque MCCCXXXIX,* in *Rerum italicarum scriptores,* 12, ed. L. A. Muratori (Milan 1728) 413-414. Also Marino Sanuto,

of reminding Dubrovnik of their privileged status, and never ceased to demand its observance, as they did once again in 1351.[54]

There are many indications that the Venetians retained their advantageous position in Dubrovnik even after 1358, when they no longer held dominion over the city. Continued demands for proof of Venetian citizenship in matters relating to customs is one such indication.[55] Another is the near panic state of the Ragusans on hearing in Dubrovnik in 1360 that the Venetians had forbidden every non-Venetian from loading their goods on Venetian ships lying in Dalmatian ports, for export beyond the Adriatic area. This automatically placed the Venetians in Dubrovnik in a far superior position, as they were now free to ship the highly valuable Balkan materials from Dubrovnik on Venetian ships, the Ragusans being forbidden to do so. In a complaint made on this subject the Ragusan government explicitly mentioned that lead was shipped by Venetian merchants from Dubrovnik.[56]

In 1372 we find the first mention of a Venetian consul in Dubrovnik. He was Nicoletto Miorato (Milloratus), a merchant active in Dubrovnik from 1364 to 1378.[57] Even at a time when Veneto-Ragusan relations were rapidly deteriorating, as in 1377 when foreigners were prohibited from selling textiles in Dubrovnik and its territories, an exception was made for the Venetians.[58] Soon after this, however, every Venetian in Dubrovnik was arrested — as we have already said — during the war of Chioggia, when Dubrovnik was an ally of Genoa and Hungary against Venice. Nevertheless, when that was over, a great many Venetians remained in Dubrovnik and the best proof of their strength in the city was the election in 1389 of a new Venetian consul in Dubrovnik. A group of twelve prominent Venetians convened in the Ragusan cathedral and "post maturam deliberationem" elected the goldsmith Bartholomeus de la Donna "in consulem civium venetorum." He remained consul until 1392.[59]

We have dwelt long enough on Venetians in Dubrovnik. It is time to revert to broader themes. Foreigners, although enjoying a large degree of equality with Ragusans, and considerable freedom of action in Dubrovnik, were nevertheless subjected to certain limitations and there was some discrimination in their treatment. There were no organized colonies of foreigners in Dubrovnik, nor did foreigners have

---

Vitae Ducum Venetorum italice scriptae ab origine urbis sive ab anno CCCCXXI usque ad annum MCCCCXCIII, ibid. 22 (Milan 1733) 601-605. H. Kretschmayr, *Geschichte von Venedig* 2 (Gotha 1920) 186-189. A. Battistella, *La Repubblica di Venezia ne'suoi undici secoli di storia* (Venice 1921) 214-216. R. Cessi, *Storia della Repubblica di Venezia* 1 (Milan 1944) 294-295.

[54] *Reformationes* (n. 36 above) XVI, fol. 15v.

[55] *Reformationes* XVIII, fol. 19v.

[56] *Ibid.* fols. 40v, 68. J. Tadić, *Pisma i uputstva Dubrovačke Republike* (Belgrade 1935) 29-30.

[57] *Diversa canc.* (n. 52 above) XXIII, fol. 109. I. Mitić, "Predstavnici stranih država u Dubrovniku za vrijeme Republike," *Pomorski zbornik* 4 (1966) 381, thinks that the Venetian merchant Marco Guoro, present in Dubrovnik between 1366 and 1370, had been the Venetian consul in the city in 1368, but I have not been able to find proof for this assumption.

[58] *Dubrovački zakoni* (n. 23 above) 103.

[59] *Diversa not.* (n. 53 above) X, fol. 78.

particular buildings in the city for their use. The vast majority of the foreigners, anyway, were highly mobile merchants and seafarers, who spent but a short time in Dubrovnik minding their affairs, and then continued their journeys to other regions and other places. There were, however, also foreigners whose stay in the city was prolonged, or even permanent. Such was the case with most craftsmen and professional men, as well as with many Slavs engaged in lowlier occupations. To all of these people it was certainly desirable to obtain Ragusan citizenship, or, at least, the status of resident — "habitator."

"Habitatores" were those foreigners who had usually spent a prolonged period in Dubrovnik and had acquired standing in the city. Among them one finds prominent Italian and Dalmatian merchants, Slavs from the hinterland, Albanians, Levantines and Greeks, Catalans, and others. Not all the "habitatores" were rich or prominent people. There were among them many small merchants, craftsmen, shipowners, fishermen, priests and others. For many, being a resident was the first step towards obtaining citizenship. To become a citizen was the highest achievement for a foreigner in Dubrovnik, but the granting of citizenship was a matter that the government handled with considerable caution because of Dubrovnik's delicate political and geographical position, lying always between two different worlds.

Already in the thirteenth century the Ragusans had admitted to the ranks of their nobility a number of foreign noble families, especially from Kotor, who immediately became part of the local patriciate, participating fully in the Major Council and in the government of the city. Furthermore, Ragusan nobility was granted sometimes to the Bosnian rulers and their most prominent noblemen. In such cases it was explicitly stated "quod recipiatur in nostrum civem de consilio." Thus, in 1397 nobility was given to the neighboring Bosnian prince Pavle Radenović. In 1399 Dubrovnik granted the rank of hereditary Ragusan noblemen to the king of Bosnia, Stjepan Ostoja, and to the most powerful Bosnian nobleman of the period, Duke Hrvoje Vukčić. Along with the status of Ragusan noblemen, each was also given a palace in the city worth fifteen hundred ducats. All of this was done for good reason: the king and the duke had just given to Dubrovnik a piece of Bosnian land, which, although poor, was essential to the rounding out of the Ragusan territories north of the city itself. To keep in the good graces of the former lord of that land, the duke Radič Sanković, he, too, was granted nobility by Dubrovnik.[60] Another Bosnian king, Tvrtko II, and the very powerful Bosnian duke Sandalj Hranić, were granted Ragusan nobility in 1405 (Sandalj visited Dubrovnik in 1426), while still another important Bosnian nobleman and Ragusan neighbor, the duke Radosav Pavlović, obtained it in 1423.[61]

In essence, however, these grants of nobility were much more a political gesture than a political reality. Although these noblemen were given palaces in Dubrovnik and were legally members of the Ragusan Major Council, they did not move into or

[60] S. Ćirković, *Istorija srednjovekovne bosanske države* (Belgrade 1964) 186. Mijušković (n. 8 above) 93-94, 99.
[61] HAD, *Consilium Rogatorum* III, fol. 139v; *Consilium Maius* II, fol. 116. Mijusković (n. 8 above) 101.

reside in the city, nor did they take an active part in its life, or in the legislation of the local patriciate. For the most part, granting Ragusan nobility to Balkan potentates was an insurance for them should they need to leave their countries because of internal upheavals or, as later on, because of the external Ottoman threat (the same is true of similar grants by Venice). On the other hand, in granting nobility to foreign dignitaries, Dubrovnik was always guided by political considerations. This is why these grants were made only to those who had contributed beneficially to Dubrovnik, or who could be useful to Ragusan interests, for example, the protection of roads, of merchants, of mining privileges, and so on. In refusing initially to grant nobility to Duke Radosav Pavlović, in 1423, the Ragusans explained that his predecessors and himself "non aiutarono allo crescimento di Ragusa."[62]

One consequence of such a policy was that most grants were made to the nearby powerful Bosnian lords, whose attitude could affect Ragusan interests very directly. The only two non-Bosnian personalities granted nobility by the Ragusans — as far as is now known — were the famous Albanian hero, George Kastriotes-Scanderbegh in 1439 (he visited Dubrovnik and in 1450 and 1462),[63] and the Croatian prince Grgur Blagajski in 1464.[64] It is noteworthy in this connection to observe that there were no Serbian rulers or noblemen among those granted Ragusan nobility, although Dubrovnik's links with them were very close and friendly. Several from among them visited Dubrovnik and were most warmly and magnificently received (Emperor Stefan Dušan in 1350; Despot George Branković in 1426, 1440 and 1441).[65] Certain Serbian personalities, however, were granted Ragusan citizenship (Prince Lazar Hrebeljanović, the tragic hero of Kosovo who visited Dubrovnik in 1362;[66] his son Despot Stevan Lazarević; the Balšić family;[67] and so on). Like similar grants of nobility to Bosnian personalities, these grants of citizenship to Serbs were more honorary than tangible.

It should be mentioned that Dubrovnik did not hesitate to use its grants of nobility and citizenship as a very effective tool against its enemies. In 1378, during the Chioggia war, Dubrovnik sent an envoy to lure the citizens of Kotor — then under Venetian rule — with the promise of Ragusan citizenship.[68] This attempt does not seem to have been particularly successful, but a later attempt did succeed. In 1451, the very powerful, nearby Bosnian regional lord Herzeg Stjepan Vukčić-Košaca (of Herzegovina) attacked Dubrovnik and laid siege to the city. Stjepan had earlier been made a Ragusan nobleman and, consequently, the Ragusan government now proclaimed him a traitor and offered a reward to anyone who would kill him. This

---

[62] Mijušković (n. 8 above) 101.

[63] K. Jireček, *Geschichte der Serben* 2 (Gotha 1918) 184, 193. J. Tadić, "Johannes Gazulus, dubrovački humanista XV veka," *Zbor. Filos. fak. u Beogradu* 8.1 (1964) 442, 443.

[64] *Consilium Maius* (n. 61 above) XII, fol. 175v. Mijušković (n. 8 above) 102.

[65] J. Tadić, *Promet putnika u starom Dubrovniku* (Dubrovnik 1939) 49, 72-88. M. Medini, *Dubrovnik Gučetića* (Belgrade 1953) 95-96.

[66] *Monumenta ragusina*, ed. G. Gelcich, 3 (Zagreb 1895) 212.

[67] K. Jireček, *Istorija Srba* 1 (Belgrade 1952) 243. Tadić (n. 65 above) 53. Mijušković (n. 8 above) 104-105.

[68] Mahnken (n. 3 above) 1.80.

reward, in addition to 15,000 ducats, a palace in Dubrovnik worth 2000 ducats, and an annual income of 300 ducats, also held the promise of hereditary Ragusan nobility for whoever did the deed. In fact, Stjepan was so scared by the threat that he raised the siege,[69] and this was the last time until 1806 that foreign troops stood outside the walls of Dubrovnik.

Most of the new citizens were, naturally, of a much lower rank than those just mentioned: merchants, craftsmen and professional men of various sorts. Even though patricians from other Dalmatian cities were sometimes granted Ragusan citizenship, they did not join the ranks of the local patriciate, but became plain, ordinary citizens. For all these people, becoming a Ragusan citizen was a very real occurrence, and they took full advantage of their new situation. For Dubrovnik, granting citizenship to them was a means of strengthening the city by attracting new men and new families, especially those whose skills it needed. The Ragusan government did not make any secret of this aspect of its citizenship grants. In many instances, it was stated explicitly that citizenship was given "pro bono et augmento civitatis et districtus Ragusii," or "pro comodo et utilitate comunis Ragusii." There is nothing to indicate, for example, that foreign craftsmen were restricted from becoming members of Ragusan fraternities.[70] Although vertical mobility was very limited in Dubrovnik, some of the naturalized citizens founded families that later became very rich and prominent in the city and joined the ranks of the Fraternity of Saint Anthony (Antunini),[71] which constituted the richest and, after the patricians, the most politically influential group in the city, whose importance in Dubrovnik's life persisted for centuries.

To become a citizen, a foreigner was required to submit a "supplicatio," usually to the Minor Council. When approved, the foreigner had to swear, personally or through a representative, an oath of allegiance, which until 1358 contained the words: "Semper ero fidelis et obediens excellentissimi domini Ducis et comunis Veneciarum et comitis et comunis Ragusii ero fidelis et obediens civis et terrigena, sicut ceteri cives de Ragusio sunt."[72] In the register it was usually briefly stated: so-and-so "factus fuit civis Ragusii, qui juravit fidelitatem domini Ducis Veneciarum, domini Comitis Ragusii et comunis Ragusii."[73] After 1358 the formula was: so-and-so "factus fuit civis Ragusii, qui juravit esse fidelis comunis Ragusii et facere omnes angaridias reales et personales, sicut quilibet alius Raguseus,"[74] or, simply, "juravit

---

[69] Jireček (n. 63 above) 2,200. Ćirković (n. 60 above) 300. S. Ćirković, *Herceg Stefan Vukčić-Kosača i njegovo doba* (Belgrade 1964) 165-166, points out that the Herceg had yet another reason to lift the siege of Dubrovnik hurriedly: he was called to Kotor, which had been attacked by the Albanians.

[70] *Bratovštine i obrtne korporacije u Republici Dubrovačkoj,* ed. K. Vojnović (Zagreb 1899). On restrictions in Venice see Lane (n. 12 above) 319. On Genoa's liberalism see Lopez (n. 5 above) 45-46.

[71] Mijušković (n. 8 above) 103.

[72] HAD, *Acta Sanctae Mariae Maioris,* Prep. 14.5. *Diplomatički zbornik Kraljevine Hrvatske, Dalmacije i Slavonije,* ed. T. Smičiklas, 10 (Zagreb 1912) 419-420.

[73] *Reformationes* (n. 36 above) XV, fol. 12.

[74] *Reformationes* XVII, fol. 99v.

fidelitatem et obedientiam dominationi Ragusii."[75] The fact that after 1358 there is
no mention of allegiance to the king of Hungary and Croatia, the new protector of
Dubrovnik, is in itself an indication of Dubrovnik's new independence and of its
different relationship towards the king, compared with its previous dependence upon
Venice. True, there were special cases, when a naturalized citizen wished to keep his
previous allegiance, too. Thus, in 1350, "Comes Dionisius, baronus domini Regis
Ungarie," was made a Ragusan citizen. He swore the usual oath to the Doge, Venice,
Count and Dubrovnik, but with the addition, "semper salva fidelitate domini Regis
Ungarie."[76] After making the oath, the new citizen was issued a "littera (carta)
civilitatis," bearing the seal of the city as proof of his new status.[77]

We know with certainty that many of those who became citizens had been earlier
"habitatores" of Dubrovnik, but that was not a necessary precondition, nor do we
see a fixed length of residence in Dubrovnik as a precondition for citizenship.[78]
There are cases where it is said that the new citizen "diu Ragusii stetit" or "pluribus
ac pluribus annis habitavit in civitate nostra,"[79] but only as a statement of fact, not
as a condition of citizenship. There is one text, however, from which one might infer
that twenty-five years of residence were required to permit integration into the
community and enjoyment of its advantages, but this is a very peculiar text. On
25 January 1358, a short time before Dubrovnik ceased to recognize Venetian
supremacy, Venice, in a desperate effort to keep the fidelity of the Ragusans, granted
them – at this late hour – the extraordinary privilege "quod omnes Ragusei nati in
Ragusio et ex eis de cetero nascituri sint cives nostri Veneciarum et possint mercari
tamquam cives Veneti, navigando cum navigiis nostris." As for foreigners, they would
be included in this privilege, provided they had resided in Dubrovnik for twenty-five
years and had shared all the burdens of the citizens.[80] What we have here is, in fact,
the Venetian view of residence as a precondition for enjoying the advantages of
citizenship, not the Ragusan position on the matter.

To be born in Dubrovnik, or to have a Ragusan father was of use, as was being
married and having children in the city, and paying taxes and other dues. Personal
merit and powerful intervention were also helpful. In 1464 a man from Cremona was
granted Ragusan citizenship, "ad requisitionem et instantiam illustrissimi principis et
serenissimi domini, domini Francisci Sforce, vicecomitis Ducis Mediolani."[81]

However, citizenship could be lost, especially if a naturalized Ragusan moved

[75] Reformationes XXX, fol. 42. Mijušković (n. 8 above) 122.

[76] Reformationes XV, fol. 76. Mahnken (n. 3 above) 1.92.

[77] Consilium Maius (n. 61 above) II, fol. 13v. Mijušković (n. 8 above) 123.

[78] Venice required twenty-five years of residence before granting citizenship. See Ljubić
(n. 43 above) 4.87. Genoa, on the other hand, was very liberal until 1404, when it began requiring three years' residence. Lopez (n. 5 above) 31, 41, 45-46. In Split foreigners who spent there
less than six months were exempt from local duties, but those who spent three years in the city
were not considered as foreigners in criminal cases. See Novak (n. 27 above) 1.262, 263.

[79] Consilium Maius (n. 61 above) VII, fol. 110v; IX, fol. 7. Mijušković (n. 8 above) 116.

[80] Liber statutorum (n. 22 above) 227-228.

[81] Consilium Maius XII, fol. 176. Mijušković (n. 8 above) 117-118.

away from Dubrovnik for a protracted period of time, if he refused to obey governmental orders, or if he took part in hostile activities against Dubrovnik.[82] But prominent individuals who had lost Ragusan nobility or citizenship could regain it (King Ostoja, Duke Radosav Pavlović; and Herzeg Stjepan Vukčić, who has a price on his head in 1451, not only reestablished good relations with Dubrovnik, but even visited the city in 1466).[83]

Interestingly enough, there is nothing in the city statutes on the subject of granting nobility or citizenship, and only three general decrees have been found in the records of the governmental councils (1364, 1395 and 1449). Parallels with other cities, on the other hand, are difficult. Either there is no sufficient evidence (for example, for Kotor, Split and other Dalmatian cities), or the similarities which exist are only partial.[84] The obvious parallel would be with Venice. While Venice had the "cives de intus" and "cives de intus et de foris, de extra,"[85] in Dubrovnik one finds, apart from "cives," also those called "cives de foris"; but there are only two such cases concerning six persons. There is, also, in Dubrovnik the mention of "cives albi," "blanchi," but again only twice; and to compare them with the Genoese "cives albi" would be certainly too risky. Thus, the only thing one can venture to say about these two groups of naturalized Ragusans is that they do not seem to have been required to live in the city, but could live elsewhere, provided they paid their taxes and took care to "manutenere honorem et bonum statum civitatis et civium Ragusii." The other, ordinary new citizens were required to live in Dubrovnik, to bring their families there and to own property. Frequently, strict time limitations were imposed for the fulfillment of these requirements.[86]

We have just mentioned three decrees concerning citizenship preserved in Ragusan documents. The first was from 1364. It stated that noblemen from Kotor, Ulcinj and Bar (cities on the Serbian coast, south of Dubrovnik), could not be granted Ragusan citizenship, unless they moved their families to Dubrovnik. As for others, the Minor Council could act "secundum antiquam consuetudinem."[87] This meant that nobility from other cities, even when not moving their families to Dubrovnik, could be granted citizenship by a decision of the Major Council, or of the Senate. The obstacles thus created for the acceptance of noblemen from Serbian maritime cities

---

[82] Native Ragusans could renounce their citizenship. On 30 December 1326, the Major Council allowed one of the five (or more) daughters of Margaritus Krusić (de Crosio) "illa . . . que placuerit dicto Margarito" to renounce her Ragusan citizenship. One of them did so on 8 January 1327; *Reformationes* (n. 36 above) VIII, fol. 75v. Mahnken (n. 3 above) 1.228 thinks that this might have been because she wanted to marry outside of Dubrovnik. However, in 1333 the same girl married a Ragusan patrician.

[83] Tadić (n. 65 above) 132. Mijušković (n. 8 above) 96-97. Ćirković (n. 69 above) 266.

[84] For Kotor see I. Sindik, *Komunalno uredjenje Kotora* (Belgrade 1950) 38, 40. For Split: Novak (n. 27 above) 1.263-264.

[85] Lane (n. 12 above) 62, 140. Lopez (n. 5 above) 38-39.

[86] Mijušković (n. 8 above) 118-119. For Byzantine regulations see R. Lopez, "Foreigners in Byzantium," *Bulletin de l'Institut historique belge de Rome* 44, Miscellanea Charles Verlinden (1974) 341-352.

[87] *Dubrovački zakoni* (n. 23 above) 79. Mijušković (n. 8 above) 109-110.

were, no doubt, the result of Dubrovnik's fear of competition and, also, the reaction
to the attitude of many of these men during a recent war between Dubrovnik and a
nearby Serbian lord (Vojislav Vojinović).[88]

In 1395 new rules were drawn up concerning the granting of citizenship. Persons
from Dalmatia and from the maritime areas of Serbia could become citizens from
that time on only with the approval of the Ragusan Major Council. For the Slavs
from the hinterland it was enough to have the approval of the Minor Council, but
"quaecumque alie libertates quas hactenus habuisset Minus consilium volendi facere
et creare cives Ragusii per aliquos ordines vel consuetudines sint irrite et nullius
vigoris."[89]   Obviously, the Major Council was taking on itself a growing role in the
granting of citizenship. In addition, the decision of 1395 clearly oriented
Dubrovnik's immigration policy towards acceptance in the first place of people from
the hinterland. This contributed considerably to the slavicization and population
growth of the city. Such an attitude probably reflected the Ragusan preference for
people whose minor skills, insufficient experience in business and limited available
capital prevented them from becoming dangerous competitors, as could happen with
large numbers of Italians. Still, the city did not hesitate to grant citizenship to a man
of great skills and experience whom Dubrovnik needed, such as Pietro Pantella in
1430.

In 1449, the conditions governing the acceptance of hinterland Slavs were drastically stiffened (two-thirds of the Minor Council and then two-thirds of the Major
Council must approve). The reason given for this change was the introduction of new
customs laws, according to which foreigners, including Balkan Slavs, were levied
double the fees paid by Ragusans. To prevent Slavic attempts to evade the law by
obtaining citizenship, new citizenship regulations were enacted.[90]   Their effect was a
dramatic decrease in new grants of Ragusan citizenship to people from the hinterland. I am inclined to believe that in all of this the Ragusans had an ulterior motive:
they wanted, I suspect, to reduce the chances of irritating the Ottomans, the new
masters of the hinterland. By preventing a massive drainage of the population from
areas newly conquered by the Ottomans they hoped that such irritation could be
avoided. Indeed, large movements of the hinterland population to the west, the
Adriatic coast and even to Italy, were already under way, and Dubrovnik, while
helping the refugees, certainly did not wish to offer a pretext to the all-powerful
Ottomans to take a hostile attitude towards the city.

IV

The last question we must attempt to answer is the most important one: just what
was the contribution of foreigners to Dubrovnik's life and development in the late

[88] Jireček (n. 63 above) 1.422. M. Zečević, *Ratovanje Vojislava Vojinovića sa Dubrovnikom*
(Belgrade 1908).

[89] HAD, *Liber viridis* fols. 96v-97. Mahnken (n. 3 above) 1.80-81. Mijušković (n. 8 above)
111.

[90] *Consilium Maius* (n. 61 above) IX, fol. 83v. *Liber viridis* fols. 264-265. Mijušković (n. 8
above) 112, 115.

Middle Ages? The answer to this question touches upon many things, but I shall concentrate on, in my opinion, the essential aspect of the foreigners' role in Dubrovnik — the economic one.

The importance of foreigners in Dubrovnik's economic growth is obvious. At one time, in the thirteenth century, when Dubrovnik captured the lion's share of the Serbian mining market (and a little later the Bosnian one also), Ragusan merchants certainly did not yet have enough capital to invest in such vast and risky ventures. Although we do not have any documents for the earliest period, it is safe to assume that foreigners played a big role as early investors in the mining trade. They probably also played a major role in the transportation of minerals by sea from Dubrovnik to the West. This situation continued into the fourteenth century, as can be seen from many documents. It should be pointed out, however, that foreigners (Italians in the first place) rarely went personally into the rough and inhospitable Balkan hinterland. They organized companies with the Ragusans, invested their money, and provided the ships, but stayed mostly in Dubrovnik themselves or traveled elsewhere by sea, while letting the Ragusans go to the hinterland and transact the business. For the Ragusans this was considerably easier, not only because they had ancient contacts with those areas, but, above all, because they spoke the same language as the Balkan population.

As it turned out, this kind of arrangement proved to be more advantageous to the Ragusans in the long run. In taking these journeys they came to learn a great deal about mining, about Serbia and Bosnia, about the people and their habits, about the political structure and the functioning of those states. All of this was a great asset to the Ragusan state and its merchants, once their economic strength increased and allowed them to develop their own investments and enterprises in the hinterland. This process has not yet been sufficiently studied, but it seems possible to conjecture that the change from predominantly foreign-financed to predominantly domestic-financed enterprises took place in the mid-fourteenth century.

Somewhat later a similar process began in the Ragusan naval trade. This trade was vital for Dubrovnik, especially because through it the city obtained — among many other things — all the grain it needed to feed its population.[91] The cessation of the Venetian domination, and of the Venetian-imposed limitations on Ragusan shipping, in 1358; the unstable conditions in Serbia after Emperor Stefan Dušan's death, in 1355; and the growing interest of the Ragusans in naval trade, together with the new availability of funds to invest into it — all of this led to an upsurge in Ragusan shipbuilding and maritime commerce in the seventies of the fourteenth century. The maritime and shipbuilding tradition, at least a hundred years old already,[92] now got a big boost.

This, of course, does not mean that, by this time, the foreigners had lost their

[91] D. Dinić-Knežević, "Trgovina žitom u Dubrovniku u XIV veku," *Godišnjak Fil. fak. u Novom Sadu* 10 (1967) 79-131. The same, "Promet žitarica izmedju Dubrovnika i zaledja u srednjem veku," *ibid.* 12.1 (1969) 73-87.

[92] As witnessed by the seventh book of the *Liber statutorum* (n. 22 above) 151-172. See also J. Jučić, "Pomorsko-trgovački dometi Dubrovnika u XIII stoljeću," *Spomenica Josipa Matasovića* (Zagreb 1972) 151-161.

importance. It is enough to look at the participation of the Pratesi and other Italians in the organization and development of the Ragusan textile production; it is enough to see the contribution the Catalan merchants made in providing raw materials for that production, to realize how important the role of the foreigners in Dubrovnik continued to be in the fifteenth century. Indeed, the textile production — which was started in response to the growing needs of the Ragusan textile exports towards the Balkan hinterland — became one of the most vigorous branches of the Ragusan economy in the fifteenth century. In short, there is no doubt that foreigners continued to play a vital role in Dubrovnik's economy. It could not be otherwise. Dubrovnik was a city whose prosperity did not depend on some narrow, local production or natural resources of any kind. Its whole existence and success was built on its position as intermediary between East and West, North and South. To keep that role and to safeguard its own importance, Dubrovnik had to be open to foreigners and to offer them continuously new opportunities and chances of success. Through their success, Dubrovnik achieved a large portion of its own progress and prosperity.

Department of History
University of California
Los Angeles, California 90024, U.S.A.

THE LÜBECKERS BARTHOLOMÄUS GHOTAN AND NICOLAUS BÜLOW IN NOVGOROD AND MOSCOW AND THE PROBLEM OF EARLY WESTERN INFLUENCES ON RUSSIAN CULTURE

•

by David B. Miller

Over seventy-five years ago Vasilii Kliuchevskii in a famous lecture characterized Russia's relations with western Europe in the fifteenth and the sixteenth centuries as "*intercourse*, and not influence."[1] He meant that Russian society was unconscious of cultural inferiority and concomitant need to study or adopt Western culture. Traditional cultures integrate values and beliefs into a unified world view. They express them in a complex of symbols which ritualize life and define norms of behavior. And they can absorb alien strains so long as they do not threaten unifying assumptions. Kliuchevskii doubted that Russians assimilated significant elements of the culture of Catholic Europe and he denied that contact with Westerners caused Russians to reconsider their own cultural values.

We know a good deal about Russia's relationship with western Europe in the period to which Kliuchevskii referred. In our time we are also aware that cultural interrelationships are more complex than Kliuchevskii's model, which held intercourse and influence to be the only variables. Cultural changes under external stress, for example, have resulted in curious amalgams of the alien and new with vigorous reassertions of the traditional. In the process conservative reaction within traditional cultures must be understood to have been as much the product of cultural interaction as were emulation or unconscious assimilation.[2]

Bartholomäus Ghotan and Nicolaus Bülow came from a society which itself was under stress. In the late fifteenth century the Hansa metropolis of Lübeck began to lose its economic hegemony in the Baltic. The cause of its reverses was the rise of national states. Lübeck was at the same time an arena in which Renaissance ideas of man began to clash with traditional values. It in turn was an exporter of culture, including Renaissance ideas, throughout the Baltic. Among its exports were popular – often secular – literature, a preoccupation with history, a growing

---

[1] V. O. Kliuchevskii, *Sochineniia* 3 (Moscow 1957) 256.
[2] A perceptive example from the twentieth century is Frantz Fanon, *The Wretched of the Earth* (New York 1968) 148-248. See also A. Ia. Gurevich, "Nekotorye aspekty izucheniia sotsial'noi istorii," *Voprosy istorii* (1965) no. 10, pp. 59-61.

spiritual unease, and the spread of astrological "science." None was entirely new, but the manner in which they were understood and put to use, in human-centered ideological formulas, was.[3] Also new was the technology of dispersion, the printing press. Ghotan and Bülow were intellectual adventurers and missionaries of this bifurcated culture in Novgorod in the 1490s. Bülow later lived in Moscow for over thirty years where he shared his views with the court of Grand Prince Vasilii III. Recently, archival research by Harold Raab and Norbert Angermann has unearthed much new information about these men and it has attracted the analysis of Soviet historians.[4] From the new data about their lives, writings, translations, and printings,

[3] Philippe Dollinger, *The German Hansa* (Stanford 1970) 260-332 is an excellent survey. On the first Lübeck printers see Friedrich Bruns, "Lebensnachrichten über Lübecker Drucker des 15. Jahrhunderts," *Nordisk Tidskrift för Bok- och Biblioteksväsen* 2 (1915) 220-237. The new humanism of Italy never completely supplanted traditional culture at the courts and in the medieval towns of North Europe. The ambiguous results, whether in the emergence of national popular cultures or in philosophy, make the "North European Renaissance" a controversial subject. The case for decadence in the relevant age was first made with unsurpassed brilliance for France and the Netherlands by J. Huizinga, *The Waning of the Middle Ages* (English ed.: Garden City 1954) in 1924. See also Wallace K. Ferguson, *The Renaissance in Historical Thought* (New York 1948), especially chapters 9-11, and Denys Hay, ed., *The Renaissance Debate* (New York 1965).

[4] H. Raab, "Germanoslawisches im Ostseeraum an der Wende vom Mittelalter zur Neuzeit," *Wissenschaftliche Zeitschrift der Ernst Moritz Arndt-Universität Greifswald, Gesellschafts- und sprachwissenschaftliche Reihe* 6.1-2 (1956/1957) 57-60; *idem* "Zu einigen niederdeutschen Quellen des altrussischen Schrifttums," *Zeitschrift für Slawistik* 3.2-4 (1958) 323-335; *idem*, "Über die Beziehungen Bartholomäus Ghotans und Nicolaus Buelows zum Gennadij-Kreis in Novgorod," *Wissenschaftliche Zeitschrift der Universität Rostock, Gesellschafts- und sprachwissenschaftliche Reihe* 8.3 (1958/1959) 419-422; *idem*, "Novye svedeniia o pechatnike Barfolomee Gotans," *Mezhdunarodnye sviazi Rossii do XVII v. Sb. statei* (Moscow 1961) 339-351; and N. Angermann, "Bartholomäus Ghotan in Novgorod," *Zeitschrift des Vereins für Lübeckische Geschichte und Alterumskunde* (ZVLGA) 45 (1965) 141-148; *idem*, "Nicolaus Bülow: Ein Lübecker Arzt und Theologe in Novgorod und Moskau," ZVLGA 46 (1966) 88-90; *idem*, "Kulturbeziehungen zwischen dem Hanseraum und dem Moskauer Russland um 1500," *Hansische Geschichtsblätter* 84 (1966) 20-48; *idem*, "Neues über Nicolaus Bülow und sein Wirken im Moskauer Russland," *Jahrbücher für Geschichte Osteuropas* n.s. 17 (1969) 408-419. Most Soviet scholars have minimized the importance of Ghotan and Bülow in Russia. See Ia. S. Lur'e, "K voprosu o 'Latinstve' gennadievskogo literaturnogo kruzhka," *Issledovaniia i materialy po drevnerusskoi literature AN SSR, In-t mirovoi lit. im. Gor'kogo*, ed. V. D. Kuz'min (Moscow 1961) 68-77; *idem*, "O putiakh razvitiia svetskoi literatury v Rossii i u zapadnykh slavian v XV-XVI vv.," *Trudy Otdeleniia drevne-russkoi literatury* (TODRL) 19 (1963) 262-288; *idem*, *Ideologicheskaia bor'ba v russkoi publitsistike kontsa XV-nachala XVI vv.* (Moscow 1960) 66-74, 223-234, 266-284, 395-404; *idem*, "Elementy Vozrozhdeniia na Rusi v kontse XV-pervoi polovine XVI veka," *Literatura epokhi Vozrozhdeniia i problemy vsemirnoi literatury* (Moscow 1967) 183-211; and *idem*, "Cherty Vozrozhdeniia v russkoi kul'ture XV-XVI vv. (Drevnerusskaia literatura i zapadnaia 'narodnaia kniga')," *Feodal'naia Rossiia vo vsemirno-istoricheskom protsesse. Sb. statei posviashchennyi L'vu Vladimirovichu Cherepninu* (Moscow 1972) 157-171; A. A. Zimin, "Doktor Nikolai Bulev — publitsist i uchenyi medik," *Issledovaniia* (see above) 78-86 and *idem*, *Rossiia na poroge novogo vremeni: (Ocherki politicheskoi istorii Rossii pervoi treti XVI v.)* (Moscow 1974) 344-364. An exception is the expert on incunabula E. Nemirovskii, *Vozniknovenie knigopechataniia v Moskve: Ivan Fedorov* (Moscow 1964) 58-61, 70-74. Raab and such non-Soviet historians as Élie Denissoff, "Aux origines de l'église russe autocéphale," *Revue des études slaves* 23 (1947) 66-88 and Joseph L. Wieczynski, "Archbishop Gennadius and the West: The Impact of Catholic Ideas upon the Church of Novgorod," *Canadian-American Slavic*

and from contemporary writings about them, one may confidently sketch their cultural horizons and assess their impact on changes in Russian culture. It will be noted that, although few Russians responded sympathetically, their views provoked a reaction which was to help shape the beginnings of a Russian national consciousness. It was a reaction which in important respects was similar to that provoked by Renaissance influences elsewhere in northern Europe.

Bülow was born into a well-to-do Lübeck family. His father owned properties, an uncle was a church canon, one brother a municipal priest, and another became a burgher of Tallinn.[5] Between 1480 and 1483 Bülow earned a baccalaureate and a master's degree at the University of Rostock, in the Faculty of Arts.[6] By 1490 he was an authority on astronomy and sometime before 1518 he became a medical doctor, but when and where he studied medicine is uncertain.[7] Ghotan's career as one of the early printers of northern Germany is well known. He was born in Magdeburg, became a cathedral vicar, and there he established his first press. By 1479 his parents had registered as citizens of Lübeck, and by 1484 Ghotan also was there.[8] Ghotan printed for clients in Sweden as well as in northern Germany. He printed in Lübeck to 1486 and again from 1488 to 1493. In 1486/87 he established a press in Stockholm and it printed in his name after he had returned to Lübeck.[9] Among his early works were the lavish *Missale Magdeburgense*, but also possibly an early Low German edition of the Dracula legend.[10] In Latin and in vernaculars he continued to print books and broadsides in equally varied genres: holy writ, hagiography and popular religious texts, popular stories, almanacs, and popular medical compendiums. He printed the first book in Swedish. Always he printed indulgences.[11]

Studies 6 (1972) 374-389 have overstated, often uncritically, the importance of western influences in Novgorod.

[5] Angermann, "Nicolaus" 89-90.

[6] *Die Matrikel der Universität Rostock* 1: *1419-1499* (Rostock 1889) 229, 236; see also Raab, "Über die Beziehungen" 421; Angermann, "Neues" 410-412.

[7] Angermann, "Neues" 410, 412-413, 419. He was a doctor when he arrived in Moscow no earlier than 1506. No evidence has been uncovered to support the hypothesis of L. N. Maikov that he studied at Padua; "Nikolai Nemchin, russkii pisatel' kontsa XV-nachala XVI veka," *Izvestiia Otdeleniia russkogo iazyka i slovesnosti* (IORIaS) 5.1-2 (1900) 382-383.

[8] Wilhelm H. C. Gläser, *Bartel Ghotan, Domvikar und Diplomat, Schriftgiesser und Buchdrucker, Urheber des Mohnsignet von 1479-1494 in Magdeburg und Lübeck, in Stockholm und Moskau* (Lübeck 1903) 1-2. Konrad Haebler, *Die deutschen Buchdrucker des XV. Jahrhunderts im Auslande* (Munich 1924) 285-286 suggests that he was born in Magdeburg.

[9] Bruns (n. 3 above) 228-230; Raab, "Zu einigen" (n. 4 above) 323-329.

[10] Bruns (n. 3 above) 228-229; Nemirovskii (n. 4 above) 73; C. Borchling and B. Claussen, *Niederdeutsche Bibliographie: Gesamtverzeichnis der niederdeutschen Drucke bis zum Jahre 1800,* 2 vols. (Neumünster 1931-1936) 1 nos. 66, 63. In Magdeburg he also printed Martin von Mellerstadt's *Prognostikon auf das Jahr 1483* (1483), a Psalter, a Gospel table, and the *Ordinarius Verdensis.*

[11] In Lübeck and Sweden Ghotan printed in Latin Donatus's primer, *De octo partibus orationis* and religious works: the *Vita Catherinae* and missals for Bishop Conrad Rogge of Strängnäs, a missal for the bishop of Åbo, Eusebius's *Epistola de vita Hieronymi*, the *Revelationes* of St. Birgitta and the *Vita Brynolphi* for the Vadstena Monastary in Sweden, and the Uppsala Psalter. His popular religious printings in Low German were an untitled broadside of a confrontation between *dat levent* and *de dod* to which scholars have given the title *Zwiegespräch zwischen*

Here were two men of the Lübeck elite: Bülow the scholar and possibly already a doctor of medicine, and Ghotan a missionary of printing of holy and profane books. Then, for reasons still uncertain, both entered Russian service shortly before 1490.

Embassies between Moscow and both the German emperor and the papacy passed through Lübeck regularly for six years beginning in 1488. The two Western powers sought Russian religious reunion and alliances, above all against the Turks. Moscow primarily sought allies against Poland and also recruited artisans.[12] Although sources are garbled, leading some to suggest that Bülow was at this time recruited in Rome, Angermann convincingly argued that he met the Russian diplomats in Germany. Probably on the order of Emperor Maximilian, he left Lübeck for Novgorod in 1489/90 in the company of Georgios Trakhaniotes, a Greek in Muscovite service, and the imperial ambassador von Thurn.[13] Ghotan became a Muscovite agent in 1490, recruited by the same Trakhaniotes. In 1492 Grand Prince Ivan III of Moscow directed his envoy Ivan Volk Kuritsyn to give Ghotan a gift of silk brocade. In the same year Muscovite envoys intervened for Ghotan in Lübeck and in Sweden to forestall suits against his properties. A Russian dispatch of 25 August 1492 said that Ghotan, now "Ivan's servant," helped to translate into German documents of an embassy which remained several months in Lübeck waiting for Maximilian to return from campaign. Ghotan was last heard of in Lübeck in January 1493. Probably

dem Leben und dem Tod [Dialogue between Life and Death], Licht der Seelen [Light of Souls], Speygel der Doghede [Mirror of Virtue], two prayer books, and a breviary; in Swedish the Articuli abbreviati. His non-religious printings in Low German were almanacs for 1484, 1491, and 1492, and still a fourth published in Sweden; and a series of "low-brow" medical treatises: Boek der arstdien van allen Krankheyden [Book of Remedies for all Illnesses], Ortloff von Baiernland's Eyn Ghud und Doghede der branden Watere [About the Worth and Virtues of Distilled Spirits], Bartholomäus de Benevento's Etliche Kraft und Doghede der branden Watere [Considerable Potency and Virtues of Distilled Spirits], and Valascus de Taranta's Eyn Ghud bewert Regiment der Pestilencie [A Worthwhile Regimen for Avoiding Plague]. See Borchling-Claussen 1 (n. 10 above) nos. 69, 71-73, 78, 79, 82, 84, 87, 88; Bruns (n. 3 above) 228-230; Haebler (n. 8 above) 285-286; W. H. C. Gläser, Bruchstücke zur Kenntnis der Lübecker Erstdrucke von 1464 bis 1524, nebst Rückblicken in die spätere Zeit (Lübeck 1903) 9-22; Raab, "Zu einigen" (n. 4 above) 323-329; I. Collijn, "Drei neu aufgefundene niederdeutsche Einblattkalen des 15. Jahrhunderts: Ein Beitrag zur Geschichte des Lübecker Buchdrucks," Skrifter utgifna af Kungl. Humanistiska Vetenskaps-Samfundet, Uppsala 9 (1904) 1-11; and Nemirovskii (n. 4 above) 59, 72.

[12] K. V. Bazilevich, Vneshniaia politika russkogo tsentralizovannogo gosudarstva, vtoraia polovina XV veka (Moscow 1952) 255-281; P. Karge, "Kaiser Friedrichs III. und Maximilians I. ungarische Politik und ihre Beziehungen zu Moskau, 1486-1506," Deutsche Zeitschrift für Geschichtswissenschaft 9 (1893) 259-277; J. L. I. Fennell, Ivan the Great of Moscow (London 1961) 117-131; Angermann, "Kulturbeziehungen" (n. 4 above) 23-25; and N. K. Kazakova, Russko-livonskie i russko-ganzeiskie ontnosheniia (Leningrad 1975) 170-337.

[13] Both the letter of Bülow's grandnephew (1585) published by E. Pabst, "Nicolaus Bülow, Astronom, Dolmetsch, und Leibarzt beim Grossfürsten in Russland," Beiträge zur Kunde Ehst-, Liv-, und Kurlands 1 (1868) 84-85, and that of Bülow's sister (1540s), Angermann, "Neues" (n. 4 above) 418-419, stated that Bülow went to Novgorod to help recompute the paschal canon. The first, however, dated Bülow's recruitment to 1508 and said that he came from Rome. The sister also said that he came to Vasilii III from Rome, but as an interpreter. These statements suggest two trips, not one, calendar correction being a preoccupation only of the 1490s; Angermann, "Neues" 409-414.

accompanying Trakhaniotes, he was in Åbo in July, and via Tallinn came to Novgorod.[14]

On 29 May 1494 one Johann von Unckell wrote from Novgorod to the Tallinn *Rat* that Ghotan had arrived with several assistants to serve, with Bülow, Archbishop Gennadii Gonzov of Novgorod and Ivan III.[15] Bülow, according to all testimony, as one educated in astronomy was to recompute the paschal canon for Gennadii.[16] The Lübeck chronicle of 1556 of Reimar Kock said that Ghotan came to Russia to print religious books, in response to an initiative of Ivan to Rome in 1488 to have the Catholic faith introduced into Russia. The story is fanciful but reflects a diplomatic reality of papal hopes and Moscow's willingness to play on them, and the likelihood that Ghotan brought assistants to Novgorod in order to print. Kock said that Russians later looted Ghotan and drowned him. He is last known to have been alive in 1496. Bülow remained in Novgorod working for Gennadii throughout the 1490s.[17]

At some point, as Angermann shows, Bülow left Russia. He entered papal service and possibly at this time received his medical education. He was working at the papal court in Rome when the pope recommended him as a translator to a Russian embassy of Vasilii III, probably that of 1506.[18] Bülow spent the rest of his life in Moscow as physician to Vasilii, this despite his wish to leave and pleas for his return from relatives, the pope, the Hansa, and the Master of the Livonian Knights. Vasilii in 1533 on his death bed expressed fond respect for his learned slave and gave him a large sum of money. Bülow was last mentioned as alive in 1541 in records of his property in the Lübeck archive.[19]

An appreciation of Bülow's and Ghotan's work in Russia must begin with an understanding of the Gennadii circle. From the late 1480s Archbishop Gennadii of Novgorod found himself unable to rebut criticism by so-called Judaizer heretics. Grand Prince Ivan of Moscow resisted Gennadii's efforts at repression and this raised new questions regarding the relationship between clerical and princely power. To

---

[14] The documents are in *Pamiatniki diplomaticheskikh sosnoshenii s innostranami derzhavami* 1 (Moscow 1851) 82-115, esp. 88, 101-106. See Angermann, "Kulturbeziehungen" (n. 4 above) 23-25; Bruns (n. 3 above) 230-231; Karl von Stern, *Bartholomäus Ghotan in Stockholm und Moskau, nebst einer Abhandlung über die Anfänge des Buchdruckerei in Deutschland und Russland* (Lübeck 1903) 3-9; Raab, "Zu einigen" (n. 4 above) 329 and "Über die Beziehungen" (n. 4 above) 419; Nemirovskii (n. 4 above) 60-61; and A. von Brandt, "Bartholomäus Gothan in Åbo, 1493," ZVLGA 43 (1963) 85-86.

[15] *Liv- Est- und Kurländisches Urkundenbuch* 1.2 (Riga 1900) 1 no. 2. He also complained that Ghotan left debts in Lübeck.

[16] Pabst (n. 13 above) 84-85; Angermann, "Neues" (n. 4 above) 418-419.

[17] Raab, "Über die Beziehungen" (n. 4 above) 422; Nemirovskii (n. 4 above) 60-61; Bruns (n. 3 above) 231; Angermann, "Neues" (n. 4 above) 412-413 and "Kulturbeziehungen" (n. 4 above) 41.

[18] Angermann, "Neues" 412-413, 418.

[19] Angermann, "Nicolaus" (n. 4 above) 89-90 and "Neues" (n. 4 above) 411-412; Zimin, *Rossiia* (n. 4 above) 352; *Polnoe sobranie russkikh letopisei* 6 (Moscow 1853) 266, 271.

refashion the Church's spiritual defenses Gennadii recruited publicists and trans-
lators. They included the Russians Gerasim Popovka, Dmitrii Gerasimov, and Georgii
Tokmakh, and the Trakhaniotes brothers. Gennadii supplemented their efforts by
turning to Catholic publicists, an act which may have alarmed Ivan. Metropolitan
Zosima was openly hostile to Gennadii. The imperial ambassador Georg von Thurn
regaled Gennadii with a description of the Spanish Inquisition and Gennadii was
favorably impressed. Gennadii also recruited the South Slav Dominican Veniamin
who wrote a discourse on the primacy of church over state. In 1503 Gennadii joined
the monk Iosif of Volokolamsk in opposition to Ivan's attempt to confiscate
monastic properties. Shortly after, Ivan and Metropolitan Simon removed Gennadii
from office for simony and brought him to Moscow under arrest.[20]

Bülow and Ghotan were other Catholic recruits to the circle. Gennadii commissioned Bülow as a master of astronomy and mathematics to recompute the Russian
paschal canon which determined the date of Easter. In 1492, the end of the seventh
millenium since Creation according to the old calendar, the computations ended. By
tradition the date had been thought to herald Christ's second coming. There was
little indication that this would happen as the time approached and the heretics
seized on this issue to ridicule the Church. Bülow recomputed the paschal canon in
1490/91, and his result can be linked to translations of Western religious and
scientific works which were part of a collection of books with which Ghotan
enriched the circle.[21] One of them, the earliest Russian copy of which is in the same
manuscript as the canon, was the explanation of the Catholic religious calendar from
the *Rationale divinorum officiorum* of Guillaume Durand, a renowned canonist of
the Roman curia educated at Bologna. Durand wrote the *Rationale* between 1286
and 1291. It was a large and popular treatise on the liturgy and its symbols, the
eighth book of which discussed the Christian calendar. Gennadii ordered that part of
it translated in 1495. Bülow was undoubtedly the translator and his source was the
Strasbourg edition of 1486. Ghotan was experienced with calendars and may have
brought this edition to Novgorod.[22] The circle also produced a translation from Low

[20] Concerning the Gennadii circle see A. D. Sedel'nikov, "Ocherki katolicheskogo vliianiia v
Novgorode v kontse XV-nachale XVI veka," *Doklady AN SSSR*, ser. B (1929) no. 1, 16-19; Lur'e
"K voprosu" (n. 4 above) 68-77, *Ideol. bor'ba* (n. 4 above) 244-284, 409-420; Ia. S. Lur'e and
N. K. Kazakova, *Anti-feodal'nye ereticheskie dvizheniia na Rusi XIV-nachala XVI veka* (AED)
(Moscow 1955) 134-146, 195-210; Nemirovskii (n. 4 above) 70-74; Raab, "Novye" (n. 4 above)
339-351; Angermann, "Kulturbeziehungen" (n. 4 above) 29, 31-43; and A. I. Klibanov,
Reformatsionnye dvizheniia Rossii v XIV-pervoi polovine XVI vv. (Moscow 1960) 188-227.

[21] See D. O. Sviatskii, "Astrolog Nikolai Liubchanin i al'manakhi na Rusi XVI v.," *Isvestiia
Leningradskogo nauchnogo in-ta im. P. F. Lesgrafta* 15.1-2 (1929) 46-47. See also Zimin,
"Doktor" (n. 4 above) 81, 83-84 and *Rossiia* (n. 4 above) 354, and Angermann, "Neues" (n. 4
above) 414-416.

[22] The translator's name is not given. Sviatskii 46-47, Angermann, "Neues" 414-415, 418, and
Raab, "Über die Beziehungen" (n. 4 above) 421 are persuasive in attributing it to Bülow. See also
L. Hain, *Repertorium bibliographicum, in quo libri omnes ab arte typografica inventa usque ad
annum MD* (Stuttgart 1826-31) nos. 6491 or 6492. N. Beneshevich, "K istorii perevodnoi
literatury v Novgorode," *Sbornik Otdeleniia russkogo iazyka i slovesnosti* (SORIaS) 101.3 (1928)
378-380 first identified the Russian translation. He and V. P. Zubov, "Kirik Novgorodets i

German of a work called in the West the *Lucidarius*. Compiled in 1195 for Duke Heinrich of Braunschweig, the *Lucidarius* was an encyclopedia for laymen mixing Aristotelian physics with spiritual advice. Its apocryphal author, Elucidarius, "the Enlightener," answered questions about God, creation, heaven, hell, the elements, natural calamities, geography, and astronomy. Bülow did not translate it, but it is likely that Ghotan brought the text to Novgorod. The only Low German edition was that printed in 1485 in Lübeck by Ghotan's colleague Mattäus Brandis.[23]

Later Bülow translated another scientific work, an almanac which attributed to the mathematician-astronomer Johannes Stöffler of Justingen (1452-1531) the terrifying astrological prediction of a second universal deluge to come in 1524. Stöffler in 1499 at Ulm printed with Jakob Pflaum an almanac which noted that on 25 February 1524 there would occur a great conjunction of the planets in the watery sign of Pisces in the zodiac. Its magnitude foretold great events both for the elements and for man. One of many dire predictions so popular in a Europe in which previously unquestioned authorities had lost respect, it achieved wide popularity because of the momentous nature of its heavenly signs. Reprinted in Venice seven times before 1524, it spawned more specific predictions of a great flood by other astrologers. These in turn generated panic as the date approached. Judging from a citation located in a polemic against it, the Russian translation came from the Venetian edition of 1513 or that of 1518. Rumor of a general inundation may have come from Bülow, who, as we shall see, wrote a revisionist commentary and elaborated on it to Russians.[24]

Between 1493 and 1499 the Gennadii circle produced its greatest work, the first complete Slavic Bible in Russia. To answer Judaizer biblical exegesis, the circle

---

drevnerusskie deleniia chasa," *Istoriko-matematicheskie issledovaniia* 6 (1953) 201-204, suggested Veniamin as its translator; Lur'e, *Ideol. bor'ba* (n. 4 above) 269-270, proposed Dmitrii Gerasimov. On Durand see L. Falletti, "Guillaume Durand," *Dictionnaire de droit canonique* 5 (Paris 1953) 1014-1075 and G. H. Buijssen, *Durandus' Rationale in spätmittelhochdeutschen Übersetzung* (Assen 1966), 15-20.

[23] On the Brandis edition see Hain no. 8815; for the Russian text see *Letopisi russkoi literatury i drevnosti izdavaemye N. Tikhonravovym* 1 (Moscow 1859) 41-66. The translator, "Georgii," was probably Georgii Ivanovich Tokmakh who, along with the *Lucidarius,* was the object of criticism by Maxim the Greek; Nemirovskii (n. 4 above) 73-74; A. I. Ivanov, *Literaturnoe nasledie Maksima Greka* (Leningrad 1969) 129-131; and Maxim the Greek, *Sochineniia prepodobnago Maksima Greka,* 3 vols. (Kazan 1859-1862) 3.226-236. See also A. S. Arkhangel'skii, "K istorii drevnerusskogo 'Lutsidariusa'," *Uchenye zapiski Imperatorskogo kazanskogo universiteta* 65.5 (1899) 27-72; Raab, "Zu einigen" (n. 4 above) 333; Angermann, "Kulturbezeihungen" (n. 4 above) 32. Commentators have often confused the *Lucidarius* with the *Elucidarium sive Dialogus de summa totius Christianae theologiae* of Honorius of Autun (early twelfth century). It did draw on the cosmographical summary *Imago mundi* ascribed to Honorius. See George Sarton, *Introduction to the History of Science,* 3 vols. (Baltimore 1927-1948) 1.749 and 2.1.200-201, 293, 386.

[24] Hain no. 15085 for the Stöffler-Pflaum prediction. A. L. Gol'dberg, "Tri 'poslaniia Filofeia' (Opyt tekstologicheskogo analiza)," TODRL 24 (1974) 70 identified the fragment from the Venetian edition in the letter of Filofei of Pskov. Also see Lynn Thorndike, *A History of Magic and Experimental Science,* 6 vols. (New York 1923-1941) 4.483 and 5.178-233. On the Russian translation see Sviatskii (n. 21 above) 48-52; Zimin, "Doktor" (n. 4 above) 83-84 and *Rossiia* (n. 4 above) 354-355. Bülow was named as translator by Maxim (n. 23 above) 1.457-484.

supplemented a Slavic Bible with books of the Old Testament translated from a Latin Bible, a German Bible, and both a Low German and a Latin Psalter.[25] Manuscript preparations dated from 1493, suggesting that the project awaited the arrival of Ghotan with the necessary Western sources. Bülow's participation remains conjectural, but likely. In 1493 Veniamin translated from the Vulgate books of the Old Testament which were unavailable to Gennadii in Slavic Bibles. It is impossible to determine which Latin Bible he used, because ninety-four Vulgate Bibles were printed in the fifteenth century. Whichever it was, Ghotan probably brought it to Novgorod. References to those parts of the Old Testament that in the Gennadii Bible came from the Vulgate appeared in the "Dialogue between Life and Death," a work which Ghotan had printed and later translated into Russian. The German Bible has been easier to trace, and it appeared before Ghotan came to Novgorod. The preface to the Gennadii Bible said that the "Song of Songs" was not translated into German. The preface also contained fragments of biblical commentary from Nicolas de Lyra. And, indeed, the Cologne Bibles printed in 1478 in Low German by Heinrich Quentell had Latin texts of the "Song of Songs" and contained Nicolas's commentaries.[26] There were available only two Low German Psalters, one by Lukas Brandis of Lübeck printed about 1473 and a Lübeck Psalter of 1493. Ghotan himself in 1481 had printed a Latin Psalter.[27]

Ghotan and Bülow also collaborated to supply the Gennadii circle with two popular anti-Jewish polemics, Nicolas de Lyra's thirteenth-century *Quaestiones disputatae contra Hebraeos* and the *Rationes breues magni rabi Samuelis iudei nati*. Gerasimov translated Nicolas de Lyra from a Latin book, anonymous and undated, but printed before Ghotan came to Novgorod.[28] Samuel was a converted Moroccan Jew who wrote in Arabic. His tract appeared in Latin in 1339. The chapters translated into Russian contained refutations of Jewish beliefs and the Jewish calendar with theological speculation about Judeo-Christian history. One manuscript of the Russian translation said that its Latin source was printed in Cologne in 1493 by Heinrich Quentell and translated the following year. Two decades later Maxim the

[25] A. Gorskii and K. Nevostruev, *Opisanie slavianskikh rukopisei Moskovskoi Sinodal'noi biblioteki,* 5 vols. (Moscow 1855-1869) 1.1-137. See also I. E. Evseev, "Ocherki po istorii slavianskogo perevoda Biblii," *Khristianskoe chtenie* (1912) nos. 11-12, 1261-1285, 1342-1374, and *idem,* "Gennadievskaia Bibliia 1499-go goda," *Trudy XI-ogo Arkheograficheskogo s'ezda v Novgorode* 2 (Moscow 1914) 1-14; Lur'e, *Ideol. bor'ba* (n. 4 above) 271-276.

[26] *Gesamtkatalog der Wiegendrucke,* 8 vols. (Leipzig 1925-1940) 4 nos. 4307, 4308 and the Quentell editions in the Newberry Library, Chicago, Rare Book Room, nos. 227, 228; and A. I. Sobolevskii, "Perevodnaia literatura moskovskoi Rusi XIV-XVII vekov," SORIaS 74.1 (1903) 184. See also Raab, "Germanoslawisches" (n. 4 above) 58; Lur'e, *Ideol. bor'ba* (n. 4 above) 273-276; Nemirovskii (n. 4 above) 70-71; Angermann, "Kulturbeziehungen" (n. 4 above) 27-28.

[27] Hain, nos. 13519, 13520, 13484; Borchling-Claussen 1 (n. 10 above) no. 1; Sobolevskii (n. 26 above) 186; and see Nemirovskii (n. 4 above) 71 and Angermann, "Kulturbeziehungen" (n. 4 above) 31.

[28] Nemirovskii (n. 4 above) 71; Hain no. 10408. See also Angermann, "Neues" (n. 4 above) 415-416.

Greek, an Orthodox monk and former scholar in Renaissance Italy who was in Moscow, noted that Bülow was the translator.[29]

There survive as well translations of other works which Ghotan probably brought to Novgorod. About 1535 Dmitrii Gerasimov translated from the Latin the eleventh-century Psalter of Bishop Bruno of Würzburg. Of the three editions printed in the fifteenth century, one, from the press of Reiser, dated from about 1490 or before Ghotan came to Novgorod. Gerasimov might have brought Ghotan's library to Moscow when he moved there in 1518 to assist Maxim the Greek in other translations. Bülow himself might have moved it. Either way, it would explain why Maxim was well informed on the content of the translations of the Gennadii circle.[30] Ghotan brought to Novgorod and translated himself a Low German rhymed broadside, the "Dialogue between Life and Death," and he may also have introduced into Russia the "History of the Destruction of Troy" written by Guido de Columna in 1267. The "Dialogue" had its origin in medieval Latin and was popular in the vernacular. Ghotan printed a Low German edition and it was the basis for his Slavic translation in Novgorod where, perhaps, it served in Gennadii's struggle with heretics.[31] A manuscript of about 1500 of the Russian "History of the Destruction of Troy" originated in Novgorod. It was an exact translation of a Latin edition printed in Strasbourg between 1487 and 1493.[32]

Raab and E. Nemirovskii have in addition suggested that Ghotan's editions of the "Tale of the Voevoda Dracula" and of Donatus's *De octo partibus orationis* were the sources for Russian versions of these works appearing between the late 1480s and 1522, but this is unlikely. The Dracula tale survives in a Russian manuscript of 1490, and is based on an original said to have been done in 1486. In some respects it is unique, and it has been speculated that Fedor Kuritsyn or someone in his embassy to

[29] Maxim (n. 23 above) 1.55. He dated the translation incorrectly as 1504. See Ivanov (n. 23 above) 108. PL 149.338-367 has the Latin text. On the translation see Sobolevskii (n. 26 above) 191-193; Wieczynski (n. 4 above) 380-381; Nemirovskii (n. 4 above) 72; Angermann, "Neues" (n. 4 above) 415-416; and Hain no. 14268. V. S. Ikonnikov, *Maksim Grek i ego vremia,* ed. 2 (Kiev 1915) surmised much of what Élie Denissoff discovered about the person and the Italian career of Maxim, *Maxime le Grec et l'Occident* (Paris 1943). See also A. I. Ivanov, "Maksim Grek i ital'ianskoe Vozrozhdenie," *Vizantiiskii vremennik* 33 (1972) 140-157; 34 (1973) 112-123; 35 (1973) 119-136; and Jack V. Haney *From Italy to Muscovy: The Life and Works of Maxim the Greek* (Munich 1973).

[30] Hain no. 4011. See also Sobolevskii (n. 26 above) 189-191; Nemirovskii (n. 4 above) 72, 74; Ivanov (n. 23 above) 108, 129-131.

[31] See Raab, "Zu einigen" (n. 4 above) on the translation, and R. P. Dmitrieva, *Povesti o spore zhizni i smerti* (Moscow 1964) 141-142. Ghotan's edition was from a text of 1428.

[32] V. Shchepkin, "Litsevoi sbornik Imperatorskogo rossiiskogo muzeia," IORIaS 4.3-4 (1899) 1345-1385. Lur'e, "Cherty" (n. 4 above) 160 still maintains that the "Tale" derived from the South Slav "Troy Parables" in the first edition of the Russian Chronograph, although the latter is now dated no earlier than 1500. Angermann, "Kulturbeziehungen" (n. 4 above) 31 shows Raab, "Zu einigen" (n. 4 above) 333 and Nemirovskii (n. 4 above) 73 unconvincing in their suggestion that the "Tale" derived from the Low German edition of 1487 printed by the Lübecker Lukas Brandis. A text of the original edition is Guido de Columna, *Historia destructionis Troiae,* ed. N. A. Griffen (Cambridge, Mass. 1936).

Hungary and Moldavia, which returned in 1486, wrote it. It is possible, however, that in Lübeck Ghotan passed his Low German edition to Fedor's brother, the diplomat Ivan Volk Kuritsyn, and that it influenced the Russian tale as we know it.[33] Donatus was the standard Latin primer of the Middle Ages. Ghotan did print an edition in 1487, but Gerasimov noted in his translation, completed in Moscow in 1522, that he had begun it as a student in Livonia, presumably from an edition acquired there.[34]

The last translation from a Lübeck book was the *Gaerde der Suntheit,* "The Pleasant Garden of Health." Iogan von Kube wrote it in 1447 and Stefan Arndes printed it in Lübeck in 1492. Ghotan may have brought it to Novgorod and Bülow certainly translated it into Slavic for Metropolitan Daniil in 1534 in Moscow.[35]

Bülow also wrote in Moscow several works in Russian. Only his critique of a Russian icon entitled "The Descent of the Holy Ghost" survives;[36] but from polemics, sermons, and letters criticizing his views, we know that Bülow wrote to Abbot Vassian Sanin, brother of the famous Iosif Sanin of Volokolamsk, about union of Russian Orthodoxy with Rome. These sources confirm that he also talked and wrote about this, about theological differences between the faiths, and about astrology to Misiur' Mikhail Grigorievich Munekhin, a government official in Pskov, and to the court official and diplomat Fedor Karpov.[37]

An attempt to sketch the beliefs of Ghotan and Bülow primarily from titles of printed books, translations of the works of others, and from attacks upon Bülow has obvious dangers. Nevertheless, the sources and their lives suggest a world view that was familiar enough in nothern Europe to allow us to surmise some of the intellectual connections. Clearly, their world view was a composite of authorities common

[33] See the text and commentary by Ia. S. Lur'e, *Povest' o Drakule* (Moscow 1964) and "Elementy" (n. 4 above) 194-197; and Jurij Striedter, "Die Erzählung vom walachischen Vojevoden Drakula in der russischen und deutschen Überlieferung," *Zeitschrift für slayische Philologie* 29 (1961) 398-427. Nemirovskii (n. 4 above) 73 and Raab, "Zu einigen" (n. 4 above) 333-335 argued for a Low German original and referred to the broadside attributed to Ghotan by Borchling-Claussen (n. 10 above) no. 66.

[34] See Angermann's correction, "Kulturbeziehungen" (n. 4 above) 31 of Nemirovskii (n. 4 above) 59, 72 and the text of the Russian Donatus, I. V. Jagić, "Rassuzhdeniia iuzhnoslavianskoi i russkoi stariny o tserkovno-slavianskom iazyke," *Issledovaniia po russkomu iazyku: Otdeleniia russ. iazyka i slov., Imp. akad. nauk* 1 (1895) 812-911, esp. 820.

[35] In Slavic, *Blagoprokhladnyi tsvetnik.* See Hain no. 8957; Angermann, "Neues" (n. 4 above) 416; Nemirovskii (n. 4 above) 74; and L. F. Zmeev, *Russkie vrachebniki. Issledovanie v oblasti nashei drevnei vrachebnoi pis'mennosti = Pamiatniki drevnei pis'mennosti* 112 (1895) 5-24, 35-38.

[36] A. I. Sobolevskii, "Materialy i zametki po drevne-russkoi literature 7: Iz istorii ikonopisi," IORIaS 20.1 (1915) 274-277.

[37] V. Zhmakin published Vassian's reply to Bülow's letter, "Pamiatnik russkoi protivo-katolicheskoi polemiki XVI veka," *Zhurnal Ministerstva narodnogo prosveshcheniia* 211 (1880) no. 10, 319-332. Our knowledge of Bülow's letter to Munekhin comes from Filofei of Pskov and from Maxim the Greek who quotes Bülow. V. Malinin, *Starets Eleazarova monastyria Filofei i ego poslaniia* (Kiev 1901) appendix 37-47, esp. 37 n. 1, and V. F. Rzhiga, "Neizdannye sochine-niia Maksima Greka," *Byzantinoslavica* 6 (1935-1936) 90-91. See also Zimin, "Doktor" (n. 4 above).

to North German medieval tradition combined, not necessarily harmoniously, with elements of Renaissance science, humanism, and popular literature.

The family backgrounds of Ghotan and Bülow were commonplace and their educations traditional. Both were from burgher-clerical families. Ghotan was first a cathedral vicar. Bülow may have swum in humanist currents in the Faculty of Arts at Rostock, but his degrees were bestowed by a devout and conservative theologian, Albert Krantz. Somehow, in the manner of others of their time and station, they broke free of the confining hierarchical society of their fathers. Ghotan became an entrepreneur of printing. He took his book business from town to town and to a foreign country, printed all manner of works in Latin, Low German, and Swedish, and was constantly in fear of bankruptcy. Bülow entered the service of Maximilian whose court, an outpost of the Renaissance in northern Europe, must have seemed dazzling. His medical training, wherever it was, his interest in wordly astrological prediction, and the fact that somewhere he learned Greek, suggest that he embraced the new learning with a passion. In Rome he must have served the papacy of Julius II whose court was thoroughly secular and who was himself a patron of astrology. [38] What greater testimony could there have been to their adventurous individualism than that they agreed to go into Russian service, in Bülow's case not once but twice, and that both came to master Russian? In 1518 in Moscow the imperial ambassador Francesco da Collo could justly describe Bülow as a "professor of medicine and of astrology and wise in all sciences."[39]

The translations which Ghotan and Bülow helped to bring to Russia were more medieval than Renaissance. They illustrate again that in northern Europe one looks in vain for clear-cut divisions between the two periods. Nor is it possible to demonstrate that Bülow and Ghotan substituted the new Aristotle of Renaissance classicists for the scholastic Aristotle, or that they were drawn to the revival of Platonism. Yet it is justified to argue that they employed and combined traditional sources in a manner which suggested new and humanist, yet still thoroughly religious, preoccupations. The popularity of Ghotan's edition of the "Dialogue between Life and Death" attested to a current of unease in an increasingly worldly society in northern Europe over the inevitability of death and the reality of salvation. Was it not like that for Ghotan who could turn out blank indulgences, holy writ, possibly an early edition of the Dracula tale about a tyrant to whom Christian morality did not apply, and who produced predictive almanacs which marked the passage of time and religious festivals with symbols of the zodiac?[40] And if the anti-Jewish translations and the uses to which they were put in Novgorod reflect their beliefs, were not

---

[38] On Bülow at Rostock University see *Die Matrikel* (n. 6 above) 229, 236, and Karl-Friedrich Olechnowitz, *Geschichte der Universität Rostock: Festschrift zur Fünfhundertfünfzig-Jahr-Feier der Universität* 1: *1419-1789* (Berlin 1969) 17; Wallace K. Ferguson, *The Renaissance* (New York 1940) 106-125 and Thorndike (n. 24 above) 5.175 on papal astrology, and on predictive "science" under Maximilian, 4.457, 478-479; 5.339, 347-349; 6.441, 444-445, 488.

[39] *Polnoe* (n. 19 above) 6.266, Sviatskii (n. 21 above) 46.

[40] Raab, "Zu einigen" (n. 4 above) 324-326; Collijn (n. 11 above) 8-11; Borchling-Claussen (n. 10 above) nos. 63, 69, 186, 194.

then Bülow and Ghotan victims of the same spiritual crisis in northern Europe in the late Middle Ages which transformed traditional anti-Judaism into popular anti-Semitism?[41]

Bülow's spiritual solution was to infuse his religion with a daringly optimistic interpretation of history that spoke of the imminence of the coming of Christ in judgment. His criticism of the Russian icon "The Descent of the Holy Ghost" was on one hand a restatement of the Catholic argument on the *filioque*. But in it he also had his Orthodox adversary interpret the central figure of the icon wearing an imperial crown as a world darkened by sin, while he saw the figure as Christ reigning in triumph on earth with his promise of salvation for all.[42]

The computations which Bülow did for Gennadii gained him a reputation as an astronomer, but he was more than that. The shocked replies to him by the monks Maxim the Greek and Filofei of Pskov establish that astronomy was subsidiary to astrological prediction which in turn shaped Bülow's theology and history. Maxim protested that the stars had nothing to do with God's will or with history. His arguments reveal that Bülow knew both pre-Christian and Christian history and explained them according to the stars. Maxim in one polemic referred to errors in Bülow's translation of chronological chapters from Samuel the Jew. Elsewhere Maxim offered counter arguments to Bülow's astrological history, explaining that according to Thucydides, Themistocles had defeated the Persians without astrological advice, that Aristotle had not taught Alexander of Macedon astrology, and that the Gauls had been driven from Italy without astral intervention. Conversely, Maxim cited the Persians, Hannibal, and other would-be conquerors who had relied on the stars and had met ruin.[43] In Christian times, he maintained, faith and bravery rather than the stars had won victories for Constantine the Great and other Byzantine emperors and for Dmitrii Donskoi of Moscow over unbelievers.[44] As a contemporary foil Maxim noted elsewhere that the stars led Duke Ludovico the Moor of Milan to war against the French (in 1499) and, thus, false science had brought him to ruin.[45] Maxim called Bülow's astrology a Latin import, a "German deceit," and learnedly said its origins were in pagan obfuscations of Zoroaster, the Egyptians, in Epicurean philosophy, and in the writings of the "godless" Arabs. Filofei called it "Greek pedantry."[46] These retorts indicate that the German doctor had some knowledge of classical philosophy. Shrewdly, Maxim branded Bülow's unionist logic as a product of the "Italian school," that is, based on pagan philosophers Aristotle and Plato.[47]

[41] Gavin Langmuir, "Anti-Judaism as the Necessary Preparation for Anti-Semitism," *Viator* 2 (1971) 383-389, esp. 387-388.

[42] Sobolevskii (n. 36 above) 275-277.

[43] Maxim (n. 23 above) 1.55, 354-359 and Ikonnikov (n. 29 above) 260-311.

[44] Maxim 1.357-360.

[45] *Ibid.* 427-428 and the extended discussion of Maxim's arguments against astrology, Haney (n. 29 above) 154-158.

[46] Maxim (n. 23 above) 1.437, 446-447, 451, 461-466 and Malinin (n. 37 above) appendix, 37.

[47] Maxim 1.215, 247; Haney (n. 29 above) 119-120, 158.

Thus Ghotan and especially Bülow brought to Russia from Lübeck profoundly unsettling views. Maxim detected a "Pythagorean spirit" in Bülow's world view that reminds us of Renaissance visions of a new Christian age which were a mélange of arithmetic and astrological schemes for arranging human affairs.[48] Bülow's elaboration of the almanac of Stöffler in 1521 caused Maxim to write that the doctor claimed that the stars promised victory to Emperor Maximilian or his successor over the Turks, a victory that would usher in Christian unity under Catholic and imperial auspices.[49] Such hopes had been widespread at papal and imperial courts, both of which Bülow had served.[50] Although neither Maxim nor Filofei was specific, it seems that Bülow predicted that Christ's second coming was to crown the triumph of Christian brotherhood. The binding of astrological science to eschatological prediction may have been Bülow's invention. Where contemporary German soothsayers and almanac makers tended to pessimistic warnings, he insisted on the opposite. It was an affirmation of a dream that was running stubbornly counter to growing divisiveness in Europe of the 1520s. What then was the influence of these remarkable men on Russian culture?

First of all, Ghotan and Bülow contributed to translations of the Gennadii circle which were immensely important in the approved literature of Russia. The Gennadii Bible was the source of the *Ostrog* Bible which was printed in 1580/81 in the Ukraine. It, in turn, was the prototype for later Orthodox Bibles of Russia, the Ukraine, and Belorussia.[51] The Bruno Psalter entered the mainstream of Russian ecclesiastical literature when Metropolitan Makarii included it in his official compendium, the "Great Menology" [*Velikie minei chetii*] of 1552.[52] Makarii also in 1538 extended the pascal canon computed by Bülow.[53] Finally, the *Gaerde der Suntheit,* which Bülow translated in 1534, was the first medical manual in Russian.[54]

---

[48] Maxim (n. 23 above) 1.299-300; Zimin, *Rossiia* (n. 4 above) 357 and "Doktor" (n. 4 above) 86. See also Frances A. Yates, *Giordano Bruno and the Hermetic Tradition* (London 1964) 144-150 and D. P. Walker, *The Ancient Theology: Studies in Christian Platonism from the Fifteenth to the Eighteenth Century* (Ithaca 1972) 10-12ff.

[49] See Maxim (n. 23 above) 1.399-434 and Rzhiga (n. 37 above) 91. See also Ivanov (n. 23 above) 120-122; Zimin, *Rossiia* (n. 4 above) 356-357; Sviatskii (n. 21 above) 48-52.

[50] Bülow repeated his prediction of the impending unification of churches in communications to Vassian Sanin and Fedor Karpov. See Zhmakin (n. 37 above) 319-322; Malinin (n. 37 above) appendix, 37-41; Maxim (n. 23 above) 1.235-266, 267-322 (sermons to Karpov, 1519-1520), 213-234, 323-340, 455-456, 509-532 (sermons to Bülow, ca. 1518-1524). Concerning such predictive traditions in the West see Yates (n. 48 above) 113-143 and Thorndike (n. 24 above) 5.229-230, 243.

[51] Lur'e, *Ideol. bor'ba* (n. 4 above) 283; A. S. Zernova, *Nachalo knigopechataniia v Moskve i na Ukraine* (Moscow 1947) 55-65; E. I. Katsprzhak, *Pervopechatnik Ivan Federov* (Moscow 1964) 71, 75-88.

[52] Arkhimandrit Iosif, *Podrobnoe oglavlenie Velikikh chetiikh minei Vserossiiskogo Mitropolita Makariia, khraniashchikhsia v Moskovskoi Patriarshei Biblioteke* (Moscow 1892) 425-427.

[53] Nemirovskii (n. 4 above) 53.

[54] Maikov (n. 7 above) 392; Zimin, "Doktor" (n. 4 above) 82; T. Rainov, *Nauka v Rossii, XI-XVII vekov* 1-3 (Moscow 1940) 268.

One enters a speculative but more important area when one assesses the reactive qualities of a Russian culture in the process of self-definition when confronted with the world view offered by Ghotan and Bülow. The translations of western anti-Jewish tracts of Nicolas de Lyra and Samuel for Archbishop Gennadii help to substantiate the conclusion that Gennadii and not Iosif of Volokolamsk initiated charges that the Novgorod heresy was in many of its beliefs Jewish. The nature of the heresy, including the possibility of Jewish origins or influences, remains obscure and controversial.[55] But the allegations of Judaizing, to which Ghotan and Bülow contributed substantiating evidence, stand at the beginning of a long tradition of official anti-Semitism in Russia. Grand Prince Ivan III opposed Gennadii's repression of the heresy. But the church council of 1490, over which he presided, referred to some of its beliefs as Jewish. And from 1503 under Iosif's influence the charge of Judaizing carried the day.[56] One may also speculate that Iosif took the title *Prosvetitel'*, or "Enlightener," for his polemic against Judaizers and in praise of divine-right monarchy from the title of the Slavic translation of the *Lucidarius.*[57]

By contrast, few Russians were attracted to Bülow's Renaissance vision of brotherhood despite the tolerant character of Vasilii's court until the mid-1520s. Bülow impressed the well-traveled diplomat-official Munekhin with his astrological predictions and, perhaps, with his description of the glories to result from religious union; but his only intellectual conquest was Fedor Karpov, the diplomat and translator of Latin in Moscow.[58] Maxim the Greek, who would have known better than anyone, assumed Fedor's familiarity with classical philosophy and called him "most wise Fedor."[59] He could cite Aristotle and verses — as yet untranslated — of Ovid.[60] Karpov admired Bülow as a man of science and was attracted to astrology.

[55] Soviet historians, following Lur'e, *Ideol. bor'ba* (n. 4 above) 154-164 and AED (n. 20 above) 74-224, generally reject that the heresy had anything to do with Judaism. See also Charles J. Halperin, "Judaizers and the Image of the Jew in Medieval Russia: A Polemic Revisited and a Question Posed," *Canadian-American Slavic Studies* 9.2 (Summer 1975) 141-155. Others have contested this conclusion and the question of Jewish (or other) influences on the heresy remains open. See the survey of opinions and literature by Henrik Birnbaum, "On Some Evidence of Jewish Life and Anti-Jewish Sentiments in Medieval Russia," *Viator* 4 (1973) 246-252. For references to Jewish elements in the heresy by Gennadii and the Council of 1490 see AED 310, 311, 313-314, 316, 375, 383, 390, 436.

[56] On such an origin of anti-Semitism see Henry R. Huttenbach, "The Judaizing Heresy and the Origins of Russian Anti-Semitism," *Studies in Medieval Culture* 4.3 (1974) 496-506. On the popularity of the Samuel translation see Ivanov (n. 23 above) 108 n. 13, and Sobolevskii (n. 26 above) 191-193.

[57] Iosif of Volokolamsk, *Prosvetitel', ili oblichenie eresi zhidovstvuiushchikh,* ed. 2 (Kazan 1882); Ivanov (n. 23 above) 130 n. 40.

[58] We know little of Munekhin. See Malinin (n. 37 above) esp. 159-162 and Zimin, *Rossiia* (n. 4 above) 359-362.

[59] Maxim (n. 23 above) 1.371, 417ff. and Karpov's letters to Maxim, *ibid.* 3.274-277 and in N. K. Nikol'skii, "Materialy dlia istorii drevnerusskoi dukhovnoi pis'mennosti," *Khristianskoe chtenie* (August 1909) 15-16.

[60] Karpov's letter to Metropolitan Daniil published by V. G. Druzhinin, "Neskol'ko neizvestnykh literaturnykh pamiatnikov iz sbornika XVI v.," *Letopis' zaniatii Arkheograficheskoi kommissii* 21 (1909) 106-113; V. F. Rzhiga, "Boiarin-Zapadnik XVI veka (F. I. Karpov),"

He also respected how Bülow could marshal Renaissance Catholicism, so rich in classical philosophy, to support his science and his dream of religious union. In these, in his tolerance, and in his humanist political philosophy Karpov was a solitary figure at court.[61] Of the small educated and cosmopolitan elite in Moscow Dmitrii Gerasimov was the more typical. Schooled in German Livonia, he was a translator for Gennadii and later with Maxim, and a Russian diplomat. In Rome on a diplomatic mission in 1525 he impressed Paolo Giovio, bishop of Nocera, with his intelligence and curiosity. But one encounters silence when one listens for Gerasimov to discuss what he had seen, heard, or read, or for a Maxim to observe it. Gerasimov could remark about the wonders of Renaissance Italy to Giovio and return to Russia to translate traditional religious works.[62]

The fate of popular literature in Russia in the sixteenth century, some of which we have ascribed to Ghotan, supports the conclusion that few Russians were attracted to new traditions of thought. Had Ghotan set up a press, a task for which one source said that he was recruited, it would have been the first press in Russia. That he had hoped to do just that is suggested by the crew of German helpers who were in Novgorod with him. Nothing survives that would indicate a success. His patrons must have forbidden it.[63] Instead, in a reversal of technological progress, Ghotan and Bülow in their translations turned printed books back into manuscripts. The eminent Soviet historian Ia. S. Lur'e has cited the proliferation in manuscripts of popular, often secular, literature from the late fifteenth century in Russia to claim that the Renaissance spirit, evident elsewhere in northern Europe, was also at work there.[64] Admitting these important additions to Russian literature, one should remain skeptical of high opinions of the weight of such literature in Russian culture until at least the seventeenth century. Without the printing press such works were a novelty. Even in manuscript tradition the tale of Dracula stirred almost no interest in sixteenth-century Russia. Historians know of only two Slavic manuscripts of it, one of which survives, from the late fifteenth century. Russians copied it again, so far as we know, only in the seventeenth.[65] The "Tale of Troy" was only slightly more popular. An appreciation of it appeared in a writing of the 1530s by one of the disciples of Maxim the Greek, an educated official in Novgorod, V. M. Tuchkov.

Rossiiskaia assotsiatsiia nauchno-issledovatel'nykh institutov obshchestvennykh nauk: In-t istorii, Uchenye zapiski 4 (1929) 39-48.

[61] Maxim (n. 4 above) 1.247-248ff.; A. A. Zimin, "Obshchestvenno-politicheskie vzgliady Fedora Karpova," TODRL 12 (1956) 160-173 and *Rossiia* (n. 4 above) 344-350; E. N. Kimeeva, " 'Poslanie Mitropolitu Daniilu' Fedora Karpova," TODRL 9 (1953) 220-234; and I. N. Golenishchev-Kutuzov, *Gumanizm u vostochnykh slavian* (Moscow 1963) 28-29.

[62] Paolo Giovio, *Opera* 8 (Rome 1972) 449-450 no. 14; P. N. Berkov, "Ostslavische Studenten an deutschen Hochschulen in der vorpetrinischen Zeit," *Zeitschrift für slavische Philologie* 30 (1962) 351-374; Zimin, *Rossiia* (n. 4 above) 358-359; Golenishchev-Kutuzov 27-28.

[63] Angermann, "Bartholomäus" (n. 4 above) 144; Nemirovskii (n. 4 above) 58, 60-61.

[64] Lur'e, "O putiakh" (n. 4 above) 262-288; "Elementy" (n. 4 above) 183-211; "Cherty" (n. 4 above) 157-161.

[65] Lur'e (n. 33 above); Sobolevskii (n. 26 above) 41, and the review of Lur'e by John V. A. Fine, Jr., *Kritika* 2.1 (Fall 1965) 1-6.

Later it went into the "Illuminated Chronicle" [*Litsevoi svod*] prepared at court for Ivan IV "the Terrible" in the 1560s. There it became — and remained — integrated into Russian Christian historical tradition.[66] The one translation of popular literature which immediately had a rich literary history in Russia was Ghotan's religious broadside, the "Dialogue between Life and Death."[67]

But the most significant result of the thought of Bülow and Ghotan was that it provoked a reaction that was hostile, intolerant, and massive. Bülow's treatise to Vassian Sanin on the union of churches occasioned a bitter anti-Latin polemic.[68] The reaction of Maxim the Greek and its influence in Russia was more complex and more important. Maxim had rejected the intellectual world of Renaissance Italy first for a Dominican monastery and then for the most ascetic form of Orthodoxy, a monastic cell at Mount Athos. Recruited there to translate religious books from Greek into Slavic, there is little doubt that Maxim radiated a knowledge of Renaissance philosophy, science, mythology and history to a little band of *cognoscenti* at Vasilii's court. One also must recognize his respect for some of the intellectual and monastic traditions of Catholicism. Yet, he was the first and most comprehensive polemicist in Moscow of the sixteenth century against every alien faith and people. At times he was as vituperative as the most obscurantist of Russian clerical polemicists.[69] The Soviet authority on Maxim, A. I. Ivanov, counted forty-seven of Maxim's polemics. They are divided in origin roughly equally between those prompted by Bülow's writings and a later group by which Maxim hoped to prove his Orthodoxy after conviction as a heretic. Up to thirteen of the forty-seven answer Bülow or translations made in Novgorod of Samuel the Jew and the *Lucidarius*. At least five more, the majority addressed to Karpov and concerning astrology, may also be counted among works which Bülow inspired.[70] We already know Maxim's opinion of astrology, a false science which was a trait of that heretical Latin philosophy which cherished pagan Greek classics, in other words, Bülow's brand of Catholicism.[71] In similar fashion Maxim condemned Islam, Judaism, and, later, Lutheranism.[72] The Orthodox remained an uncorrupted island in a doomed world. Maxim accepted Bülow's apocalyptic vision of the imminence of the Day of Judgment, but turned it around to use it as an argument that damnation would surely

[66] See L. A. Dmitriev, ed., *Povesti o zhitii Mikhaila Klopskogo*, (Moscow 1958) 164 and Shchepkin (n. 32 above) 1364. On Tuchkov see S. O. Shmidt, "Novoe o Tuchkovykh (Tuchkovy, Maksim Grek, Kurbskii)," *Issledovaniia po sotsial'no-politicheskoi istorii Rossii: Sb. statei pamiati B. A. Romanova* (Leningrad 1971) 129-141.

[67] Dmitrieva (n. 31 above).

[68] Zhmakin (n. 37 above) 319-322.

[69] B. I. Dunaev, *Pr. Maksim Grek i grecheskaia ideia na Rusi v XVI veke* (Moscow 1916); Haney (n. 29 above) esp. 118, 124-127.

[70] Ivanov (n. 23 above) 104-133; Sviatskii (n. 21 above) 47-48. N. V. Sinitsyna, "Maksim Grek i Savonarola (o pervom rukopisnom sobranii sochinenii Maksima Greka)," *Feodal'naia Rossiia* (n. 4 above) 149-156.

[71] Ivanov describes some works which are as yet unpublished (n. 23 above) 108-114, 120-127, 129-131 and Maxim (n. 23 above) 1.180-484, 509-532, and 3.226-236.

[72] Ivanov (n. 23 above) 104-108, 114-120, 127-129, 131-133, and Maxim (n. 23 above) 1.55-180, 485-508.

follow contamination from alien faiths. This was a view and an intolerance which by 1525 was to dominate the official church and to influence strongly the court, and to which Maxim was to fall victim as a foreigner who knew his enemy too well.[73]

A recent study has established that the first of the three letters attributed to Filofei of Pskov which ennunciated the famous concept of "Moscow — the third Rome," and possibly the only one actually written by Filofei, was that which he penned to Misiur' Munekhin in 1524.[74] The internal consistency of this letter, in comparison to the disparate themes contained in the other two, makes such a conclusion all the more convincing. Filofei wrote, we may remember, in response to Munekhin's account of Bülow's use of astrology as a predictive science of religious-political history. The date of the letter was that for which elaborations of Stöffler had predicted a great flood. In addition to attacking astrology as heretical and wrongheaded, Filofei proposed an alternative theory of history based on faith. Its outlines are familiar and vivid: Old Rome and Constantinople, the second Rome, had left the faith and suffered the inevitable fate for apostasy, invasion and ruin. Moscow alone remained unsullied in its Orthodoxy; it was the third and last Rome and would stand until Christ's Second Coming and the Day of Judgment. Its ruler was the one Christian emperor.[75]

Was he in this context what Maxmilian had been in Bülow's musings? Suggestively, Filofei turned to the Slavic translation of the commentary by Andreas of Caesaria of the twelfth chapter of the Revelation to Saint John for the symbolism of his answer. And its central metaphor was that of a flood. A serpent, the devil, waited to inundate the newborn babe — the Christian czar — of a pregnant woman, the true faith. According to Filofei the flood was one of unbelief.[76] Thus Filofei consciously took up Bülow's imagery while carefully building his rebuttal from a traditional

---

[73] On Maxim's demise see *Sudnye spiski Maksima Greka i Isaka Sobaki,* ed. S. O. Shmidt (Moscow 1971).

[74] The letters are in Malinin (n. 37 above) appendix, 37-66; the textual study by Gol'dberg (n. 24 above) 68-97. The most recent statement of alternative dating is that of Frank Kämpfer, "Beobachtungen zu den Sendschreiben Filofejs," *Jahrbücher für Geschichte Osteuropas* n.s. 18 (1970) 1-46.

[75] Malinin (n. 37 above) appendix, 41-46. Assertions of Wieczynski (n. 4 above) 378-380 and others that the formulation originated in the 1490s in the *Povest' o belom klobuke* [Tale of the White Cowl] and was of Western origin rest on questionable textual conclusions and must be rejected. Texts of the *Povest'* in both of its editions contain anachronisms which make a later dating, probably as late as the second half of the sixteenth century, most likely. See Lur'e, *Ideol. bor'ba* (n. 4 above) 229-234.

[76] Compare Malinin (n. 37 above) appendix, 46 with Metropolitan Makarii, *Velikiia minei chetii* for September 25-30 (Moscow 1883) 1743-1744 and Revelation 12.1-6, 14-15. Of the three commentaries on St. John known to exist in Slavic translation, Filofei's citation resembled closely only that of Andreas. Another Filofei letter, Malinin, appendix, 61-64 contained an even more detailed exegesis of Andreas's commentary. Also, Filofei's phrase "now two Romes have fallen, but the third stands, and a fourth there shall never be" has a resonance that is reminiscent of yet another passage of Andreas's commentary on the Revelation to St. John; "[There are seven kings], five of whom have fallen, one is, and the other has not yet come." Compare Malinin, appendix, 45 with Makarii 1767. Andreas interpreted the kings to mean empires. Filofei's source was suggested to me by Professor Ihor Ševčenko in a seminar at Columbia University eighteen years ago.

Orthodox source. His conception was to serve as the foundation for a strong and particularistic national consciousness. The letter found its way into Metropolitan Makarii's "Great Menology" of 1552; by then the other Filofei letters had appeared; and thenceforth the theory turned up in official documents, historical works, and many other texts.[77] Ironically, in the same decade that Bülow's dream of Catholic and imperial renaissance collapsed in Germany, he, and to a lesser extent Ghotan, were catalysts to the emergence of the major texts which set forth a religious ideology of Russian national exclusiveness.

Department of History
Roosevelt University
Chicago, Illinois 60605, U.S.A.

[77] Arkhimandrit Iosif (n. 52 above) 501, and Gol'dberg (n. 24 above).

VIATOR Style Sheet

1. All contributions must be typewritten in *double space*, with ample margins. This applies to text, quoted material, and footnotes. Please do *not* use corrasible paper.

2. Footnotes should be typed in *double space* on separate sheets at the end of the article and numbered consecutively.

3. Bibliographical references ordinarily belong in the notes rather than in the text; the first reference to an item should contain complete and unabbreviated data (save for the sigla indicated in section 5 below):

Book:	J. K. Brown,	*Book Title* (City 1879) 234-236.
		Title [Translation of title] (City 1877) 34.
		Title, ed. John Doe and Jane Doe (City [etc.]).
		ed. 2 (City [etc.]).
		trans. John Doe (City 1876) fol. 15v.
Monograph:		John G. Black, *Monograph Title*, Title of Series (ABBRV) 21 (1786) 34.
		C. J. Smith, *Monograph in Same Series*, ABBRV 22 (1787) 345-346, esp. 345 n. 4.
Article:		John Doe, "Article," *Journal* 76 (1879) 1-22, 34ff., 50.
		Undated Journal 76.1-22.
Manuscript:		Augustine, *De musica* 3.4, Paris, Bibliothèque Nationale MS lat. 9320, fols. 4, 5v, 6rv.

4. Subsequent references may be shortened as follows, always with a view to brevity without ambiguity.

a. Smith 24-25.	(Only one Smith is cited, in a recent footnote, and there can be no possible ambiguity.)
b. Jones (n. 2 above) 245-246.	(Complete reference is in n. 2 above.)
c. Jones, "The Blue Book" (n. 2 above) 34.	(Jones has more than one reference in n. 2, so short title is necessary.)
d. Augustine 3.6 (7v).	

5. Sigla: *Acta sanctorum*: AS Apr. 3.420.
   Patrologia graeca: PG 37.96A.
   Patrologia latina: PL 129.432.
   Monumenta Germaniae historica: MGH Auctores antiquiores 5.1 (Berlin 1882) 130.

6. Titles of foreign books and articles should be capitalized according to the usages of the respective languages. In Latin and the Romance languages, only the first word and proper nouns should be capitalized.